MICROSOFT®
VISUAL C#™
.NET

Mickey Williams

PUBLISHED BY
Microsoft Press
A Division of Microsoft Corporation
One Microsoft Way
Redmond, Washington 98052-6399

Copyright © 2002 by Microsoft Corporation

Library of Congress Cataloging-in-Publication Data
Williams, Mickey.
    Microsoft Visual C# (core reference) / Mickey Williams.
        p. cm.
    Includes index.
    ISBN 0-7356-1290-0
    1. Microsoft Visual C#.   2. C# (Computer program language)   I. Title.

  QA76.736.C153 .W55235   2002
  005.26'8--dc21   2001059058

Printed and bound in the United States of America.

2 3 4 5 6 7 8 9   QWT   7 6 5 4 3 2

Distributed in Canada by H.B. Fenn and Company Ltd.

A CIP catalogue record for this book is available from the British Library.

Microsoft Press books are available through booksellers and distributors worldwide. For further information about international editions, contact your local Microsoft Corporation office or contact Microsoft Press International directly at fax (425) 936-7329. Visit our Web site at www.microsoft.com/mspress. Send comments to *mspinput@microsoft.com*.

ActiveX, Authenticode, Encarta, FrontPage, IntelliMouse, IntelliSense, JScript, Microsoft, Microsoft Press, MSDN, .NET logo, OpenType, Verdana, Visual Basic, Visual C++, Visual C#, Visual Studio, Win32, Windows, Windows NT, and Xbox are either registered trademarks or trademarks of Microsoft Corporation in the United States and/or other countries. Other product and company names mentioned herein may be the trademarks of their respective owners.

The example companies, organizations, products, domain names, e-mail addresses, logos, people, places, and events depicted herein are fictitious. No association with any real company, organization, product, domain name, e-mail address, logo, person, place, or event is intended or should be inferred.

Acquisitions Editor: Danielle Bird
Project Editor: Dick Brown
Technical Editors: Donnie Cameron and Julie Xiao

Body Part No. X08-06141

For my racing buddies Ali and Mackenzie,
and for my wife René,
who has been waiting for a trip to Banff for 10 years now.

Contents at a Glance

Table of Contents

Part V   ASP.NET and Web Services

Acknowledgments

No author can create a book of this scope working alone—the number of people who come together on a project like this is amazing. An author agrees to write a book, and as the process begins, people start coming out of the woodwork to help. It's a lot like the Microsoft Office Assistant: "Hey! It looks like you're writing a book! Want some help? How about some great graphics for the part openers in your book? This heading would be great if it was in a gerund form!"

At Microsoft Press, I'd like to thank Danielle Bird for asking me to write this book. Danielle, I promise to stop hounding you for an Xbox console. I'd also like to thank Dick Brown, who is doomed to a life of trying to get authors like me to hit deadlines. I'm sure Dick is happy to see the last bits of this book cross his desk. Jennifer Harris was responsible for turning my geeky text into readable English sentences. Jennifer, I'm sorry about forcing you to read my long-winded digression on the significance of the Battle of Agincourt. Thanks to Donnie Cameron and Julie Xiao for their excellent work as technical editors. I've never been so thoroughly reviewed and cross-checked. Thanks for your diligence and support.

A big thank you to the other authors, who provided me some much-needed help: Brad Jones, Brad Wist, Mike Pope, and Christoph Wille. Thanks, guys.

Thanks to the people I work with at Interactive Software Engineering and .NET Experts in Santa Barbara: Bertrand and Annie Meyer, Raphaël Simon, Manu Stapf, and Bill Navickas. Thanks for working around my schedule and for providing a great place for me to train and consult with other developers. Special thanks to Hal Webre, my training cohort at .NET Experts. Hal kept me well supplied with CDs and cookbooks. While we were at the ACM SIGCSE conference recently, Hal took me out for Cincinnati-style chili, which was interesting, but why it's called chili is beyond me.

And it's not just to the people who deal with me professionally that I owe thanks. Thanks to my sister, Jennifer, and her husband, Mitch, for providing a base where I could write while I was in San Diego, as well as for scheduling new additions to their family around my book writing timetable.

And finally, thanks to my daughters, Ali and Mackenzie, for remembering what I look like. And thanks to my wife, René for being far more patient than I deserve. Next year we're definitely going to Banff.

Introduction

When I first started working with Microsoft Visual C# .NET, I was immediately struck by how productive my coding sessions became. Even though I was working with the pre-beta release, the development environment and the .NET Framework simplified much of the work that I was doing. The increased productivity was due to four factors:

- The C# programming language, which is well-suited for component-based development

- The simplified programming and deployment model offered by the common language runtime

- The .NET Framework and its associated class library

- The developer automation features included in the Microsoft Visual Studio .NET environment

The tools for development that are realized today with Visual C# .NET are light-years ahead of the tools I was using in the mid-1980s when I started developing for Microsoft Windows. When I was asked to write a book about Visual C# .NET, I just couldn't refuse. I'm sure that you'll find working with Visual C# .NET a rewarding experience, and I'm pleased that you've selected this book to help get you started.

I enjoy talking to readers, and I'm happy to answer any questions you might have after reading my books. If you have any feedback or questions about this text, feel free to contact me at mickey.williams@codevtech.com. I can't always respond immediately, but I try to answer all of my e-mail.

Who Should Read This Book

This book is intended for developers who want to learn the C# programming language using Microsoft Visual C# .NET. The book is intended to provide a broad overview of programming with Visual C# .NET, so it explores a wide variety of topics. In addition to a discussion of the C# programming language, this book covers the more commonly used classes in the .NET Framework, including Windows Forms programming, ASP.NET, Extensible Markup Language (XML), XML Web services, and more.

System Requirements

To use this book, you'll need to have Visual C# .NET or Visual Studio .NET installed on your computer. Any computer that satisfies the minimum requirements for Visual C# .NET will work effectively with most of the examples in this book. Be aware that Microsoft Windows XP Home Edition and Microsoft Windows NT 4 don't support the hosting of XML Web services or ASP.NET Web applications with the .NET Framework. Although you can build these projects on these operating systems, you'll need to upload the projects to a properly configured host to execute them. I recommend that development be done on the Microsoft Windows XP Professional or Microsoft Windows 2000 Professional operating systems. For Chapter 20, you need IIS version 4 or later in order to run the sample code.

Organization

This book is arranged in five parts, with each part covering a different aspect of programming using Visual C# .NET:

- **Part I** Introduces the Visual C# .NET environment and examines the core portions of the C# programming language.

- **Part II** Describes the more advanced aspects of the C# programming language and the .NET Framework. In addition to chapters on delegates and exception handling, we'll cover topics such as collection classes, debugging, and writing multithreaded code.

- **Part III** Here you'll learn how to write graphical user interface (GUI) applications using Visual C# .NET. The .NET Framework includes extensive support for writing Windows Forms–based applications, and you'll see that many advanced controls are very easy to use.

- **Part IV** Examines ADO.NET and XML. You'll learn how to use ADO.NET for data access to databases such as SQL Server. We'll also look at the .NET Framework classes that implement a new model for manipulating XML, in which data is pulled from an XML stream. With the .NET Framework and Visual C# .NET, it's easy to manage data using either ADO.NET or XML.

■   **Part V**   The book wraps up with a discussion of creating Web applications using ASP.NET and Visual C# .NET and shows you how to use XML Web services.

Sample Files

Sample files for this book can be found at the Microsoft Press Web site at *http://www.microsoft.com/mspress/books/5029.asp*. Clicking the Companion Content link takes you to a page from which you can download the samples.

The sample files can also be found on the book's companion CD, along with other supplemental content. To access those files, insert the companion CD in your computer's CD-ROM drive and make a selection from the menu that appears. If the AutoRun feature is not enabled on your system (if a menu doesn't appear when you insert the disc in your computer's CD-ROM drive), run StartCD.exe in the root folder of the companion CD. Installing the sample files on your hard disk requires approximately 7.8 MB of disk space. If you have trouble running any of these files, refer to the text in the book that describes these programs.

Aside from the sample files that this book discusses, the book's supplemental content includes two eBook installations: a stand-alone eBook installation, and a Visual Studio Help eBook installation. The stand-alone eBook installation will allow you to access an electronic version of the print book directly from your desktop. The Visual Studio Help eBook installation will allow you to access a second electronic version of the print book directly from the Visual Studio .NET help system.

Visual Studio .NET Professional Trial Version

In addition to the companion CD, this book includes a DVD with an evaluation copy of Microsoft Visual Studio .NET Professional. This evaluation copy can help you follow the examples in this book and get you started learning Microsoft Visual C# .NET, but the software must be activated, and it will expire and stop working 60 days after you install it. Also, your computer must have a DVD-ROM drive. You can learn more about this evaluation copy and its system requirements at *http://msdn.microsoft.com/vstudio/productinfo/trial.asp*.

Support

Every effort has been made to ensure the accuracy of this book and the contents of the companion CD. Microsoft Press provides corrections for books through the World Wide Web at the following address:

http://www.microsoft.com/mspress/support

To connect directly to the Microsoft Press Knowledge Base and enter a query regarding a question or an issue that you may have, go to:

http://www.microsoft.com/mspress/support/search.asp

If you have comments, questions, or ideas regarding this book or the companion content, or questions that are not answered by querying the Knowledge Base, please send them to Microsoft Press via e-mail to:

mspinput@microsoft.com

Or via postal mail to:
Microsoft Press
Attn: *Microsoft Visual C# .NET (Core Reference)* Editor
One Microsoft Way
Redmond, WA 98052-6399

Please note that product support is not offered through the above addresses. For product support information, please visit the Microsoft Support Web site at:

http://support.microsoft.com

Part I

Introducing Microsoft Visual C# .NET

1

A Tour of Visual Studio .NET and Visual C# .NET

This chapter introduces you to Microsoft Visual Studio .NET and Microsoft Visual C# .NET. In this chapter, you'll tour Visual Studio .NET and Visual C# .NET, and you'll see how Visual C# is used to write software for the Microsoft .NET platform. Even if you have experience with earlier versions of Visual Studio, you'll be surprised at the new features in Visual Studio .NET. Visual C# .NET offers great support for rapid application development (RAD), including features that make it easy to develop the basic elements of a program with just a few mouse clicks. A large number of project templates are available, including templates for Web and Microsoft Windows applications, XML Web services, and various types of components. You'll also find cool productivity enhancements such as the Task List window, which simplifies the job of tracking the work that remains to be done on your project, and the Dynamic Help window, which automatically provides a list of relevant help topics as you're working. Visual C# .NET also includes features that are unique in the Visual Studio .NET family, such as documentation comments, which Visual C# .NET can use to automatically generate HTML pages.

This chapter also introduces the basics of writing software using the Microsoft .NET Framework. You'll write and build your first Visual C# program, using one of the project templates included with Visual C#, and then we'll look at the layout of a simple Visual C# program.

Creating Applications for the .NET Platform

All applications written with Visual C# are written using the .NET Framework. The .NET Framework provides the class libraries that simplify programming in Visual C#, and it also provides the runtime support you need to execute and manage your code. In this section, we'll look at the .NET Framework and assemblies, which are the unit of reuse, versioning, and deployment in the .NET platform.

The .NET Framework

A *framework* is commonly thought of as a set of class libraries that aid in the development of applications. The .NET Framework is more than just a set of classes. The .NET Framework is targeted by compilers using a wide variety of programming languages (over twenty at the time of this writing). These languages are used to create a wide range of applications, including everything from small components that run on handheld devices to large Microsoft ASP.NET applications that span Web farms, where multiple Web servers act together to improve the performance and fault tolerance of a Web site. The .NET Framework is responsible for providing a basic platform that these applications can share. This basic platform includes a runtime set of services that oversee the execution of applications. A key responsibility of the runtime is to manage execution so that software written by different programming languages uses classes and other types safely.

The Common Language Runtime

The *common language runtime* is responsible for managing and executing code written for the .NET Framework. Code that's compiled with the Visual C# .NET compiler always runs with the help of the runtime and is known as *managed code*. The runtime is responsible for overseeing all aspects of code execution, including the following tasks:

■   Determining how and when code should be loaded and managing the layout of objects in memory. As your code executes, the runtime determines which classes and methods are required for execution and compiles them as needed. This process is discussed later in this chapter, in the section "Compiling Assemblies for Execution."

- Handling the memory needs of managed code. The garbage collection mechanism used by the .NET Framework is discussed in more detail in Chapter 3.

- Ensuring type safety for the code the runtime executes. The runtime is responsible for guaranteeing that classes and other types are used in a safe manner.

- Handling and propagating errors in managed code using a common error-handling framework based on exceptions.

- Maintaining security for the runtime and your applications. Security in the .NET Framework takes two forms: *code access security,* which is used to ensure that code is executed in a safe context, and *role-based security,* which controls access to system resources.

Type Safety and the Runtime

The runtime ensures *type safety* for applications and components. The runtime notion of type safety extends beyond the traditional notion, which simply guarantees that types interact with each other in a predictably safe way. For example, a traditional view of type safety is that a variable that refers to a string shouldn't occasionally hold an integer value. This sort of type safety is enforced by the Visual C# .NET compiler.

The runtime enforces a broader view of type safety that guarantees that types and variables are never used in a way that's dangerous to the runtime or to neighboring applications or components. Types such as classes or structures can be accessed only in specific ways. For example, access to memory locations is allowed only at offsets that correspond to actual fields in a class or a structure. This broader view of type safety helps ensure that multiple applications and components can be executed without interfering with each other.

Type safety is an important part of the .NET security architecture, and the runtime uses type safety to keep applications working robustly. The runtime can offer greater assurances that code will execute properly when code can be verified as type-safe, a process that occurs when your code is compiled into its final machine code format. Many languages that target the .NET platform, including Visual C#, generate code that can be verified to ensure type safety. Code that can be verified as type-safe is allowed to run with a lower level of trust than code that isn't verifiable.

Understanding Assemblies

Applications built for Windows typically have dependencies on one or more dynamic-link libraries (DLLs). Often these DLLs are components that are shared with other applications, and sometimes these DLLs contain Component Object

Model (COM) classes that are registered in the system registry. Unfortunately, when these components are updated or improperly installed, existing applications can be broken—a situation commonly known as "DLL hell". The .NET Framework seeks to avoid DLL hell through the use of *assemblies*—self-describing modules that replace the notion of DLLs and executable files (EXEs).

The Visual C# .NET compiler doesn't generate machine code that can be directly executed on your computer. Instead, your project's source code is compiled into an assembly, as shown in Figure 1-1.

Figure 1-1.   The Visual C# .NET compiler generating an assembly from your source code.

As you can see in Figure 1-1, an assembly has two parts: *intermediate language* (IL) and *metadata*.

- **Intermediate language (IL)**   Contains the executable portion of the program. IL is similar to the output from the first pass of a compiler. It can't be executed directly on your computer because it hasn't been translated into the binary format that your computer's processor recognizes. Instead, it must undergo a final compilation pass by a compiler that's part of the .NET Framework, as described later in this chapter, in the section "Compiling Assemblies for Execution."

- **Metadata**   Describes the assembly contents. Embedding metadata into each assembly enables any assembly to be completely self-describing, simplifying many of the tasks that need to be performed when you're distributing components with older technologies. The .NET Framework uses metadata to eliminate the need for component registration. Each assembly includes information about references to other assemblies in metadata, enabling the runtime to bind assemblies together using a flexible approach that's discussed in the next section. Tools such as Visual C# .NET use metadata to simplify development; tools can simply inspect the assembly's metadata and determine the types and operations that are exported by the assembly.

Loading External Assemblies

When the common language runtime loads your application, it examines your program's metadata to determine which external assemblies are required for execution. There are two types of assemblies.

- **Private assemblies**   Used by a single application; typically located in the same directory as the application that uses them. This is the preferred method of using assemblies. Because a private assembly isn't shared with other applications, private assemblies can be easily updated or replaced, with no impact on any other applications.

- **Shared assemblies**   Intended for use by multiple applications. A shared assembly has restrictions placed on it by the runtime and must adhere to naming and versioning rules. More information about shared assemblies is provided later in this chapter, in the section "Using the Global Assembly Cache."

An application that depends on private assemblies is easily installed or moved. Just copy or move the application from its current location to a new location, and it will work perfectly. Applications that target the .NET platform require no registration, and an application that uses only .NET Framework assemblies and private assemblies can be run as soon as it's copied into its directory. There are a couple of caveats, however.

- If you're copying a .NET application to a new computer, that machine must have at least the redistributable version of the .NET runtime installed.

- If your application requires access to the user's desktop or Start menu, you'll need to make some entries in the system registry, just as with previous Windows development tools.

Compiling Assemblies for Execution

When the code in an assembly must be executed, the runtime compiles the assembly into machine code. However, the entire assembly isn't compiled in one step. Instead, each method in the assembly is compiled as it's needed, in a process known as *just-in-time compilation,* or *jitting.* Because each method is compiled as it's needed, this compilation process is much faster than simply interpreting the IL code.

As an option, you can elect to compile your assembly into processor-specific code that can be directly executed by the processor. This work isn't performed by the Visual C# .NET compiler; the tool used for this type of compilation is the Native Image Generator, or ngen.exe, which is included as part of the .NET Framework. The following command creates a native image from an assembly named hello.exe:

```
ngen hello.exe
```

The compiled native image is automatically installed into the native image assembly cache. Creating a native image is known as *prejitting* your assembly. Even if you prejit your assembly, you must deploy your nonjitted assembly; this deployment is necessary because the nonjitted assembly contains the assembly metadata and might be required if recompilation is needed due to an update in dependent assemblies.

Working with Multi-Module Assemblies

An assembly in its simplest form looks just like any EXE or DLL module that you might have developed using earlier development tools. It's possible for an assembly to consist of multiple modules, although the assembly is always the versioning unit for .NET programs. You can't upgrade a single module in a multi-module assembly; the entire assembly must be deployed or versioned as a single unit. Visual C# .NET supports building single-module assemblies using Visual Studio .NET. To build a multi-module assembly, you can use the Assembly Linker tool, al.exe, included as part of the .NET Framework.

> **Note**   There are two situations in which you might consider using multi-module assemblies. Assemblies that are downloaded from a Web site are downloaded module by module, with unused modules never requiring a download. Some efficiency can be achieved by placing rarely used classes in separate modules that most clients can avoid downloading. It's also possible to compile modules written in different programming languages, which can result in one assembly built using different language tools. However, multi-module assemblies are more difficult to compile, build, deploy, and version. Instead of building multi-module assemblies, you can achieve a similar effect with less work by simply factoring large assemblies into smaller assemblies.

Using the Global Assembly Cache

Assemblies that are employed by multiple projects can be placed in the global assembly cache, which serves as both a storage location and a registry for shared .NET components. The global assembly cache offers much more flexibility than the registration used by COM, enabling multiple versions and cultures (previously known as *locales*) of an assembly to be stored.

Although a private assembly has few restrictions on its naming, versioning, and deployment, the global assembly cache places stringent requirements on assemblies to properly identify each assembly image it stores. An assembly that meets these requirements is known as a *strong-named assembly*. The identity of a strong-named assembly consists of the following four components:

- The name of the assembly

- The assembly's version number

- A public/private key pair that uniquely identifies the assembly's creator

- An optional cultural designation for localization purposes

Assemblies are installed in the global assembly cache using Microsoft Windows Installer 2 or later. On a development machine, the .NET Framework includes the Global Assembly Cache Utility tool, gacutil.exe, which is used to add, remove, and view assembly components. Only assemblies with a strong name can be installed into the global assembly cache. Creating assemblies with strong names and installing them in the global assembly cache is discussed in Chapter 6.

Overview of Visual Studio .NET

Microsoft Visual C# is just one of the languages that uses Visual Studio .NET as its development environment. Other programming languages supplied by Microsoft that use Visual Studio .NET include Visual Basic .NET and Visual C++ .NET. In addition, companies other than Microsoft are supplying compilers for Visual Studio .NET, which will enable you to develop solutions that include Eiffel, COBOL, and other languages. All programming using these languages can take advantage of the same set of tools and features offered by Visual Studio .NET, including all of the designers and tool windows that are part of the integrated development environment (IDE) as well as the integrated help system. Although this chapter focuses on how you can use and customize Visual Studio .NET with the Visual C# programming language, most of this information will apply to all Visual Studio .NET languages.

The Start Page

The Visual Studio .NET Start Page, shown in Figure 1-2, provides a home base for obtaining information and services that extend beyond your machine. Many of the tabs available to you on the Start Page require an Internet connection. These tabs provide late-breaking information about Visual Studio .NET, provide links to new downloads, and enable you to host Web services with just a couple of mouse clicks.

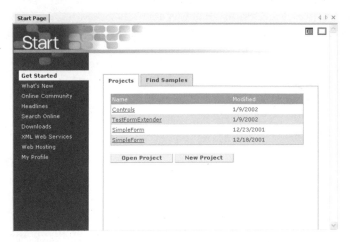

Figure 1-2.   The Visual Studio .NET Start Page.

Specifically, the Visual Studio .NET Start Page contains the following tabs:

- **Get Started** The Get Started tab is displayed initially and includes a list of solutions that you've worked with recently. (See the section "Creating Visual C# Solutions" later in this chapter for a description of a solution.) When you first launch Visual C# .NET, the list of solutions will be empty. Later the list will contain links to your most recent projects. This tab also includes a link for reporting Visual Studio .NET bugs. If you have a connection to the Internet, Visual Studio .NET will check for service packs and add a link to the update page when a service pack is available.

- **What's New** The What's New tab is a Web page that has the latest updates and information about Visual Studio .NET. This tab includes additional up-to-date content that's downloaded from the Microsoft Web site if you have an Internet connection.

- **Online Community** The Online Community tab has a selection of newsgroups and Web sites for Visual Studio .NET developers.

- **Headlines** The Headlines tab contains information from the Microsoft Developer Network (MSDN) Web site, including the latest features, technical information, news, and links to relevant knowledge base articles. To use this tab, you must have a connection to the Internet.

- **Search Online**   The Search Online tab provides access to online searching of the MSDN database. To use this tab, you must have a connection to the Internet.

- **Downloads**   The Downloads tab provides links to downloads and code samples that are related to developing with Visual C# .NET and Visual Studio .NET. To use this tab, you must have a connection to the Internet.

- **XML Web Services**   The XML Web Services tab allows you to search for XML Web services you want to use in your current project. To use this tab, you must have a connection to the Internet.

- **Web Hosting**   The Web Hosting tab provides information about Web hosting options that are available to you as a .NET developer using Visual C# .NET. Visual Studio .NET includes *one-click hosting,* a simplified way to host your applications. (One-click hosting is described in the next section.) To use this tab, you must have a connection to the Internet.

- **My Profile**   The My Profile tab is used to configure the Visual Studio .NET user interface according to predefined profile elements. This tab is discussed in the section "Changing Your User Profile."

Taking Advantage of One-Click Hosting

One-click hosting enables you to upload Web applications and services to a service provider with a single mouse click, which allows you to easily upload a Web application or a Web service to a central location that can easily be used by others. One-click hosting is useful for demonstration or testing purposes, as well as for deploying small applications. The Web Hosting tab on the Visual Studio .NET Start Page includes a current list of companies that are participating in one-click hosting and offering free trial periods.

Changing Your User Profile

The Visual Studio .NET user interface can be adjusted to suit your preferences by modifying settings on the My Profile tab on the Visual Studio .NET Start Page. By selecting a user profile, you can identify yourself as a developer experienced with Visual C++, Visual Basic, or other tools. Visual Studio .NET will use this information to orient toolbars and other windows in a way that's more familiar to you. You also can set the keyboard and windows schemes separately to match earlier versions of Microsoft programming tools. For example, you can set your keyboard mapping to match Visual C++ 2 and your window layout to match Visual C++ 6.

The My Profile tab also enables you to define a default help filter so that help results are returned for a specific programming language or technology that you use (or ask questions about) most often. You also can choose to have help shown in an external window instead of in the default internal window.

Visual Studio .NET Windows

Visual Studio .NET has a large number of windows, toolbars, and Toolbox windows that you'll use when developing your Visual C# applications. The environment is completely customizable, and the location and appearance of most windows can be easily modified to suit your needs. The default Visual Studio .NET layout is shown in Figure 1-3.

Figure 1-3.   The Visual Studio .NET development environment.

Visual Studio .NET has two modes for managing its child windows, as follows:

■   By default, child windows are tabbed and are stacked to conserve screen real estate. (Figure 1-3 shows Visual Studio .NET in tabbed-document mode.) Open files are selected by clicking on tabs that identify each open file.

■   Optionally, you can display child windows using the Multiple Document Interface (MDI), which manages child windows as overlapped windows that are contained within the main Visual Studio .NET window. In this mode, child windows are allowed to overlap, as shown in Figure 1-4.

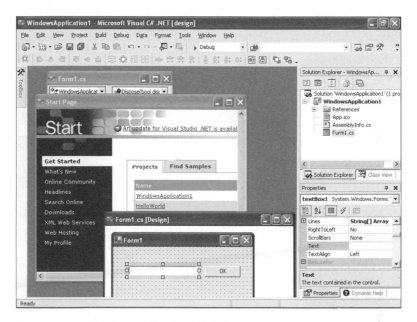

Figure 1-4.   The Visual Studio .NET development environment in MDI mode.

In addition to the child windows used for editing text and forms, Visual Studio .NET has a number of windows that are located around the edges of its main window. The following sections discuss those windows.

Solution Explorer

Solution Explorer displays a tree of the current Visual Studio .NET solution. Using Solution Explorer, you can browse through all the projects that make up the current solution, as well as the files that belong to each project.

Double-clicking a project file will open the file for editing. Opening a file will change the menu and toolbar items that are available. For example, if you open an XML file, a top-level menu item for XML operations will be added to the main menu. Right-clicking on any element in Solution Explorer will display a shortcut menu with actions that you can perform on that element. For example, the shortcut menu for the solution icon allows you to perform tasks such as adding a new project to the solution, whereas the shortcut menu for a project enables you to add new items to the project and perform other project-related activities.

Class View

The Class View window displays the class and type hierarchy for the current project and is used to traverse the project's type hierarchy. Clicking an element that's declared in your project will open the source code editor at the point of declaration. If you click on an element that's part of the .NET Framework, the Object Browser window will open for that element.

Resource View

The Resource View window is used to view resource files associated with a project. If your project contains resources such as menus, string tables, and dialog boxes, those resources can be accessed in this window. The Resource View window is normally displayed only for projects that have an associated resource (.rc) file.

Properties

The Properties window is used to declaratively set properties for different elements of your solution. The contents of this window vary depending on the type of item you're currently working with. If you click an icon in Solution Explorer, properties for the selected item will be displayed. If you're working with user interface controls or forms, many of the control and form properties can be set through this window. Likewise, if you're working with an HTML or XML document, object model properties for these documents can be set in this window.

Task List

The Task List window provides a running list of tasks that must be completed. This window is hidden by default. To display the Task List window, choose Other Windows from the View menu and choose Task List, or press Ctrl+Alt+K. Each item in the task list includes a category, a description, a file name, and a line number; double-clicking a task will open the source editor at the location indicated by the file name and line number. Depending on the task's category, the entry can also have a priority that can be used to sort the tasks or a check box that can be used to indicate whether the task has been completed.

Initially, the task list contains only build errors; however, it can be used to display a wide range of other tasks, including the following categories:

■   **Comment tasks**   These tasks are defined inside comment marks and are useful for tagging sections of code that require further attention. Visual Studio .NET defines the tokens *TODO*, *HACK*, and *UNDONE*. Comments that begin with these tokens will be displayed in the task list.

- **Shortcut tasks**   These tasks are created by right-clicking in the source code editor and choosing Add Task List Shortcut from the shortcut menu. Shortcut tasks are easy to create and useful when you don't need to associate a comment with the new task. You can specify a priority for a shortcut task by clicking in the leftmost column of the task and then choosing one of the displayed priorities. After the task has been completed, select the task's check box to mark the task as finished.

- **User-defined tasks**   These tasks are created by defining a comment token, as described later in this chapter, in the section "The Environment Category."

To specify the categories of items that will be shown in the task list, choose Show Tasks from the View menu. Alternatively, you can right-click in the Task List window, select Show Tasks from the shortcut menu, and then select the task category you want the task list to show. In addition to specifying a task category to be displayed, you can display all tasks or show only tasks that are checked or only tasks that are unchecked. Click on the task list header to sort the tasks based on priority, category, checked state, or any other displayed field.

Server Explorer

Server Explorer provides access to system services that are available on your machine as well as on other machines on your network. Normally, Server Explorer is tucked away under the edge of the Visual Studio .NET window, with just a small icon visible, as shown earlier in Figure 1-3. If you position the mouse pointer over the Server Explorer icon, the window expands to display a list of servers available on your network, as shown in Figure 1-5. To lock the Server Explorer window in place, click the pin icon in the upper-right; this will prevent the window from auto-hiding until the pin icon is clicked again.

Figure 1-5.   The Server Explorer window, which provides access to system services.

Server Explorer provides easy access to event logs, databases, performance counters, and other system services. Server Explorer is more than just a console for viewing information; you can drag objects from Server Explorer into your project, and Visual C# .NET will automatically generate code to make use of the new objects in your project. For example, to add a database connection to a Windows application, you can simply drag a database icon from Server Explorer to an open form in the Visual Studio .NET Windows Forms Designer. Adding database connections will be covered in detail in Chapter 18.

Toolbox

The Toolbox window contains items that can be easily added to your projects. Each tool category is located on a separate tab in the Toolbox window; clicking a tab displays the items in that category. For example, in Figure 1-6, the Web Forms tab is open, showing a number of controls and elements that are useful when you're creating a Web form.

Figure 1-6.   The Web Forms tab of the Toolbox window, which provides easy access to commonly used items.

Visual Studio .NET will populate the Toolbox window with tool categories that are relevant to your current project. For example, a Web application will have Toolbox items that provide data access and controls for Web Forms. You can control the behavior of the Toolbox window through a shortcut menu that appears when you right-click in the Toolbox window.

Other Windows

Visual Studio .NET includes a number of additional windows that you might find useful on occasion. You can display each of these windows by choosing Other Windows from the View menu and selecting the window you want Visual Studio .NET to show. Some of the windows available in the Other Windows menu are described here:

- **Object Browser** The Object Browser window is used to explore the types that are available in your solution. All projects in the current solution are listed as top-level nodes in the Object Browser window, as are all explicitly referenced assemblies from the .NET Framework. By expanding the nodes in the Object Browser window, you can view the enclosed namespaces, classes, structures, and all other types, as well as type members. In addition to basic structural information, the Object Browser window provides documentation for the elements it displays.

- **Stack Trace** The Stack Trace window is used during debugging to display the current call stack. The call stack includes information such as the method names in the stack, the current line number within each method, and parameter-related data.

- **Output** The Output window contains information about the most recent build status of your solution and displays output information during debugging.

- **Command Window** The Command Window is used to issue commands to the Visual Studio .NET IDE, as well as to evaluate statements while debugging your Visual C# projects. For example, to display the Find In Files dialog box, simply type the following line in the Command Window, followed by a carriage return:

```
>Edit.FindInFiles
```

  Using the Command Window while debugging is discussed in Chapter 9.

- **Favorites** The Visual Studio .NET Favorites window is an extension of the Internet Explorer Favorites window. Items in the Visual Studio .NET Favorites window are shared with the Internet Explorer Favorites folder. The Favorites window includes two icons that you can use to add the current item to your Favorites window and to manage items in your Favorites folder.

Docking and Tabbing Windows

By default, Visual Studio .NET child windows are initially docked—that is, the windows are attached to one of the edges of the main Visual Studio .NET window. Many of the windows contain tabs and appear to be stacked on top of each other. Visual Studio .NET allows you to change the size, docking state, and tabbing for all child windows by simply dragging the windows to new locations.

To undock a window, simply drag it by its title bar away from its docked position. The window will undock and follow the mouse pointer. As you drag the window, an outline will show its new size and location. If you drag a tabbed window by its title bar, the entire set of tabbed windows will undock together. Double-clicking the title bar will restore the window to its previous location; dragging the window close to the edge of the main Visual Studio .NET window will cause it to dock in that position.

To untab a window from its current collection of windows, drag the window away from its current position by dragging its tab. The window will revert to an untabbed state and will follow the mouse pointer. As with docking operations, the outline of the dragged window is displayed to assist you in positioning the window. To force a window to be tabbed with other windows, drag the window over the window with which it will be tabbed. Position the mouse pointer over the target window's title bar, and when the dragging outline changes to include the outline of a tab, drop the window to complete the dragging operation. If the target window already has tabs, you can target an existing tab instead of the window's title bar.

Visual Studio .NET Options

Customization of the Visual Studio .NET environment is performed through the Options dialog box, shown in Figure 1-7, which is opened by choosing Options from the Tools menu.

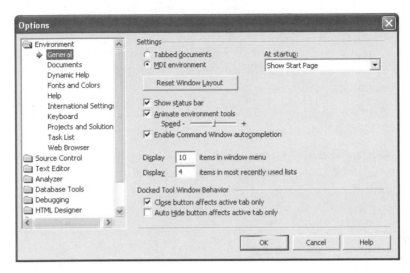

Figure 1-7.   The Visual Studio .NET Options dialog box, which allows you to customize the behavior and appearance of Visual Studio .NET.

You can use the Options dialog box to customize the behavior and appearance of Visual Studio .NET. Configuration options are grouped into categories and subcategories that appear in a tree view. To modify a particular option, you first navigate to the category and subcategory of the option, and then update the settings shown on that specific dialog box page. The Visual Studio .NET Options dialog box includes a large number of settings, many of which are outside the scope of this chapter. In this section, we'll look at some of the more common Environment and Text Editor category options.

The Environment Category

The Environment category includes configuration options that affect the Visual Studio .NET development environment. Options in this category are not related to a specific programming language. Some of the more commonly used configuration settings are described here:

■ **General**   The General page includes settings to specify whether child windows should be tabbed or use MDI, as well as menu and status bar behavior.

■ **Documents**   The Documents page is used to control how documents are handled in Visual Studio .NET. For example, you can specify how Visual Studio .NET handles open documents that are changed by external programs.

- **Dynamic Help**   The Dynamic Help page is used to enable or disable dynamic help for specific categories or types of help. Although Dynamic Help is a useful feature, disabling it will improve the performance of Visual Studio .NET, especially on underpowered machines.

- **Fonts And Colors**   The Fonts And Colors page is used to set the fonts used for various windows in Visual Studio .NET.

- **Help**   The Help page allows you to configure the settings for online help, such as the help collection that's used by default, the preferred language for online help, and whether online help is displayed in an internal window or in a separate window external to Visual Studio .NET.

- **International Settings**   The International Settings page is used to select the default language when multiple languages are installed on your computer.

- **Keyboard**   The Keyboard page is used to control the keyboard bindings for Visual Studio .NET. You can choose from predetermined mapping schemes or specify new custom key mappings for commands.

- **Projects And Solutions**   The Projects And Solutions page sets the default location for Visual Studio .NET projects. This page also specifies build behavior, such as the treatment of open files and whether the Output or Task List windows should be displayed.

- **Task List**   The Task List page is used to configure how task list items are managed within Visual Studio .NET. Visual Studio .NET is initially configured to warn you before a task item is deleted or if a new task item is initially hidden. You can override that behavior on this page. You can also define new comment tokens that identify particular types of tasks. New comment tokens are case-sensitive. For example, if your new comment token is *FIXME*, a comment that begins with *FixMe* won't be added to the task list.

- **Web Browser**   The Web Browser page enables you to set options for the Home and Search pages and configure Internet Explorer options.

The Text Editor Category

The Text Editor category includes options for editing source files inside Visual Studio .NET. Configuration settings that apply to all types of source files are set on the General page. This page includes basic settings that relate to how the editor margins are displayed, as well as generic settings such as the setting that allows drag-and-drop editing within the Text Editor window.

Each type of source file has its own configuration page. For example, Visual C# and XML files can have different configuration settings. Language-specific settings pages enable you to configure settings such as word wrap (off by default) and line numbers (also off by default).

Visual Studio .NET Help

The online help system in Visual Studio .NET is based on the MSDN Library and is significantly better than online help systems in earlier versions of Visual Studio. Improved filtering and searching options make this version of online help much more useful. In addition, vendors of tools and components that integrate with Visual Studio .NET can now safely integrate their product documentation with the online help system, making it much easier to get help for third-party tools and components.

Using Dynamic Help

Dynamic help is a great new feature in Visual Studio .NET. As you work with the various tools in Visual Studio .NET, the dynamic help system searches through the MSDN Library for relevant help topics. The list of help topics is updated as you use different tools or windows in Visual Studio .NET. As you edit a Visual C# source file, the Dynamic Help window is automatically updated to include help on the keywords or classes that you're typing.

Searching with Online Help

You can display the Search window for online help by choosing Search from the Help menu. A predefined set of filters can be used to narrow your search. For example, if you're interested in searching only through .NET Framework Software Development Kit (SDK) topics, you can easily narrow your search to include only those items. The Results window, which opens automatically when you conduct a search, displays the results of the search.

Using the Online Help Index

The online help keyword index is displayed by choosing Index from the Help menu. Using the index is sometimes faster than searching when you know the title of the item you're looking for. When the index search returns multiple topics, the list of results will be displayed in the Results window.

Creating Visual C# Solutions

New projects are created by choosing New Project from the File menu. Visual Studio .NET displays the New Project dialog box, as shown in Figure 1-8. This dialog box gives you access to all available project types, including Database, Setup, and Deployment projects. If you have Visual Basic .NET or other languages installed, you can create new projects in those languages from this dialog box.

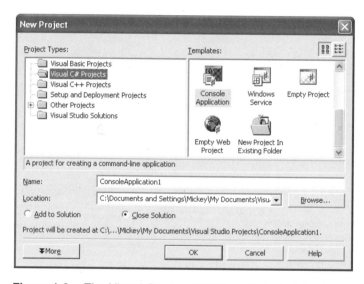

Figure 1-8. The Visual Studio .NET New Project dialog box, which is used to create new projects and solutions.

All projects are created as part of a solution, which can contain multiple projects of different types. A solution ties together all the projects and files that you're working with in an instance of the Visual Studio .NET IDE. By default, when you create a new project, the current solution is closed and a new solution is created to house your project. To override this behavior and add a new project to the current solution, select the Add To Solution radio button instead of the Close Solution radio button in the New Project dialog box.

Using Project Templates

A number of templates are available for creating new Visual C# projects. Each template will create a project skeleton, usually with an initial set of source files added to the project. Each project includes an AssemblyInfo.cs source file, which is used to configure properties for your compiled assembly.

Each Visual C# project template will provide a default name for the project. In most cases, you should override the suggested project name unless you're happy with names like ConsoleApplication1. The New Project dialog box also allows you to specify a location for your project.

The available templates for Visual C# projects are listed here:

- **Windows Application**   Creates a Windows Forms application that initially consists of a single form. The class that supports the initial form also provides the main entry point to the application.

- **Class Library**   Creates a project containing a single Visual C# class, with no specified inheritance. You can use this class as a starting point to create new class libraries of any type.

- **Windows Control Library**   Creates a project that you can use to develop reusable user interface controls for Windows applications. The project includes one class, which is derived from *System.Windows.Forms.UserControl*.

- **ASP.NET Web Application**   Creates an ASP.NET project, including all the necessary files for a simple Web application. The project includes a number of files specific to Web applications that will be discussed in greater detail in Chapter 20.

- **ASP.NET Web Service**   Creates a special type of Web application that uses the Simple Object Access Protocol (SOAP) to expose services that can be invoked by SOAP clients.

- **Web Control Library**   Creates a project that you can use to develop reusable user interface controls for Web applications. This type of project is discussed in more detail in Chapter 20.

- **Console Application**   Creates a command-line application for Windows. This type of project includes one Visual C# .NET class that includes the main entry point for the application.

- **Windows Service**   Creates a Windows service application, a special type of long-running process that runs on Microsoft Windows NT, Microsoft Windows 2000, and Microsoft Windows XP. This type of application runs in its own Windows session and will continue to run even if the user logs off.

- **Empty Project**   Creates a Windows project with no source files. This type of project is useful if you're planning to add existing files to the project.

- **Empty Web Project**   Creates a Web application project with no source files. This type of project is useful if you'll be using files that already exist.

- **New Project In Existing Folder**   Creates a new, empty project in an existing folder, instead of creating a new project folder.

When you create a project using the ASP.NET Web Application, ASP.NET Web Service, or Empty Web Project template, the location of a machine that's running Microsoft Internet Information Services (IIS) 5.1 or later is specified as the project location. If your development machine has IIS installed, you can specify *localhost* as the project location.

Generating a New Solution

Each project template creates its own unique set of files used to compile your project. A subdirectory with the same name as the project is created to contain the project's files; by default, its location is under My Documents\Visual Studio Projects. All project files are located in the project directory except for Web applications and Web services. For these projects, most files are uploaded into a virtual directory accessible to your Web server, with only a solution file remaining in the project directory.

The first project we'll look at is the classic Hello World program written in Visual C#.

> **Note**   This project, like all the projects discussed in this book, is available on the companion CD.

To create a basic HelloWorld project, open the New Project dialog box, and select the Visual C# Projects folder in the Project Types list. Next select Console Application from the Templates list, and change the project name to HelloWorld. It's not necessary to change the default location of the project; however, you might want to make note of the location so that you can access the project later. When you're happy with the name and location of the project, click OK, and Visual Studio .NET will create the project for you.

The files generated for the HelloWorld solution fall into two categories: files that define the solution and the project, and source files that are compiled to generate the project assembly.

Solution and Project Files

When a new project such as HelloWorld is created, it's usually created as part of a new solution. The solution will have the same name as the project, although each can be renamed after the project is created. The project and solution files for the HelloWorld project include the following:

- **HelloWorld.suo**   A hidden binary file that contains current user options for the solution

- **HelloWorld.sln**   A text file that contains information about the solution

- **HelloWorld.csproj**   An XML file that defines the Visual C# project

- **HelloWorld.csproj.user**   An XML file that contains user-specific project information

Source Files

The source files generated for a project vary for each type of project template. The specific files that are generated will be discussed throughout this book as we examine each project type. All the project types share a few similarities, however. For example, all Visual C# projects include an AssemblyInfo.cs file, which is used to define assembly characteristics. Each project's source files also define a default namespace that encloses all classes and other types in the project. This default namespace is initially set to the name of the project but should be changed to a more unique name if your project is to be distributed to others.

Layout of a Typical Visual C# Program

Let's take a closer look at the HelloWorld project created in the previous section. Although this program is quite simple, it demonstrates the basic principles of developing programs using Visual C#. As mentioned, the HelloWorld solution includes one project, also named HelloWorld. The HelloWorld project contains a Visual C# source file named Class1.cs, which is shown here:

```
using System;
namespace HelloWorld
{
    /// <summary>
    /// Summary description for Class1
    /// </summary>
    class Class1
    {
```

```
        static void Main(string[] args)
        {
            //
            // TODO: Add code to start application here.
            //
        }
    }
}
```

This Visual C# code listing shows Class1.cs as it's generated by the Visual C# project template. This is a basic Visual C# console-mode program; as written, it does nothing except start and exit. We'll add some enhancements to the program in the following sections. For now, let's look at the program as is.

Commenting Your Source

One of the first things you might notice is that comment lines in C# begin with two or more slashes. It is also possible to use comment blocks as in C and C++. Comment blocks begin with /* and end with */. The region inside a comment block can span multiple lines, like this:

```
/*
    HelloWorld - a simple C# example by Mickey Williams
*/
```

Comment blocks can't be nested.

Using Documentation Comments

You might have noticed that one section of the source code has comments that begin with three slashes. This is a *documentation comment*. Documentation comments are one of the new features of the Visual C# .NET editor. These comments can be extracted during compilation to create documentation for your project.

Two types of documentation can be generated, as follows:

- An XML document that includes detailed information about the current solution. This XML can be processed using standard XML techniques to perform searches or even transformation into other documentation formats.

- A set of HTML pages that describe your solution, including cross-references among the different solution elements, with separate files for different solution elements.

To create documentation comments, simply move to the line above any type, namespace, method, or variable declaration and type three slashes above the program element you're commenting about, as shown here:

```
///
```

The editor will automatically create a comment block for you. A comment block for a public or an internal method declaration will include parameter names and return values. The editor inserts comment tags in XML format, with each tag identifying some part of the source element that's documented by the comments.

Extracting Documentation Comments

To generate documentation pages for your solution, choose Build Comment Web Pages from the Tools menu. By default, the Build Comment Web Pages dialog box is configured to generate comments for the entire solution. If your solution has multiple projects, you can pick one or more projects from the solution to have its comments generated. You also can specify a directory that will receive the generated Web pages.

The Build Comment Web Pages dialog box also enables you to add the start page for the documentation to your Internet Explorer Favorites list. Click OK to generate the documentation. The documentation start page will be displayed inside Visual Studio .NET, and you can immediately start browsing your documentation pages.

Extracting the raw XML documentation is slightly more complex. You must first open the Property Pages dialog box for the project by right-clicking the project's icon in Solution Explorer and choosing Properties from the shortcut menu. Select the Build category in the Configuration Properties folder. Enter the name of the XML file as the XML Documentation File property. This path is project-relative. Each time your project is compiled, this file will be rebuilt if required. The XML file will be rebuilt whenever changes to your source code should be reflected in the XML documentation.

Using Namespaces

Namespaces are used two ways in the HelloWorld project. The following line enables simplified use of types found in the .NET Framework's *System* namespace:

```
using System;
```

Additionally, a new namespace for the HelloWorld project is created with this code:

```
namespace HelloWorld
{
    ⋮
}
```

The Visual C# project template creates a namespace that contains all of your project's types. This helps to insulate any types you create from types that might exist elsewhere in the .NET Framework. When you declare new types in your applications, you should declare them within a unique namespace, as the Console Application template did here. Namespaces are discussed in more detail in Chapter 2.

Declaring a Class

When you're programming in C#, all code executes within a class—there are no global functions or methods in C#. The Visual C# project template has created a class for us and named it *Class1*. (We'll rename it with a more meaningful name later in this chapter, in the section "Providing Output for Hello World.")

Classes are declared using the *class* keyword, followed by the name of the class, as shown here:

```
class Class1
{
    ⋮
}
```

All declarations of methods, types, and member variables made within the curly braces that follow the class name are *members* of the class. Classes and their declaration syntax are discussed in more detail in Chapter 2. For now, it's enough to understand that a C# class usually contains data members and methods. In this case, *Class1* defines a single method named *Main*.

Defining a *Main* Method

Every console-mode application has a *Main* method that serves as the entry point (or starting point) for your application. Although it's possible to have more than one method named *Main* in a project, there's no reason to do so, and you'd be required to specify which of the methods is the real entry point for your application.

Main can be defined in any of the following ways:

```
static void Main(string[] args)
{
    // No return value; accepts command-line parameters
}


static int Main(string[] args)
{
    // Returns integer value; accepts command-line parameters
}


static void Main()
{
    // No return value; no command-line parameters
}


static int Main()
{
    // Returns integer value; no command-line parameters
}
```

Keep in mind that C# is a case-sensitive language—although *Main* is a valid name, *main* and *MAIN* aren't. The two versions of *Main* that accept command-line arguments include a parameter declaration for a variable named *args*. Using command-line arguments as parameters passed to *Main* is discussed in Chapter 5.

Compiling Your Project

At this point, you can compile your solution by choosing Build Solution from the Build menu or by pressing Ctrl+Shift+B. The compilation should be successful, as shown in the output window, which should look something like this:

```
Build started: Project: HelloWorld, Configuration: Debug .NET

Preparing resources...
Updating references...
Performing main compilation...

Build complete -- 0 errors, 0 warnings
Building satellite assemblies...

--------------------- Done ------        ----------

    Build: 1 succeeded, 0 failed, 0 skipped
```

This output shows that a debug compilation, or build, of the HelloWorld project was started and that the build was completed with no warnings or errors. The output assembly is placed in the bin\debug subdirectory of your project's directory and will be named HelloWorld.exe.

You can execute this program either on the command line or through Windows Explorer; however, the Hello World program doesn't actually do anything yet. In the next section, we'll add an output statement.

Providing Output for Hello World

The first step I take with my projects is to give the classes meaningful names. *Class1* is a perfectly valid name for a C# class, but it doesn't really help describe the class's purpose. Because the class contains the entry point for the Hello World application, I've renamed it HelloWorldApp. The following code also has additional comments and an output statement that displays *Hello World* on the console:

```
using System;

namespace HelloWorld
{
    /// <summary>
    /// A C# version of Hello World!
    /// </summary>
    class HelloWorldApp
    {
        static void Main(string[] args)
        {
            // Display a hello message.
            Console.WriteLine("Hello, World!");
        }
    }
}
```

This version of Hello World displays a message in the command-line screen or console by executing the following line:

```
Console.WriteLine("Hello, World!");
```

This line of code invokes the *WriteLine* method of the *Console* class and passes a string as a parameter. String literals such as "Hello, World!" are always enclosed in quotation marks. The *WriteLine* method offers many options for displaying and formatting text output. In the next few chapters, you'll use the *Console* class for accepting input from the user as well as writing output to the user.

Conclusion

Visual C# .NET and Visual Studio .NET include a number of features that simplify .NET development. Visual Studio .NET offers an improved online help system and improved form designers, and it can be easily customized to suit your needs. Visual C# .NET also includes the ability to extract documentation comments, which can be used to automatically generate HTML documents.

The .NET Framework includes a large number of classes and other types that are used to develop your application, but the .NET Framework is more than just a class library. It also includes the common language runtime, which manages and supports code written for the .NET platform.

Visual C# is a new object-oriented language in the C family of languages, and it's easily understood by existing C and C++ programmers. In addition, its clean syntax and simple programming model (much simpler than C++) make it an easy language to learn, even if you're not currently using C or C++.

2

C# Basics

Microsoft Visual C# .NET provides a rich environment for developing object-oriented applications and components using the C# programming language. Visual C# .NET leverages the Microsoft .NET Framework to provide a rich set of built-in types that you can use when building your own classes. A subset of these types can be used for interacting with other .NET languages. The .NET Framework also provides an extensive class library that you can use and extend with Visual C# .NET.

The basic types that you can create in C# include the following:

- **Classes**   Define new types and methods for interacting with those types

- **Exceptions**   Describe errors that occur in your classes

- **Interfaces**   Group related methods together

■ **Structures**   Aggregate other types into a new type

■ **Enumerations**   Define a range of named values for a type

Each of these basic types is similar to types available in other languages. In many cases, C# includes additional features that make these language constructions more useful to the component or application developer.

Note   If you're familiar with some of these features in other languages, you'll want to at least skim this material to ensure that you understand how C# compares to your previous programming language.

Basic Data Types

The C# language works seamlessly with the .NET Framework, so it should come as no surprise that the built-in data types available to you as a C# developer are also part of the .NET platform. For example, C# has a built-in *string* type that's identical to the *System.String* class included in the .NET Framework. The *string* type supports various string manipulation operations such as concatenation. Table 2-1 describes the built-in data types that are part of the C# language, along with their equivalent .NET Framework types.

Table 2-1.   Built-In C# Types and Equivalent .NET Framework Types

C# Type	.NET Framework Type	Description
bool	*System.Boolean*	Logical value that's either *true* or *false*. The default value is *false*.
byte	*System.Byte*	Unsigned byte that stores values from *0* through *255*. The default value is *0*.
sbyte	*System.SByte*	Signed byte that stores values from − *128* through *127*. The default value is *0*.
char	*System.Char*	Unsigned 16-bit Unicode character. The default value is *'\0'*.
decimal	*System.Decimal*	Decimal number not subject to rounding; often used for financial calculations. The default value is *0.0m*.

(continued)

Table 2-1.   Built-In C# Types and Equivalent .NET Framework Types *(continued)*

C# Type	.NET Framework Type	Description
double	*System.Double*	Double-precision floating-point type. The default value is *0.0d*.
float	*System.Single*	Single-precision floating-point type. The default value is *0.0f*.
int	*System.Int32*	Signed 32-bit integer type. The default value is *0*.
uint	*System.UInt32*	Unsigned 32-bit integer type. The default value is *0*.
long	*System.Int64*	Signed 64-bit integer type. The default value is *0*.
ulong	*System.UInt64*	Unsigned 64-bit integer type. The default value is *0*.
object	*System.Object*	Reference to a class instance. The default value is *null*.
short	*System.Int16*	Signed 16-bit integer type. The default value is *0*.
ushort	*System.UInt16*	Unsigned 16-bit integer type. The default value is *0*.
string	*System.String*	Reference to a string object. The default value is *null*.

Although the C# types and the types found in the .NET Framework are equivalent, you should stick with using the C# names for these types. Your code will look cleaner and be easier to read. However, if you're required to work with component developers who use other languages, you should keep Table 2-1 in mind, as it will aid in mapping types between languages.

The .NET Common Type System

The *common type system* is a specification that defines type usage in the .NET Framework common language runtime and is a key part of the .NET Framework. When you use a *string* in C#, you're using the same *string* that a Visual Basic .NET developer uses. When you use a *bool* in C#, that's the same *BOOLEAN* type used by Eiffel programmers. A big win for all .NET developers is the simplicity with which we can now share data and types, without the need for the specialized conversion layers required prior to .NET.

Another big advantage of the common type system is that the runtime can guarantee type safety for many of the .NET languages, including C#. This means that the runtime can guarantee that programs will execute safely, without accidentally overwriting memory addresses, corrupting the stack, or accidentally writing into random areas of memory.

The Common Language Specification

Rules about how languages for the .NET platform such as C# should interact with each other are specified in the Common Language Specification (CLS). The CLS contains rules about how data types should be exposed and organized so that developers employing multiple languages can reuse data types. The CLS isn't concerned with how your code is organized internally; it specifies only the behavior that's publicly exposed. If you build a component that follows all of the CLS rules, your component is said to be *CLS-compliant*. If your code breaks any of the CLS rules, the component isn't compliant and you might find that your component is unusable by programs written in languages other than the language used for your component.

CLS compliance is desirable, but it limits both the types that are exposed by your components and the way in which the components are exposed. Some programming languages don't properly handle both signed and unsigned types of the same size. For that reason, most of the unsigned C# scalar data types, other than the *byte* type, aren't CLS-compliant. Table 2-2 lists the primitive C# types and indicates whether each is CLS-compliant.

Table 2-2.   C# Primitive Types and Their CLS Compliance

C# Type	CLS Compliance
bool	Yes
byte	Yes
sbyte	No
char	Yes
decimal	Yes
double	Yes
float	Yes
int	Yes
uint	No
long	Yes
ulong	No
object	Yes
short	Yes
ushort	No
string	Yes

Classes

C# is a modern object-oriented language that encourages good object-oriented design practices. Many aspects of the C# language will be familiar to you if you've used C or C++. C# is different in some fundamental ways, however. For example, the C# language doesn't permit functions to exist outside of class declarations, which is allowed in C++. The C# language also includes a much richer class library than C++, has a unified type system, and utilizes garbage collection to free the programmer from the low-level details of memory management.

As with all object-oriented languages, C# promotes reuse through classes. A class defines a type as well as the methods and properties that are used to interact with instances of the type. For example, a class that represents an animal might include methods that represent the animal's activities (such as eating and sleeping) and properties that represent its characteristics (such as color or size).

Adding a Class in Visual C#

To add a class to an existing project in Visual C#, right-click the project icon in Solution Explorer and choose Add and then Add Class from the shortcut menu. (Alternatively, you can select the project in Solution Explorer and choose Add Class from the Project menu.) The Add New Item dialog box will be displayed, as shown in Figure 2-1.

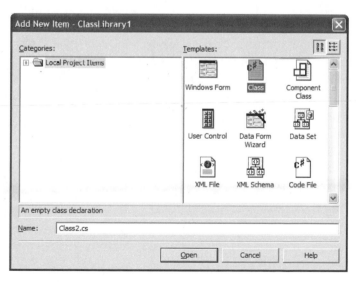

Figure 2-1.   The Add New Item dialog box, which is used to add classes and other types to a Visual C# project.

The Add New Item dialog box is used to add new classes or other types to a Visual C# project. To add a new class, click the Class icon, supply a name for the new class source file, and then click the Open button. Visual C# .NET will create the source file and open it for editing.

Declaring a Class

The following example demonstrates the syntax for declaring a class in C#:

```
public class Cat
{
    public Cat(string aName)
    {
        _name = aName;
    }
    public void Sleep()
    {
        _sleeping = true;
    }
    public void Wake()
    {
        _sleeping = false;
    }
    // Member variables
    protected bool    _sleeping;
    protected string _name;
}
```

The *Cat* class is defined using the *class* keyword. Declarations for member variables and methods that form the class are enclosed inside the outermost curly braces and make up the class declaration. Unlike C++, in C# the declaration and implementation of your class occur in the same file. This simplifies the programming model—you always know exactly which file contains the implementation of your class. By convention, each source file contains one class. You can implement multiple classes in a single source file, but there's no reason to do so and it's considered bad programming style.

There are other differences between a C# class and a C++ class, including the following:

■ In C#, every class member should have a specified accessibility level. Any member that doesn't declare its accessibility defaults to *private*.

■ There are no *#include* directives. The C# compiler will globally analyze the project and automatically resolve dependencies.

■ No semicolon is required after the class declaration. The C# compiler is intelligent enough to determine where the class ends without the need for extra punctuation.

In our example, each member of a class is preceded by the *public* or *protected* keyword, which specifies whether the member is visible and available for use outside the class. Defining the accessibility of members and classes is discussed later in this chapter, in the section "Accessibility."

Keep in mind that in the previous example, *Cat* is not an object, but a class. A class is a definition of a type, whereas an object is a particular instance of that type. To create an object from a class, use the *new* keyword, which allocates storage for an object and assigns the object reference to a variable, as in this statement:

```
Cat anastasia = new Cat();
```

This statement has two parts. The first part declares a variable of type *Cat* named *anastasia*. The second part creates a *Cat* object and stores a reference to the object in the variable named *anastasia*. The parentheses after *Cat* are required.

After creating an object, you can use member variables and methods that are exposed by the class, as shown here:

```
anastasia.Sleep();
```

Access to members is always made through the *dot* operator (.) (as shown in the preceding code). C++ sometimes requires the use of the -> or :: operator for member access. In C#, the -> and :: operators don't exist—the dot operator is the only way to access the member of a type.

Objects are never created on the stack; they're always created in an area of memory that automatically frees unused resources in a process known as *garbage collection* (discussed in detail in Chapter 3). When an object reference variable isn't attached to an object, its default value is *null* and it can't be used as a valid reference. C# won't allow a variable to be used before it's assigned a value, which eliminates many common error cases found in other programming languages. If you insist on attempting to use a null reference, as in the following code, the common language runtime will detect the null reference and generate a *NullReferenceException*:

```
Cat c = null;

// Not OK; generates a null reference exception.
c.Eat();
```

An Introduction to Inheritance

When using an object-oriented language, you're encouraged to create classes that attempt to model the real world. Continuing with our animal classes example, one approach to organizing the many types of animals would be to completely describe each animal in a separate class. To represent five types of animals, you would create five classes, with each class fully describing the characteristics of each animal, as shown in Figure 2-2.

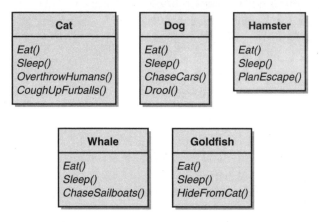

Figure 2-2.   A simple set of classes to model animals.

Figure 2-2 is a Unified Modeling Language (UML) diagram that shows five classes that model animals. UML is a common modeling tool used to describe relationships between classes. In this static class diagram, each box represents a class, and inside each is the class name and its members. As you can see, the five classes provide a simplified model of some basic animals. However, each class implements some of the same functions found in the other classes. Object-oriented design gives us a way to take advantage of the similarity between types: *inheritance.*

Inheritance enables you to look for similarities between classes and factor those similarities out into base classes that are shared by descendent classes. For example, all of our animal classes share the common characteristics *Eat* and *Sleep.* Even though some animals move on land and some swim, their common characteristics can be moved into a single class that each of the other classes can share, as shown in Figure 2-3.

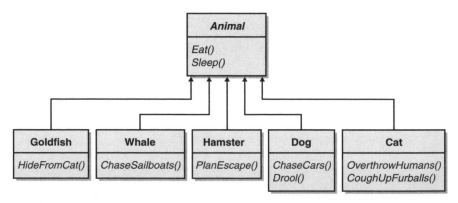

Figure 2-3.   Modeling animals using inheritance.

In Figure 2-3, a new class is introduced. The *Animal* class contains methods that are common to all of our animals. We can further categorize these animals by dividing them into types, as shown in Figure 2-4.

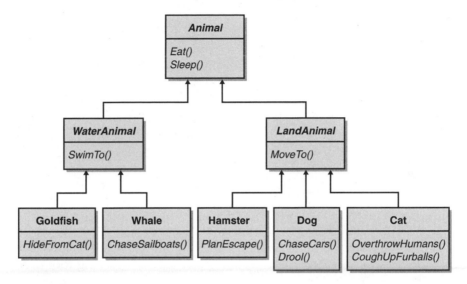

Figure 2-4. Multiple levels of inheritance.

In Figure 2-4, two new classes are introduced. The *WaterAnimal* and *Land-Animal* classes are specializations of the *Animal* class that include methods unique to those particular types of animals. As shown in Figure 2-4, the relationship between a base class and its subclasses is indicated with an arrow drawn from the subclass to the base class. Finally, each of the five original classes is a further specialization that implements only the methods unique to each particular animal.

Defining base classes in this way allows us to more easily introduce new animals into our set of classes. To add a *Penguin* class, for example, we would simply derive the new class from *WaterAnimal* and perhaps add a *RentTuxedo* method.

Declaring a Class as *abstract*

When you're declaring a hierarchy of classes such as the animal classes, the base classes are often incomplete and shouldn't be directly instantiated. Instead of directly creating an object from the *Animal* or *WaterAnimal* class, it's more appropriate to create an instance of the *Whale* or *Goldfish* class.

In C#, base classes that aren't to be directly instantiated are tagged with the *abstract* keyword, as follows:

```
abstract class Animal
{
    ⋮
}
```

Using the *abstract* keyword with your base classes allows the compiler to enforce proper use of your class hierarchy by preventing base classes from being directly instantiated.

If a method signature is defined in an abstract base class but not implemented in the class, it is marked as *abstract*, as shown here:

```
abstract class Horse
{
    abstract public void ChaseAfterBadGuys();
}
```

Abstract methods are discussed in more detail later in this chapter, in the section "Abstract Methods."

Declaring a Class as *sealed*

C# also supports the opposite of the abstract class—a class that isn't available as a base class. By declaring a class as *sealed*, you notify the compiler that the class must never be used as a base class, as follows:

```
sealed class Horse
{
}
```

Classes aren't normally sealed because doing so prevents the class from being extended in the future. However, you might want to seal a class for exactly that reason—because you want only one specific class to be used, with a specific implementation, and with no subclasses permitted. This can be for reliability reasons or for commercial purposes. Another reason to seal a base class is for performance. When a sealed class is loaded, the runtime can perform optimizations for method calls to the sealed class because it knows that no virtual method calls will be required for subclasses.

C# also permits an individual method to be declared as *sealed*, preventing that method from being overridden in a subclass.

Communicating with the Base Class

Like C++, C# allows you to access the current object through the *this* keyword. In addition, C# allows you to access the members of the immediate base class through the *base* keyword. The following example calls the *PreDraw* method of the *CommandWindow* class:

```
class MyCommandWindow: CommandWindow
{
    public void DrawShape()
    {
        base.PreDraw();
        Draw();
    }
    ⋮
}
```

The *base* keyword gives access to the immediate base class only. Returning to our animals example (as shown in Figure 2-4), you couldn't use the *base* keyword within the *Whale* class to call a method from the *Animal* class, as shown here:

```
class Whale : WaterAnimal
{
    ⋮
    // Won't work; the following line calls a WaterAnimal
    // method rather than a method from Animal.
    base.Eat();
    ⋮
}
```

The *base* keyword also is available only from within the class—it can't be called from outside the class, as shown here:

```
// Won't work; base is not allowed in this context.
BessieTheCow.base.GetPlansForWorldDomination();
```

Inheritance vs. Ownership

Inheritance is a great tool for modeling real-world problems with classes, but you should take care to use inheritance only when appropriate. Inheritance is useful when modeling what are known as *IS-A relationships,* as in the following examples:

- A Cow IS-A LandAnimal.

- A Whale IS-A WaterAnimal.

- An Airplane IS-A Vehicle.

All these cases are great prospects for inheritance. Watch out for cases in which inheritance is used to model ownership—known as *HAS-A relationships*—such as the ones shown here:

- A BaseballTeam HAS-A HomeStadium.

- A House HAS-A Foundation.

The HAS-A relationship indicates a need for a member variable instead of inheritance. These cases are not suitable for inheritance, and trying to use inheritance will likely lead to implementation difficulty.

The *object* Base Class

All types in C# are ultimately derived from the *object* class. Of course, not all classes derive directly from *object*, but if you follow the inheritance hierarchy for any type, you'll eventually come to *object*. In fact, deriving from *object* is such a fundamental aspect of programming in C# that the compiler will automatically generate the necessary code to inherit from *object* if you don't specify any inheritance for your class. This means that the following two class definitions are identical:

```
class Cat
{
    ⋮
}

class Cat: object
{
    ⋮
}
```

> **Note**   The C# *object* type is identical to the *System.Object* class found in the .NET Framework. It's considered good C# programming style to use the C# name rather than the .NET Framework name, but you can use either name freely—both refer to the same types.

Even the built-in types available to you as a C# programmer are derived from the *object* class. Because all types are based on a common base class, you can perform some useful operations on all types—unlike C++, where the built-in types missed out on some benefits of an object-oriented language. For example, in C# all types can be easily converted to string values by calling their *ToString* method, as shown here:

```
int n = 32;
string stringValue = n.ToString()
```

Or you can skip using the *int* type and just apply *ToString* to the value, as follows:

```
string stringValue = 32.ToString()
```

Other methods available through the *object* class include *GetType*, which returns a *Type* object that can be used to determine the type of an object at runtime. Still other methods deal with garbage collection, testing for equality, and cloning objects.

Members

Most C# classes have one or more members. Members in C# classes expose functionality and maintain the state of an instance. Members fall into the following categories:

- **Fields** Locations for storing data—similar to C++ member variables. Fields are described in more detail in the next section.

- **Constants** Class members with values that don't change. Constants are discussed later in this chapter, in the section "Constants."

- **Methods** Functions that perform tasks for an object or a class. Methods are described later in this chapter, in the section "Methods."

- **Constructors** Functions that are used to initialize an object when it's first created. Constructors are described later in this chapter, in the section "Constructors."

- **Destructors** Functions that are used to clean up an object as it's destroyed. Destructors are discussed later in this chapter, in the section "Destructors."

- **Properties** Functions that appear to be instance variables to clients, decoupling the client from the implementation details of the class, while providing the simplicity of direct public member access. Properties are discussed in Chapter 4.

- **Operators** Functions that define how common expression operators will interact with objects. Operators are discussed in Chapter 4.

- **Events** Used to provide notifications to clients, without the difficulties found in implementing callbacks. Events are discussed in Chapter 6.

- **Indexers** Used to enable a class instance to appear to be an array to a client. Indexers are discussed in Chapter 7.

The following sections discuss the class members you're likely to find in most C# programs. More specialized member types, such as operators and indexers, will be covered in upcoming chapters.

Fields

As mentioned, a field is a lot like a C++ member variable. A field is declared in a class by specifying its type, its name, and if necessary, its accessibility, as shown here:

```
public int _age;
```

The declaration of a field can optionally include an initial value, as follows. This value is useful when the type's default value isn't appropriate.

```
public int _answer = 42;
```

By default, each object has its own copy of every field. Fields modified in one object don't affect fields of the same name in other objects. By marking a field with the *static* modifier, the field is shared among all instances of a class, as shown here:

```
static public int _objectCount;
```

Although a static field is shared and accessible by multiple objects, there's no synchronization provided automatically. If multiple threads attempt to modify the field simultaneously, the results are undefined.

Because static fields are specific to a class rather than an object, they can't be accessed through an object reference. Instead, they must be referenced through the class name, as shown here:

```
class Cat: Animal
{
    public static int mouseEncounters;
}

static void Main()
{
    Cat c = new Cat();
    // Not allowed; must use class name for static member.
    c.mouseEncounters = 0;
    // OK
    Cat.mouseEncounters = 0;
}
```

Fields can also be declared as *readonly*, as shown here:

```
public readonly int _age;
public static int _maxClasses;
```

Marking a field as *readonly* prevents any code from modifying the field after the object has been constructed. The compiler will flag any field assignment that occurs after construction as an error. A *readonly* field declaration can include an assignment, and it can optionally be marked as *static*. A *readonly* field can be assigned a value only when it's first declared or within the constructor of its class. (More on constructors later in this chapter, in the section "Constructors.")

Constants

A constant is similar to a field, but its value isn't allowed to change from a value specified at compile time. The constant doesn't take up space in the object; instead, it's compiled into the executable where required. To declare a constant, use the *const* modifier, as follows:

```
public const int _maxSize = 9;
```

If you attempt to declare a constant member as *static*, the C# compiler will flag it as an error. A *const* member can be assigned a value only when it's first declared. Members declared as *const* behave like *static* members because they aren't associated with a particular object. There's no need to define a *const* member as *static*—just define the member as *const*, and use it via the class name.

```
ClearRange(MyClass._maxSize);
```

Methods

Methods in C# classes contain the code executed on behalf of the class. All methods in C# exist as class members because C# doesn't support stand-alone or global functions. Methods are always declared as part of the class declaration. Unlike C++, there's no way to declare a C# method implementation separately from the class declaration.

Except for constructors and destructors (which we'll look at later in this chapter, in the sections "Constructors" and "Destructors"), method declarations in C# consist of an accessibility level, a return type, a method name, and a list of zero or more formal parameters passed to the method, as shown here:

```
public int GetNextRecordId(string TableName)
{
    ⋮
}
```

If the accessibility level is omitted, the level is private by default.

Like fields, methods can be declared as *static*, and just as with fields, a static method must be called using the class name rather than using an object reference:

```
class Cat: Animal
{
    public static void ChaseMouse()
    {
```

(continued)

```
        ⋮
    }
}
class CatApp
{
    static void Main()
    {
        Cat c = new Cat();
        // Not allowed; must use class name for static member.
        c.ChaseMouse();
        // OK
        Cat.ChaseMouse();
    }
        ⋮
}
```

Method Parameters   C# doesn't support default parameters. (A default parameter allows a default value to be defined as part of the method declaration and then inserted automatically when a client invokes a method with the parameter omitted.) This feature is disallowed due to component versioning. The default parameter is injected in the caller's code—updating the default parameter would cause versioning issues for clients compiled against older versions of the class. Much of the benefit of default parameters can be obtained via method overloading or other design patterns.

By default, parameters are passed to a method by value, meaning that the method doesn't have access to the actual parameter, but only a copy of the parameter's value, as follows:

```
static void Main()
{
    int testValue = 12;
    Console.WriteLine("The test value is {0}", testValue);
    TrainInVain(testValue);
    Console.WriteLine("The test value is {0}", testValue);
}
public static void TrainInVain(int param)
{
    param = 42;
}
```

In this example, both calls to *WriteLine* display *testValue* as 12. The *TrainInVain* method changes the value of *param*, but this is only a copy of the actual parameter passed from the *Main* method. After *TrainInVain* returns to the caller, the original parameter is unchanged. When object references are passed by value, the value of the reference is passed to the method, allowing the method to have complete access to the object. However, the method can't change the value of the object reference itself.

Parameter Modifiers   The *ref* keyword is used to pass a parameter by reference, enabling the parameter's value to be updated by the called method, as shown here:

```
static void Main()
{
    int testValue = 12;
    Console.WriteLine("The test value is {0}", testValue);
    ChangeValue(ref testValue);
    Console.WriteLine("The test value is {0}", testValue);
}
public static void ChangeValue(ref int param)
{
    param = 42;
}
```

Here the first instance of *WriteLine* displays *testValue* as 12, but the second instance displays it as 42. The *ref* keyword modifies the type of the parameter and must be used by the caller as well as in the called method's parameter list. If the caller omits the *ref* keyword, the compiler will flag it as an error.

The *out* keyword is similar to *ref*, except that you can't pass a value in to a method in a parameter defined as *out*. Modifying a parameter with *out* indicates that the method will pass a value from the method back to the caller:

```
static void Main()
{
    int testValue;
    GetValue(out testValue);
    Console.WriteLine("The test value is {0}", testValue);
}
public static void GetValue(out int param)
{
    param = 42;
}
```

This output to *WriteLine* shows that *testValue* is 42. Unlike *ref*, the *out* modifier places a burden on the called method. The C# compiler will insist that a method called with an *out* parameter assign a value to the parameter; this is a quality assurance measure similar to the rule that variables must be assigned a value before use. Parameters marked as *ref* must be assigned a value by the caller.

The final modifier for parameters is used to pass a variable number of parameters to a method. The *params* keyword must be associated with a single-dimensional array, it must be the last entry in the parameter list, and there can be only one *params* modifier for each method declaration, as follows:

```
static void Main()
{
    PrintValues(42);
    PrintValues(1, 2, 3, 5, 7, 11, 13);
```

(continued)

```
}
public static void PrintValues(params int[] aListToPrint)
{
    foreach(int val in aListToPrint)
    {
        Console.WriteLine(val);
    }
}
```

In this example, *PrintValues* is called with parameter lists of two different lengths, and the method simply walks the length of the array, printing the value for each array element. Arrays are discussed in detail in Chapter 3. The *foreach* expression is a simplified version of the C/C++ *for* expression and is discussed in Chapter 4.

Overloading Methods   C# permits method overloading, whereby multiple variations of a method are defined within a class. All versions of an overloaded method declaration have the same name, but differ in their parameter lists, as shown here:

```
public void Eat(CatFood food)
{
    :
}

public void Eat(Bird theBird)
{
    :
}

public void Eat(Bird theBird, int howMany)
{
    :
}
```

When an overloaded method is called, the compiler must determine the best match for the method call. If no acceptable match is found, the compiler will flag the method call as an error.

```
Duck aDuck = GetDuck();

// Error; no overload of Eat accepts a duck.
theCat.Eat(aDuck);
```

The process of resolving exactly which overloaded method is invoked consists of the following two steps:

1.   Methods are inspected to determine whether they're potentially callable using the actual parameter list.

2.   Methods are ranked according to the quality of the match for each parameter.

If one member function is ranked as the best acceptable match, that method is invoked. If there's no acceptable method, the method call is rejected by the compiler as invalid. If more than one method is ranked equally acceptable, the method call is rejected by the compiler as ambiguous.

Constructors

A constructor is a special type of method that's called to initialize an object. Constructors always have the same names as their enclosing class and never have a return value. There are two types of constructors, as follows:

- **Instance constructors**   Used to initialize a specific object instance

- **Static constructors**   Also called *class constructors*; called before the first use of a class

An instance constructor is invoked as part of the creation of an object. The call to create an object with *new* causes the constructor to be invoked, as shown here:

```
class Orangutan: LandAnimal
{
    public Orangutan()
    {
        _bugCount = 100;
    }

        ⋮

}


static void Main()
{
    Orangutan tan;

    // Invokes constructor
    tan = new Orangutan();
}
```

Constructors can be overloaded just like other methods, and the process of overloading is the same as with ordinary methods—each constructor must have a different parameter list. When the object is created, parameters passed as part of the creation expression are used to determine which overloaded constructor should be called.

```
class Orangutan: LandAnimal
{
    public Orangutan()
    {
```

(continued)

```
            _bugCount = 100;
        }

        public Orangutan(int StartingBugCount)
        {
            _bugCount = StartingBugCount;
        }

        public Orangutan(string Name)
        {
            _name = Name;
        }

            ⋮
    }

    static void Main()
    {
        // Calls Orangutan()
        Orangutan tan1 = new Orangutan();

        // Calls Orangutan(int)
        Orangutan tan2 = new Orangutan(100);

        // Calls Orangutan(string)
        Orangutan tan3 = new Orangutan("Stan");
    }
```

Base Class Initialization   As part of the object construction process, the constructor in a subclass will invoke a constructor in the base class. This process can be implicit, with the call injected by the C# compiler, as shown here:

```
class LandAnimal
{
    ⋮
}

class Orangutan: LandAnimal
{
    public Orangutan()
    {
        _bugCount = 100;
    }

    ⋮
}
```

The C# compiler will inject a call to the *LandAnimal* base class before executing any code in the *Orangutan* constructor. The call can also be made explicitly using a constructor initializer.

```
public Orangutan(): base()
{
    _bugCount = 100;
}
```

An overloaded constructor doesn't automatically search for a base class constructor that matches its parameter list; it will implicitly call the default base class constructor, which isn't always the preferred execution path. A constructor initializer is normally used to invoke a non-default base class constructor, as shown in the following code. Using a constructor initializer is useful when a subclass and a base class share a set of overloaded constructors, especially because the constructor initializer has access to all the parameters passed to the constructor.

```
class Orangutan: LandAnimal
{
    // Initialize base class using the Name parameter.
    public Orangutan(string Name): base(Name)
    {
        _bugCount = 100;
    }

       ⋮
}
```

The constructor initializer doesn't have access to the *this* pointer because the current object hasn't yet been constructed. Attempting to access *this* or any members will be rejected by the compiler.

```
class Orangutan: LandAnimal
{
    // Doesn't work; _bugCount can't be referenced.
    public Orangutan(string Name): base(_bugCount)
    {
        _bugCount = 100;
    }
    protected long _bugCount;
       ⋮
}
```

Member Initializers   Much of the code in a constructor is used to initialize member variables; this is true in many languages, including C#, C++, and Visual Basic. C# also provides the *member initializer*, a simple way for instance fields to be initialized before the body of the constructor is executed. Instance members are initialized in the order of declaration. To create a member initializer, simply provide an assignment expression with the member declaration, as follows:

```
class AnimalReport
{
    public string _name = "unknown";
    public static int _counter;
    ⋮
}
```

You can't refer to other member fields or methods in an initializer expression. A member initializer reduces the amount of code you're required to write and reduces the possibility of errors because all member initialization can take place in one location.

Static members can be initialized in the same way as instance members, but they're always initialized before any of the instance members. Here's the exact order of initialization:

1.   Any static fields are initialized.

2.   The static constructor is invoked.

3.   Any instance fields are initialized.

4.   An instance constructor is invoked.

Static Constructors   Static constructors are similar to instance constructors, but they're invoked automatically before an instance of the class is created, and they're typically used to interact with static class members. Static constructors are implicitly public and have no access specifiers. A static constructor looks like a default instance constructor with an added *static* modifier, as shown here:

```
class Player
{
    static Player()
    {
        _counter = -1;
    }
    public Player(string Name)
    {

        ⋮
    }
    ⋮
}
```

The exact timing for the invocation of a static constructor might vary. In particular, there's no way to ensure the ordering of static constructors in unrelated classes. Regardless of their exact order, you can be sure that static constructor invocation will occur as follows:

- The static constructor will be invoked before the first instance of the class is created.

- The static constructor will be invoked only once.

- The static constructor will be invoked *after* the static members are initialized.

- The static constructor will be invoked before any static members are referenced.

Destructors

A *destructor* is an optional member function that contains the code necessary to destroy an instance of a class. In C#, destructors are declared using the familiar C++ syntax, with the destructor using the class name prefixed with a tilde (~), as shown here:

```
~Orangutan()
{
    StopGrooming();
}
```

Unlike in C++, a destructor in C# isn't guaranteed to be called. The C# destructor isn't called when a reference goes out of scope, as in C++; rather, it's called later, when the object is reclaimed during garbage collection. Garbage collection is automatically handled for you, and there's rarely a need for you to invoke it. Garbage collection is described in detail in Chapter 3, but for now, it's important to understand that a C# destructor might be called long after the last reference has been removed, and might not be called at all. Classes that need to clean up scarce resources should release their resources by other methods. A common design pattern discussed in Chapter 3 is the implementation of a *Close* or *Dispose* method that explicitly releases resources.

Inheritance and Methods

Inheritance alters the way methods are declared and invoked. When a subclass derives from a base class, it might be useful for the subclass to implement or redefine methods that exist in the base class. In some cases, a subclass might want to hide a base class implementation of a method.

Abstract Methods

Abstract methods are useful when the base class can't supply any meaningful implementation for a method. Unlike in C++, in C# an abstract method can't have a method body. If the abstract method isn't implemented by a subclass, the subclass can't be instantiated directly.

To implement the abstract method, the client must clearly indicate its intention by using the *override* keyword, as shown in the following code. This helps avoid several error cases that might occur if base classes and subclasses are versioned or developed separately. (For an example error case, see the following section.) By forcing the subclass and base class to explicitly indicate their intentions, the chances for error are greatly reduced.

```
class Palomino: Horse
{
    override public void ChaseAfterBadGuys()
    {
        ⋮
    }
}
```

Virtual Methods

As mentioned, the *abstract* keyword allows a base class to require the implementation of a method in a derived class. A method declared as *virtual* in C# serves a similar purpose—allowing, but not requiring, that a subclass provide a new implementation. Here's an example of declaring a virtual method:

```
class LandAnimal
{
    public virtual void Eat()
    {
        Chew();
        Swallow();
    }
}
```

After a method is declared as *virtual* in a base class, a subclass indicates its intent to override the base class version of the class by using the *override* keyword. The *override* keyword is used with virtual methods exactly as it is used with the abstract methods discussed earlier, as shown here:

```
class Cat: LandAnimal
{
    public override void Eat()
    {
        PlayWithFood();
        Chew();
        Swallow();
    }
}
```

When a virtual method is called, the most-derived version of the method is invoked. The most-derived method is determined by looking through the inheritance tree from the actual runtime class to the base classes. The first method discovered is invoked. This is usually, but not always, the desired result. Occasionally, it's desirable to hide a base class method due to an issue widely known as the "fragile base class problem." The following chain of events demonstrate this type of problem:

1.   A base class, *LandAnimal*, is created and deployed.

2.   A subclass, *Orangutan*, is created and deployed, along with other subclasses of the *LandAnimal* class.

3.   This framework is wildly successful, so a second version is developed. In this second version, the developers responsible for *LandAnimal* introduce a new virtual method named *Groom*.

4.   Unfortunately, the *Orangutan* class already has a method named *Groom* and will no longer compile because *Groom* isn't declared with the *override* keyword.

In this example, a change to the base class has caused a maintenance problem in a subclass. The original version of *Groom* probably looks something like this:

```
class Orangutan: LandAnimal
{
    public void Groom(Orangutan other)
    {
        other.CleanFur();
        other.LookForBugs();
        other.EatBugs();
    }
}
```

You can solve this problem in C# by creating the *Groom* method in *Orangutan* using the *new* keyword. In C#, the *new* keyword is used to hide a virtual base class method. When a method is declared as *new*, the compiler is notified that this method doesn't participate when looking for a virtual method, so if a virtual method is added to the base class, the existing code will continue to work correctly:

```
class Orangutan: LandAnimal
{
    new public void Groom(Orangutan other)
    {
```

(continued)

```
        other.CleanFur();
        other.LookForBugs();
        other.EatBugs();
    }
}
```

Calls made to the *Groom* method through a base class reference will call the most-derived version of the *Groom* method that isn't decorated with *new*. Calling *Groom* through an *Orangutan* reference will call the original *Orangutan.Groom* method.

Accessibility

Types and members in C# programs have a specific level of accessibility. Five levels of accessibility are available to class members, as described in Table 2-3.

Table 2-3.   Accessibility Options for C# Class Members

Access Level	Description
public	Completely open for access.
protected	Access granted to the enclosing class and subclasses.
internal	Access granted to classes in the enclosing assembly. (Assemblies are described later in this chapter, in the section "Adding References.")
protected internal	Access granted to classes in the enclosing assembly and subclasses of the enclosing class.
private	Access granted to the enclosing class only.

You must provide an accessibility level for each member, as in the example that follows, or the compiler will use the default level:

```
public class Employee
{
    // Name has public accessibility.
    public string Name;

    // EmployeeId has private accessibility.
    string EmployeeId;

    ⋮
}
```

Accessibility Options for Types

Every type has some degree of access tuning available—if you declare nothing for that particular type, a default level of accessibility is defined for it. In some cases, the default accessibility changes depending on where the type is declared. Types that are defined at the highest level, the so-called top-level types, have public accessibility by default. Types that are defined inside of a class are given private accessibility by default, as shown here:

```
// Access level is public by default for top-level classes.
class MilkFactory
{
    public MilkFactory()
    {
        Console.WriteLine("Milk factory");
    }
}
class Cow
{
    // Access level is private by default for embedded classes.
    class MilkFactory
    {
        public MilkFactory()
        {
            Console.WriteLine("Cow milk factory");
        }
    }
}
```

The assumption is that a type defined inside a class is likely to be an implementation detail, and the most appropriate access level is likely to be private. This means that simply moving a class definition will affect its accessibility unless you take the reasonable step of prefixing all class declarations with your desired level of access.

> **Note**   If you create a project using Visual C# .NET, top-level classes are automatically adorned with the *public* accessibility keyword even though this is the default access level.

Another option for a top-level type is to define it as *internal*, thus granting access only to code in the assembly that contains the class, as shown here:

```
// Accessible only from within the assembly
internal class Cow: ITemperamental
{
    ⋮
}
```

It just makes sense to define top-level types as either *public* or *internal*, as none of the other access levels apply. Types that are nested inside of other types often have other accessibility options.

Members of Interfaces and Enumerated Types   Members of interfaces (discussed later in this chapter, in the section "Interfaces") are always public. Because the purpose of an interface is to declare public methods, there's no option to reduce the visibility of interface methods. Likewise, enumerated types (discussed later in this chapter, in the section "Enumerations") provide a mechanism for naming scalar values. The members of an enumerated type are always public, and their accessibility can't be reduced. However, an *enum* variable can be given any of the five accessibility levels in Table 2-3.

Members of Structures   The default accessibility for structure members is *private*. This is contrary to the custom in C++, in which members are *public* by default. A structure member can have *public*, *private*, or *internal* accessibility. You can't grant a member of a structure *protected* accessibility because you're not able to inherit from a *struct*. The following example shows a structure with public and internal members:

```
struct Sailboat
{
    // Completely visible to all clients
    public int Length;

    // Visible only within the assembly
    internal int Beam;

    // Only visible within struct
    private string _secretName;
}
```

Members of Classes   The default accessibility for class members is private. Class members can be given any of the five accessibility levels in Table 2-3. In object-oriented programming, it's considered good practice to hide the implementation details of your class from clients, which can be achieved by using any of the accessibility options except *public*.

Nested Accessibility   The accessibility options granted to a member of a class or structure aren't absolute because they're also dependent on the accessibility of the enclosing type. For example, if a field that refers to a class is declared as *protected*, the accessibility of its members is always protected or lower, even if the class has public members, as shown here:

```
class Horse
{
    public void ChaseAfterBadGuys()
    {
    ⋮
    }
}
class Cowboy
{
    protected Horse _myHorse;
    public Cowboy()
    {
        _myHorse = new Horse();
    }
}
public class CowboyApp
{
    static void Main(string[] args)
    {
        Cowboy cowboyBill = new Cowboy();

        // Won't compile; _myHorse is not accessible.
        cowboyBill._myHorse.ChaseAfterBadGuys();
    }
}
```

In this example, methods for the *Horse* class aren't accessible through the *Cowboy* class, even though the methods are given public accessibility. Because the *_myHorse* member variable has protected accessibility, none of the *Horse* members can have more open access.

Allowing Access to Known Friends

The C# language doesn't include the oft-misused *friend* keyword from C++. The protection levels in Table 2-3 expand on the protection levels offered in C++. C# enables you to specify that protected or private members of a class should be visible within an assembly, by declaring them as *internal*. This is a useful feature that allows a component developer to expose members internally within a component without granting access to users of the component.

Namespaces

As outlined in Chapter 1, all types, even the main application class, are defined inside namespaces. Types that appear to be declared outside of a namespace are placed into the default *global* namespace. The namespaces used in C# are similar to namespaces used in other languages, such as C++. At the .NET

Framework level, the name of a type includes the namespace. For example, consider the following class:

```
namespace RailRoad
{
    public class Train
    {
        ⋮
    }
}
```

C# types are declared using namespaces as shown in this example, but the .NET Framework sees the name of the type declared above as *RailRoad.Train*. In C#, you can refer to the type as *Train* or *Railroad.Train*. The latter name works, but it can be somewhat unwieldy.

Creating a New Namespace

As you saw in Chapter 1, a new namespace is created with the *namespace* keyword, as shown here:

```
namespace MSPress.CSharpCoreRef.Animals
{
    ⋮
}
```

Members of a namespace can be defined in multiple files—it isn't necessary for the entire namespace to be located in a single source file. When the compiler encounters multiple source files that use the same namespace, they're simply added together.

As a style issue, the namespace should reflect a hierarchy, with your company name or other unique identifier at the namespace root. Creating a namespace with your company name as its root node helps to ensure that your namespaces don't accidentally clash with namespaces from other developers. Most of the source code for this book is placed in the *MSPress.CSharpCoreRef* namespace.

Unlike C++ namespaces, an entire C# namespace can be defined on a single line, as follows:

```
YourCompanyName.ComponentArea.ClassCluster
```

It isn't necessary for all of your classes to exist within a single namespace. In large projects, it's a good idea to create hierarchies of namespaces. For example, when creating reusable components for an application, you might organize your namespaces as shown in Figure 2-5:

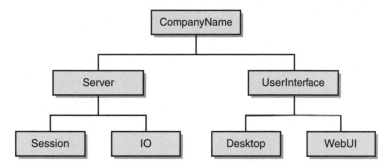

Figure 2-5. Typical namespace organization for a large project.

Using a Namespace

By default, a Visual C# class created using any of the wizards will include a reference to the *System* namespace. When using data types from other namespaces in the .NET Framework, you have two options. The first option is to use the full name of the type including the namespace, as shown here:

```
System.Xml.XmlTextReader tr;
```

The second option is to add the namespace to your current namespaces with the *using* keyword:

```
using System.Xml;
```

Now when you declare an instance of the type, you can simply use the type name:

```
XmlTextReader tr;
```

If two types have the same names within their respective namespaces, you'll need to manually solve the ambiguity for the compiler. For instance, consider an example program that uses two classes named *Id*, each in a separate namespace, as shown here:

```
namespace BankTypes
{
    public class Id
    {
        string _identifier;
        public Id(string Identifier)
        {
            _identifier = Identifier;
        }
        string GetId()
        {
            return _identifier;
```

(continued)

```
            }
        }
    }
namespace ClubTypes
{
    public class Id
    {
        string _identifier;
        public Id(string Identifier)
        {
            _identifier = Identifier;
        }
        string GetId()
        {
            return _identifier;
        }
    }
}
```

The *ClubTypes* and *BankTypes* namespaces each contain classes named *Id*. You're free to use both namespaces in any of your source files, but if you attempt to create an *Id* object, you'll get a compilation error due to the ambiguity. The compiler will return an error because the name *Id* could refer to either of the two classes—either *ClubTypes.Id* or *BankTypes.Id*.

If you have IntelliSense enabled, Visual Studio .NET will warn you of this problem as you're editing your source file. Given namespaces and types as declared in the previous example, if you insert the following line into your code, IntelliSense will warn that the *Id* type name is ambiguous and must be further qualified:

```
Id myId = new Id("CSharpCoreRef");
```

If one of the *Id* types is to be used, it must be fully qualified:

```
ClubTypes.Id myClubId = new ClubTypes.Id("CSharpCoreRef");
```

Adding References

In the .NET Framework, available types are packaged into *assemblies*. Assemblies are the unit of versioning and deployment for .NET applications and components. In its most basic form, an assembly is a single EXE or DLL module that contains a type.

Before you can make use of a type, you must add a reference to the assembly that contains the type. If you're building a project from the command line, use the */reference* or the shorter */r* switch to add a reference to the proper assembly, as shown here:

```
csc /reference:system.xml.dll; animals.cs
```

To add a reference to an assembly in Visual Studio .NET, right-click the References icon in Solution Explorer and choose Add References from the shortcut menu. The Add Reference dialog box will be displayed, as shown in Figure 2-6.

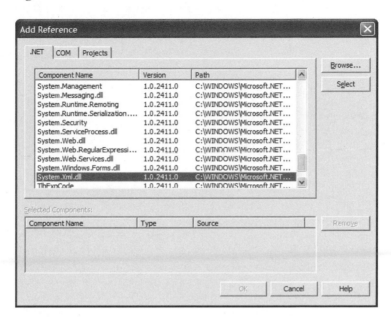

Figure 2-6.   The Visual C# Add Reference dialog box.

The .NET tab contains all assemblies that are available for use in the global assembly cache. The Select button is used to select specific assemblies to be referenced by the project. To select an assembly that isn't in the global assembly cache, you can use the Browse button to navigate to a private assembly.

The compiler will add the reference to the external assembly to a portion of your assembly known as the *manifest*, which includes a list of all external dependencies for the DLL. The .NET Framework uses the dependency list in the manifest to load the types used by your code. You can determine the assembly for a particular .NET Framework type using the MSDN documentation. The documentation of each type includes information about both its namespace and its assembly.

Interfaces

An interface in C# is similar to a pure abstract class in C++. An interface is similar to a class, but it has no member variables and no implementation of any interface methods. An interface is simply a description of work that a derived class can perform.

Using Interfaces

An interface can never be instantiated.

```
// Won't work; can't be instantiated directly.
ISpeak speaker = new ISpeak();
```

You must create a class that's derived from the interface and create an instance of the class, as in the following example:

```
class Cat: ISpeak
{
    ⋮
}


Cat anastasia = new Cat();
```

Likewise, it's incorrect to say that you have an *ISpeak* object—it's more accurate to say that you have an object that implements the *ISpeak* interface.

Classes that implement an interface are responsible for implementing all methods that are part of the interface. If one or more methods in an interface aren't implemented, the class can't be instantiated, as shown here:

```
interface ISpeak
{
    void StringToSpeech(string Message);
    void TextFileToSpeech(string FileName);
}

class SpeechEngine: ISpeak
{
    public void StringToSpeech(string Message)
    {
        ⋮
    }

    // TextFileToSpeech not implemented.
}
```

In this example, the *SpeechEngine* class doesn't implement the *TextFileTo-Speech* method inherited from the *ISpeak* interface. The C# compiler will flag this as an error because a non-abstract class that inherits from an interface must provide an implementation for all members. If *SpeechEngine* were declared as abstract, it could declare the nonimplemented member method as abstract, and the compiler would be happy; by declaring the class and the nonimplemented method as abstract, the intent to defer implementation has been made clear.

Classes and Interfaces

So far, we've examined how classes are created in C# and we've looked at inheritance. As noted in the previous section, the C# language doesn't support inheritance from multiple base classes, but it does support implementing multiple interfaces. In some cases, implementing multiple interfaces can enable your classes to have some of the benefits of multiple inheritance.

In the .NET Framework, you often have a choice of either implementing an interface or deriving directly from a base class. For example, when creating a new collection class, you can either derive from the *CollectionBase* class, which implements the *IList*, *ICollection*, and *IEnumerable* interfaces, or you can implement those interfaces directly. Classes that implement these three interfaces can be used like any of the basic collection classes offered by the .NET Framework.

In many cases, it makes sense to take advantage of the functionality of the base class provided by the .NET Framework. However, if your new class is so specialized that it can't take advantage of the functionality offered by the base class, it might make sense for you to spend the time required to implement the interfaces in your class.

Managing Errors with Exceptions

All nontrivial software programs are subject to errors. These errors can come in many forms, such as coding errors, runtime errors, or errors in cooperating systems. Regardless of the form that an error takes or where it's detected, each of these errors must be handled in some way. In C#, all errors are considered exceptional events that are managed by an exception handling mechanism.

Exception handling provides a robust way to handle errors, transferring control and rich error information when an error occurs. When an exception is raised, control is transferred to an appropriate exception handler, which is responsible for recovering from the error condition.

Code that uses exceptions for error handling tends to be clearer and more robust than code that uses other error handling methods. Consider the following code fragment that uses return values to handle errors:

```
bool RemoveFromAccount(string AccountId, decimal Amount)
{
    bool Exists = VerifyAccountId(AccountId);
    if(Exists)
    {
        bool CanWithdraw = CheckAvailability(AccountId, Amount);
        if(CanWithdraw)
        {
            return Withdraw(AccountId, Amount);
        }
    }
    return false;
}
```

Code that depends on return values for error detection has the following problems:

■   In cases in which a *bool* value is returned, detailed information about the error must be provided through additional error parameters or by calling additional error handling functions. This is the approach taken by much of the Win32 API.

■   Returning an error or a success code requires each programmer to properly handle the error code. The error code can be easily ignored or interpreted incorrectly, and an error condition might be missed or misinterpreted as a result.

■   Error codes are difficult to extend or update. Introducing a new error code might require updates throughout your source code.

In C#, error information is passed with exceptions. Rather than return a simple error code or a *bool* value, a method that fails is expected to raise an exception. The exception is a rich object that contains information about the failure condition.

Handling Exceptions

To handle an exception, you must protect a block of code using a *try* block and provide at least one *catch* block to handle the exception, as shown here:

```
try
{
    Dog d;
    // Attempt to call through a null reference.
```

```
    d.ChaseCars();
    ⋮
}
catch
{
    // Handle any exception.
    ⋮
}
```

When an exception is raised, or thrown, within a *try* block, an exception object of the proper type is created and a search begins for an appropriate *catch* clause. In the preceding example, the *catch* clause doesn't specify an exception type and will catch any type of exception. Program execution is transferred immediately to the *catch* clause, which can perform one of these actions:

- Handle the exception and continue execution after the *catch* clause
- Rethrow the current exception

To catch only a specific exception, the *catch* clause supplies a parameter that serves as a filter, specifying the exception or exceptions that it's capable of handling, as shown here:

```
try
{
    Dog d;
    // Attempt to call through a null reference.
    d.ChaseCars();
    ⋮
}
catch(NullReferenceException ex)
{
    // Handle only null reference exceptions.
    ⋮
}
```

If the *catch* clause can recover from the error that caused the exception, execution can continue after the *catch* clause. If the *catch* clause can't recover, it should rethrow the exception so that another exception handler can try to recover from the error.

To rethrow an exception, the *throw* keyword is used with the exception object passed to the *catch* clause, as in the following example:

```
try
{
    Dog d;
    // Attempt to call through a null reference.
    d.ChaseCars();
```

(continued)

```
        }
    catch(NullReferenceException ex)
    {
        // (ex);
Log error information.
        LogError (ex);
        // Rethrow the exception.
        throw(ex);
    }
```

To rethrow the current exception, the *throw* keyword can be used without specifying an exception object, as shown here:

```
    catch(NullReferenceException ex)
    {
        ⋮
        // Rethrow the current exception.
        throw;
    }
```

In a general *catch* block, *throw* must be used by itself, as there is no exception object to be rethrown:

```
    catch
    {
        ⋮
        // Rethrow the current exception.
        throw;
    }
```

If an exception is rethrown, a search is performed for the next *catch* clause capable of handling the exception. The call stack is examined to determine the sequence of methods that have participated in calling the current method. Each method in the call stack can potentially handle the exception, with the exception being offered first to the immediate calling method if an acceptable *catch* clause exists. This sequence continues until the exception is handled, or until all methods in the call stack have had an opportunity to handle the exception. If no handler for the exception is found, the thread is terminated due to the unhandled exception.

Using Exception Information

A reasonable description of the exception can be retrieved from any of the .NET Framework exceptions by calling the exception object's *ToString* method, as shown here:

```
    catch(InvalidCastException badCast)
    {
        Console.WriteLine(badCast.ToString());
    }
```

Other information is available from exception objects, as described here:

- **StackTrace**   Returns a string representation of a stack trace that was captured when the exception was thrown

- **InnerException**   Returns an additional exception that might have been saved during exception processing

- **Message**   Returns a localized string that describes the exception

- **HelpLink**   Returns a URL or Universal Resource Name (URN) to more information about the exception

If you create your own exception types that are exposed to others, you should provide at least this information. By providing the same information included with .NET Framework exceptions, your exceptions will be much more usable.

Providing Multiple Exception Handlers

If code is written in such a way that more than one type of exception might be thrown, multiple *catch* clauses can be appended, with each clause evaluated sequentially until a match for the exception object is found. At most, one of the *catch* clauses can be a general clause with no exception type specified, as shown here:

```
try
{
    Dog d = (Dog)anAnimal;
}
catch(NullReferenceException badRef)
{
    // Handle null references.
    ⋮
}
catch(InvalidCastException badCast)
{
    // Handle a bad cast.
    ⋮
}
catch
{
    // Handle any remaining type of exception.
    ⋮
}
```

The *catch* clauses are evaluated sequentially, which means that the more general *catch* clauses must be placed after the more specific *catch* clauses. The Visual C# compiler enforces this behavior and won't compile poorly formed catch clauses such as this:

```
try
{
    Dog d = (Dog)anAnimal;
}
catch(Exception ex)
{
    // Handle any exception.
}
catch(InvalidCastException badCast)
{
    // Handle a bad cast.
}
```

In this example, the first *catch* clause will handle all exceptions, with no exceptions passed to the second clause, so an invalid cast exception won't receive the special handling you expected. Because this is obviously an error, the compiler rejects this type of construction.

It's also possible to nest exception handlers, with *try-catch* blocks located within an enclosing *try-catch* block, as shown here:

```
try
{
    Animal anAnimal = GetNextAnimal();
    anAnimal.Eat();
    try
    {
        Dog d = (Dog)anAnimal;
        d.ChaseCars();
    }
    catch(InvalidCastException badCast)
    {
        // Handle bad casts.
        :
    }
}
catch
{
    // General exception handling
    :
}
```

When an exception is thrown, it's first offered to the most immediate set of *catch* clauses. If the exception isn't handled or is rethrown, it's offered to the enclosing *try-catch* block.

Guaranteeing Code Execution

When you're creating a method, sometimes there are tasks that must be executed before the method returns to the caller. Often this code frees resources or performs other actions that must occur even in the presence of exceptions or other errors. C# allows you to place this code into a *finally* clause, which is guaranteed to be executed before the method returns, as shown here:

```
try
{
    Horse silver = GetHorseFromBarn();
    silver.Ride();
}
catch
{
    ⋮
}
finally
{
    silver.Groom();
}
```

In this example, the *finally* clause is executed after the exception is thrown. A *finally* clause is also executed if a *return, goto, continue,* or *break* statement attempts to transfer control out of the *try* clause.

As you can see, you can have a *finally* clause and *catch* clauses attached to the same *try* clause. If a *catch* clause rethrows an exception, control is first passed to the *finally* clause before it's transferred out of the method.

.NET Framework Exceptions

The .NET Framework includes a large number of exception classes. Although all exceptions are eventually derived from the *Exception* class in the *System* namespace, the design pattern used in .NET is to include exceptions in the namespaces that generate the exceptions. For example, exceptions that are thrown by IO classes are located in the *System.IO* namespace.

Exceptions in the .NET Framework are rarely directly inherited from the *System.Exception* class. Instead, they're clustered into categories, with a common subclass that enables clients to group similar exceptions together. For example, all IO exceptions are subclasses of the *System.IO.IOException* class, which is derived from *System.Exception*. This hierarchical relationship enables clients to write exception handlers that handle IO-specific errors in a single *catch* block without the need to write separate handlers for each exception, as shown here:

```
catch(IOException ioError)
{
    // Handle all IO exceptions here.
    ⋮
}
```

When developing your own exception classes, consider following this pattern and deriving your classes from one of the many subclasses rather than deriving directly from the *System.Exception* class. Doing so will make your exceptions more usable by client code and might enable clients to handle exceptions thrown by your classes without requiring any new code.

Casting

In C#, a *cast* is used to explicitly convert a value or a reference to a different type. A cast is performed with a cast operator, which is a type enclosed in parentheses, as shown here:

```
Type T2 newType = (T2)oldType;
```

Casting isn't required when you're assigning a subclass to a base class reference because subclasses can always be substituted for a base class. However, the reverse is not true.

```
// OK; assignment to base reference.
Animal a = aDog;

// Error; requires a cast.
Dog d = anAnimal;

// Conversion OK with a cast.
Dog d2 = (Dog)anAnimal;
```

Explicit casting is required in this case because, in general, a client that expects functionality found in a subclass can't assume that the base class also contains the same functionality. If you're sure that a reference to a base class is actually a reference to the derived class, a cast will perform the conversion for you. But what if the cast can't be performed, perhaps because an unexpected subclass has been encountered? Performing a cast is inherently unsafe—any attempt to perform a conversion can fail if the conversion isn't allowed. When a conversion fails, an *InvalidCastException* is raised, as shown in this somewhat contrived example, in which a *Cat* object is passed to a method that was expecting a *Dog* object:

```
class Animal
{
    public void Eat()
    {
        Console.WriteLine("Eating");
    }
}

class Cat: Animal
{
    public void ChaseBirds()
    {
        Console.WriteLine("Chasing birds");
    }
}
```

```
class Dog: Animal
{
    public void ChaseCars()
    {
        Console.WriteLine("Chasing cars");
    }
}

class TestAnimal
{
    static void ChaseACar(Animal anAnimal)
    {
        Dog d = (Dog)anAnimal;
        d.ChaseCars();
    }

    static void Main()
    {
        Cat c = new Cat();
        ChaseACar(c);
    }
}
```

To handle invalid cast exceptions, casts that aren't absolutely safe should provide the necessary exception handling, as shown here:

```
static void ChaseACar(Animal anAnimal)
{
    try
    {
        Dog d = (Dog)anAnimal;
        d.ChaseCars();
    }
    catch(InvalidCastException badCast)
    {
        // Error-recovery code
    }
}
```

The compiler can't, in general, catch invalid casting errors during compilation—these errors can be detected reliably only at runtime. Sometimes raising an exception is too drastic, however; often it's more appropriate to attempt a conversion and take alternative actions if the conversion fails. In C#, you can attempt a conversion without raising an exception by using the *as* keyword, as follows:

```
Dog d = anAnimal as Dog;
```

Like a cast, *as* will attempt to convert a source type to a different target type, but unlike a cast, the *as* keyword won't raise an exception if the conversion fails. Instead, the reference will be set to *null* so that the failure is easily detected programmatically.

```
static void ChaseACar(Animal anAnimal)
{
    Dog d = anAnimal as Dog;
    if(d != null)
        d.ChaseCars();
    else
        Console.WriteLine("Not a dog");
}
```

Structures

Like C and C++, C# includes support for creating structure types. A structure is an aggregate type that combines members of multiple types into a single new type. As with classes, members of a structure are private by default and must be explicitly made public to grant access to clients. A structure is declared using the *struct* keyword, as shown here:

```
struct Point
{
    public int x;
    public int y;
}
```

Structures and Inheritance

Structures can't be inherited.

```
struct Point
{
    public int x;
    public int y;
}
// Not allowed; can't inherit from a struct.
class ThreeDPoint: Point
{
    public int z;
}
```

This is in contrast to C++, in which there's very little real difference between a class and a structure. In C#, structures can inherit from interfaces, but they're not allowed to inherit from classes or other structures.

Allocating Structures

Unlike instances of classes, structures are never heap-allocated; they're allocated on the stack. Staying out of the heap makes a structure instance much more efficient at runtime than a class instance in some cases. For example, creating large numbers of temporary structures that are used and discarded within a single method call is more efficient than creating objects from the heap. On the other hand, passing a structure as a parameter in a method call requires a copy of the structure to be created, which is less efficient than passing an object reference.

Creating an instance of a structure is just like creating a new class instance, as shown here:

```
Point pt = new Point();
```

Always use the dot operator to gain access to members of a structure.

```
pt.y = 5;
```

Member Functions

Structures can have member functions in addition to member fields. Structures can also have constructors, but the constructor must have at least one parameter, as shown here:

```
struct Rect
{
    public Rect(Point topLeft, Point bottomRight)
    {
        top = topLeft.y;
        left = topLeft.x;
        bottom = bottomRight.y;
        right = bottomRight.x;
    }
    // Assumes a normalized rectangle
    public int Area()
    {
        return (bottom - top)*(right - left);
    }
    // Rectangle edges
    int top, bottom, left, right;
}
```

Structures aren't allowed to declare a destructor.

Enumerations

An enumeration is a list of enumerated values that are associated with a specific type. Enumerations are declared using the *enum* keyword, as shown here:

```
enum Color
{
    Red, Yellow, Green
}
```

An enumeration value is accessed using the dot operator.

```
Color background = Color.Red;
```

Unlike C++ enumerators, C# enumerators must be used with the *enum* type name. This reduces the likelihood of name clashes between enumerations and improves readability.

An enumeration assigns scalar values to each of the enumerators in the enumerated list. By default, the base type used to store enumerated values is *int*, which can be changed to any of the scalar types, as shown here:

```
enum Color : byte
{
    Red, Yellow, Green
}
```

The values of enumerators begin at 0 unless an initial value is specified—in this case, 1:

```
enum Color : byte
{
    Red = 1, Yellow, Green
}
```

Enumerators are assigned sequential values unless an initializer is specified for the enumerator. The value of an enumerator must be unique, but need not be sequential or ordered.

```
enum Color : byte
{
    Red = 1, Yellow = 42, Green = 27
}
```

Although an enumerator is based on the *int* type (or another scalar value), you can't assign an enumerator to or from an *int* value without being explicit about your intentions, as shown here:

```
Color background = (Color)27;
int oldColor = (int)background;
```

Conclusion

Visual C# gives you access to a rich set of built-in types based on the common type system as well as the .NET Framework class library. As with all object-oriented languages, in C# you leverage built-in types and class libraries to build new types for your applications. When exposing your new types for consumption by others, your types should conform to the Common Language Specification (CLS) to maximize their reuse by developers using other programming languages.

C# shares many of the features of other object-oriented languages, such as C++. C# includes support for virtual methods, abstract classes, and method overloading. C# offers additional features that promote more reusable and more robust classes, such as a superior model for overriding methods in derived classes and an improved exception handling model.

Chapter 3 introduces and discusses value types and references. We'll examine the important differences between value types and references, including object lifetime, storage, and garbage collection. Chapter 3 also discusses properties and how they can make your classes more user-friendly

3

Value Types and Reference Types

As you saw in Chapter 2, all Visual C# objects are derived from the *object* type. Unlike some other object-oriented languages, in C# even the primitive types such as integers and floating-point variables are derived from *object*. Visual C# isn't the first language to unify the type system—Smalltalk is an early example of a language in which all objects are derived from a single base class and are allocated from a single heap. This unified type system provides for consistent interaction with all objects, albeit at a performance cost—allocating every object in a system dynamically (including integers and similar primitive types) places a significant load on the runtime. The challenge for the developers of the .NET platform and Visual C# was to develop a type system unified around a common base class that would be efficient enough for general-purpose programming.

In C or C++, the programmer can decide on a case-by-case basis whether an object should be allocated on the heap or the stack. A heap-allocated object costs slightly more to allocate but offers benefits: a heap-allocated object is easily shared with other classes and can have a lifetime that exceeds the life of the current method. On the other hand, the heap-allocated object's lifetime must be explicitly managed—a mistake will lead to memory leaks or program failure.

In contrast, a stack-allocated object is more efficient in terms of performance and memory allocation but isn't easily shared with other methods, as its lifetime is strictly bound by the method that declares it. When the enclosing method returns, the object is automatically destroyed. Remember, the stack is an area of memory that's allocated when a method or statement block is entered and freed when the method or statement block is exited.

The approach taken for .NET languages was to optimize the runtime for types with short lifetimes that are frequently used. These types are allocated with the same scope as their surroundings. A value type declared as a field in an enclosing reference type is allocated "in-line" for objects of the reference type. A value type declared in a method call is always allocated on the temporary execution stack rather than on the managed heap, offering performance gains for these temporary objects. The term *value types* indicates that objects of these types are always used directly by value, without references. Types allocated on the managed heap are known as *reference types*, to emphasize that objects of these types are always indirectly referenced. In this chapter, we'll look at these two type categories and how to use them and at how Visual C# and the common language runtime allocate, treat, and destroy them.

Understanding Value Types

Value types in Visual C# include the primitive types such as *int*, *float*, and *decimal*. Value types also include *enum* and *struct* types (discussed in Chapter 2). Other types in the .NET Framework are also explicitly declared to be value types, such as the *Rectangle*, *Point*, and *Size* structures found in the *System.Drawing* namespace. These types often have short lifetimes and are rarely shared between multiple clients, so declaring them as value types improves performance and reduces the memory pressure on the garbage collection mechanism. The garbage collection mechanism is described in detail later in this chapter, in the section "Reference Type Lifetime and Garbage Collection."

When a value type variable is declared in Visual C#, the variable contains the actual type instance. For example, an integer named *Age* is declared as follows:

```
int Age = 42;
```

The Visual C# .NET compiler will allocate 4 bytes of stack area for the *Age* variable, making it available for direct access without any indirection to the managed heap. For consistency, value type variables can also be declared using the *new* syntax, as shown here:

```
int Age = new int(42);
```

The effect of this statement might be surprising to C++ programmers. piler will detect that the variable is an instance of a value type and allocate the stack. In Visual C#, the allocation policy for an object depends on the type definition.

Value Type Lifetime

Value types have a lifetime that's limited by their scope. Unlike an object allocated on the heap, a value type variable declared in a method call is allocated on the stack, as shown in Figure 3-1.

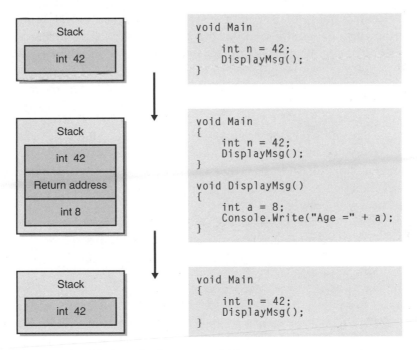

Figure 3-1.   Lifetime of value type variables.

Value type variables live on the stack and are destroyed with the stack when a method returns. In Figure 3-1, the *Main* method calls the *DisplayMsg* method. As *DisplayMsg* begins executing, two values are added to the stack: the return address inside the *Main* method and a temporary stack variable. When the *DisplayMsg* method returns, the stack values are destroyed.

By default, parameters in Visual C# are passed by value. Local copies are made for each value type parameter—only the copy is used by the called method. Passing parameters by value can cause performance penalties when large value types are passed as parameters. Although the primitive types don't carry a high cost when passed by value, the cost of copying every value stored in a structure can quickly add up, especially if the method is called frequently.

To avoid performance penalties when passing large value types as parameters, consider passing the parameters by reference. The *ref* and *out* parameter modifiers discussed in Chapter 2 can be used with value types to reduce the cost of passing a value type parameter. Instead of creating and copying a large structure, you'll pass only a reference to the value, as shown here:

```
BigStruct s1, s2;
  :
CompareBigStructs(ref s1, ref s2);
```

Keep in mind that when a value type is passed by reference, the called method can change the value of the variable. The called method is accessing the original variable, not a copy. It's up to you to determine whether the possible side effects justify the performance gains.

Boxing

All types are derived from the *object* class, but the value types aren't allocated on the managed heap. Value type variables actually contain the bits required to represent their values, so how then can these types be stored in arrays and used in methods that expect reference variables? The answer lies in a Visual C# feature known as *boxing*.

Visual C# enables you to box your value type variables so that they can be used exactly like reference types. Boxing effectively places the value type variable in a reference "box," which is then used as a reference type variable, as shown in Figure 3-2.

Figure 3-2.   A value type variable that's been boxed to make it appear to be a reference object.

Boxing usually occurs implicitly—for example, when a value type is assigned to an object or passed as a parameter that expects the *object* type. When a conversion from a value type to a reference type is required, the compiler will perform the boxing operation for you implicitly, as follows:

```
int Age = 42;
object obj = Age; // Implicitly boxed
```

In contrast, when a conversion from reference type to value type is required, you must explicitly state your intentions because the conversion, known as *unboxing*, can easily result in lost data or an improper conversion. For example, if an *int* is boxed and stored in a reference to *object*, the following code will recover the value of the *int*:

```
object obj;
⋮
int Age = (int)obj;
```

An unboxing attempt that might lead to data loss will cause an exception to be thrown. For example, the following code will cause an *InvalidCast-Exception* to be thrown:

```
long feetPerLightYear;
⋮
object obj = feetPerLightYear;
int Age = (int)obj; // Not OK; overflows.
```

Declaring New Value Types

New value types are declared as *struct* types. The Visual C# .NET compiler will automatically derive new *struct* types from the *System.ValueType* class rather than directly from the *object* class. The *System.ValueType* class provides extra functionality for comparing value types for equality. By default, types derived from the *object* class compare for equality by testing for the location of the compared instances. Because two value type variables never have the same location, value type equality is determined by comparing the values stored by the variable.

A new value type requires a structure that contains the data used to store the data for your new type as well as a definition of the operations that can be performed on the type. Defining those operations requires a technique known as *operator overloading*, which is discussed in Chapter 4.

Understanding Reference Types

As mentioned, a variable declared as a reference type serves as a reference to an object located on the heap. As illustrated in Figure 3-3, multiple reference variables can be attached to a single object, and some reference variables might not be attached to any object. When a reference type variable is declared without assigning it to an object, its default value is *null*.

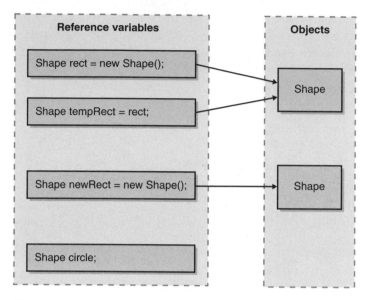

Figure 3-3. Objects on the managed heap, accessed through reference variables.

In Visual C#, objects are always created using the *new* keyword, but the objects aren't explicitly released as they are in C or C++. The .NET Framework's garbage collector will automatically free the memory used by unreferenced objects. In some situations, however, you must take explicit action when you've finished using an object—for example, when objects hold scarce resources and you can't wait for the garbage collector to act. Such situations have implications for how you write code, as you'll see later in this chapter, in the section "Reference Type Lifetime and Garbage Collection."

Working with Arrays

An *array* is a reference type that contains a sequence of variables of a specific type. An array is declared by including index brackets between the type and the name of the array variable, as shown here:

```
int [] ages;
```

This example declares a variable named *ages* that's an array of *int*, but it doesn't attach that reference variable to an actual array object. To do so requires that the array be initialized, as shown here:

```
int [] ages = {5, 8, 39};
```

Arrays are reference types that the Visual C# .NET compiler automatically subclasses from the *System.Array* class. When an array contains value types, the space for the types is allocated as part of the array. When an array contains reference elements, the array contains only references—the objects are allocated elsewhere on the managed heap, as shown in Figure 3-4.

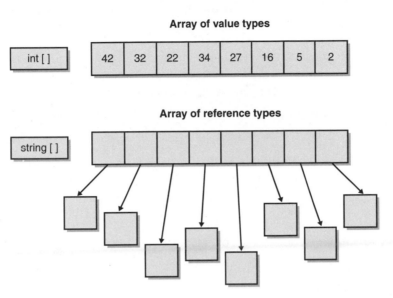

Figure 3-4.   An array of value types and an array of reference types.

The individual elements of an array are accessed through an index, with *0* always referring to the first element in the array, as follows:

```
int currentAge = ages[0];
```

You can determine the number of elements in an array by using the *Length* property:

```
int elements = nameArray.Length;
```

An array can be cloned with the *Clone* method, which returns a new copy of the array. Because *Clone* is declared as returning an array of *object*, you must explicitly state the type of the new array, as follows:

```
string [] secondArray = (string[])nameArray.Clone();
```

Cloning an array creates a shallow copy. All the array elements are copied into a new array; the objects referenced by array elements aren't copied.

Clear is a static method in the *Array* class that removes one or more of the array elements by setting the removed array elements to *0* (for value types) or *null* (for reference types). The array to be cleared is passed as the first parameter, along with the index of the first element to clear and the number of elements be removed. To eliminate all the elements of the array, pass 0 as the start element and the array length as the third parameter, as shown here:

```
Array.Clear(nameArray, 0, nameArray.Length);
```

Reverse is a static method in the *Array* class that reverses the order of array elements, operating on either the complete array or just a subset of elements. To reverse an entire array, simply pass the array to the static method, as shown here:

```
Array.Reverse(nameArray);
```

To reverse a range within the array, pass the array along with the start element and the number of items to be reversed.

```
Array.Reverse(nameArray, 0, nameArray.Length);
```

Sort is a static method that sorts an array. There are several versions of *Sort*; the simplest version accepts an array as its only parameter and sorts the elements in ascending order.

```
Array.Sort(nameArray);
```

Other overloads of the *Sort* method allow you to exercise more control over the sorting process. The interfaces and methods used when sorting are discussed in more detail in Chapter 8.

The following example manipulates an array containing the names of the month. The array is examined, reversed, sorted, cloned, and finally cleared.

```
using System;
namespace MSPress.CSharpCoreRef.ArrayExample
{
    class ArrayExampleApp
    {
        static void Main(string[] args)
        {
            string [] months = { "January", "February", "March",
                                  "April", "May", "June", "July",
                                  "August", "September", "October",
                                  "November", "December"};
            Console.WriteLine("The array has a rank of {0}.",
                        months.Rank);
            int elements = months.Length;
            Console.WriteLine("There are {0} elements in the array.",
                        elements);
```

```
Console.WriteLine("Reversing...");
Array.Reverse(months);
PrintArray(months);

Console.WriteLine("Sorting...");
Array.Sort(months);
PrintArray(months);

string [] secondArray = (string[])months.Clone();
Console.WriteLine("Cloned Array...");
PrintArray(months);

Console.WriteLine("Clearing...");
Array.Clear(months, 0, months.Length);
PrintArray(months);
}
/// <summary>
/// Print each element in the names array.
/// </summary>
static void PrintArray(string[] names)
{
    foreach(string name in names)
    {
        Console.WriteLine(name);
    }
}
}
}
```

This example uses the *foreach* statement to iterate over each of the array elements. You can use this type of statement in Visual C# to simplify loop programming when working with arrays. The *foreach* statement allows you to declare a variable that's used to represent the currently indexed element in the array. This element will be updated for every loop iteration, with bounds checking performed automatically. Use of the *foreach* statement with arrays and other types is discussed in more detail in Chapter 7.

Arrays can be multidimensional, meaning that instead of extending in a simple sequence, they extend in multiple dimensions. A multidimensional array can be either rectangular, meaning that array dimensions are consistent, or jagged, meaning that array dimensions can have varying lengths. Some examples of different array types are shown in Figure 3-5.

Single-dimensional array

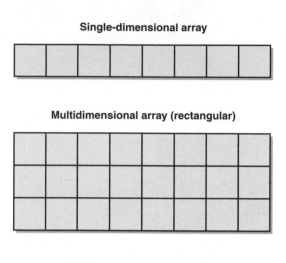

Multidimensional array (rectangular)

Multidimensional array (jagged)

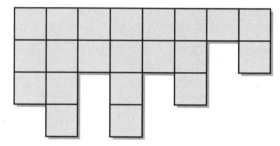

Figure 3-5. A single-dimensional array, a rectangular multidimensional array, and a jagged multidimensional array.

To create a rectangular multidimensional array, the array declaration simply separates each dimension with commas, as shown here:

```
string [,] location = new string[5,2]; // 2-dimensional array
string [,,] locationsWithZipCode;       // 3-dimensional array
```

If the *Length* property is used with a multidimensional array, it returns the number of elements in the entire array, not just one of the dimensions. To determine the number of elements in one dimension of a multidimensional array, use the *GetLength* method, passing the dimension that you want tested, as follows:

```
int locations = names.GetLength(0); // Length of first dimension
```

A jagged array is declared using multiple index brackets:

```
double[][] polygons;
```

Dimensions within a jagged array are allocated just like new arrays of simpler rank.

```
double[][] shapes = new double[4][];
shapes[0] = new double[1] {10};              // Circle
shapes[1] = new double[4] {3, 4, 3, 4};      // Quadrilateral
shapes[2] = new double[3] {3, 4, 5};         // Triangle
shapes[3] = new double[5] {5, 5, 5, 5, 5};   // Pentagon
```

Jagged arrays are more flexible because any dimension can be made up of arrays with differing lengths, but allocating and navigating jagged arrays is potentially more difficult. Each edge in a jagged array must be tested for its length and navigated separately. The *foreach* statement can be used to simplify iteration over a jagged array, as shown here:

```
static void DisplayShapeInfo(double[][] shapes)
{
    int rankNumber = 0;
    foreach(double[] shape in shapes)
    {
        int totalLength = 0;
        foreach(int side in shape)
        {
            totalLength += side;
        }
        Console.WriteLine("Shape {0} perimeter length is {1}",
                        rankNumber,
                        totalLength);
        ++rankNumber;
    }
}
```

This example uses the *foreach* statement to iterate over each dimension of the array. Even though the second dimension of the array is jagged, the *foreach* statement allows you to write a simpler loop than is possible with other loop constructions.

Working with Strings

Visual C# includes a built-in string reference type that simplifies string manipulation. Strings can be created with the *new* operator. However, because strings are built-in types, the compiler also allows a simpler syntax, in which a string literal provides an initial value to a string reference variable, as shown here:

```
string name = "Mickey";
```

String literals are always enclosed within double quotation marks. Slashes are escaped with a preceding slash, so the string literal with the value *C:\Windows* would be as follows:

```
string path = "C:\\Windows";
```

Alternatively, the @ operator can be used to indicate to the compiler that a string literal is to be evaluated without escaping, allowing you to use a simpler syntax.

```
string path = @"C:\Windows";
```

Conceptually, a string is an array of characters, so the *string* class allows you to access individual characters as if you are accessing an array element. This example assigns the third character from *name* to the *char* variable *c*:

```
char c = name[2];
```

If *name* is empty or doesn't have at least three characters, an *IndexOutOf-RangeException* exception will be thrown.

When testing strings for equality, you have two options: value comparisons and reference comparisons. To test strings for value equality, simply use the Visual C# equality operator (==), as shown here:

```
if(name1 == name2)
{
    // Strings match.
}
```

This code performs a case-sensitive test for string equality; two string variables that are set to *null* will always test as equivalent. Strings can also be relatively compared using the relational operators, which will be discussed in detail in Chapter 4.

To determine whether two string references point to the same object, you must explicitly test for equality using the *object* base class, as shown here:

```
if((object)path == (object)name)
{
    // The path and name variables refer to the same string object.
}
```

Strings are concatenated using the addition operator (+), just like other built-in types. However, Visual C# strings are immutable—once a string is created, its value never changes. The simple act of concatenating a string results in the creation of a new string object, as shown here:

```
path += fileName; // Concatenation
string fullPath = path + fileName; // Addition
```

In both examples, adding *fileName* to *path* causes a new string to be created. In the first line, the new string object is assigned to the *path* string reference. In the second example, the *path* string reference isn't modified and the new string is assigned to the *fullPath* string reference.

Reference Type Lifetime and Garbage Collection

As you've seen in Chapter 2 and Chapter 3, Visual C# uses the *new* keyword to create new instances of reference types. You usually don't take any action to explicitly release an object because the .NET Framework uses a process known as garbage collection to automatically free objects that are no longer in use. For the most part, this process occurs automatically, and you'll rarely be aware of it. However, garbage collection is such a fundamental part of the .NET Framework that understanding the mechanics of garbage collection will help you to write much more efficient code.

Understanding Garbage Collection

The basic ideas behind garbage collection are simple enough, and many types of systems today use some form of garbage collection. All garbage collection mechanisms have one thing in common: they absolve the programmer from the responsibility of tracking memory usage. Although most garbage collectors require that applications occasionally pause to reclaim memory that's no longer used, the garbage collector used to manage memory in the .NET Framework is highly efficient.

Assumptions Made by the Garbage Collector

As with all modern garbage collectors, the .NET garbage collector is optimized for the following assumptions, which hold true for most applications:

- Objects that have been recently allocated are most likely to be freed. When methods are executed, objects are often allocated for the use of that method; searching the subset of objects that were most recently allocated will yield the most free memory for the smallest amount of work.

- Objects that have lived the longest are least likely to be become free. Objects that have survived a few passes of the garbage collector are much less likely to be temporary objects that will be free for the next collection pass; searching these memory blocks tends to yield a smaller amount of free memory for the amount of work required.

- Objects allocated together are often used together. Keeping objects allocated together in close proximity to each other improves cache performance.

The garbage collector in .NET is known as a *generational garbage collector*, meaning that allocated objects are sorted into three groups, or generations. Objects that have been most recently allocated are placed in generation zero. Generation zero provides fast access to its objects because the size of generation zero is small enough to fit into the processor's L2 cache. Objects in generation zero that survive a garbage collection pass are moved into generation one. Objects in generation one that survive a collection pass are moved into generation two. Generation two contains long-lived objects that have survived at least two collection passes.

The details of the garbage collection pass will be discussed in the next section, but the basic idea is simple: look for unused objects, remove them from memory, and compact the managed heap to recover the space that the unused objects were occupying. After the heap is compacted, all object references are adjusted to point to the new object locations.

Understanding Memory Allocation and Collection

When an object is allocated by a Visual C# program, the managed heap will almost instantly return the memory required for the new object. The reason for the extremely fast allocation performance is that the managed heap is not a complex data structure. The managed heap resembles a simple byte array, with a pointer to the first available memory location, as shown in Figure 3-6.

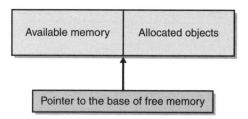

Figure 3-6.   Memory allocation in .NET.

When a block of memory is requested for an object, the value of the pointer is returned to the caller, and the pointer is adjusted to point to the next available memory location. Allocation of a managed block of memory is only slightly more complex than simply incrementing a pointer. This is one of the performance wins that the managed heap offers you. In an application that doesn't require much garbage collection, the managed heap will outperform a traditional heap.

Due to this linear allocation method, objects that are allocated together in a Visual C# application tend to be allocated near each other on the managed heap. This arrangement differs significantly from traditional heap allocation, in which memory blocks are allocated based on their size. For example, two objects allocated at the same time might be allocated far apart from each other on the heap, reducing cache performance.

So allocation is very fast, but in a nontrivial program, the memory available in generation zero will eventually be exhausted. Remember, generation zero fits inside the L2 cache and no unused memory is being spontaneously returned. Until now, you've seen only how .NET simply increments a pointer when a program needs more memory. Although this approach is very efficient, it obviously can't continue forever.

When no more memory can be allocated in generation zero, a garbage collection pass will be initiated on generation zero, which removes any objects that are no longer referenced and moves currently used objects into generation one. Promoting referenced objects into generation one frees up generation zero for new allocations. A collection pass for generation zero is the most common type of collection, and it's very fast. A generation one collection pass is performed if a generation zero collection pass isn't sufficient to reclaim memory. As a last resort, a generation two collection pass is performed only when collections on generations zero and one haven't freed enough memory. If no memory is available after a complete collection pass of all generations, an *OutOfMemoryException* is thrown.

Using Finalizers

A class can expose a finalizer that executes when the object is destroyed, subject to conditions that we'll look at later in this section. In Visual C#, the finalizer is a protected method named *Finalize*, as shown here:

```
protected void Finalize()
{
    base.Finalize();
    // Clean up external resources.
}
```

If you implement a finalizer, you should always declare it as protected. Never expose your finalizer as a public method because it is called only by the .NET Framework. In your finalizer, you must follow a pattern whereby you call the finalizer for your base class before executing any of your own code, as shown in the previous example.

The Visual C# .NET compiler will generate code equivalent to a well-formed finalizer if you declare a destructor, as shown here:

```
~ResourceConnector()
{
    // Clean up external resources.
}
```

Attempting to declare a destructor and a *Finalize* method in the same class will result in an error.

Keep in mind that finalizers, and therefore Visual C# destructors, aren't guaranteed to execute at any specific time, and they might not even execute at all in some circumstances. The .NET Framework can't guarantee that it will call an object's destructor or finalizer in a timely fashion because of the way it executes the finalization process. When an object with a finalizer is collected, it's not immediately removed from memory. Instead, a reference to the object is placed in a special queue that contains objects waiting for finalization.

A dedicated thread is responsible for executing the finalizer for each object in the finalization queue. This thread then marks the object as no longer requiring finalization and removes the object from the finalization queue. Until finalization is complete, the queue's reference to the object is sufficient to keep the object alive. After finalization has been completed, the object will be reclaimed during the next garbage collection pass.

There's no guaranteed order for finalization. When an object is finalized, other objects that it refers to might have already been finalized. During finalization, you can safely free external resources such as operating system handles or database connections, but objects on the managed heap shouldn't be referenced.

Avoid creating finalizers whenever possible. Objects with finalizers are more costly to the .NET Framework than objects without finalizers. They also maintain their existence through at least two garbage collection passes, increasing the memory pressure on the runtime.

Instead of including a finalizer, consider exposing a *Dispose* method that can be called to properly free your object's resources, as shown in the following code. Classes that handle files and connections often name this method *Close*. You can use this method to free any resources that you're holding, including any managed object references.

```
public void Dispose()
{
    // Clean up owned resources.
}
```

If you clean up your object using a *Dispose* or *Close* method, you should indicate to the runtime that your object no longer requires finalization by calling *GC.SuppressFinalize*, as shown here:

```
public void Dispose()
{
    tools.Dispose();
    statusBar.Dispose();
    dbConnection.Dispose();
    GC.SuppressFinalize(this);
}
```

If you're creating and using objects that have *Dispose* or *Close* methods, you should call these methods when you've finished using the objects. A good place to make these calls is in a *finally* clause, which guarantees that the objects are properly handled even if an exception is thrown.

If you implement a *Dispose* or *Close* method, you still need to implement a finalizer if your class has external resources that aren't allocated from the managed heap. In the ideal case, your public *Dispose* method will properly clean up resources and suppress finalization, resulting in efficient cleanup of your object. If a user of your class forgets to call *Dispose*, the finalizer might be called and will act as a safety net to ensure that your external resources will be freed.

Implementing the *IDisposable* Interface

Creating and properly disposing of an object requires several lines of correctly written code. A mistake in implementing this code can cause errors that are difficult to trace, so the Visual C# language offers a more automated solution based on using the *IDisposable* interface.

IDisposable defines one method: *Dispose*. Implementing this interface is the preferred way for a class to advertise that it's exposing a method for proper object cleanup. A typical implementation of *IDisposable* is shown here:

```
public class ResourceConnector: IDisposable
{
    ~ResourceConnector()
    {
        Dispose(false);
    }

    public void Dispose()
    {
        Dispose(true);
    }

    protected void Dispose(bool disposing)
    {
        if(disposing)
        {
            GC.SuppressFinalize(this);
            // Dispose of managed objects if disposing.
        }
        // Release our external resources here.
        ⋮
    }
    ⋮
}
```

When the *Dispose* method is called, the object is being properly freed by a client. External resources are freed, and *GC.SuppressFinalize* is called as an optimization step to prevent finalization. If the object is disposed by command, it's also appropriate for an object to dispose of objects it owns.

If the finalizer is called by the .NET Framework, the call to *GC.Suppress-Finalize* isn't needed because the object is already being finalized. In addition, it's not appropriate to reference any managed objects because these objects may have been finalized or even collected already.

Using the *IDisposable* Interface

Classes that implement *IDisposable* can take advantage of a Visual C# language feature that assists in proper disposal. The *using* statement works with the *IDisposable* interface to simplify the process of writing client code that correctly cleans up objects that require finalization. The *using* statement guarantees that the *Dispose* method is called even if exceptions occur. Consider the following code:

```
using(ResourceConnector rc = new ResourceConnector())
{
    rc.UseResource();
    // rc.Dispose called automatically.
}
```

The *using* statement has two sections: the allocation expression is located between the parentheses, and the code block that follows provides scoping. After the code block has finished executing, the *Dispose* method will be called for the allocated object.

The Visual C# .NET compiler will generate code equivalent to the following code written without the *using* statement:

```
ResourceConnector rc = null;
try
{
    rc = new ResourceConnector();
    // Use rc here.
    ⋮
}
finally
{
    if(rc != null)
    {
        IDisposable disp = rc as IDisposable;
        disp.Dispose();
    }
}
```

As you can see, the code written with the *using* statement is more clear and less error-prone.

Multiple objects of a single type can be allocated in a single *using* expression by simply separating the allocation expressions with commas, as shown here:

```
using(SolidBrush greenBrush = new SolidBrush(Color.Green),
    redBrush = new SolidBrush(Color.Red))
{
    ⋮
}
```

Using the *System.GC* Class

The *System.GC* class contains static methods that are used to interact with the garbage collection mechanism, including methods to initiate a garbage collection pass, to determine an object's current generation, and to determine the amount of allocated memory.

The most frequently used *System.GC* method is *SuppressFinalize*, shown in the following code.

```
GC.SuppressFinalize(this);
```

The *SuppressFinalize* method prevents an object from being finalized and optimizes the performance of the garbage collector. You should call this method when your object is disposed of via a *Dispose* or *Close* method.

Collect is used to programmatically initiate a garbage collection pass. There are two versions of *Collect*. The version with no parameters, shown here, performs a full collection:

```
GC.Collect();
```

The more useful version of *Collect* allows you to specify the generation to be collected. This flexibility enables you to quickly reclaim generation zero if you've recently used and freed a number of temporary objects:

```
GC.Collect(0);
```

A generation one or two collection pass always includes any lower generations, so calling *Collect(2)* will cause a full garbage collection pass.

The *GetGeneration* method will return the current generation of an object passed as a parameter:

```
int myGeneration = GC.GetGeneration(this);
```

GetGeneration is useful for tracking objects as they interact with the garbage collector and for auditing memory usage. Like the *GetTotalMemory* method, however, *GetGeneration* has limited value in code not dedicated to tracing or debugging.

GetTotalMemory returns the amount of memory allocated on the managed heap. Depending on the parameter you pass to the function, the function's return value might not be a precise number, due to the way the managed heap works. If unreferenced objects that the garbage collector hasn't yet reclaimed exist on the heap, *GetTotalMemory* might return a number that's larger than the number of currently allocated bytes. To get a more exact number, this method allows you to pass a *bool* parameter that specifies whether a collection is to be initiated before the measurement, as follows:

```
long totalMemory = GC.GetTotalMemory(true);
```

Passing *true* as a parameter causes a full garbage collection pass before the managed heap's size is calculated. Passing *false* simply returns the size of the heap without attempting to collect or compact any unused space.

Conclusion

Types used in Visual C# applications fall into two categories: value types and reference types. Value types include the primitive types such as integers and other numeric types. Other types can be explicitly defined to be value types, such as the *Rectangle* and *Point* types found in the *System.Drawing* namespace. These value types typically have short lifetimes, and declaring them as value types improves efficiency by causing them to be allocated on the stack rather than on the managed heap.

Reference types are always allocated on the managed heap and are reclaimed by the garbage collector. Classes that need to be cleaned up immediately should implement the *IDisposable* interface to enable clients to use the *using* statement.

In Chapter 4, we'll look at operators and type conversions. These features help make your types behave more like the primitive types built into the Visual C# language.

4

Operators, Type Conversions, and Properties

This chapter discusses several of the methods you can use to make your classes and other types more user-friendly. By taking advantage of operator overloading and type conversion operators and by supplying properties for your classes and structures, you can simplify the code required to use your types.

As you'll see in this chapter, operators are symbols or keywords that are used to construct the computations that your C# program performs. Like many object-oriented languages, C# allows you to overload operators to define how operators interact with types that you have defined. (Overloading an operator consists of changing the default behavior of the operator.) C# also has strict rules about how values can be converted to a different type, and in C#, you can overload the behavior of type conversion operators so that your types are as easy to use as the built-in types.

In this chapter, a value type, named *BattingAverage*, is created and used as an example to demonstrate how operators, type conversions, and properties can be used to enhance user-defined types. The *BattingAverage* value type implements the basic behavior required for a new value type, including overriding the *ToString* method to properly format a string that displays a batting average in the expected format. You'll also see how the *BattingAverage* structure overrides operators so that it can be used much like the built-in types.

Examining Operators

Operators are used in different ways in C# and can be divided into three groups, depending on the number of *operands* (the variables or constants that operators act on) used with the operator, as follows:

- **Unary operators**   Used with a single operand. Examples of unary operators include the increment operator (++), which is used to increment scalar values, and the negation operator (/), which is used to invert a Boolean value.

- **Binary operators**   Used with two operands. Examples of binary operators include the multiplication operator (*) and the division operator (/).

- **Ternary operator**   The lone ternary operator (?:) works with three operands to form a conditional expression.

In addition to categorizing operators by the number of operands they work with, you can categorize them by the type of work they perform, as follows:

- Relational operators

- Logical operators

- Arithmetic operators

- Bitwise operators

- Assignment operators

- Conditional operator

- Type-information operators

- Direct memory access operators

- Other operators

The following sections describe these operator categories in more detail.

Comparing Objects with the Relational Operators

The relational operators are used to create expressions that compare two objects and return a Boolean value, as in the following code snippet:

```
int peopleYears = 1;
int dogYears = 7;
// Compare and store the result in a Boolean variable.
bool result = dogYears > peopleYears;
```

This expression tests *dogYears* and *peopleYears* to determine whether they're equal, creating an expression that has a Boolean value. The result of the expression can be stored, as in this example, or combined with other expressions.

The six relational operators defined in C# are listed in Table 4-1.

Table 4-1.   Relational Operators in C#

Operator	Description
==	Equality
!=	Inequality
<	Less than
>	Greater than
<=	Less than or equal to
>=	Greater than or equal to

The comparison operator (==) tests for equality between two operands, as shown here:

```
bool result = (myAge == yourAge);
```

A common mistake is to use the assignment operator (=) instead of the == operator. The Microsoft Visual C# .NET compiler will usually detect inappropriate use of the = operator and flag it as an error. For example, the following code will compile in C++, but not in Visual C# .NET:

```
// Valid C++, not C#
bool result = myAge = yourAge;
```

The error message returned by the compiler complains that the result of the assignment (an *int* value) can't be implicitly converted to a *bool*. This is an example of how the more restrictive rules governing type conversion found in C# protect you from common programming mistakes. Type conversion is discussed in more detail later in this chapter, in the section "Converting Types."

The inequality operator (!=) tests two operands for inequality, returning *true* if the operands aren't equal and *false* if they're equal, as shown here:

```
bool notMaximumHeight = (height != maxHeight);
```

The less than (<) and greater than (>) relational operators compare the relative order of two operands, as follows:

```
bool isLess = (height < maxHeight);
bool isGreater = (height > minHeight);
```

The less than or equal to (<=) and greater than or equal to (>=) operators are similar to the < and > operators, except that they'll evaluate as *true* when the operands are equal.

Forming Logical Expressions with the Logical Operators

The logical operators work with Boolean operands to form logical expressions. C# defines eight logical operators, listed in Table 4-2.

Table 4-2.   Logical Operators in C#

Operator	Description
!	NOT (negation)
&&	AND (short-circuit)
&	AND (full evaluation)
||	OR (short-circuit)
|	OR (full evaluation)
^	XOR (exclusive OR)
true	Tests for a *true* value (used when overloading)
false	Tests for a *false* value (used when overloading)

The NOT (negation) operator (*!*) works with a single operand and inverts a Boolean value, as shown here:

```
bool notTrue = !true;
```

C# shares the AND (short-circuit) operator (*&&*) with C and C++. This operator works with two operands, evaluating as *true* if both operands are *true*:

```
bool hasTwoWheels = true;
bool hasPedals = true;
bool isBicycle = (hasTwoWheels && hasPedals);
```

The OR (short-circuit) operator (*||*) works with two operands, like the *&&* operator, but evaluates to *true* if any of the operands are *true*.

An interesting property of the *&&* operator and the *||* operator is that they *short-circuit*, meaning that if the result can be determined from the first operand, the second operand isn't evaluated. Short-circuiting isn't normally a problem, as the following code illustrates:

```
bool hasAge = (testAge && GetAge());
```

In this code, the *&&* operator will short-circuit if *testAge* is *false*. Because the *&&* operator requires both operands to be *true*, if the first operand is *false*, there's no need to continue to evaluate the expression and invoke the *GetAge* method.

But what if you require all of your operands to be evaluated? C# includes operators that work exactly like *&&* and *| |*, except that they guarantee full evaluation of both operands. The AND (*full evaluation*) operator (*&*) is a logical AND with full evaluation, and the OR (full evaluation) operator (*|*) is a logical OR with full evaluation. In the following code, the methods *IsWindow* and *IsVisible* are always called:

```
bool windowReady = (IsWindow() & IsVisible());
```

The XOR (exclusive OR) operator (^) is used to determine whether exactly one of two operands is *true*, as shown in the following code. If neither of the operands is *true*, or if both are *true*, the expression evaluates as *false*.

```
bool decisionReady = (IsGoingLeft() ^ IsGoingRight());
```

This brings us to the *true* and *false* operators. These operators are rarely invoked directly. If you're implementing your own types, however, you can overload these operators to control how logical operations are evaluated against your type. The section "Creating a New Value Type," later in this chapter, discusses creating your own types and overloading these operators in more detail.

As mentioned, implicit conversion from scalar to Boolean types isn't allowed in C#. This means that common C and C++ constructions such as the following aren't allowed:

```
int answer = 42;
if(answer){ ... }
```

To prevent a host of common programming errors, C# requires you to be slightly more explicit about your intentions, as shown here:

```
int answer = 42;
if(answer != 0){ ... }
```

Doing Math with the Arithmetic Operators

The arithmetic operators are used to create expressions that perform math operations. The operators for creating basic math expressions such as addition, multiplication, division, and other operations are listed in Table 4-3.

Table 4-3.   Arithmetic Operators in C#

Operator	Description
+	Addition
-	Subtraction
*	Multiplication
%	Modulo (Remainder)
/	Division
++	Increment
--	Decrement

The addition operator (+) is used to add two operands. The resulting expression contains the value of the operation, as follows:

```
int answer = 5 + 37;
```

When the operands have different types, the C# compiler must apply type conversion rules to ensure that the operation occurs in a predictable manner. In the following example, the first operand is converted to the *float* type, and then the + operator is called. The resulting expression has the *float* type.

```
float answer = 5 + 37.5;
```

The subtraction operator (-) is used to subtract the second operand from the first, as shown here:

```
int answer = 52 - 5;
```

The multiplication operator (*) is used to multiply two operands:

```
int answer = 21 * 2;
```

The division operator (/) is used to divide the first operand by the second, as shown here, with the resulting expression containing the operation result:

```
int answer = 84 / 2;
```

When two scalar operands are encountered, the / operator returns a scalar result, rounded down to the lower whole number. To determine the remainder, if any, use the modulo operator (%).

The % operator is used to divide the first operand by the second, with the resulting expression containing the remainder of the operation, as shown here:

```
int answer = 142 % 50;
```

The ++ and -- operators work with a single operand, incrementing or decrementing the value of the operand. You can use either the prefix or postfix versions of these operators. The difference is subtle but important if you're testing for the resulting value of the expression. A prefix increment or decrement operation increments the value of the operand, and the resulting expression is the changed value of the operand, as shown here:

```
int n = 41;
int answer = ++n; // answer = 42, n = 42;
```

Although a postfix increment or decrement operation increments the value of the operand, the resulting expression has the value of the operand before the operator was applied, as shown here:

```
int n = 41;
int answer = n++; // answer = 41, n = 42;
```

In some cases, the prefix increment and decrement operations will be more efficient than the postfix versions, because the implementation of those methods doesn't require that a temporary value be created.

The arithmetic operators can cause your program to throw an exception. An attempt to divide by 0 will result in a *DivideByZeroException* exception being thrown. Other operations that result in an overflow condition, in which a variable is assigned a value outside the range of values that the variable can hold, might result in an *OverflowException* exception being thrown if the code is running in a checked context.

Managing Bit Patterns with the Bitwise Operators

The bitwise operators are used to manipulate bit patterns for scalar types. These operations are useful when you're interacting directly with the operating system or with legacy code that depends on masking values stored in a scalar type.

Table 4-4 lists the bitwise operators offered in C#.

Table 4-4.   Bitwise Operators in C#

Operator	Description
>>	Right shift
<<	Left shift
&	AND
|	OR
^	XOR (exclusive OR)
~	Complement

> **Note**   Several of the operators in Table 4-4 are shared with the logical operators discussed earlier and shown in Table 4-2. When the Visual C# .NET compiler detects that one of these operators is being used, it invokes the correct operator based on the types of the surrounding operands.

The left-shift operator (<<) shifts the bits of the scalar value a specified number of bits to the left, as shown in Figure 4-1.

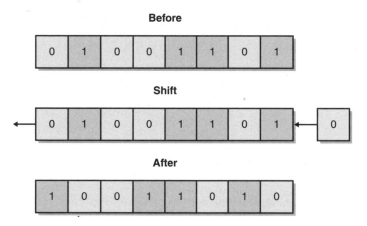

Figure 4-1.   The << operator, which moves the bit pattern to the left.

Any bits that are shifted out of the variable are discarded. New bits with 0 values are inserted to fill in the space left by the shift operation, as follows:

```
int answer = 21 << 1; // answer = 42
```

The right-shift operator (>>) shifts the bits of a scalar value to the right, in a manner similar to the << operator, as shown here:

```
int answer = 84 >> 1; // answer = 42
```

The bitwise AND operator (&) combines a scalar value and a bit mask by performing a logical AND operation on a bit-by-bit basis. This operation results in a new bit pattern, as shown in Figure 4-2.

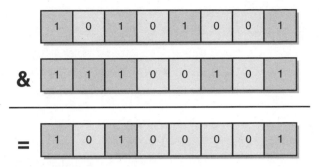

Figure 4-2.   The & operator, which is used to mask bits in a scalar value by performing bitwise AND operations.

Where the original value and the bit mask both have a corresponding bit enabled, the resulting bit pattern will have that bit enabled. All other bits will be set to 0, as shown here:

```
int n = 0x007F;
int x = 0x00AA;
int answer = n & x;
Console.WriteLine(answer); // Displays 42
```

The bitwise OR operator (|) combines a scalar value and a bit mask much like the & operator does, except that the | operator performs a logical OR operation, as shown in Figure 4-3.

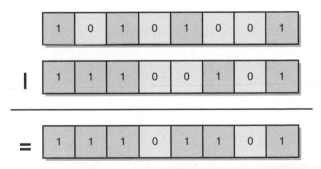

Figure 4-3.   The / operator, which is used to combine bits in a scalar value by performing bitwise OR operations.

Where the original scalar value *or* the bit mask have a bit enabled, the resulting bit pattern will have the corresponding bit enabled, as shown here:

```
int n = 0x0020;
int x = 0x002A;
int answer = n | x;
Console.WriteLine(answer); // Displays 42
```

The bitwise XOR (exclusive OR) operator (^) is similar to the & and | operators, except that the ^ operator performs an XOR operation on each bit, and the resulting bit pattern has a bit set only if the original scalar value or the bit mask has its corresponding bit set, as shown in Figure 4-4.

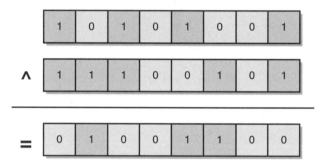

Figure 4-4.   The ^ operator, which is used to perform bitwise XOR operations.

If both (or neither) have the bit set, the resulting bit pattern has its bit cleared.

The bitwise complement operator (~) generates a bitwise complement for a scalar value. Any bits that are enabled in the original scalar value are disabled in the resulting bit pattern, and any bits that are disabled are enabled.

Setting Variables with the Assignment Operators

Several types of assignment operators are available in C#, the most common of which is the simple assignment operator (=). Table 4-5 lists these assignment operators, which provide a concise method for combining common operations with the = operator.

Table 4-5.   Assignment Operators in C#

Operator	Description
=	Assignment
+=	Addition assignment
-=	Subtraction assignment

(continued)

Table 4-5. **Assignment Operators in C#**   *(continued)*

Operator	Description
*=	Multiplication assignment
/=	Division assignment
%=	Remainder assignment
<<=	Left-shift assignment
>>=	Right-shift assignment
&=	Bitwise-AND assignment
|=	Bitwise-OR assignment
^=	Bitwise-XOR assignment

The = operator is used to assign the value of one operand (the right operand) to a second operand (the left operand). The value of the resulting expression is the value of the right operand, so assignment operations can be chained together as shown here:

```
y = x = n = 42;
```

In this expression, *y* is set to the value *42*. All assignment operations are subject to rules regarding type conversions, which are discussed later in this chapter in the section "Converting Types."

The addition assignment operator (+=) combines addition and assignment, adding the first operand to the second and then storing the result in the first operand, as shown here:

```
y = 40;
y += 2;
```

This example is equivalent to the following code:

```
y = 40;
y = y + 2;
```

The other operators that combine arithmetic operations with assignment work much like the += operator. The subtraction assignment (-=), multiplication assignment (*=), division assignment (/=), and remainder assignment (%=) operators provide a convenient and concise way to show that a value is being applied to an existing operand.

The left-shift assignment (<<=) and right-shift assignment (>>=) operators combine a shift operation with an assignment operation, storing the result of the shift operation in the first operand, as shown here:

```
int n = 21;
n <<= 1;
Console.WriteLine(n); // Displays 42
```

The remaining assignment operators are based on operators that are shared between logical and bitwise operations. These assignment operators behave differently depending on whether they're used with scalar or Boolean operands.

The bitwise-AND assignment operator (*&*=) combines an AND operation with assignment. When used with Boolean operands, the first operand and the second operand are combined to form a logical AND expression, and the resulting value is stored in the first operand. When *&*= is used with scalar values, a bitwise AND operation is performed, as is done for the *&* operator. The resulting value is stored in the first operand. The following code demonstrates the use of the *&*= operator:

```
int n = 0x007F;
n &= 0x00AA;
Console.WriteLine(n); // Displays 42
```

The bitwise-OR assignment operator (|=) and bitwise-XOR assignment operator (^=) have characteristics that are similar to the *&*= operator. The |= operator combines an OR operation with an assignment, and the ^= operator combines XOR and an assignment. Both of these operators tailor their behavior to suit the type to which they are applied.

Using the Conditional Operator

The conditional operator (*?:*) works with three operands, as shown here:

```
bool isTrue = true;
string result = isTrue? "true": "false";
Console.WriteLine(result); // Displays true
```

Because it's the only operator that works with three operands, the *?:* operator is sometimes called the *ternary operator*. The first operand must be a Boolean value or expression. If *true*, the value of the conditional expression is the second operand; otherwise, the conditional expression's value is the third operand.

When used judiciously, the *?:* operator can result in concise, expressive code. Used to the extreme, it can result in code that's difficult to maintain and read. For example, the following code compiles and runs as expected, but it's not as clear as the preceding example:

```
bool isTrue = true;
Console.WriteLine(isTrue? "true": "false");
```

Obtaining Type Information

C# includes operators that are used to determine information about the type of an object at runtime. These operators are listed in Table 4-6.

Table 4-6.   Type Information Operators in C#

Operator	Description
is	Tests for a specific type
typeof	Tests for type information
sizeof	Tests for the size of a value type

The *is* operator is used to test an object to determine whether the object is a specific type, as shown in the following code. The resulting expression has a Boolean value.

```
public void DisplayObject(object obj)
{
    if(obj is BattingAverage)
    {
        // obj refers to a BattingAverage object.
        ⋮
    }
}
```

The *typeof* operator is used to represent runtime type information about a class, as shown in the following code. This operator is applied to a type name rather than to an object. The resulting expression is a *System.Type* object.

```
Type theType = typeof(BattingAverage);
```

The *sizeof* operator returns the size of a value type, as shown in the following code. (You can't determine the size of a reference type.) To use *sizeof*, your code must be executing in the unsafe context. The *unsafe* keyword, which you can apply as a modifier to the callable members of a type, denotes an unsafe context that extends from the parameter list to the end of the function. Unsafe code is described in more detail in Chapter 10.

```
int size = sizeof(BattingAverage);
```

Addressing Memory Directly

C# also provides operators that are used to address memory directly. These operators can be used only in code executing in the unsafe context. The operators used for direct memory access are listed in Table 4-7.

Table 4-7.   Direct Memory Access Operators in C#

Operator	Description
*	Pointer indirection
->	Member access
[]	Index
&	Address of

> **More Info**   Chapter 10 describes the use of direct memory access operators in more detail.

Using Other Operators

Several additional operators are used with C#. The first of these is the dot operator (.). The dot operator is used to access members of a namespace, class, structure, or enumeration, as in *System.Console.WriteLine*.

The dot operator is used much as it is in C or C++. But unlike in those languages, in C# the dot operator is the only member access operator offered. The member access operator (->), which combines pointer dereferencing and member access, is never used except when you're working with unsafe code, and the scope resolution operator (::) doesn't exist in C#.

As you saw in Chapter 3, the index operator ([]) is used to access a member element in an array. It's also used to access an indexer, if one is provided by a class. Declaring an indexer for your class enables you to use the class like an index. Providing indexers for your classes is discussed in Chapter 7. The cast operator (()) is used to attempt to coerce a type change for a value, as shown in the following code. To use the () operator, enclose the new type in parentheses to the left of the value to be cast. If the value can't be cast into the new type, an *InvalidCastException* exception is thrown.

```
public void DisplayObject(object obj)
{
    try
    {
        BattingAverage avg = (BattingAverage)obj;
        ⋮
    }
    catch(InvalidCastException exc)
    {
        ⋮
    }
}
```

Working with Operators

C# provides you with a large set of operators and gives you a great deal of control over the behavior of those operators in an expression. This section focuses on how to control the behavior of operators. First we'll look at operator precedence and executing code in a checked context, and then we'll look at an example that shows you how to overload operators to work with a new value type.

Understanding Operator Precedence

Each operator has a defined precedence. When you combine multiple operators to create a single expression, it's important to understand how operator precedence will affect the evaluation of the expression. Table 4-8 lists the C# operators, categorized according to precedence, from highest to lowest.

Table 4-8.   Operator Precedence in C#

Category	Operators
Primary	.f(x) a[x] x++ x-- new typeof checked unchecked
Unary	+ - ! ~ ++x --x (T)x
Multiplication	* / %
Addition	+ -
Shift	<< >>
Relational and type testing	< > <= >= is as
Equality	== !=
Logical AND	&
Logical XOR	^
Logical OR	|
Conditional AND	&&
Conditional OR	||
Ternary (conditional)	?:
Assignment	= *= /= %= += -= <<= >>= &= ^= |=

The Primary category refers to basic expressions that form a tight binding between operator and operand. The notation *f(x)* refers to a function call invocation, where *x* is passed as an argument. As you saw in Chapter 2 and Chapter 3, the *new* operator is used to allocate an object. The *checked* and *unchecked* operators, discussed in the next section, are used to mark whether an expression tests for math overflow conditions.

In the Unary category, the *(T)x* notation signifies a cast expression, where a value *x* is cast to type *T*.

Tip   You can use parentheses to alter the order in which operators are evaluated. Expressions within parentheses are always evaluated first. If you need an operator with lower precedence to be evaluated ahead of an operator with higher precedence, just group the necessary expression using parentheses, like this:

```
decimal first = 3.2M;
decimal second = 4.3M;
decimal pi = 3.1415926535M;
decimal answer = pi * (first + second);
```

Another property of operators is the way they're associated with their operands. Most unary operators are associated with the operands to their right; the only exception is the unary postfix operators.

The binary operators are usually left-associative, meaning that operations are carried out from left to right. The exception is the assignment operator, which is associated with the operand to its right. This exception allows assignment operators to be chained together, as shown earlier in this chapter in the section "Setting Variables with the Assignment Operators." The conditional ternary operator is also right-associative.

Using the *checked* and *unchecked* Keywords

Math operations can sometimes result in overflow or underflow errors. Some languages check every math operation to guard against these errors, but this type of runtime checking increases the cost of every math operation. Some languages perform no runtime checking, expecting that error checking will be inserted by the programmer wherever such checks are warranted. This approach often leads to errors at runtime. C# offers keywords that are used to explicitly enable or disable automatic checking of math operations.

The *checked* keyword is used to mark a block or an expression as checked for arithmetic overflow errors, as shown in the following code. If an operation overflows its destination, an *OverflowException* exception will be thrown.

```
try
{
    checked
```

```
    {
        short max = 32767; // Maximum value for a short
        ++max;
    }
}
catch(OverflowException exc)
{
    ⋮
}
```

The *unchecked* keyword marks a block or an expression as not checked for overflow errors. If no keyword is present, the behavior depends on the current compiler settings—normally set to *unchecked*.

Defining Operators for Your Types

When defining your own class or structure types, you also can define how operators work with those types. Providing operators for your types allows them to be used more like the built-in types. It also helps make your types more intuitive. For example, the default behavior of the = operator is to test for object equality rather than value equality. As discussed in Chapter 3, the *string* type overloads the relational operators and tests the *string* value instead of the object location. This is the behavior that most users would expect of a *string* class, and it's a good example of providing a useful set of operators for a class.

Many of the operators, such as the dot operator, can't be overloaded. Table 4-9 lists the operators that are available for overloading in C#.

Table 4-9. Operators That Can Be Overloaded in C#

Operator Type	Operators
Unary	+ - ! ~ ++ -- *true* *false*
Binary	+ - * / % & | ^ << >> == != > < >= <=

The ternary operator can't be overloaded, nor can the index or cast operator. (In C#, you define how the index operator works by providing an indexer for your class.) Instead of overloading the cast operator, in C# you provide explicit type conversion methods, as discussed later in this chapter, in the section "Performing Explicit Conversions."

You're free to implement specialized versions of the comparison operators; however, operators must be implemented in pairs. The > operator must be implemented together with the < operator. The >= operator must be implemented in tandem with the <= operator. The == and != operators must always be implemented together. In addition, if you implement == and !=, the Visual C# .NET compiler will issue a warning if you don't override the *Object.Equals* and *Object.GetHashCode* methods.

By default, the *Object.Equals* method tests reference equality. If you override this method to test for logical equivalence, you're expected to implement the following basic behavior:

- If *Equals* is passed a reference to the current object, it should return *true*, except for some specific floating-point cases.

- If *Equals* is passed a null reference, it must return *false*.

- If the objects *Equals* works with are unmodified, *Equals* must return the same result.

- For floating-point types, when comparing two objects that evaluate as *NaN, Equals* will return *true*.

- The *Equals* method must be reflexive—that is, if *x.Equals(y)* is *true*, *y.Equals(x)* must be *true*.

- The *Equals* method is transitive—that is, if *x.Equals(y)* is *true*, and *y.Equals(z)* is *true*, *x.Equals(z)* must be *true*.

The *GetHashCode* method is a hash function used to enable proper distribution in a hash table or similar collection type. When implementing this method, keep in mind that an ideal hash function is one that returns the same hash value for logically equivalent objects. In the example in the next section, the hash function calls *ToString* to generate a string representation of the object and then uses the string type's implementation of *GetHashCode* to generate a hash value.

Caution   If your implementation of *GetHashCode* returns different values during the lifetime of an object, you must take steps to avoid storing the object in certain types of collections. Some .NET collection classes, such as *HashTable,* use the object's hash code to determine how the object is stored. If the hash code for an object changes, it might be impossible to locate the object in the collection. This isn't a problem when you're storing objects in arrays or simple collection classes such as *List* or *Stack*. Collections that depend on stable hash codes document this requirement in their online documentation.

Understanding Hashing

A hash function is used to translate input, such as a string or other data, into a numeric value called a *hash code,* or simply a *hash*. Given identical inputs, a hash function always returns the same hash, which makes it ideal for a common use—as an index key to an object stored in a table. To search for the data object, you can apply the hash function to the query to produce the index key to the table. This can be much more efficient than searching through every data object in a table until a match is found for the query.

Hashes also play a role in security systems. For example, they can be used to verify the integrity of data that's been transmitted. If the data is transmitted together with a hash of the data, the recipient can apply the hash function to the data and compare the resulting hash to the hash that was transmitted with the data. If the two hash values are equal, the chances that the data suffered corruption or that someone tampered with the data are extremely unlikely.

In the .NET Framework, hashes are used in two ways: First, some collection classes use the hash code returned by an object to organize their internal storage of objects. Hash codes are also used to perform a presumptive test to determine object equivalence. Testing hash codes is often faster than performing a complete test for equality—if two objects have the same hash code, they're likely to be equivalent.

Hash codes are also used to ensure that assemblies with *strong names* aren't compromised. A hash of the assembly's contents is created and stored with the assembly. When an assembly is loaded, the hash is recalculated, and the runtime will not allow the assembly to load if the hash has changed. Strong-named assemblies are discussed in more detail in Chapter 1.

Creating a New Value Type

To demonstrate how operators can be redefined for a type, let's consider a new value type that models (in a simplified way) a baseball batting average. The basic idea behind a batting average is that it represents the number of hits divided by the number of at bats for a baseball player. (Of course, like so many things in baseball, an explanation of exactly what constitutes a hit or an at bat could take hours, and sometimes seems to depend on the mood of the official scorer, but that's another story.)

The following code shows an initial version of the *BattingAverage* value type. Like all value types, it's declared as a *structure*.

```
using System;
namespace MSPress.CSharpCoreRef.BattingAverageExample
{
    public struct BattingAverage
    {
        // Constructs a new BattingAverage value type instance
        public BattingAverage(int atBats, int hits)
        {
            TestValid(atBats, hits);
            _atBats = atBats;
            _hits = hits;
        }
        /// Returns the batting average, subject to floating-
        /// point rounding
        public float Average()
        {
            if(_atBats == 0)
                return 0.0f;
            else
                return (float)_hits / (float)_atBats;
        }
        /// Tests for valid hits and at bats, throwing an exception
        /// if the parameters are invalid
        private static void TestValid(int testAtBats, int testHits)
        {
            if(testAtBats < 0)
            {
                string msg = "At bats must not be negative";
                throw new ArgumentOutOfRangeException(msg);
            }
            if(testAtBats < testHits)
            {
                string msg = "Hits must not exceed at bats";
                throw new ArgumentOutOfRangeException(msg);
            }
        }
        public int _atBats;
        public int _hits;
    }
}
```

The *BattingAverage* value type uses two private fields to represent the number of at bats and hits used to calculate the batting average. Methods are used to validate and calculate the batting average.

As defined in the preceding code, the *BattingAverage* type can be used to calculate and store batting average information. However, comparing *Batting-Average* objects is awkward in this first version of the class, as shown here:

```
if(firstBatter.Average() < secondBatter.Average())
{
    // secondBatter's average is higher...
}
```

Instead of requiring clients of the *BattingAverage* class to explicitly invoke the *Average* method and compare the results, it's more intuitive to overload the comparison operators and allow for a simplified syntax that's similar to the built-in types, as follows:

```
if(firstBatter < secondBatter)
{
    // secondBatter's average is higher...
}
```

The following methods overload all of the relational operators and the *object* class's *Equals* and *GetHashCode* methods: The complete code listing is available on the companion CD.

```
// Equality operator for batting averages
public static bool operator ==(BattingAverage left,
                                BattingAverage right)
{
    if((object)left == null)
        return false;
    else
        return left.Equals(right);
}


// Inequality operator for batting averages
public static bool operator !=(BattingAverage left,
                                BattingAverage right)
{
    return !(left == right);
}


// Override of the Object.Equals method; returns
// true if the current object is equal to another
// object passed as a parameter
public override bool Equals(object other)
{
    bool result = false;
    if(other != null)
    {
        if((object)this == other)
        {
            result = true;
        }
        else if(other is BattingAverage)
```

(continued)

```
            {
                BattingAverage otherAvg = (BattingAverage)other;
                result = Average() == otherAvg.Average();
            }
        }
        return result;
    }

    // Converts the batting average to a string, and then
    // uses the string to generate the hash code
    public override int GetHashCode()
    {
        return ToString().GetHashCode();
    }

    // Compares two operands using the greater than operator
    public static bool operator >(BattingAverage left,
                                  BattingAverage right)
    {
        return left.Average() > right.Average();
    }

    // Compares two operands using the less than or equal to
    // operator
    public static bool operator <=(BattingAverage left,
                                   BattingAverage right)
    {
        return left.Average() <= right.Average();
    }

    // Compares two operands using the less than operator
    public static bool operator <(BattingAverage left,
                                  BattingAverage right)
    {
        return left.Average() < right.Average();
    }

    // Compares two operands using the greater than or
    // equal to operator
    public static bool operator >=(BattingAverage left,
                                   BattingAverage right)
    {
        return left.Average() >= right.Average();
    }

    // Returns true if the object is logically false
    public static bool operator false(BattingAverage avg)
    {
        return avg.Average() == 0;
    }
```

```
// Returns true if the object is logically true
public static bool operator true(BattingAverage avg)
{
    return avg.Average() != 0;
}


// Performs an AND operation on two batting averages
public static BattingAverage operator &(BattingAverage left,
                                         BattingAverage right)
{
    if(left.Average() == 0 || right.Average() == 0)
        return new BattingAverage();
    else
        return new BattingAverage(left._atBats + right._atBats,
                                  left._hits + left._hits);
}


// Performs an OR operation on two batting averages
public static BattingAverage operator |(BattingAverage left,
                                         BattingAverage right)
{
    if(left.Average() != 0)
        return new BattingAverage(left._atBats, left._hits);
    else if(right.Average() != 0)
        return new BattingAverage(right._atBats, right._hits);
    else
        return new BattingAverage();
}
```

The relational operators for *BattingAverage* encapsulate the *Average* method and allow clients to compare *BattingAverage* objects with each other naturally, just like built-in types such as *int* or *string*.

Controlling the Behavior of *&&* and *||*

Now that we've covered the basics of operator overloading, let's take on a more advanced topic: overloading the *&&* and *||* operators. Although the *&&* and *||* operators can't be overloaded directly, you can affect how they're evaluated. When the *&&* operator is encountered in an expression, the C# compiler generates code that calls the *true, false,* and *&* operators. We'll examine the way these operators are invoked in a minute. For now, let's look at how the *true, false,* and *&* operators work.

The *true* and *false* operators return Boolean values that indicate whether an object has the value specified by the operator. The *true* operator returns *true* when the object has a logically *true* value; otherwise, it returns *false*. The *false* operator returns *true* if the object has a *false* value; otherwise, it returns *false*. The *&* operator returns a new object of the same type as the operands; this object is the result of performing a logical AND with the operands. For the *BattingAverage* value type, the *true* and *false* operators are defined as follows:

```
public static bool operator false(BattingAverage avg)
{
    return avg.Average() == 0;
}


public static bool operator true(BattingAverage avg)
{
    return avg.Average() != 0;
}
```

The operators consider any batting average greater than 0 to be logically *true*; a batting average of 0 is considered logically *false*.

The *&* operator for the *BattingAverage* type looks like this:

```
public static BattingAverage operator &(BattingAverage left,
                                         BattingAverage right)
{
    if(left.Average() == 0 || right.Average() == 0)
        return new BattingAverage();
    else
        return new BattingAverage(left._atBats + right._atBats,
                                  left._hits + right._hits);
}
```

If either of the *BattingAverage* objects has a 0 average, a new, empty *Batting-Average* object is created and returned. Otherwise, a new *BattingAverage* object that combines the two operands is created and returned.

For the purpose of tracing how the Visual C# .NET compiler creates the *&&* expression, consider the following code:

```
BattingAverage a;
BattingAverage b;
:
bool isTrue = (a && b);
```

Behind the scenes, the compiler combines the *true*, *false*, and *&* operators in the following way to evaluate the *&&* operator:

```
if(BattingAverage.false(a) != true)
{
    return BattingAverage.true(BattingAverage.operator&(a, b));
}
else
{
    return BattingAverage.true(a);
}
```

The first operand, *a*, is tested by invoking the *false* operator. If the operand isn't *false*, the & operator is invoked to combine both *a* and *b* operands in an AND operation. The result of that operation is passed to the type's *true* operator, and the result of that operation is kept as the result of the && expression. If the first operand is *false*, the operand is passed to the type's *true* operator, and the result of that operation is used as the result of the && expression.

In a similar way, when the || operator is used like this:

```
bool isTrue = (a || b);
```

the Visual C# .NET compiler will generate code equivalent to the following:

```
if(BattingAverage.true(a) == true)
{
    return BattingAverage.true(a);
}
else
{
    return BattingAverage.true(BattingAverage.operator|(a, b));
}
```

Converting Types

The C# programming language puts a high value on type safety. Every value in a C# program has a specific type, and each type has a unique contract to which the type adheres. When a value is assigned to a variable that has a different type, a type conversion is required.

Type conversion is used to migrate values from one type to another. When a new type is defined, such as the *BattingAverage* type in the previous section, type conversion is often used to integrate the new type into existing code. For example, later in this section we'll add some type conversion operators to simplify converting a *BattingAverage* object to a *string* or *float* value. Understanding how C# type conversion works can make your types much easier to use.

Performing Implicit Conversions

Some type conversions are inherently safe and are allowed to occur automatically, without any conversion code required. When you're converting between scalar types, some conversions are guaranteed to succeed. For example, scalar types such as *short*, *int*, and *long* differ only in the range of values they can store. A *short* value can always be stored in an *int*, and an *int* can always be stored in a *long*, without writing any conversion code, as shown here:

```
short s = 32767;
int n = s;
```

One characteristic of these implicit conversions is that they are inherently asymmetrical, meaning that you can implicitly store a *short* value in an *int*, but a conversion in the other direction can potentially result in the loss of data, and can't be done implicitly by the compiler.

Performing Explicit Conversions

Conversions that result in a loss of data require you to write code that explicitly demands that a conversion take place. Examples of conversions that must be managed explicitly are a conversion that results in a loss of precision or a conversion to a scalar type with a smaller range.

Many times, a conversion that might result in a loss of data is actually harmless. For example, a conversion from a *double* to a *float* results in a loss of precision; in your application, however, the degradation in precision might be a harmless conversion. A value stored as a *long* can be safely converted to an *int* if you know that its value will always fall into the range permitted for an *int*.

The brute-force way to explicitly convert a value from one type to a type that might result in a loss of data is to use the cast operator. As discussed earlier in this chapter in the section "Using Other Operators," to use the cast operator, you enclose the new type in parentheses and place it to the left of the value to be cast, as shown here:

```
int longVal = 32767;
short s = (short)longVal;
```

Another method that can be used to convert types is to use the *System.Convert* class, as discussed in the next section.

String conversion can be accomplished in multiple ways, one of which is to override the *ToString* method. The *object* base class implements a default version of *ToString*, and most types override that implementation and provide a new version of *ToString* that converts the object's value to a *string*. For the *BattingAverage* type, the *ToString* method has been overridden first to calculate the batting average and then to format the text as a string in the traditional batting average format, with three digits to the left of the decimal point, as shown here:

```
// Convert the batting average to a string.
public override string ToString()
{
    float average = Average();
    string result = string.Format("{0:#.000}", average);
    return result;
}
```

Overriding the *Object.ToString* method simplifies the use of the *Batting-Average* type when you're formatting text. For example, when a *BattingAverage* object is passed to the *Console.WriteLine* method, the *Console* class will use the

ToString method to retrieve the text that's sent to the console. With the following code, a batting average of *.333* is displayed to the user:

```
// 30 at bats, 10 hits
BattingAverage ba = new BattingAverage(30, 10);
Console.WriteLine(ba);
```

Using the *Convert* Class

The *Convert* class offers a convenient way to convert values to different types, even if the types are unrelated. The *Convert* class has an added feature: the current culture settings are respected, so symbols such as the decimal separator are formatted correctly.

All methods in the *Convert* class are static, so you never need to create a *Convert* object. The following code uses the *Convert* class to convert a *string* value to an *int* value:

```
string stringValue = "1542";
int intValue = Convert.ToInt32(stringValue);
```

Each of the *ToXxxx* methods is used to convert a value to one of the primitive .NET types, where *Xxxx* is a .NET type name such as *Int16*, *Int32*, or *String*. The class overloads these methods for ease of use (the *ToInt32* method, for example, can convert several different types to an *Int32*), with some methods offering dozens of overloads.

Performing User-Defined Conversions

A *user-defined conversion* is a type-conversion method supplied by a class or structure that defines how an object of that type can be converted to another type. In C#, user-defined conversions serve a role similar to that of the C++ cast operator, but they allow more flexibility. A user-defined conversion can be defined as either *implicit* or *explicit*. Implicit conversions can occur automatically when a parameter is passed to a method or during an assignment. Explicit conversions take place only if the cast operator is used. If a conversion can result in a loss of data, you should define the conversion as explicit.

All conversions must abide by the following rules:

■ A user-defined conversion isn't allowed to convert a type to the same type, or to a subclass or superclass of the type.

■ User-defined conversions must be to or from the type defining the conversion.

■ Conversion can't be attempted to or from an interface or the *object* type.

These rules help provide predictable behavior for user-defined conversions as well as prevent interference with built-in conversions.

User-defined conversion operators accept a single type as a parameter. An explicit user-defined conversion for the *BattingAverage* type to *float* looks like this:

```
public static explicit operator float(BattingAverage avg)
{
    return avg.Average();
}
```

To define an implicit conversion, simply use the *implicit* keyword instead of *explicit* as was done in this example. Here the choice of an implicit or explicit conversion is a judgment call, as the conversion doesn't actually cause any data loss. However, because an implicit conversion would allow the *Batting-Average* type to be substituted for the *float* type for any method parameters or assignment, the preceding code requires the caller to use a cast operator for the conversion.

Basic String Formatting for Numeric Values

String formatting is used in many places when you develop with C#. For example, the *Console.WriteLine* method uses the same string formatting rules as the *string* type's *Format* method. This section provides an introduction to string formatting, using the *BattingAverage* class as an example.

The format strings passed to methods such as *Console.WriteLine* control how optional parameters are formatted. When we've used *Console.WriteLine* in earlier examples, we've always passed fairly basic strings such as this:

```
string name = "Mickey";
Console.WriteLine("Hello, {0}.", name);
```

The *{0}* notation in this example is used to identify the first parameter, with the number inside the placeholder used to specify the parameter index.

It's possible to have multiple parameters in a single call to *WriteLine*, as in the following code:

```
string name1 = "Mickey";
string name2 = "Ali";
Console.WriteLine("Hello, {0} and {1}.", name1, name2);
```

By default, the *WriteLine* method calls the *ToString* method for each parameter, substituting the returned string for each placeholder. Alternatively, you can specify width, format, and precision information inside the placeholders. This allows you to apply specific formatting rather than relying on the object's *Write-Line* method.

To specify the width used by a parameter, add a comma after the parameter number, followed by the minimum number of characters to be reserved for the parameter, as shown here:

```
int n = 42;
Console.WriteLine("{0,4},{0,8},{0,12},{0,16}", n);
```

The format and precision for numeric types can be controlled by using one of eight format characters in the format $0{:}Sn$, where 0 is a number specifying the parameter index, S is a format character, and n is an optional value specifying the precision of the displayed value. Table 4-10 lists the standard .NET formatting characters for numeric types.

Table 4-10.   String Formatting Characters for Numeric Types in C#

Character	Description
C	Displayed as currency using the current culture settings, such as *$12.00*. If no precision is specified, two digits after the decimal separator are displayed.
D	Displayed in a decimal format. This format can be used only by scalar types. The precision can be used to specify the minimum number of digits to be displayed.
E	Displayed in an exponential form, such as *1.012e+004*, with the precision specifying the number of digits to be displayed after the decimal point. The case of the exponent symbol will match the case of the formatting character.
F	Displayed in fixed-point form, with the precision specifying the number of digits to be displayed after the decimal separator. If no precision is specified, two digits are displayed after the decimal separator.
G	Displayed using the general format, which delegates to either the decimal or fixed-point format, depending on which can display the most compact and accurate representation.
N	Displayed in number format, with the precision specifying the number of zeros to append to the number after a decimal separator. If no precision is specified, two digits are displayed after the decimal separator.
P	Displayed in a percentage format, with the precision specifying the number of digits to be displayed after the decimal separator.
R	Displayed in a round-trip format that most accurately represents the value. This is useful for floating-point values that must be reconstituted from the string later.
X	Displayed in a hexadecimal format such as *0x4A*, with the case of the displayed hexadecimal characters matching the case of the formatting character. If no precision is specified, the precision defaults to the minimum number of characters needed to display the value.

The case of the formatting character is insignificant except for *X* and *E*, where some portion of the output matches the case of the formatting character.

Alternatively, the formatting string can also include picture information that controls how a number is displayed. In the *BattingAverage.ToString* method, the string is formatted as follows so that the average will be displayed correctly:

```
{0:#.000}
```

This formatting string is passed to the *string* type's *Format* method, which uses the same mechanism employed by *Console.WriteLine*, as follows:

```
float average = Average();
string result = string.Format("{0:#.000}", average);
```

Passing the initial *#* as the picture specification will cause a digit to be displayed only if it's significant. This prevents the display of a leading zero for the batting average, in keeping with the customary format. The next character is a decimal, which causes the decimal separator to be displayed using the proper symbol in the current culture. Finally, the three zeros after the decimal point force exactly three digits to be displayed after the decimal separator.

Using Properties as Smart Fields

Properties are a useful way for a user-defined type to expose data to clients. From the client's viewpoint, a property appears to be a public field. By implementing a property instead of a field, you can insulate users from the details of your implementation, as well as provide additional processing such as validation or tracing when a property is accessed.

For example, *BattingAverage* has two public fields: *_hits* and *_atBats*. Exposing these fields publicly makes them easily accessible by clients. However, it's difficult to change the types of these fields, and it's impossible to perform validation processing when a client updates one of the values.

The *_hits* and *_atBats* fields are marked as private in the final version of *BattingAverage*, shown in the following code, and access to the fields is provided through the *Hits* and *AtBats* properties:

```
public int AtBats
{
    get
    {
        return _atBats;
    }
    set
```

```
    {
        TestValid(value, _hits);
        _atBats = value;
    }
}

public int Hits
{
    get
    {
        return _hits;
    }
    set
    {
        TestValid(_atBats, value);
        _hits = value;
    }
}
```

A property is defined by specifying its access protection (*public* in this case), the type for the property value, and the property name. Within the property definition, a *get* method is used to return the property value, and a *set* method is used to provide a new value for the property. The *set* method has a hidden parameter named *value* that contains the new property value. A read-only property is defined by eliminating the *set* method.

Conclusion

A wide array of operators are provided with the C# language, including many operators that are familiar to C and C++ programmers. C# also provides operators that go beyond C and C++, such as operators for performing full logical evaluations and operators for obtaining type information. C# also provides several techniques for enhancing your user-defined types so that they're easier to use. By overloading operators for your types, you can give your types behavior that matches that of built-in types.

When values are converted to a new type, the process is managed by a type conversion operator. When you define conversion operators for your types, they can be declared as either *implicit* or *explicit*. Implicit operators can be invoked silently and shouldn't result in a loss of data; explicit operators must be explicitly invoked and are used when a conversion might result in data loss.

Properties look like fields to the user, but they look like methods when added to your class or structure. This versatility simplifies the programming model for the consumer, because the consumer can access the property using the same syntax as is used to directly access a field. Meanwhile, the supplier is able to decouple the property name from the implementation of the property, much like access methods provided in other languages.

Chapter 5 introduces statements used to control the flow of execution, which enable you to write more sophisticated code than we've written thus far. C# includes a number of statements that support iteration, conditional execution, and transferring control within your application.

5

Flow of Control

In previous chapters, we've examined the basic syntax you use when developing C# programs. Most of the code developed thus far has been relatively simple, focusing on basic construction techniques, such as creating classes, declaring fields and variables, and using properties. Beginning with this chapter, we'll begin to use statements and expressions to build control structures in your programs.

In this chapter, you'll see how using selection statements to control the flow of execution in a program allows you to write code that executes conditionally based on user input. There are two selection statements used in C#:

■ The *if* statement is used to execute blocks of code conditionally, based on the value of an expression that's evaluated as your program executes.

■ The *switch* statement allows you to select from among multiple execution paths by matching the value of an expression with possible values, each of which has a code path associated with it.

This chapter also discusses the statements used to create iteration and looping algorithms in C#, as follows:

■ The *for* loop is used to perform a number of iterations over a statement or statement block. The *for* loop allows you to define the behavior of the loop in a compact format at the beginning of the loop.

- The *foreach* loop has a simple structure and is designed for iterating over all members of a collection, such as an array or any of the collection classes in the Microsoft .NET Framework.

- The *while* loop is used to repeat a statement or statement block for as long as an expression evaluates as *true*.

- The *do* loop is similar to a *while* loop, except that it always executes at least once.

We'll also look at jump statements, which are used to transfer control unconditionally to another part of your program. In previous chapters, you've seen and used *return* and *throw* statements. In this chapter, we'll look at these statements in more detail and also examine the *break*, *continue*, and *goto* statements.

Selecting Code Paths Conditionally

The first type of control statements we'll cover are the selection statements. Selection statements give you the ability to execute specific sections of your code based on conditions you specify. Using selection statements, you can choose to execute code if a specific condition is true, if a value is less than a predefined value, or if a specific menu selection has been made.

The *if* Statement

The *if* statement is used to test an expression and execute one or more statements if the expression evaluates as *true*, as follows:

```
if(condition)
    controlled-statement;
```

The *if* statement can be thought of as guarding or controlling execution of a statement, only allowing execution if a specific expression is evaluated as *true*.

To conditionally execute multiple statements, a statement block must be created by enclosing the controlled statements within curly braces ({}), as shown here:

```
if(name.Length > 0)
{
    Console.WriteLine("Your name is:");
    Console.WriteLine(name);
}
```

The expression tested by the *if* statement must have a Boolean value. Unlike C or C++, C# doesn't implicitly convert a numeric value of *0* to *false*, with all other values implicitly converted to *true*. The following code is valid C or C++ code, but it won't be allowed by the C# compiler:

```
// Valid C or C++, not valid C#
if(name.Length)
{
    Console.WriteLine(name);
}
```

Although popular in C and C++, implicit conversions for Boolean tests are often a source of programming errors. C# requires that you provide a Boolean expression, as in the previous examples, where *name.Length* was explicitly compared to a value of *0*.

The *if* statement can be extended to execute one of two statements by adding an *else* statement, as shown here:

```
if(name.Length > 0)
    Console.WriteLine(name);
else
    Console.WriteLine("Please enter your name.");
```

An *else* statement is always associated with a specific *if* statement. Although C# doesn't have an *else-if* statement as is found in Microsoft Visual Basic, an *else* and an *if* can be combined to provide the same effect:

```
if(name.Length > 0)
    Console.WriteLine(name);
else if(retries < 3)
    Console.WriteLine("Please enter your name.");
else
    DisplayHelp();
```

When using nested *if* and *else* statements, watch out for cases in which indentation provides misleading information about which statements will be executed for a particular expression, as shown here:

```
if(name == "Jen")
    DisplayName();
else if(ageChecked == true)
    if(age < 40)
        DisplayAge();
else
    age = GetAge();
```

In this example, the indentation implies that *GetAge* is invoked if *name* isn't equal to *Jen* when *ageChecked* is *false*. However, the *else* statement always binds to the most recent *if* statement that isn't already bound to an *else* statement. Therefore, *GetAge* is actually associated with the test of *age < 40*, which is quite different from the implied ordering.

To avoid problems of this sort, it's a good idea to use statement blocks and curly braces to make your intent clear. Rewriting the preceding example using statement blocks, as shown here, makes it possible for the C# compiler to generate the code as you intended:

```
if(name == "Jen")
{
    DisplayName();
}
else if(ageChecked == true)
{
    if(age < 40)
    {
        DisplayAge();
    }
}
else
{
    age = GetAge();
}
```

In C and C++, it's common practice to reuse variable names by declaring variables with the same names in nested blocks. To prevent a host of common programming errors, C# doesn't permit you to redeclare a variable name in a nested block. For example, the following code contains a nested statement block that declares the string variable *name*:

```
static void Main(string[] args)
{
    string name = Console.ReadLine();
    if(name.Length == 0)
    {
        // Not allowed in C#; can't declare
        // a variable with the same name.
        string name = Console.ReadLine();
        Console.WriteLine(name);
    }
}
```

The *name* variable in the nested statement block clashes with a variable with an enclosing scope, and the compiler will reject the variable redeclaration as an error.

The rule preventing nested declarations using the same variable name applies even if the variable in the outer block is declared after the inner block. Therefore, this code also is rejected by the compiler:

```
static void Main(string[] args)
{
    if(args.Length == 0)
    {
        string name = Console.ReadLine();
        Console.WriteLine(name);
    }
    // Redeclaration not allowed in C#.
    string name = "Rene";
}
```

The *switch* Statement

The *if* and *else* statements are useful when you're conditionally selecting from a small group of options. However, these statements become unwieldy when you must choose from among a large number of cases. The *switch* statement is used to select among multiple choices, offering a more elegant syntax for situations that would otherwise require cascading *if* statements, as shown here:

```
string name = Console.ReadLine();
⋮
switch(name)
{
    case "Mickey":
        Console.WriteLine("Hello Mickey");
        break;

    case "Mackenzie":
        Console.WriteLine("Hello Mackenzie");
        break;

    default:
        Console.WriteLine("Hello World");
        break;
}
```

The *switch* statement uses the following three keywords:

■   ***switch***   The *switch* clause introduces the expression that's used to determine the branch value for the statement. This expression can be a variable, as in the preceding example, a method call, or any other expression.

■   ***case***   One or more *case* labels are used to specify a constant value that's compared to the *switch* expression. The constant value included in the *case* label must have a type that's compatible with the *switch* expression. Each *case* label is usually followed by one or more optional statements that are executed if the value in the *case* label matches the *switch* expression. Later in this section, you'll learn how to combine *case* labels to execute the same statements for multiple conditions.

- **default**   The *default* clause is used to define statements that will be executed if none of the *case* labels have values that match the *switch* expression.

In addition, each *case* label must terminate its group of controlled statements by using a jump expression, such as the *break* statement in the preceding example. The C# jump statements are discussed later in this chapter, in the section "Using Jump Statements to Transfer Control."

When multiple *case* levels require the same work to be done, the *case* labels can be combined, like this:

```
switch(name)
{
    case "Ali":
    case "Mackenzie":
        PlaySoccer();
        break;

        ⋮

    default:
        break;
}
```

The practice of "falling through" *case* labels is common C and C++ idiom but isn't allowed in C#. If there are any statements under a *case* label, the compiler won't allow you to write code that simply falls through to the next *case*. For example, this code is legal in C and C++, but not in C#:

```
switch(name)
{
    case "Ali":
        LookForSocks(); // Implicit fall-through
                        // Not allowed in C#
    case "Mackenzie":
        PlaySoccer();
        break;
    ⋮
    default:
        break;
}
```

The reason for barring this type of construction is that it's a common source of programming errors. If you need this behavior, you can use a *goto* statement to explicitly transfer control to another *case* label, as shown here:

```
switch(name)
{
    case "Ali":
        LookForSocks();
        goto case "Mackenzie"; // Explicit fall-through OK.

    case "Mackenzie":
        PlaySoccer();
        break;
    :
    default:
        break;
}
```

Unlike in C and C++, a *case* label in C# can specify a string value, with each *case* label specifying a separate string value that will be compared with the *switch* expression. This feature makes the C# *switch* statement usable in situations where a C or C++ programmer would be forced to use nested *if* and *else* statements.

When the statements executed for a particular *case* label require the use of temporary variables, you must create a statement block that scopes the lifetime and visibility of the variables, as shown here:

```
switch(name)
{
    case "Ali":
    {
        int sockCount = GetCurrentSockCount();
        if(sockCount < 2)
            LookForSocks();
        goto case "Mackenzie";
    }

    case "Mackenzie":
        PlaySoccer();
        break;
    :
    default:
        break;
}
```

If you have *case* clauses that require multiple statements, it's a good idea to break out the statements into individual methods, as shown in the following code. This practice helps make your code easier to read and maintain by reducing the size and complexity of the *switch* statement.

```
switch(name)
{
    case "Ali":
        HandleAliSoccer();
        break;

    case "Mackenzie":
        HandleMackenzieSoccer();
        break;
    ⋮
    default:
        break;
}
```

Building Loops Using Iteration Statements

The next set of statements we'll look at are the iteration statements, which are used to build loops in C#. Loops enable you to execute one or more statements multiple times. You can specify that your loop is to be executed a specific number of times, or you can iterate until a specified condition occurs. C# offers four iteration statements, each of which is well-suited for a specific kind of loop.

The *for* Loop

The *for* loop is used to execute a loop until a specified condition becomes true, as follows:

```
for(initialization; condition; iteration)
    controlled-statement;
```

One of the benefits of using the *for* loop is that all the conditions for initializing and maintaining the loop are located in one place, at the top of the loop.

The *for* loop has four components: the *initialization expression,* the *conditional expression,* the *controlled statement,* and the *iteration expression.* These components are executed in the following order:

1. The initialization expression is run once when the *for* loop begins execution.

2. The conditional expression is evaluated to determine whether the *for* loop should continue executing; if the expression has a value of *false*, control passes to the statements after the *for* loop.

3. The controlled statement is executed if the conditional expression evaluates to *true*.

4. The iteration expression is executed once after each execution of the controlled statement.

The algorithm for the *for* loop is shown in Figure 5-1.

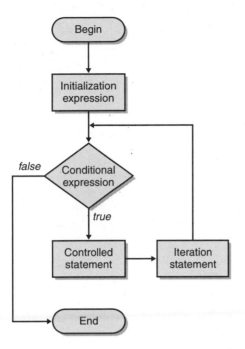

Figure 5-1.   Flowchart illustrating the operation of the *for* loop.

In general, the *for* loop is used when a loop is executed a specific number of times, such as iterating over all of the elements in an array, as shown here:

```
int [] intArray = {1, 2, 3};
for(int i = 0; i < intArray.Length; ++i)
{
    Console.WriteLine(intArray[i]);
}
```

This *for* loop prints each element of *intArray*, as shown here:

```
1
2
3
```

Each of the four expressions that constitute a *for* loop can be replaced by an empty expression. An empty conditional expression is considered to be *true*, which means that any *for* loop can safely omit any expressions that aren't needed. The minimal *for* loop—an infinite loop with no terminating condition—looks like this:

```
for(;;);
```

A variable declared in the initialization portion of the *for* loop remains visible and in scope for the lifetime of the *for* loop and isn't accessible after the end of the loop. This arrangement allows you to reuse variable names in successive loops. In the following example, two *for* loops initialize an *int* named *i*, which is used as an index for array indexing:

```
int [] intArray = {1, 2, 3};
for(int i = 0; i < intArray.Length; ++i)
{
    Console.WriteLine(intArray[i]);
}
int [] ageArray = {5, 8, 39, 40};
for(int i = 0; i < ageArray.Length; ++i)
{
    Console.WriteLine(ageArray[i]);
}
```

In keeping with the C# restriction against redeclaring variable names in nested blocks, any variables declared in the initialization expression must have unique names that don't conflict with names in the outer block, as shown here:

```
int count = 42;
string [] names = new string[] {"Ali", "Kenzie"};
// Won't compile; count isn't a unique name.
for(count = 0; count < names.Length; ++count)
{
    ⋮
}
```

The following example shows a typical use of a *for* loop, iterating over the contents of an array of Shakespeare quotations and displaying each quotation using *Console.WriteLine*:

```
class QuoteArrayApp
{
    static string [] quotes = new string []
    {
        // Henry V
        "We few, we happy few, we band of brothers.",
        // Hamlet
        "Alas, poor Yorick!",
        // Titus Andronicus
        "I know them all, though they suppose me mad.",
        // Twelfth Night
        "Some are born great, some achieve greatness, " +
        "and others have greatness thrust upon them."
    };
    static void Main(string[] args)
    {
        for(int i = 0; i < quotes.Length; ++i)
        {
            Console.WriteLine(quotes[i]);
        }
    }
}
```

> **Note**   This project and other example projects in this chapter are available on the companion CD.

The *foreach* Loop

As you saw in the previous section, a common use of the *for* loop is to iterate over items in an array. C# includes another looping statement, *foreach*, that's optimized for iterating over every item in a collection such as an array. The *foreach* statement is similar to the *For Each* loop long used by Visual Basic programmers to simplify the building of loops.

The algorithm for the *foreach* loop is shown in Figure 5-2.

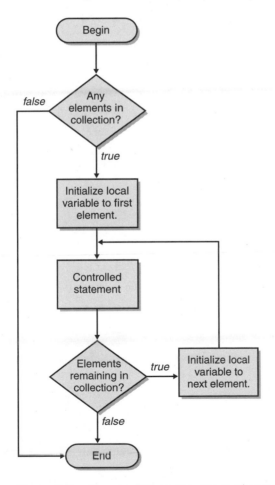

Figure 5-2.   Flowchart illustrating the *foreach* loop, which is used to iterate over each member of a collection.

As shown in Figure 5-2, the C# *foreach* statement allows you to define a variable that's updated for each iteration of the loop, as follows:

```
foreach(type local-variable in collection)
    statement;
```

Each time the controlled statement or statement block for a *foreach* loop is executed, the locally declared variable is updated to refer to the next member in the collection, simplifying the code in the loop body, as shown here:

```
int [] rg = {1, 2, 3, 4};
foreach(int i in rg)
{
    Console.WriteLine(i);
}
```

This *foreach* loop generates the following output:

```
1
2
3
4
```

The *foreach* loop isn't intended to be used to change the value of items stored in a collection. The compiler will enforce this condition when possible. For example, when primitive types are stored in an array, you can't change the value of array elements via the local variable:

```
int [] rg = {1, 2, 3, 4, 5, 6, 7};
foreach(int i in rg)
{
    // Not allowed; array elements are read-only.
    i = 0;
}
```

As you can see, it's not possible to overwrite or clear elements in a collection using a *foreach* loop. However, when nonprimitive types are stored in a collection, it's possible to call methods that update the state of individual objects.

The following example loops over the command-line arguments passed to the application's *Main* method:

```
class AverageApp
{
    static void Main(string[] args)
    {
        decimal total = 0;
        foreach(string arg in args)
        {
```

```
            total += Convert.ToDecimal(arg);
        }
        if(args.Length > 0)
        {
            decimal average = total / args.Length;
            Console.WriteLine("Average is {0}", average);
        }
    }
}
```

Command-line arguments for C# applications are passed as an array of strings, with the first argument passed as the first array element, the second argument passed as the second array element, and so on. Unlike the standard behavior in C and C++ applications, the name of the application isn't passed as the first argument; the array contains only parameters passed on the command line.

In this example, a *foreach* loop is used to visit each element in the array of command-line arguments and the *Convert.ToDecimal* method is used to convert each of the arguments to a decimal value. After the decimal values for all command-line parameters are combined, the average is calculated and displayed by calling *Console.WriteLine*.

The *foreach* loop can be used with any of the built-in collection types in the .NET Framework. If you create your own collection classes, you must implement specific methods that will be used to iterate over your collection. (An example demonstrating the implementation of a *foreach*-friendly collection will be presented in Chapter 8.) The use of these iteration methods impacts performance slightly, and you can often write a faster loop by using a *for* loop. However, the C# compiler detects when *foreach* is used with an array and performs code optimizations to bring the performance of the *foreach* statement more in line with the performance of a *for* loop.

The *while* Loop

The *while* statement is used to create a loop that executes a statement or block of statements repeatedly for as long as a supplied expression evaluates as *true*, as follows:

```
while(condition)
    statement;
```

Because the condition is tested before the loop statement is executed, a *while* loop will execute zero or more times, as illustrated in Figure 5-3.

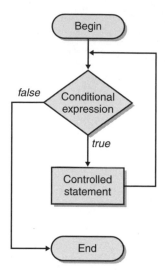

Figure 5-3. Flowchart illustrating the *while* loop, which is used to execute a statement while an expression remains *true*.

The *while* statement is well-suited for loops in which the number of iterations isn't known in advance. For example, when you create code to read an Extensible Markup Language (XML) stream using the *XmlTextReader* class, you'll often use the *while* loop to read all the data in the stream, as follows:

```
XmlTextReader reader = new XmlTextReader("books.xml");
while(reader.Read())
{
    switch(reader.NodeType)
    {
        ⋮
    }
}
```

To create a loop that executes until it's explicitly exited, use *true* as the conditional expression, as shown here:

```
while(true)
{
    ⋮
}
```

As with the other iteration statements, it's important to ensure a terminating condition for a *while* loop, either in the conditional statement or by adding a jump statement such as a *break* statement to the body of the loop, as will be discussed later in this chapter, in the section "Using Jump Statements to Transfer Control."

The *do* Loop

The *do* statement is similar to the *while* statement, but the conditional test is performed after each iteration of the *do* loop, as shown here:

```
do
    statement;
while(condition);
```

Unlike the *while* loop, the controlled statements associated with a *do* loop must execute at least once, as shown in Figure 5-4.

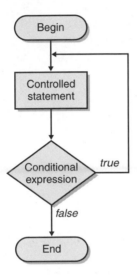

Figure 5-4.   Flowchart illustrating the *do* loop, which executes at least once, even if the conditional expression evaluates to *false*.

Loops that require at least one pass are sometimes written using a *while* statement, which leads to duplicate code. An example of such a code fragment is shown here:

```
Console.WriteLine("Enter your name:");
string name = Console.ReadLine();
while(name.Length > 0)
{
    AddNameToDatabase(name);
    Console.WriteLine("Enter your name:");
    name = Console.ReadLine();
}
```

In this example, the calls to *Console.WriteLine* and *Console.ReadLine* are duplicated, resulting in code that's difficult to maintain. This code could be rewritten to use a *do* statement, placing all of the controlled statements within the loop body, like this:

```
string name;
do {
    Console.WriteLine("Enter your name:");
    name = Console.ReadLine();
    if(name.Length > 0)
        AddNameToDatabase(name);
} while(name.Length > 0);
```

The second version is easier to maintain because there are no controlled statements that execute outside the loop body. The loop could be simplified still further by providing an explicit *break* statement inside the loop and replacing the conditional expression with *true*, as follows:

```
string name;
do {
    Console.WriteLine("Enter your name:");
    name = Console.ReadLine();
    if(name.Length == 0)
        break;
    AddNameToDatabase(name);
} while(true);
```

The following program recursively lists the contents of a directory, beginning at a path specified by the user. At the heart of this example is a *do* statement that requests a path from the user and then calls *DisplayDirectoryInfo* to display information about the directory.

```
class DirListApp
{
    static void Main(string[] args)
    {
        string directoryPath;
        do {
            Console.WriteLine("Enter path, or <return> to quit.");
            directoryPath = Console.ReadLine();
            if(directoryPath.Length == 0)
                break;
            // Get a DirectoryInformation array for the
            // specified path.
            DirectoryInfo info = new DirectoryInfo(directoryPath);
            DisplayDirectoryInfo(info);
        } while(true);
    }
    static void DisplayDirectoryInfo(DirectoryInfo info)
    {
        try
```

```
    {
        DirectoryInfo[] directories = info.GetDirectories();
        foreach(DirectoryInfo directory in directories)
        {
            DisplayDirectoryInfo(directory);
        }
        FileInfo[] files = info.GetFiles();
        foreach(FileInfo file in files)
        {
            Console.WriteLine(file);
        }
    }
    catch(DirectoryNotFoundException exc)
    {
        Console.WriteLine("Could not find the directory.");
    }
    catch(Exception exc)
    {
        Console.WriteLine(exc);
    }
}
}
```

In this example, the program begins by requesting a directory path from the user. As long as the user continues to supply directory paths, the program will continue to execute its main loop. Because at least one iteration is always required, the *do* statement is a good choice for this sort of loop.

Using Jump Statements to Transfer Control

Jump statements are used to transfer control from one location in your code to another. Unlike selection statements, jump statements transfer control unconditionally. Some jump statements, such as the *return* statement, allow you to pass additional context information that can be used when control is obtained at the new location. Other statements, such as *break* and *goto*, simply transfer control to a new location.

Jump statements also differ in the context in which they're used. The *break* and *continue* statements are used to control the flow of execution within other constructions, such as loops or selection statements. In contrast, the *goto*, *return*, and *throw* statements can be used in almost any part of your program. Used properly, jump statements make your code more readable and maintainable. Used improperly, jump statements not only make your code difficult to maintain, they can also make your program less robust.

The *break* Statement

The *break* statement is used to break out of a control structure, such as a loop or a *switch* statement, as shown here:

```
int n = 0;
while(true)
{
    ⋮
    if(++n == 3)
        break;
}
```

In this example, the *while* loop is terminated after three items have been displayed, even though the *while* statement would potentially allow the loop to run forever.

The most common use of the *break* statement is to terminate the processing of *case* labels in a *switch* statement, as follows:

```
switch(name)
{
    case "Ali":
        PlaySoccer();
        break;
    ⋮
}
```

When multiple control structures are nested, a *break* statement will terminate processing of only the most immediate control structure. For example, if a *while* loop is located inside a *foreach* loop, a *break* statement will stop the processing of only the innermost loop, as shown here:

```
int [] rg = {1, 2, 3, 4, 5};
foreach(int i in rg)
{
    int n = 1;
    int factorial = 1;
    while(true)
    {
        factorial *= n;
        if(n++ == i)
            break;
    }
    Console.WriteLine("{0}! is {1}", i, factorial);
}
```

If you must completely break out of nested loops, you have two options: you can either use a *goto* statement, as will be discussed later in this chapter, in the section "The *goto* Statement," or use a flag to indicate that control should break out of both loops.

The *continue* Statement

The *continue* statement is used to return to the beginning of a loop statement, short-circuiting any further processing of the current iteration, as shown here:

```
for(int i = 0; i < 20; ++i)
{
    if(i % 2 == 0)
        continue;
    Console.WriteLine("{0}", i);
}
```

This code prints only the odd numbers, bypassing display of the even values.

Although the *continue* statement is useful, in most cases it can be replaced by more structured code. For example, the preceding loop could be rewritten as follows:

```
for(int i = 1; i < 20; i += 2)
{
    Console.WriteLine("{0}", i);
}
```

Another common scenario for employing a *continue* statement is when a special case is detected within a loop, as in the following code:

```
for(int user = 0; user < lastUser; ++user)
{
    if(SessionExpired(nameList[user]) == true)
        continue;

    ProcessUser(nameList[user]);
}
```

This code could be rewritten as follows:

```
for(int user = 0; user < lastUser; ++user)
{
    if(SessionExpired(nameList[user]) == false)
    {
        ProcessUser(nameList[user]);
    }
}
```

Of course, your goal should always be to write code that clearly conveys the algorithm that you're implementing. In some cases, a *continue* statement is the best choice. If you find yourself creating a loop with multiple *continue* statements, however, you can probably rewrite your loop in a more structured manner.

The *goto* Statement

Like many programming languages, C# offers a *goto* statement, which is used to transfer control to a label elsewhere in the current method, as shown here:

```
label:
  :
    goto label;
```

One of the most common uses for *goto* in C# is in a *switch* statement, where a *goto* can be used to explicitly continue processing at another label, as follows:

```
switch(name)
{
    case "Ali":
        LookForSocks();
        goto case "Mackenzie";
      :
}
```

The *goto* statement has a reputation for leading to the destruction of otherwise well-structured code. It's true that, in most cases, a *goto* statement can be replaced by a more structured control element. It's possible to write quite large applications in C# without ever touching a *goto*, and many people do.

In C#, the capability of the *goto* statement to ruin code, lives, and property is mitigated by the restriction that a *goto* can jump only to a label within the current method. One good example of the usefulness of *goto* is breaking out of deeply nested loops, as follows:

```
private string [,] table = new string [4,5];
  :
for(int i = 0; i < table.GetLength(0); ++i)
{
    for(int j = 0; j < table.GetLength(1); ++j)
    {
        if(name == table[i,j])
            goto found;
    }
}
  :
found:
    UseName(name);
```

In this example, a *goto* allows you to completely break out of the nested loop easily. Without a *goto* statement, writing equivalent code would be much more difficult; as mentioned, you'd have to set up a flag for each loop to test to determine whether the loop needs to exit.

The *return* Statement

The *return* statement is used to initiate a return from a method call, passing control back to the caller. A *return* statement in a constructor, a destructor, or a method that's prototyped as returning *void* specifies no return value, as shown here:

```
public void f()
{
    ⋮
    return;
}
```

In a method that specifies a return value, the *return* statement must include a return value, which will be passed to the method's caller, as shown here:

```
public int Cube(int n)
{
    return n * n * n;
}
⋮
int result = Cube(5);
Console.WriteLine(result);
```

When executing inside a *try* block that has an associated *finally* clause (see Chapter 2 for a detailed discussion of exception handling), the return value doesn't immediately transfer control out of the method. Instead, control is first passed to the *finally* block and then passed back to the method's caller.

The *throw* Statement

As discussed in Chapter 2, the *throw* statement is used to throw an exception. When an exception is thrown, control is immediately passed to the first *catch* block capable of handling the exception, which can be supplied by the caller. The following code shows how to throw an exception using the *throw* statement:

```
bool SessionExpired(string userName)
{
    if(UserExists(userName) == 0)
        throw new InvalidOperationException("Not a current user");
    ⋮
}
```

An exception shouldn't be used as a general-purpose flow control statement because an exception is relatively expensive to create and propagate. Reserve the use of exceptions to error handling or other truly exceptional conditions.

Transferring Control out of an Exception Handling Block

Jump statements behave in specific ways in the presence of *try* and *finally* blocks. When an exception attempts to transfer control out of a *try* block, control is first offered to the associated *catch* block, if one exists. If there's no *catch* block associated with the *try* block, or if the *catch* block isn't capable of handling the thrown exception, control is first transferred to the *finally* block. After the *finally* block executes, control is transferred according to the intent of the jump statement.

Consider the following example:

```
string [] table;
⋮
static void WriteNames(string filename)
{
    FileStream fs = new FileStream(filename, FileMode.Create);
    StreamWriter writer = new StreamWriter(fs);
    try
    {
        if(table == null || table.Length == 0)
            throw new InvalidOperationException();
        foreach(string name in table)
        {
            ⋮
        }
    }
    finally
    {
        if(writer)
            writer.Close();
    }
}
```

In this example, *FileStream* and *StreamWriter* objects are created to handle text output to a file. However, if *table* (an array of *string*) isn't properly allocated, an exception is thrown. Because the *try* block isn't associated with a *catch* block to catch the exception, control is passed to the *finally* block, which will properly close the *StreamWriter* instance (as well as the underlying instance of *FileStream*). After the *finally* block has executed, the exception will be passed to the first appropriate *catch* block in the calling functions, using the search algorithm discussed in Chapter 2.

An interesting aspect of the *finally* block is that it must be allowed to run to completion. No jump statements can be invoked in order to leave the *finally* block early. This restriction is due to the fact that a *finally* statement might be executing due to a pending jump statement; that jump statement is currently on hold and must be allowed to execute immediately after the *finally* block has completed. Allowing a new jump statement inside a *finally* block would significantly complicate error handling for C# programmers.

Conclusion

C# includes a rich set of statements that are used to control the flow of execution in your code. These statements fall into three categories:

- **Selection statements (*if* and *switch*)**   Used to select a statement or statement block to be executed. These statements are used to select from among multiple paths of execution. The *if* statement is typically used to execute statements if a specific condition evaluates as *true*. The *if* statement is optionally coupled with the *else* statement in order to force a selection from one of two possible execution paths. Although the *switch* statement can be used to select from one or two possible execution paths, it's most often used when there are more than two possible execution branches.

- **Iteration statements (*for*, *foreach*, *while*, and *do*)**   Used to build loops. Each of these loops has different characteristics that make it more or less useful in specific situations. The *for* loop is most useful when statements must be executed a specific number of times; the *foreach* loop is used to iterate over each item in a collection. The *while* loop executes statements for as long as a controlling expression evaluates as *true*; the *do* loop is similar to the *while* loop but guarantees that the controlled statements execute at least once.

- **Jump statements (*break*, *continue*, *goto*, *return*, and *throw*)**   Used to transfer control to a new location in your program. The *break* and *continue* statements are used only with control structures. The *break* statement is used to transfer control out of the current control structure. The *continue* statement is used to immediately return to the beginning of a loop statement. The *return* statement is used to transfer control to the invoker of the method, and the *throw* statement is used to raise an exception. C# also includes the notorious *goto* statement, which can be used to transfer control to a label within the current method.

Selection and iteration statements use the values of expressions to control their execution. (Expressions are discussed in Chapter 4.) Jump statements transfer control unconditionally.

Chapter 6 discusses additional C# language features that are used to structure your code: delegates and attributes. Delegates are similar to function pointers used in C++ and other languages, with additional type-safety features. Attributes are a convenient way for you to declaratively add functionality to your application and are widely used to add support for transactions, security, and other runtime features.

Part II
Advanced C#

6

Delegates and Attributes

If you have a background in C or C++, the material in Part I of this book has probably had a familiar feel. Many of the C# language features discussed thus far are similar to features that are available in C or C++. This chapter introduces three C# features that may be new to you: *delegates*, *events*, and *attributes*.

Delegates are the C# way to enlist methods contained in other classes. As you'll see, a delegate is similar to a function pointer or callback function in C or C++, but it's type-safe and more flexible. Delegates also work well with the C# language and can target both static and non-static methods—something that's difficult to do in C++. In this chapter, we'll examine how events extend delegates to provide a well-defined idiom for client subscription to event notifications.

This chapter will also cover attributes, how they're used to declaratively add functionality to your code, and how you can create your own attributes. This discussion of attributes will include reflection, a common language runtime feature that enables you to inspect and extract information about types at runtime.

Using Delegates

Delegates are used to encapsulate functions into callable function objects that are used much as function pointers are used in C, C++, and other languages. Like function pointers, delegates enable you to separate a function reference from its implementation, allowing the implementation to exist in a separate module. Unlike function pointers, delegates are type-safe, enabling the compiler and the Microsoft .NET Framework to ensure that code called via a delegate is executed safely.

The most common use of delegates is in those cases in which a traditional C or C+ programmer would use a function pointer. For example, in Chapter 10, we'll use delegates to provide thread handling methods in multithreaded applications. A thread handling function is created as a delegate, which is called in a separate thread by the runtime, as shown in Figure 6-1.

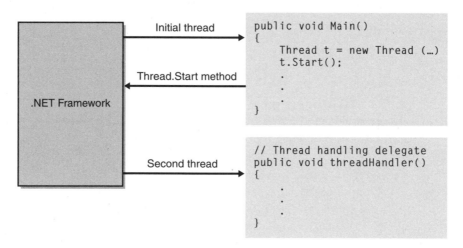

Figure 6-1.   Thread delegate invoked by a new thread.

Delegates are widely used in C# to provide event handlers when you're developing Windows Forms applications or when you're using Web Forms with Microsoft ASP.NET. Multiple delegates can be automatically chained together, as shown in Figure 6-2, making it easy to build applications that use layers of delegates to handle events. (Using delegates for event handling is discussed later in this chapter, in the section "Handling Events.")

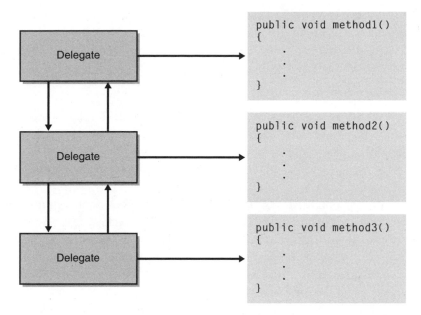

Figure 6-2. Delegates chained together to allow multiple functions to be called through a delegate, which improves event handling.

Creating Delegates

Delegates in C# are declared in a two-step process. First a delegate type is declared, and then instances of the delegate type are created, as shown in the following code. A delegate type is declared using the *delegate* keyword along with the method signature of the delegate.

```
public delegate void OpDelegate(int First, int Second);
```

Any method that conforms to the declared signature can be used as a delegate. Unlike function pointers in C++, any static or non-static member method can be used for your delegate in C#, as long as the signature matches. Here are some examples of methods that can be used with the preceding delegate declaration:

```
static public void Subtract(int First, int Second)
{
    ⋮
}

public void Add(int First, int Second)
{
    ⋮
}
```

To create a delegate, use the *new* keyword to create a new instance of the delegate type, passing the method name as an argument. In the following code, the method name passed as a parameter serves as the delegate's target method. When the delegate is invoked, the target method will be called.

```
new MathOp.OpDelegate(AddFunc.Add);
```

When a delegate is created, the C# compiler actually generates a great deal of code behind the scenes for you. All delegates written in C# are actually types derived from the *System.MulticastDelegate* class. When you create a new instance of a delegate, you're creating new objects that are subclassed from *MulticastDelegate*.

The *System.MulticastDelegate* class is derived from *System.Delegate*, a more limited delegate type. The *MulticastDelegate* class extends *Delegate*, adding methods and internal data structures that allow delegates to be chained together. When a delegate type is created using the C# *delegate* keyword, it's always a subclass of *MulticastDelegate* rather than *Delegate*.

Although the simplest way to declare a delegate is to use the C# *delegate* keyword, you also can create classes that derive from *System.MulticastDelegate* or *System.Delegate* directly. In most cases, however, you'll get no benefit from using a handcrafted delegate class, especially because you can use the *delegate* keyword and still gain access to the methods declared for the *MulticastDelegate* class. Later in this chapter, in the section "Combining Delegates," we'll use methods from *MulticastDelegate* to manage types created using the *delegate* keyword.

Using Delegates as Callback Methods

The most common use of a delegate is to call back to a method that will perform a required task. A delegate used to perform callback operations is typically passed as a parameter to a constructor or another method and invoked when the callback is executed. The following example uses a delegate when performing a bubble sort on an array:

```
public class BubbleSort
{
    /// <summary>
    /// A delegate is used to define the sort order for two
    /// elements in the table.
    /// </summary>
    public delegate bool Order(object first, object second);

    /// <summary>
    /// Sort elements in an Array object, using the Order
    /// delegate to determine how items should be sorted.
```

```
///  </summary>
///  <param name="table">Array to be sorted</param>
///  <param name="sortHandler">Delegate to manage
///  sort order.</param>
public void Sort(Array table, Order sortHandler)
{
    if(sortHandler == null)
        throw new ArgumentNullException();

    bool nothingSwapped = false;
    int pass = 1;
    while(nothingSwapped == false)
    {
        nothingSwapped = true;
        for(int index = 0; index < table.Length - pass; ++index)
        {
            // Use an Order delegate to determine the sort order.
            if(sortHandler(table.GetValue(index),
                table.GetValue(index + 1)) == false)
            {
                nothingSwapped = false;
                object temp = table.GetValue(index);
                table.SetValue(table.GetValue(index + 1), index);
                table.SetValue(temp, index + 1);
            }
        }
        ++pass;
    }
}
}
```

The *BubbleSort* class defines a delegate type named *Order* that's used to determine the relative sort order for elements in an array. Methods that are associated with the *Order* delegate type accept the two objects that are compared to determine their relative sort order as parameters. The method is expected to return *true* if the first item should be sorted into a lower position than the second item and return *false* otherwise.

The *BubbleSort.Sort* method accepts two parameters: an array to be sorted, and an instance of the *Order* delegate that will be invoked to perform the sort. The *Sort* method uses the bubble sort algorithm to iterate over the array to be sorted. Part of the bubble sort algorithm requires that adjacent items in the array be compared to determine whether they're in the correct order. If they're not, the items are swapped. In the *Sort* method, the comparison is done using the delegate passed as a parameter. Enabling a client of the *Sort* method to define a sort order delegate allows the *Sort* method to be used with any type of object, because only the delegate needs to understand how array elements are sorted.

> **Tip**   If a delegate is invoked through a null reference, a *NullReference-Exception* is thrown by the runtime. For this reason, it's a good idea to test a delegate reference before attempting to invoke the delegate. In the *BubbleSort.Sort* method, the *Order* delegate is tested; if *null*, an *ArgumentNullException* is thrown to the caller.

An application that uses the *BubbleSort* class to sort an array of integers is shown here:

```
class DelegateSortApp
{
    static int [] sortTable = {5,4,6,2,8,9,1,3,7,0};
    static void Main(string[] args)
    {
        DelegateSortApp app = new DelegateSortApp();

        // Print array in original order.
        foreach(int i in sortTable)
            Console.WriteLine(i);

        Console.WriteLine("Sorting");
        BubbleSort sorter = new BubbleSort();
        BubbleSort.Order order = new BubbleSort.Order(SortOrder);
        sorter.Sort(sortTable, order);

        foreach(int i in sortTable)
            Console.WriteLine(i);
        Console.WriteLine("Done");
    }

    // Delegate method; returns true if first is less than second
    static public bool SortOrder(object first, object second)
    {
        int firstInt = (int)first;
        int secondInt = (int)second;
        return firstInt < secondInt;
    }
}
```

The *DelegateSortApp* class shown here defines the type of elements stored in the array as well as the method used to compare elements in the array. In this example, the array contains *int* values, but it could easily contain any other type. The *DelegateSortApp.SortOrder* method is used for comparing array elements. This method matches the signature of the *BubbleSort.Order* delegate, which is invoked by the *BubbleSort* class to determine the relative sort order of array elements. The algorithms used to sort the array are encapsulated in the *BubbleSort* class, whereas the array definition as well as the knowledge required to manage the array elements are kept in the *DelegateSortApp* class.

Using Delegates as Functors

Another way to use delegates is as *functors,* or classes that implement methods that can be "plugged in" to provide functionality for other classes. For example, consider a delegate declaration that defines a math operation:

```
public delegate void OpDelegate(int First, int Second);
```

The *AddFunc* class in the following code implements a single method, *Add*, which conforms to the signature of *OpDelegate*:

```
public class AddFunc
{
    static public void Add(int First, int Second)
    {
        int res = First + Second;
        Console.WriteLine("{0}+{1}={2}", First, Second, res);
    }
}
```

The following class, *MathOp*, exposes a public field named *Op*, which is an instance of *OpDelegate*. When *MathOp.Invoke* is called by a client, the *Op* delegate is called to perform a math operation on operands stored in the *MathOp* object.

```
public class MathOp
{
    public delegate void OpDelegate(int First, int Second);
    public OpDelegate Op;

    public MathOp(int First, int Second)
    {
        _first = First;
        _second = Second;
    }
    public void Invoke()
    {
        if(Op != null)
            Op(_first, _second);
    }

    protected int _first;
    protected int _second;
}
```

This example code illustrates how the *MathOp* class is used:

```
class MathDelegateApp
{
    static void Main(string[] args)
    {
        MathOp mo = new MathOp(42, 27);
        mo.Op = new MathOp.OpDelegate(AddFunc.Add);
        mo.Invoke();
    }
}
```

An instance of the *MathOp* class is created by passing two operands as parameters to the constructor. An instance of *OpDelegate* is created and assigned to the public field *Op*. Finally the *MathOp.Invoke* method is called, which invokes the delegate and calls *AddFunc.Add*. The *MathOp* class is completely generic and doesn't track the details of the math operations performed. The implementation of math operations is encapsulated in *OpDelegate* objects, which can be plugged in to the *MathOp* class as needed.

Combining Delegates

As mentioned, delegates can be linked together easily, enabling you to combine multiple delegate objects into a chain of delegates. This capability is built into the .NET Framework's *System.MulticastDelegate* class. Each delegate can track the delegates located ahead of and behind it in the delegate chain. Invoking a method on a delegate implicitly causes each delegate in the chain to be invoked sequentially.

The *System.MulticastDelegate* class includes member functions that are used to chain delegates together. The *Delegate* class also overrides a number of operators that simplify the task of managing chains of delegates. To combine two or more delegates, you can use the same addition operators (+ and +=) that you would use on primitive types, as shown here:

```
mo.Op = new MathOp.OpDelegate(AddFunc.Add) +
        new MathOp.OpDelegate(SubtractFunc.Subtract);
mo.Op += new MathOp.OpDelegate(MultFunc.Multiply);
```

Delegates are removed from a delegate chain using the subtraction operators (− and −=), as follows:

```
mo.Op = mo.Op - new MathOp.OpDelegate(MultFunc.Multiply);
mo.Op -= new MathOp.OpDelegate(MultFunc.Multiply);
```

You must have a reference to the delegate to remove it. If you plan to remove a delegate, you can keep a reference to the delegate when it's originally created, or you can create a new instance of the delegate specifically for the removal operation.

An example of using a chain of delegates is shown in the following code. The *MultFunc* and *SubtractFunc* classes implement methods that can be used with the *MathOp* class (and its *OpDelegate* member) shown in the example in the preceding section, "Using Delegates as Functors."

```
public class MultFunc
{
    static public void Multiply(int First, int Second)
    {
        int res = First * Second;
        Console.WriteLine("{0}*{1}={2}", First, Second, res);
    }
}

public class SubtractFunc
{
    static public void Subtract(int First, int Second)
    {
        int res = First - Second;
        Console.WriteLine("{0}-{1}={2}", First, Second, res);
    }
}
```

The enhanced version of the *MathDelegateApp* class shown here creates three delegate objects, with each delegate targeting one of the *AddFunc.Add*, *SubtractFunc.Subtract*, and *MultFunc.Multiply* methods:

```
class MathDelegateApp
{
    static void Main(string[] args)
    {
        MathOp mo = new MathOp(42, 27);
        mo.Op += new MathOp.OpDelegate(AddFunc.Add);
        mo.Op += new MathOp.OpDelegate(SubtractFunc.Subtract);
        mo.Op += new MathOp.OpDelegate(MultFunc.Multiply);
        mo.Invoke();
    }
}
```

In this example, when *mo.Invoke* is called, each of the delegates will be called in turn. The output from this version of the *MathDelegate* project is shown here:

```
42+27=69
42-27=15
42*27=1134
```

Remember, inside the *MathOp.Invoke* method, the *Op* delegate is called directly, without any iteration statements, as follows:

```
public void Invoke()
{
    if(Op != null)
        Op(_first, _second);
}
```

When *Op* is called, the delegate automatically takes care of iterating over the list of delegates, calling each in turn. This behavior raises an issue when you're dealing with multiple return values or when exceptions are thrown by a delegate. When multiple delegates are invoked, any exceptions thrown by a delegate that aren't handled in the delegate are first passed to the method that invoked the delegate, just as if the method had invoked the delegate directly. Because the exception transfers control back to the method that invoked the delegate, no delegates farther down in the invocation list will be executed.

Iterating Manually over the Delegate Chain

If you're using delegates that must throw exceptions, you can take advantage of a delegate invocation technique that manually iterates over the delegate list and invokes each delegate separately. This is a useful way to execute your delegates if you need fine-grained control over exception handling or managing return values. First let's look at a simple version of *MathOp.Invoke*, rewritten with manual iteration over the delegate chain:

```
public void Invoke()
{
    object[] args = new object[2];
    args[0] = _first;
    args[1] = _second;

    Delegate [] operators = Op.GetInvocationList();
    foreach(Delegate d in operators)
    {
        d.DynamicInvoke(args);
    }
}
```

This example retrieves a list of the delegate instances by calling the delegate's *GetInvocationList* method. *GetInvocationList* returns an array of *System.Delegate* objects that make up the delegate chain. The .NET Framework *Delegate* class is used in this context because, as shown in the following code, you can't use the C# *delegate* keyword to declare an object, only a type:

```
// Error; won't compile. Must use Delegate class.
delegate [] operators = Op.GetInvocationList();
```

The *foreach* statement is then used to iterate over the invocation list. Because delegates can have any number of parameters, delegate parameters are passed as an object array to the *DynamicInvoke* method. The *Delegate* class then manually binds to the method associated with the delegate, throwing a runtime exception if the parameters don't match the called method.

The following version of *MathOp.Invoke* expands on the preceding example by handling any exceptions thrown by delegate methods. When an exception is thrown, the exception is logged, and a recovery action is taken before the next delegate in the list is invoked.

```
public void Invoke()
{
    object[] args = new object[2];
    args[0] = _first;
    args[1] = _second;

    Delegate [] operators = Op.GetInvocationList();
    foreach(Delegate d in operators)
    {
        try
        {
            d.DynamicInvoke(args);
        }
        catch(Exception exc)
        {
            LogException(exc);
            Recover(exc);
        }
    }
}
```

Exception handling is just one reason to explicitly manage the delegate invocation list. Other scenarios include explicit management of reference parameters or return values.

By default, reference parameters are passed to each delegate method in turn. If a method changes the state of a reference parameter, delegates farther down in the invocation list will receive the changed parameter. Explicit management of delegate invocation allows you to alter this behavior.

The return value for a delegate chain is the return value of the last delegate method. The return values from methods called earlier in the delegate chain are simply discarded. If you explicitly manage the invocation of delegates, you have the opportunity to examine the return value for each method in the delegate chain.

Using Delegates with Non-Static Methods

The delegate examples presented up to now have been associated with static methods. It's often useful to associate a delegate with a non-static method, providing the method with easy access to fields defined for a class. When creating a new delegate that's associated with a non-static method, you must provide a specific instance of the class when passing the method to the delegate constructor, as shown here:

```
delegate bool ScoringPolicy(int questionCount, int correct);

class TestScore
{
    public TestScore(decimal minimumScore)
    {
        _minimum = minimumScore;
    }

    public bool PassOrFail(int questions, int correct)
    {
        decimal score = (decimal)correct/(decimal)questions;
        return _minimum <= score;
    }
    ⋮
    protected decimal _minimum;
}
ScoringPolicy midTermPolicy = null;
ScoringPolicy finalPolicy = null;

// Create a delegate that uses a minimum score of 70.
TestScore midTermExam = new TestScore(70);
midTermPolicy = new ScoringPolicy(midTermExam.PassOrFail);
// Create a delegate that uses a minimum score of 75.
TestScore finalExam = new TestScore(75);
finalPolicy = new ScoringPolicy(finalExam.PassOrFail);
```

The following code presents a more complete example of using a delegate with non-static methods. The *Account* class models a bank account that provides overdraft protection for individual accounts. The class includes methods for handling deposits and withdrawals, as well as tracking the current account balance.

```
public class Account
{
    public delegate bool DebitPolicy(decimal aWithdrawal);
    public Account(decimal anInitialBalance,
                DebitPolicy aDebitPolicy)
    {
        _balance = anInitialBalance;
```

```
            _debitPolicy = aDebitPolicy;
        }

        public decimal Balance
        {
            get
            {
                return _balance;
            }
        }

        public void Deposit(decimal aDeposit)
        {
            if(aDeposit < 0)
                throw new ArgumentOutOfRangeException();
            _balance += aDeposit;
        }

        public bool Withdrawal(decimal aWithdrawal)
        {
            if(aWithdrawal < 0)
                throw new ArgumentOutOfRangeException();
            if(aWithdrawal < _balance)
            {
                _balance -= aWithdrawal;
                return true;
            }
            else
            {
                // If no debit policy, no overdrafts are permitted.
                if(_debitPolicy == null)
                    return false;

                aWithdrawal -= _balance;
                if(_debitPolicy(aWithdrawal))
                {
                    _balance = 0;
                    return true;
                }
                else
                {
                    return false;
                }
            }
        }

        protected DebitPolicy _debitPolicy;
        protected decimal _balance;
    }
```

The *DebitPolicy* delegate is declared in the *Account* class and is used to manage overdrafts. The *DebitPolicy* delegate is invoked by the *Account.Withdrawal* method when a withdrawal is larger than the current balance. If the overdraft is allowed, the delegate returns *true*; if denied, the delegate returns *false*. Because the overdraft debit policy is managed via delegates, multiple types of overdraft management can be defined, allowing different accounts to use different debit management policies while maintaining the same code in the *Account* class.

One overdraft policy class is shown in the following code. The *Overdraft-Protection* class accepts an initial loan amount as a parameter during construction, and tracks the amount of overdraft protection currently available.

```
public class OverdraftProtection
{
    public OverdraftProtection(decimal initialLoan)
    {
        _availableLoan = initialLoan;
        _currentLoan = 0;
    }

    public decimal AvailableLoan
    {
        set { _availableLoan = value; }
        get { return _availableLoan; }
    }
    public decimal CurrentLoan
    {
        set { _currentLoan = value; }
        get { return _currentLoan; }
    }

    // Method used with instances of WithdrawalPolicyDelegate
    // to manage debits to an account. Overdrafts are covered
    // up to a fixed amount specified at construction.
    public bool HandleDebit(decimal debit)
    {
        if(debit > 0)
        {
            if(debit <= _availableLoan)
            {
                _availableLoan -= debit;
                _currentLoan += debit;
            }
            else
                return false;
        }
        return true;
    }
```

```
    // Loan available for use in case of overdraft
    protected decimal _availableLoan;
    // Current overdraft loan amount
    protected decimal _currentLoan;
}
```

The *OverdraftProtection.HandleDebit* method matches the signature of the *DebitPolicy* delegate and is used to manage overdraft debit requests. The *OverdraftProtection* and *Account* classes are used as follows:

```
OverdraftProtection op = new OverdraftProtection(500);
Account.DebitPolicy policy;
policy = new Account.DebitPolicy(op.HandleDebit);
Account myAccount = new Account(100, policy);
```

In this sample code, an *OverdraftProtection* object named *op* is created, with an initial overdraft loan limit of $500. Next an instance of the *DebitPolicy* delegate is created, using *op.HandleDebit* as the target method. Last the *Account* object is created, with an initial balance of $100 and a reference to the newly created *policy* delegate. This code is part of the Bank example on the companion CD, which contains code that allows you to interactively overdraw the account and cause the overdraft debit policy delegate to be invoked.

Handling Events

In C and C++ programs, callback functions and function pointers are often used for event notification. In C#, a specific type of delegate known as an *event* provides event notifications to clients. Event handling is a common idiom for developing applications with C#. For example, Windows Forms applications consume events to receive notifications about mouse movement and behavior, menu selection, button clicks, and similar occurrences.

Events simplify the task of event notification in C# applications. Because they're based on delegates, events are type-safe and have a well-defined model for connecting a single producer with multiple consumers. Events also have specific programming guidelines that simplify their use as one-way notification methods. Some of the usage conventions for delegates are mandatory and are enforced by the compiler; other usage patterns are simply recommended and exist to make your events more usable.

The C# compiler enforces a key restriction for events: outside the class that declares an event, very little access is granted to an event field. A client of the enclosing class can add or remove event handling methods using the overloaded += and −= operators, as follows:

```
mainForm.MouseMove += new MouseEventHandler(OnMouseMove);
```

It's reasonable for a client to use the += or −= operators with events, as this is the basic way for a client to manage event notifications. However, the client isn't allowed any other access to the event. Other than the operations shown here, client classes have no access to the events in a class. Although a delegate can be invoked by any client with access, an event can be raised only by the class that contains the event.

Because events are used as one-way notifications to (potentially) many interested parties, the event delegate is typically declared as returning *void*. If you find that your event needs to pass information as a return value, you should use a delegate as described in the previous section instead of using the event pattern.

By convention, event handling delegates are declared with names ending with *EventHandler* and have two parameters, *sender* and *e*, as shown here:

```
public delegate void OverdraftEventHandler(object sender, EventArgs e);
```

The first parameter, *sender*, is a reference to the object that raised the event. This parameter is always declared as *object*—even when a more specialized type is known to be the sender. The second parameter, *e*, is an *EventArgs* object that describes the event. *EventArgs* is a base class for event argument classes and doesn't carry any useful information to event subscribers.

If your event must pass additional information to event subscribers, subclass the *EventArgs* class and embed your additional information as properties in that class, as shown here:

```
public class DepositEventArgs: EventArgs
{
    public DepositEventArgs(decimal aDeposit)
    {
        _deposit = aDeposit;
    }

    public decimal Deposit
    {
        get { return _deposit; }
    }

    protected decimal _deposit;
}
```

This example follows the convention for naming *EventArgs* subclasses with names that end with *EventArgs*.

Using Event Fields

Events are used much like delegates, with a few differences. First, the *event* keyword is used to declare a field for the event, as follows:

```
public delegate void OverdraftEventHandler(object sender,
                                            OverdraftEventArgs e);
public event OverdraftEventHandler OnOverdraftHandler;
```

The *event* keyword signals to the C# compiler that this delegate is used as an event, causing the compiler to place restrictions on its use, as described earlier.

If your event field is public, a client can subscribe to an event using the += operator to concatenate a new event handling delegate to the existing delegates. A useful design pattern is to provide methods that add and remove event handling delegates. The *AddOnEventName* method is used to add event handlers, like this:

```
myAccount.AddOnDeposit(new Account.DepositHandler(OnDeposit));
```

The *RemoveOnEventName* method is used to remove an event handler, like this:

```
myAccount.RemoveOnDeposit(new Account.DepositHandler(OnDeposit));
```

The implementation of the *AddOnEventName* and *RemoveOnEventName* methods simply uses the += and − = operators, like this:

```
public void AddOnOverdraft(OverdraftEventHandler handler)
{
    OnOverdraftHandler += handler;
}

public void RemoveOnOverdraft(OverdraftEventHandler handler)
{
    OnOverdraftHandler -= handler;
}
```

Raising Events

As mentioned, an event can be raised only from within the class that declares the event. By convention, events have two parameters that must be properly initialized when the event is raised:

- ■ **Sender**   The object that has raised the event
- ■ *e*   An object that contains event arguments

Raising an event is much like invoking a delegate callback, as shown here:

```
EventArgs args = new EventArgs();
if(OnStrikeoutHandler != null)
    OnStrikeoutHandler(this, args);
```

In this code, a new instance of *EventArgs* is created and passed with the event. This example shows an event that has no event-specific event arguments and uses the *EventArgs* base class as a placeholder. In a case like this, it's reasonable to create one *EventArgs* object, maintain a reference to it, and send the same *EventArgs* object each time the event is raised.

It's a good idea to encapsulate your event-raising code in a method, as shown in the following example. This isolates the code in a single method and makes it possible for subclasses to raise events. By convention, this method is named *OnEventName*.

```
protected void OnStrikeout()
{
    EventArgs args = new EventArgs();
    if(OnStrikeoutHandler != null)
        OnStrikeoutHandler(this, args);
}
```

When an event is raised, the client can invoke operations on your object. Keep in mind that an event handler can raise exceptions when handling an event, so you might want to use *try*, *catch*, and *finally* blocks around the code that raises the event.

An Example Using Events

To demonstrate using events with C#, let's revisit the Bank example presented earlier, this time using an event instead of a callback delegate. The new version of the Bank example will raise an event when an overdraft occurs rather than invoke a delegate method.

The following code presents a new version of the *Account* class. In this version, the *DebitPolicy* delegate has been replaced by *OverdraftEventHandler*.

```
public class Account
{
    public delegate void OverdraftEventHandler(object sender,
                                              OverdraftEventArgs e);

    public event OverdraftEventHandler OnOverdraftHandler;

    public Account(decimal anInitialBalance)
    {
        _balance = anInitialBalance;
    }
```

```csharp
public decimal Balance
{
    get
    {
        return _balance;
    }
}

public void Deposit(decimal aDeposit)
{
    if(aDeposit < 0)
        throw new ArgumentOutOfRangeException();
    _balance += aDeposit;
}

public bool Withdrawal(decimal aDebit)
{
    if(aDebit < 0)
        throw new ArgumentOutOfRangeException();
    if(aDebit < _balance)
    {
        _balance -= aDebit;
        return true;
    }
    OverdraftEventArgs args = new OverdraftEventArgs(_balance,
                                                    aDebit);
    OnOverdraft(args);
    return false;
}

public void AddOnOverdraft(OverdraftEventHandler handler)
{
    OnOverdraftHandler += handler;
}

public void RemoveOnOverdraft(OverdraftEventHandler handler)
{
    OnOverdraftHandler -= handler;
}

protected void OnOverdraft(OverdraftEventArgs e)
{
    if(OnOverdraftHandler != null)
        OnOverdraftHandler(this, e);
}

protected decimal _balance;
}
```

This new version of *Account* implements a new event named *OnOverdraftHandler* that uses the *OverdraftEventHandler* delegate type. Clients subscribe to the event by calling the *AddOnOverdraft* method and can unsubscribe by calling *RemoveOnOverdraft*. Internally, the overdraft event is raised by calling *OnOverdraft*.

The overdraft event includes an *OverdraftEventArgs* object that describes the nature of the overdraft. The declaration of the *OverdraftEventArgs* class is shown here:

```
public class OverdraftEventArgs: EventArgs
{
    public OverdraftEventArgs(decimal balance, decimal withdrawal)
    {
        _balance = balance;
        _withdrawal = withdrawal;
    }

    public decimal Balance
    {
        get { return _balance; }
    }

    public decimal Withdrawal
    {
        get { return _withdrawal; }
    }
    protected decimal _balance;
    protected decimal _withdrawal;
}
```

The *OverdraftEventArgs* class is derived from *EventArgs* and adds two fields: the current balance and the attempted withdrawal amount.

To use the new version of the *Account* class and subscribe to the overdraft event, a client can use code like this:

```
Account myAccount = new Account(100);
Account.OverdraftEventHandler handler = null;
handler = new Account.OverdraftEventHandler(OnOverdraft);
myAccount.AddOnOverdraft(handler);
```

After creating an *Account* object, the client subscribes to the overdraft event by creating an event handler and calling *AddOnOverdraft*. The method used as a target for the event handler is shown here:

```
static void OnOverdraft(object sender, OverdraftEventArgs e)
{
    Console.WriteLine("An overdraft occurred.");
    Console.WriteLine("The account balance is {0}.", e.Balance);
    Console.WriteLine("The withdrawal was {0}.", e.Withdrawal);
}
```

The *OnOverdraft* method uses the *OverdraftEventArgs* class to obtain information about the overdraft.

Working with Attributes

Like delegates and events, attributes provide a method for adding code to classes; unlike those approaches, however, the functionality is contributed in a more opaque manner. The source code behind the functionality exposed by attributes is usually hidden from view. Instead, attributes are used in a declarative way to decorate assemblies, classes, and other source code elements.

Attributes are classes, and all attributes are derived from the *System.Attribute* class. The .NET Framework includes many attributes that are used when developing applications for the .NET platform. For example, the *Obsolete* attribute is used to mark source code elements that are no longer favored, like this:

```
[Obsolete("Use the new BubbleSorter class")]
class BubbleSort
{
    ⋮
}
```

If you use a class, method, or other element marked with the *Obsolete* attribute, the compiler will issue a warning (or optionally, an error). During compilation, the compiler inspects all types used by your program, and if it detects the *Obsolete* attribute in a type or method used by your code, it issues a warning (or an error).

Later in this section, you'll learn how to define custom attributes as well as how to write code to detect those attributes after compilation. But first we'll take a detailed look at the C# syntax used with attributes.

Using Attributes

Attributes are placed within a set of square brackets, immediately before their associated programming element. The preceding example illustrated the *Obsolete* attribute attached to a class declaration. This attribute also can be associated with methods, as follows:

```
[Obsolete()]
public void Hide()
{
    ⋮
}
```

The syntax for an attribute is similar to that for a constructor, with the parameters passed as arguments within parentheses. Parameters passed as shown in the following code are known as *positional parameters* because they're identified by their position in the list of parameters:

```
[Obsolete("This class is obsolete", true)]
```

An attribute can also include *named parameters,* in which properties and public fields are passed by name rather than position, as follows:

```
[WebService(Namespace="http://www.microsoft.com")]
```

Named parameters are always passed after any positional parameters; a named parameter passed before a positional parameter is flagged by the compiler as an error.

Resolving Attributes

When an attribute is attached to a class or other programming element, no executable code is generated as a result of that association. Instead, metadata is added to the assembly that identifies the attributes, as shown in Figure 6-3.

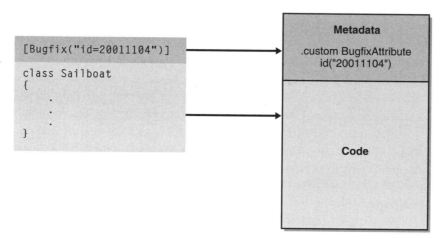

Figure 6-3. Compilation of attributes into assembly metadata.

The attribute is instantiated and potentially used only when the attribute is examined by a class that is expressly searching for the attribute. In the case of the *Obsolete* attribute, the compiler performs the search. For other attributes, such as the attributes that control connection pooling and transactioning, the attributes are detected by classes in the .NET Framework at runtime.

For example, as you'll see in Chapter 19, any types that you create can potentially be serialized into an XML document. (*Serializing* a type involves generating a stream or file from an instance of the type.) The default behavior of the XML serializer is sufficient to properly serialize objects to and from XML for most types. The .NET Framework also includes a number of attributes that provide fine-grained control over the XML serialization process. To prevent a field or property from being serialized, the *XmlIgnore* attribute is used, like this:

```
[XmlIgnore()]
public int Size;
```

In addition to specifying code elements that are to be ignored, attributes can be used to specify namespaces and alternative element names to the XML serializer. You don't need to write code to manage the serialization process; you simply adorn your existing code with attributes that control how the serializer works.

As the serializer examines objects that are passed to it, it uses a .NET feature known as *reflection* to search the metadata for relevant serialization attributes. (Reflection is discussed in more detail later in this chapter, in the section "Determining Whether an Attribute Is Used.") When an attribute is found, the XML serializer creates an instance of the attribute and uses the attribute object to control the serialization process. At least three classes are involved in the interaction with even the simplest attribute, as follows:

- The class that defines the attribute
- The class or other type that uses the attribute
- The class that detects that attribute and performs work based on the attribute's existence

As you'll see in the next section, most of the work performed for an attribute takes place in the code that detects the presence of the attribute. The actual attribute class is used only to collect the properties that are stored by the attribute.

Defining Custom Attributes

In addition to the wide variety of attributes that are defined as part of the .NET Framework, you can define your own custom attributes derived from the *System.Attribute* class. By convention, all attribute classes end with *Attribute*, so the *Obsolete* attribute used earlier is actually named *ObsoleteAttribute*. When the C# compiler encounters an attribute, it will look first for the name specified within the square brackets—in this case, *Obsolete*. If that type name isn't found, or if that type name isn't derived from the *System.Attribute* class, the compiler will automatically append *Attribute* to the name and search again.

Declaring an *AuthorAttribute* Class

The *AuthorAttribute* class shown here provides a means of tracking the author of various program elements in your source code:

```
public class AuthorAttribute: Attribute
{
    public AuthorAttribute(string name)
    {
        _name = name;
    }

    public string Name
    {
        get { return _name; }
    }

    public string Notes
    {
        set { _notes = value; }
        get { return _notes; }
    }

    protected string _name;
    protected string _notes;
}
```

The *AuthorAttribute* class includes the following two fields:

- ■ ***_name*** Contains the name of the author of a particular class, method, or other code element that's adorned with the attribute. The value of this member is set in the constructor and is accessible through the *Name* property.

- ■ ***_notes*** Contains optional notes that are associated with a code element. This member is accessible only through the *Notes* property.

The *AuthorAttribute* class contains no code that detects the usage of its attribute or that takes action based on the presence of the *Author* attribute. We'll write that code shortly; first let's look at how the *Author* attribute is used.

Using the *Author* Attribute

To use the *Author* attribute defined in the preceding section, just add the attribute before a program element such as a class, passing the class author's name as a parameter to the attribute, as shown here:

```
[Author("Mickey Williams")]
public class Sailboat
```

```
{
    ⋮
}
```

The *Author* attribute also can be used with a field, property, or other class member, as shown here:

```
[Author("Mickey Williams")]
public string Name
{
    ⋮
}
```

```
[Author("Mickey Williams")]
protected string _name;
```

An interesting issue arises when you tag an assembly with an attribute. Unlike program elements that exist in your source code, an assembly is compiled, so there's no clear location for an assembly attribute. For this reason, Microsoft Visual C# .NET automatically creates the AssemblyInfo.cs source file, which contains assembly attributes. Each assembly attribute uses the following format:

```
[assembly:attribute()]
```

The first part of the assembly annotation, *assembly*, is an attribute target. The attribute identifier notifies the compiler that the attribute is intended for a specific program element. To use the *Author* attribute with an assembly, the proper syntax is as follows:

```
[assembly: Author("Mickey Williams")]
```

The ability to specify a target for an attribute is useful in other situations in which the compiler can't determine the intended target for an attribute. For example, attributes can be declared for return values or methods. Given the following attribute usage, the C# compiler will assume that the attribute is intended for the method declaration:

```
[SerializationName("BOOL")]
public bool AvoidWhale()
{
    ⋮
}
```

If your intent was to annotate the method return value, however, you must explicitly provide an attribute target.

There are nine attribute types, as follows:

- *assembly*
- *event*
- *field*
- *method*
- *module*
- *param*
- *property*
- *return*
- *type*

For example, to specify that an attribute targets the return value rather than the method, the syntax would look like this:

```
[return:SerializationName("BOOL")]
public bool AvoidWhale()
{
    ⋮
}
```

Determining Whether an Attribute Is Used

As mentioned, attributes add no executable code to your assembly. Instead, information about an attribute is added to the assembly's metadata, and you must write code that examines the metadata to determine whether an attribute is being used. We'll use classes from the *System.Reflection* namespace to query metadata and retrieve information about custom attributes. Reflection is a powerful technique that allows you to determine, at runtime, information about types that are available to you.

A common starting point when using the reflection classes is to retrieve a *System.Type* object that describes the type of object you're interested in. In a C# program, all objects expose a *GetType* method that returns an instance of the *System.Type* class, as follows:

```
CSharpAuthor me = new CSharpAuthor();
Type myType = me.GetType();
```

Alternatively, if you don't have an instance of the type, you can use the *typeof* operator with the type name, like this:

```
Type myType = typeof(CSharpAuthor);
```

Armed with a *System.Type* object, you can use the reflection classes to retrieve the custom attributes that annotate the type, as shown in the following code:

```
public class AuthorAttributeCheck
{
    public AuthorAttributeCheck(Type theType)
    {
        _type = theType;
    }

    public string GetAuthorName()
    {
        foreach(Attribute attrib in _type.GetCustomAttributes(true))
        {
            AuthorAttribute auth - attrib as AuthorAttribute;
            if(auth != null)
            {
                return auth.Name;
            }
        }
        return null;
    }

    public string GetNotes()
    {
        foreach(Attribute attrib in _type.GetCustomAttributes(true))
        {
            AuthorAttribute auth = attrib as AuthorAttribute;
            if(auth != null)
            {
                return auth.Notes;
            }
        }
        return null;
    }
    protected Type _type;
}
```

The *AuthorAttributeCheck* class accepts a *System.Type* object as a parameter and then caches the type as a member field. The methods used to retrieve attribute information work in similar ways: first the array of custom attributes is retrieved by calling *_type.GetCustomAttributes*, and then each attribute is tested to determine whether it's an instance of *AuthorAttribute*. If the attribute has the proper type, properties are retrieved from the attribute and returned to the caller, as shown on the following page.

```
foreach(Attribute attrib in _type.GetCustomAttributes(true))
{
    AuthorAttribute auth = attrib as AuthorAttribute;
    if(auth != null)
    {
        // Use auth attribute here.
        ⋮
    }
}
```

The *AuthorAttributeCheck* class determines whether the *Author* attribute is used, retrieving information if the attribute is present. To use the *AuthorAttribute* class, first pass the type to be checked as a constructor parameter, and then call methods to retrieve the author name and notes properties, as shown here:

```
Type t = typeof(Sailboat);
AuthorAttributeCheck check = new AuthorAttributeCheck(t);
string name = check.GetAuthorName();
if(name != null)
    Console.WriteLine("The author's name is: {0}", name);
```

The preceding version of *AuthorAttributeCheck* detects when an *Author* attribute is attached to a type, but it doesn't detect cases in which the *Author* attribute is attached to a field, method, or other type member. It's reasonable to attach an *Author* attribute to a field, because several authors might have been involved in creating the code for a class. An attribute attached to a field is detected using slightly different reflection code, as shown here:

```
public string[] GetAllMemberAuthorInfo()
{
    MemberInfo[] members = _type.GetMembers();
    string [] result = new string[members.Length];
    int n = 0;
    foreach(MemberInfo info in members)
    {
        string name = info.Name;
        string memberType = info.MemberType.ToString();
        string author = MemberToAuthor(info);
        if(author == null)
            author = "Not known";
        result[n] = memberType + ": " + name + ", author:" + author;
        ++n;
    }
    return result;
}


protected string MemberToAuthor(MemberInfo info)
{
    foreach(Attribute attrib in info.GetCustomAttributes(true))
```

```
    {
        AuthorAttribute auth = attrib as AuthorAttribute;
        if(auth != null)
        {
            return auth.Name;
        }
    }
    return null;
}
```

The methods described here are part of the final version of *AuthorAttributeCheck*. They make it possible to determine whether any members of a type are adorned with the *Author* attribute. *GetAllMemberAuthorInfo* calls the *_type.GetMembers* method to retrieve the array of members defined for the type. This array contains constructors, methods, fields, properties, and other program elements that are declared for a particular type. The custom attributes for each member are then checked for the presence of the *Author* attribute.

It's also possible to use reflection to examine a specific member, instead of retrieving an array containing information for all members. The *GetMember* method returns an array of *MemberInfo* for a specific member name that's passed as a parameter. The *GetMemberAuthorInfo* method shown here uses *GetMember* to return author information for a specific member:

```
public string[] GetMemberAuthorInfo(string memberName)
{
    MemberInfo[] members = _type.GetMember(memberName);
    string [] result = new string[members.Length];
    int n = 0;
    foreach(MemberInfo info in members)
    {
        string name = info.Name;
        string memberType = info.MemberType.ToString();
        string author = MemberToAuthor(info);
        if(author == null)
            author = "Not known";
        result[n] = memberType + ": " + name + ", author:" + author;
        ++n;
    }
    return result;
}
```

Reflection can also be used to retrieve custom attribute information for assemblies, as shown in the following *GetAssemblyAuthorName* method:

```
public string GetAssemblyAuthorName(string asmName)
{
    Assembly asm = Assembly.Load(asmName);
    if(asm != null)
```

(continued)

```
    {
        foreach(Attribute attrib in asm.GetCustomAttributes(true))
        {
            AuthorAttribute auth = attrib as AuthorAttribute;
            if(auth != null)
            {
                return auth.Name;
            }
        }
    }
    return null;
}
```

This *GetAssemblyAuthorName* method starts by retrieving an instance of the *Assembly* class that refers to an assembly passed as a parameter. As with the previous examples, the array of custom attributes is retrieved, and if an *AuthorAttribute* instance is detected, the *Name* property is returned to the caller.

Controlling Custom Attribute Usage

As a practical matter, you'll often want to control the usage of your custom attributes. The usage restrictions for custom elements are specified by using the *AttributeUsage* attribute, as follows:

```
[AttributeUsage(AttributeTargets.All)]
public class AuthorAttribute: Attribute
{
    ⋮
}
```

The *AttributeUsage* attribute has the following three parameters:

- ■ *ValidOn* Positional parameter that defines the program elements that are eligible to use the attribute

- ■ *AllowMultiple* Named parameter that specifies whether an attribute can be used multiple times in the same program element

- ■ *Inherited* Named parameter that indicates whether the attribute should be inherited by subclasses of the type

The *ValidOn* parameter's value must use one of the values from the *AttributeTargets* enumeration, listed here:

- ■ *All*
- ■ *Assembly*
- ■ *Class*
- ■ *Constructor*

■ *Delegate*

■ *Enum*

■ *Event*

■ *Field*

■ *Interface*

■ *Method*

■ *Module*

■ *Parameter*

■ *Property*

■ *ReturnValue*

■ *Struct*

Values can be combined using the OR (|) operator. For example, to allow an attribute to be used on classes or structs, combine two values from the enumeration like this:

```
[AttributeUsage(AttributeTargets.Class|AttributeTargets.Struct)]
```

Custom attributes aren't inherited in subclasses by default. If you want your attribute to be inherited when its target is subclassed or overridden, set the *Inherited* parameter to *true*, as follows:

```
[AttributeUsage(AttributeTargets.All, Inherited=true)]
```

By default, attributes can be attached to a target only once. To allow your custom attribute to be used multiple times on the same attribute target, set the *AllowMultiple* parameter to *true*, as follows:

```
[AttributeUsage(AttributeTargets.All, AllowMultiple=true)]
```

In most cases, it makes sense to limit an attribute to a single use per target. However, consider the case in which an attribute is used to trace bug fixes. Because a class or method can have multiple bug fixes in its lifetime, you should allow the attribute to be used multiple times, as shown here:

```
[Bug(id="20011004", fixedby="mw")]
[Bug(id="20011001", fixedby="mw")]
class ScoopBinder
{
    ⋮
}
```

Creating a Strong Name

A common use of attributes is to provide a strong name for an assembly. As discussed in Chapter 1, assemblies that have a strong name can be placed in the global assembly cache. The global assembly cache enables a single assembly to be shared among multiple projects. The global assembly cache can be used to share multiple copies of the same assembly, as long as the copies differ in their version number or culture. The global assembly cache can store multiple copies of an assembly because it uses an assembly's unique strong name, instead of its file name, as an identifier. There are four components to a strong name, as follows:

- The file system's name for the assembly

- The assembly's version number

- A cryptographic key pair used to sign the assembly

- An optional culture designation that's used for localized assemblies

> **Note** A strong name ensures that an assembly hasn't been tampered with and protects the version path for a specific assembly. You can be sure that the assembly was created by the same company or individual that provided the original assembly, because the cryptographic keys must match. However, a strong name doesn't guarantee that the assembly was created by a specific trustworthy individual, as does the guarantee provided by an Authenticode signature.

Creating a Cryptographic Key Pair

As part of the strong-naming process, the assembly is digitally signed using a cryptographic key pair. There are two portions to the cryptographic key: a public portion, which is exposed to everyone, and a private portion, which remains secret. A hash of the assembly's contents is combined with the private portion of the key pair; the hash value is written into the assembly, along with the public portion of the key pair. A hash of the public portion of the key, commonly known as the *public key token,* is written into any assemblies that reference an assembly with a strong name.

The runtime calculates the proper hash value when loading the assembly and guarantees that the assembly contents have not been tampered with by a third party. Additionally, when a new version of a strong-named assembly is stored in the global assembly cache, the runtime ensures that the same key pair was used to sign the new version of the assembly.

So how do you create a cryptographic key pair? Although a cryptographic service provider (CSP) can be used as a source for your key pair, there's no need to use one. The simplest way to obtain a key pair is to run the Strong Name utility (sn.exe), which is part of the .NET Framework. The following command generates a key pair and stores it in a file named MyKeys.snk. (You must execute this command from the Microsoft Visual Studio .NET command prompt.)

```
sn -k MyKeys.snk
```

Although you can use the Assembly Linker (al.exe) to sign an assembly with a key pair, the simplest technique is to reference the key pair file using an attribute in your source code, enabling Visual C# to sign the assembly when it is compiled. The key pair is referenced using the *AssemblyKeyFile* attribute, which is located in the AssemblyInfo.cs source file included in every Visual C# project. By default, the *AssemblyKeyFile* attribute is provided a default empty value, as shown here:

```
[assembly: AssemblyKeyFile("")]
```

To sign your assembly, pass the key pair's file path to the *AssemblyKeyFile* attribute. The path is relative to the assembly binary, rather than to the project. If the file containing the key pair is located in the project directory, you must adjust the path accordingly, like this:

```
[assembly: AssemblyKeyFile(@"..\..\MyKeyPair.snk")]
```

Deploying Assemblies into the Global Assembly Cache

The preferred method for deploying an assembly into the global assembly cache is to use Microsoft Windows Installer 2.0 or later, which is fully aware of the global assembly cache and will properly install assemblies into it. For development and debugging purposes, you can use the Global Assembly Cache Utility tool (gacutil.exe). To register an assembly, use a command such as this from the Visual Studio .NET command prompt:

```
gacutil /i myctrl.dll
```

To remove an assembly from the global assembly cache, use the following command:

```
gacutil /u myctrl.dll
```

This command removes all copies of myctrl.dll. To remove a specific version, pass the version and public key token, as shown here:

```
gacutil /u myctrl.dll,Version=1.2.3.4,PublicKeyToken=8e091308dafe6804
```

The Global Assembly Cache Utility tool isn't meant to be distributed to end users. As you've seen, it's easy to remove items from the global assembly cache, and the tool is meant for use only on your development and test computers.

Conclusion

Delegates provide a type-safe and object-oriented way to manage callbacks into methods that have a specific signature. Situations that called for function pointers or callback methods in C and C++ are perfect candidates for delegates, which are type-safe and more flexible than function pointers. Delegates used in C# are based on the .NET Framework's *MulticastDelegate* class, which allows delegate methods to be multiplexed into a chain of methods that are invoked sequentially.

Events are used for one-way notifications between an event supplier and a client. Although events are based on delegates, they're not appropriate for cases in which the client needs to pass a return value or a reference parameter back to the supplier.

Finally, attributes provide a unique way for you to declaratively add functionality to your code by adorning your program's elements. By subclassing the *System.Attribute* class, you can create your own attributes.

7

Indexers and Enumerators

As you've seen in previous chapters, C# allows you to declare arrays, which are accessed using the subscript operator ([]), as shown here:

```
int [] Ages = { 5, 8, 40, 42 };
```

Members of the array are accessed using the [] operator, passing the zero-based index of the element to be retrieved:

```
int firstAge = Ages[0];
```

Accessing subelements of an array through the [] operator is a common idiom in C and C++ programming. C++ classes that act as containers for other types often provide their own implementation of the *operator* [] method, allowing access to contained objects using the [] operator, as shown here:

```
// This is a C++ class, not valid C#.
class SmartArray
{
public:
    int operator[](int item)
    {
        if(item >= 0 && item < arraySize)
        {
            return _values[item];
        }
        // Handle error.
        throw new range_error("invalid index");
    }
    :
};
```

Unlike C++, the C# programming language doesn't allow you to override the *operator* [] method. Instead, C# allows you to define indexers, which permit your classes and structures to be indexed like arrays. In this chapter, you'll see how indexers offer a much more powerful and flexible mechanism than the *operator* [] overloading found in C++. In C#, you can define indexers that accept any number and type of parameters. An indexer is responsible for resolving the arguments passed as subscript parameters and determining the course of action to be taken. As you'll see later in this chapter, subscript parameters are typically used to identify a contained object. We'll also look at enumeration, which is another common technique used for accessing collections of objects. By providing support for enumeration, you make your types more usable. For example, enumerable types can be used in the C# *foreach* statement, as shown here:

```
foreach(Camper camper in CampingTroop)
{
    camper.MakeMarshmallowVolcano();
}
```

Classes that support enumeration provide enumeration classes that act as cursors, enabling you to iterate over subitems. In the Microsoft .NET Framework, two interfaces provide a standard infrastructure for enabling enumeration. *IEnumerable* is implemented by all types that allow themselves to be enumerated, and *IEnumerator* is implemented by enumeration classes.

Using Indexers

As mentioned, indexers are used to provide index-like access to an object. In C++, this effect is achieved by overloading *operator* []; however, the C# language was designed to offer a wider range of functionality than the simple [] operator overloading offered by C++. In this section, we'll examine the syntax used to create indexers using C# and look at the scenarios where it makes sense to supply indexers with your classes. We'll also look at the features offered by C# indexers that make them more compelling than the similar [] operator in C++. As you'll see later in this chapter, in the section "Providing Multidimensional Indexers," C# indexers can easily accept multiple index parameters to simulate multidimensional arrays—a feature that's difficult to achieve in C++.

Indexers are useful in situations in which single objects must appear to be an array of objects. For example, classes that serve as containers for other objects can implement an indexer to provide a natural way to access the contained objects, such as the .NET Framework's *ArrayList* class, shown here:

```
ArrayList train = new ArrayList();
:
string name = train[42].ToString();
```

The *ArrayList* class combines the flexibility of a list with the ease of use found in an array. Although the *ArrayList* class includes more traditional methods and properties to access contained objects, accessing contained objects as if they're stored in an array often leads to cleaner code.

Declaring an Indexer

Indexers are declared much like properties, except that the declaration includes the *this* keyword, along with a declaration for the index key, as shown here:

```
public object this[int key]
{
    get{ return _items[key]; }
    set{ _items[key] = value; }
}
```

Just like properties, the *get* and *set* accessors are used to define the methods that implement the indexer, with the *value* keyword representing the parameter passed as the new element value to the *set* accessor. As with properties, a read-only index is defined by omitting the *set* accessor, as shown here:

```
public object this[int key]
{
    // Read-only indexer
    get{ return _items[key]; }
}
```

An indexer declaration can be declared as virtual or abstract by adding the appropriate keyword to the indexer declaration, as follows:

```
public virtual object this[int key]
{
    get{ return _items[key]; }
    set{ _items[key] = value; }
}
```

When declaring an indexer as abstract, you must provide empty *get* and *set* accessor declarations:

```
public abstract object this[int key]
{
    get;
    set;
}
```

As with other abstract declarations, such as properties or methods, a class that contains an abstract indexer must also be marked as abstract.

Overloading Indexers

Just as classes can define multiple properties, they can also define multiple
indexers. Although the compiler differentiates properties by their names, it dis-
tinguishes between multiple indexers by their signatures. For example, a class
can define indexers that use both string or integer keys, as shown here:

```
// Index by string value.
public object this[string key]
{
    get{ ... }
    set{ ... }
}

// Index by int value.
public object this[int key]
{
    get{ ... }
    set{ ... }
}
```

Multiple indexers enable the user to select the most convenient indexing type.
Given the preceding index definitions, the user could write code such as this:

```
gradeIndex[42] = 100;
gradeIndex["Nicolette"] = 100;
```

When multiple indexers are provided for a class, the compiler determines
the proper index to invoke based on the signature of the index parameter.
When required, the compiler will apply the usual conversion rules for the index
parameters. For example, a short integer used as an index argument in the previous example will use the integer indexer, as follows:

```
short id = 0;
gradeIndex[id] = 75;    // Uses [int]
```

Providing Multidimensional Indexers

A class also can declare multidimensional indexers, which is useful when you're
modeling tables or other multidimensional structures. An interesting twist to
multidimensional indexers is that each index dimension can have a different
type, as shown here:

```
public class TestScore
{
    public object this[string name, int testNumber]
    {
        get
        {
            return GetGrade(name, testNumber);
```

```
        }
        set
        {
            SetGrade(name, testNumber, value);
        }
    }
    ⋮
}
```

In the preceding code, test results are indexed by student ID and test number. Providing indexes that follow the natural order of included items can make your classes easier to use. To retrieve test scores using the previous example, you can use code like this:

```
string studentId = "ALI92";
for(testNumber = 0; testNumber < maxTest; ++testNumber)
{
    decimal score = gradeIndex[studentId, testNumber];
    ⋮
}
```

Declaring Indexers for Interfaces

In Chapter 2, interfaces were presented as a way to provide a template for behavior that's implemented by a type. For example, classes that support the dispose pattern implement the *IDisposable* interface. In addition to methods and properties, interfaces can also define indexers as part of the contract to be implemented by a type. Including an indexer provides a standard method for accessing objects stored by type. For example, the *IDictionary* interface, implemented by some of the collection classes that will be discussed in Chapter 8, implements an indexer that's used to access stored objects.

Indexers can be declared as interface members; however, there are some differences in the declaration syntax when compared to an index declared as a class member. An indexer declaration in an interface doesn't include any access modifiers such as *public* or *private*. Because interfaces never include program statements, the *get* and *set* accessors have no bodies. An example of an interface declaration that includes an indexer is shown here:

```
interface IGradeIndex
{
    object this[string name, int testNumber]
    {
        get;
        set;
    }
}
```

When a class or structure inherits an interface such as *IGradeIndex*, the access modifier for the index must be specified and the accessors must be implemented, as shown here:

```
class GradingTable: IGradeIndex
{
    public object this[string name, int testNumber]
    {
        get
        {
            return GetGrade(name, testNumber);
        }
        set
        {
            SetGrade(name, testNumber, value);
        }
    }
    :
}
```

An Indexer Example

Let's look at a concrete example of how an indexer can be used to add value to your classes. In this section, we'll build an associative array, a data structure that allows strings to be used as index values, like this:

```
loveInterests["Romeo"] = "Juliet";
loveInterests["Beatrice"] = "Benedick";
loveInterests["Cyrano"] = "Roxanne";
```

We'll use an indexer for the associative array class so that each instance of the class can be used much like the built-in C# array type, except that the indexing will be done using strings rather than scalar values. The *AssociativeArray* class shown here implements an associative array:

```
public class AssociativeArray
{
    // Create an array and specify its initial size.
    public AssociativeArray(int initialSize)
    {
        _items = new object[initialSize];
    }
    // Declare the indexer used to access individual array items.
    public object this[string key]
    {
        get{ return KeyToObject(key); }
        set{ AddToArray(key, value); }
    }
    // Mimic the Length property found in other .NET arrays.
    public int Length
```

```
{
    get { return _count; }
}
// Helper method used to add an item to the array. If the
// key already exists, the existing item is replaced. If the
// array is full, the array size is increased.
protected void AddToArray(string key, object item)
{
    if(KeyExists(key))
    {
        // Scroll through the item array and replace the
        // existing item associated with the key with the
        // new item.
        for(int n = 0; n < _count; ++n)
        {
            KeyItemPair pair = (KeyItemPair)_items[n];
            if(key == pair.key)
                _items[n] = new KeyItemPair(key, item);
        }
    }
    else
    {
        if(_count == _items.Length)
        {
            IncreaseCapacity();
        }
        _items[_count] = new KeyItemPair(key, item);
        _count++;
    }
}
// Returns true if a specific key exists in the array;
// otherwise, returns false.
protected bool KeyExists(string key)
{
    for(int n = 0; n < _count; ++n)
    {
        KeyItemPair pair = (KeyItemPair)_items[n];
        if(key == pair.key)
            return true;
    }
    return false;
}
// Given a key in the array, returns the associated object, or
// returns null if the key isn't found.
protected object KeyToObject(string key)
{
    for(int n = 0; n < _count; ++n)
    {
        KeyItemPair pair = (KeyItemPair)_items[n];
```

(continued)

```
            if(key == pair.key)
                return pair.item;
        }
        return null;
    }
    // Increases the size of the item array.
    protected void IncreaseCapacity()
    {
        int size = _items.Length + 5;
        object [] oldArray = _items;
        _items = new object[size];
        oldArray.CopyTo(_items, 0);
    }
    // The array that stores items in the associative array
    protected object[] _items;
    // The number of items in the array
    protected int _count = 0;
    // A structure that contains the item and key pair stored in
    // each array element
    protected struct KeyItemPair
    {
        public KeyItemPair(string k, object obj)
        {
            key = k;
            item = obj;
        }
        public object item;
        public string key;
    }
}
```

Internally, objects are stored in _items, an array of objects that's automatically grown as needed when additional items are added to the array. The AddToArray method is used to add an item to the _items array; if additional storage is required, the IncreaseCapacity method is used to grow the array, preserving any existing items.

The indexer calls the AddToArray method when adding items and uses the KeyToObject method to retrieve items. If the key isn't found in the array, KeyToObject returns a null value, which the indexer returns to the caller.

The KeyItemPair structure is used to provide mapping between item keys and the objects associated with the keys. This structure is strictly for internal use only and is never exposed outside the AssociativeArray class.

As mentioned, the AssociativeArray class is used much like the array types that are included in the .NET Framework class library. To use this class to store favorite foods, you can use code like this:

```
static void Main(string[] args)
{
    AssociativeArray foodFavorites = new AssociativeArray(4);
    foodFavorites["Mickey"] = "Risotto with Wild Mushrooms";
    foodFavorites["Ali"] = "Plain Cheeseburger";
    foodFavorites["Mackenzie"] = "Macaroni and Cheese";
    foodFavorites["Rene"] = "Escargots";

    Console.WriteLine(foodFavorites["Ali"]);
    Console.WriteLine(foodFavorites["Mackenzie"]);
    Console.WriteLine(foodFavorites["Mickey"]);
    Console.WriteLine(foodFavorites["Rene"]);
}
```

Using Enumerators

Although the version of the *AssociativeArray* class presented in the previous section is useful, it has a limitation that restricts its use in a C# application. Because it doesn't support the standard enumeration pattern used by classes in the .NET Framework, iterating over all elements in the array is difficult and requires client code to know the key for each element stored in the collection.

There are multiple ways that iteration over an associative array collection could be supported. One approach would be to expose an indexer that supports numerical indexing, allowing a loop similar to the following to be written:

```
for(int n = 0; n < foodFavorites.Length; ++n)
{
    string favorite = foodFavorites[n];
    ⋮
}
```

The problem with this approach is that it can't be generalized to all types of collections. For example, consider a collection class that stores items in a tree-based data structure. Although it would be possible to expose an indexer that provides indexing based on integer keys, it wouldn't result in a natural access method for the container.

The .NET Framework offers a different approach for iterating over all items in a collection—the enumerator. Enumerators are classes used to provide a standard iteration method over all items stored in a collection. By specifying the standard interfaces used to implement enumerators, the .NET Framework formalizes a design pattern that's used for all collection types. In this section, we'll examine the standard interfaces used to build enumerators, and we'll add enumerator support to the *AssociativeArray* class.

Understanding Enumeration Interfaces

Enumerators are classes that implement the *IEnumerator* interface, which is part of the *System.Collections* namespace. The *IEnumerator* interface, shown in the following code, is used to define a cursor-style iteration over a collection:

```
interface IEnumerator
{
    object Current
    {
        get;
    }
    void   Reset();
    bool   MoveNext();
}
```

The *IEnumerator* interface exposes two methods and one property:

- **Reset**   Returns the enumerator to its initial state
- **MoveNext**   Moves to the next item in the collection, returning *true* if the operation was successful or *false* if the enumerator has moved past the last item
- **Current**   Returns the object to which the enumerator currently refers

The *IEnumerator* interface isn't implemented directly by collection classes; instead, it's implemented by separate enumerator classes that provide enumeration functionality. Decoupling enumeration classes from the collection class makes it easy to support multiple simultaneous enumeration objects for one collection, as shown in Figure 7-1. If *IEnumerator* was to be implemented by a collection class, it would be difficult for a collection class to support more than one client using enumeration at any given time.

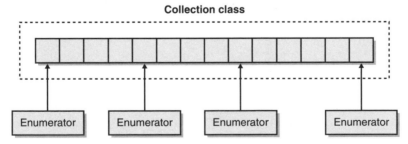

Figure 7-1   Multiple enumeration objects acting on a collection class concurrently.

Classes that support enumeration and want to expose enumerators to their clients implement the *IEnumerable* interface. *IEnumerable* includes a single method, *GetEnumerator*, which returns an enumerator object for the current object. The declaration for *IEnumerable* is shown here:

```
interface IEnumerable
{
    IEnumerator GetEnumerator();
}
```

When enumerators are newly minted, the enumerator's *Current* property can't be used because it's positioned just prior to the first item. To advance the enumerator to the first item in the collection, you must call *MoveNext*, which will return *true* if the enumerator is positioned at a valid collection item. This behavior allows you to write a very compact loop when iterating over a collection, as shown here:

```
IEnumerator enumerator = enumerable.GetEnumerator();
while(enumerator.MoveNext())
{
    MyObject obj = (MyObject)enumerator.Current;
    ⋮
}
```

Enumerators are always tightly bound to a specific collection object. If the collection is updated, any enumerators associated with the collection are invalidated and can't be used. If you attempt to use an enumerator after it's been invalidated or when it's positioned before the first element or after the last element, an *InvalidOperationException* exception will be thrown.

Implementing Enumeration Interfaces

The first step in implementing enumeration interfaces is to create an internal or embedded class that implements *IEnumerator*. Although you'll create a concrete class derived from *IEnumerator* to implement the enumerator, you probably won't expose this class as public. To prevent clients from depending on your specific enumerator declaration, it's a much better idea to keep your enumerator class protected or private and expose functionality only through the *IEnumerator* interface.

Creating an Enumerator Class

In addition to implementing the *IEnumerator* interface, your enumerator class must be able to access individual items in the underlying collection. For the enumerator example presented in this section, the *AssociativeArray* class has been modified to make the *_items* field internal, granting access to any classes in the assembly, as shown here:

```
internal object[] _items;
```

Another approach is to implement an enumerator as a class that's embedded in the collection class, as follows:

```
public class AssociativeArray: IEnumerable
{
    ⋮
    public class AssociativeArrayEnumerator : IEnumerator
    {
        ⋮
    }
}
```

When an enumerator is implemented as a class embedded within the collection, it can access all members of the collection class, which can provide for better encapsulation. However, embedding the enumerator also increases the size and complexity of the collection class. For the purposes of this example, the enumerator class is broken out separately.

Regardless of the implementation of the enumerator, you'll need to pass a reference to the collection to the enumerator when the enumerator is constructed and initialized, as shown here:

```
public IEnumerator GetEnumerator()
{
    return new AssociativeArrayEnumerator(this);
}
```

Remember that you must provide a mechanism that enables the collection to invalidate any enumerators that are associated with the collection. This is the only way that users of the enumerator can determine that the collection has been updated. A good way to invalidate the enumerator is to provide an event that's raised when the collection is updated. By subscribing to the event during construction, enumerators can receive an event notification and mark themselves invalid when their associated collection is changed.

An example of an enumerator that provides iteration access to the *AssociativeArray* class is shown here:

```
// An enumerator for the AssociativeArray class
public class AssociativeArrayEnumerator : IEnumerator
```

```
{
    public AssociativeArrayEnumerator(AssociativeArray ar)
    {
        _ar = ar;
        _currIndex = -1;
        _invalidated = false;
        // Subscribe to collection change events.
        AssociativeArray.ChangeEventHandler h;
        h = new AssociativeArray.ChangeEventHandler(InvalidatedHandler);
        ar.AddOnChanged(h);
    }
    // Property that retrieves the element in the array that this
    // enumerator instance is pointing to. If the enumerator has
    // been invalidated or isn't pointing to a valid item, throw
    // an InvalidOperationException exception.
    public object Current
    {
        get
        {
            AssociativeArray.KeyItemPair pair;
            if(_invalidated ||
                _currIndex == -1 ||
                _currIndex == _ar.Length)
                throw new InvalidOperationException();
            pair = (AssociativeArray.KeyItemPair)_ar._items[_currIndex];
            return pair.item;
        }
    }
    // Move to the next item in the collection, returning true if the
    // enumerator refers to a valid item and returning false otherwise.
    public bool MoveNext()
    {
        if(_invalidated || _currIndex == _ar._items.Length)
            throw new InvalidOperationException();
        _currIndex++;
        if(_currIndex == _ar.Length)
            return false;
        else
            return true;
    }
    // Reset the enumerator to its initial position.
    public void Reset()
    {
        if(_invalidated)
            throw new InvalidOperationException();
        _currIndex = -1;
    }
    // Event handler for changes to the underlying collection. When
    // a change occurs, this enumerator is invalidated and must be
```

(continued)

```
    // re-created.
    private void InvalidatedHandler(object sender, EventArgs e)
    {
        _invalidated = true;
    }
    // Flag that marks the collection as invalid after a change to
    // the associative array
    protected bool _invalidated;
    // The index of the item this enumerator applies to
    protected int _currIndex;
    // A reference to this enumerator's associative array
    protected AssociativeArray _ar;
}
```

Providing Access to the Enumerator

You should create new enumerator objects in response to a call to the collection class's *GetEnumerator* method. Although you'll return your enumerator object, the client code that retrieves your enumerator has access to your object only through *IEnumerator* because *GetEnumerator* is typed to return only an *IEnumerator* interface. The version of *GetEnumerator* for the *AssociativeArray* class is shown here:

```
public class AssociativeArray: IEnumerable
{
    ⋮
    public IEnumerator GetEnumerator()
    {
        return new AssociativeArrayEnumerator(this);
    }
    ⋮
}
```

In response to the call to *GetEnumerator*, the *AssociativeArray* class creates a new enumerator object, passing the *this* pointer so that the enumerator can initialize itself to refer to this *AssociativeArray* object.

Other changes made to the *AssociativeArray* class to provide enumerator support are shown here:

```
public class AssociativeArray: IEnumerable
{
    // Event delegate
    public delegate void ChangeEventHandler(object sender, EventArgs e);
    ⋮
    public AssociativeArray(int initialSize)
    {
        _count = 0;
        _items = new object[initialSize];
        _eventArgs = new EventArgs();
```

```
}
⋮
public void AddOnChanged(ChangeEventHandler handler)
{
    Changed += handler;
}
// Remove an event handler for the changed event.
public void RemoveOnChanged(ChangeEventHandler handler)
{
    Changed -= handler;
}
// Raise a changed event to subscribed enumerators.
protected void OnChanged()
{
    if(Changed != null)
        Changed(this, _eventArgs);
}
⋮
// Event handler for distributing change events to enumerators
public event ChangeEventHandler Changed;
// A member that holds change event arguments
protected EventArgs _eventArgs;
}
```

In addition to implementing *IEnumerable*, several changes have been made to the *AssociativeArray* class. First, an event delegate type has been declared to propagate events to enumerators. Next, the *AddOnChanged* and *RemoveOnChanged* methods have been added to assist in subscribing and unsubscribing to the *Changed* event. Each enumerator subscribes to this event so that the enumerators can be invalidated after changes to the *AssociativeArray* object. Instead of creating new *EventArgs* objects when each *Changed* event is raised, a single *EventArgs* object is created and passed for all events raised during the object's lifetime.

Consuming Enumeration Interfaces

There are two ways to use the .NET Framework's enumerator interfaces. The first method is to request the enumerator directly and explicitly iterate over the collection using the *IEnumerator* interface, like this:

```
public void Iterate(object obj)
{
    IEnumerable enumerable = obj as IEnumerable;
    if(enumerable != null)
    {
        IEnumerator enumerator = enumerable.GetEnumerator();
        while(enumerator.MoveNext())
```

(continued)

```
    {
        object theObject = enumerator.Current;
        Console.WriteLine(theObject.ToString());
    }
    }
}
```

A more useful and common way to make use of the enumeration interfaces is to use a *foreach* loop, as shown in the following code.

```
static void Main(string[] args)
{
    AssociativeArray foodFavorites = new AssociativeArray(4);
    foodFavorites["Mickey"] = "Risotto with Wild Mushrooms";
    foodFavorites["Ali"] = "Plain Cheeseburger";
    foodFavorites["Mackenzie"] = "Macaroni and Cheese";
    foodFavorites["Rene"] = "Escargots";

    try
    {
        foreach(string food in foodFavorites)
        {
            Console.WriteLine(food);
        }
    }
    catch(InvalidOperationException exc)
    {
        Console.WriteLine(exc.ToString());
    }
}
```

Behind the scenes, the C# compiler will generate the code required to make use of *IEnumerable* and *IEnumerator*. When the preceding code is compiled and executed, the output looks like this:

```
Risotto with Wild Mushrooms
Plain Cheeseburger
Macaroni and Cheese
Escargots
```

Conclusion

Indexers are used to provide array-like access for structures, arrays, and interfaces. Multiple indexers can be provided for a type, and indexers can easily support multiple dimensions. Indexers can be declared as virtual or abstract, and they're declared with an access protection level, such as public or internal, except when declared as part of an interface.

Enumerators are used to provide a standard navigation mechanism over a set of objects. Types that expose enumerators do so through the *IEnumerable* interface, which provides a standard way to retrieve an enumerator. All enumerators are derived from the *IEnumerator* interface, which includes methods for forward-only cursor-style iteration.

In Chapter 8, we'll expand our examination of indexers and enumerators to look at the various types of collections that are included as part of the .NET Framework class library.

8

Collections and Sorting

In this chapter, we'll examine the classes and interfaces used for comparing, sorting, and storing objects in collections in the Microsoft .NET Framework. We'll begin by looking at two interfaces: *IComparable* and *IComparer*. By implementing the *IComparable* interface with your types, you can provide them with a standard comparison mechanism that's interoperable with classes in the .NET Framework. The *IComparer* interface is implemented by classes that provide comparison services to other types. These two interfaces are frequently used for comparison and sorting in the .NET Framework and enable you to easily leverage the built-in support for sorting provided by many other types in the .NET Framework, including the *Array* class.

This chapter also examines the collection classes included with the .NET Framework. Up to now, we've used only arrays as containers for other objects. This chapter explores the more advanced classes that can be used to manage collections of objects, such as the *Queue*, *Stack*, and *Hashtable* classes.

Later chapters, including the chapters on programming Microsoft Windows Forms, will use collection classes extensively. Understanding the similarities and differences between the collection classes will help you determine the type of collection best suited for a particular purpose.

Comparing and Sorting

The .NET Framework includes a standard set of interfaces that are used for comparing and sorting objects. Although implementing these interfaces is optional, any class that does implement them can interact with other .NET Framework classes to achieve greater functionality. In this section, you'll see how these interfaces make it possible to compare and sort instances of your types, in the same way the built-in types are used.

Creating Comparable Types with the *IComparable* Interface

The *IComparable* interface can be implemented by types to provide a standard way of comparing multiple objects. By implementing *IComparable*, types can maintain reference equality semantics while providing a standard method for value comparison.

The *IComparable* interface is declared as follows:

```
interface IComparable
{
    int CompareTo(object obj);
}
```

The *CompareTo* method returns one of the following three possible values:

- Less than 0 if the current object compares as less than *obj*
- 0 if the current object compares as equal to *obj*
- Greater than 0 if the current object compares as greater than *obj*

The following code shows an example of a simple value type that implements *IComparable*. The *ZipCode* structure models a U.S. postal ZIP Code, including the optional "plus 4" digits that help further define the destination. The *IComparable.CompareTo* method is used to enable comparison of multiple *ZipCode* objects.

```
public struct ZipCode: IComparable
{
    public ZipCode(string zip, string plusFour)
    {
        _zip = zip;
        _plusFour = plusFour;
    }

    public ZipCode(string zip)
    {
        _zip = zip;
        _plusFour = null;
    }

    public int CompareTo(object obj)
    {
        if(obj == null)
            return 1;
```

```
        if(obj.GetType() != this.GetType())
            throw new ArgumentException("Invalid comparison");

        ZipCode other = (ZipCode)obj;
        int result = _zip.CompareTo(other._zip);
        if(result == 0)
        {
            if(other._plusFour == null)
                result = _plusFour == null? 1: 0;
            else
                result = _plusFour.CompareTo(other._plusFour);
        }
        return result;
    }

    public override string ToString()
    {
        string result;
        if(_plusFour != null && _plusFour.Length != 0)
            result = string.Format("{0}-{1}", _zip, _plusFour);
        else
            result = _zip;
        return result;
    }

    string _zip;
    string _plusFour;
}
```

The *ZipCode* class has two fields that are used to store the components that make up a U.S. ZIP Code. The *ZipCode.ToString* method is overridden to provide string formatting in the customary format of, for example, 92653 or 92653-8204 if a "plus 4" code is present. The method of most interest in the *Zip-Code* class is *CompareTo*. Although the details of how two objects are compared will differ, all implementations of *CompareTo* will follow this general pattern:

```
public int CompareTo(object obj)
{
    // If the other object is null, this object sorts as greater.
    if(obj == null)
        return 1;
    // If there's a type mismatch, throw an exception.
    if(obj.GetType() != this.GetType())
        throw new ArgumentException("Invalid comparison");
    // Return a result based on a comparison of the two objects.
    ⋮
}
```

An implementation of the *CompareTo* method should first test to see whether *null* was passed as a parameter. If so, the comparison should be short-circuited and a result greater than 0 should be returned to indicate that the current object compares as greater than *null*. It's also important to test that the objects being compared have the same type or are of a comparable type. Otherwise, you can run into a scenario such as this one:

```
Orange anOrange;
Apple  anApple;
int result = anOrange.CompareTo(anApple);
```

After adding support for *IComparable* to a class or a structure, you can make use of the type's support for comparison in two ways. The first way is to directly call the *CompareTo* method to determine the relative sort order for two objects, as shown here:

```
ZipCode lagunaHills = new ZipCode("92653", "8204");
ZipCode redmond = new ZipCode("98052");
ZipCode phoenix = new ZipCode("85044");

int comparison = lagunaHills.CompareTo(redmond);
```

The second way to take advantage of *IComparable* is to leverage other types and methods in the .NET Framework that are aware of the *IComparable* interface. These types offer increased functionality when they're used with classes and structures that implement *IComparable*. For example, the *Array.Sort* static method can be used to sort an array of types that implement *IComparable*, as shown here:

```
ZipCode [] codes = { lagunaHills, redmond, phoenix };
Array.Sort(codes);
foreach(ZipCode code in codes)
{
    // Display sorted array of ZIP Codes.
    Console.WriteLine(code);
}
```

The version of the *Array.Sort* method used here detects and uses the *IComparable* interface to determine the relative sort order of objects in the array. If you attempt to use this version of *Sort* with an array of objects that don't implement *IComparable*, an *InvalidOperationException* will be thrown.

Building Comparison Classes with the *IComparer* Interface

The *IComparable* interface is useful for those cases in which there's a clear ordering method for class instances. However, there are times when a number of possible sort methods are available for a collection of objects. The *IComparer* interface enables you to build classes that are specialized to compare instances of other classes.

The *IComparer* interface is declared as follows:

```
interface IComparer
{
    int Compare(object x, object y);
}
```

The *Compare* method works much like the *CompareTo* method discussed in the previous section, returning one of the following values:

- Less than 0 if the first object compares as less than the second object

- 0 if the first object compares as equal to the second object

- Greater than 0 if the first object compares as greater than the second object

As with the *IComparable.CompareTo* method, if an object reference is *null*, it compares as less than any object.

Implementing *IComparer* in Pluggable Classes

The *IComparer* interface makes it possible for you to create multiple comparison classes, each of which performs a different type of comparison. The following class implements the *IComparer* interface and sorts *ZipCode* objects in ascending order:

```
public class AscendingComparer: IComparer
{
    public int Compare(object x, object y)
    {
        int result = 0;
        if(x == null && y == null)
            result = 0;
        else if(x == null)
            result = -1;
        else if(y == null)
            result = 1;
        else
        {
            if(x.GetType() != y.GetType())
            throw new ArgumentException("Invalid comparison");
            IComparable comp = x as IComparable;
            if(comp == null)
                throw new ArgumentException("Invalid comparison");
            result = comp.CompareTo(y);
        }
        return result;
    }
}
```

This code shows a common pattern for implementing *IComparer.Compare*. In much the same way as in the earlier *IComparable* example, any reference to *null* is sorted as less than object references. If two valid object references are compared, the types of the objects are tested to ensure that they're comparable. In this case, the *AscendingComparer* class tests to verify that both objects have the same type.

The following code implements the *DescendingComparer* class, which works exactly like *AscendingComparer* except that it sorts its objects in reverse order:

```
public class DescendingComparer: IComparer
{
    public int Compare(object x, object y)
    {
        int result = 0;
        if(x == null && y == null)
            result = 0;
        else if(y == null)
            result = -1;
        else if(x == null)
            result = 1;
        else
        {
            if(x.GetType() != y.GetType())
            throw new ArgumentException("Invalid comparison");
            IComparable comp = y as IComparable;
            if(comp == null)
                throw new ArgumentException("Invalid comparison");
            result = comp.CompareTo(x);
        }
        return result;
    }
}
```

When sorting is required, you can simply plug in an instance of the preferred comparison class, allowing multiple sort options to be used for a single type. For example, the following code uses both of the previous comparison classes to sort *ZipCode* objects:

```
Array.Sort(codes, new AscendingComparer());
foreach(ZipCode code in codes)
{
    Console.WriteLine(code);
}
Array.Sort(codes, new DescendingComparer());
foreach(ZipCode code in codes)
{
    Console.WriteLine(code);
}
```

In the preceding examples, the *AscendingComparer* and *DescendingComparer* classes are exposed as public classes. Another alternative is to expose the classes that perform the comparison through properties, as shown here:

```
Array.Sort(codes, codes.AscendingComparer);
⋮
Array.Sort(codes, codes.DescendingComparer);
⋮
```

The advantage of this approach is that the comparison classes are more completely encapsulated, thus hiding more implementation details from the user.

Using the Built-In Comparison Classes

The .NET Framework includes two classes that implement the *IComparer* interface and can be leveraged in your own classes to simplify comparisons. The *Comparer* and *CaseInsensitiveComparer* classes provide basic implementations of *IComparer* that are suitable for many comparison classes. Both of these classes respect the culture preferences of the user, providing proper comparisons based on the locale and language settings associated with the current thread.

You never directly create an instance of the *Comparer* class using the *new* operator. Instead, you call the *Default* method, which returns a properly initialized *Comparer* object, as shown here:

```
Comparer theComparer = Comparer.Default;
```

After you have a *Comparer* object, you can delegate comparison calls to its *Compare* method. The following code illustrates a simplified version of *AscendingComparer* implemented using the *Comparer* class:

```
public int Compare(object x, object y)
{
    return Comparer.Default.Compare(x, y);
}
```

In this code, *ZipCode* objects are passed to the *Comparer* class, which is able to properly compare the objects through their *IComparable* interface. This is the only way that *Comparer* can perform comparisons on arbitrary objects. If your classes don't implement *IComparable*, you can't pass instances of the classes to *Comparer.Compare*.

The *CaseInsensitiveComparer* class works much like the *Comparer* class, comparing any two objects through the *IComparable* interface, except that it performs a case-insensitive comparison on strings that it encounters. Like the *Comparer* class, the static *Default* method is used to obtain a reference to a properly initialized *CaseInsensitiveComparer* object, as shown here:

```
CaseInsensitiveComparer aComparer = CaseInsensitiveComparer.Default;
```

Unlike the *Comparer* class, you can use the *new* operator to create *CaseInsensitiveComparer* objects. The default constructor has little advantage over the *Default* method, other than enabling you to cache a specific *Case-InsensitiveComparer* object. An overloaded version of the constructor allows you to specify the culture to be used for the comparison. (The culture of the current thread is used by default.) The following code performs a string comparison using the Swedish culture definition:

```
public class SwedishNameComparer: IComparer
{
    public int Compare(object x, object y)
    {
        CultureInfo ci = new CultureInfo("sv");
        CaseInsensitiveComparer aComparer = null;
        aComparer = new CaseInsensitiveComparer(ci);
        return aComparer.Compare(x, y);
    }
}

    ⋮

public Main()
{
    string [] places = { "Kista", "Älvsjö", "Stockholm" };
    Array.Sort(places, new SwedishNameComparer());
    foreach(string place in places)
    {
        Console.WriteLine(place);
    }
}
```

The preceding code sorts the strings according to the ordering used in Swedish, where Ä is placed after Z, as shown here:

```
Kista
Stockholm
Älvsjö
```

If the en-US (English as spoken in the United States) culture is used to sort the strings, the strings are sorted as follows:

```
Älvsjö
Kista
Stockholm
```

Which comparison is most appropriate? The answer depends on the expectations of the user, which are expressed in the culture settings associated with the current thread. Because the comparison classes included with the .NET Framework take the culture settings into account, they handle these sorting issues correctly.

Storing Objects in Collection Classes

The .NET Framework includes specialized classes known as collection classes, or simply collections, which are used to store objects. Like arrays, collections enable you to place objects into a container for later retrieval. However, collections differ from arrays in the way they're used, as well as in the techniques used for interaction. Some collection classes, such as the *Stack* and *Queue* classes, have specialized methods for inserting and removing items. Other collection classes, such as the *StringCollection* class, are dedicated for use with a certain type of object. In this section, you'll see how the *Queue*, *Hashtable*, and *Stack* classes are used. You'll also be introduced to the interfaces commonly implemented by all collection classes in the .NET Framework.

Commonly Used Collection Interfaces

A wide variety of collection classes are included in the .NET Framework. Each class has unique features that separate it from other collection classes, but a few interfaces (*ICollection*, *IEnumerable*, *ICloneable*, *IDictionary*, and *IList*) are consistently implemented by most collection classes. This section examines those interfaces in detail.

ICollection—The Root of All Collections

The *ICollection* interface is implemented by all collection classes in the .NET Framework. This interface defines the minimum contract for a collection class and is declared as follows:

```
interface ICollection
{
    int     Count{ get; }
    bool    IsSynchronized{ get; }
    object  SynchRoot{ get; }
    void    CopyTo(Array array, int index);
}
```

The members of the *ICollection* interface are described here:

- **Count**   Returns the number of objects stored in the collection

- **IsSynchronized**   Returns true if the collection is thread-safe; otherwise, returns false

- **SynchRoot**   Returns an object used to synchronize multithreaded access to the collection

- **CopyTo**   Copies the objects in the collection to an array

By factoring the common properties and methods for collections into the *ICollection* interface, a basic contract is defined for all collection classes in the .NET

Framework. All collections must implement the *Count* property so that clients can determine the number of objects in a collection. All collections expose the *CopyTo* method to provide a standard way for a collection to copy its contents to an array.

All collection classes also implement the *IsSynchronized* and *SynchRoot* properties to support basic multithreaded programming. The use of these properties is covered, along with other multithreaded programming topics, in Chapter 10.

> **Note**   Keep in mind that *ICollection* is the minimum interface for collection classes. All collection classes support the methods listed in this section, as well as methods and other interfaces that define their behavior.

Providing Enumerators with the *IEnumerable* Interface

The *IEnumerable* interface, which was discussed in Chapter 7, is implemented by all collection classes in the .NET Framework. To review, *IEnumerable* is the standard interface implemented by classes that support iteration over contained objects. *IEnumerable* is declared as follows:

```
interface IEnumerable
{
    IEnumerator GetEnumerator();
}
```

Some classes forego returning *IEnumerator* in favor of a more specialized interface suited for their particular type of collection. For example, the *Hashtable* class (discussed later in this chapter, in the section "Using the *Hashtable* Class") returns an enumerator that implements the *IDictionaryEnumerator* interface, which is more suited for enumerating that type of collection. The *IDictionaryEnumerator* interface will be discussed later in this chapter, in the section "Mapping Keys to Values with the *IDictionary* Interface."

Copying Objects with the *ICloneable* Interface

The *ICloneable* interface is used to provide a standard way to create copies of existing objects. The *ICloneable* interface is declared as follows:

```
interface ICloneable
{
    object Clone();
}
```

The *Clone* method returns a new instance that is of the same type as (or occasionally a derived type of) the current object. As the method's name implies, the returned object is initialized with the same contents as the current object.

An interesting aspect of cloning is that the type that's being cloned can provide a shallow copy or a deep copy of the current object. A shallow copy copies the current object; however, no new instances of any fields are created. Instead, the shallow copy maintains references to the same objects as the original, as shown in Figure 8-1.

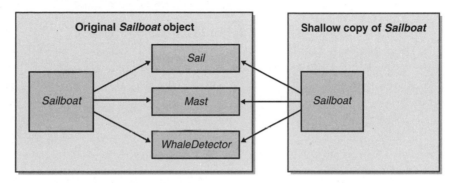

Figure 8-1.   A shallow copy, which copies only contained references.

In contrast, a deep copy creates a new object that includes references to completely new objects, as shown in Figure 8-2.

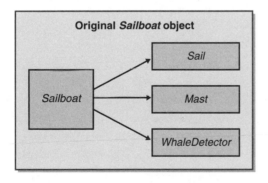

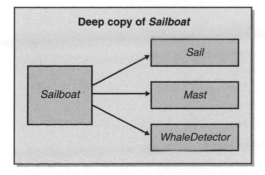

Figure 8-2.   A deep copy, which creates new objects for field references.

Although a deep copy is more costly to execute, it results in a copy that's more isolated from its original. Thus, if your code makes changes to an object's deep copy, the original object (as well as any items that the original object references) remains the same. The execution cost for a deep copy can be especially significant for collections because many items can be stored in a collection object. For this reason, most collection classes provide shallow copy semantics.

Mapping Keys to Values with the *IDictionary* Interface

The *IDictionary* interface is exposed by collection classes that support mapping keys to values, much like the *AssociativeArray* class presented in Chapter 7. Classes that support *IDictionary* can be defined as having a fixed size, which prevents adding new keys to the collection while allowing existing keys to be associated with new values. Classes also can be specified as read-only, which prevents the contents of the collection from being modified in any way.

The *IDictionary* interface is declared as follows:

```
interface IDictionary
{
    bool IsFixedSize { get; }
    bool IsReadOnly { get; }
    ICollection Keys { get; }
    ICollection Values  { get; }
    object this[object key] { get; set; }
    void Add(object key, object value);
    void Clear();
    bool Contains(object key);
    IDictionaryEnumerator GetEnumerator();
    void Remove(object key);
}
```

IDictionary specifies an indexer that uses the collection key as the index parameter. A *get* operation on the indexer returns the value mapped to the key and a *set* operation overwrites the item currently associated with the key. If the collection exposing *IDictionary* doesn't have a fixed size, a new item can be added to the collection using the indexer. If the collection has a fixed size, attempting to add a new item will result in a *NotSupportedException* exception being thrown.

The other methods and properties declared by *IDictionary* are listed here:

- ■ ***IsFixedSize***   Returns *true* if the size of the collection is fixed or *false* if new keys can be added.

- ■ ***IsReadOnly***   Returns *true* if the collection is read-only or *false* if items can be added to the collection.

- ■ ***Keys***   Returns an *ICollection* interface that can be used to interact with all keys in this collection.

- **Values**   Returns an *ICollection* interface that can be used to interact with all values in this collection.

- **Add**   Adds a new key/value pair to the collection. If the key already exists, an *ArgumentException* exception is thrown.

- **Clear**   Removes all key/value pairs from the collection.

- **Contains**   Returns *true* if a specified key exists in the collection or *false* if the key isn't found.

- **GetEnumerator**   Returns an *IDictionaryEnumerator* interface for the collection. *IDictionaryEnumerator* provides a richer interface than *IEnumerator* and is discussed in more detail shortly.

- **Remove**   Removes a specific key and its associated value from the collection.

Classes that implement *IDictionary* often have a nonlinear method of associating keys with values. For example, many data structures based on trees or hashing are difficult to iterate using the *IEnumerator* interface. The *IDictionaryEnumerator* interface, shown in the following code, is a specialized version of the *IEnumerator* interface that's well-suited for enumerating dictionary-style collections:

```
interface IDictionaryEnumerator: IEnumerator
{
    DictionaryEntry Entry { get; }
    object Key { get; }
    object Value { get; }
}
```

Using the *IList* Interface

Collections that implement the *IList* interface offer listlike semantics, including access to individual items and insertion and removal of items at any point in the list. The *IList* interface is declared as follows:

```
interface IList
{
    bool IsFixedSize { get; }
    bool IsReadOnly { get; }
    object this[object key] { get; set; }
    int Add(object value);
    void Clear();
    bool Contains(object value);
    int IndexOf(object value);
    Insert(int index, object value);
    void Remove(object key);
    void RemoveAt(int index);
}
```

The *IList* interface is implemented by several of the collection classes included in the .NET Framework, including the following:

- *ArrayList*
- *ListDictionary*
- *StringCollection*
- *StringDictionary*

As discussed in Chapter 7, the *ArrayList* class combines the properties of an array and a list. The *StringCollection*, *ListDictionary*, and *StringDictionary* classes are discussed later in this chapter, in the section "Using the Specialized Collection Classes."

Using the *Queue* Class

The *Queue* class implements a first-in, first-out data structure that places objects into a waiting list, or queue, as shown in Figure 8-3. Conceptually, objects are inserted into a queue at one end and removed at the other end. Queues are useful for processing objects sequentially because they can store objects (for later processing) in the order in which the objects were inserted.

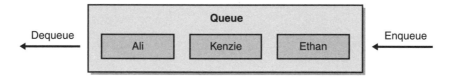

Figure 8-3.   A queue, which is a first-in, first-out collection.

Queue Interfaces and Methods

Like most collection classes, the *Queue* class implements the three major collection interfaces: *ICollection*, *IEnumerable*, and *ICloneable*. In addition to the methods exposed by those interfaces, the most commonly used methods exposed by the *Queue* class are as follows:

- **Enqueue**   Adds a new item to the back of the queue
- **Dequeue**   Removes and returns an item from the front of the queue
- **Peek**   Returns the object at the front of the queue but doesn't remove it from the queue
- **Clear**   Removes all objects from the queue
- **Contains**   Returns *true* if a specified object exists in the queue or *false* if the object isn't found

> **Note**   Attempting to call the *Dequeue* or *Peek* methods on an empty queue will cause the collection to throw an *InvalidOperationException* exception.

Internally, the items in a queue are stored as elements in a buffer, and the buffer expands as needed to accommodate additional items. Operations performed on a queue are relatively inexpensive, unless the internal buffer must be enlarged, which requires that a new, larger buffer be allocated and all existing items be copied to the new array.

If the performance cost of resizing the *Queue* object's internal array is a concern, there are some steps you can take to reduce the likelihood of frequent resizing. The default size of the internal array allows it to store 32 objects. You can specify the initial size of the array by passing a value to the *Queue* constructor, as shown here:

```
Queue aQueue = new Queue(50);   // The initial capacity is 50 objects.
```

During construction, you also can define the growth factor for the *Queue* object, which is used when determining the size of the object's new internal array. By default, the growth factor is *2.0*, which means that the internal array is doubled whenever it must be grown. One of the constructors for the *Queue* class allows you to specify the initial capacity for the *Queue* as well as its growth factor, as shown here:

```
// Set the growth factor to 3.0.
Queue aQueue = new Queue(50, 3.0);
```

The growth factor can be as large as *10.0*. By providing a growth factor larger than the default value, you can reduce the number of times your *Queue* objects are resized. However, this added runtime efficiency adds to the total memory footprint of your collection object.

A Queuing Example

To illustrate how the *Queue* collection class can be used in an application, this section presents a simple simulation of a ski lift, named *SkiLiftQueue*. The *SkiLiftQueue* application places *Skier* objects into a queue that represents a ski lift and removes *Skier* objects from the queue to simulate the skiers reaching the end of the lift.

The *Skier* structure is a simple value type that demonstrates that nonprimitive types can be stored in a queue. The *Skier* structure is basically a *struct* wrapper around a single *string* field, as shown on the following page.

```
struct Skier
{
    public Skier(string name)
    {
        Name = name;
    }
    public string Name;
}
```

Although the *Skier* structure is simplified to reduce the complexity of the example, keep in mind that arbitrarily complex objects can be stored in a queue.

The *Main* method for the *SkiLift* example is also quite basic—it simply creates an instance of the *SkiLift* class and calls its *Run* method, as shown here:

```
static void Main(string[] args)
{
    SkiLift lift = new SkiLift();
    lift.Run();
}
```

Most of the code in the *SkiLiftQueue* example is found in the *SkiLift* class, which is declared as follows:

```
public class SkiLift
{
    public SkiLift()
    {
        _theLift = new Queue();
    }

    public void Run()
    {
        bool done = false;
        while(!done)
        {
            DisplayStatus();
            SkiAction choice = GetNextAction();
            switch(choice)
            {
                case SkiAction.AddSkier:
                    string name;
                    do
                    {
                        Console.Write("Skier's name: ");
                        name = Console.ReadLine();
                    } while(name.Length == 0);
                    Skier newSkier = new Skier(name);
                    _theLift.Enqueue(newSkier);
                    break;
```

```csharp
                case SkiAction.RemoveSkier:
                    if(_theLift.Count == 0)
                    {
                        Console.WriteLine("The lift is empty.");
                    }
                    else
                    {
                        Skier nextSkier = (Skier)_theLift.Dequeue();
                        Console.WriteLine("{0} has left the ski lift.",
                            nextSkier.Name);
                    }
                    break;

                case SkiAction.Quit:
                    Console.WriteLine("Goodbye.");
                    done = true;
                    break;

                default:
                    break;
            }
        }
    }

    protected void DisplayStatus()
    {
        Console.WriteLine("There are currently {0} skiers on the lift.",
            _theLift.Count);
        if(_theLift.Count > 0)
        {
            Skier nextSkier = (Skier)_theLift.Peek();
            Console.WriteLine("The next skier will be {0}.",
                nextSkier.Name);

            Console.WriteLine("Skiers on the lift:");
            Array skiers = _theLift.ToArray();
            foreach(Skier aSkier in skiers)
            {
                Console.WriteLine("\t" + aSkier.Name);
            }
        }
    }

    protected SkiAction GetNextAction()
    {
        SkiAction result = SkiAction.Quit;
        bool done = false;
        while(!done)
```

(continued)

```
        {
            Console.WriteLine("A) Add a skier to the lift");
            Console.WriteLine("R) Remove a skier from the lift");
            Console.WriteLine("Q) Quit");
            Console.Write("Choice: ");

            switch(Console.ReadLine().ToUpper())
            {
                case "A":
                    result = SkiAction.AddSkier;
                    done = true;
                    break;

                case "R":
                    result = SkiAction.RemoveSkier;
                    done = true;
                    break;

                case "Q":
                    result = SkiAction.Quit;
                    done = true;
                    break;

                default:
                    break;
            }
        }
        return result;
    }
    protected enum SkiAction { AddSkier, RemoveSkier, Quit };
    protected Queue _theLift;
}
```

When an instance of the *SkiLift* class is constructed, it creates a *Queue* object that will be used to store *Skier* instances. The *Run* method calls the following two methods that provide the primary interaction with the user:

■ **GetNextAction** Prompts the user for the next action to be performed by the ski lift

■ **DisplayStatus** Displays the current state of the ski lift's *Queue* object, including the current number of items in the collection as well as the names of *Skier* objects in the queue

If the user chooses to add a skier to the ski lift, a new *Skier* object is created and added to the collection with the *Enqueue* method. If the user chooses to remove a skier from the ski lift, a *Skier* object is removed by calling the *Dequeue* method.

Using the *Stack* Class

The *Stack* class implements a last-in, first-out data structure that stores its objects such that the last object inserted appears to be at the top of the stack, as shown in Figure 8-4.

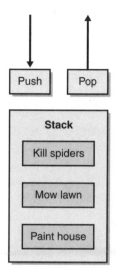

Figure 8-4.   A stack, which is a last-in, first-out collection.

In addition to the *ICollection*, *IEnumerable*, and *ICloneable* interfaces, the most commonly used methods implemented by the *Stack* class are as follows:

- ■   *Push*   Adds a new object to the top of the stack

- ■   *Pop*   Removes and returns the object at the top of the stack

- ■   *Peek*   Returns the object at the top of the stack but doesn't remove it from the stack

- ■   *Clear*   Removes all objects from the stack

- ■   *Contains*   Returns *true* if a specified object exists in the queue or *false* if the object isn't found

Like the *Queue* class, the *Stack* class stores its objects in an array. As long as the array is large enough to store new objects, a call to the *Push* method is very efficient. If the internal array must be resized, however, a new array must be allocated and existing objects copied into it. To avoid this performance cost, you can take the same steps outlined in the previous section for the *Queue* class: either preallocate a large internal array, or define an appropriate growth factor that meets your performance needs.

The following source code provides an example of how the *Stack* class is used. The *StackApp* class uses a *Stack* object to store several strings representing various colors.

```
class StackApp
{
    static void Main(string[] args)
    {
        Stack colorStack = new Stack();

        colorStack.Push("Red");
        colorStack.Push("Green");
        colorStack.Push("Blue");
        colorStack.Push("Yellow");
        colorStack.Push("Orange");

        Console.WriteLine("Contents of stack...");
        foreach(string color in colorStack)
        {
            Console.WriteLine(color);
        }

        while(colorStack.Count > 0)
        {
            string color = (string)colorStack.Pop();
            Console.WriteLine("Popping {0}", color);
        }
        Console.WriteLine("Done");
    }
}
```

When the preceding code is compiled and executed, the output looks like this:

```
Contents of stack...
Orange
Yellow
Blue
Green
Red
Popping Orange
Popping Yellow
Popping Blue
Popping Green
Popping Red
Done
```

Using the *Hashtable* Class

The *Hashtable* class implements a data structure that supports associating objects, known as keys, with other objects, known as values. The *Hashtable* class gets its name from the way it stores objects internally, which is based on the hash code for keys stored in the collection.

Keys and objects stored in a *Hashtable* object are arranged in a series of smaller collections, as shown in Figure 8-5.

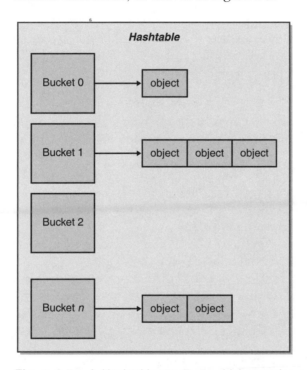

Figure 8-5.   A *Hashtable* structure, which contains multiple subcollections called buckets.

The hash bucket associated with a particular key is determined based on the hash code for the key. If two keys have the same hash code, the keys are always sent to the same hash bucket. When searching for an object, the *Hashtable* class uses the hash code of the object's key to search for the object in only one bucket, thus making the search significantly more efficient.

The Fine Print of Hashing

It's possible, and even likely, that some objects with different hash codes will be placed into the same hash bucket. For example, when a default *Hashtable* object is constructed, it has 11 hash buckets. As each key/value pair is added to the *Hashtable object*, the key is transformed from a 32-bit value into the index of one of the 11 hash buckets. If multiple keys are resolved into the same hash bucket index, a *collision* is said to occur and the entries are stored in an array. Although some collisions are inevitable, too many collisions degrade performance because they increase the likelihood of a linear search and increase the cost of inserting an item into the collection.

The *Hashtable* load factor controls the ratio of hash buckets to keys. When the number of keys exceeds the load factor, the number of hash buckets is increased. By default, the load factor is 1.0, which keeps the number of buckets and objects approximately equal and strikes a balance between unused hash buckets and collisions. The load factor can be defined when the *Hashtable* object is initially constructed, as follows:

```
Hashtable elements = new Hashtable(118, 0.1f);
```

The load factor must be between 0.1 and 1.0, with 0.1 offering the best possible performance and 1.0 providing the most compact memory footprint.

The implementation of the key's *GetHashCode* method can greatly impact the performance of the collection. The worst possible case for *Hashtable* performance occurs when a poorly implemented hash code returns the same value for all keys in the collection, resulting in performance that's worse than an array, and with much greater complexity.

Even worse than an inefficient hash code is a hash code that changes. If a key stored in a *Hashtable* is modified in such a way that its hash code varies, it might be impossible to retrieve the object from the collection at a later time. If you override *GetHashCode* in one of your classes, take care either to base your implementation of *GetHashCode* on a value that doesn't change or to not change the value of keys while they're stored in a *Hashtable*.

Interfaces Implemented by the *Hashtable* Class

The *Hashtable* class implements a number of interfaces. In addition to the commonly implemented collection interfaces *ICollection, IEnumerable,* and *ICloneable*, the *Hashtable* class implements the *IDictionary* interface. (The *IDictionary* interface was described earlier in this chapter, in the section "Mapping Keys to Values with the *IDictionary* Interface.") The *Hashtable* class also implements the *ISerializable* and *IDeserializationCallback* interfaces, which are used when serializing instances of the class. Refer to **MSDN** for a detailed discussion about these two interfaces.

The *Hashtable* class offers a number of ways to interact with objects stored in the collection. Because the *Hashtable* class exposes an enumerator, the *foreach* statement can be used to iterate over all objects stored in the collection, as shown here:

```
struct Element
{
    public Element(string itsName, string itsSymbol)
    {
        Name = itsName;
        Symbol = itsSymbol;
    }
    public string Name;
    public string Symbol;
}

static void Main(string[] args)
{
    Hashtable elements = new Hashtable(118, 0.1f);
    Element sodium = new Element("Sodium", "Na");
    Element lead = new Element("Lead", "Pb");
    Element gold = new Element("Gold", "Au");
    elements.Add(sodium.Symbol, sodium);
    elements.Add(lead.Symbol, lead);
    elements.Add(gold.Symbol, gold);

    foreach(DictionaryEntry entry in elements)
    {
        string symbol = (string)entry.Key;
        Element elem = (Element)entry.Value;
        Console.WriteLine("{0} - {1}", symbol, elem.Name);
    }
}
```

In this code, the *DictionaryEntry* type is used inside the *foreach* statement. *DictionaryEntry* is a structure that contains the key/value pair for a *Hashtable* entry.

Another way to access the objects in a *Hashtable* class is to use keys as indexers, as follows:

```
Element anElement = (Element)elements["Na"];
Console.WriteLine(anElement.Name);
```

The difficulty with this approach is that you must know the values of each key. Fortunately, the *Hashtable* class exposes the keys stored in the collection through its *Keys* property. The following code provides index-based access to every object in a *Hashtable* object by iterating over the collection returned by the *Keys* property and then using each key as an index to the *Hashtable class*:

```
foreach(object key in elements.Keys)
{
    Element e = (Element)elements[key];
    Console.WriteLine(e.Name);
}
```

Using the Specialized Collection Classes

The .NET Framework class library includes a number of specialized collection classes in the *System.Collections.Specialized* namespace. Some of these classes, such as the *StringCollection* class, are dedicated to holding specific types. Other classes solve a specific need, such as the *ListDictionary* class, which is optimized for small collection sets. This section introduces these two specialized classes and the *StringDictionary* class.

The *StringCollection* Class

The *StringCollection* class is a collection class that's strongly typed to hold string objects. In addition to the *ICollection* and *IEnumerable* interfaces, the *String-Collection* class implements the *IList* interface, so it supports listlike access to the strings that it contains, as shown here:

```
static void Main(string[] args)
{
    StringCollection stringBag = new StringCollection();
    stringBag.Add("Mickey");
    stringBag.Add("Rene'");
    stringBag.Add("Ali");

    int index = stringBag.IndexOf("Ali");
    Console.WriteLine("Ali's index is {0}", index);
    stringBag.Insert(0, "Kenzie");
    foreach(string name in stringBag)
    {
        Console.WriteLine(name);
    }
}
```

The *StringCollection* class supports multiple strings with the same value, so using the *Remove* or *IndexOf* methods will affect only the first string encountered in the collection.

The *ListDictionary* Class

The *ListDictionary* class is a lightweight collection that implements *IDictionary*. Unlike the *Hashtable* class, *ListDictionary* is implemented as a simple linked list of items that offers improved performance for small dictionaries of 10 or fewer items. As shown in the following code, the *ListDictionary* class is used just like the *Hashtable* class presented earlier:

```
struct Element
{
    public Element(string itsName, string itsSymbol)
    {
        Name = itsName;
```

```
            Symbol = itsSymbol;
    }
    public string Name;
    public string Symbol;
}
:
ListDictionary dictionary = new ListDictionary();

Element sodium = new Element("Sodium", "Na");
Element lead = new Element("Lead", "Pb");
Element gold = new Element("Gold", "Au");
dictionary.Add(sodium.Symbol, sodium);
dictionary.Add(lead.Symbol, lead);
dictionary.Add(gold.Symbol, gold);

Element anElement = (Element)dictionary["Na"];
Console.WriteLine(anElement.Name);
foreach(DictionaryEntry entry in dictionary)
{
    string symbol = (string)entry.Key;
    Element elem = (Element)entry.Value;
    Console.WriteLine("{0} - {1}", symbol, elem.Name);
}
```

Because the *ListDictionary* class is manipulated using the same *IDictionary* interface exposed by the *Hashtable* class, the code used for both collections is similar. The *ListDictionary* class isn't suitable for collections with more than ten items, however.

The *StringDictionary* Class

The *StringDictionary* class is similar to the *Hashtable* class except that it's strongly typed to accept string keys and values. Internally, the *StringDictionary* class uses a private *Hashtable* field to contain keys and values in the collection. The *StringDictionary* class simply acts as a wrapper around the *Hashtable* class to provide strong typing.

As shown in the following code, the *StringDictionary* class works with string keys and values without the need for explicit casting:

```
StringDictionary elements = new StringDictionary();
elements.Add("Na", "Sodium");
elements.Add("Pb", "Lead");
elements.Add("Au", "Gold");

foreach(string key in elements.Keys)
{
    Console.WriteLine("{0} - {1}", key, elements[key]);
}
```

Although *StringDictionary* supports the same properties and methods found in interfaces such as *ICollection* and *IDictionary*, it doesn't implement those interfaces. *IEnumerable* is the only interface *StringDictionary* implements. The keys in a *StringDictionary* collection are compared without regard to their case and are automatically converted to lowercase when they're inserted into the collection. If you require high fidelity for your keys, you'll need to use a different type of collection.

Conclusion

The .NET Framework includes a standard set of interfaces used for sorting and comparison. By implementing the *IComparable* interface, classes and structures can advertise their ability to be sorted by their containers. The .NET Framework provides two classes that implement the *IComparer* interface, which is used to compare other objects. The *Comparer* class is used for basic comparisons and assumes that the compared types implement *IComparable*. The *CaseInsensitive-Comparer* class is similar, except it performs a case-insensitive comparison for string objects.

The .NET Framework also includes a wide variety of collection types, including types that implement queues, stacks, and hash tables. The *System.Collections* namespace includes both concrete types and interfaces that can be used to create new collection types. The *System.Collections.Specialized* namespace includes a set of types that are used for specific purposes.

9

Debugging Techniques

This chapter examines the debugging and diagnostic techniques that you can use when developing with Microsoft Visual C# .NET. The C# language and the Microsoft .NET Framework include a number of features that not only simplify debugging but also make it extremely easy to take advantage of sophisticated diagnostic techniques. For example, with Visual C# .NET, it's easy to send debug and trace messages to the event log, a disk file, or the console. Adding this functionality requires less than a dozen lines of Visual C# code. To achieve similar functionality using the C language would require a significantly larger effort, probably a thousand lines or more.

With Visual C#, you can also take advantage of classes that enable you to inspect and display the call stack. (See the section "Using the Call Stack," later in this chapter.) This information can be invaluable during debugging. This chapter also discusses how to create a custom trace listener to display output messages as XML and closes with a section that describes the debugger integrated into Microsoft Visual Studio .NET.

Compiling Code Conditionally

Visual C# .NET includes a useful feature known as *conditional compilation,* which allows you to define methods that will be compiled when specific symbols are defined. Conditional compilation is commonly used with methods that are used only for debug builds. If code is useful only during debugging, conditional compilation can be used to automatically remove the code for release builds.

Prior to the advent of the Microsoft .NET platform, the traditional method of compiling conditionally using C++ or Visual Basic was to explicitly mark the regions of conditional code. The following code is an example of conditional compilation using C++:

```
// C++, not C#
class BankAccount
{
public:
#ifdef DEBUG
    void DumpAccountDetail()
    {
        // Display account information.
    }
#endif
    :
};

void HandleTransaction()
{
    BankAccount* account = new BankAccount();
    :
#ifdef DEBUG
    // Call conditional method.
    account->DumpAccountDetail();
#endif
}
```

The C++ preprocessor scans the source file and removes the conditional code in the initial steps of compiling a C++ project. The disadvantage of using the preprocessor is that both the method and the method caller must mark the code for conditional compilation. Additionally, the syntax is awkward, especially when client code must invoke a number of conditional methods.

When developing code with conditional methods using Visual C# .NET, you can take advantage of a much simpler and more flexible conditional compilation technique—the *Conditional* compilation attribute, which is part of the *System.Diagnostics* namespace. To mark a method as conditionally compiled, apply the *Conditional* attribute to the method, as shown here:

```
[Conditional("DEBUG")]
public void DumpAccountDetail()
{
    // Display account information.
}
```

In the preceding code, the *DumpAccountDetail* method is compiled only when the *DEBUG* symbol is defined. By default, a Visual C# project defines

DEBUG and *TRACE* for debug builds and defines *TRACE* only for release builds. There are two ways to define a new symbol. The first method is to simply define the conditional compilation symbol at the top of any source file that calls the conditionally compiled method, as shown here:

```
#define TEST
```

The second way to define a new conditional compilation symbol for a project is through the Build property page for the project, as shown in Figure 9-1. The Property Pages dialog box is displayed by right-clicking the project icon in Solution Explorer. Individual property pages are displayed by selecting a node in the tree control in the left pane; the Build property page is located in the Configuration Properties folder.

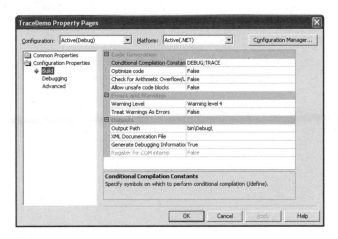

Figure 9-1. The Build property page for a project, on which new symbols are defined.

The project's conditional compilation symbols are separated by semicolons. You can append new symbols to the existing items, but you must separate the symbols with semicolons. Before making changes to the property page, make sure that the changes will be applied to the proper project configuration. In the Configuration drop-down list, you can select the currently active configuration or any of the other build configurations or you can apply a change to all build configurations.

A method can be tagged with multiple *Conditional* compilation attributes, as shown here:

```
[Conditional("DEBUG")]
[Conditional("TEST")]
public void SetValue(int newValue)
{
    ⋮
}
```

This method will be compiled if either the *DEBUG* or the *TEST* symbol is defined.

Conditional methods are subject to the following restrictions:

- The *Conditional* attribute can't be applied to a method within an interface—it can be applied only to a method implementation. Methods declared in an interface and implemented in a class or structure can't be annotated with the *Conditional* attribute.

- The *Conditional* attribute can't be applied to a method marked with the *override* modifier. It can be applied to a virtual method, which has the effect of conditionally compiling all overridden versions of the method.

- The *Conditional* attribute can be applied only to methods with a void return type.

In most cases, it doesn't make sense to conditionally compile a method with a non-void return type. Because the return value is often used to set the value of variables, if conditional compilation of these methods were allowed, it would often result in variables left unassigned, as shown here:

```
static void Main(string[] args)
{
    string secretWord = GetSecretWord();
    Console.WriteLine("The secret word is {0}", secretWord);
}


// Won't compile due to non-void return type
[Conditional("TEST")]
public static string GetSecretWord()
{
    return "Fulminate";
}
```

You can work around this restriction by conditionally compiling methods that mark their parameters with the *out* or *ref* keyword. Keep in mind that when a conditional method with an *out* or a *ref* parameter isn't compiled, as might be the case in the following code, a compiler error can occur if a variable is used before it's assigned a value.

```
[Conditional("TEST")]
public void GetSecretWord(out string secretWord)
{
    secretWord = "Fulminate";
}
```

Tracing the Stack

The call stack is a useful tool during debugging. The .NET Framework includes classes in the *System.Diagnostics* namespace that provide access to the call stack, enabling you to examine or display this information in trace or logging messages, much like the call stack information available in exception objects, which were discussed in Chapter 2.

Displaying the Call Stack

The *StackTrace* class is used to gain access to the call stack and represents the call stack for a specific thread. Each *StackTrace* object provides access to one or more *StackFrame* objects, each of which represents one method call in the stack. The relationship between *StackTrace* and *StackFrame* objects is shown in Figure 9-2.

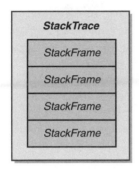

Figure 9-2.   A *StackTrace* object, which can contain one or more *Stack-Frame* objects.

As you can see, the *StackTrace* class serves primarily as a container for *StackFrame* objects. The following *StackTrace* property and methods are the most commonly used (refer to the Microsoft Developer Network (MSDN) Library for the other methods of *StackTrace*):

- **FrameCount**   This property holds the number of *StackFrame* objects associated with this *StackTrace* instance.

- **GetFrame**   This method returns one *StackFrame* object specified by passing the stack frame index as a parameter, with *0* referring to the most recent frame.

- **ToString**   This method returns a string that describes the call stack.

There are two commonly used constructors for the *StackTrace* class. The default constructor is used to create a *StackTrace* object for the current thread, without file information, as shown here:

```
StackTrace callstack = new StackTrace();
```

File information can be useful for debugging purposes, as it adds both the file name and line numbers to your stack tracing information. To create a *Stack-Trace* object for the current thread that includes file information, pass a Boolean *true* value to a second version of the constructor, as shown here:

```
StackTrace callstack = new StackTrace(true);
```

The *ToString* method from the *StackFrame* class can be used to generate a string that describes the call stack, using code such as the following:

```
StackTrace callStack = new StackTrace();
string traceInfo = callStack.ToString();
```

This code is easy to use, and it provides basic information that can help you determine the sequence of method calls that resulted in the call to the current method. If you need more detailed information, such as line offset information to aid in your tracing efforts, you can take advantage of methods and properties in the *StackFrame* class. The most commonly used methods in the *StackFrame* class are shown here:

- **GetFileLineNumber** Returns the line number for the code being executed for this frame, if debug symbols are available

- **GetFileName** Returns the file name containing the code being executed, if debug symbols are available

- **GetMethod** Returns a *MethodBase* object that describes the method executing this frame

- **ToString** Returns a string that describes the stack frame

In many cases, simply calling the *StackFrame.ToString* method will provide you with a reasonable string describing the stack frame. The following method uses *StackFrame.ToString* to display a stack trace with more detailed information than the previous example, including more detailed information for each stack frame:

```
protected string GetStackTrace()
{
    StringBuilder result = new StringBuilder();
    // Create a call stack trace with file information.
    StackTrace trace = new StackTrace(true);
    int frameCount = trace.FrameCount;
```

```
    for(int n = 0; n < frameCount; ++n)
    {
        StackFrame frame = trace.GetFrame(n);
        result.Append(frame.ToString());
    }
    return result.ToString();
}
```

The *GetStackTrace* method iterates over each *StackFrame* object in the current stack by calling *GetFrame*. As each *StackFrame* object is retrieved, its *ToString* method is called to assemble a string describing the entire call stack.

Although the *StackFrame.ToString* method returns a reasonable string that describes the stack frame, you might want to exercise more control over the information displayed for the trace. Instead of relying on a call to the *ToString* method from each stack frame, you can access properties and methods to build up a string manually, as you'll see in the next section.

Accessing Detailed Method Information

The source file name and offset information provided by a *StackFrame* object includes file names and line numbers instead of method names or parameter data. Although this is enough information to look up the method names manually, a stack trace is much easier to use if it includes more detailed information about the methods that are invoked for each frame in the call stack.

The *StackFrame.GetMethod* method returns a *MethodBase* object that represents the method that was executing code in the stack frame. By using reflection (discussed in Chapter 6), you can obtain information about the method, including the method name and any parameters associated with it. The following method uses the *MethodBase* class to provide detailed information about the call stack:

```
protected string GetStackTraceWithMethods()
{
    StringBuilder result = new StringBuilder();
    StackTrace trace = new StackTrace(true);
    int frameCount = trace.FrameCount;
    for(int n = 0; n < frameCount; ++n)
    {
        StringBuilder frameString = new StringBuilder();
        StackFrame frame = trace.GetFrame(n);

        int lineNumber = frame.GetFileLineNumber();
        string fileName = frame.GetFileName();
        MethodBase methodBase = frame.GetMethod();
        string methodName = methodBase.Name;
        ParameterInfo [] paramInfos = methodBase.GetParameters();
```

(continued)

```
        result.AppendFormat("{0} - line {1}, {2}",
                            fileName,
                            lineNumber,
                            methodName);
        if(paramInfos.Length == 0)
        {
            // No parameters for this method; display
            // empty parentheses.
            result.Append("()\n");
        }
        else
        {
            // Iterate over parameters, displaying each parameter's
            // type and name.
            result.Append("(");
            int count = paramInfos.Length;
            for(int i = 0; i < count; ++i)
            {
                Type paramType = paramInfos[i].ParameterType;
                result.AppendFormat("{0} {1}",
                                    paramType.ToString(),
                                    paramInfos[i].Name);
                if(i < count - 1)
                    result.Append(",");
            }
            result.Append(")\n");
        }
    }
    return result.ToString();
}
```

The *GetStackTraceWithMethods* method uses the reflection namespace to gather more information about the call stack and presents it in a specialized format. Each method in the call stack is displayed, along with source file line numbers and parameter information. This is achieved by retrieving a *MethodBase* object for each *StackFrame* object that exists in the call stack. Parameter information is retrieved by calling the *GetParameters* method, which returns an array of *ParameterInfo*. Each parameter in the array is inspected and then added to the result string.

Using the *Trace* and *Debug* Classes

It's often useful to have your application generate information in the form of debugging or trace messages while it executes. Prior to the release of the .NET Framework and Visual C# .NET, creating an infrastructure for displaying this information was a difficult and time-consuming task.

With Visual C# .NET, you can take advantage of the .NET Framework's excellent support for handling tracing and debugging messages. The .NET Framework includes classes to control trace and debug output messages and to write output messages to files, streams, and the event log. This section discusses these classes in detail.

Generating Program Trace Information

Trace and debug messages are handled by classes found in the *System.Diagnostics* namespace; these classes provide easy access to basic tracing functionality. For example, the following code sends a debug message to the debug console:

```
Debug.WriteLine("Hello Debugger");
```

When the *Debug* class is used to generate an output message, output is sent to an output device only for Visual C# .NET debug builds. The *Trace* class is similar to the *Debug* class and is used to generate output messages for all builds, as follows:

```
Trace.WriteLine("Hello Debugger");
```

When you create a new project configuration setting, define the *DEBUG* symbol to enable output with the *Debug* class and the *TRACE* symbol to enable output with the *Trace* class.

Displaying Messages with the *Trace* and *Debug* Classes

The *Trace* and *Debug* classes are composed of static methods, so you never create an instance of these classes. Both classes expose the same methods and behave in the same manner, except that they're enabled by different conditional compilation symbols. The commonly used methods and properties from the *Trace* and *Debug* classes are listed here:

- **Assert** Generates an assertion violation message if a supplied expression is *false*
- **AutoFlush** Gets or sets a Boolean value that indicates whether each listener should be flushed automatically after every write operation
- **Close** Flushes the message buffer and closes all listeners
- **Fail** Generates an assertion violation message
- **Flush** Flushes the message buffer
- **Listeners** Returns the *TraceListenerCollection* object associated with trace and debug message output

- **Write** Generates an output message without appending a newline character

- **WriteIf** Generates an output message without appending a newline character if a supplied expression is true

- **WriteLine** Generates an output message and appends a newline character

- **WriteLineIf** Generates an output message and appends a newline character if a supplied expression is true

Several of the methods in this list display output messages; however, each of these methods is used in different scenarios. The following sections discuss these methods in more detail.

Asserting That Expressions Are True

The *Assert* method is used to display an error message when a condition that's expected to evaluate as *true* evaluates as *false*. When displayed to the user, the message is clearly defined as an assertion failure. When encountered in an interactive process, such as a Microsoft Windows Forms or console application, instances of the *DefaultTraceListener* class display a dialog box similar to the one shown in Figure 9-3. You'll find a detailed discussion of the *DefaultTraceListener* class later in this chapter, in the section "Consuming Trace Messages with Trace Listeners."

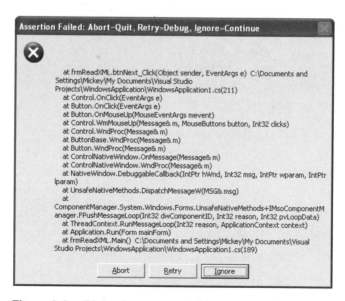

Figure 9-3. Dialog box generated by trace and debug output with the *Assert* method.

As you can see, this dialog box includes call stack information when available. Where debug symbols are available, the stack trace includes file name and line number information.

When a *DefaultTraceListener* object detects that the *Assert* method has been called from a server process, the listener doesn't display a dialog box because there's no interactive user to observe and dismiss the dialog box. Instead, it writes the output message to the Visual Studio Output window and any other debuggers currently accepting output from the Microsoft Win32 *OutputDebugString* function.

The *Assert* method has three versions. The most basic version simply accepts an expression that triggers an assertion failure message if the expression evaluates as *false*, as shown here:

```
Debug.Assert(ceilingHeight > 0);
```

The second version of *Assert* accepts a second parameter that serves as a short error message describing the assertion violation:

```
Debug.Assert(ceilingHeight > 0, "The sky is falling");
```

The third version of *Assert* accepts a third parameter that includes detailed information about the assertion violation:

```
Debug.Assert(ceilingHeight > 0,
            "The sky is falling",
            ChickenLittle.ToString());
```

Displaying Failure Messages

The *Fail* method is similar to the *Assert* method, except that messages are always sent to the *Listeners* collection. Trace and debug messages that are generated using the *Fail* method are displayed as assertion violations, in the same way as failed assertions generated with the *Assert* method.

The *Fail* method has two versions, as shown in the following code:

```
Debug.Fail("Allocation failure");
Debug.Fail("Allocation failure",
            "Could not allocate a new port for the session");
```

The first version of *Fail* accepts a description of the failure. The second version of the *Fail* method accepts a second parameter that provides a more detailed description of the failure.

Writing General-Purpose Output Messages

The *Trace* and *Debug* classes offer four additional methods that are used to generate output messages to the *Listeners* collection: *Write*, *WriteIf*, *WriteLine*, and *WriteLineIf*. Unlike the *Assert* and *Fail* methods described earlier, the methods described in this section are used to generate informational messages that don't necessarily indicate that an error exists. The *DefaultTraceListener* class never uses dialog boxes to display messages that have been created using these methods.

The first two of these methods, *Write* and *WriteIf*, create messages without appending a line terminator. The *WriteIf* method includes a parameter that controls output. If the expression passed as a parameter evaluates as *true*, the trace or debug message is displayed. If the expression evaluates as *false*, the message isn't generated.

The *Write* and *WriteIf* methods each have four overloaded versions. The first version generates an output message using the string passed as a parameter, as shown here:

```
// Display trace message.
Trace.Write("Close button clicked");
// Conditionally display trace message.
Trace.WriteIf(count > 3, "Clicked " + count.ToString() + "times.");
```

The second version accepts any object as a parameter. The *ToString* method for the object is used to generate the output message sent to the *Listeners* collection:

```
private void HandleOverdraft(object sender, System.EventArgs e)
{
    Trace.Write(sender);
    Trace.WriteIf(sender.GetType() == typeof(BankAccount), sender);
    ⋮
}
```

In this version, the *Trace.Write* method unconditionally displays the string returned from the *sender.ToString* method, whereas the *Trace.WriteIf* method displays a trace message only if the *sender* object is an instance of *BankAccount*.

The third and fourth overloaded versions of *Write* and *WriteIf* are similar to the first two versions, except that they each accept an additional string parameter used to specify a category name for the message, as shown here:

```
private void HandleOverdraft(object sender, System.EventArgs e)
{
    Trace.Write(sender, "Overdraft");
    Trace.WriteIf(sender.GetType() == typeof(BankAccount),
                sender,
                "Overdraft");
    ⋮
}
```

The *Trace* and *Debug* classes also include *WriteLine* and *WriteLineIf* methods, which are comparable to *Write* and *WriteIf*, except that a line terminator (typically \r\n for text messages) is added by the listener objects that handle each message.

Controlling Output with Switches

In addition to controlling trace and debug output through symbols injected into your code during compilation, fine-grained control over output can be achieved by using classes derived from the *Switch* class. The interesting and useful feature shared by *Switch* objects is that each instance can be controlled by an application's configuration file, and therefore by an administrator, without recompiling your code. *Switch* objects are used to provide Boolean values that are used in conjunction with the *WriteIf* and *WriteLineIf* methods.

Switch objects are always given a display name and description. The name of the *Switch* object is used to look up the value for the object in the configuration file. By default, all *Switch* objects are disabled, so if the runtime can't locate configuration information about a particular *Switch* object, the *Switch* object is turned off. The following sections describe how the classes derived from *Switch* are used to control trace and debug output.

Using the *BooleanSwitch* Class

The *BooleanSwitch* class is used to create simple *Switch* objects that can be either enabled or disabled. The following code creates a *BooleanSwitch* object with a display name of *mySwitch*:

```
BooleanSwitch theSwitch = new BooleanSwitch("mySwitch",
                                            "Application tracing");
theSwitch.Enabled = true;
```

This code also enables the *mySwitch* object programmatically. The switch can be used to control tracing or debugging output using code such as this:

```
Trace.WriteLineIf(theSwitch.Enabled, "An overdraft occurred");
```

The *BooleanSwitch.Enabled* property returns either *true* or *false*, which you can use to control message output with *WriteIf* or *WriteLineIf* methods.

As an alternative to enabling the switch statement in your code, you can control the switch object in an application's configuration file. An application's configuration file is always placed in the application's directory and has the same name as the application, with *.config* added to the configuration file name. For example, an application named SwitchTest.exe would have a configuration file named SwitchText.exe.config. The following configuration file enables the *mySwitch* object discussed earlier:

```
<configuration>
    <system.diagnostics>
        <switches>
            <add name="mySwitch" value="1" />
        </switches>
    </system.diagnostics>
</configuration>
```

Switches are controlled by adding XML element nodes inside the *switches* element. Multiple switch objects can be configured through a configuration file by adding additional elements to the *switches* node. An *add* element, as shown in this example, configures a switch object with a specific value. *BooleanSwitch* objects are disabled by default and are enabled if they're assigned a nonzero value in a configuration file.

Providing Multiple Trace Levels with the *TraceSwitch* Class

The *TraceSwitch* class is used to provide multiple tracing levels instead of the simple on/off control offered by the *BooleanSwitch* class. The *TraceSwitch* class uses the *TraceLevel* enumeration to control the output of trace and debug messages, as described in Table 9-1.

Table 9-1.   *TraceLevel* Enumeration Members

Member	Description
Off	Outputs no messages to listeners
Error	Outputs only error-handling messages
Warning	Outputs error-handling and warning messages
Info	Outputs error-handling, warning, and information messages
Verbose	Outputs all messages

An instance of the *TraceSwitch* class is constructed just like the *BooleanSwitch* objects described in the previous section. Tracing is enabled for a *TraceSwitch* object through the *Level* property, however, as shown here:

```
TraceSwitch theSwitch = new TraceSwitch("mySwitch",
                                  "Application tracing");
theSwitch.Level = TraceLevel.Verbose;
```

This code enables all types of tracing through the switch. To prevent the output of any messages, set the *Level* property to *TracingLevel.Off*, as shown here:

```
theSwitch.Level = TraceLevel.Off;
```

The *TraceSwitch* class exposes four trace-level properties that return Boolean values that depend on the currently defined trace level:

■   *TraceError*

■   *TraceWarning*

■   *TraceInfo*

■   *TraceVerbose*

If the trace level is enabled for a particular tracing category, the property returns *true*. For example, if the trace level is set to *TracingLevel.Warning*, the *Trace-Error* and *TraceWarning* properties will return *true*, whereas the *TraceInfo* and *TraceVerbose* properties will return *false*.

To send controlled output messages to any of the available listeners, use the *WriteIf* or *WriteLineIf* method and pass one of the trace-level properties as the controlling parameter, as shown here:

```
Trace.WriteLineIf(mySwitch.TraceError, "An overdraft occurred");
```

In this example, the *mySwitch.TraceError* property will return *true* if error-level tracing is enabled, allowing the trace message to be output. Otherwise, the *TraceError* property will return *false*, and the trace message won't be sent to any of the listeners.

When using a configuration file to control a *TraceSwitch* object, you must provide a scalar value that corresponds to a *TraceLevel* using the values from Table 9-2.

Table 9-2.   *TraceLevel* Enumeration Members

TraceLevel Member	Configuration Value
Off	0
Error	1
Warning	2
Info	3
Verbose	4

The following application configuration file sets the tracing level for *mySwitch* to *TraceLevel.Verbose*:

```
<configuration>
    <system.diagnostics>
        <switches>
            <add name="mySwitch" value="4" />
        </switches>
    </system.diagnostics>
</configuration>
```

The ability to control trace output in a configuration file makes it practical to add sophisticated tracing to your application. During normal operation, tracing can be turned off, and your application can execute with very little performance cost. When tracing is required, it can be enabled from the configuration file.

Consuming Trace Messages with Trace Listeners

Visual C# .NET and the .NET Framework provide excellent support for consuming the trace output messages that are generated by the *Trace* and *Debug* classes. Your output messages are sent to *TraceListener* objects, which are responsible for handling output messages, as shown in Figure 9-4.

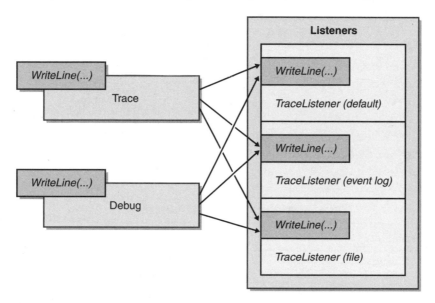

Figure 9-4.   Output sent from the *Trace* and *Debug* classes to *TraceListeners*.

By default, trace and debug messages are sent to an instance of the *DefaultTraceListener* class. This class routes output messages to the Visual Studio Output window, as well as passing the output to any applications that receive output from the Win32 *OutputDebugString* function, such as third-party debuggers or monitoring tools.

All trace listeners are instances of classes derived from the abstract *TraceListener* class. The .NET Framework includes three nonabstract listener classes:

- ■   **DefaultTraceListener**   As mentioned, sends messages to Visual Studio and applications that receive output through the *OutputDebugString* function

- ■   **EventLogTraceListener**   Sends messages to the Windows event log

- ■   **TextWriterTraceListener**   Sends messages to a *TextWriter* or *Stream* object

In addition to these three classes, you can derive new classes from the *Trace-Listener* class to provide custom trace listener functionality.

Listener objects are stored in a collection that's shared by the *Trace* and *Debug* classes. Any listeners associated with either class are available to both classes. The following code creates a new listener attached to the console and adds the listener to the *Listeners* collection:

```
TextWriterTraceListener listener = null;
listener = new TextWriterTraceListener(System.Console.Out);
Trace.Listeners.Add(listener);
```

To remove all listeners from the *Listeners* collection, call the *Clear* method exposed by the collection, as shown here:

```
Trace.Listeners.Clear();
```

Sending Trace Information to *TextWriter*s and *Stream*s

The *TextWriterTraceListener* class is used to write trace information to a *TextWriter* or *Stream* object, such as a log file, network stream, or console. *TextWriterTraceListener* is the most flexible of the listener classes, enabling you to send output to a wide variety of destinations. Because of this flexibility, the *TextWriterTraceListener* class has seven constructors.

The default constructor for the *TextWriterTraceListener* class creates a listener object that uses a *TextWriter* instance for output. The *TextWriterTraceListener* class exposes a *Writer* property that's used to access the associated *TextWriter* object, as shown here:

```
StringWriter sw = new StringWriter(new StringBuilder());
TextWriterTraceListener listener = null;
listener = new TextWriterTraceListener();
listener.Writer = sw;
```

In this example, an instance of *StringWriter*, a subclass of *TextWriter*, is used for output. Instead of working through the two-step process required in the example, you can pass the *TextWriter* object as a parameter to a second constructor:

```
TextWriterTraceListener listener = null;
listener = new TextWriterTraceListener(writer);
```

A third constructor for *TextWriterTraceListener* creates a listener that sends output to any *Stream* instance. This enables you to send trace and debug output to a wide variety of destinations, including network streams, file streams, and the console. An earlier example (see the previous section, "Consuming Trace Messages with Trace Listeners") demonstrated associating a *TextWriterTraceListener* object with the console. The code on the following page binds a *TextWriterTraceListener* object to a file stream.

```
FileStream stream = new FileStream("TraceOutput.txt",
                                   FileMode.Create);
TextWriterTraceListener listener = null;
listener = new TextWriterTraceListener(stream);
Trace.Listeners.Add(listener);
```

Although the preceding code can be generalized for any type of stream, the *TextWriterTraceListener* class offers a fourth constructor, which simplifies the code required to send output to a file. Instead of creating an instance of *FileStream*, you can simply pass the name of the file to the *TextWriterTraceListener* constructor, as shown here:

```
TextWriterTraceListener listener = null;
listener = new TextWriterTraceListener("TraceOutput.txt");
```

For each of these three constructors (for *TextWriter*, *Stream*, and *string*), an additional overloaded constructor allows you to name the listener by passing its name as a second parameter, as shown here:

```
listener = new TextWriterTraceListener("TraceOutput.txt", "filetrace");
```

Providing a name for the listener makes it easy to remove the listener from the *Listeners* collection later. To turn off output for the listener, call its *Flush* and *Close* methods, like this:

```
listener.Flush();
listener.Close();
```

Using the *EventLogTraceListener* Class

The *EventLogTraceListener* class is used to route trace and debug messages to the Windows event log. The event log can be located on a different machine, which makes the *EventLogTraceListener* class useful even on machines running an operating system that doesn't support the event log, such as Microsoft Windows Me.

There are several ways to create and use the instances of the *Event-LogTraceListener* class. The default constructor creates an instance of the class that isn't associated with a specific event log. Before output can be sent to the event log, you must explicitly affiliate an *EventLog* object with the listener, as shown in the following code:

```
EventLogTraceListener logListener = null;
⋮
EventLog myEventLog = new EventLog(evLogName);
logListener = new EventLogTraceListener();
logListener.EventLog = myEventLog;
```

A second constructor for *EventLogTraceListener* allows you to pass an *EventLog* object during construction, reducing the number of steps required to create and initialize the listener, as follows:

```
logListener = new EventLogTraceListener(myEventLog);
```

Alternatively, you can take advantage of the third constructor for *Event-LogTraceListener*, which accepts the name of an event source as a parameter:

```
logListener = new EventLogTraceListener("MyEventLog");
```

When sending trace and debug output to the event log, keep in mind that the event log isn't designed to be a boundless repository for output. Instead, it's designed to serve as a container for essential log messages. If you use an *Event-LogTraceListener* object, consider restricting the number of messages sent to the listener.

Creating a Custom Trace Listener

As an example of how to create a custom trace listener, the companion CD includes the XMLListener application. The *XmlStreamTraceListener* class contained in this application formats trace and debug messages in XML and then sends the output to any *Stream* object. Although classes from the .NET Framework's XML namespace are used to provide the XML output, the interesting parts of the class can be appreciated without any knowledge of XML. (The XML classes used in this example are covered in detail in Chapter 19.)

The following code implements the *XmlStreamTraceListener* class:

```
public class XmlStreamTraceListener: TraceListener
{
    public XmlStreamTraceListener(){}

    public XmlStreamTraceListener(Stream stream, string name)
        : base(name)
    {
        Open(stream);
    }

    public override void Close()
    {
        if(_writer != null)
        {
            _writer.Close();
            _writer = null;
        }
        else
            throw new InvalidOperationException();
    }

    public void Open(Stream stream)
    {
        _writer = new XmlTextWriter(stream, Encoding.UTF8);
        _writer.Formatting = Formatting.Indented;
        WriteDocumentHeader();
    }
```

(continued)

```csharp
public void Dispose()
{
    Dispose(true);
}

protected override void Dispose(bool disposing)
{
    if(disposing)
    {
        if(_writer != null)
        {
            _writer.Close();
        }
    }
}

public override void Fail(string message)
{
    WriteFailNode(message, null);
}

public override void Fail(string message, string detailMessage)
{
    WriteFailNode(message, detailMessage);
}

public override void Flush()
{
    _writer.Flush();
}

public override void Write(object o)
{
    WriteTraceNode(o.ToString(), null);
}

public override void Write(string message)
{
    WriteTraceNode(message, null);
}

public override void Write(object o, string category)
{
    WriteTraceNode(o.ToString(), category);
}

public override void Write(string message, string category)
{
    WriteTraceNode(message, category);
}
```

```
public override void WriteLine(object o)
{
    WriteTraceNode(o.ToString(), null);
}

public override void WriteLine(string message)
{
    WriteTraceNode(message, null);
}

public override void WriteLine(object o, string category)
{
    WriteTraceNode(o.ToString(), category);
}

public override void WriteLine(string message, string category)
{
    WriteTraceNode(message, category);
}

protected void WriteFailNode(string message, string detail)
{
    _writer.WriteStartElement("AssertionViolation", traceNamespace);
    if(_stackTrace == true)
    {
        WriteStackTrace();
    }
    if(message != null && message.Length != 0)
    {
        _writer.WriteElementString("Message",
            traceNamespace,
            message);
    }
    if(detail != null && detail.Length != 0)
    {
        _writer.WriteElementString("DetailedMessage",
            traceNamespace,
            detail);
    }
    _writer.WriteEndElement(); // AssertionViolation
}

protected void WriteTraceNode(string message, string category)
{
    _writer.WriteStartElement("Trace", traceNamespace);
    if(_stackTrace == true)
    {
        WriteStackTrace();
    }
```

(continued)

```csharp
        _writer.WriteStartElement("Message");
        if(category != null)
        {
            string prefix = _writer.LookupPrefix(traceNamespace);
            _writer.WriteStartAttribute(prefix,
                                        "Category",
                                        traceNamespace);
            _writer.WriteString(category);
            _writer.WriteEndAttribute();
        }
        _writer.WriteString(message);
        _writer.WriteEndElement(); // Message
        _writer.WriteEndElement(); // Trace
    }

    protected void WriteStackTrace()
    {
        _writer.WriteStartElement("Stack", traceNamespace);
        _writer.WriteStartElement("StackFrames", traceNamespace);

        StackTrace trace = new StackTrace(true);
        int frameCount = trace.FrameCount;
        for(int n = 0; n < frameCount; ++n)
        {
            StackFrame frame = trace.GetFrame(n);
            MethodBase methodBase = frame.GetMethod();

            // Don't display ourselves or internal tracing
            // methods in the call stack.
            if(methodBase.ReflectedType == this.GetType() ||
               methodBase.ReflectedType == typeof(Trace)   ||
               methodBase.ReflectedType.Name == "TraceInternal")
               continue;

            // If part of the call stack lacks debug symbols, we
            // won't have valid data for these values.
            string fileName = frame.GetFileName();
            if(fileName == null)
                fileName = "Not available";
            string lineNo = frame.GetFileLineNumber().ToString();
            string methodName = methodBase.Name;
            if(methodName == null)
                methodName = "Not available";

            _writer.WriteStartElement("StackFrame", traceNamespace);
            _writer.WriteElementString("FileName",
                traceNamespace,
                fileName);
            _writer.WriteElementString("LineNumber",
```

```
                      traceNamespace,
                      lineNo);
                _writer.WriteElementString("MethodName",
                      traceNamespace,
                      methodName);
                _writer.WriteEndElement(); // StackFrame
        }
        _writer.WriteEndElement(); // StackFrames
        _writer.WriteEndElement(); // Stack
    }

    protected void WriteDocumentHeader()
    {
        _writer.WriteStartDocument(true);
        _writer.WriteStartElement(tracePrefix,
                                 "TraceInformation",
                                 traceNamespace);
        _writer.WriteStartElement("Traces",
                                 traceNamespace);
    }

    protected void CloseDocument()
    {
        _writer.WriteEndDocument();
        _writer.Close();
    }

    bool StackTrace
    {
        set { _stackTrace = value; }
        get { return _stackTrace; }
    }

    protected bool _stackTrace = true;
    protected XmlTextWriter _writer = null;

    private const string traceNamespace = "urn:csharpcoreref";
    private const string tracePrefix   = "cscr";
}
```

The *XmlStreamTraceListener* class exposes a Boolean property named *StackTrace* that specifies whether a stack trace is to be included with messages. The default value for *StackTrace* is *true*, and it can be changed at any time during execution.

In addition to a protected member variable that tracks the current state of the *StackTrace* property, the listener has an instance of *XmlTextWriter* named *_writer* that's used to generate the XML document. The *Open* method is used to create and initialize *_writer* and is called during construction if the user passes a

Stream object as a constructor parameter. Alternatively, the default constructor can be used to create a listener instance, followed by a call to the *Open* method.

Much of the code in *XmlStreamTraceListener* overrides methods declared in the *TraceListener* base class. Methods such as *Write*, *WriteLine*, *Fail*, *Close*, and *Flush* are called by the *Trace* and *Debug* classes to generate output messages or otherwise manage message output. The *Write* and *WriteLine* methods are implemented in the same way—they simply call *WriteTraceNode*. This listener doesn't inject any sort of line terminator for messages, because all messages are serialized as an XML document. The *Close* and *Flush* methods call the appropriate methods on the *XmlTextWriter* object associated with the listener.

The implementations of *WriteTraceNode* and *WriteFailNode* have a small bit of code that's used to provide proper XML formatting for each new trace node in the XML document. If the *StackTrace* property is *true*, these methods call *WriteStackTrace* to inject stack trace information into the document. Otherwise, the message is formatted and serialized to the XML document.

The *XmlStreamTraceListener* class is used much like any other listener. The following code creates an instance of the listener, adds it to the *Listeners* collection, generates trace messages, and flushes and closes the listener:

```
using MSPress.CSharpCoreRef.XmlListener;
⋮
class TestXmlListenerApp
{
    static void Main(string[] args)
    {
        FileStream stream = new FileStream("TraceInfo.xml",
                                           FileMode.Create);
        XmlStreamTraceListener xstl = new
            XmlStreamTraceListener(stream,
                                   "XML application tracing");
        Trace.Listeners.Add(xstl);

        GenerateAssertion();

        Trace.Flush();
        Trace.Close();
    }

    static void GenerateAssertion()
    {
        Trace.Assert(false);
    }
}
```

When you run this code, an XML document named *TraceInfo.xml* that contains an assertion violation will be generated. Included as part of the assertion violation is a stack trace that consists of two frames. *XmlStreamTraceListener* is just one example of how the *TraceListener* class can be extended to create new classes that handle trace and debug messages.

Debugging with Visual Studio .NET

Microsoft Visual Studio .NET includes an integrated debugger that can be used to debug your Visual C# projects. Because the debugger is integrated into the same tool used to edit and compile your Visual C# code, the compile/test/debug cycle is greatly simplified.

When your Visual C# project is created, it has two configurations: Debug and Release. The Debug configuration generates symbolic information that's used by the debugger; this information isn't included when building a project with the default Release configuration.

Setting Breakpoints

Breakpoints are code locations that cause the debugger to pause (or break) execution of your program. A breakpoint is typically used to halt the debugger in an interesting location. For example, let's say your application isn't responding correctly after receiving user input. By setting a breakpoint at the location in your code that handles input from the user, you cause the debugger to pause execution at the specified point. While stopped at a breakpoint, you can inspect the program variables, change the path of program execution, or step through your program's instructions.

Breakpoints can be added on any line of your Visual C# source code that contains a program statement. A breakpoint is set by pressing F9 while the insertion point is on a line in your program. If the breakpoint is set successfully, a red dot will be displayed in the left margin of the Text Editor window. Each time you press F9, the breakpoint will be toggled on or off. The other function keys often used during debugging are listed in Table 9-3.

Table 9-3.   Function Keys Commonly Used in Debugging

Function Key	Description
F5	Launches debugging session
Shift+F5	Stops debugging session
F10	Steps to next instruction
F11	Steps into current instruction

While your program is stopped at a breakpoint, you can inspect and modify variables in several ways. If you hover the mouse pointer over a variable, the type and value of the variable will be displayed in a ToolTip. Alternatively, you can take advantage of the following windows, which display variables while debugging:

- **Autos**   Contains variables referenced on the current or previous line.

- **Locals**   Contains variables defined in the current method.

- **This**   Displays the member variables for the current object.

- **Watch**   Contains variable names that you define while debugging. Up to four Watch windows can be open at one time.

The Autos, Locals, and This windows are automatically populated by the debugger. You can drag and drop variables into a Watch window or add a new variable name by clicking on the first empty line in the window and typing the variable name. To change the value of a variable, simply click the value to be updated and enter the new value.

Managing Breakpoints

The current breakpoints for your project can be managed through the Breakpoints window, shown in Figure 9-5. To open this window, choose Windows from the Debug menu and then choose Breakpoints.

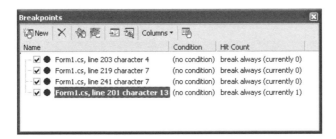

Figure 9-5.   The Breakpoints window, which is used to manage project breakpoints.

Breakpoints that are enabled appear selected, and disabled breakpoints have an empty check box. The Breakpoints window includes the file name and location for each breakpoint, as well as any breakpoint conditions and the number of times that the breakpoint has been hit.

Breaking Conditionally

The breakpoints described in the previous section are known as *unconditional breakpoints,* which means that the debugger will break whenever they are encountered. The Visual Studio .NET debugger also allows you to set breakpoints that include conditions—if the condition evaluates as *true*, the debugger will stop at the breakpoint.

Conditional breakpoints are useful when a breakpoint is set in a location that is hit often, but the debugger doesn't need be stopped each time. By setting a breakpoint condition, you can look for a specific test case before stopping execution.

Breakpoint conditions are defined using the Breakpoint Properties dialog box, shown in Figure 9-6. To display the dialog box, right-click a breakpoint in the Breakpoints window, and choose Properties from the shortcut menu.

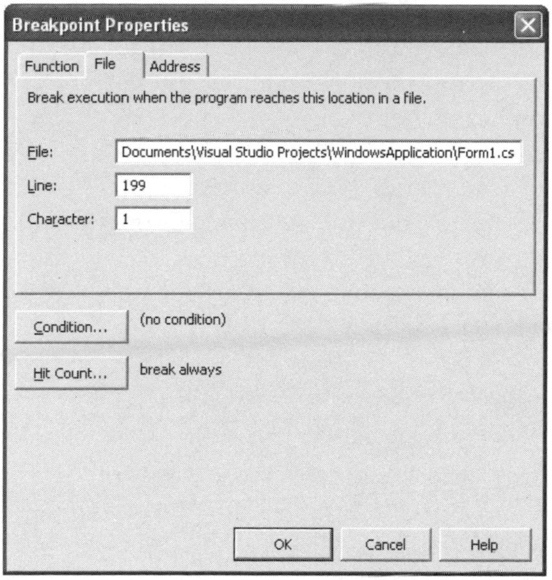

Figure 9-6.   The Breakpoint Properties dialog box.

Click the Condition button on the File tab to display the Breakpoint Condition dialog box, shown in Figure 9-7.

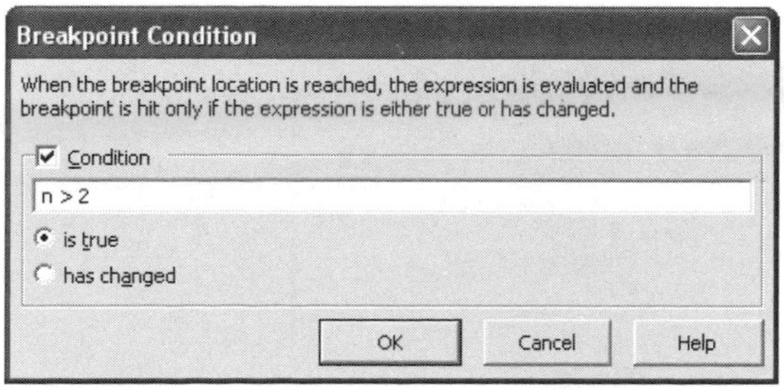

Figure 9-7.   The Breakpoint Condition dialog box.

To define an expression to be used as a breakpoint condition, enter an expression in the Condition text box. By default, the breakpoint stops execution if the expression is true. Alternatively, you can elect to have execution stop when the value of the expression changes.

Using the Call Stack

As your code executes, the operating system and CPU maintain a record of the chain of callers that have worked together to cause the current instruction to be executed. This record is stored in a temporary stack data structure known as the call stack that grows and shrinks as your program executes.

The contents of the call stack can be very useful when debugging, because the call stack provides information about the current execution context. Although breakpoints can help you break at a specific location in your code, only the call stack tells you the path taken to arrive at a specific location in your code. If you're currently executing in a method that's called from many locations, the call stack can provide the sequence of methods in the calling chain that were invoked prior to the current method.

When you're debugging, the Debug Location toolbar, shown in Figure 9-8, is displayed by default.

Figure 9-8.   The Debug Location toolbar.

When you stop at a breakpoint, the contents of the call stack are displayed in the Stack Frame combo box. Selecting an entry from the combo box will navigate to the code location referred to in the call stack.

You can also display the call stack in the Call Stack window, which is opened by choosing Windows from the Debug menu and then choosing Call Stack. The Call Stack window contents are valid only when your program is stopped at a breakpoint, as shown in Figure 9-9.

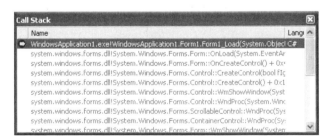

Figure 9-9.   The Call Stack window.

> **Tip** If you're stopped at a breakpoint, you can add breakpoints to the Call Stack window by selecting an entry and pressing F9. This is a useful way to quickly return to a location in the call stack without manually single-stepping the debugger.

Conclusion

Visual C# .NET includes a number of enhancements that make debugging and diagnostics much simpler. Conditional compilation in Visual C# programs is achieved through use of the *Conditional* attribute. Default Visual C# projects define the *DEBUG* and *TRACE* symbols for debug builds and define only the *TRACE* symbol for release builds.

The call stack can be manipulated using the *StackTrace* and *StackFrame* classes. These classes can be used to determine the methods that conspired to call a specific location in your code. Other classes in the .NET Framework provide support for sophisticated output of trace and debug messages.

10

Advanced Topics

In this chapter, we'll look at two advanced features that you can take advantage of as a Microsoft Visual C# developer: writing multithreaded code and using unsafe code. The first section of the chapter demonstrates how to write multithreaded programs that perform work asynchronously. Multithreaded applications are often more efficient than applications that use a single thread, especially when they're executed on more advanced hardware with multiple processors. You'll learn how to create and manage threads with the classes in the .NET Framework, as well as use classes and techniques to safely synchronize the work performed by multiple threads.

The second section of this chapter discusses how you can gain direct access to memory locations via pointers in C#. The C# language allows you to designate portions of your code as unsafe; any code in these regions is allowed to use pointers, much as is done in a C or C++ program. Although you rarely need to take advantage of unsafe code, it's a good tool to have available if you need it.

Writing Multithreaded Code

Visual C# .NET and the common language runtime provide built-in support for writing multithreaded code. Threads are the execution path through your code, and they're the atoms of application scheduling and priority. Each application has at least one thread that executes code. Multiple threads can be launched and used to execute your Visual C# application. The C# language includes key-words to assist in thread safety, and classes in the .NET Framework simplify the task of writing code that has multiple threads of execution.

Understanding Application Domains

The common language runtime executes applications in logical processes known as *application domains,* or *AppDomains.* AppDomains provide isola-tion boundaries for the applications they host, in much the same way that pro-cesses provide isolation boundaries in Microsoft Windows. However, an AppDomain is much easier to manage than a Windows operating system pro-cess. Also, multiple AppDomains can execute within a single Windows operat-ing system process. Because Visual C# programs are verifiably type-safe, the runtime can execute multiple logical processes within a single operating system process without worrying that one application will interfere with another.

> **Note**   As you read through this discussion of writing multithreaded applications using Visual C#, keep in mind that each application runs within an AppDomain and can share a physical process with another AppDomain.

Working with Threads

One or more threads run in an AppDomain. The *System.Threading.Thread* class encapsulates a thread made available by the runtime. At first, each App-Domain has an initial thread. A *Thread* object that represents the current thread can be obtained by calling the static *CurrentThread* property, as shown here:

```
Thread currentThread = Thread.CurrentThread;
```

To cause the current thread to pause for a specified period of time, call the *Thread* class's static *Sleep* method, as follows:

```
Thread.Sleep(5000);
```

Starting and Stopping Threads

To create a new thread, first create a new *Thread* object, as shown in the fol-lowing code:

```
static void Main(string[] args)
{
    Thread currentThread = Thread.CurrentThread;
```

```
    Thread workThread = new Thread(new ThreadStart(Work));
    ⋮
}
static void Work()
{
    Console.WriteLine("Hello");
}
```

The *Thread* constructor accepts a *ThreadStart* delegate as a parameter. This delegate is invoked when the thread is started and serves as the method where the thread begins execution. If the thread exits this method, the thread is terminated.

The method associated with the *ThreadStart* delegate can be static, as shown in the preceding example, or nonstatic. Using a nonstatic method enables the thread procedure to have access to instance variables that can serve as input, as shown in the following *Worker* class:

```
public class Worker
{
    protected string _message;
    public string Message
    {
        set { _message = value; }
        get { return _message; }
    }
    public void PrintMessage()
    {
        Console.WriteLine("Message from worker: {0}.", _message);
    }
}
```

When you create a new *Thread* object that uses the *Worker* class, the *Worker* instance is created and initialized first, as shown here:

```
static void Main(string[] args)
{
    Worker w = new Worker();
    w.Message = "Hello from the worker thread";
    Thread workerThread = new Thread(new ThreadStart(w.PrintMessage));
    ⋮
}
```

After a *Thread* object has been created, calling the *Start* method causes it to begin executing, as shown here:

```
workerThread.Start();
```

The thread will be scheduled to run by the operating system and will execute until it exits its *ThreadStart* method or until the thread is forced to stop by other means.

To suspend execution of a thread, call its *Suspend* method, as shown here:

```
workerThread.Suspend();
```

If the thread hasn't been started or has finished executing, a *ThreadStateException* will be generated. The current state of a thread can be determined through the *ThreadState* property, which returns a *ThreadState* enumeration member. Table 10-1 describes the members of the *ThreadState* enumeration.

Table 10-1.   *ThreadState* Enumeration Members

Member Name	Description
Aborted	The thread has been stopped due to an abort request.
AbortRequested	Another thread has requested that this thread be terminated.
Background	The thread is executing as a background thread.
Running	The thread is executing, or at least is eligible for execution by the operating system.
Stopped	The thread has stopped executing.
StopRequested	The thread has been requested to stop.
Suspended	The thread is suspended.
SuspendRequested	Another thread has requested that this thread be suspended.
Unstarted	The thread has been created but hasn't yet started.
WaitSleepJoin	The thread has been blocked while waiting for another object to be signaled, has called *Sleep*, or is waiting to join another thread.

The *ThreadState* members listed in Table 10-1 are often combined. To determine whether a thread is in a particular state, use code such as the following to ensure that the thread is not in the *Unstarted* or *Stopped* state before attempting to suspend the thread:

```
if(IsThreadStarted(workerThread))
{
    workerThread.Suspend();
}
⋮
static bool IsThreadStarted(Thread aThread)
{
    bool result = ((aThread.ThreadState & ThreadState.Unstarted) != 0
              && (aThread.ThreadState & ThreadState.Stopped) != 0);
    return result;
}
```

The *ThreadState* property can't be used to absolutely determine a thread's state in every case. Because threads run asynchronously, the thread state could easily change between the point in time when the thread state is sampled and the time when the state is tested. *ThreadState* can be used for testing obvious problems, however, such as an attempt to suspend a thread that has already been terminated.

The *Resume* method is used to restart a thread that's currently suspended, like this:

```
workerThread.Resume();
```

The *Interrupt* method causes a thread to cut short any blocking behavior in which it's currently involved, effectively waking up any threads in the *Wait-SleepJoin* state. A *ThreadInterruptedException* exception is generated and must be handled if you want the thread to be able to continue execution after *Interrupt* has been called, as shown in the following code:

```
for(int loop = 0; loop < MaxIterations; ++loop)
{
    try
    {
        Thread.Sleep(SleepInterval);
        ⋮
    }
    catch(ThreadInterruptedException e)
    {
        Console.WriteLine("I've been interrupted");
    }
    ⋮
}
```

To terminate a thread, use the *Abort* method, as shown here:

```
workerThread.Abort();
```

When *Abort* is called for a thread, a *ThreadAbortException* exception is generated. Unlike the *ThreadInterruptedException* exception discussed earlier, you can't stop this exception from terminating the current thread. The following code illustrates how the exception can be handled to clean up resources owned by the thread. The thread will always be terminated, however.

```
public void ThreadProc()
{
    try
    {
        Thread.Sleep(sleepInterval);
    }
    catch(ThreadAbortException e)
```

(continued)

```
    {
        // Clean up resources.
    }
}
```

The *Join* method is used to wait until a thread has terminated. This method blocks the current thread until the referenced thread has completed its work, as shown here:

```
workerThread.Join();
```

This code will wait unconditionally until the other thread completes its work. Two other overloads of the *Join* method enable you to specify a time-out period. These versions of *Join* return a *bool* that indicates the success or failure of the *Join* attempt. If a time-out occurs before the *Join* method succeeds, these methods return *false*. The following code uses a *Join* method with a time-out of 5 seconds:

```
workerThread.Join(5000);
```

Managing Thread Properties

Every thread runs at a specific priority level, which can be retrieved or altered with the *Priority* property. The thread's priority determines how the operating system will schedule the thread for execution, with higher priority threads always scheduled ahead of threads with lower priority. Values for the *Priority* property are taken from the *ThreadPriority* enumeration. The members of the *ThreadPriority* enumeration are listed here:

- *Lowest*

- *BelowNormal*

- *Normal*

- *AboveNormal*

- *Highest*

Threads initially have *Normal* priority. In the majority of cases, you shouldn't need to change a thread's priority. The operating system will always execute the thread with the highest priority, while sharing time equally among threads with the same priority. If a thread performs background work that can be deferred until all normal threads are idle, setting the priority to *BelowNormal* will prevent the worker thread from regularly preempting threads performing more important work. If a thread must be able to interrupt other threads to carry out its work, set the priority to *AboveNormal* or *Highest*.

The following code demonstrates the use of the *Priority* property to adjust a thread's priority:

```
workerThread.Priority = ThreadPriority.BelowNormal;
```

This example sets the thread's priority level to *BelowNormal*, which means that this thread will be scheduled after the threads with *Normal* priority and before those with *Lowest* priority.

Threads that run in the runtime are designated as running in the foreground or background. A process will run as long as it includes at least one foreground thread. Background threads can perform the same work as foreground threads, but they'll be terminated automatically when the last foreground thread terminates. The *IsBackground* property is used to get or set the background status for the thread, as shown here:

```
workerThread.IsBackground = true;
⋮
protected bool DumpThreadInfo(Thread aThread)
{
    bool background = aThread.IsBackground;
    ⋮
}
```

Synchronizing Access to Shared Objects

By using multiple threads in your applications, you can partition work into multiple asynchronous pieces, which enables you to write more efficient code. However, the ability to have multiple threads executing in a single process also adds risk and complexity. If multiple threads don't synchronize their access of shared data, the data will become corrupted. Often, these failures are difficult to detect, especially on single-processor systems.

On a multiple-processor system, several threads can execute at exactly the same time. If these threads attempt to simultaneously change the value of a variable, the results are unpredictable. Even if your code runs only on single-processor machines, you can't escape the problem. If a thread is preempted by the operating system while it's updating a variable and another thread updates the variable while the first thread is interrupted, the results are, again, unpredictable.

> **Note**   The C# language specification guarantees that some operations are uninterruptible—also known as *atomic operations*. Simple reads and writes of 32-bit or smaller scalar values are guaranteed to be atomic, as are reference assignments. More complex operations, such as reading and writing floating-point or 64-bit scalar values, aren't atomic and can be interrupted. In addition, ++ and --, the innocent-looking operators used to increment and decrement scalar values, aren't atomic, because they require a value to be read, updated, and written.

Consider the following code, in which the *Broken* class includes a method that updates a field named *dangerousVariable*:

```
public class Broken
{
    const int MaxLoops = 20000;
    protected long dangerousVariable = 0;

    protected void UpdateMethod()
    {
        dangerousVariable++;
    }

    public long Result
    {
        get { return dangerousVariable; }
    }

    public void ThreadProc()
    {
        for(int n = 0; n < MaxLoops; ++n)
        {
            UpdateMethod();
            Console.Write(".");
        }
    }
}
```

The following code creates an instance of the *Broken* class and creates two threads that execute inside the *Broken.ThreadProc* method. On a single-processor system, the code fails occasionally. On a machine with multiple processors, the code fails every time.

```
Broken broken = new Broken();
Thread bw1 = new Thread(new ThreadStart(broken.ThreadProc));
Thread bw2 = new Thread(new ThreadStart(broken.ThreadProc));
bw1.Start();
bw2.Start();
bw1.Join();
bw2.Join();
Console.WriteLine("Total = {0}.", broken.Result);
```

In the two preceding code fragments, the *UpdateMethod* is used to increment *dangerousVariable*, a field in the *Broken* class. Two threads are created, and they attempt to increment the field a number of times. If the program executes correctly, the final result displayed should be *40000*. On a system with multiple processors, the problem will be obvious. However, on a single-processor system, the fault might not be immediately apparent. Remember, on a single-processor machine, one thread must be preempted while it's updating the *dangerousVariable* field. The problem will occur if you iterate the tests long enough. On a single-processor system, you can simply add a loop around the main test, like this:

```
for(int n = 0; n < 20; ++n)
{
    Broken broken = new Broken();
    Thread bw1 = new Thread(new ThreadStart(broken.ThreadProc));
    Thread bw2 = new Thread(new ThreadStart(broken.ThreadProc));
    bw1.Start();
    bw2.Start();
    bw1.Join();
    bw2.Join();
    Console.WriteLine("Total = {0}.", broken.Result);
}
```

> **Tip**   It's a good idea to invest in a multiple-processor machine if you're developing multithreaded software for commercial use. This test illustrates the expected behavior for synchronization problems in multithreaded applications. Faults seem to occur at random, especially on single-processor machines. A multiple-processor machine can save a lot of testing and debugging time by exposing synchronization issues before your software is released.

To avoid synchronization problems, you must provide synchronization when multiple threads access shared objects. Fortunately, it's easy to provide synchronization when developing with Visual C# .NET.

Synchronizing Threads with the *Monitor* Class

The .NET Framework includes the *Monitor* class, which is part of the *System.Threading* namespace. The *Monitor* class is used to guard access to a reference variable or a section of code. A section of code that's protected by the *Monitor* class is known as a *critical section*. As shown in Figure 10-1, a critical section can be accessed by a single thread at any given time.

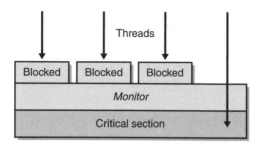

Figure 10-1. Threads blocked by a *Monitor* class guarding a critical section.

The *Monitor* class has only static methods. You never directly create an instance of the *Monitor* class, and because the class is sealed, other classes can't inherit from it either. The *Monitor* class exposes the following two primary methods:

- **Enter** Takes possession of a lock on an object passed as a parameter if the lock is available

- **Exit** Releases possession of an object's lock

The *Monitor* class is typically used as follows:

```
protected void UpdateMethod()
{
    Monitor.Enter(this);
    dangerousVariable++;
    Monitor.Exit(this);
}
```

Before entering a region of code that's been designated as a critical section, the thread makes a call to *Monitor.Enter*, passing an object reference as a parameter. If another thread has already called *Monitor.Enter* with the same object reference and hasn't yet called *Monitor.Exit*, this thread will be blocked and won't continue until the other thread has called *Monitor.Exit*.

When you use *Monitor.Enter* to take possession of an object-wide lock, you don't protect any static members. To protect static type members, pass a *typeof* reference to the *Monitor.Enter* method, like this:

```
Monitor.Enter(typeof(Broken));
```

Locking Objects

It's very easy to implement coarse-grained synchronization for a method using the *Monitor* class. One problem with using *Monitor* to guard regions of your code is that you're required to properly manage *Monitor.Enter* and *Monitor.Exit* pairs. For example, the following code is broken:

```
public void TakeALock()
{
    try
    {
        Monitor.Enter(this);
        ThrowAnException();
        Monitor.Exit(this);
    }
    catch
    {
        Console.WriteLine("Caught an exception");
    }
}
private void ThrowAnException()
{
    throw new InvalidOperationException("Bypass monitor code");
}
```

When the exception flows through the *TakeALock* method, the call to *Monitor.Exit* is bypassed. No other thread can take possession of the object's synchronization lock until the thread that owns the lock has called *Monitor.Exit* or until the thread that owns the lock has been destroyed.

To properly use the *Monitor* class in the presence of exceptions, you must write code such as the following:

```
public void ImprovedTakeALock()
{
    try
    {
        Monitor.Enter(this);
        ThrowAnException();
    }
    finally
    {
        Monitor.Exit(this);
    }
}
```

In this code, the *Monitor.Exit* method is placed in a *finally* block, guaranteeing that the monitor will be released, even in the presence of exceptions.

Caution   If you use the *Monitor* class directly, you should protect calls to *Monitor.Exit* by placing them in a *finally* block.

A simpler approach is to use the locking support that's built into the C# language, as shown in the following code. The *lock* keyword is used to enact a coarse-grained lock on a reference variable, using a much simpler coding pattern than is required with the *Monitor* class. The most commonly used form of the *lock* keyword accepts a reference variable as a parameter and creates a guarded region.

```
public void SimpleLock()
{
    lock(this)
    {
        DoWork();
    }
}
```

As with the *Monitor* class in the preceding section, you can lock static members for a class by locking the class type, like this:

```
public void SimpleLock()
{
    lock(typeof(Broken))
    {
        DoWork();
    }
}
```

Synchronizing Threads with Wait Handles

The *lock* keyword can be used to implement relatively coarse synchronization that relies on your ability to identify a single object that can be used for synchronization purposes. The .NET Framework also includes the following event and mutual exclusion classes that can be used to synchronize threads:

- ***ManualResetEvent***   Provides an event object that's signaled when a specific action occurs

- ***AutoResetEvent***   Provides an automatically resetting event object that's signaled when a specific action occurs

- ***Mutex***   Provides interprocess resource synchronization

All the classes in this list are derived from the *WaitHandle* class, which generalizes the process of acquiring, releasing, and waiting for a synchronization object. Each class uses operating system resources to synchronize thread access. In keeping with the recommended design pattern for classes that have external references, the *WaitHandle* class (and the three derived classes) implements the *IDisposable* interface. This allows you to take advantage of the *using* statement when employing these classes, as shown here:

```
using(Mutex instanceMutex = new Mutex(false, mutexName))
{
    ⋮
}
```

Every *WaitHandle* object is in one of the following two states:

- **Signaled**   Indicates that the *WaitHandle* object can be acquired by any thread.

- **Not Signaled**   Indicates that the *WaitHandle* object isn't available for acquisition. Any threads attempting to acquire the object will be blocked until the synchronization object is signaled.

The *WaitHandle* class has the following three methods that are commonly used for synchronization in derived classes:

- **WaitAll**   Static method that blocks the calling thread until all handles in an array are signaled

- **WaitAny**   Static method that blocks the calling thread until any handle in an array is signaled

- **WaitOne**   Virtual method that blocks the calling thread until the current *WaitHandle* object is signaled

Each of these methods includes overloaded versions that allow you to specify a time limit for the wait attempt and specify whether to exit the synchronization domain before the wait.

Synchronizing with event classes   As mentioned, the .NET Framework includes two classes that are used to provide event-based synchronization: *Auto-ResetEvent* and *ManualResetEvent*. Both of these classes are used to block threads until a specific event has occurred. Instances of the *AutoResetEvent* class will automatically be reset to an unsignaled state after a wait request is satisfied, whereas instances of the *ManualResetEvent* remain signaled until explicitly reset.

Both event classes are created in much the same way, by passing the initial signaling state to the constructor, as shown here:

```
AutoResetEvent automaticEvent = new AutoResetEvent(true);
ManualResetEvent manualEvent = new ManualResetEvent(false);
```

In this code, *automaticEvent* is initially signaled and *manualEvent* isn't signaled. In addition to the *WaitOne* method, the following two methods from the *AutoResetEvent* and *ManualResetEvent* classes are commonly used to control event objects:

- **Set**   Causes an event object to be signaled

- **Reset**   Causes an event object to be not signaled

Synchronization events are used to block a thread until a particular event occurs elsewhere in your code. For example, if another thread is carrying out a task, an event can be used to indicate that the task has been completed.

The *AutoResetEvent* is best suited to cases in which a signaled event should be automatically reset after a thread is notified of the completion, as in the preceding code. A *ManualResetEvent* is like an open door—once the event is signaled, it remains signaled, no matter how many threads test the event. As shown in the following code, a *ManualResetEvent* is well-suited for indicating that a state transition has occurred—in this case, indicating that the application has been initialized:

```
public class EventApp
{
    protected ManualResetEvent initializationEvent = null;
    public EventApp()
    {
        initializationEvent = new ManualResetEvent(false);
    }

    static void Main()
    {
        Thread workerThread = new Thread(ThreadStart(this.Work));
        workerThread.Start();
        // Wait for initialization.
        initializationEvent.WaitOne();
        // Initialization complete.
        DoOtherWork();
        ⋮
    }

    protected void Work()
    {
        // Perform initialization.
        ⋮
        initializationEvent.Set();
        // Perform other work.
        ⋮
    }
}
```

Using the *Mutex* class   The *Mutex* class, which gets its name from *mutual exclusion,* is used to allow at most one thread to access a resource. A *Mutex* object works by allowing only one thread to acquire ownership at any given time.

Although a *Mutex* object can be used to protect code regions, its primary use is to guard resources that must be shared between AppDomains or processes. A *Mutex* object can be given a name, and multiple processes can use the name to acquire references to the *Mutex* in any process. To name a *Mutex* object, use code such as this:

```
Mutex instanceMutex = new Mutex(false, "MyApp.Initialization");
```

Here the first parameter is a Boolean value that specifies whether the creator of the *Mutex* object also acquires ownership of the exclusion lock. In this code, the *Mutex* object is initially free to be acquired by any thread. The second parameter is optional and is the name of the *Mutex*. Like many objects that are managed by the Windows kernel, a *Mutex* object can be given a name, which enables it to be shared between multiple processes.

Named *Mutex* objects can be used to ensure that only one copy of your application can run at any given time. In the following code, the main thread tries to acquire ownership of a named *Mutex*. If the attempt is successful, the main thread continues with the main execution path. If the attempt fails, another copy of the application has previously acquired the *Mutex* and a message is displayed to the user before the program is exited. The complete code listing is contained in the SingleInstance project on the companion CD.

```
static void Main(string[] args)
{
    string mutexName = "MSPress.CSharpCoreRef.SingleInstance";
    using(Mutex instanceMutex = new Mutex(false, mutexName))
    {
        if(instanceMutex.WaitOne(1, true) == false)
        {
            Console.WriteLine("Another instance is executing");
            return;
        }
        Console.Write("Enter your name: ");
        string name = Console.ReadLine();
        Console.WriteLine("Hello, {0}.", name);
    }
}
```

In addition to *WaitOne*, the *Mutex* class exposes the *ReleaseMutex* method, which releases ownership of a *Mutex* object, allowing another waiting thread to acquire the *Mutex*. The *ReleaseMutex* method has no parameters and is used as follows:

```
portMutex.ReleaseMutex();
```

A thread that owns the *Mutex* object can call *WaitOne* multiple times without blocking. However, the thread must call *ReleaseMutex* a corresponding number of times before any waiting threads can take control of the *Mutex* object. If a thread that owns a *Mutex* object is destroyed, the *Mutex* is released.

Creating a Thread-Safe Collection

One of the most common places where thread safety is needed is in collection objects. When multiple threads contend for access to a collection object, you must provide some type of synchronization or the collection will become corrupted. By default, collection classes in the .NET Framework aren't synchronized. If multiple threads attempt to change the state of a collection object simultaneously, the object's internal data structures won't be synchronized and the behavior of the collection object will be unpredictable.

Leaving collections unsynchronized provides the best possible performance for single-threaded use, which is the most common scenario. If you're writing multithreaded code, however, you're not left out in the cold. The collection classes in the .NET Framework provide an easy way to create thread-safe collection objects.

As mentioned in Chapter 8, the *ICollection* interface includes the following two properties that are used for synchronization:

- **IsSynchronized**   Returns *true* if the collection is thread-safe
- **SyncRoot**   Returns an object that can be used for synchronization

The object returned by the *SyncRoot* property can be used with the *lock* statement to synchronize access to the collection object, like this:

```
lock(SyncRoot)
```

The following code implements a thread-safe wrapper around a *Stack* object by locking the object returned by the *SyncRoot* property for each access attempt:

```
public class SafeStack : Stack
{
    public SafeStack() :base() {}
    public SafeStack(ICollection col) :base(col) {}
    public SafeStack(int initialCapacity) :base(initialCapacity) {}

    public override object Pop()
    {
        lock(SyncRoot)
        {
            return base.Pop();
        }
    }

    public override object Peek()
    {
        lock(SyncRoot)
        {
            return base.Peek();
        }
    }
```

```
public override void Push(object obj)
{
    lock(SyncRoot)
    {
        base.Push(obj);
    }
}

public override object[] ToArray()
{
    lock(SyncRoot)
    {
        return base.ToArray();
    }
}

public override int Count
{
    get
    {
        lock(SyncRoot)
        {
            return base.Count;
        }
    }
}

public override void Clear()
{
    lock(SyncRoot)
    {
        base.Clear();
    }
}

public override bool Contains(object obj)
{
    lock(SyncRoot)
    {
        return base.Contains(obj);
    }
}
}
```

In addition to the properties exposed by *ICollection*, most collection classes expose a static method named *Synchronized* that returns a thread-safe wrapper such as the one outlined in the preceding code. A collection object must be passed as a parameter to *Synchronized*. For example, to create an instance of a thread-safe *Stack* object such as the one shown in Figure 10-2, you use code such as the following:

```
Stack safeStack = Stack.Synchronized(new Stack());
```

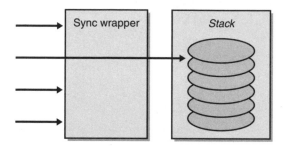

Figure 10-2.   Synchronization wrappers, which enable safe access to collections.

If you need a collection object that's fully synchronized so that any thread can be used to access any method or property, creating a thread-safe collection with the static *Synchronized* method is the simplest approach. If you need to occasionally synchronize a collection, or if you need to protect just a few methods for the collection, the collection's *SyncRoot* property can be used to provide fine-grained synchronization, without the overhead of synchronization each time the collection is accessed.

Working Asynchronously Using the Thread Pool

Threads can also be used to carry out individual tasks asynchronously. For example, instead of executing a task on the main thread, a new thread can be created to carry out the work, as shown in the following code. When the work is completed, the thread can be destroyed.

```
public class Calculate
{
    double _radius;
    double _result;
    public Calculate(double radius)
    {
        _radius = radius;
    }
    public void Circumference()
    {
        _result = 2 * _radius * 3.1415926535d;
    }
```

```
    public double Result
    {
        get { return _result; }
    }
}
class ThreadPoolTestApp
{
    ⋮
    static void SimpleThread()
    {
        Calculate calc = new Calculate(2.0d);
        Thread worker = new Thread
            (new ThreadStart(calc.Circumference));
        worker.Start();
        worker.Join();
        Console.WriteLine("{0}", calc.Result);
    }
}
```

In this code, the *SimpleThread* method creates a new thread and uses the *Calculate* class to calculate the circumference of a circle. After the thread has been created, the creating thread waits for the worker thread to complete its work.

The preceding approach has a few problems.

■ Thread creation isn't free, and spinning up a thread to carry out small units of work can increase the processing costs of these smaller tasks.

■ Context switching and scheduling costs for threads add to the cost of executing your application.

■ Every thread increases resource costs for your application, including stack space and local storage. These costs are incurred for each thread you create, even threads with a short lifetime.

Multithreaded systems that require the highest possible performance often implement a pool of threads that are used to carry out short tasks. By maintaining a collection of threads that are capable of handling tasks on demand, much of the overhead associated with creating individual threads can be avoided. The construction of a thread pool from scratch is a difficult task, however, and requires an in-depth knowledge of Windows multithreading internals. Fortunately, as a Visual C# developer, you can take advantage of the thread pool provided by the runtime.

> **Note**   The thread pool has multithreaded semantics, so in some cases, a thread pool isn't appropriate. For example, if you require thread affinity for a task, meaning that a specific thread will always perform the work, a thread pool won't work for you. The thread pool will dispatch threads as required, and you have no control over which threads will carry out a particular task. In a similar vein, you have no control over thread priority in a thread pool, as all threads run at the default thread priority. If you require fine-grained management of threads or have tasks that will degrade the performance of the thread pool by blocking for long periods of time, you should manually create a thread to handle the task.

Queuing Work Items to the Thread Pool

Using the thread pool to queue asynchronous tasks is a great way to handle specific types of asynchronous work. For example, a work queue is perfectly suited for cases in which work must be performed but you don't require notification when the work has been completed. Work items are added to a work queue, and the thread pool asynchronously removes items from the queue, as shown in Figure 10-3.

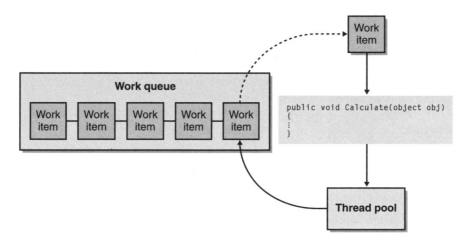

Figure 10-3.   The thread pool, which services items in the work queue.

To take advantage of the thread pool to execute work items, you must define a method that will be invoked by the thread pool to execute your work. This method, which will be bound to a *WaitCallback* delegate, is always declared as accepting an *object* parameter. Although the *object* parameter must be declared for every method associated with a *WaitCallback* delegate, it's used only in scenarios in which arguments are provided to the method. One way to associate state information with your queued work item is to create a work object class that includes the necessary state as well as a method that's invoked to carry out the work, as shown in the following code:

```
public class FibonacciWorkItem
{
    int _maxIterations;
    public FibonacciWorkItem(int maxIterations)
    {
        _maxIterations = maxIterations;
    }
    public void Calculate(object obj)
    {
        int x = 0;
        int y = 0;
        int fib = 0;
        for(int n = 0; n < _maxIterations; ++n)
        {
            Console.WriteLine(fib);
            x = y;
            if(fib == 0)
                y = 1;
            else
                y = fib;
            fib = x + y;
        }
    }
}
```

This code declares a *FibonacciWorkItem* class that includes an upper limit for a Fibonacci sequence and a *Calculate* method that will be invoked by the thread pool. As the Fibonacci sequence is calculated, the result is written to the console.

> **Note**   A Fibonacci sequence is a series of numbers originally used by the thirteenth-century mathematician Leonardo Fibonacci to describe the breeding characteristics of rabbits.

To queue a *FibonacciWorkItem* object for execution by the thread pool, the static *QueueUserWorkItem* method is called, as shown here:

```
FibonacciWorkItem fwi = new FibonacciWorkItem(25);
ThreadPool.QueueUserWorkItem(new WaitCallback(fwi.Calculate));
```

Another approach is to use a separate object that contains state information and pass the object as a parameter when calling *QueueUserWorkItem*, as shown here:

```
class Fibonacci
{
    public static void Calculate(object obj)
    {
        int iterations = (int)obj;
        ⋮
    }
} .
⋮
ThreadPool.QueueUserWorkItem(new WaitCallback(Fibonacci.Calculate), 25);
```

In this example, the *Calculate* method is stateless, and each invocation requires that necessary parameters be passed to it. This approach avoids the overhead of creating a new object to house the *WaitCallback* delegate and parameter state.

Waiting for Handles with the Thread Pool

The thread pool also comes in handy when you're waiting for *WaitHandle* objects to become signaled. A common, albeit inefficient, design pattern is to create a new thread that's used to wait for a system handle to be signaled. The thread pool enables you to designate a method that will be invoked when a *WaitHandle* is signaled.

The *RegisterWaitForSingleObject* method is used to associate a *WaitHandle* with a method to be invoked when the handle is signaled, as shown here:

```
string activePort = "2555";
int portTimeout = 5000;
RegisteredWaitHandle regHandle;
regHandle = ThreadPool.RegisterWaitForSingleObject(portOpenedEvent,
                      new WaitOrTimerCallback(PortOpened),
                      activePort,
                      portTimeout,
                      true);
```

The following five parameters are passed to *RegisterWaitForSingleObject*:

- ■ ***WaitHandle***   The *WaitHandle* object to be monitored.

- ■ ***WaitOrTimerCallback***   The delegate to be invoked when the *WaitHandle* object is signaled.

- ■ ***object***   An object passed as a parameter when the delegate is invoked.

- ■ ***int***   The length of time to wait for the *WaitHandle* object to be signaled before a time-out occurs. Pass a value of −*1* to disable time supervision.

- **bool**   A Boolean value that's set to *true* if the *WaitHandle* should be supervised only once. Pass *false* to enable continuous supervision.

A *RegisteredWaitHandle* object is returned from the call to *RegisterWait-ForSingleObject*. To remove the association between the *WaitHandle* object and the callback delegate, call the *RegisteredWaitHandle* object's *Unregister* method, like this:

```
regHandle.Unregister(portOpenedEvent);
```

The callback method associated with the *WaitHandle* object is declared as shown in the following code. If a time-out occurs before the *WaitHandle* object is signaled, the *timedOut* parameter will be *true*.

```
protected void PortOpened(object state, bool timedOut)
{
    ⋮
}
```

There are three additional overloaded versions of *RegisterWaitForSingle-Object*, differing only in how the time-out period parameter is passed. Where the example discussed in this section uses an *int* value, these additional overloads enable the use of *long*, *uint*, or *TimeSpan* values.

Using Unsafe Code

The C# language doesn't generally allow you to perform certain operations considered to be unsafe. For example, accessing memory locations directly and performing pointer arithmetic are considered to be unsafe operations. Rather than completely barring these operations, C# permits them, but it requires that such code be explicitly marked as unsafe.

The unsafe context prevents code verification. Therefore, any executable code that includes an unsafe context requires a higher level of trust. This restriction might prevent your code from being executed in some scenarios. This section will discuss the need for unsafe code and how to declare unsafe contexts.

Examining the Need for Unsafe Code

Do you need unsafe code? Unsafe code is rarely necessary, but here are a few cases when unsafe code is useful:

- You're using platform invoke (P/Invoke) to interoperate with existing COM or Microsoft Win32 code, and you have data structures with embedded pointers. In this case, using unsafe code might be the simplest and safest way to manage the legacy data structures.

- Similarly, if you're dealing with legacy data structures that are written directly to a disk or a socket stream, the simplest course of action might be to use unsafe code.

- Occasionally, you can write more efficient code using direct memory access instead of using purely managed code.

When you're working exclusively with the classes in the .NET Framework, there's little need for unsafe code. The capability is included in the language for those rare situations in which you must manipulate memory directly, such as when you're working with legacy code and data structures. For example, when you're working with files that use an existing file format, you might need to read the contents of the file into a buffer and access the memory directly.

Declaring Unsafe Contexts

An unsafe code region is declared with the *unsafe* keyword. The unsafe region consists of code enclosed in curly braces that follows the *unsafe* keyword. Unsafe code is permitted within this code region, as shown here:

```
unsafe
{
    ⋮
}
```

The *unsafe* keyword can be used only when you're compiling with the */unsafe* compiler switch. If you don't set the */unsafe* switch, the compiler will generate an error and refuse to compile your code. This restriction is intended to make your decision to move to unsafe code an explicit one. The */unsafe* switch is enabled on the project's Build property page in the Configuration Properties folder, as shown in Figure 10-4.

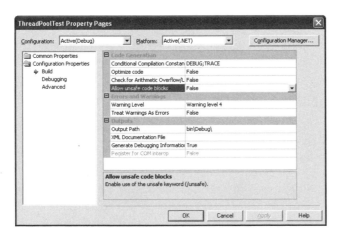

Figure 10-4.   Enabling the */unsafe* compiler switch on the project's Build property page.

In addition to declaring code regions as unsafe, you can also declare types as unsafe. Declaring a type as unsafe enables you to use pointer declarations as fields or parameters. Any use of unsafe types in externally visible portions of your code makes it noncompliant with the Common Language Specification (CLS).

To declare a type as unsafe, simply add the *unsafe* keyword to the type declaration, as shown here:

```
unsafe public struct IntNode
{
    public IntNode* pNext;
    public int  x;
    ⋮
}
```

Declaring a class or a structure as unsafe enables the use of pointers as fields. In addition, pointers can be declared in method parameters, as follows:

```
unsafe public class Tree
{
    public void CopyNode(TreeNode* node)
    {
        ⋮
    }
    ⋮
}
```

Individual methods can be declared as unsafe, marking the method, but not the enclosing type, as unsafe:

```
public class Tree
{
    unsafe public void CopyNode(TreeNode* node)
    {
        ⋮
    }
    ⋮
}
```

An interface can be marked as unsafe, enabling you to use pointers in the interface declaration as shown here:

```
unsafe interface INode
{
    void CopyNode(TreeNode* node);
    ⋮
}
```

Operators Used in Unsafe Code

C# offers a number of operators that can be used only in an unsafe context, as described in Table 10-2. These operators enable you to directly access objects and memory using pointers, to determine the addresses of objects, and to use pointer arithmetic to calculate addresses. Although they can be useful, remember that these operations are potentially dangerous and can be used only in an unsafe context.

Table 10-2.   Operators Used Only in the Unsafe Context

Operator	Description
sizeof	Returns the size of the value type or value type object
&	Returns the address of an object
– >	Provides indirect member access
*	Provides pointer declaration or indirection

Reflecting the heritage of the C# language, the operators listed in Table 10-2 are shared with the C and C++ languages. The C# versions of these operators work almost exactly like their C and C++ counterparts. For example, the following code declares a pointer and assigns an address to it:

```
int n = 42;
int *pn = &n;
```

Although you can determine the address of a value type object, you can never calculate the address of a managed object with the *&* operator. To dereference an address, the *** operator is used, as shown here:

```
Console.WriteLine("{0}", *pn);
int k = *pn;
```

To access members of a structure via a pointer, use the *– >* operator, as shown here:

```
public void RemoveNode()
{
    pNext->pPrev = pPrev;
    ⋮
}
```

Locking Memory Blocks

Memory that's allocated on the managed heap is subject to being relocated as part of the heap's garbage collection process. Before manipulating blocks of managed memory, the memory locations must be locked using the *fixed* statement, as shown here:

```
MyType mt = new MyType();
fixed(int *pmt = &mt.x)
{
    ⋮
}
```

The *fixed* statement consists of two parts: an expression that can be converted to an unmanaged type, and a declaration of an unmanaged type variable that's assigned the value of the expression. The address is locked until the statement or statement block that follows the *fixed* statement has finished executing.

The *fixed* statement can target any managed memory block, including instance or static class fields, but the variable that's the target of the *fixed* statement must be a value type, an array, or a string. The following code shows how a single *fixed* statement can lock multiple memory blocks, as long as they are of the same type:

```
fixed(int *pmt = &mt.x, pmy = &mt.y)
{
    ⋮
}
```

Locking a memory block potentially degrades heap performance because it interferes with the heap compacting mechanism. Any blocks that are locked can't be moved and must remain locked in place until they're unlocked. When you lock a memory block, take care to lock it for as short a time as possible.

Allocating Temporary Memory

When running code in an unsafe context, you can allocate memory from the call stack. The *stackalloc* keyword allocates enough storage space from the stack to accommodate a specified number of objects of a specific type, as shown here:

```
int* pn = stackalloc int[42];
```

In the preceding code, the *stackalloc* keyword allocates an array of 42 integers. The memory allocated by *stackalloc* isn't initialized, so you must explicitly initialize it to a default value, as follows:

```
int* pn = stackalloc int[42];
for(int n = 0; n < 42; n++)
{
    pn[n] = 0;
}
```

The space allocated from the stack is allocated along with automatic variables for the current method. When the current method returns, the call stack unwinds and the memory allocated by *stackalloc* is reclaimed.

Using an Unsafe Code Block

The UnsafeSort project, included on the companion CD, provides an example of how you can use unsafe code blocks. UnsafeSort implements the QuickSort sorting algorithm using direct memory manipulation and pointer arithmetic.

QuickSort is a recursive algorithm that progressively divides an array into smaller subarrays, refining the order as the array is subdivided. The basic algorithm works like this:

1. Take the value of the array's midpoint element.

2. Starting at the lower bound of the array, look for the first element that has a value larger than the midpoint element. If the element is discovered prior to reaching the midpoint, this element is out of position.

3. Starting at the upper end of the array, look for the first element that has a value smaller than the midpoint element. If the element is discovered prior to reaching the midpoint, this element is out of position.

4. Exchange the elements found in steps 2 and 3.

5. Repeat steps 2 through 4 until every element in the array is tested.

6. Restart the algorithm twice, using the array below the midpoint for the first iteration and the array above the midpoint for the second iteration. Continue recursively until the array subsection that's tested has two sorted elements.

The QuickSort algorithm is implemented in the *UnsafeQuickSort* method, which is part of the *Sorter* class, shown in the following code:

```
public unsafe void UnsafeQuickSort(int* pLower, int* pUpper)
{
    if(pLower < pUpper)
    {
        int* pOriginalLower = pLower;
        int* pOriginalUpper = pUpper;
        long elements = pUpper - pLower;
        int  midpointValue = *(pLower + (elements/2));
        while(pLower <= pUpper)
        {
            // Find the first unsorted element below the midpoint.
            while((pLower < pOriginalUpper)&&(*pLower < midpointValue))
                ++pLower;

            // Find the last unsorted element above the midpoint.
            while((pUpper > pOriginalLower) && (*pUpper > midpointValue))
                --pUpper;

            if(pLower < pUpper)
            {
                // Sneaky trick that quickly swaps two scalar
                // values in place
                *pLower ^= *pUpper;
```

```
            *pUpper ^= *pLower;
            *pLower ^= *pUpper;
        }
        if(pLower <= pUpper)
        {
            ++pLower;
            --pUpper;
        }
    }
    // Recursively call method again to sort the remaining
    // unsorted portion of the array.
    if(pLower < pOriginalUpper)
        UnsafeQuickSort(pLower, pOriginalUpper);
    if(pUpper > pOriginalLower)
        UnsafeQuickSort(pOriginalLower, pUpper);
    }
}
```

As you can see, this method uses a lot of pointer arithmetic, beginning on the first line, where the addresses passed to the method are compared. The *pLower* and *pUpper* addresses mark the range of addresses in the array that are to be sorted. If these addresses are equal or *pLower* is greater than *pUpper*, no sorting is performed.

If the array range appears to be valid, the midpoint for the array is calculated and the value of the midpoint element is cached in *midpointValue*. Next the *UnsafeQuickSort* method looks for unsorted elements on the wrong side of the midpoint and exchanges them. After *UnsafeQuickSort* iterates over the entire array, the array is roughly sorted into the following subsections:

- Elements smaller than the midpoint element are located below the midpoint.

- Elements larger than the midpoint element are located above the midpoint.

To complete the sorting process, the array is split into two subarrays, which are recursively sorted. Because the *pLower* and *pUpper* pointers have either met or crossed, *pLower* is used as the lower bound of the subarray with higher values and *pUppser* is used as the upper bound of the subarray with lower values for the next sorting iteration.

The *UnsafeQuickSort* method is invoked by the *Sorter.Sort* method shown in the following code. The *Sort* method exposes a managed signature that's callable by managed code that isn't executing in an unsafe context.

```
public void Sort(int [] numberArray)
{
    unsafe
```

(continued)

```
    {
        fixed(int* p = numberArray)
        {
            UnsafeQuickSort(p, &p[numberArray.Length-1]);
        }
    }
}
```

The *Sort* method establishes an unsafe code block, pins the array to prevent relocation by the garbage collector, and invokes the *UnsafeQuickSort* method, as shown here:

```
static void Main(string[] args)
{
    int [] ar = {3,7,2,1,6,8,5,4,9,12,6,3,14,7,2,2,13,10,11,1,1,1,11,2};
    Sorter s = new Sorter();
    s.Sort(ar);

    Console.WriteLine("Array contents:");
    foreach(int n in ar)
    {
        Console.WriteLine(n.ToString());
    }
    Console.WriteLine("Done");
}
```

This code creates an array of integers and an instance of the *Sorter* class. After the *Sort* method is called to sort the array, the array contents are written to the console.

Conclusion

The .NET Framework includes a number of classes that simplify multithreaded programming. The *Thread* class is used to represent threads that execute code in an application that targets the .NET Framework. The framework also includes classes that are used for thread synchronization. Applications that target the .NET Framework can also take advantage of the common language runtime thread pool, which is accessed through the *ThreadPool* class.

The C# language offers the ability to directly access memory through pointers in code regions explicitly marked as unsafe. Designating an unsafe code region has some disadvantages, such as requiring a higher level of security trust and rendering the code unverifiable. However, the ability to access memory directly can be advantageous when dealing with legacy code or when performance is a concern.

Part III

Programming
Windows Forms

11

An Introduction to Windows Forms

In this chapter, you'll learn about Windows Forms, the classes within the Microsoft .NET Framework that are used to create traditional Microsoft Windows GUI desktop applications. The key class in the *System.Windows.Forms* namespace is *Form*, the base class used for most windows in a Windows Forms application. The *Form* class serves as a base class for all top-level windows, including your application's main window, view windows, and any dialog boxes that you create. This chapter introduces you to the *Form* class, as well as to three other key classes in the *System.Windows.Forms* namespace:

- **■** ***Application***   Used to manage application-level characteristics of your program

- **■** ***ApplicationContext***   Used to manage the behavior of an application, such as how it is launched and closed

- **■** ***MessageBox***   Used to display simple dialog boxes known to the user as message boxes

In addition, this chapter discusses many of the commonly used properties and methods associated with the *Form*, *Application*, and *MessageBox* classes.

In this chapter, we'll also look at the Microsoft Visual C# Forms Designer and examine the source code generated by the Forms Designer that's injected into your source code. The forms and controls included in the .NET Framework expose a wide variety of properties that affect every aspect of forms and controls' behavior. The Forms Designer provides a visual interface to those properties. As you manipulate controls visually and set properties in the Properties window, the Forms Designer serializes the required properties directly into your source code.

This chapter focuses on the core classes used for programming Windows Forms applications. Subsequent chapters in Part III will expand on that programming, describing the controls that are available to you, how to collect user input, and other advanced programming techniques.

Understanding Windows Forms

Windows Forms is a rich programming framework for building client applications that provides improved ease-of-use, tool support, and lower deployment costs. Traditional Windows desktop applications are often referred to as *rich-client applications* to differentiate them from browser-based Web applications that are downloaded from a central location. Classes used to create rich-client applications are found in the *System.Windows.Forms* namespace and are collectively known as the Windows Forms classes. This namespace includes the *Form* class, which is used as a base class for all dialog boxes and top-level windows in a .NET desktop application. In addition, the *System.Windows.Forms* namespace includes classes that manage controls, interaction with the clipboard, menus, printing, and more.

Using Forms as Dialog Boxes

A common way to use forms is as dialog boxes that interact with the user. Dialog boxes can range from basic forms that contain a simple text box control to elaborate forms with large numbers of controls. The .NET Framework includes a wide variety of controls that can be used with dialog boxes. Much of the discussion of Windows Forms in this book will focus on the controls available to you.

Some types of dialog boxes are used so often they're included as part of the operating system. These dialog boxes, known collectively as the *common dialog boxes,* include prebuilt dialog boxes that handle tasks such as selecting files, specifying colors, choosing fonts, and configuring printer settings. The .NET Framework includes classes that provide access to these common dialog boxes; these classes will be covered throughout the next few chapters.

Dialog boxes are often used to display notification messages to the user. Instead of requiring each programmer to develop dialog boxes used for generic notification messages, the Windows operating system provides a message box control. The message box is a specialized dialog box that simplifies the task of displaying a simple text message to the user, using a variety of predefined icons and button layouts. The .NET Framework wraps the Windows message box in the *MessageBox* class. (The *MessageBox* class is discussed later in this chapter, in the section "Displaying Information with Message Boxes.")

Using Forms as Views

A typical Windows Forms application is made up of more than just top-level windows and dialog boxes; Windows Forms applications can also include child windows that allow interaction between the user and the application. If you're familiar with the Microsoft Foundation Classes (MFC) library included with Microsoft Visual C++, you'll remember that this type of window is called a *view* and is derived from the *CView* class. In the .NET Framework, top-level windows, modal dialog boxes, and nonmodal application windows all share *Form* as their base class.

Forms used as views typically differ from dialog boxes in that they usually don't have button controls that are used to dismiss the form. To use a form as a view, call its *Show* method, as shown here:

```
UserView userView = new UserView();
userView.Show();
```

When the view is no longer needed, use the *Close* method to dismiss the form:

```
userView.Close();
```

As you'll see later in this chapter, in the section "Modal Forms vs. Modeless Forms," the *Show* command is used to display a modeless dialog box. In most cases, a dialog box is modal, meaning that no work can be done with the rest of the application while the dialog box is displayed. Using a nonmodal form to interact with the user allows several forms to be open simultaneously, which can provide a richer experience for some types of applications.

Developing a Simple Windows Forms Project

To create a Windows Forms project, begin by opening the New Project dialog box and selecting Windows Application, as shown in Figure 11-1. Clicking the OK button will cause Microsoft Visual C# .NET to automatically generate a basic Windows Forms project for you, including a simple main form for the top-level window and other associated files.

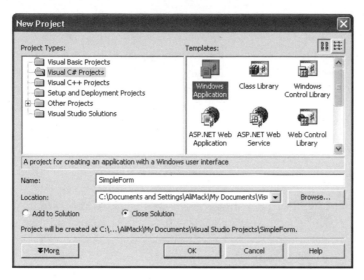

Figure 11-1. Creating a Windows Forms project with Visual C# .NET.

> **Note** The examples shown in this section are created using a project named SimpleForm. This project, like all the other examples discussed in this chapter, is included on the companion CD.

Examining Files Created by Visual C# .NET

The project directory contains a number of files that are used to create the compiled assembly for your application. For a basic project such as SimpleForm, the generated files are as follows:

- **App.ico**   The default icon for the application
- **AssemblyInfo.cs**   A C# source file that contains attribute declarations that target the assembly generated by the project
- **Form1.cs**   The primary C# source file for the project
- **Form1.resx**   An XML file that stores some resource information associated with Form1.cs
- **SimpleForm.csproj**   The primary Visual C# project file
- **SimpleForm.csproj.user**   A Visual C# project file that contains user-specific settings

- **SimpleForm.sln**   The primary Visual C# solution file

- **SimpleForm.suo**   A Visual C# solution file that contains user-specific information

Of these files, only the Form1.cs and AssemblyInfo.cs files contain C# source code. As with the console applications discussed in Part I and Part II, the AssemblyInfo.cs file contains only assembly attributes that define the characteristics of the compiled assembly. Most of the C# code for a new project is found in the Form1.cs file. When a source file that implements a form is opened, the form is initially displaycd in design mode, as shown in Figure 11-2.

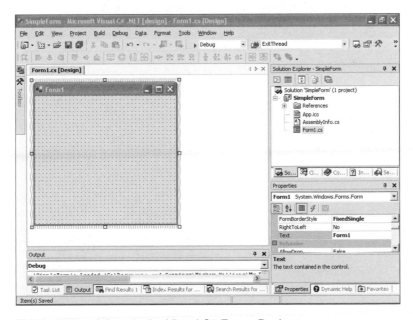

Figure 11-2.   A form in the Visual C# Forms Designer.

To view the C# source code for a form, press F7, or right-click the form and choose View Code from the shortcut menu. Either action will cause the source code to be displayed for editing while Visual C# .NET keeps your form open in design mode on a separate tab. The contents of Form1.cs are shown here, with some comments removed for clarity:

```
using System;
using System.Drawing;
using System.Collections;
using System.ComponentModel;
using System.Windows.Forms;
using System.Data;
```

(continued)

```csharp
namespace SimpleForm
{
    public class Form1 : System.Windows.Forms.Form
    {
        private System.ComponentModel.Container components = null;

        public Form1()
        {
            InitializeComponent();
        }

        /// <summary>
        /// Clean up any resources being used.
        /// </summary>
        protected override void Dispose( bool disposing )
        {
            if( disposing )
            {
                if (components != null)
                {
                    components.Dispose();
                }
            }
            base.Dispose( disposing );
        }

        #region Windows Form Designer generated code
        /// <summary>
        /// Required method for Designer support - do not modify
        /// the contents of this method with the code editor.
        /// </summary>
        private void InitializeComponent()
        {
            this.components = new System.ComponentModel.Container();
            this.Size = new System.Drawing.Size(300,300);
            this.Text = "Form1";
        }
        #endregion

        /// <summary>
        /// The main entry point for the application.
        /// </summary>
        [STAThread]
        static void Main()
        {
            Application.Run(new Form1());
        }
    }
}
```

The preceding source code looks a lot like the source code used in the console applications presented earlier in this book, with a few differences. One of these differences is that the *using* statements at the top of the file reference a number of namespaces that are commonly used in Windows Forms applications, including the following:

- **System.Collections**   As discussed in Chapter 8, the *Collections* namespace includes classes that provide collection-style containment for other types.

- **System.ComponentModel**   Includes classes that implement container and control behavior. A form uses an instance of *System.ComponentModel.Container* to track the components used by the form.

- **System.Data**   Includes classes that are used for Microsoft ADO.NET database access. This namespace isn't used in a default application, so you can safely remove the *using* statement for this namespace if you're not programming with ADO.NET.

- **System.Drawing**   Includes classes that provide access to basic GDI+ drawing functions. The use of classes in this namespace and GDI+ are discussed in more detail in Chapter 14.

- **System.Windows.Forms**   Includes all of the Windows Forms classes, enabling you to call the types in this namespace by their shorter, friendlier names.

Another difference between a Windows Forms application and a console application is that the *Form1* class is derived from the *System.Windows.Forms.Form* base class. As mentioned, this class serves as a base class for all form windows that you create in a .NET application.

One section of the source file is protected by *#region* and *#endregion* preprocessor directives, which define collapsible code regions for the Code Editor. This particular region includes source code that's used by the Forms Designer to store properties and other configuration information for the form, as well as any child controls owned by the form. When the designer-related code is enclosed in a region, it can be collapsed by default and protected from inadvertent editing. To view this code in the Code Editor, click the small plus sign (+) adjacent to the highlighted region labeled *Windows Form Designer generated code*.

The *Main* method in a Windows Forms application includes a call to *Application.Run*, as shown here:

```
static void Main()
{
    Application.Run(new Form1());
}
```

As you'll see later in this chapter, in the section "Starting an Application," the *Run* method will start the message loop required by all Windows applications and will display the main form for the application. When the application's main form is closed, the *Run* method will return.

Finally, because all form classes interact with operating system handles (specifically window handles), every form class implements the *Dispose* method. If you add resources that require disposal to a form class, you should arrange for their disposal inside the *Dispose* method.

> **Note**   Remember, you can reference managed resources only if *disposing* is *true*. If *disposing* is *false*, there's no way to safely touch a managed reference, because the object might have already been reclaimed by the garbage collector.

Executing a Windows Forms Project

Windows Forms projects are compiled just like other C# projects: you simply press Ctrl+Shift+B to build the project or choose Build Solution from the Build menu. To launch a Windows Forms project in the debugger, press F5, or choose Start from the Debug menu. If you execute the *SimpleForm* application, a simple form with no buttons or other controls will be displayed, as shown in Figure 11-3.

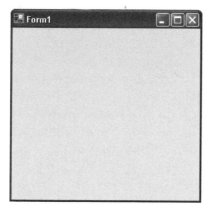

Figure 11-3.   The *SimpleForm* application.

One big difference between Windows Forms projects and the console applications from earlier chapters is that Windows Forms projects are easier to debug. Because Windows Forms projects are event driven—meaning that they respond to events—you'll probably find it easy to examine the behavior of a Windows Forms application in the debugger. To do so, just set a breakpoint in a particular event handler, and you'll be ready to go.

Adding a New Form to a Project

Most Windows Forms projects consist of multiple forms that handle various aspects of the application. In general, a new form is just a class that's a descendant of the *System.Windows.Forms.Form* class.

There are two ways to add a new form class to your project: you can choose Add Windows Form from the Project menu, or you can right-click on the project name in Solution Explorer and then choose Add Windows Form from the shortcut menu. Either method will open the Add New Item dialog box, shown in Figure 11-4.

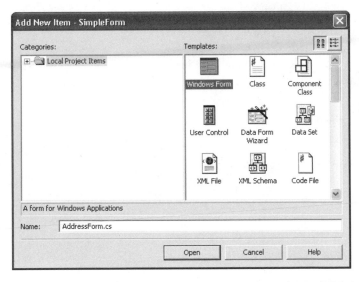

Figure 11-4.   Adding a new form with the Add New Item dialog box.

To add a new form, type a name for the class, and click Open. Visual C# .NET will create a new form class and add it to your project. Forms that are added to your project include a *Dispose* method, as well as the *Initialize-Component* method used by the Forms Designer.

Modal Forms vs. Modeless Forms

You can display a form to the user in one of two ways:

- A *modal form* prevents access to any other portions of the application while the form is displayed. This type of form is useful when you're displaying a dialog box that must be acknowledged by the user before proceeding.

- A *modeless form* allows other parts of your application to be used while the modeless form is displayed. This type of form is useful for situations in which a form can be used over a long period of time.

Examples of modal forms are message boxes, dialog boxes that are used to open or save files, and dialog boxes that display error information. Modeless forms are used when interaction with an application is required, such as when displaying a child form in Microsoft Word. In most cases, a modeless form is preferred over a modal form, as it enables the user to control the flow of an application. However, when information must be acknowledged by the user or input must be supplied by the user before the execution of your application can proceed, a modal form is perfectly acceptable.

A form is displayed as either modal or modeless depending on the method that was called to display the form. To display a modeless form, use the *Show* method, as shown here:

```
Form addressForm = new AddressForm();
addressForm.Show();
```

As mentioned, when a form is displayed using *Show*, you use the *Close* method to destroy the form programmatically:

```
addressForm.Close();
```

Alternatively, you can use the *Hide* method to simply make the form invisible:

```
addressForm.Hide();
```

To display a modal form, use the *ShowDialog* method, as shown here:

```
addressForm.ShowDialog();
```

The call to *ShowDialog* doesn't return until the dialog box has been dismissed by the user.

Determining the *DialogResult* Value

Modal dialog boxes supply a return value that provides a way to determine how the dialog box was dismissed. One reason you should be concerned about the return value is that the code that invoked the dialog box can easily determine whether the dialog box contains valid data, as shown here:

```
Form addressForm = new AddressForm();
DialogResult result = addressForm.ShowDialog();
if(result == DialogResult.OK)
{
    // Dialog box contents are valid.
}
```

The *DialogResult* return value generally indicates which button was clicked by the user to close the dialog box. The return value is taken from the *DialogResult* enumeration, which contains the following values:

- *Abort*
- *Cancel*
- *Ignore*
- *No*
- *None*
- *OK*
- *Retry*
- *Yes*

The return value is usually, but not always, the value of the button that was clicked by the user. For example, if the user presses Esc, a value of *Dialog-Result.Cancel* will be returned. As you'll see in Chapter 12, you also can specify the *DialogResult* value returned by a form, regardless of the button clicked by the user.

Passing Values to Forms

Often when you're using a form as a dialog box, you'll need to pass information to and from the dialog box. Typically, you need to populate the dialog box with the initial information that's displayed to the user, and later collect the user's input after the dialog box has been dismissed.

In general, the simplest way to pass information to and from a form is to define properties that provide access to the input provided by the user. For example, the following code shows how properties can be used to pass name and address information to a dialog box that displays information to a user:

```
public void DisplayAddress(Address userAddress)
{
    AddressForm addressForm = new AddressForm();
    addressForm.UserName = userAddress.user;
    addressForm.StreetAddress = userAddress.StreetAddress;
    addressForm.ShowDialog();
}
```

Each property can be associated with a member variable that's used to initialize dialog box controls. When the *AddressForm* class is used, the properties can be employed to populate the dialog box with appropriate values, as shown in the preceding example. When used with the *DialogResult* value returned from *ShowDialog*, property values can be retrieved only in cases in which the user has clicked the OK button, as shown here:

```
public Address GetAddressForUser(string user)
{
    Address userAddress = null;
    AddressForm addressForm = new AddressForm();
    addressForm.UserName = user;

    DialogResult result = addressForm.ShowDialog();
    if(result == DialogResult.OK)
    {
        userAddress = new Address();
        userAddress.StreetAddress = addressForm.StreetAddress;
        userAddress.City = addressForm.City;
        ⋮
    }
    return userAddress;
}
```

In Chapter 12, various controls will be used to collect input from the user. Properties enable you to easily obtain values from a form such as a dialog box. When the user attempts to close the form, you can validate input and store control values in member variables.

> **Note**   Throughout the remainder of this chapter, properties will be used to pass values to and from the example forms. Although it's possible to achieve a similar effect by using public fields, it's generally considered bad practice to expose internal implementation details publicly. By using properties instead of exposing members directly, you retain the option of calculating values instead of returning them directly, and you can also easily validate the initial values passed to your form.

Displaying Information with Message Boxes

The *MessageBox* class is used to provide simple interaction with the user by displaying a message box, which is a specialized type of dialog box containing a message, optional icons, and one or more buttons. Message boxes are often used to present information that can be formatted in a simple text message.

Unlike with other forms that you'll use in your application, you never create an instance of the *MessageBox* class. Instead, you call the static *Show* method to display the message box, like this:

```
MessageBox.Show("A simple message box");
```

This version of *Show* displays the most basic message box, containing the string passed as a parameter and an OK button, as shown in Figure 11-5. There are 12 overloaded versions of the *Show* method, which provide a great deal of flexibility in specifying message box behavior, including the buttons and icons that are displayed. The following sections describe the options available through these overloaded versions.

Figure 11-5.   A simple message box, including a text message, a button, and an optional icon.

To include a caption or title for the message box, pass a second string to *MessageBox.Show*, as shown here:

```
MessageBox.Show("A simple message box", "MessageBox demo");
```

Specifying Message Box Buttons

Message boxes can be populated with buttons other than the OK button, enabling you to collect a response from the user in response to a question posed in the message box. Although up to three buttons can be displayed in a message box, you don't have free rein in defining these buttons. Instead, you must select from the predefined button groups found in the *MessageBoxButtons* enumeration, listed in Table 11-1.

Table 11-1. *MessageBoxButtons* Enumeration Values

Member	Buttons Included
AbortRetryIgnore	Abort, Retry, Ignore
OK	OK
OKCancel	OK, Cancel
RetryCancel	Retry, Cancel
YesNo	Yes, No
YesNoCancel	Yes, No, Cancel

The following code demonstrates how you can specify an alternative button layout for a message box by passing a value from the *MessageBoxButtons* enumeration as a parameter:

```
DialogResult result = MessageBox.Show("A message box with 3 buttons",
                          "MessageBox demo",
                          MessageBoxButtons.YesNoCancel);
switch(result)
{
    ⋮
}
```

As you can see, the return value from the *Show* method is one of the *DialogResult* return values shown in Table 11-1.

Adding Icons to Message Boxes

The *MessageBoxIcon* enumeration is used to specify which of four icons is displayed in the message box. Although there are only four possible icons, there are nine members in the *MessageBoxIcon* enumeration, as described in Table 11-2.

Table 11-2. *MessageBoxIcon* Enumeration Values

Member	Description
Asterisk	Displays a circle containing a lowercase *i*.
Error	Displays a red circle containing a white *X*.
Exclamation	Displays a yellow triangle containing an exclamation point.
Hand	Displays a red circle containing a white *X*.
Information	Displays a circle containing a lowercase *i*.
None	No icon is displayed.
Question	Displays a circle containing a question mark.

(continued)

Table 11-2. *MessageBoxIcon* **Enumeration Values**   *(continued)*

Member	Description
Stop	Displays a red circle containing a white *X*.
Warning	Displays a yellow triangle containing an exclamation point.

To specify the icon displayed in a message box, pass one of the values from the *MessageBoxIcon* enumeration to the *Show* method, in addition to specifying the button layout and other parameters, as shown here:

```
DialogResult result = MessageBox.Show("A message box with an icon",
                      "MessageBox demo",
                      MessageBoxButtons.YesNoCancel,
                      MessageBoxIcon.Asterisk);

switch(result)
{
    ⋮
}
```

Defining Default Buttons for Message Boxes

The *MessageBoxDefaultButton* enumeration enables you to specify the button in a dialog box that will be the default button, and thus will be returned to the user as a *DialogResult* return value if the user presses Enter. The enumeration has three values: *Button1*, *Button2*, and *Button3*. The following code demonstrates using the *MessageBoxDefaultButton* enumeration to specify a default button:

```
DialogResult res = MessageBox.Show("The default button is Ignore",
                   "MessageBox demo",
                   MessageBoxButtons.AbortRetryIgnore,
                   MessageBoxIcon.Asterisk,
                   MessageBoxDefaultButton.Button3);

switch(res)
{
    ⋮
}
```

This code displays a message box that contains three buttons: Abort, Retry, and Ignore, with the Ignore button specified as the default button.

Controlling Special Cases for Message Boxes

The *MessageBoxOptions* enumeration is used to control how a message box is displayed to the user, as well as to define some special-case behavior. The members of the *MessageBoxOptions* enumeration are described in Table 11-3.

Table 11-3. *MessageBoxOptions* Enumeration Values

Value	Description
DefaultDesktopOnly	Displays the message box on the default desktop of the interactive window station, even if no interactive user is logged on. This option is used for services that don't normally run in the context of an interactive user.
RightAlign	Right-aligns text in the message box, including message text and the caption.
RtlReading	Displays message box text in right-to-left reading order.
ServiceNotification	Displays the message box on the currently active desktop, even if no interactive user is logged on. This option is used for services that don't normally run in the context of an interactive user.

The values in Table 11-3 can be combined using the bitwise OR operator (|). The following code demonstrates combining values from the *MessageBox-Options* enumeration:

```
DialogResult res = MessageBox.Show("The service has not\nstarted\n.",
                        "Service demo",
                        MessageBoxButtons.AbortRetryIgnore,
                        MessageBoxIcon.Exclamation,
                        MessageBoxDefaultButton.Button3,
                        MessageBoxOptions.RightAlign |
                        MessageBoxOptions.DefaultDesktopOnly);
switch(res)
{
    ⋮
}
```

This code creates a message box suitable for use by a Windows service, with right-aligned text.

Specifying a Parent Window for a Message Box

To ensure that a message box is displayed in front of a specific form, you can specify a reference to the form when calling the *MessageBox.Show* method. Each of the overloaded versions of the *Show* method discussed earlier in this chapter has a similar overload that allows you to specify the message box parent. In most cases, you can simply pass a pointer to the parent form as the first parameter, as shown here:

```
MessageBox.Show(this, "Just a message", "MessageBox demo");
```

The first parameter can be a reference to any object that implements the *IWin32Window* interface. This interface is implemented by all controls and forms in the .NET Framework and is a standard interface for types that encapsulate Win32 window handles.

Controlling a Windows Forms Application

The *Application* class is used to provide basic application-level behavior for a Windows Forms application. You never create an instance of the *Application* class directly; instead, you invoke static methods and properties exposed by the *Application* class. The static methods provided by the *Application* class, such as *Run* and *Exit*, enable you to control how your application starts and stops. The static properties exposed by the *Application* class enable you to determine information such as the path used to store application data. As mentioned, you can't create an instance of the *Application* class, but the following sections will show you how to supply context objects and event handlers that collaborate with the *Application* class to control the behavior of your application.

Starting an Application

A Windows Forms application is started by calling the static *Application.Run* method, as shown here:

```
Application.Run(new Form1());
```

There are three overloaded versions of the *Run* method. This example shows the most commonly used version of *Run*, which accepts the top-level form for the application as a parameter. The *Run* method will create a message loop and display the form passed as a parameter. This version of *Run* is called for you automatically in Windows Forms projects created by Microsoft Visual Studio .NET.

Alternatively, you can call *Run* with no parameters, as shown here:

```
Application.Run();
```

When *Run* is called with no parameters, the *Application* class will create a Windows message loop on the current thread but won't display an initial form. This version of *Run* is useful if you'll be displaying the form at a later time, or perhaps not displaying a form at all.

The third version of the *Run* method accepts an *ApplicationContext* object that will be used by the *Application* class. The default *ApplicationContext* object used with the previous versions of the *Run* method will automatically exit the application when the main form is closed. By deriving a new class from *ApplicationContext*, you can define your own specialized behavior. The following code is an example of a class derived from *ApplicationContext* that overrides the built-in behavior for closing the application:

```
public class QueryApplicationContext: ApplicationContext
{
    private string _saveMessage = "Exit and discard changes?";
    private string _caption = "Application Exit";

    public QueryApplicationContext(MainForm form)
    {
        form.Show();
        form.Closing += new CancelEventHandler(FormClosing);
    }

    private void FormClosing(object sender, CancelEventArgs e)
    {
        DialogResult result = MessageBox.Show(saveMessage,
                                _caption,
                                MessageBoxButtons.YesNo,
                                MessageBoxIcon.Question,
                                MessageBoxDefaultButton.Button1);
        if(result == DialogResult.Yes)
        {
            ExitThread();
        }
        else
        {
            e.Cancel = true;
        }
    }
}
```

In this code, the *FormClosing* method is used to handle the *Closing* event for the application's main form. The *Closing* event is raised when a form is closed, enabling its handler to prevent closure through the *CancelEventArgs* object passed as a parameter. In the *FormClosing* method, a confirmation message box is displayed to the user. If the user clicks the Yes button, *ExitThread* is called, which causes the application to terminate. If the user clicks No, the *Closing* event is canceled.

To use a specialized version of the *ApplicationContext* class, you pass an instance of the class to *Application.Run*, as shown here:

```
static void Main()
{
    MainForm form = new MainForm();
    QueryApplicationContext appContext;
    appContext = new QueryApplicationContext(form);
    Application.Run(appContext);
}
```

Determining Application Path Information

When locating files needed by your Windows Forms application, you often need to determine the path information. The *Application* class includes properties that simplify the task of determining commonly used paths, such as your application path, and folders used for storing application data.

The path to the executable that launched the current application can be obtained through the *ExecutablePath* property, as shown here:

```
string executablePath = Application.ExecutablePath;
```

To retrieve the start-up directory path, use the *StartupPath* property, as shown here:

```
string startupPath = Application.StartupPath;
```

According to Windows application design guidelines, application data should be stored in specific ways to simplify the way users interact with applications. Application data should always be stored in a subdirectory of the Documents And Settings folder, with user-specific data stored in a path under My Documents (which maps to *Documents And Settings\\<user_name>*). Storing data in this way allows users to have a single location for their data and allows applications to be used in roaming profiles. The *Application* class helps you do the right thing by calculating these paths for you.

> **Note**   At the time of this writing, two sets of guidelines describe how applications written for Windows should perform. The first of these guidelines, "*Application Specification for Microsoft Windows 2000 for Desktop Applications*," defines the expected behavior of applications written for the desktop. The second, "*Application Specification for Microsoft Windows 2000 Server*," describes the expected behavior for server applications. Both guidelines are available in the MSDN documentation that accompanies Visual C# .NET.

Common data that's shared by all users of a Windows Forms application should be stored in an application-specific subdirectory of the Documents And Settings folder. To determine the location of this subdirectory, use the *CommonAppDataPath* property, as shown here:

```
string commonDataPath = Application.CommonAppDataPath;
```

The location for this directory is in the ***<company_name>\\<product_name>\\<version>*** subdirectory of the Documents And Settings\All Users\Application Data folder. The company name and product name are determined by inspecting the assembly attributes in the AssemblyInfo.cs file. If these attributes are empty, as they are when a project is initially created by Visual C# .NET, the company name and product name will be set to the name of the Visual C# project.

This directory won't be created unless you access the property to ask for its location. At that point, the *Application* class will assume that you have an interest in storing information in the common application data directory and will create a directory if it doesn't already exist.

The path for user-specific information is obtained through the *UserApp-DataPath* property, as shown here:

```
string userDataPath = Application.UserAppDataPath;
```

The path for per-user information follows the same rules as common application data, except that the path is composed using the current user's identity. For example, a user named Ali would have a per-user path located in the Documents And Settings\Ali\Application Data folder.

Performing Idle Work

The *Application* class includes an event that's raised when the message loop is performing no work. This event, known as the *Idle* event, is used to trigger low-priority tasks that are performed when no other work is being done. For example, you can use the *Idle* event to trigger an update of user interface elements such as status bars or other informational displays.

The first step in handling the *Idle* event is to define a method that conforms to the *EventHandler* delegate signature, as shown here:

```
private void OnIdle(object sender, EventArgs e)
{
    // Perform idle processing here.
}
```

Before your *Idle* event handler will be called, you must subscribe to *Idle* events by creating an *EventHandler* delegate and appending it to any existing *Application.Idle* delegates, as shown here:

```
MyForm()
{
    ⋮
    Application.Idle += new EventHandler(OnIdle);
}
```

Closing an Application

By default, an application will exit when the main form is closed. As discussed in the previous section, you can override this behavior through the *Application-*

Context class. Another approach is to interact with the *Application* class directly.

The *Application* class provides the *Exit* method, which can be used to initialize shutdown for an application. The *Exit* method can be called by any thread, as shown here:

```
Application.Exit();
```

The *Exit* method doesn't cause the application to close immediately. Instead, all of the message pumps are closed and the *Run* method returns. Returning from the *Run* method will typically cause the application to terminate, as the application's *Main* method usually contains only code used to clean up application resources after *Run*, as shown here:

```
static void Main()
{
    ⋮
    Application.Run(new Form1());
    appMutex.Close();
    stream.Close();
    ⋮
}
```

You generally won't call *Exit* directly because it immediately closes any forms that are currently open. The preferred way to close an application is to call the main form's *Close* method.

To close a specific thread in a Windows Forms application, call the *ExitThread* method, as shown here:

```
if(Application.MessageLoop == true)
    Application.ExitThread();
```

Here the *MessageLoop* property is used to determine whether a message loop exists on the current thread before calling *ExitThread*. If the current thread has a message loop, calling *ExitThread* causes the message loop to close. If the *Run* method has been called for the current thread, calling *ExitThread* causes *Run* to return to its caller.

To receive notification when an application is exiting, add a handler for the *ApplicationExit* event. As shown in the following code, you can use this event handler to clean up resources owned by the application:

```
// Form constructor
AddressForm()
{
    ⋮
    Application.ApplicationExit += new EventHandler(OnAppExit);
}
```

(continued)

```
private void OnAppExit(object sender, EventArgs e)
{
    appMutex.Close();
    stream.Close();
}
```

When handling the *ApplicationExit* event, you can clean up resources that haven't yet been disposed of; however, you can't control the exit of the application. When your *ApplicationExit* event handler is invoked, the application has already begun to shut down.

Using Form Properties to Affect Form Behavior

All of the form and control objects that are created using the Visual C# Forms Designer have properties that control their behavior. These properties can be accessed in two ways: either programmatically in your C# application or through the Properties window for the form or control, which is shown in Figure 11-6.

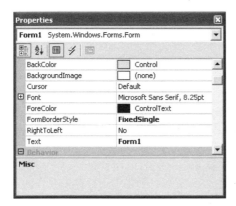

Figure 11-6.   The Visual C# Properties window.

When property values are updated through the Properties window, the Visual C# Forms Designer will generate the necessary code and inject it into your C# source file. There's no hidden property configuration file that controls the behavior of your forms and controls; instead, your forms and controls are always governed by C# source code.

Setting Border Styles

A variety of border styles can be defined for forms. This is an important property for a form, because the form's border provides the initial visual cues to the user about the type of interaction possible with the form. For example, if a window appears to allow resizing, the user will expect to be able to resize the window, and your code must be able to render the window properly. The border style is defined by the *FormBorderStyle* property, which must be set to one of the values from the *FormBorderStyle* enumeration, listed in Table 11-4.

Table 11-4.   *FormBorderStyle* Enumeration Values

Property	Description
Fixed3D	Displays a three-dimensional border that can't be resized.
FixedDialog	Displays a thick border that can't be resized.
FixedSingle	Displays a thin border that can't be resized.
FixedToolWindow	Displays a fixed tool window that can't be resized.
None	No border is displayed, and the form can't be resized.
Sizable	Displays a sizable form border.
SizableToolWindow	Displays a sizable tool window border.

The following code demonstrates setting the *FormBorderStyle* property programmatically:

```
FormBorderStyle = FormBorderStyle.FixedToolWindow;
```

Form border properties can affect more than a form's resizing behavior and edge rendering. If a form has its *FormBorderStyle* property set to *FormBorderStyle.None*, no caption is displayed, because no title bar is provided. If the border style is set to one of the tool window styles, the height of the title bar area is reduced, and the system menu isn't displayed.

By default, forms created with the Visual C# Forms Designer have their *FormBorderStyle* property set to *FormBorderStyle.Sizable*. This style usually isn't suitable for forms that are used as dialog boxes, which typically have a fixed size.

Defining Other Form Properties

In addition to the form's border style, the *Form* class includes a number of properties that can be used to control many aspects of the form's appearance and behavior. Some of the more commonly used properties exposed by the *Form* class are listed here:

- **BackColor** Specifies the background color for the form. By default, this value is set to *Control*, which specifies that the form should use the background color specified in the current Windows color scheme.

- ■   ***Size***   Specifies the dimensions of the form.

- ■   ***StartPosition***   Specifies the location where the form will be created.

- ■   ***Text***   Specifies the form's caption. By default, this value is set to the name of the form; however, the default is usually changed to a more meaningful caption for the form.

- ■   ***WindowState***   Specifies the current state of the form, which is taken from the *WindowState* enumeration.

The *Color* structure is used to represent 32-bit color values in the .NET Framework. The color is specified as a 32-bit value made up of alpha, red, green, and blue (ARGB) components. (The alpha component specifies transparency.) The *Color* type includes dozens of predefined colors, including common color values such as *Red*, *Green*, and *White* as well as more exotic values such as *AliceBlue*, *BurlyBrown*, and *SeaGreen*. The following code demonstrates using the *Color* type to change a form's background color:

```
BackColor = Color.AliceBlue;
```

> **Note**   The *Color* type is discussed in detail in Chapter 14.

The *StartPosition* property specifies the position of a newly created form. By default, *StartPosition* is set to *WindowsDefaultLocation*. This property must be set to one of the values from the *FormStartPosition* enumeration, listed in Table 11-5.

Table 11-5.   *FormStartPosition* Enumeration Values

Property	Description
CenterParent	Form is centered within its parent's rectangle.
CenterScreen	Form is centered on the screen.
Manual	Form's size and location determine its starting position.
WindowsDefaultBounds	Form's size and location are determined by Windows defaults.
WindowsDefaultLocation	Form's location is determined by Windows defaults.

The *FormWindowState* property is updated as your application executes. *FormWindowState* is set to one of the following values, depending on the current state of the form:

- **Minimized**   Form is currently minimized.

- **Maximized**   Form is currently maximized.

- **Normal**   Form is currently at its normal size.

The following code sets several of the form's properties, including *Back-Color*, *Text*, and *StartPosition*:

```
public Form1()
{
    InitializeComponent();
    FormBorderStyle = FormBorderStyle.FixedToolWindow;
    BackColor = Color.AliceBlue;
    Text = "Basic Form Demo";
    StartPosition = FormStartPosition.CenterScreen;
}
```

Conclusion

Classes in the *System.Windows.Forms* namespace are used to create rich-client applications using C#. The *Form* class is the base class for most windows in a Windows Forms application. When you add a new form to your Visual C# project, the class will be created with a number of necessary methods already defined. The *Form* class exposes a number of properties that can be changed programmatically or through the Forms Designer's Properties window.

The *MessageBox* class is used to display message boxes to users and includes a wide variety of options that control the appearance of the message box. Using the *MessageBox* class, you can control the display of icons, button placement, and other properties.

A Windows Forms application is controlled by the *Application* class, which is responsible for starting the application's message loop and displaying the top-level window. The *Application* class also includes properties that calculate the proper locations for storing per-user or application data. Instead of creating an instance of the *Application* class, you call static methods exposed by the class, such as *Application.Run* and *Application.Exit*. You can also use form properties to control form behaviors such as setting a form's border style and defining its background color.

12

Adding Controls to Forms

Chapter 11 examined the Form class, the central unit of programming a rich client application with Microsoft Visual C# .NET. This chapter introduces many of the basic controls that are used with Windows Forms, including buttons, list boxes, combo boxes, and labels, as well as the event handling mechanism used by controls to pass notifications to their parents. This chapter also covers containment, which allows specific controls, such as group box and panel controls, to contain other controls.

The classes in the *System.Windows.Forms* namespace provide a new way to develop forms-based applications for Windows. When I first started programming for the Windows platform, I had to write large amounts of code to route and handle messages sent from the operating system to control the application. Any error in the message routing code would break the application and lead to hours, if not days, of debugging. Copious amounts of C code were required to change even the simplest of control attributes. For example, creating a push button control with a specific color required hundreds of lines of code.

Windows Forms change all of that. With Windows Forms and the .NET Framework, building a rich client application is greatly simplified. You can build applications that are far richer than ever before, while writing less code. In fact, one of the great things about the Windows Forms Designer is how little code you actually need to write. All properties are exposed through the Properties window, enabling you to define the appearance and behavior of controls declaratively, rather than requiring you to write code. By reducing the amount of code you must write, Visual C# .NET and Windows Forms enable you to concentrate on what really counts—adding real functionality to your application.

An Introduction to Controls

Many types of controls are used to create Windows Forms applications. Some of these controls are complex, such as the tree view and list view controls. Others are simpler and more fundamental, such as the status bar and push button controls. Whether simple or complex, all controls share a set of common properties that can be manipulated to affect the controls' appearance and behavior. In addition, each control raises events to notify you that an interesting thing has occurred inside the control.

All Windows Forms controls are derived from the *Control* class. This class includes all Windows Forms components that present a user interface, including the *Form* class. The *Control* class includes a basic implementation of many properties, events, and methods that are common to all controls. In fact, most of the properties and events discussed in this chapter are defined in the *Control* base class.

Because *Control* is an abstract class, you can't create an instance of it directly. Instead, we'll start this chapter by looking at a simple, yet very common, set of controls: the button classes.

Using the Button Classes

The following classes fall into the button category:

- *Button*
- *RadioButton*
- *CheckBox*

Each of these classes is used to represent one of the standard types of buttons offered by Windows. In addition, each of these classes inherits its basic behavior from a common base class: the *ButtonBase* class.

The *ButtonBase* Class

Many of the methods and properties available in the *Button*, *RadioButton*, and *CheckBox* classes are actually inherited from the *ButtonBase* class. Although you rarely interact with the *ButtonBase* class directly, the concrete *Button*, *RadioButton*, and *CheckBox* classes depend on the *ButtonBase* class to provide basic behavior that's common to all three classes. If you're new to Windows programming, you might be surprised that the radio button and check box controls are considered buttons, but they do share some characteristics with common buttons:

- They can be clicked.
- They have labels.

Radio buttons and check boxes are really just monostable buttons. You can think of a radio button or check box control as a button that stays depressed when you click it.

The *Button* Class

The *Button* class represents a Windows push button control and includes properties, methods, and events that simplify the task of interacting with the button. The *Button* class exposes properties and methods that make it easy to provide advanced behavior, which can be difficult in other languages, such as C++. In this section, we'll look at how the *Button* class is used to manage push button controls.

Using the Windows Forms Designer to Add Buttons to a Form

As you saw in Chapter 11, the Windows Forms Designer is used to create the forms that make up a Windows Forms application. When a form is open in the Windows Forms Designer, the Toolbox will include a tab that contains available controls, as shown in Figure 12-1.

Figure 12-1.   The Visual Studio .NET Toolbox, which contains controls available for Windows Forms.

You can add buttons and other controls to a form using any of the following techniques:

- Draw a control on a form by clicking the control in the Toolbox and then clicking and dragging a rectangle in the control's desired location on the form.

- Drag a control onto a form by clicking the control in the Toolbox and dragging it to the desired position on the form.

- Add a control to the upper left corner of a form by double-clicking the control's icon in the Toolbox. You can then reposition the control as needed.

Every control has a set of default properties that are generated automatically. In addition, some properties are created by the Forms Designer, such as the default name of the control. When you add a control to your form, the Windows Forms Designer serializes information about the control into your form's source file, including the control's default name, size, and position. As you update properties for a control using the Properties window, the code necessary to update the properties is added to your form.

Controlling Button Appearance with Properties

The *Button* class exposes several properties that enable you to manage the appearance of a control. The most commonly used properties that affect the appearance of push buttons are listed here:

- *FlatStyle*   Defines how the control's edges are drawn
- *BackColor*   Specifies the color for the control's background
- *ForeColor*   Specifies the text color for the control
- *Text*   Controls the caption displayed in the control

The *FlatStyle* property enables you to change the appearance of buttons and other controls to match the Web look offered by products such as recent versions of Microsoft Money. You also can create buttons and other controls that are initially displayed as flat but become three-dimensional as the mouse pointer moves over them. The *FlatStyle* property must be set to a value from the *FlatStyle* enumeration, provided in Table 12-1.

Table 12-1.   *FlatStyle* Enumeration Values

Value	Description
Flat	The button is flat.
Popup	The button is normally flat but is raised when the mouse pointer moves over it.
Standard	The button is drawn with three-dimensional edges.
System	The button's style is determined by the operating system.

Figure 12-2 shows a series of push buttons with their *FlatStyle* property set to *Flat*, *Popup*, and *Standard*.

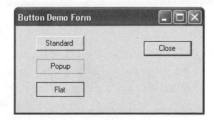

Figure 12-2.   Push button controls with various *FlatStyle* settings.

Like other properties, the *FlatStyle* property for a control can be set programmatically, as shown in the following code, or through the Properties window. Because the style of a control rarely changes at run time, it's usually more convenient to set the style using the Properties window.

```
closeButton.FlatStyle = FlatStyle.Flat;
```

> **Note**   Although it might be unusual to change the style of a control at run time, you can still do so with Windows Forms controls. All Windows Forms controls are stateless, which makes it possible to change properties that affect the appearance or behavior of the control at run time. The ability to change properties dynamically enables you to create very flexible user interfaces. Later in this chapter, in the section "Using the *ComboBox* Class," we'll look at an example program that allows a combo box to dynamically change its drop-down style.

The *BackColor* property is used to set the background color for the control. By default, this property is set to *KnownColor.Control*, which is the system-wide default color for controls defined by the operating system. The following code sets the background color of a button to dark red:

```
okButton.BackColor = Color.DarkRed;
```

Recall that in Chapter 11 we used similar code to specify the background color for a form. Because forms and all controls share *Control* as a common base class, the technique for manipulating common properties is exactly the same.

The *ForeColor* property for a control is used to specify the color used to draw the caption text. For button controls, this property is by default set to *KnownColor.ControlText*, which is the system-wide color defined by the operating system and used for control captions. To change the color of the caption text for a button, use code such as this:

```
okButton.ForeColor = Color.AntiqueWhite;
```

> **Tip**   It's easy to manipulate the colors of Windows Forms objects such as forms and controls. Keep in mind, however, that the user might not share your love of alternative color schemes. It's a good idea to consider respecting the default background and foreground control colors, as these colors can be configured by users. Projecting your own color scheme might cause difficulties when users try to run your application.

Sometimes it's useful to change a button's caption. For example, a button that opens a window might have the caption *Open Window*. After the window has been opened, it's reasonable to change the function of the button to close the open window and change the button's caption to *Close Window*, using code such as this:

```
private void ToggleWindow()
{
    if(openButton.Text == "Open Window")
    {
        reservationForm = new ReservationForm();
        reservationForm.Show();
        openButton.Text = "Close Window";
    }
    else
    {
        reservationForm.Close();
        openButton.Text = "Open Window";
    }
}
```

As shown in the preceding code, the caption displayed by a button control is managed through the control's *Text* property. All forms and controls that include a label or caption expose the *Text* property to enable you to provide a new caption. To allow a user to use the keyboard to select a button, prefix one of the characters with an ampersand (&), as shown here:

```
openButton.Text = "&Close Window";
```

When a character in the caption text is prefixed with an ampersand, the user can click the button by pressing the ALT key in conjunction with the character. It's customary to provide this type of shortcut with all push button controls except the OK and Cancel buttons.

Controlling Button Behavior with Properties

The *Button* class also includes properties that control the behavior of a push button control. The properties discussed in this section aren't unique to the *Button* class. These properties are inherited from the *Control* base class and are exposed by all Windows Forms controls.

When it's not appropriate for a control such as a button to be selected by a user in the current context, the control should be disabled. A disabled control provides a visual cue to the user that the control can't be used, which is a more user-friendly approach than enabling the control only to display an error message after the button is clicked. Controls expose the *Enabled* property, which is used to enable or disable the button or other Windows Forms controls. When disabled, button controls can't be selected by the user, and the button label is drawn using the system's disabled text color. The following code illustrates how to disable a button control:

```
removeItem.Enabled = false;
```

To enable a control that's currently disabled, set its *Enabled* property to *true*, as shown here:

```
removeItem.Enabled = true;
```

Sometimes it's more appropriate to completely hide a control instead of simply disabling it. Controls are typically hidden when it's unlikely that they'll be used. For example, controls used only for special cases can be hidden and displayed only when the special case occurs. Hiding controls that aren't likely to be used reduces clutter on your forms and makes the forms easier to use.

To hide a control such as a push button, set its *Visible* property to *false*, as shown here:

```
removeItem.Visible = false;
```

Alternatively, you can hide the control using the *Hide* method, like this:

```
removeItem.Hide();
```

Using Control Properties with Forms

The properties and methods discussed in this section apply to all Windows Forms controls. In addition, because the *Form* class is a descendant of *Control*, these properties can be used with any form in your application. For example, to disable an entire form, set its *Enabled* property to *false*, as follows:

```
reservationForm.Enabled = false;
```

In a similar vein, to hide a form, you can set its *Visible* property to *false* (or call its *Hide* method), as shown here:

```
private void CloseButton_Click(object sender, System.EventArgs e)
{
    Visible = false;  // Or Hide();
}
```

This code hides the form when the user clicks the Close button. This is a useful technique when a form is costly to initialize. By creating the form only once and hiding instead of closing the form, the form can be displayed more quickly.

To display a control that's currently hidden, set its *Visible* property to *true*, as shown here:

```
removeItem.Visible = true;
```

Or, if you prefer to invoke a method rather than set a property, you can use the *Show* method, like this:

```
removeItem.Show();
```

Associating a Button with a *DialogResult* Value

As you saw in Chapter 11, a form's *DialogResult* property provides a way to determine how a modal form was dismissed by the user. When a form is used as a dialog box, a *DialogResult* value should be associated with the form before the form is closed. This value is available as a property after the dialog box has been dismissed, and it's also returned as a result when *ShowDialog* is called, as shown here:

```
private void newItem_Click(object sender, System.EventArgs e)
{
    AddComboItemForm dlg = new AddComboItemForm();
    DialogResult result = dlg.ShowDialog(this);
    if(result == DialogResult.OK)
    {
        ⋮
    }
}
```

There are two ways to set the *DialogResult* property for a form. One way is to set the property explicitly while processing events in the form, as shown here:

```
private void CloseButton_Click(object sender, System.EventArgs e)
{
    DialogResult = DialogResult.OK;
    Close();
}
```

Another approach is to set the *DialogResult* property for a button control used to close the form. Each push button control has a *DialogResult* property; the value of *DialogResult* will be passed through to the form if the button is used to close the form. Although the *DialogResult* property for a push button control can be set in code, as shown here, it's most often set declaratively using the Properties window:

```
closeButton.DialogResult = DialogResult.OK;
```

The *RadioButton* Class

The *RadioButton* class is used to create a radio button control. A radio button control is used when the user must make one selection from multiple options—for this reason, the radio button control is sometimes referred to as the *option button control*. When multiple radio button controls exist in the same group on a form, the control will automatically enforce *mutual exclusion*, meaning that when the user selects one radio button, all other radio buttons are guaranteed to be cleared.

The radio button control shares many properties with the push button control, including the *FlatStyle*, *BackColor*, *ForeColor*, and *Text* properties discussed earlier in this chapter, in the section "Controlling Button Appearance with Properties." In addition, the *Checked* property is used to determine whether a radio button is selected, as shown here:

```
if(standardRadio.Checked == true)
{
    ⋮
}
```

You can also use the *Checked* property to select a radio button, like this:

```
standardRadio.Checked = true;
```

When the user selects a radio button, a *Click* event is raised. To handle the *Click* event, you must provide an event handler; this technique is discussed later in this chapter, in the section "Basic Event Handling."

An unusual property exposed by the *RadioButton* class is the *Appearance* property. The *Appearance* property has two possible values, which are taken from the *Appearance* enumeration, shown in Table 12-2.

Table 12-2.   *Appearance* Enumeration Values

Value	Description
Button	The radio button is drawn as a push button.
Normal	The radio button is drawn normally.

When the *Appearance* property is set to *Appearance.Button*, radio button controls look like those shown in Figure 12-3. The Red, Blue, and Green buttons are actually radio buttons, and in this case, the Blue button is checked, so it's drawn like a button that's pressed. The Red and Green radio buttons aren't selected, so they're drawn as normal push buttons.

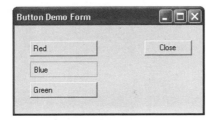

Figure 12-3.   A group of radio buttons with the *Appearance* property set to *Appearance.Button*.

The *CheckBox* Class

The *CheckBox* class is used to create a check box control. The check box control is similar to the radio button control except that no mutual exclusion is enforced by check box controls—meaning that the user can select several or none of the check boxes on a form.

The *CheckBox* class shares many characteristics with the *RadioButton* class. Like *RadioButton*, the *CheckBox* class exposes the *BackColor*, *ForeColor*, *FlatStyle*, *Text*, and *Checked* properties. Like the *RadioButton* class, the *CheckBox* class exposes the *Appearance* property, which can be used to force the check box control to be drawn as a button. Also, as with other button controls, when the user selects a check box, a *Click* event is generated and can be handled by supplying an event handler delegate.

As with the radio button control, you can use the *Checked* property to retrieve or set the value of a two-state check box. Unlike the radio button control, a check box control can optionally support three states rather than just two. The third state is useful when a check box must reflect a state that's neither *true* nor *false*. This ability to reflect three states isn't enabled by default; you must set the control's *ThreeState* property to *true*, as shown here:

```
subscribeCheckBox.ThreeState = true;
```

Once the *ThreeState* property is enabled, you should use the *CheckState* property to determine or set the state of the control. The *CheckState* property must be set to one of the values from the *CheckState* enumeration, shown in Table 12-3.

Table 12-3.   *CheckState* Enumeration Values

Value	Description
Checked	The check box is selected.
Unchecked	The check box is cleared.
Indeterminate	The check box is neither selected nor cleared and is drawn with a disabled check mark.

When the check box control is drawn as a button, the indeterminate state is rendered as a flat push button, the checked state appears as a depressed push button, and the unchecked state appears as a raised push button.

Basic Event Handling

All controls raise events that are used to notify you when something of interest has occurred within the control. Many events are generated when the user interacts with the control. For example, when the user clicks a button or enters characters in a text box, events are generated. By handling these events, Windows Forms applications interact with the user and respond to the user's actions.

An application indicates its interest in handling an event by supplying an event handler delegate with an appropriate signature and associating the delegate with an event exposed by the control. Any events that aren't handled by the application are provided with default handling by the class associated with the control. The behaviors that are common to all controls are implemented by base classes. For example, the *Control* base class provides a basic implementation of everything a Windows Forms control is required to do, including managing a window handle from the operating system and providing a user interface. As mentioned, the *ButtonBase* class implements the default behavior for all button controls.

Event Handling Architecture

Each control class in the .NET Framework exposes a large number of events that are used to send event notifications to a Windows Forms application. Many of these events are defined by the *Control* base class, and most of the descendants of *Control* add events that are specific to each type of control.

Although Windows Forms controls expose dozens of events, you'll probably handle only a few of these events routinely. Some events, such as the *Click* event raised by a button control, almost always will be handled each time the control is used. Many of the other events are exposed to enable you to properly subclass controls and provide appropriate behavior. For example, whenever control properties such as the background color, location, and size are changed, an event is raised. Although you'll rarely need to handle these events in a form that contains only *Button* or *TextBox* objects, derived classes can use these events to update their appearance to properly reflect underlying properties.

The button control is one of the most commonly used controls in a Windows Forms application. The most commonly handled events raised by the *Button* class are as follows:

- ■ **_Click_** Fires when the user has clicked the control or selected the control using other means

- ■ **_Disposed_** Fires when the _Dispose_ method of the control has been invoked

- ■ **_DoubleClick_** Fires when the user has double-clicked the control

- ■ **_GotFocus_** Fires when the control has acquired keyboard input focus

- ■ **_LostFocus_** Fires when the control has lost keyboard input focus

- ■ **_TextChanged_** Fires when the control's _Text_ property has changed

- ■ **_Validated_** Fires when the control's contents have been validated

- ■ **_Validating_** Fires when the control's contents are being validated

Keep in mind that this is only a partial list of the events available to Windows Forms controls. Many of the control classes provide additional events specific to the characteristics of each control. These additional events will be discussed with the relevant controls in later sections and in the remainder of Part III. There are also additional events that are used to implement specific functionality. For example, if you implement drag and drop for one or more controls, a number of events must be handled. In a similar way, interaction using the mouse involves the management of various mouse movement events. Although these events aren't discussed in this chapter, the remaining chapters in Part III will introduce the events required to interact with various Windows Forms features.

Adding New Event Handlers

You subscribe to an event by creating an event handler and associating it with a specific event. You can use several approaches to handle events. One straightforward approach is to define a method that conforms to the event handler signature and then programmatically add the event handler to the control, as shown here:

```
public ButtonForm()
{
    ⋮
    closeButton.Click += new EventHandler(OnButtonClicked);
}

private void OnButtonClicked(object sender, EventArgs e)
{
    MessageBox.Show("I've been clicked");
}
```

The Windows Forms Designer can be used to automatically define an event handler method and wire it to an appropriate event. If you double-click on a form or control in the Forms Designer, an event handler method will be created for you and will automatically be wired to handle the default event for the control. The source code editor will be opened automatically, with the insertion point positioned in the new event handler method. If an event handler is already defined for the default event, the source code editor will be opened with the insertion point positioned in the existing event handler.

Because each control handles a large number of events, the Windows Forms Designer will automatically generate an event handler for the control's default event, which is the event that you're most likely to handle. For example, if you double-click any of the button controls, a handler for the *Click* event will be created. If you double-click a text box control, an event handler for the *Text-Changed* event will be created. If you double-click the form surface, the Forms Designer will create a handler for the form's *Load* event.

When the Forms Designer creates an event handler method for you, it follows the naming convention *objectname_eventname* for the new method. So a method that handles the *Click* event for a *Button* object named *closeButton* is named *closeButton_Click*. To wire the event handler, the Windows Forms Designer adds code to your Visual C# source file in two places. First it creates a method that conforms to the event's delegate signature, as shown here:

```
private void closeBtn_Click(object sender, System.EventArgs e)
{
    ⋮
}
```

Next the Windows Forms Designer creates an event handler delegate and assigns it to the relevant object, as shown here:

```
this.closeBtn.Click += new System.EventHandler(this.closeBtn_Click);
```

This code is located in the form's *InitializeComponent* method, which is found in the code region that's collapsed by default when the source file is viewed in the Visual C# Code Editor.

The Windows Forms Designer isn't limited to creating handlers for default events; it can be used to create event handler methods for any event raised by a control. To view the events that are exposed by the control, click the Events icon in the Properties window, as shown in Figure 12-4.

As you can see in the figure, event names are shown on the left side of the Properties window and the names of any event handlers are shown on the right side. Double-click any event handler listed on the right side of the window, and the source code editor will open with the insertion point positioned at the event handler method.

Figure 12-4.   The Properties window, displaying events as well as properties.

To add a new event handler, enter the event handler's name in the space adjacent to the event with which it should be associated. Using the name entered in the Properties window, the Windows Forms Designer will create an event handler for you and will take care of wiring the method to the control or form's event through a delegate. Alternatively, you can double-click the event listed in the Properties window, and an event handler will be created using *objectname_eventname* as the name of the event handler. Using the Properties window to add an event guarantees that the event handler will have the proper signature and will be correctly subscribed to the desired event with just a few keystrokes.

When a form contains multiple controls of the same type, it's a simple matter to use a single event handler for all of the controls. The event handler's *sender* parameter can be used to determine the control that sent the event, as shown here:

```
private void OnClick(object sender, System.EventArgs e)
{
    Button clickedButton = (Button)sender;
    switch(clickedButton.Name)
    {
        case "standardButton":
            MessageBox.Show("Standard button clicked");
            break;

        case "popupButton":
            MessageBox.Show("Popup button clicked");
            break;
```

(continued)

```
         case "flatButton":
             MessageBox.Show("Flat button clicked");
             break;

         default:
             MessageBox.Show("Unknown button clicked");
             break;
     }
 }
```

In this code, three push buttons—*standardButton*, *popupButton*, and *flatButton*—are using the *OnClick* method as the event handler for their *Click* event. The *OnClick* method begins by casting the *sender* parameter to a *Button* reference; it then displays different messages based on the sending button control's *Name* property.

To route additional events to an existing handler, simply create a new delegate and associate it with the desired method, as shown here:

```
EventHandler clickHandler = new EventHandler(OnClick);
standardButton.Click += clickHandler;
popupButton.Click += clickHandler;
flatButton.Click += clickHandler;
```

The Properties window can be used to easily assign multiple events to a single handler. When an event is selected in the Properties window, a drop-down button is displayed on the right side of the cell. Click the drop-down button to display a list of all event handler methods that are capable of handling the event, and then select an event handler from the list to route the event to an existing method.

Removing Event Handlers

Removing an event handler at run time follows the steps outlined in Chapter 6 for removing any delegate or event handler. You must use the subtraction with assignment operator (− =), passing an instance of the delegate to be removed, as shown here:

```
flatButton.Click -= new EventHandler(OnClick);
```

Although the code to remove a delegate is somewhat counterintuitive at first glance, it follows the delegate and event handler view of equality: two delegates are equivalent if they're associated with the same method.

Translating Key Presses into Button Clicks

One way that Windows Forms differ from Win32 dialog boxes is that forms don't automatically route key presses when the user presses the Enter and

Esc keys. As part of the default behavior that all Win32 modal dialog boxes share, pressing the Enter key is translated into a click of the OK button, and pressing the Esc key is translated into a click of the Cancel button. Although the default behavior for Windows Forms doesn't perform this translation, the following properties can be used to achieve the same result:

- ***AcceptButton***   Specifies a button that will be clicked when the user presses Enter

- ***CancelButton***   Specifies a button that will be clicked when the user presses Esc

Assuming that your form has an OK button named *okButton*, you can use code such as the following to enable a user to click the button by pressing the Enter key:

```
AcceptButton = okButton;
```

The following code causes a *Click* event for a button named *cancelButton* when the user presses Esc:

```
CancelButton = cancelButton;
```

Validating the Contents of Controls

All Windows Forms controls expose events that enable you to easily validate their contents. As mentioned, every control exposes two validation events: *Validating* and *Validated*.

Because the *Form* class is a descendant of *Control*, all forms also expose the validation events. For a validation event to be raised for a control, its *CausesValidation* property must be set to *true*, which is the default value. You can take advantage of control validation in either of two ways: you can manage the validation events for each control that requires validation, or you can manage the validation events at the form level.

The first approach requires you to provide validation event handlers for each control that requires validation. By explicitly providing an event handler for the *Validating* event, you indicate your interest in validating input for a specific control. A typical event handler for the *Validating* event is shown here:

```
private void OnValidating(object sender, CancelEventArgs e)
{
    if(itemTextBox.Text.Length == 0)
    {
        e.Cancel = true;
        MessageBox.Show("You must provide a value for the new item.",
                "Validation failure",
```

(continued)

```
                        MessageBoxButtons.OK,
                        MessageBoxIcon.Hand);
    }
    else
    {
        _newItem = itemTextBox.Text;
    }
}
```

As shown in this code, the validation handler tests the user's input and displays an error message if the input is invalid. In addition, the handler interacts with the *CancelEventArgs* object passed to it as a parameter. By setting the object's *Cancel* property to *true*, the event handler prevents further processing of the event. This has the effect of keeping the keyboard input focus unchanged and will prevent the user from dismissing the form.

One problem with tying a validation event handler to a particular control is that it tends to complicate the user's interaction with your form. The event handler for *Validating* will be called whenever focus is removed from the control or when the form is dismissed. If the user simply tabs away from the control, your validation handler will be called; if this behavior is what you're looking for, tie your validation handler to the specific control you want to validate. Another problem is that you must handle validation for each control separately, which leads to more complex validation code.

The second approach to handling validation events is used to perform validation at the form level instead of at the control level. In the majority of validation scenarios, you're interested in validating input only when the user is dismissing the form and explicitly accepts the current control values, usually by clicking an OK or Apply button. When the user clicks the Cancel button in a modal dialog box, there's usually no reason to perform validation.

By attaching a validation handler to a central location, you can validate user input for the entire form rather than a specific control, which allows users to provide input as they see fit, with validation occurring only when the user is ready to submit. If the user dismisses a modal form with an OK button to confirm input, you can attach the validation handler to the form. Alternatively, if the user clicks an Apply or a Confirm button that leaves the form displayed, you should attach the validation handler to the button control clicked by the user.

Any controls that shouldn't trigger validation events must have their *CausesValidation* property set to *false*, as shown here:

```
cancelButton.CausesValidation = false;
```

As with other properties, you can simply set the *Validation* property for the control to *false* through the Properties window.

In a similar vein, if the user clicks the Close icon in the form's caption to cancel the dialog box, you'll also want to prevent validation. To prevent validation in this case, you must inhibit validation for the form, as shown here:

```
// Form constructor
public AddListBoxItemForm()
{
    ⋮
    CausesValidation = false;
}
```

Alternatively, you can set the *Validation* property to *false* for the form using the Properties window, as is done with other controls.

Using the *TextBox* Class

Other commonly used controls include the text box control, the list box control, and the combo box control. Although these controls present a different appearance than the button controls described earlier in this chapter, they share many of the same characteristics. Many of the properties exposed by button controls are used with other controls, and most events raised by the button control are also raised by the controls we'll examine in this section and the following sections.

The text box control is used to create a standard Windows edit control, also known as a text box. The text box control is most often used to accept text input from the user and is probably the most commonly used control after the ubiquitous push button control. The *TextBox* class is used to manage text box controls and is a subclass of the *TextBoxBase* class. The *TextBoxBase* class serves as the parent class for the *TextBox* and *RichTextBox* classes and contains the properties and methods common to all text input controls. (The *RichText-Box* class will be discussed in Chapter 15.)

The text entered in a text box control by the user is available through the *Text* property, as shown here:

```
string newItem = itemTextBox.Text;
int itemLength = itemTextBox.TextLength;
```

As shown in this example, you can retrieve the length of the text stored in the text box control by using the *TextLength* property. You also can set the text displayed in the control by assigning a string value to the *Text* property of the *TextBox* instance, as shown here:

```
itemTextBox.Text = "Elvis has left the building";
```

To remove the text in a text box control, call the *TextBox.Clear* method, as shown here:

```
itemTextBox.Clear();
```

In addition to the *Clear* method, the *TextBox* class also offers full support for interaction with the clipboard, including the ability to cut, copy, and paste. Using the cut and paste functions exposed by the *TextBox* class is discussed in Chapter 17.

The text box control exposes the *TextChanged* event, which is raised each time the text in the control is changed. This event is useful when another control must be updated based on the current contents of the text box, as shown here:

```
public TextBoxForm()
{
    ⋮
    textBox.TextChanged += new EventHandler(textBox_TextChanged);
}
private void textBox_TextChanged(object sender, System.EventArgs e)
{
    label.Text = "Contents: " + textBox.Text;
}
```

In this example, the value of the *label* control is updated whenever the contents of the *textBox* control are updated.

Hiding Passwords in a Text Box Control

When a password or other sensitive information is entered in a text box control, the user's input is typically hidden to protect the information from prying eyes. To mask the characters entered in a text box control, use the *PasswordChar* property to specify a masking symbol for the text box. The following code sets the *PasswordChar* property to an asterisk (*):

```
passwordTextBox.PasswordChar = '*';
```

Working with Multiline Text Box Controls

When a text box control is dropped on a Windows Form using the Windows Forms Designer, initially the control can be resized horizontally but not vertically. This is because the default behavior for a text box control is to support the entry of a single line of text. To accept multiple lines, the *TextBox* class's *Multiline* property must be set to *true*, as shown here:

```
multilineTextBox.Multiline = true;
```

When working with an instance of the *TextBox* class that supports multiple lines, you can elect to have the text for each line extend past the far edge of the control or wrap automatically to the next line at the control boundary. This behavior is controlled by the control's *WordWrap* property, which will wrap long text lines into paragraphs if set to *true* or extend long lines if set to *false*, as shown in the following code. The default value is *true*.

```
multilineTextBox.WordWrap = false;
```

Scroll bars aren't automatically provided for *TextBox* objects. Although the user can use the keyboard's arrow keys to navigate a multiline control, in most cases you'll want to provide at least a vertical scroll bar to assist in navigation. Scroll bars are specified using the *TextBox* class's *ScrollBars* property, which must be assigned a value from the *ScrollBars* enumeration, shown in Table 12-4.

Table 12-4.   *ScrollBars* Enumeration Values

Value	Description
None	No scroll bars are displayed.
Horizontal	A horizontal scroll bar is displayed.
Vertical	A vertical scroll bar is displayed.
Both	Both horizontal and vertical scroll bars are displayed.

A horizontal scroll bar is never displayed if the control's *WordWrap* property is set to *true*.

There are two ways to retrieve the text from a multiline *TextBox* object. The first approach, shown here, is to use the *Text* property, as is done with single-line *TextBox* objects:

```
string str = multilineTextBox.Text;
MessageBox.Show(str);
```

Another way to extract the text from a multiline control is to use the *Lines* property, which returns an array of strings, with each array element referring to a text line, as shown here:

```
private void getContents_Click(object sender, System.EventArgs e)
{
    string [] strs = multilineTextBox.Lines;
    foreach(string line in strs)
    {
        MessageBox.Show(line, "Line-by-line display");
    }
}
```

The elements in the *Lines* array don't necessarily reflect the physical lines in the control. If word wrapping is enabled, a single line of text can occupy multiple physical lines in the control but is only one element in the *Lines* array.

You also can use the *Lines* property in the Properties window to provide the initial text for a multiline text box control. If you select the *Lines* property in the Properties window, a small push button will be displayed, with a caption that consists of an ellipsis (…). If you click this button, the String Collection Editor dialog box will be displayed, in which you can enter the initial text for the control.

Using Other Text Box Properties

When you're working with a multiline text box, it's not unusual to use the Tab and Enter keys to format the text input. By default, however, these keys have special meaning in a form. If a button is specified in the form's *AcceptButton* property, that button will be clicked when the user presses the Enter key, which usually results in closing the form. If the user presses the Tab key, the input focus will move to the next control in the tab order. The *TextBox* class exposes two properties that enable you to override this default behavior, as follows:

- **AcceptsReturn**   If set to *true*, this property specifies that pressing the Enter key in the control will create a new line of text in the control. If set to *false*, this property specifies that pressing the Enter key will activate the default button for the form. The default value is *false*.

- **AcceptsTab**   If set to *true*, this property specifies that pressing the Tab key in the control will enter a tab character in the control. If this property is set to *false*, the user can move the focus by pressing the Tab key. The default value is *false*.

> **Note**   If the *AcceptsReturn* property is *false*, the user can create a new line in a control by pressing Ctrl+Enter. When the *AcceptsTab* property is *true*, the user can move to the next control in the tab order by pressing Ctrl+Tab. These properties have no effect if the text box doesn't support multiple lines.

As with the button control, described earlier in this chapter, in the section "Using the Button Classes," you can control the appearance of a text box control. The appearance of a text box control is managed through the *BorderStyle* property, which must be set to one of the values from the *BorderStyle* enumeration, shown in Table 12-5.

Table 12-5. *BorderStyle* **Enumeration Values**

Value	Description
None	The control has no border.
Fixed3D	The control has a three-dimensional border.
FixedSingle	The control has an outline border.

By default, the *BorderStyle* property of *TextBox* objects is set to *Fixed3D*. The following code changes the *BorderStyle* property to *FixedSingle*, resulting in a control that has a flat appearance:

```
printerTextBox.BorderStyle = BorderStyle.FixedSingle;
```

Using the *Label* Class

The *Label* class is used to create a descriptive label that's placed on a form. *Label* controls are typically associated with specific controls and are used to name controls such as text boxes that don't have their own captions. Although the *Label* class has many of the same properties exposed by other controls— such as *BackColor*, *ForeColor*, and *Text*—the *Label* class is typically used as a static control. You'll rarely program against the *Label* class directly, except perhaps to change the control's caption text, as shown here:

```
label.Text = "Contents have been updated";
```

A Windows Forms label control has one unusual feature—it can never receive the input focus. Instead, it passes the focus to the next control in the tab order. For this reason, label controls associated with a text box or other control are usually placed immediately ahead of their associated control and are provided with a caption that includes an ampersand before the character that is to be the shortcut key. This enables a user to use Alt + the shortcut key to select the control associated with the label.

Using the *LinkLabel* Class

The *LinkLabel* class is similar to the *Label* class. Instead of providing only a descriptive label, however, a *LinkLabel* object has the appearance of an HTML hyperlink on a Web page. This control is often used to provide a link to a relevant Web page or as a navigation control for forms that employ a Web-like user interface.

Handling the *Click* Event

A *LinkLabel* object has some of the same properties exposed by the *Button* and *Label* classes. For example, the caption displayed by the *LinkLabel* object is set with the *Text* property, as shown here:

```
linkLabel.Text = "Support Page";
```

The *LinkLabel* class raises a *LinkClicked* event when the user clicks the label control. To open a Web page in response to the event, use the *Process.Start* method from the *System.Diagnostics* namespace, as shown here:

```
private void linkLabel_LinkClicked(object sender,
                                   LinkLabelLinkClickedEventArgs e)
{
    Process.Start("http://www.microsoft.com");
}
```

In this example, the *Process.Start* method will open the user's Web browser and navigate to the specified URL.

Of course, you're not limited to simply navigating to a URL. In the *Link-Clicked* event handler, you also can open another form or take some other action, as shown here:

```
private void linkLabel_LinkClicked(object sender,
                                   LinkLabelLinkClickedEventArgs e)
{
    reservationForm = new ReservationForm();
    reservationForm.ShowDialog();
}
```

Unique *LinkLabel* Properties

The *LinkLabel* class has several properties that enable it to have the same characteristics as an HTML hyperlink. For example, you can define specific colors that will be used when drawing the link's text, depending on the link's state. The properties used to define the link colors are listed here:

- **ActiveLinkColor** Used to specify the color of a link that's in the process of being clicked
- **DisabledLinkColor** Used to specify the color of a link that's been disabled by setting the control's *Enabled* property to *false*
- **LinkColor** Used to specify the color of a link in its normal state, before it's been clicked or visited
- **VisitedLinkColor** Used to specify the color of a link that's been visited, which is specified via the *LinkVisited* property

The colors used by a *LinkLabel* object are typically set to different values, using either the Properties window or through code, as shown here:

```
public WebLookForm()
{
    ⋮
    linkLabel.ActiveLinkColor = Color.Lime;
    linkLabel.DisabledLinkColor = Color.DarkOrange;
    linkLabel.LinkColor = Color.DarkGreen;
    linkLabel.VisitedLinkColor = Color.DarkOliveGreen;
}
```

The default colors provided by the *LinkLabel* class are listed in Table 12-6.

Table 12-6.   *LinkLabel* **Default Colors**

Property	Enumeration Value	RGB Value
LinkColor	*Blue*	0, 0, 255
ActiveLinkColor	*Red*	255, 0, 0
DisabledLinkColor	(none)	143, 140, 127
VisitedLinkColor	*Purple*	128, 0, 128

The default color used for *DisabledLinkColor* is a variation of gray that isn't included in the *Color* enumeration.

A *LinkLabel* object has no built-in ability to know whether a link has been visited. Because navigation behavior for the control is really specified by the *LinkClicked* event handler that you implement, you're responsible for specifying whether the link has been visited. The following code is an example of setting the *LinkVisited* property to *true* inside the *LinkClicked* event handler:

```
private void linkLabel_LinkClicked(object sender,
                          LinkLabelLinkClickedEventArgs e)
{
    ⋮
    linkLabel.LinkVisited = true;
}
```

If you prefer not to provide a different link color for visited link label controls on your forms, simply refrain from setting the *LinkVisited* property.

By default, when you drop a *LinkLabel* control on a form, the entire control is clickable. Although this is often a reasonable way to use the *LinkLabel* control, there are times when it make sense to have just a portion of the control serve as a clickable link. The *LinkArea* property is used to define the portion of the control that's clickable and is set using the *LinkArea* class, as follows:

```
public WebLookForm()
{
    ⋮
    LinkArea range = new LinkArea(8, 4);
    linkLabel.LinkArea = range;
}
```

As shown in this code, the *LinkArea* class is initialized by passing two values to its constructor: the index where the clickable area begins and the clickable area's length.

In addition to specifying the region of the *LinkLabel* control that serves as the clickable region, you also can specify the appearance of the link using the *LinkBehavior* property. For example, you can specify that the link will be underlined only when the mouse pointer is over the control, as is done for many Web pages. Alternatively, you can elect to turn the underline off altogether, which is useful if you intend to stop processing *Click* events. The *Link-Behavior* property must be set to a value from the *LinkBehavior* enumeration, shown in Table 12-7.

Table 12-7.   *LinkBehavior* Enumeration Values

Value	Description
AlwaysUnderline	The clickable portion of the control is always underlined.
HoverUnderline	The clickable portion of the control is underlined only when the mouse pointer is over the control.
NeverUnderline	The control is never underlined.
SystemDefault	The control follows the system's default settings.

The default value for the *LinkBehavior* property is *SystemDefault*.

Using the *ListBox* Class

The *ListBox* class is used to create a list box control and provides access to all of the features that are available to a standard Win32 list box. In addition, the *ListBox* class neatly wraps up much of the functionality required to create an *owner-drawn list box*, so you can easily take over the task of rendering the list box and its items if you want to provide a different user interface for your control. An owner-drawn list box can include list items that contain information other than, or in addition to, text strings.

You don't directly interact with items stored in the list box control—instead, you'll usually work with the following list box collection classes, which are used to represent items stored in the list box:

- **ListBox.ObjectCollection**   Contains all items displayed in the list box control

- **ListBox.SelectedIndex**   Contains the index of each selected item in the list box control

- **ListBox.SelectedObjectCollection**   Contains a reference to each selected item in the list box control

- **ListBox.SelectedIndexCollection**   Contains the indexes to the selected items in the list box control

Of these classes, the one you'll most often use is *ListBox.ObjectCollection* because it contains an entry for each item in the list box. A reference to the collection is obtained through the *Items* property, like this:

```
private void RemoveItems(ListBox listBox)
{
    ListBox.ObjectCollection items = listBox.Items;
    if(items.Count != 0)
    {
        ⋮
    }
}
```

Typically, you won't extract and hold a reference to *ObjectCollection*; instead, you'll just use the *Items* property as if it were the actual collection, as shown in the following code, which determines the number of items in the list box:

```
private void RemoveItems(ListBox listBox)
{
    if(listBox.Items.Count != 0)
    {
        ⋮
    }
}
```

Adding Items to a List Box

To add an item to a list box, you must add a reference to the item to the *Object-Collection* object maintained by the *ListBox* class. To add an item at the end of the list box, use the *Add* method, as shown here:

```
private void newItem_Click(object sender, System.EventArgs e)
{
    AddListBoxItemForm dlg = new AddListBoxItemForm();
    DialogResult result = dlg.ShowDialog(this);
    if(result == DialogResult.OK)
```

(continued)

```
    {
        string newItem = dlg.NewItem;
        listBox.Items.Add(newItem);
    }
}
```

To add an item at a specific position in the list box, use the *Insert* method, passing a 0-based index for the new item, like this:

```
private void newItem_Click(object sender, System.EventArgs e)
{
    ⋮
    listBox.Items.Insert(0, newItem);
}
```

You must be sure that the index passed to *Insert* is a valid index for inserting items into the list box. The index must be no smaller than 0 and no larger than the number of items currently in the list box. If you pass a smaller or larger value as the index, an *ArgumentOutOfRangeException* exception will be thrown.

When adding multiple items to a list box, you can optimize your interaction with the *ListBox* class by using the *AddRange* method, which enables you to add multiple items at once. There are two overloaded versions of *AddRange*. The following code passes an array of objects to *AddRange*, which will insert each array element into the list box:

```
private void InitListBox()
{
    string [] names = {"Rob", "John", "Alice", "Jen", "Gwen" };
    listBox.Items.AddRange(names);
}
```

You also can pass a reference to an existing *ListBox.ObjectCollection* instance, which simplifies the task of copying list box contents from one control to another, as shown here:

```
private void CopyLeftToRight()
{
    rightListBox.Items.AddRange(leftListBox.Items);
}
```

You're not limited to adding simple strings to a list box. Instances of more complex types can be added. As long as the types override the *ToString* method, the *ListBox* class will insert the string returned from the *ToString* method into the list box control. For example, consider a class declaration such as the following:

```
public class Sailboat
{
    public Sailboat(string name, int length)
    {
        _name = name;
        _length = length;
    }
    public string Name
    {
        set { _name = value; }
        get { return _name; }
    }
    public int Length
    {
        set { _length = value; }
        get { return _length; }
    }
    override public string ToString()
    {
        return _name;
    }
    string _name;
    int    _length;
}
```

Because the *Sailboat* class overrides the *ToString* method, *Sailboat* objects can be added to the list box, as shown here:

```
private void newBoat_Click(object sender, System.EventArgs e)
{
    Sailboat larrysBoat = new Sailboat("Sayonara", 65);
    Sailboat phillipesBoat = new Sailboat("Pegasus", 40);
    listBox.Items.Add(larrysBoat);
    listBox.Items.Add(phillipesBoat);
}
```

The *ListBox* class will invoke *Sailboat.ToString* and add the sailboat's name to the list box control.

Removing Items from a List Box

To remove an item from a list box, you must remove the item from the *ListBox* object's collection of items. To remove an item at a specific location, pass the item's index to the *RemoveAt* method, as shown here:

```
listBox.Items.RemoveAt(index);
```

The index passed to *RemoveAt* must be within the valid range for the current list box, with a value not less than 0 and no larger than the index of the last item in the list box. If an invalid index is passed to *RemoveAt*, an *ArgumentOutOf-RangeException* exception will be thrown.

If you have a reference to the object to be removed, you can pass an object reference to the *Remove* method, which will search through the items stored in the collection and remove the first object in the collection that's equivalent to the object passed as a parameter, as shown here:

```
listBox.Items.Remove(larrysBoat);
```

The *Clear* method provides an efficient way to remove every item in the list box:

```
listBox.Items.Clear();
```

Preventing Repainting When Updating a List Box

When an item is added to or removed from a list box, the list box is repainted. The preferred way to add multiple items to a list box is to use the *AddRange* method, which enables you to add multiple items in a single operation. However, you might need to add items to the list box one at a time and call *Add* or *Insert* once for each item to be added. Also, there's no method to remove multiple items in a single call. This can be a problem if you're adding or removing multiple items from the list box, as the repainting can become distracting.

To avoid unnecessary repainting, use the *BeginUpdate* and *EndUpdate* methods, as shown here:

```
private void updateListBox()
{
    listBox.BeginUpdate();
    foreach(SailboatSlip slip in Marina)
    {
        listBox.Items.Add(slip.boat);
    }
    listBox.EndUpdate();
}
```

As shown in this example, the *BeginUpdate* method turns off the redrawing of the list box control. After all of the items have been updated, the *EndUpdate* method is called to redraw the list box and restore its default behavior.

Selecting List Box Items

There are a number of ways to interact with the selected items in a list box. You can elect to retrieve either index information about the items selected in a list box or references to the objects that underlie the selected items.

> **Note**   The default behavior for a list box is to allow at most one item to be selected at any given time. As you'll see later in this chapter, in the section "Using Other List Box Properties," a list box can easily be made to accept multiple selections.

Retrieving the Selected Index

To retrieve the index of the currently selected item, use the *SelectedIndex* property. This property will return *−1* if no item is selected; otherwise, it returns the index value of the selected item. The following code illustrates how the *SelectedItem* property is typically used to determine which item should be affected by an operation on the list box—in this case, the selected item is removed:

```
if(listBox.Items.Count != 0)
{
    int index = listBox.SelectedIndex;
    if(index != -1)
    {
        listBox.Items.RemoveAt(index);
    }
    else
    {
        MessageBox.Show("You must select an item to remove",
                    "Can't remove item",
                    MessageBoxButtons.OK,
                    MessageBoxIcon.Hand);
    }
}
else
{
    MessageBox.Show("The list box is empty",
                "Nothing to remove",
                MessageBoxButtons.OK,
                MessageBoxIcon.Hand);
}
```

If the list box supports multiple selections, the *SelectedIndex* property will return the index of one of the selected items. The *SelectedIndex* property is useful when further work on the control is anticipated, such as removing the currently selected item based on its index. However, there are times when you really want to retrieve the object stored in the list box rather than its index—in these cases, you can use the *SelectedItem* property.

Retrieving a Reference to the Selected Item

The *SelectedItem* property returns a reference to the object that underlies the selected item in the list box. For example, if a list box contains *Sailboat* objects, the following code returns the *Sailboat* object that's currently selected by the user:

```
Sailboat boat = (Sailboat)listBox.SelectedItem;
if(boat)
{
    ⋮
}
```

As with the *SelectedIndex* property, *SelectedItem* will return one of the selected items if the list box supports multiple selections.

Working with Multiple-Selection List Boxes

When dealing with a list box that supports multiple selections, you can choose to retrieve the set of selected indexes or items. To fetch the selected indexes for a list box, use the *SelectedIndices* property, as shown here:

```
ListBox.SelectedIndexCollection indices = listBox.SelectedIndices;
```

Because many items can be selected in a multiple-selection list box at any given time, the *SelectedIndices* property returns an instance of *SelectedIndex-Collection*, which contains the indexes of all items currently selected in the list box. The following code provides an example of how you can use the *Selected-IndexCollection* object to determine the currently selected indexes:

```
ListBox.SelectedIndexCollection indices = listBox.SelectedIndices;
foreach(int index in indices)
{
    Trace.WriteLine("Selected index - " + index.ToString());
}
```

Watch out for code such as the following. If you modify the contents of the list box, the *SelectedIndexCollection* is updated as the loop progresses, and you won't remove the items you expect.

```
ListBox.SelectedIndexCollection indices = listBox.SelectedIndices;
int selected = indices.Count;
if(indices.Count > 0)
{
    foreach(int index in indices)
    {
        listBox.Items.RemoveAt(index);
    }
}
```

In this code, the first iteration of the loop removes the first selected item and then sets index to the value of the second selected item. Because one selected item has already been removed, however, one item has been skipped. As items are removed from the list box, the *foreach* loop skips past every second selected item. You can avoid this problem by removing items in reverse order, as shown in the following code:

```
ListBox.SelectedIndexCollection indices = listBox.SelectedIndices;
int selected = indices.Count;
if(indices.Count > 0)
{
    for(int n = selected - 1; n >= 0; n--)
    {
        int index = indices[n];
        listBox.Items.RemoveAt(index);
    }
}
```

By removing indexes in reverse order, as shown here, the collection ordering remains valid and the proper items are removed from the list.

Another way to reference multiple selected items in a list box is to use the *SelectedItems* property. This property returns an instance of *SelectedObjectCollection*, which is used much like *SelectedIndexCollection* except that it stores a reference to each selected item instead of its index. As shown in the following code, this enables you to perform operations on the objects stored in the list box:

```
ListBox.SelectedObjectCollection selectedItems = listBox.SelectedItems;
foreach(Sailboat boat in selectedItems)
{
    DisplayBoatInfo(boat);
}
```

Selecting Items Programmatically

Although items in a list box are typically selected by the user, you can also select items programmatically. A simple way to set an item as selected is to use the *SelectedIndex* property, as shown here:

```
listBox.SelectedIndex = 3;
```

You can't clear the selection state of a single item in a multiple-selection list box using the *SelectedIndex* property, but you can clear all of the selected items for any type of list box by setting the *SelectedIndex* property to −1, as shown here:

```
listBox.SelectedIndex = -1;
```

A more flexible way to select or deselect an item is to use the *SetSelected* method, passing the item's index and a Boolean value that represents the selection state, as shown in this example:

```
listBox.SetSelected(0, true);
```

The *SetSelected* method works with the current selection mode of the list box. For single-selection list boxes, a selection of a new item will deselect any currently selected item. For list boxes that support multiple selections, selecting a new item doesn't automatically deselect any currently selected items.

Handling Selection Events

It's often useful to know exactly when selections in a list box control have changed. For example, if you provide help text or populate additional controls based on the current list box selection, you can immediately update your user interface when the user selects a new item. Three selection events are raised by the *ListBox* class, as follows:

- *SelectedIndexChanged*
- *SelectedValueChanged*
- *DoubleClick*

The first two events are raised whenever an item is selected or deselected in the list box control. These events receive the generic *EventArgs* parameter, with no information about the newly selected or deselected items. Instead, you're expected to use these events to trigger a reexamination of the list box to determine which item or items are currently selected.

A *DoubleClick* event is generated when an item in the list box is double-clicked by the user. *DoubleClick* is often used as shown in the following code:

```
private void listBox_DoubleClick(object sender, System.EventArgs e)
{
    Sailboat boat = (Sailboat)listBox.SelectedItem;
    string message = string.Format("Sailboat: {0}, length: {1}",
                                   boat.Name,
                                   boat.Length);
    MessageBox.Show(message);
}
```

In this example, the *MessageBox.Show* method displays a new form that contains information based on the selected item. This is a common shortcut that helps to simplify navigation for experienced users.

Using Other List Box Properties

The *ListBox* class exposes a number of other useful properties that simplify your interaction with list box controls. The more commonly used *ListBox* properties are listed here:

- **MultiColumn**   Enables the display of items in multiple columns
- **SelectionMode**   Enables you to define how items are selected in the list box
- **Sorted**   Enables automatic sorting of list box items
- **TopIndex**   Sets or returns the topmost visible item in the list box

The *MultiColumn* property enables the list box to display items in multiple columns within the list box. When this property is set to *true*, as shown in the following code, items will be displayed in as many columns as required to avoid the need for vertical scrolling:

```
listBox.MultiColumn = true;
```

Normally, the width of each column is set to a default value. You can specify a value using the *ColumnWidth* property, however, passing the number of pixels required for the width, as shown here:

```
listBox.ColumnWidth = 100;
```

The *SelectionMode* property determines how list box items are selected. Values for this property are taken from the *SelectionMode* enumeration, shown in Table 12-8.

Table 12-8.   *SelectionMode* Enumeration Values

Value	Description
None	No items can be selected.
One	One item at a time can be selected.
MultiExtended	Multiple items can be selected by using the mouse with the Ctrl, Shift, and arrow keys.
MultiSimple	Multiple items in the list box can be selected by simply clicking them; they're deselected if clicked again.

The *SelectionMode* property has a default value of *SelectionMode.One*.

By default, items in a list box aren't sorted. However, it's often convenient to sort the items in a list box. If the user is expected to select items in a list box, the task is generally much easier when the items are ordered. The *ListBox* class exposes the *Sorted* property, which, when set to *true*, automatically keeps a list box control properly sorted alphabetically, as shown here:

```
private void sortCheckBox_CheckedChanged(object sender,
                                         System.EventArgs e)
{
    listBox.Sorted = sortCheckBox.Checked;
}
```

In this example, a *CheckedChanged* event handler for a check box control is used to specify the sorting behavior for the list box. When the user selects the check box, the list box is sorted. When the check box is cleared, the order of items in the list box is no longer preserved.

Using the *CheckedListBox* Class

The *CheckedListBox* class creates a list box control that includes a check box to the left of each list box item, as shown in Figure 12-5.

Figure 12-5.   A checked list box, which includes a check box for each list box item.

The *CheckedListBox* class is derived from *ListBox*, adding functionality that enables you to interact with the check boxes in the list box.

The *CheckedListBox* class is similar to the *ListBox* class, and any code that targets a *ListBox* object should work with an instance of *CheckedListBox*. Because the *CheckedListBox* class is derived from *ListBox*, all of the properties, collections, events, and methods associated with the *ListBox* class described earlier in this chapter are exposed and available to you through the *CheckedListBox* class.

Checking Items in a Checked List Box

The appearance of the check boxes associated with each item in a checked list box is controlled by the *ThreeDCheckBoxes* property. By default, this property is set to *false*, which results in a check box that has a flat appearance. If the *ThreeDCheckBoxes* property is set to *true*, as shown in the following code, the check box is given a chiseled, three-dimensional look.

```
listBox.ThreeDCheckBoxes = true;
```

By default, the user must click once to select an item and then click again to toggle the status of the check box, effectively requiring two clicks to check an item. The *CheckOnClick* property can be used to alter this behavior. The following code enables the check box status for an item in the control to be toggled each time the user selects an item with the first click:

```
listBox.CheckOnClick = true;
```

The *CheckedListBox* class maintains collections that can be used to interact with the checked items in the control, as follows:

- **CheckedListBox.CheckedItemCollection**   Stores references to all items that have a checked or an indeterminate state

- **CheckedListBox.CheckedIndexCollection**   Stores the indexes of all items that have a checked or an indeterminate state

To retrieve a reference to *CheckedItemCollection*, use the *CheckedItems* property, as shown here:

```
CheckedListBox.CheckedItemCollection ci = checkedListBox.CheckedItems;
```

The *CheckedIndices* property is used to retrieve a reference to *CheckedIndexCollection*, as shown here:

```
CheckedListBox.CheckedIndexCollection ci = null;
ci = checkedListBox.CheckedIndices;
```

To determine whether a particular item is checked, use the *GetItemChecked* property, as shown here:

```
bool isChecked = checkedListBox.GetItemChecked(index);
```

The *GetItemChecked* property returns the value *true* or *false*. If an item's check box is checked or in the indeterminate state, the property returns *true*. Because all items in a checked list box can reflect three states, you can use the *GetItemCheckState* property to return a high-fidelity view of the check box state, as shown here:

```
CheckState chkState = checkedListBox.GetItemCheckState(index);
```

The *GetItemCheckState* property returns a value from the *CheckState* enumeration, shown earlier in this chapter, in Table 12-3.

Handling Events from the Checked List Box

In addition to the commonly handled events discussed earlier for the list box control, a checked list box will raise an *ItemCheck* event when the state of an item's check box changes. A handler for the *ItemCheck* event receives an *ItemCheckEventArgs* object as a parameter. Derived from *EventArgs*, this class has three properties related to the event, as follows:

- **Index**   The index of the item that raised the event ,

- **CurrentValue**   The *CheckState* value representing the current state of the check box

- **NewValue**   The *CheckState* value representing the new state of the check box

These properties can be used as shown in the following code when handling the *ItemCheck* event:

```
private void OnItemCheck(object sender,
                        System.Windows.Forms.ItemCheckEventArgs e)
{
    int index = e.Index;
    if(e.NewValue == CheckState.Checked)
    {
        Sailboat boat = (Sailboat)checkedListBox.Items[index];
        string msg = string.Format("Add {0} to the list of sold boats?",
                                    boat.Name);
        DialogResult result = MessageBox.Show(msg,
                                    "Confirm",
                                    MessageBoxButtons.YesNo,
                                    MessageBoxIcon.Question);
        if(result == DialogResult.Yes)
        {
            // Sell the boat.
            listBox.Items.Add(boat);
        }
    }
}
```

In this example, the *ItemCheckEventArgs* object, *e*, is passed with information about the object that's been checked in the list box. The *OnItemCheck* event handler extracts the index and new *CheckState* value for the clicked item. After the object has been extracted from the list box, the user is asked to confirm by clicking the check box control. If the user confirms by clicking the message box's Yes button, the item is added to a second list box.

Using the *ComboBox* Class

The *ComboBox* class is used to create a combo box control, a control that combines a text box control with a list box. The *ComboBox* class is derived from *List-Control*, which is the parent class of the *ListBox* control discussed earlier in this chapter. The combo box control is often used in cases in which it's convenient to offer the user a selection from multiple choices in the list box portion of the control, without requiring the space used by a list box. The combo box control also offers a variety of styles that control its behavior, such as whether the list box is shown or whether the text in the text box control can be modified.

Using Combo Box Properties

Because a combo box control consists of a list box and a text box control, it comes as no surprise that many of the properties exposed by the *ComboBox* class are shared with either the *ListBox* or the *TextBox* class. For example, the *ComboBox* class maintains a collection of items stored in the list box portion of the control. Although this is technically a different class from the collection used by the *ListBox* class—the type is *ComboBox.ObjectCollection* in this case—the collection is referenced through the *Items* property, just as with the *ListBox* control. The following code contains methods that add and remove items stored in a combo box control:

```
private void newItem_Click(object sender, System.EventArgs e)
{
    AddComboItemForm dlg = new AddComboItemForm();
    DialogResult result = dlg.ShowDialog(this);
    if(result == DialogResult.OK)
    {
        string newItem = dlg.NewItem;
        combo.Items.Add(newItem);
    }
}
private void removeItem_Click(object sender, System.EventArgs e)
{
    int index = combo.SelectedIndex;
    if(index != -1)
    {
        combo.Items.RemoveAt(index);
    }
    else
```

(continued)

```
        {
            MessageBox.Show("You must select an item to remove",
                            "Can't remove item",
                            MessageBoxButtons.OK,
                            MessageBoxIcon.Hand);
        }
    }
}
```

As with the *ListBox* class, the *ComboBox* class exposes the *SelectedItem* and *SelectedIndex* properties for determining which item is selected in the combo box control, as shown here:

```
int index = combo.SelectedIndex;
string name = (string)combo.SelectedItem;
```

Unlike the *ListBox* class, *ComboBox* doesn't support multiple selection of items in its list box.

As with a text box, the text displayed in the text box section of the combo box is retrieved using the *Text* property, as shown here:

```
string name = combo.Text;
```

The combo box offers a flexible appearance that's controlled by properties and can be changed at run time. The default style for a combo box is to supply a drop-down list box with the text box control. The *DropDownStyle* property is used to define the style for the combo box, and it's set to one of the values from the *ComboBoxStyle* enumeration, shown in Table 12-9.

Table 12-9.   *ComboBoxStyle* **Enumeration Values**

Value	Description
Simple	The list box portion of the control is always visible, and the text box control can be edited by the user.
DropDown	The list box portion of the control is normally hidden, and the text box control can be edited by the user. This is the default style.
DropDownList	The list box portion of the control is normally hidden, and the text box control can't be edited by the user.

The control's style can be changed at run time because of the stateless nature of Windows Forms, as discussed earlier in this chapter, in the section "Controlling Button Appearance with Properties." Other properties that affect the appearance of the control are as follows:

■ **_DropDownWidth_**   Specifies the width in pixels of the drop-down portion of the combo box

- ■ ***DroppedDown***   Specifies a Boolean value that indicates whether the drop-down list should be shown

- ■ ***Height***   Specifies the height in pixels of a simple combo box

- ■ ***MaxDropDownItems***   Specifies the number of items to be shown in the drop-down portion of the combo box

The following code uses many of the property styles to change the style of a combo box at run time. This code is taken from the Controls example project included on the companion CD.

```
private void dropDownRadio_CheckedChanged(object sender,
                                          System.EventArgs e)
{
    combo.DropDownStyle = ComboBoxStyle.DropDown;
}

private void dropDownListRadio_CheckedChanged(object sender,
                                              System.EventArgs e)
{
    combo.DropDownStyle = ComboBoxStyle.DropDownList;
}

private void simpleRadio_CheckedChanged(object sender,
                                        System.EventArgs e)
{
    combo.DropDownStyle = ComboBoxStyle.Simple;
    combo.Height = 80;
}
```

In this code, the *Height* property for the combo box is set when the style is changed to the simple combo box style. The default height for other combo box styles is the height of the text box control. When the style is switched to a simple combo box, the height is used to determine the height of the entire control. If you change from one of the other combo box styles to a simple style combo box and keep the default height, the items in the drop-down portion of the simple combo box won't be visible.

Handling Combo Box Events

Most of the events raised by a combo box control are also raised by the list box and text box controls. For example, the *SelectedIndexChanged* and *SelectedValueChanged* events are raised when a new item is selected in the list box portion of the control. The *TextChanged* event fires when the contents of the text box are changed.

In addition to these commonly used events, the *ComboBox* class exposes its own set of unique events. The most commonly handled of these events are listed here:

- **DropDown**   The drop-down list has been displayed.

- **SelectionChangeCommitted**   The user has committed changes to an item from the list box portion of the control.

The following code uses the *SelectionChangeCommitted* event to determine when the user has selected an item in the combo box:

```
private void combo_SelectionChangeCommitted(object sender,
                                            System.EventArgs e)
{
    string message = string.Format("The new selection is {0}",
                                   combo.SelectedItem.ToString());
    MessageBox.Show(message);
}
```

In this example, the *SelectedItem* property is used to retrieve a reference to the selected item rather than simply calling *combo.Text*. This is because the *OnCommitted* event is raised before the text box control has been updated, and the *Text* property will return the old value of the control.

Scrolling Controls with the *ScrollBar* Classes

It's common practice for Windows applications to provide scroll bars as needed to display a control or form that's larger than the area provided. This is commonly done for forms that contain documents, as seen in Microsoft Word or Microsoft Excel, or in controls such as list boxes and tree view controls.

Although the scroll bars that are embedded in controls such as the list box control don't require programming support from you, you must manage any scroll bars that you add to forms or custom controls. Prior to the release of Visual C# .NET and the .NET Framework, using scroll bars in an application wasn't a trivial task. However, with Visual C#, you can easily leverage the scroll bar classes included in the .NET Framework and easily add scrolling capabilities to your application.

The .NET Framework includes two scroll bar implementations. The *HScrollBar* class is used to create horizontal scroll bars, and the *VScrollBar* class is used to create vertical scroll bars. These classes are both derived from a common base class, *ScrollBar*.

Most of the time, you won't need to create scroll bars explicitly. Many Windows Forms classes support automatic scrolling; these classes are derived from the *ScrollableControl* class. This class provides built-in support for scroll bars, allowing complete scroll bar functionality simply by setting a property. One of the classes derived indirectly from *ScrollableControl* is the *Form* class. Enabling basic automatic scrolling functionality for a form is as simple as setting the form's *AutoScroll* property to *true*, as shown in the following code:

```
AutoScroll = true;
```

In addition to *AutoScroll*, two other properties affect scrolling behavior:

- **AutoScrollMargin**   The minimum margin that's required between child controls and the container's edge. Scroll bars are created if needed to preserve this margin.

- **AutoScrollMinSize**   The minimum size for the scrollable form or control. Scroll bars will be created automatically if the form or control is resized below this minimum size, even if no child controls have been obscured.

The *AutoScrollMargin* and *AutoScrollMinSize* properties have *Size* values. The *Size* structure is frequently used in Windows Forms classes to represent the dimensions of a rectangle, exposing two properties: *Height* and *Width*. A *Size* object is typically constructed as shown here:

```
Size minimumSize = new Size(150, 200);
```

The *Size* structure is discussed in more detail in Chapter 14. For now, it's enough to understand that the *Size* structure is used with a form's scrolling properties. By default, the *AutoScrollMargin* and *AutoScrollMinSize* properties have sizes with a height and width of 0. This triggers the creation of scroll bars only when a control is clipped by the edge of the form during a resizing operation.

If you prefer to establish some padding around the controls on your form, you can adjust the *AutoScrollMargin* property, as shown here:

```
AutoScrollMargin = new Size(50, 50);
```

Alternatively, you can use the following code to set the *AutoScrollMinSize* property to a minimum size for the scrolled region. If the dimensions of the form fall below this minimum size, scroll bars are displayed, even if no controls have been obscured.

```
AutoScrollMinSize = new Size(400, 400);
```

Controls That Act as Containers

A form acts as a container for any child controls located on the form's surface. When you use the Windows Forms Designer to place a control on the form's surface, two things happen. First the location and size of the control are saved and used as control properties, and these properties are serialized into the form's *InitializeComponents* method, generating code that looks something like this:

```
button1 = new System.Windows.Forms.Button();
button1.Location = new System.Drawing.Point(200, 24);
```

Second the control is added to the *Controls* collection, which keeps a reference to every child control that is contained by the form by using code similar to the following:

```
Controls.AddRange(new System.Windows.Forms.Control[] {button1});
```

Once a containment relationship has been established, the child control assumes the ambient properties of its container. For example, the background color of the container is used by default by the child control. If the container is hidden, child controls are hidden; if the container is disabled, the child controls are disabled.

Although the *Form* class is the most common container for controls, it isn't the only container available. Two other control classes can act as containers:

- **GroupBox** Provides logical grouping for a collection of controls with or without a caption
- **Panel** Provides logical grouping with scroll bar support

These controls act as containers for other controls, supplying their child controls with a separate tab order, ambient properties, and a logical separation from other parts of the form.

Embedding Controls

A typical use for control containment is to serve as a logical grouping for radio buttons. Radio buttons automatically provide exclusion within each group of radio buttons. When multiple radio button controls are placed on a form, the radio buttons are placed in a single group by default. However, by adding a group box or panel control to a form, you can create separate groups for radio buttons, with each group providing its own mutual exclusion.

To create a control and embed it in a container, you must either draw or drag and drop the control directly from the Toolbox into the container. If you reposition an existing control over a group box, no containment will be changed. You can use the clipboard, however, by cutting the existing control to the clipboard (Ctrl+X), selecting the container, and pasting the control into the container (Ctrl+V).

The *GroupBox* Class

The *GroupBox* class is used to create a control container that can have a caption, as shown in Figure 12-6.

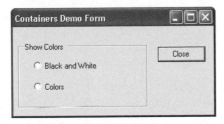

Figure 12-6.   A group box control as a container that can have a caption.

To create a caption for a group box control, use the *Text* property, as shown here:

```
reservationGroup.Text = "&Reservations";
```

In this example, a group box caption is prefixed with an ampersand. Although the group box doesn't receive the focus directly, the focus is delegated to controls inside the group box when the user activates the shortcut.

The *Panel* Class

The *Panel* class is used to create a panel control. Like a group box control, a panel can act as a container for other controls. However, unlike a group box, a panel never has a caption. Also unlike a group box, a panel control can be associated with a scroll bar. For this reason, the *Panel* class is often used when child controls must be visibly set apart, either by providing a different *Back-Color* property or by supplying a scroll bar to enable multiple controls to be placed in a constrained space.

By default, a panel control is drawn with no border. To create a visible boundary for the control, set its *BorderStyle* property to one of the values from the *BorderStyle* enumeration listed earlier in this chapter, in Table 12-5. The following code uses the *BorderStyle* property to create a three-dimensional border around a panel control:

```
panel.BorderStyle = BorderStyle.Fixed3D;
```

Automatic scrolling is disabled by default for panel controls. To enable scrolling for a panel, set its *AutoScroll* property to *true*, as shown here:

```
panel.AutoScroll = true;
```

Conclusion

The Windows Forms classes include a number of fundamental controls that are used with Forms classes, such as *Button*, *TextBox*, *Label*, *LinkLabel*, *ListBox*, *CheckedListBox*, *ComboBox*, *ScrollBar*, *GroupBox*, and *Panel*. All controls, including the *Form* class itself, are derived from the *Control* base class, which defines the basic functionality for all visible Windows Forms components. Most properties, methods, and events are defined by the *Control* class. Individual classes derived from the *Control* class add the properties, methods, and events to make them unique.

The Windows Forms Designer and its Properties window greatly simplify the task of writing a rich client application with Visual C# .NET. All properties and events can be accessed either through code or through the Properties window, making it a simple matter to define functionality either programmatically or declaratively.

In Chapter 13, we'll move on to collecting user input and providing feedback, including working with the keyboard and mouse to obtain input from the user. You'll learn how to add menus to your application and use status bars to provide feedback.

13

User Input and Feedback

The Microsoft Windows Forms platform offers a rich environment for interaction with the user and provides two principle methods of input: the keyboard and the mouse. The keyboard is used primarily for text and navigation, and the mouse is typically used to manipulate menus and controls. Although much of the input in an application is provided through controls, it's important to understand how to accept input directly from the keyboard and the mouse. This chapter addresses this issue and also examines how feedback can be provided to a user who's navigating using a mouse—by altering the default mouse pointer, you can provide direct feedback to the user.

In this chapter, we'll also look at the menu classes that are part of the Microsoft .NET Framework, and you'll learn how to use the Microsoft Visual C# .NET Forms Designer to easily create menus for your applications. You'll also create shortcut menus that are dynamically updated to provide relevant menu options to the user. The chapter closes with a section on status bars, describing how you can use them to provide helpful feedback.

Working with the Mouse

In a Windows Forms application, a great deal of user interaction occurs through the mouse. As the mouse is moved and clicked by the user, events are raised and sent to your application. Although you can create an application that doesn't use the mouse for user input, the mouse is the preferred method of input for most Windows users. The following subsections describe how you can use the mouse as an alternative to keyboard input.

Handling Mouse Movement Events

The mouse communicates with your application through events that are raised as the user interacts with the mouse. As the mouse pointer moves over a control or a form, events are raised to enable you to track the current mouse position. Events are passed only to a single form or control; normally, this is the object that's located under the mouse pointer. Table 13-1 lists the events related to mouse movement.

Table 13-1. Mouse Movement Events

Event	Description
MouseEnter	The mouse pointer has entered the control or form region.
MouseHover	The mouse pointer has stopped moving over a control or a form. This event is not sent each time the mouse pointer pauses over a control; rather, it's sent the first time the mouse pointer stops moving after a *MouseEnter* event has been raised.
MouseLeave	The mouse pointer has left the control or form region.
MouseMove	The mouse pointer has moved to a new position.
MouseWheel	The user has moved the mouse wheel while the control or form has the input focus.

Although most of the events listed in Table 13-1 accept *EventHandler* delegates, the event handler for the *MouseMove* and *MouseWheel* events must be an instance of the *MouseEventHandler* class rather than *EventHandler*. Instances of the *MouseEventHandler* delegate are created as shown here:

```
MouseMove += new MouseEventHandler(form_MouseMove);
private void form_MouseMove(object sender, MouseEventArgs e)
{
    ⋮
}
```

As shown in the preceding example, a method associated with a *MouseEventHandler* delegate accepts a *MouseEventArgs* reference as its second parameter, instead of a reference to an *EventArgs* object. The *MouseEventArgs* class provides additional information about the location and state of the mouse. The *MouseEventArgs* class exposes the following properties:

■ **Button**   A value from the *MouseButtons* enumeration that indicates which mouse button was clicked by the user

■ **Clicks**   The number of times the mouse button has been clicked recently

■ **Delta**   The number of positions, or *detents*, that the mouse wheel has been rotated

■ **X**   The x-coordinate of the mouse, in client coordinates

■ **Y**   The y-coordinate of the mouse, in client coordinates

So what happens if you're handling an event that provides a simple *EventArgs* parameter and you need the mouse coordinates? You're in luck, because the *Form* class includes the *MousePosition* property, which returns the current mouse position, as shown here:

```
private void main_Click(object sender, System.EventArgs e)
{
    Point mousePoint = PointToClient(MousePosition);
    string msg = string.Format("Mouse click at X:{0}, Y:{1}",
                                mousePoint.X,
                                mousePoint.Y);
    MessageBox.Show(msg);
}
```

The location returned from *MousePosition* is a *Point* structure, which consists of the xy-coordinates for a specific location on the desktop. The *Point* structure returned by *MousePosition* is relative to the entire screen rather than to the current form or control. The preceding code uses the *PointToClient* method to transform the location into client coordinates.

The *MouseButtons* enumeration, shown in Table 13-2, is used to determine the current state of the mouse buttons. Values in the *MouseButtons* enumeration can be combined as necessary to provide an accurate picture of the mouse state.

Table 13-2. *MouseButtons* **Enumeration Values**

Value	Description
None	No mouse button was pressed.
Left	The primary (usually left) mouse button was pressed.
Middle	The middle mouse button was pressed.
Right	The secondary (usually right) mouse button was pressed.
XButton1	The first XButton on a Microsoft IntelliMouse Explorer was pressed.
XButton2	The second XButton on an IntelliMouse Explorer was pressed.

The last two entries in Table 13-2 refer to extra buttons that are present on the IntelliMouse Explorer mouse. These mice have five mouse buttons; the two additional XButtons are typically used for navigation.

All of the mouse movement events can be accessed through the Forms Designer's Properties window, except for the *MouseWheel* event. In most cases, controls that can be manipulated with the *MouseWheel* event will already provide default handling for this event. To explicitly handle *MouseWheel* events, you must manually add an event handler delegate to your form or control, as shown here:

```
nameListBox.MouseWheel += new MouseEventHandler(list_MouseWheel);
private void list_MouseWheel(object sender, MouseEventArgs e)
{
    ⋮
}
```

Handling Mouse Selection Events

The most common use of the mouse is for item selection. In most cases, you don't need to detect mouse clicks directly. Most controls and other objects that accept user input generate *Click* events, as discussed in Chapter 12. Table 13-3 lists the mouse selection events.

Table 13-3. **Mouse Selection Events**

Event	Description
MouseDown	A mouse button was pressed over the control or form.
MouseUp	A mouse button was released over the control or form.
Click	The control or form was clicked.
DoubleClick	The control or form was double-clicked.

The *MouseDown* and *MouseUp* events are associated with *MouseEvent-Handler* delegates, which enable them to pass a reference to a *MouseEventArgs* object as a parameter. The *Click* and *DoubleClick* events are associated with *EventHandler* delegates, however, and don't provide any additional information about the mouse position or state.

Although mouse events are raised asynchronously and can come at any time, there's a guarantee with regard to the relative order of mouse events: The *MouseEnter* and *MouseLeave* mouse events bracket other mouse events, such as *MouseHover, MouseMove*, and any mouse selection events. A *Click* event occurs only after *MouseDown* and *MouseUp* events, and a *DoubleClick* event occurs only after a *Click* event.

The companion CD includes MouseEvents, an example project that demonstrates how mouse events are raised and handled. The main form from MouseEvents is shown in Figure 13-1.

Figure 13-1.   The MouseEvents main form.

As you can see, the main form includes a list box control and a label control that are used to display mouse-related events that are handled by the application. The constructor for the main form is shown here:

```
public MainForm()
{
    InitializeComponent();
    MouseEventHandler wheelHandler = null;
    wheelHandler = new MouseEventHandler(listBox_MouseWheel);
    eventListBox.MouseWheel += wheelHandler;
}
```

The call to *InitializeComponent* was inserted by the Forms Designer to initialize the form and the user interface controls. After the call to *Initialize-Component*, an event handling delegate is created for the list box's *MouseWheel* event. The implementation of the *listBox_MouseWheel* method that handles the wheel events from the mouse is shown on the following page.

```
private void listBox_MouseWheel(object sender,
                                MouseEventArgs e)
{
    UpdateEventLabels("(ListBox)MouseWheel", e.X, e.Y, e);
}
```

When mouse-related events are received by the MouseEvents application, the event handler calls the *UpdateEventLabels* method, shown here:

```
private void UpdateEventLabels(string msg,
                               int x,
                               int y,
                               MouseEventArgs e)
{
    string message = string.Format("{0} X:{1}, Y:{2}",
                                    msg,
                                    x,
                                    y);
    positionLabel.Text = message;
    string eventMsg = DateTime.Now.ToShortTimeString();
    eventMsg += " " + message;
    eventListBox.Items.Insert(0, eventMsg);
    eventListBox.TopIndex = 0;

    string mouseInfo;
    if(e != null)
    {
        mouseInfo = string.Format("Clicks: {0}, Delta: {1}, " +
                                  "Buttons: {2}",
                                  e.Clicks,
                                  e.Delta,
                                  e.Button.ToString());
    }
    else
    {
        mouseInfo = "";
    }
    mouseEventArgsLabel.Text = mouseInfo;
}
```

The *UpdateEventLabels* method accepts the following parameters:

- ***msg***   A string that describes the event
- ***x***   The mouse pointer's x-coordinate
- ***y***   The mouse pointer's y-coordinate
- ***e***   An optional reference to a *MouseEventArgs* object

The *UpdateEventLabels* method uses these parameters to format messages that are displayed in the dialog box. After every mouse-related event, a summary of the event is added to the list box, which is then reset so that the most recent messages are always displayed. The current position of the mouse pointer is displayed in the *positionLabel* label control. When a reference to a *MouseEventArgs* object is passed as a parameter, additional information is displayed in the *mouseEventArgsLabel* label control.

For events that pass a reference to *EventArgs* instead of a reference to *MouseEventArgs*, the *MousePosition* property is used to specify the current mouse coordinates, as shown here:

```
private void listBox_MouseEnter(object sender, System.EventArgs e)
{
    Point mousePoint = PointToClient(MousePosition);
    UpdateEventLabels("(ListBox)MouseEnter",
                    mousePoint.X,
                    mousePoint.Y,
                    null);
}
```

Table 13-4 lists the events that are handled by the MouseEvents application and the controls that handle them.

Table 13-4.   Mouse-Related Events Handled by the MouseEvents Application

Event	Form	List Box
Click	X	
DoubleClick	X	X
MouseDown	X	X
MouseEnter	X	X
MouseHover	X	X
MouseLeave	X	X
MouseMove	X	X
MouseUp	X	X
MouseWheel		X

To use the MouseEvents application, move the mouse pointer over the dialog box and child controls. Messages are generated as the mouse pointer passes over the form and the list box control. When the mouse pointer passes over child controls other than the list box, no messages appear; to see event messages for other child controls, you must add additional event handlers.

There are situations in which you need to know exactly where the mouse pointer is located, even if the mouse events would normally be sent to another form or control. In these cases, such as when you're performing a drag-and-drop operation, you can capture the mouse pointer, which will result in all mouse events being sent to your form or control. The *Capture* property is used to capture the mouse pointer as well as to determine whether the mouse is currently captured, as shown here:

```
if(Capture == false)
{
    Capture = true;
    if(Capture == true)
    {
        // Mouse captured.
        ⋮
    }
}
```

Providing Feedback with the Mouse Pointer

A common way to provide feedback to the user is through the mouse pointer. Because the mouse is often the primary method of user input in a Windows Forms application, altering the shape of the mouse pointer is an effective way to provide immediate feedback to the user. In most cases, the operating system and the .NET Framework will provide a mouse pointer that's appropriate. For example, the default mouse pointer is normally set to the arrow shape over most controls and forms. The following subsections describe how you can enhance the built-in support within Windows and the .NET Framework to provide additional feedback to users.

Using Standard Mouse Pointers

Windows provides many standard mouse pointers, with each mouse pointer intended to be used in specific situations. The standard arrow mouse pointer is replaced by the hourglass when an application is busy or unable to accept mouse input. In most applications, you'll want the mouse pointer to change to the I-beam when it's moved over a control that accepts text input.

The mouse pointer is changed through the *Cursor* property, which is exposed by the *Control* class and all of its subclasses, including the *Form* class, as shown here:

```
Cursor = Cursors.WaitCursor;
```

The *Cursor* property must be set to an instance of a *Cursor* object. The *Cursors* class includes static properties that return the predefined mouse pointers described in the following tables. Table 13-5 lists the general-purpose mouse pointer values.

Table 13-5.   General-Purpose Mouse Pointer Values

Value	Description
AppStarting	The mouse pointer displayed as an application is being launched
Arrow	The default mouse pointer displayed over most controls
Cross	The crosshair mouse pointer, which is commonly used when the mouse pointer is used to select small areas, such as in bitmap editors
Default	The default mouse pointer, usually the arrow mouse pointer

The mouse pointers listed in Table 13-6 are frequently used to indicate that specific actions can be taken with the mouse. These mouse pointers are context-sensitive and are typically displayed only while the mouse pointer is over a specific object that supports the action suggested by the mouse pointer.

Table 13-6.   Action-Related Mouse Pointer Values

Value	Description
Hand	The mouse pointer typically used to indicate a hyperlink in Web pages
Help	The mouse pointer typically used when invoking help on a specific user interface object
HSplit	The mouse pointer used to indicate a horizontal splitter
IBeam	The mouse pointer used to indicate a control that displays text or accepts text as input, such as a text box
No	The mouse pointer shape used when the mouse pointer is over an area that's invalid in the current context; often used in drag-and-drop operations to indicate that a target isn't a valid drop target
UpArrow	The mouse pointer used to mark an insertion point
VSplit	The mouse pointer used to indicate a vertical splitter
WaitCursor	The mouse pointer used to indicate that the application or system is busy and no input is allowed; typically shaped like an hourglass

Each of the mouse pointers described in Table 13-7 is related to mouse wheel operations. Mice that include a wheel typically allow you to change the behavior of the mouse such that the mouse pointer is locked in place; any movement of the mouse causes the window to be scrolled.

Table 13-7.   Mouse Wheel–Related Pointer Values

Value	Description
NoMove2D	The mouse pointer shape displayed when the mouse pointer can't be moved but the window can be scrolled vertically and horizontally
NoMoveHoriz	The mouse pointer shape displayed when the mouse pointer can't be moved but the window can be scrolled horizontally
NoMoveVert	The mouse pointer shape displayed when the mouse pointer can't be moved but the window can be scrolled vertically
PanEast	The mouse pointer shape displayed when the mouse pointer can't be moved and the mouse is used to scroll the window to the right
PanNE	The mouse pointer shape displayed when the mouse pointer can't be moved and the mouse is used to scroll the window up and to the right
PanNorth	The mouse pointer shape displayed when the mouse pointer can't be moved and the mouse is used to scroll the window up
PanNW	The mouse pointer shape displayed when the mouse pointer can't be moved and the mouse is used to scroll the window up and to the left
PanSE	The mouse pointer shape displayed when the mouse pointer can't be moved and the mouse is used to scroll the window down and to the right
PanSouth	The mouse pointer shape displayed when the mouse pointer can't be moved and the mouse is used to scroll the window down
PanSW	The mouse pointer shape displayed when the mouse pointer can't be moved and the mouse is used to scroll the window down and to the left
PanWest	The mouse pointer shape displayed when the mouse pointer can't be moved and the mouse is used to scroll the window to the left

There are also standard mouse pointers that are displayed for sizing operations. For example, if the mouse pointer is moved over the edge of a sizable window, the mouse pointer is changed to indicate to the user that the window can be resized. Table 13-8 provides a list of the standard mouse pointers displayed for sizing operations.

Table 13-8.   Sizing Mouse Pointer Values

Value	Description
SizeAll	A four-way sizing mouse pointer, with arrows that point up, down, left, and right.
SizeNESW	A two-way sizing mouse pointer, with arrows that point diagonally. One arrow points to the upper right, and the other arrow points to the lower left.
SizeNS	A two-way sizing mouse pointer, with arrows that point up and down.
SizeNWSE	A two-way sizing mouse pointer with arrows that point diagonally. One arrow points to the upper left, and the other arrow points to the lower right.
SizeWE	A two-way sizing mouse pointer, with arrows that point left and right.

The descriptions of mouse pointers in the preceding tables refer to the default mouse pointers provided with Windows. Although the specific shapes can vary according to the user's current desktop theme, any of the specified mouse pointers will be displayed consistently by all applications on the user's computer.

The *Cursor* property can also be used to retrieve the mouse pointer, which enables you to cache the current mouse pointer and restore it at a later time, as shown here:

```
Cursor oldCursor = Cursor;
⋮
Cursor = oldCursor;
```

Using Custom Mouse Pointers

You can also create custom mouse pointers for your application using the *Cursor* class, as shown here:

```
smileyCursor = new Cursor("..\\..\\smiley.cur");
Cursor = smileyCursor;
```

In this code, the *Cursor* constructor takes the file path to the mouse pointer file and uses it to create a custom mouse pointer object, *smileyCursor*. The *smileyCursor* object is then assigned to the form's *Cursor* property. Mouse pointer objects use an operating system handle. When the mouse pointer is no longer used, it should be disposed of to prevent resource leaks, as shown here:

```
smileyCursor.Dispose();
```

Although a custom mouse pointer that's currently used by a form will be cleaned up when the form is closed, some situations will result in resource leaks or will cause external resources to be consumed in greater numbers than necessary and released more slowly than desired. For example, if you simply create a new instance of your custom mouse pointer every time you need it, you'll probably create too many underlying resource handles. Consider this code, which creates a local version of the mouse pointer and assigns it to the form:

```
private void SetSmileyCursor();
{
    Cursor _smileyCursor = new Cursor("..\\..\\smiley.cur");
    Cursor = _smileyCursor;
}
```

Later, if a standard mouse pointer such as *Cursors.Wait* is assigned to the form in response to another event, you'll have a resource leak unless you first call *Dispose* on the current custom mouse pointer, like this:

```
Cursor oldCustomCursor = Cursor;
oldCustomCursor.Dispose();
Cursor = Cursors.Wait;
```

But there's a problem with this code. How do you know whether the previous mouse pointer really is a custom mouse pointer? If you can't be sure, the best approach is to create a single instance of all custom mouse pointers when your application or form starts, as shown here:

```
public class MainForm: System.Windows.Forms.Form
{
    Cursor _handCursor;
    Cursor _embeddedCursor;
    Cursor _smileyCursor;
    ⋮
    public MainForm()
    {
        ⋮
        _handCursor = new Cursor(externalHand);
        _embeddedCursor = new Cursor(this.GetType(), "Smiley2.cur");
        _smileyCursor = new Cursor("..\\..\\smiley.cur");
    }
    protected override void Dispose( bool disposing )
    {
        if( disposing )
        {
            if (components != null)
            {
                components.Dispose();
            }
```

```
            _handCursor.Dispose();
            _embeddedCursor.Dispose();
            _smileyCursor.Dispose();
        }
        base.Dispose( disposing );
    }
      ⋮
}
```

As shown in this code, when the main form is created, the custom mouse pointers are created. Later, when *Dispose* is called on the form, *Dispose* is called for each custom mouse pointer.

Using Microsoft Win32 Mouse Pointer Resource Handles

Three other constructors for the *Cursor* class enable you to create custom mouse pointers from a variety of sources. The *Cursor* constructor used in the following code accepts an *IntPtr* parameter, which is typically a Win32 resource handle obtained through a set of services called P/Invoke that allows managed code to work with unmanaged code:

```
private void SetExternalCursor(IntPtr handle)
{
    Cursor externalCursor = new Cursor(handle);
    Cursor = externalCursor;
}
```

The following code is similar to the code in the CursorSwap sample application, included on the companion CD. It includes a P/Invoke declaration that enables loading a mouse pointer through the Win32 *LoadCursor* API call and a method that uses the external resource handle to create a mouse pointer.

```
// Platform Invoke method to load
// a standard mouse pointer using Win32
[DllImport("user32.dll", EntryPoint="LoadCursor")]
private static extern IntPtr InteropLoadCursor(int instance,
                                               int resource);

// From the Platform SDK winuser.h header file
const int IDC_HAND = 32649;

private void externalRadioButton_CheckedChanged(object sender,
                                               System.EventArgs e)
{
    IntPtr externalHand = InteropLoadCursor(0, IDC_HAND);
    Cursor handCursor = new Cursor(externalHand);
    Cursor = handCursor;
}
```

Although this code is concise, it tends to hold external resources longer than necessary. As mentioned, when you're explicitly creating a resource externally using code such as this, you should aggressively use the *Dispose* pattern if possible. Otherwise, you run the risk of leaking resources until enough garbage collection passes have occurred to free the external resource handles. The source code for the CursorSwap example provided on the companion CD allocates the external mouse pointer object and resources when the application starts and employs the *Dispose* pattern to clean up when the application closes, as shown here:

```
public class MainForm: System.Windows.Forms.Form
{
    Cursor _handCursor;
    ⋮
    public MainForm()
    {
        _handCursor = new Cursor(externalHand);
        ⋮
    }
    ⋮
    protected override void Dispose( bool disposing )
    {
        if( disposing )
        {
            if (components != null)
            {
                components.Dispose();
            }
            _handCursor.Dispose();
        }
        base.Dispose( disposing );
    }
    ⋮
    private void externalRadioButton_CheckedChanged(object sender,
                                                    System.EventArgs e)
    {
        Cursor = _handCursor;
    }
    ⋮
}
```

Avoiding External Mouse Pointer Files

Creating a custom mouse pointer using the mouse pointer's file name is a simple, straightforward approach; however, it's often undesirable to distribute multiple files with your application. It's much more convenient to embed resources such as mouse pointers, icons, and bitmaps into your assembly and then load the resources directly from the assembly when required.

To embed a mouse pointer resource into your assembly, you must change the mouse pointer's *BuildAction* property. The default value for this property is *Content*, which results in a mouse pointer file that's used as and considered part of the project's output. The mouse pointer isn't compiled or stored as a resource, however. To embed the resource into your assembly, select the Cursor file in Solution Explorer, and change the *BuildAction* property to *Embedded Resource*.

One of the overloaded versions of the *Cursor* constructor works with mouse pointer resources embedded in assemblies. The constructor accepts two parameters:

- A type name in the assembly that's used to determine the namespace for the mouse pointer resource

- The name of the mouse pointer resource

The following code demonstrates how to create a mouse pointer from an embedded resource:

```
Cursor embeddedCursor = new Cursor(this.GetType(), "Smiley2.cur");
```

When a mouse pointer is embedded in the assembly during compilation, the mouse pointer's name is prefixed with the project's default namespace. Initially, the default prefix will be the project's name. The project's namespace can be viewed or set in the project's Property Pages dialog box. For the CursorSwap example, the default namespace was changed to *MSPress.CSharpCoreRef.CursorSwap*.

In the preceding code, the type of the current object is part of the project's default namespace, so *this.GetType* is passed for the constructor's first parameter and the mouse pointer resource is named Smiley2.cur. This is similar to code used in the CursorSwap project except that the code in the CursorSwap project is structured so that custom mouse pointers are properly disposed of when *Dispose* is called for the application's main form.

Accepting Keyboard Input

Generally speaking, you'll rarely need to accept keyboard input directly from the user. In most cases, the user provides keyboard input to a control that's designed to accept input from the keyboard, such as a text box or a rich text control. However, the .NET Framework includes support for handling user input directly. The following subsections describe how you can add support for keyboard input to your programs.

Obtaining the Input Focus

Input through the keyboard isn't available to all applications and controls simultaneously; instead, it always flows to the control or form that currently has the input focus. Controls generally change their appearance slightly as an indication that they have the input focus—for example, the text box and rich text controls display a vertical bar (|) at the point where text will be inserted, the button control displays a dashed line around its border, and other controls display similar cues to the user.

To switch focus to a specific control, use the *Focus* method, which is exposed by the *Control* class. The *Focus* method returns *true* if the input focus was switched to the control or *false* if the input focus couldn't be obtained. The following code demonstrates how to use the *Focus* method:

```
if(nameTextBox.Focus() == false)
{
    Trace.WriteLine("Couldn't set focus to text box");
}
```

The *Control* class exposes the following three properties related to the input focus:

- **CanFocus**   Returns *true* if the input focus can be switched to the control or *false* if the input focus can't be obtained

- **ContainsFocus**   Returns *true* if the control or a child control has the input focus or *false* if the input focus is owned by another control

- **Focused**   Returns *true* if the control has the input focus; otherwise, returns *false*

In addition to being exposed by all controls, these properties are available for forms because the *Form* class is derived from the *Control* class.

A control can obtain the input focus only if it's on an active, top-level form. You can test a control to see whether it can get the input focus by using the *CanFocus* property, as shown here:

```
if(nameTextBox.CanFocus)
{
    ⋮
}
```

The *ContainsFocus* property is useful when you need to know whether the control or one of its contained child controls has the input focus, as shown in the following code:

```
if(this.ContainsFocus)
{
    ⋮
}
```

The *Focused* property is used much like *ContainsFocus*, except that it doesn't test child controls.

Instead of testing for the input focus, you can also set up event handlers for the following two events related to the input focus:

- **Enter**   Raised when a control or one of its children receives the input focus
- **Leave**   Raised when a control or one of its children loses the input focus

You can use the *Enter* and *Leave* events to change portions of your user interface to reflect that a specific control has the input focus. For example, you can display help text when a control is able to accept input, as shown here:

```
private void nameTextBox_Enter(object sender, System.EventArgs e)
{
    helpLabel.Text = "Enter the user's first and last name";
}

private void nameTextBox_Leave(object sender, System.EventArgs e)
{
    helpLabel.Text = "";
}
```

> **Note**   Two related events, *GotFocus* and *LostFocus*, generally aren't used by controls or forms. To determine when a form receives and loses the input focus, you should use the *Activated* and *Deactivated* events.

Using the *Keys* Enumeration

The *Keys* enumeration contains constants for all values that can be sent to your application via the keyboard. The enumeration has 183 values and so is too long to list in full here; a complete list is available in the Microsoft Visual C# .NET online help. Table 13-9 lists some examples of keys representative of the values in the *Keys* enumeration.

Table 13-9.   Example Values from the *Keys* Enumeration

Value	Description
A	The letter *A*
F5	The F5 function key
D9	The digit *9* (not on the numeric keypad)
LShiftKey	The Left Shift key

As you can see, the values in the *Keys* enumeration follow some basic patterns. All keys that are associated with characters are available directly, as shown in the following code, which checks to see whether the user has pressed the Q key:

```
private bool TestForQuitKey(Keys pressedKey)
{
    if(pressedKey == Keys.Q)
        return true;
    else
        return false;
}
```

The *Keys* enumeration makes no distinction between uppercase and lowercase characters. The *TestForQuitKey* method will return the same value, regardless of the state of the Shift or Caps Lock key. In addition to characters and numbers, function keys and Shift keys are included in the enumeration, as are non-English keyboard keys.

The companion CD includes a program named DisplayKeys that displays all of the values from the enumeration. The source code for DisplayKeys is shown here:

```
using System;
using System.Windows.Forms;
namespace MSPress.CSharpCoreRef.DisplayKeys
{
    class DisplayKeysApp
    {
        [STAThread]
        static void Main(string[] args)
        {
            string [] keyNames = Enum.GetNames(typeof(Keys));
            foreach(string name in keyNames)
            {
                Console.WriteLine(name);
            }
        }
    }
}
```

This program retrieves the names of all enumerators in the *Keys* enumeration and then displays each one.

Handling Events from the Keyboard

Three events are generated when a user presses a key, as follows:

- **KeyDown**   Provides raw information about the state of keys and modifiers (Ctrl, Shift, and Alt keys) when a key is pressed.

- **KeyPressed**   Provides information about the key character that might result from a pressed key. This event isn't sent for every pressed key.

- **KeyUp**   Provides raw information about the state of keys and modifiers when a key is released.

The *KeyUp* and *KeyDown* events receive a parameter of type *KeyEventArgs*, a subclass of the *EventArgs* class. *KeyEventArgs* includes several properties that simplify the task of processing keyboard input directly, as follows:

- **Alt**   Returns *true* if the Alt key was pressed; otherwise, returns *false*.

- **Control**   Returns *true* if the Ctrl key was pressed; otherwise, returns *false*.

- **Handled**   Returns a Boolean value that specifies whether the message has been handled.

- **KeyCode**   Returns the key code for the primary key that's associated with the event, taken from the *Keys* enumeration. The *KeyCode* property doesn't combine the key's value with any modifier keys that were also pressed, such as the Shift, Ctrl, or Alt keys.

- **KeyData**   Returns the key code, taken from the *Keys* enumeration, for the key that was pressed, combined with the values of any Alt, Shift, and Ctrl keys that were pressed.

- **KeyValue**   Returns the integer equivalent of the *KeyData* property.

- **Modifiers**   Returns the key codes for any of the Alt, Shift, or Ctrl keys that were pressed.

- **Shift**   Returns *true* if the Shift key was pressed; otherwise, returns *false*.

The *Alt*, *Control*, and *Shift* properties return *true* if the user has pressed any of the corresponding keys. These keys receive special treatment because they're often used to modify the meaning of a key press. For example, in

Microsoft Visual Studio .NET, pressing F5 starts an executable in a debugging session, whereas pressing Shift+F5 launches the executable without debugging. One approach to testing for the presence of modifier keys is to use code such as this:

```
if(e.KeyCode == Keys.Q)
{
    if(e.Shift == true)
    {
        ⋮
    }
    if(e.Control == true)
    {
        ⋮
    }
}
```

Another approach to testing the state of modifier keys is to use the *Modifiers* property. This property will contain multiple values if multiple modifier keys are pressed. To determine exactly which keys are pressed, test for the desired modifier keys, as shown here:

```
if(e.KeyCode == Keys.B)
{
    if(e.Modifiers == (Keys.Control | Keys.Shift)
    {
        ⋮
    }
}
```

If you're testing for multiple modifier keys, use the *Modifiers* property as shown here. If you're testing for a single modifier key, it's often easier to test the individual properties exposed by the *KeyEventArgs* class.

The *KeyPress* event is sent between the *KeyDown* and *KeyUp* events. Unlike the *KeyDown* and *KeyUp* events, the *KeyPress* event includes a parameter of type *KeyPressEventArgs* instead of *KeyEventArgs*. The *KeyPressEventArgs* class doesn't provide information about the key code or modifier keys; instead, it exposes the following properties:

- **Handled** Boolean value that specifies whether the event has been handled

- **KeyChar** Character value that represents the pressed key

The value returned by the *KeyChar* property will properly reflect the state of the Shift key. The *KeyPress* event is useful when you're accepting simple text input and you're not concerned about modifier keys. The *KeyDown* and *KeyUp* events are best suited for handling navigation and function keys.

Using a Main Menu with Forms

Menus are a common user interface element in Windows applications. With the exception of simple dialog box–based applications, practically all applications written for Windows provide a menu that enables users to interact with the application. The menu that often appears along the top edge of a Windows application is known as the application's *main menu*, or *menu bar*. Menus that are displayed when you right-click a control are known as *shortcut menus*, or sometimes *context menus*.

Menus can be viewed as a series of parent-child relationships. An application's main menu will usually consist of a number of top-level menu items. Typically, these top-level menu items have associated popup child windows that are displayed when the relevant top-level menu item is clicked. Further nesting is possible, as each menu item in a popup menu can have an associated child menu.

In general, the .NET Framework will automatically render your menus in a way that's consistent with the Windows user interface guidelines. However, there are a few user interface conventions for menus that you should follow:

- Menu items should be associated with a mnemonic character—that is, a character that's part of the menu item name and that when pressed with the Alt key will invoke the menu item. For example, the top-level File menu is usually associated with *F* as a mnemonic character; pressing Alt+F on the keyboard typically invokes the File menu. The steps required to provide a mnemonic character are discussed later in this section.

- Any top-level menu items that invoke commands and don't create a popup child menu should have an exclamation mark after their name. This alerts the user to the fact that selecting the menu item will result in a command being invoked.

- Popup menu items that will require additional input from the user, such as populating a dialog box, should have an ellipsis (...) after the menu item name.

The following subsections describe the steps required to create both top-level menus and shortcut menus and show you how to use menus to make your programs more user-friendly.

Creating a Main Menu

There are two basic approaches to creating menus for your applications. The first approach is to use the Visual C# .NET Menu Designer. This is the simplest and most straightforward way to add a basic menu to your application. We'll also examine how to add menus programmatically, the second approach, so that you can gain a better understanding of the code the Menu Designer generates.

Creating a Menu Using the Menu Designer

To use the Menu Designer, drag a *MainMenu* control from the Toolbox to your form. The *MainMenu* control will automatically be attached to the top edge of your form and will also add an icon that represents the menu to an area under your form, as shown in Figure 13-2.

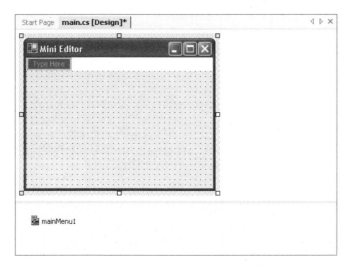

Figure 13-2.   The Forms Designer after a *MainMenu* control has been added.

As you can see, the menu initially includes a box labeled *Type Here*. To add a top-level menu item, click on the box, and enter the text for the menu item. After the new menu item has been added to the menu, two boxes will be labeled *Type Here*: one box on the top level of the menu, and one box that's a child of the new menu item. You can continue adding menu items until the menu is populated with all the menu items you want. Figure 13-3 shows an example of a menu after several menu items have been added.

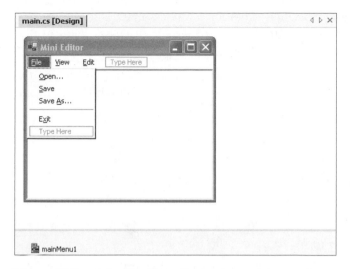

Figure 13-3.   Using the Menu Designer to create a main menu.

> **Tip**   If you click on the form or another control before adding at least one menu item to the *MainMenu* control, the menu will disappear. To make the main menu visible again, click the MainMenu icon under the form.

To add a mnemonic character to a menu item, prefix a letter in the menu item's text caption with an ampersand (&). The mnemonic character must be unique within its parent menu, so it's not always possible to use the first letter in each menu item. When the menu is displayed, pressing the Alt key and the mnemonic character will select the menu item.

A menu will often include a horizontal line known as a separator that serves to group related menu items. To add a separator to a menu, enter a dash (–) as the menu item's *Text* property, or right-click a menu item and choose Add Separator from the shortcut menu. You also can rearrange the position of a separator or other menu items by dragging them to the desired position.

The Properties window enables you to manipulate the properties for each menu item. Simply click the menu item you want to manage, and the Properties window will be updated with the properties for that menu item. The most commonly used properties for menu items are listed on the following page.

- **Checked**   Specifies whether a check mark should be displayed next to the menu item. This property is discussed later in this chapter, in the section "Adding Check Marks to Menu Items."

- **Enabled**   Enables or disables a menu item. This property is discussed later in this chapter, in the section "Disabling Menu Items."

- **Mnemonic**   Returns the mnemonic character for the menu item, or returns *0* if no mnemonic character exists.

- **Name**   Returns the identifier for the menu item.

- **Parent**   Returns a reference to the *Menu* object that's the current item's parent.

- **RadioCheck**   Specifies whether the check mark for a menu item should be replaced by a radio button.

- **Shortcut**   Specifies a keyboard sequence that executes the associated event handler just as if the menu item were clicked.

- **Text**   Specifies the text caption associated with the menu item.

- **Visible**   Specifies whether the menu item is visible.

As with other controls in the .NET Framework, all properties that can be accessed through the Properties window can also be accessed through code. In the next section, you'll learn how to create a menu directly in your code.

Creating a Menu Programmatically

Although you can easily create a menu using the Windows Forms Menu Designer, it's a good idea to understand the steps required to create a menu programmatically. A menu bar is created in two steps: first you create *MenuItem* objects and assemble them into a collection of child menu items, and then you create an instance of the *MainMenu* class and add the *MenuItem* objects to it.

The following four classes are used to create menus in the *System.Windows.Forms* namespace:

- **Menu**   Represents the base class for all other menu and menu item classes

- **MenuItem**   Represents a menu item in a *MainMenu* or *Context-Menu* instance

- **MainMenu**   Represents a main top-level menu for a form

- **ContextMenu**   Represents a shortcut menu for a form or control

As mentioned, the first step in creating a menu is to create the menu item objects that will populate the menu. After the menu items have been created, they're assembled to form a menu. Each menu item is the child of a *MainMenu* or *ContextMenu* object (for top-level items) or the child of another *MenuItem* object (for nested menus).

The *MenuItem* class, which has six constructors, is used to create menu items. The commonly used constructor shown here enables you to specify the menu item's text caption, as well as the event handler that takes care of the *Click* event:

```
EventHandler fileOpenHandler = new System.EventHandler(fileOpen_Click);
MenuItem fileOpen = new MenuItem("&Open...",
                                 fileOpenHandler);

private void fileOpen_Click(object sender, System.EventArgs e)
{
    ⋮
}
```

Two other forms of the constructor create menu items that require additional work before they're usable. The simplest of these constructors creates a menu item with an empty caption and no *Click* event handler, as shown here:

```
MenuItem fileOpen = new MenuItem();
```

The other simple *MenuItem* constructor enables you to pass just the menu item's caption as a parameter, as shown here:

```
MenuItem fileOpen = new MenuItem("&Open...");
```

A slightly more complex version of the *MenuItem* constructor enables you to specify a shortcut in addition to the text caption and event handler, as follows:

```
EventHandler fileOpenHandler = new System.EventHandler(fileOpen_Click);
MenuItem fileOpen = new MenuItem("&Open...",
                                 fileOpenHandler,
                                 Shortcut.CtrlO);
```

One *MenuItem* constructor allows you to specify a caption and an array of submenu items, as the following code shows:

```
// Create an array of menu items
MenuItem [] fileMenuItems = {
    new MenuItem("&Open"),
    new MenuItem("&Save"),
    new MenuItem("Save &As"),
    new MenuItem("E&xit")
};
// Create a menu item from the array of submenu items
MenuItem fileMenu= new MenuItem("&File", fileMenuItems);
```

The sixth constructor is used in Multiple Document Interface (MDI) applications, which aren't discussed in this book, and allows you to specify how menu items should be merged.

After creating your menu items, you assemble them and add them to a *MainMenu* object. The *MainMenu* object is then assigned to your form's *Menu* property. There are two constructors for the *MainMenu* class. The simplest version of the constructor creates a *MainMenu* object without associating it with any menu items, as shown here:

```
MainMenu mainMenu = new MainMenu();
```

The second version of the *MainMenu* constructor enables you to create a main menu that's associated with an array of *MenuItem* children that are passed as a parameter to the constructor:

```
MenuItem fileMenuItem = new MenuItem("&File")
MenuItem viewMenuItem = new MenuItem("&View");
MenuItem editMenuItem = new MenuItem("&Edit");
MenuItem [] topLevelMenuItemArray = new MenuItem[] { fileMenuItem,
                                                     viewMenuItem,
                                                     editMenuItem };
MainMenu mainMenu = new MainMenu(topLevelMenuItemArray);
```

As you'll recall, the *Menu* class serves as the base class for all other menu classes. One of the features implemented by the *Menu* class is its ability to store child menu items in an instance of *MenuItemCollection*. However, you'll seldom need to create a reference to this class directly because it's typically accessed through the *MenuItems* property, as shown here:

```
Menu.MenuItemCollection items = mainMenu.MenuItems;
```

A more common use of the *MenuItemCollection* class is simply to use the *MenuItems* property as an array of *MenuItem* objects, as shown here:

```
foreach(MenuItem item in mainMenu.MenuItems)
{
    item.Enabled = false;
}
```

The *Add* method is used to add a menu item to the collection. There are five versions of the *Add* method. The simplest version just adds a menu item to the end of the current menu and returns the index position of the new item, as shown here:

```
MenuItem helpMenuItem = new MenuItem("&Help");
int position = mainMenu.MenuItems.Add(helpMenuItem);
```

Another version of the *Add* method creates a new menu item at the end of the current menu, using the string passed as a parameter for the menu item's *Text* property, and returns a reference to the new menu item:

```
MenuItem helpMenuItem = mainMenu.MenuItems.Add("&Help");
```

You can also use the *Add* method to create a new menu item that's associated with a *Click* event handler, as shown here:

```
EventHandler indexHandler = new EventHandler(helpIndex_Click);
MenuItem indexItem = helpMenuItem.MenuItems.Add("&Index", indexHandler);
```

The fourth version of the *Add* method, shown in the following code, enables you to specify the index that the menu item will occupy. Any menu items currently in the menu will be shifted down if needed.

```
int position = helpMenuItem.MenuItems.Add(0, indexItem);
```

The fifth and final version of the *Add* method enables you to add a menu item that contains a submenu. For this version of the *Add* method, you pass the *Text* property for the new menu item and an array of menu items that will form the submenu.

```
EventHandler helpIndexHandler = new EventHandler(index_Click);
EventHandler helpContentsHandler = new EventHandler(contents_Click);
EventHandler helpSearchHandler = new EventHandler(search_Click);
MenuItem helpIndex = new MenuItem("&Index", helpIndexHandler);
MenuItem helpCont = new MenuItem("&Contents", helpContentsHandler);
MenuItem helpSearch = new MenuItem("&Search", helpSearchHandler);
MenuItem [] helpMenuArray = new MenuItem [] { helpIndex,
                                              helpCont,
                                              helpSearch };
MenuItem helpMenuItem = mainMenu.MenuItems.Add("&Help", helpMenuArray);
```

The *AddRange* method is used to add an array of menu items to the collection. This method enables you to potentially add a large number of child menu items with one method call. The *AddRange* method is similar to the last version of the *Add* method discussed in the preceding paragraph, except that *AddRange* appends an array of menu items to the current menu, rather than creating a new submenu, as shown here:

```
MenuItem helpMenuItem = mainMenu.MenuItems.Add("&Help");
helpMenuItem.MenuItems.AddRange(helpMenuArray);
```

The *Count* method is used to retrieve the number of menu items in the collection, as shown here:

```
int topLevelItemCount = Menu.MenuItems.Count;
int helpItemCount = helpMenuItem.MenuItems.Count;
```

To remove an item from the collection, pass a reference to the item to be deleted to the *Remove* method, as shown here:

```
editMenuItem.MenuItems.Remove(editWrap);
```

To remove an item at a specific index, you can use the *RemoveAt* method, as shown here:

```
editMenuItem.MenuItems.RemoveAt(1);
```

To remove all menu items from the collection, use the *Clear* method:

```
editMenuItem.MenuItems.Clear();
```

The following code creates a main menu that has three top-level menu items, each associated with a popup submenu:

```
// Top-level menu
MenuItem fileMenuItem = new MenuItem("&File");
MenuItem viewMenuItem = new MenuItem("&View");
MenuItem editMenuItem = new MenuItem("&Edit");
MainMenu mainMenu = new MainMenu( new MenuItem[] { fileMenuItem,
                                                   viewMenuItem,
                                                   editMenuItem });
// Event handlers for the File popup menu
EventHandler fileOpenHandler = new EventHandler(fileOpen_Click);
EventHandler fileSaveHandler = new EventHandler(fileSave_Click);
EventHandler fileSaveAsHandler = new EventHandler(fileSaveAs_Click);
EventHandler fileExitHandler = new EventHandler(fileExit_Click);
// File popup menu
MenuItem fileOpen = new MenuItem("&Open...", fileOpenHandler);
MenuItem fileSave = new MenuItem("&Save", fileSaveHandler);
MenuItem fileSaveAs = new MenuItem("Save &As...", fileSaveAsHandler);
MenuItem fileSeparator = new MenuItem("-");
MenuItem fileExit = new MenuItem("E&xit", fileExitHandler);
MenuItem [] fileMenuItemArray = new MenuItem [] { fileOpen,
                                                  fileSave,
                                                  fileSaveAs,
                                                  fileSeparator,
                                                  fileExit };
fileMenuItem.MenuItems.AddRange(fileMenuItemArray);
// Event handlers for the View popup menu
EventHandler viewHorizHandler =
    new EventHandler(viewHorizontal_Click);
EventHandler viewVertHandler = new EventHandler(viewVertical_Click);
// View popup menu
MenuItem viewScroll = new MenuItem("&Scroll bars");
MenuItem viewHorizontal =
    new MenuItem("&Horizontal", viewHorizHandler);
MenuItem viewVertical = new MenuItem("&Vertical", viewVertHandler);
```

```
MenuItem [] scrollMenuItemArray = new MenuItem [] { viewHorizontal,
                                                    viewVertical };
viewScroll.MenuItems.AddRange(scrollMenuItemArray);
viewMenuItem.MenuItems.Add(viewScroll);
// Event handlers for the Edit popup menu
EventHandler editClearHandler = new EventHandler(editClear_Click);
EventHandler editWrapHandler = new EventHandler(editWrap_Click);
// Edit popup menu
MenuItem editClear = new MenuItem("&Clear", editClearHandler);
MenuItem editWrap = new MenuItem("&Word Wrap", editWrapHandler);
MenuItem [] editMenuItemArray = new MenuItem [] { editClear,
                                                  editWrap };
editMenuItem.MenuItems.AddRange(editMenuItemArray);
// Assign new MainMenu object to the form's Menu property.
Menu = mainMenu;
```

This code begins by creating three menu items and adding them to a *MainMenu* object as its top-level menu items. Next event handler delegates are created for menu items in the File popup menu and are used in the construction of the individual menu items. After the File menu items have been created, they're packed into a *MenuItem* array and added to the menu item collection of *fileMenuItem*. Because *fileMenuItem* is a top-level menu item, its child menu items will form the popup menu displayed when the menu item is clicked. This process is repeated for the View and Edit popup menus. After all menu items have been created and relationships have been established, the *mainMenu* object is assigned to the form's *Menu* property.

Note   The code generated by the Menu Designer is located in the same code region as the code generated by the Forms Designer. If you examine the code that the Menu Designer generates, you'll see that it's written in a slightly different style than the code presented here. In general, the Menu Designer creates *MenuItem* and *MainMenu* instances using the default constructor and then sets each property. This approach works well for the Menu Designer because the code is easy for the tool to update, but the code it creates is more verbose.

Handling Menu Events

There are two ways to handle events for menu items: programmatically and using the Forms Designer. As shown in the previous section, event handler delegates for the *Click* event can be attached to menu items programmatically during construction. In this section, you'll learn how to write code to handle additional events from menu items. You'll also learn how to use the Forms Designer to write the code required to handle menu-related events.

Three events are raised by *MenuItem* objects in response to user actions, as follows:

- **Popup**   The menu item is about to be displayed. This event is useful when you need to update the status of a menu item dynamically, as will be done in the next section.

- **Select**   The menu item has been highlighted as a selection but has not yet been clicked. This event is useful when help text is displayed for a potential menu choice, such as text displayed in a status bar. Using the *Select* event to update status bars is discussed later in this chapter, in the section "Using Status Bar Panels."

- **Click**   The menu item has been chosen by the user. Of all the menu-related events, this is the one that you'll probably use the most, as it indicates that the user has clicked an item on the menu and expects the application to take some sort of action.

These menu item events tell you when individual menu items are selected or clicked; however, there's no menu item event to tell you that a menu has been dismissed. Instead, the *Form* class raises two events that tell you when the menu is initially displayed and dismissed:

- **MenuStart**   Raised when a menu initially receives the input focus
- **MenuComplete**   Raised when the menu loses the input focus

The *MenuStart* event is typically used to manage the form's user interface. When a menu item is selected, you might want to disable specific controls. Alternatively, you might want to enable controls that are used to provide feedback about the menu selection. For example, the *MenuStart* event can be used to display a help balloon control that describes the currently selected menu item.

The *MenuComplete* event is used to reverse the action taken during the *MenuStart* event. *MenuComplete* is raised when the user has finished using the menu, either because a menu item has been clicked or because the user has abandoned the menu and selected a different object.

Updating Menu Items

Menu items can be updated dynamically to reflect the current state of the application. You can enable and disable items, add check marks, and even add and remove menu items at run time. Updating menu items dynamically is an effective way to provide feedback to the user. For example, instead of displaying an error message if the user selects a menu item that's not allowed in the current context, a more user-friendly approach is to simply disable the menu item.

Adding Check Marks to Menu Items

When a menu item is used to enable or disable a property or a feature of your application, a common user interface pattern is to supply a check mark to indicate that the item has been enabled. For example, applications that display a status bar typically provide a menu item that controls the status bar's visibility. When the status bar is visible, the menu item is checked; when the status bar is hidden, the menu item is unchecked.

As mentioned, the *MenuItem* class exposes the *Checked* property, which is used to add a check mark to the left of the menu item text, as shown here:

```
statusBarMenuItem.Checked = statusBar.Visible;
```

A common pattern is to set the state of menu items when the parent's menu item raises the *Popup* event, as shown here:

```
private void editMenuItem_Popup(object sender, System.EventArgs e)
{
    editWordWrap.Checked = textBox.WordWrap;
}
```

In this code, the check mark on the *editWordWrap* menu item is set or cleared depending on the status of the *WordWrap* property of the *textBox* object.

Disabling Menu Items

Menu items that aren't available due to the current state of your application should be disabled to indicate that they can't be selected. You can use the *Enabled* property provided by the *MenuItem* class to enable and disable menu items, as shown here:

```
private void fileMenuItem_Popup(object sender, System.EventArgs e)
{
    fileSave.Enabled = textBox.Modified;
}
```

In this code, the *Save* menu item is disabled if no changes have been made to the *textBox* object.

Using Multiple Menus

You're not limited to using a single main menu for your application. When applications support multiple tasks or multiple document types, it's common practice to provide multiple menus, with the proper menu displayed according to the context. Because a menu is associated with your main form through the form's *Menu* property, switching to a new menu can be done simply by assigning a new menu to the *Menu* property, as shown here:

```
private void SwitchToBasicMenu()
{
    Menu = basicMainMenu;
}
private void SwitchToTextDocumentMenu()
{
    Menu = textDocumentMainMenu;
}
```

To add an additional menu for use by your application, drag a menu control from the Toolbox to your form. An additional menu icon will be added under your form in the Forms Designer. To work with a specific menu using the Menu Designer, click the appropriate icon in the Forms Designer.

Creating a Simple Editor

As an example of how menus are used in an application, the companion CD includes SimpleEdit, a small Notepad-like editor. Although this example is fairly small, it illustrates the various ways menus are used in a dynamic application.

The Basic SimpleEdit Application

The SimpleEdit project is a Windows Forms application with two controls on its main form, as follows:

- A main menu control named *mainMenu* that provides access to application commands

- A text box control named *textBox* that fills the form's client area and serves as the container for edited text

The properties of the top-level menu items in the SimpleEdit project are listed in Table 13-10.

Table 13-10. **Top-Level Menu Item Properties in SimpleEdit**

Text	Name
&File	*fileMenuItem*
&View	*viewMenuItem*
&Edit	*editMenuItem*

Each of the three top-level menu items has an associated popup menu that's displayed when the top-level menu item is selected. Table 13-11 lists the properties for the menu items on the File, View, and Edit popup menus.

Table 13-11.   Popup Menu Properties in SimpleEdit

Parent Menu	Text	Name
File	&Open...	fileOpenMenuItem
	&Save	fileSaveMenuItem
	Save &As...	fileSaveAsMenuItem
	Separator	N/A
	E&xit	fileExitMenuItem
View	&Scroll Bars	viewScrollBarMenuItem
Scroll Bars	&Horizontal	hScrollMenuItem
	&Vertical	vScrollMenuItem
Edit	&Clear	editClearMenuItem
	&Word Wrap	editWrapMenuItem

The View menu has one child menu item, Scroll Bars; this menu item is in turn the parent of two submenus, Horizontal and Vertical, as shown in Figure 13-4.

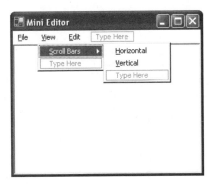

Figure 13-4.   The Scroll Bars menu item, which has two child items.

The *textBox* control used by the SimpleEdit project is just a basic text box control from the Toolbox, with a few properties set to nondefault values, as listed in Table 13-12.

Table 13-12.   Text Box Control Properties in SimpleEdit

Property	Value
Multiline	true
Name	textBox
Dock	DockStyle.Fill

The *Dock* property is used to attach a control to the edge of its container. By default, this property is set to *DockStyle.None*. Setting the property to *DockStyle.Fill* causes the control to expand to fill the entire container. Docking is simply a characteristic that specifies which edge of the current form the control will attach to. Values for the *Dock* property must be set to one of the *DockStyle* enumeration values, listed in Table 13-13. Many controls expose the *Dock* property; this feature will be discussed in more detail in Chapter 15. For now, it's enough that you simply understand that the text box control uses the *Dock* property to completely fill the client area of the form.

Table 13-13.   *DockStyle* Enumeration Values

Value	Description
Bottom	Docks to the bottom edge of the form
Fill	Docks to all edges, filling the client area of the form
Left	Docks to the left edge of the form
None	Not docked to any edge
Right	Docks to the right edge of the form
Top	Docks to the top of the form

Dynamically Updating SimpleEdit Menu Items

The File, View, and Edit popup menus each contain menu items that are updated dynamically as the menus are displayed. The *Popup* event for each top-level menu item is managed by the event handlers listed in Table 13-14.

Table 13-14.   Popup Event Handlers for SimpleEdit

Menu Item	Event Handler
fileMenuItem	fileMenuItem_Popup
editMenuItem	editMenuItem_Popup
viewScrollBarMenuItem	viewScrollBarMenuItem_Popup

The event handler methods from Table 13-14 are shown in the following code:

```
private void fileMenuItem_Popup(object sender, System.EventArgs e)
{
    fileSaveMenuItem.Enabled = textBox.Modified;
}

private void editMenuItem_Popup(object sender, System.EventArgs e)
{
    editWordWrapMenuItem.Checked = textBox.WordWrap;
}

private void
viewScrollBarMenuItem_Popup(object sender, System.EventArgs e)
{
    // Horizontal scrolling is n/a if the text box control
    // has word-wrapping enabled.
    hScrollMenuItem.Enabled = !textBox.WordWrap;
    switch(textBox.ScrollBars)
    {
        case ScrollBars.Both:
            hScrollMenuItem.Checked = true;
            vScrollMenuItem.Checked = true;
            break;
        case ScrollBars.Vertical:
            hScrollMenuItem.Checked = false;
            vScrollMenuItem.Checked = true;
            break;
        case ScrollBars.Horizontal:
            hScrollMenuItem.Checked = true;
            vScrollMenuItem.Checked = false;
            break;
        default:
            hScrollMenuItem.Checked = false;
            vScrollMenuItem.Checked = false;
            break;
    }
}
```

The handler for the File menu *Popup* event, *fileMenuItem_Popup*, enables or disables the Save menu item, depending on the state of the text box control. If the text box control's *Modified* property returns *true*, changes have been made to the contents of the text box, and the Save menu item is enabled. If the *Modified* property returns *false*, the contents of the text box control haven't been modified, and the Save item is disabled.

The *editMenuItem_Popup* method, the handler for the Edit menu's *Popup* event, controls whether a check mark is placed next to the Word Wrap menu item. If the text box control has its *WordWrap* property enabled, the check mark is set. If the property is disabled, the check mark is cleared.

The final handler for a *Popup* event, *viewScrollBarMenuItem_Popup*, is more complex than the previous two handlers because it updates two menu items based on the value of the text box control's *ScrollBars* property. The value of the *ScrollBars* property is tested to determine its value, and then check marks are either set or cleared for the *vScrollMenuItem* and *hScrollMenuItem* objects. In addition, the text box control doesn't support horizontal scrolling if the *WordWrap* property is set to *true*, so the *hScrollMenuItem* object is enabled or disabled based on this property.

Handling Menu Commands

As you'll recall, the *Click* event is raised when the user chooses a menu item. The SimpleEdit application exposes eight commands through its main menu, as listed in Table 13-15.

Table 13-15.   *Click* Event Handlers in SimpleEdit

Menu Item	Event Handler	Description
fileOpenMenuItem	*fileOpenMenuItem_Click*	Opens a file
fileSaveMenuItem	*fileSaveMenuItem_Click*	Saves the current text to a file
fileSaveAsMenuItem	*fileSaveAsMenuItem_Click*	Saves the current text to a new file
fileExitMenuItem	*fileExitMenuItem_Click*	Exits the application
hScrollMenuItem	*hScrollMenuItem_Click*	Enables the horizontal scroll bar
vScrollMenuItem	*vScrollMenuItem_Click*	Enables the vertical scroll bar
editClearMenuItem	*editClearMenuItem_Click*	Clears the contents of the text box
editWrapMenuItem	*editWordWrapMenuItem_Click*	Enables word wrap

Most of the commands available to users of the SimpleEdit application are mapped directly to properties exposed by the text box control. The only exceptions are the menu items in the File popup menu, which are discussed in the next section. The following code includes the *Click* event handlers for menu items on the Edit and View popup menus:

```
private void
editClearMenuItem_Click(object sender, System.EventArgs e)
{
    _fileName = "";
    _pathName = "";
```

```
        Text = _appName + " - " + "[Empty]";
        textBox.Clear();
    }
private void
editWordWrapMenuItem_Click(object sender, System.EventArgs e)
{
        textBox.WordWrap = !textBox.WordWrap;
    }
private void
hScrollMenuItem_Click(object sender, System.EventArgs e)
{
        if(hScrollMenuItem.Checked)
        {
            // Clear horizontal scroll bars.
            if(textBox.ScrollBars == ScrollBars.Both)
                textBox.ScrollBars = ScrollBars.Vertical;
            else
                textBox.ScrollBars = ScrollBars.None;
        }
        else
        {
            // Set horizontal scroll bars.
            if(textBox.ScrollBars == ScrollBars.Vertical)
                textBox.ScrollBars = ScrollBars.Both;
            else
                textBox.ScrollBars = ScrollBars.Horizontal;
        }
    }
private void vScrollMenuItem_Click(object sender, System.EventArgs e)
{
        if(vScrollMenuItem.Checked)
        {
            // Clear vertical scroll bars.
            if(textBox.ScrollBars == ScrollBars.Both)
                textBox.ScrollBars = ScrollBars.Horizontal;
            else
                textBox.ScrollBars = ScrollBars.None;
        }
        else
        {
            // Set vertical scroll bars.
            if(textBox.ScrollBars == ScrollBars.Horizontal)
                textBox.ScrollBars = ScrollBars.Both;
            else
                textBox.ScrollBars = ScrollBars.Vertical;
        }
    }
```

In the *editClearMenuItem_Click* method, the text box control's *Clear* method is called to remove the contents of the control. In addition, member variables that track the current file name are reset, and the application's caption is reset to indicate that no file is currently open. The *editWordWrapMenuItem_Click* method toggles word wrapping by simply inverting the property's current value.

The *hScrollMenuItem_Click* and *vScrollMenuItem_Click* methods are used to manage the scroll bars attached to the text box control. The process of enabling and disabling scroll bars requires some additional code because the *ScrollBars* property is used to control the vertical and horizontal scroll bars.

Opening and Saving Text Files

The File popup menu is used primarily for opening and saving files, as well as for closing the application, which is traditionally included as an item on this menu. The following code includes the *Click* event handlers for the File menu:

```
private void fileOpenMenuItem_Click(object sender,
                                    System.EventArgs e)
{
    OpenFileDialog dlg = new OpenFileDialog();
    dlg.Filter = _fileFilter;
    dlg.InitialDirectory = Application.CommonAppDataPath;
    dlg.CheckFileExists = false;
    if(dlg.ShowDialog() == DialogResult.OK)
    {
        string path = dlg.FileName;
        if(File.Exists(path) != true)
        {
            StreamWriter writer = File.CreateText(path);
            writer.Close();
        }
        _fileName = Path.GetFileName(path);
        _pathName = path;
        Text = _appName + " - " + _fileName;
        StreamReader reader = new StreamReader(path);
        textBox.Text = reader.ReadToEnd();
        reader.Close();
    }
}
private void SaveTextToPath(string path)
{
    StreamWriter writer = new StreamWriter(path);
    writer.Write(textBox.Text);
    writer.Close();
    textBox.Modified = false;
}
private void SaveTextToNewPath()
```

```
    {
        SaveFileDialog dlg = new SaveFileDialog();
        dlg.Filter = _fileFilter;
        dlg.InitialDirectory = Application.CommonAppDataPath;
        if(dlg.ShowDialog() == DialogResult.OK)
        {
            string path = dlg.FileName;
            if(File.Exists(path) == true)
            {
                DialogResult result = MessageBox.Show(_overwriteWarning,
                                            _appName,
                                            MessageBoxButtons.OKCancel,
                                            MessageBoxIcon.Question);
                if(result == DialogResult.Cancel)
                    return;
            }
            _fileName = Path.GetFileName(path);
            _pathName = path;
            Text = _appName + " - " +  _fileName;
            SaveTextToPath(path);
        }
    }
    private void fileSaveMenuItem_Click(object sender,
                                        System.EventArgs e)
    {
        if(_fileName != null && _fileName != "")
            SaveTextToPath(_pathName);
        else
            SaveTextToNewPath();
    }
    private void fileSaveAsMenuItem_Click(object sender,
                                          System.EventArgs e)
    {
        SaveTextToNewPath();
    }
    private void fileExitMenuItem_Click(object sender,
                                        System.EventArgs e)
    {
        Close();
    }
```

The SimpleEdit project uses common dialog boxes to enable users to select files used by the application. As discussed in Chapter 11, the *Application.CommonAppData* property is used as a starting location for all file operations; when a common file dialog box is displayed to the user, the initial directory is set to that path.

The *fileOpenMenuItem_Click* method creates an instance of *OpenFile-Dialog*, which enables the user to use a common file dialog box to select a file that's to be loaded into the text box control. If the user selects a file and clicks OK, the file path is tested to determine whether the file exists by passing the path to the *File.Exists* method. If the file exists, an instance of *StreamReader* is created from the selected file's path, and the *ReadToEnd* method is called to retrieve the file's contents. If the file doesn't exist, it's assumed that the user wants to work with a new file, and the file is created.

The *SaveTextToPath* and *SaveTextToNewPath* methods are used by *Click* event handlers to save the contents of the text box. The *SaveTextToPath* method is used by SimpleEdit to write the contents of the text box to a disk file. The method accepts a destination file path as a parameter. It then creates an instance of *StreamWriter* using the path, which is used to write the contents of the text box to the destination file. After the file has been closed, the text box control's *Modified* flag is reset to indicate that all changes have been saved. The *SaveTextToNewPath* method creates an instance of *SaveFileDialog*, which enables the use of a common file dialog box to select a destination for the text box control's contents. After a destination file has been selected, the *SaveText-ToPath* method is called to actually write the contents to the file.

The *fileSaveMenuItem_Click* event handler will call the *SaveTextToPath* method if a destination file has already been determined. This will be the case when a file has previously been opened for editing. If no file has been previously selected, the *SaveTextToNewPath* method will be called, and the user must select a destination path before the contents are saved. The *fileSaveAsMenuItem_Click* method always calls the *SaveTextToNewPath* method.

Implementing Shortcut Menus

Unlike a main menu, which is displayed at all times, a shortcut menu is a special menu that's displayed only when the user requests it by right-clicking a form or control or by pressing the shortcut menu key that's found on some newer keyboards. This menu appears as a popup menu, usually near the insertion point or the mouse pointer. A shortcut menu typically provides access to specific, context-sensitive operations that can be performed on the object that was clicked, rather than accessing general tasks that are carried out by the application. For example, when you right-click in Internet Explorer, the shortcut menu changes based on the type of object that was clicked—the shortcut menu displayed for a hyperlink is different from the shortcut menu displayed for an image. In this section, we'll look at how to create and use shortcut menus in an application.

Creating Basic Shortcut Menus

The *ContextMenu* class is used to create a shortcut menu. As with *MainMenu* objects, an instance of the *ContextMenu* class must contain one or more instances of the *MenuItem* class to be usable. And as with main menus, you can build shortcut menus programmatically or by using the *ContextMenu* control and the Menu Designer.

All controls and forms expose the *ContextMenu* property, which is used to associate the form or control with a shortcut menu. The following code creates an instance of a shortcut menu and assigns it to a list box control:

```
EventHandler helloHandler = new EventHandler(hello_Click);
EventHandler goodbyeHandler = new EventHandler(goodbye_Click);
ContextMenu listboxContextMenu = new ContextMenu();
MenuItem helloMenuItem = new MenuItem("&Hello", helloHandler);
MenuItem goodbyeMenuItem = new MenuItem("&Goodbye", goodbyeHandler);

MenuItem[] contextMenuItemArray = new MenuItem [] { helloMenuItem,
                                                    goodbyeMenuItem };
listboxContextMenu.MenuItems.AddRange(contextMenuItemArray);
listBox.ContextMenu = listboxContextMenu;
```

As this code shows, the *ContextMenu* class is used much like the *MainMenu* class. The menu items are represented by *MenuItem* objects, and the menu items are stored in a collection that's accessed through the *MenuItems* property. Just as with items in a *MainMenu* object, the items stored in a shortcut menu will raise *Click*, *Popup*, and *Selected* events.

The *ContextMenu* control can be used much like the *MainMenu* control. The only difference you'll notice is that the Menu Designer doesn't allow you to add new menu items to the top level of the menu. Because shortcut menus are just popup menus, there's no need to have any top-level menu items.

Programming with Shortcut Menus

Although you can associate a shortcut menu with a form, it's most often associated with a control. For example, a text box control has a built-in shortcut menu that enables a user to interact with the Windows clipboard. Many controls can benefit greatly from the added functionality and user-friendliness that a shortcut menu provides. The ControlContextMenu project on the companion CD, shown in Figure 13-5, has a list box control that provides a shortcut menu.

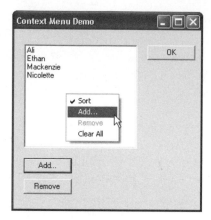

Figure 13-5.   The ControlContextMenu example application.

The list box control on the main form of ControlContextMenu provides a shortcut menu that's displayed when the user right-clicks the control. This shortcut menu enables the user to add, remove, clear, and sort items in the list box. Properties for the shortcut menu are listed in Table 13-16.

Table 13-16.   Shortcut Menu Properties in ControlContextMenu

Text	Name	Event Handler
Sort	*sortMenuItem*	*sortMenuItem_Click*
Add	*addMenuItem*	*addMenuItem_Click*
Remove	*removeMenuItem*	*removeMenuItem_Click*
Clear All	*clearMenuItem*	*clearMenuItem_Click*

The following code contains the *Click* event handlers for the shortcut menu:

```
private void sortMenuItem_Click(object sender, System.EventArgs e)
{
    listBox.Sorted = !listBox.Sorted;
}
private void addMenuItem_Click(object sender, System.EventArgs e)
{
    AddItem();
}
private void removeMenuItem_Click(object sender, System.EventArgs e)
{
    listBox.Items.RemoveAt(listBox.SelectedIndex);
}
private void clearMenuItem_Click(object sender, System.EventArgs e)
```

```
{
    listBox.Items.Clear();
}
private void AddItem()
{
    ⋮
}
```

Most of the *Click* event handlers shown in this code are mapped directly to methods exposed by the *ListBox* class. The exception is the handler for adding a new menu item, which invokes another form and isn't fully shown here.

Shortcut menus can also be updated dynamically. In this example, when the list box control is empty, the menu items that enable sorting or removal of the list box contents should be disabled. The *Popup* event handler method from the ControlContextMenu project is shown in the following code:

```
private void listBoxMenu_Popup(object sender, System.EventArgs e)
{
    if(listBox.Items.Count == 0)
    {
        sortMenuItem.Enabled = false;
        removeMenuItem.Enabled = false;
        clearMenuItem.Enabled = false;
    }
    else
    {
        if(listBox.SelectedIndex == -1)
            removeMenuItem.Enabled = false;
        else
            removeMenuItem.Enabled = true;

        sortMenuItem.Enabled = true;
        clearMenuItem.Enabled = true;
    }
    sortMenuItem.Checked = listBox.Sorted;
}
```

This code starts by determining the number of items in the list box control. If there's at least one item in the control, the Sort and Clear All menu items are enabled. A further test is made before enabling the Remove menu item, which is used to remove individual items from the list box control; it's enabled only if an item is selected. A check mark is provided for the Sort menu item that follows the list box control's *Sorted* property and is set independently of whether the menu item is enabled or disabled. If the list box is sorted, the menu item is checked; if the control is unsorted, the menu item is unchecked.

Providing Feedback with Status Bars

Status bars are used to provide feedback in several ways. A common use for status bars is to provide additional descriptions of menu items as the user selects each item. Status bars often serve as dashboards, providing feedback about the current status of the application and computer.

Unlike the top-level menu discussed earlier in this chapter, in the section "Using a Main Menu with Forms," a status bar doesn't change the size of a form's client area. Instead, the status bar control is placed on top of the form, as shown in Figure 13-6.

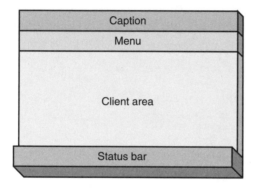

Figure 13-6.   A status bar control, which is placed above the form's client area.

The distinction between reducing the size of the form and being placed on top of it is important if you're working directly with the form surface, either by drawing on it, as will be discussed in Chapter 14, or by dynamically positioning controls.

Creating Status Bars

Status bars are created using the *StatusBar* class. A relatively small amount of code will create a simple but serviceable status bar, as shown here:

```
StatusBar status = new StatusBar();
Controls.Add(status);
```

This status bar will automatically dock itself to the bottom edge of its form, as its *Dock* property is, by default, set to *DockStyle.Bottom*. As mentioned, docking is simply a characteristic that specifies to which edge of the current form the control will attach itself; this feature will be discussed in more detail in Chapter 15.

When using a simple status bar, such as the one created in the preceding code fragment, a message can be displayed with the *Text* property, as shown here:

```
status.Text = "This is the status bar.";
```

By default, status bars include a *sizing grip* in the lower-right corner. A sizing grip simplifies the task of resizing a form because it increases the region that the user drags for resizing. Sometimes the sizing grip is undesirable, however, because it conflicts with other user interface elements (or maybe you just don't like the sizing grip). You can control the visibility of the sizing grip with the *SizingGrip* property, as follows:

```
status.SizingGrip = false;
```

Although a status bar can be created using just source code, an easy way to add a status bar to a form is to use the Forms Designer. When a form is open in the Forms Designer, the Toolbox includes a status bar control. When you add a status bar control to a form, the following properties are set by default:

- The *Dock* property is set to *DockingStyle.Bottom*.

- The *SizingGrip* property is set to *true*.

- The *Text* property is set to the name of the control.

If your application has a menu, it's traditional to provide an option for users to hide user interface elements such as status bars. Like most controls, the *StatusBar* class exposes the *Visible* property, which hides the status bar when set to *false*, as shown here:

```
status.Visible = false;
```

You can also use the *Visible* property to determine the current state of the status bar, as follows:

```
if(status.Visible == false)
{
    ⋮
}
```

Using Status Bar Panels

A common way to use a status bar is to segment the display area into multiple panels, with each panel used for a specific type of information. Each panel can be updated separately, and often each has its own display characteristics. Typically, panels that are dedicated to a specific type of information—such as the status of locking keyboard keys, the time, or other status information—have a three-dimensional, sunken style. Panels that provide general feedback text—such as descriptions of selected menu items—are often drawn in a flat style.

The *StatusBarPanels* class represents the panels displayed on a status bar. The most commonly used *StatusBarPanel* properties are as follows:

- **Alignment**   A value from the *HorizontalAlignment* enumeration that specifies how items are aligned in the panel.

- **AutoSize**   A value from the *StatusBarPanelAutoSize* enumeration that specifies how the panel handles automatic sizing.

- **BorderStyle**   A value from the *StatusBarBorderStyle* enumeration that specifies the panel's border.

- **MinWidth**   The minimum width for the panel. If the *AutoSize* property is set to *None*, this property is automatically set equal to the *Width* property. For other *AutoSize* scenarios, the value of this property is used to ensure a minimum usable size for the panel.

- **Style**   Specifies whether the panel is drawn by the .NET Framework or by the owner of the control. By default, this property is set to *StatusBarPanelStyle.Text*, causing the panel to be drawn by the .NET Framework. To take control over drawing the panel, set this property to *StatusBarPanelStyle.OwnerDraw*.

- **Text**   The message displayed in the panel.

- **Width**   The width of the panel.

Values from the *HorizontalAlignment* enumeration are provided in Table 13-17. The default value for *StatusBar* objects is *HorizontalAlignment.Left*.

Table 13-17. *HorizontalAlignment* Enumeration Values

Value	Description
Left	Items are aligned to the left.
Center	Items are aligned in the center.
Right	Items are aligned to the right.

Values from the *StatusBarPanelAutoSize* enumeration are provided in Table 13-18. The default value is *StatusBarPanelAutoSize.None*. Using panels that support automatic sizing is discussed later in this section.

Table 13-18.   *StatusBarPanelAutoSize* **Enumeration Values**

Value	Description
None	No auto-sizing is done; the width of the panel is specified by the *Width* property.
Contents	The width of the panel is auto-sized to fit its contents.
Spring	The panel expands to fill space not taken up by other panels. All panels that have their *AutoSize* property set to *Spring* will share the available space.

Values from the *StatusBarPanelBorderStyle* enumeration are provided in Table 13-19. The default value for *BorderStyle* is *StatusBarPanelBorderStyle.None*.

Table 13-19.   *StatusBarPanelBorderStyle* **Enumeration Values**

Value	Description
None	The panel has a flat appearance.
Raised	The panel has a three-dimensional raised border.
Sunken	The panel has a three-dimensional sunken border.

Each status bar maintains a collection of the *StatusBarPanel* objects it owns; this collection is accessible through the *Panels* property. The *Panels* property returns a reference to a *StatusBarPanelCollection* object, which is typically used directly, just like the *MenuItemCollection* class discussed earlier in this chapter, in the section "Creating a Menu Programmatically." For example, to add a panel to a status bar, you can use code like this:

```
StatusBarPanel mainPanel = new StatusBarPanel();
status.Panels.Add(mainPanel);
```

To remove a panel, use the collection's *Remove* or *RemoveAt* properties, as shown here:

```
status.Panels.Remove(mainPanel);
status.Panels.RemoveAt(0);
```

The *StatusBarPanelCollection* class exposes an indexer, which enables you to use the *Panels* property as an array of *StatusBarPanel* objects, like this:

```
foreach(StatusBarPanel panel in status.Panels)
{
    panel.AutoSize = StatusBarPanelAutoSize.Contents;
}
status.Panels[0].AutoSize = StatusBarPanelAutoSize.Spring;
status.Panels[0].BorderStyle = StatusBarPanelBorderStyle.None;
status.Panels[1].BorderStyle = StatusBarPanelBorderStyle.Sunken;
```

The *StatusBar* class exposes the *ShowPanels* property, which is used to enable the display of status bar panels and is set to *false* by default. The following code enables the use of panels, creates two status bar panels, and adds them to the status bar:

```
StatusBar status = new StatusBar();
status.ShowPanels = true;
StatusBarPanel mainPanel = new StatusBarPanel();
StatusBarPanel timePanel = new StatusBarPanel();
status.Panels.Add(mainPanel);
status.Panels.Add(timePanel);
```

Visual C# .NET includes the StatusBarPanel Collection Editor, which can be used to easily manage status bar panels. You can launch this editor by clicking the button adjacent to the *Panels* property in the Properties window. Initially, the editor is empty, as shown in Figure 13-7.

Figure 13-7.   The StatusBarPanel Collection Editor before any panels have been added.

Panels are added to the status bar's collection of panels by clicking the Add button. After a panel is added to the collection, its properties can be managed from within the editor. A list of the panels in the collection is provided on the left side of the editor, and the selected panel's properties are displayed on the right, as shown in Figure 13-8.

Figure 13-8.   Editing status bar panels using the StatusBarPanel
Collection Editor.

The size of each panel in the status bar depends on several factors—
primarily, the value of each panel's *AutoSize* and *Width* properties. Taken
together, these properties enable panels to be sized in a cooperative way, and
in many cases there's no need to specify an explicit size for status bar panels.
The status bar adjusts the width of its panels using the following rules:

■   Any panels that have their *AutoSize* property set to *StatusBarPanel-
    AutoSize.None* will be sized according to their *Width* property.

■   Any panels that have their *AutoSize* property sct to *StatusBarPanel-
    AutoSize.Contents* will have their width set to a size large enough to
    display their contents, but not less than their *MinWidth* property.

■   Any panels that have their *AutoSize* property set to *StatusBarPanel-
    AutoSize.Spring* will divide the remaining space on the status bar.

When a status bar is too small to display all panels, the panels are displayed in
the order in which they were stored in the status bar's collection of panels.

Displaying the Time and Date

The companion CD includes an example project named StatusBars that creates a status bar with two panels, shown in Figure 13-9: one panel for menu help text, and another panel that displays the time.

Figure 13-9.   The StatusBars example project.

Three controls have been added to the main form in the StatusBars project:

■   A *MainMenu* control is used to display commands available to the user.

■   A *Timer* control is used to generate timer events at 10-second intervals so that the time on the status bar can be updated.

■   A *StatusBar* control with two panels is used to provide feedback to the user.

The first status bar panel is named *helpPanel* and is used to display help text for menu items selected by the user. Its *AutoSize* property is set to *StatusBarPanelAutoSize.Spring* to enable it to grow to the maximum available size. The second status bar panel is named *timePanel* and is used to display the current time. Its *AutoSize* property is set to *StatusBarPanelAutoSize.Contents*, which properly sizes the panel to contain the current time.

Updating the Status Bar for Menu Events

As mentioned, a *Select* event is raised for each menu item selected by the user. The StatusBars application displays help text for each menu item by implementing handlers for these events, as shown here:

```
private void fileMenuItem_Select(object sender, System.EventArgs e)
{
    helpPanel.Text = "File Menu";
}

private void openMenuItem_Select(object sender, System.EventArgs e)
{
    helpPanel.Text = "Open file for editing";
}

private void closeMenuItem_Select(object sender, System.EventArgs e)
{
    helpPanel.Text = "Close the current file";
}

private void exitMenuItem_Select(object sender, System.EventArgs e)
{
    helpPanel.Text = "Exit the application";
}

private void statusBarMenuItem_Select(object sender, System.EventArgs e)
{
    helpPanel.Text = "Toggle the status bar";
}
```

These events aren't sufficient to properly update the status bar because the status bar would always contain the help text for the last menu item that was selected. To clear the status bar after an item has been selected or the menu has been dismissed, the StatusBars application provides a handler for the form's *MenuComplete* event, as follows:

```
private void MainForm_MenuComplete(object sender, System.EventArgs e)
{
    helpPanel.Text = "";
}
```

Displaying the Time in the Status Bar

The time panel in the status bar is refreshed periodically based on a timer control on the main form. Each time the timer raises a *Tick* event, it's handled by the StatusBars application's main form, as shown here:

```
private void timer_Tick(object sender, System.EventArgs e)
{
    timePanel.Text = DateTime.Now.ToShortTimeString();
}
```

For each *Tick* event that's raised, the current time is retrieved through the *Now* static property exposed by the *DateTime* class. This property returns a *DateTime* object, which is then converted to a string with the *ToShort-TimeString* method.

Conclusion

The Windows Forms namespace provides a great deal of support for interaction with the user. In addition to the classes provided in the .NET Framework, Visual C# .NET includes designers that simplify the task of building menus and status bars.

In applications developed for Windows Forms, the mouse and keyboard are the primary conduits for user input. The .NET Framework includes classes that simplify interaction with these devices and provides a comprehensive set of events that are raised as input is provided.

Most nontrivial applications have at least one menu that enables the user to invoke commands. The .NET Framework includes classes that represent the main menu for an application, shortcut menus for forms or controls, and menu items that represent individual items in menus. Visual C# .NET includes a Menu Designer that can be used to create both main menus and shortcut menus.

The *StatusBar* class is used to provide feedback in a status bar docked to the bottom edge of a Windows Forms application. A status bar is often divided into multiple sections known as panels, with each panel used for a different type of feedback message.

In Chapter 14, we'll look at the Windows Graphics Device Interface (GDI+) and explore how you can use the .NET Framework to easily work with fonts, bitmaps, pens, and brushes.

14

GDI+

GDI+ is a new way of drawing graphical images for Microsoft Windows applications. GDI+ improves on the Graphical Device Interface (GDI) included with earlier versions of Windows. Up to now, we've been developing the user interface by adding controls to forms; in this chapter, we'll draw directly on the form, using the methods and properties provided by the *Graphics* class.

This chapter begins with an examination of Windows Forms geometry, including the *Point*, *Size*, and *Rectangle* structures—three structures that are used to define shapes and locations when programming with Windows Forms. We'll also look at the *Color* structure and how it's used to define the colors used by your application. You'll also learn how to use *Brush* objects to fill areas such as rectangles. The Microsoft .NET Framework provides a range of brushes, including brushes used to create gradients and brushes used to fill areas with a pattern from a bitmap. The *Graphics* class includes methods that enable you to draw lines, figures, and other shapes using a *Pen* object. Pens can be created in a variety of colors, styles, and patterns, but you can also request a reference to one of the standard pens available through the *SystemPens* class. We'll finish up by looking at how the Font class is used to define the fonts used to display text.

Understanding Windows Forms Geometry

This section examines the basic structures used to define position and size in a Windows Forms application. Although we've made it through a couple of chapters on Windows Forms without describing these structures in more detail, it's impossible to draw a line or fill a rectangle unless you specify the precise location of the object to be filled or drawn.

Specifying Locations with the *Point* Structure

The *Point* structure represents a location on a two-dimensional surface in a Windows Forms application. This structure is frequently used to define locations used for forms or controls; it's also used to define boundaries when drawing lines, rectangles, and other shapes.

The *Point* structure is built around the following two properties:

- **X** Defines the x-coordinate, or horizontal position, of the *Point* structure

- **Y** Defines the y-coordinate, or vertical position, of the *Point* structure

The default constructor for a *Point* structure creates an empty *Point* structure with both the x-coordinate and the y-coordinate set to 0, as shown here:

```
Point pt = new Point();
```

An empty *Point* structure can be detected through the *IsEmpty* property, which returns *true* for empty *Point* structures.

```
if(pt.IsEmpty)
{
    // pt is an empty Point structure.
}
```

The most common way to create a *Point* structure is to pass the xy-coordinates to the constructor, as shown here:

```
int x = 10;
int y = 20;
Point pt = new Point(x, y);
```

In this constructor, the first parameter is the x-coordinate and the second parameter is the y-coordinate. Other, less commonly used overloads of the constructor enable you to create *Point* values from a *Size* structure (the *Size* structure is discussed in the next section) or an integer that specifies both *X* and *Y* values.

The *PointF* structure is similar to *Point*, except that its coordinates are composed of floating-point values that provide greater precision. The *PointF* structure also can be created by passing a pair of *float* coordinates to the constructor, as shown here:

```
float x = 22.4f;
float y = 17.8f;
Point pt = new PointF(x, y);
```

The *Point* structure includes three static methods that enable conversion from *PointF* to *Point* values, as follows:

- **Ceiling**   Converts from *PointF* to *Point* by rounding up each coordinate value to the next higher integer value

- **Round**   Converts from *PointF* to *Point* by rounding each coordinate value to the nearest integer value

- **Truncate**   Converts from *PointF* to *Point* by rounding each coordinate value to the next lower integer value

An implicit conversion operator converts *Point* values to *PointF* values without the requirement for explicit casts or method calls.

Defining the Size of Visual Elements

The *Size* structure is used to define the size of windows, forms, controls, and other rectangular regions in a Windows Forms application. The *Size* structure has two nondefault constructors. The first constructor accepts a *Point* value, as shown here:

```
Point pt;
⋮
Size mySize = new Size(pt);
```

This constructor uses the x-coordinate from the *Point* parameter to initialize the *Size* structure's length. The y-coordinate from the *Point* parameter is used to initialize the *Size* structure's height.

The second *Size* constructor accepts discrete integer values for the width and the height of the new *Size* structure, as follows:

```
int width = 20;
int height = 10;
Point pt = new Point(width, height);
```

The *Size* structure exposes its width and height through two properties: *Width* and *Height*.

As with the *Point* structure, *IsEmpty* can be used to test for empty *Size* values, as shown here:

```
if(mySize.IsEmpty)
{
    // mySize is an empty Size structure.
}
```

The *SizeF* structure is similar to *Size*, except that it uses floating-point values instead of integers to represent size dimensions. Just as with the *Point* and *PointF* structures described in the previous section, the *Size* structure includes *Ceiling*, *Round*, and *Truncate* methods for conversion from *SizeF* to *Size* values. Additionally, there's an implicit conversion operator for conversions from *Size* to *SizeF*.

Defining Rectangles

The *Rectangle* structure defines the location and size of a rectangle and is the traditional data structure used to describe controls and forms (although strictly speaking, forms and controls aren't limited to rectangular shapes). The *Rectangle* structure is organized much like the *Point* and *Size* structures, providing methods and properties to get and set the underlying coordinates on which the structure is based. The *Rectangle* structure differs somewhat from *RECT*, the equivalent Microsoft Win32 data structure. The *RECT* structure is based on four coordinates that represent the edges of the rectangle; the *Rectangle* structure consists of a *Point* structure that defines the upper-left corner of the rectangle and a *Size* structure that specifies the dimensions of the rectangle.

Two constructors are used to create *Rectangle* structures. The first constructor accepts a *Point* structure and a *Size* structure as parameters, as shown here:

```
Size  mySize = new Size(200, 300);
Point startPoint = new Point(10, 10);
Rectangle myRect = new Rectangle(startPoint, mySize);
```

The second version of the *Rectangle* constructor accepts four integers that describe its boundaries, as shown here:

```
int left = 10;
int top = 10;
int width = 200;
int height = 300;
Rectangle myRect = new Rectangle(left, top, width, height);
```

The four parameters in this example aren't the edges of the rectangle; the first two parameters define the xy-coordinates of the rectangle's upper-left corner, and the last two parameters define the width and height of the rectangle.

The *Rectangle* structure is commonly used when you're drawing or manipulating a control's client area—that is, the "main" portion of the control, minus extra nonclient elements such as scroll bars. The client area of a form is the portion of the control that's located below the title bar and menu bar (if any) and within the boundaries of the form. The *Form* class exposes a *Client-Rectangle* property that can be used to retrieve the location of the client area, as shown here:

```
Rectangle myRect = ClientRectangle;
```

As you saw in Chapter 13, the status bar overlays the client area without reducing the overall size of the client area, unlike the menu and scroll bars. When calculating the visible area of a form, remember to reduce the client area's size by the dimensions of the status bar.

The *Rectangle* structure exposes several properties that are used to get and set rectangle coordinates, listed here:

- *Left*
- *Right*
- *Top*
- *Bottom*
- *Width*
- *Height*

The *RectangleF* structure is similar to the *Rectangle* structure, except that it works with floating-point values instead of integers. In addition, *RectangleF* uses *SizeF* and *PointF* structures as parameters instead of *Size* and *Point*. And just like *PointF* and *SizeF*, the *RectangleF* structure will implicitly convert *Rectangle* values to *RectangleF* values. The *Rectangle* structure also exposes *Ceiling*, *Round,* and *Truncate* methods that convert *RectangleF* values to *Rectangle* values.

Using the *Graphics* Class

The *Graphics* class is one of the fundamental classes used in programming with Windows Forms and GDI+. Through the *Graphics* class, you gain access to information about the display resolution and device capabilities. In this section, you'll learn about the *Paint* event and how it supplies you with a reference to a properly initialized *Graphics* object. This section also covers the most common operations performed using the *Graphics* object, including drawing text and drawing and filling shapes such as rectangles and ellipses.

Handling the *Paint* Event

In a Windows Forms application, controls and forms are updated in response to *Paint* events. Much of the time, you might not even be aware that a *Paint* event has occurred. In the examples presented in Chapter 12 and Chapter 13, the user interface for each application consisted entirely of controls that encapsulated their own drawing code. Internally, however, the controls were responding to *Paint* events.

Paint events are handled by *PaintEventHandler* delegates, which are defined as follows:

```
Paint += new PaintEventHandler(this.Form_Paint);
    ⋮
private void Form_Paint(object sender,
                    System.Windows.Forms.PaintEventArgs e)
{
    ⋮
}
```

PaintEventHandler delegates accept a *PaintEventArgs* parameter that contains the event data. The *PaintEventArgs* parameter contains the following additional properties that are essential for handling the *Paint* event:

- **Graphics**   Returns an instance of the *Graphics* class to be used for output

- **ClipRectangle**   Returns the invalid rectangle to be painted

The *Graphics* class is used throughout the remainder of this chapter to display output. This class defines all the methods and properties used to draw lines, text, and shapes on the display. It also can be used to gather information about the display's characteristics, such as screen resolution and color depth.

Drawing Text with GDI+

The console programs created in Part I and Part II of this book used the *Console.Write* and *Console.WriteLine* methods to display text output. Windows Forms applications don't send output to a simple console—their output is displayed on forms in a much richer format than the display options permitted by the *System.Console* class.

When text is displayed on a Windows form or control, the text display is generated in a *Paint* event handler, using one of the six overloaded versions of the *DrawString* method. Each overloaded version of *DrawString* enables you to specify the string to be displayed, the font used to display the text, and a brush that defines the text color and pattern. The first form of the *DrawString* method is the simplest and uses a *PointF* value to specify the location of the text, as shown here:

```
PointF textPoint = new PointF(12.0f, 12.0f);
e.Graphics.DrawString("Text location specified by a PointF value",
                      Font,
                      SystemBrushes.WindowText,
                      textPoint);
```

The second version of *DrawString* enables you to pass floating-point values that specify the location of the text, as shown here:

```
e.Graphics.DrawString("Text location specified by float values",
                      Font,
                      SystemBrushes.WindowText,
                      12.0f,
                      12.0f);
```

The problem with these two versions of *DrawString* is that text is drawn in a single line from the specified point, without regard for the enclosing form. When you're drawing a longer string, as in the following example, which uses a portion of text from Shakespeare's *Henry V*, the string simply runs off the edge of the form:

```
string crispinSpeech =
    "We few, we happy few, we band of brothers. " +
    "For he today that sheds his blood with me " +
    "shall be my brother, be he ne'er so vile, " +
    "this day shall gentle his condition. " +
    "And gentlemen in England now abed " +
    "shall think themselves accursed they were not here, " +
    "and hold their manhoods cheap whiles any speaks " +
    "that fought with us upon Saint Crispin's day.";

PointF textPoint = new PointF(12.0f, 12.0f);
e.Graphics.DrawString(crispinSpeech,
                      Font,
                      SystemBrushes.WindowText,
                      textPoint);
```

The third version of *DrawString* allows you to pass a *RectangleF* value to *DrawString* that defines a bounding rectangle for the text, which will force the text to be wrapped within it, as shown here:

```
string crispinSpeech =
    "We few, we happy few, we band of brothers. " +
    "For he today that sheds his blood with me " +
    "shall be my brother, be he ne'er so vile, " +
    "this day shall gentle his condition. " +
```

(continued)

```
            "And gentlemen in England now abed " +
            "shall think themselves accursed they were not here, " +
            "and hold their manhoods cheap whiles any speaks " +
            "that fought with us upon Saint Crispin's day. ";

RectangleF boundingRect = new RectangleF(12.0f,
                                         100.0f,
                                         180.0f,
                                         180.0f);
e.Graphics.DrawString(crispinSpeech,
                      Font,
                      SystemBrushes.WindowText,
                      boundingRect);
```

The remaining three versions of the *DrawString* method are similar to the first three versions except that they include a *StringFormat* parameter that supplies text layout options. For example, in addition to a *StringFormat* object, the fourth version of *DrawString* uses a *PointF* value to define the upper-left coordinate of the text's bounding rectangle, as shown here:

```
StringFormat stringFormat = new StringFormat();
stringFormat.Alignment = StringAlignment.Center;
stringFormat.LineAlignment = StringAlignment.Center;
e.Graphics.DrawString(crispinSpeech,
                      Font,
                      SystemBrushes.WindowText,
                      textPoint,
                      stringFormat);
```

The *StringFormat* class is used to specify text layout options for *Draw-String* and other methods. The *StringFormat* class has four constructors. The simplest version accepts no parameters and creates an object with default properties, as shown here:

```
StringFormat format = new StringFormat();
```

When this constructor is used, any nondefault characteristics must be set using properties or methods exposed by the *StringFormat* class.

The second *StringFormat* constructor accepts an existing *StringFormat* object as a parameter and creates a new *StringFormat* object with the same characteristics, as shown here:

```
StringFormat format = new StringFormat(otherFormat);
```

The third *StringFormat* constructor accepts a value from the *StringFormatFlags* enumeration, as shown here:

```
StringFormat format = new StringFormat(StringFormatFlags.NoClip);
```

The fourth version of the constructor is used to specify the language used when determining the string formatting and won't be discussed here. (Refer to the Microsoft Developer Network (MSDN) Library for a detailed discussion of this version.)

The *StringFormatFlags* enumeration is used to specify formatting options for *StringFormat* objects. The enumeration values are listed in Table 14-1 and can be combined with the *OR* operator.

Table 14-1.   *StringFormatFlags* **Enumeration Values**

Value	Description
DirectionRightToLeft	Specifies text that extends from right to left
DirectionVertical	Specifies text that extends vertically
DisplayFormatControl	Displays special format characters as a formatting glyph
FitBlackBox	Specifies that text must always be drawn within the bounding rectangle, even if that causes the text edge to appear jagged
LineLimit	Displays only lines that can be shown in their entirety
MeasureTrailingSpaces	Specifies that text measurements include the trailing space at the end of a line
NoClip	Doesn't clip overhanging characters that extend beyond the bounding rectangle
NoFontFallback	Prevents automatic fallback to an alternative font if a character isn't available
NoWrap	Disables line wrap when a line extends beyond the bounding rectangle horizontally

The *StringFormat* class exposes properties that are used to control the formatting options. The most commonly used properties are listed here:

- **Alignment**   A value from the *StringAlignment* enumeration that specifies horizontal text alignment

- **FormatFlags**   A value from the *StringFormatFlags* enumeration (see Table 14-1) that specifies formatting options

- **LineAlignment**   A value from the *StringAlignment* enumeration that specifies vertical text alignment

Table 14-2 lists the values from the *StringAlignment* enumeration.

Table 14-2. *StringAlignment* **Enumeration Values**

Value	Description
Near	Aligns the text toward the origin position of the bounding rectangle. In a left-to-right layout, the near position is left. In a right-to-left layout, the near position is right.
Center	Centers the text within the bounding rectangle.
Far	Aligns the text away from the origin position of the bounding rectangle. In a left-to-right layout, the far position is right. In a right-to-left layout, the far position is left.

Drawing Lines

The *Graphics* class includes methods that are used to draw lines and curves. The simplest of these is *DrawLine*, which is used to connect two points. There are four versions of *DrawLine*; these versions differ only in the way that line endpoints are specified. The following version of *DrawLine* uses two *Point* values:

```
Point topLeft = ClientRectangle.Location;
Point bottomRight = new Point(ClientRectangle.Right,
                              ClientRectangle.Bottom);
e.Graphics.DrawLine(SystemPens.WindowText,
                    topLeft,
                    bottomRight);
```

This example draws a line from the upper-left corner of the client rectangle to the lower-right corner. The line is described with a *Pen* object, which includes properties that specify the line's style, color, and width. The call to *SystemPens.WindowText* obtains a reference to a *Pen* object that has the color selected by the user for window text. *Pen* objects will be discussed later in this chapter, in the section "Drawing with Pens."

The second version of *DrawLine* uses *PointF* values to define endpoints, as shown here:

```
PointF topLeft = new PointF(0.0f, 0.0f);
PointF bottomRight = new PointF(208.5f, 306.2f);
e.Graphics.DrawLine(SystemPens.WindowText,
                    topLeft,
                    bottomRight);
```

The remaining two versions of *DrawLine* enable you to define endpoints using discrete floating-point or integer values.

The *DrawLines* method is used to draw multiple line segments with a single method call, with the endpoints passed as an array of *Point* or *PointF* values, as shown here:

```
Point [] pointArray = new Point [] {
                                new Point(10, 10),
                                new Point(10, 200),
                                new Point(200, 200),
                                new Point(200, 10),
                                new Point(10, 10)
                        };
e.Graphics.DrawLines(SystemPens.WindowText,
                pointArray);
```

Drawing Rectangles

The *Graphics* class provides the following two methods that are used to draw rectangles:

- ■   **DrawRectangle**   Draws a single rectangle

- ■   **DrawRectangles**   Draws multiple rectangles

These two methods are similar; the advantage of the *DrawRectangles* method is that it enables you to incur the overhead of a single method call when you're drawing multiple rectangles at the same time.

The three overloaded versions of *DrawRectangle* each accept a *Pen* object and the dimensions of the rectangle to be drawn as parameters. The difference between the versions is in how the rectangle dimensions are communicated to the *DrawRectangle* method. The first version of *DrawRectangle* accepts a *Rectangle* structure as a parameter, as shown here:

```
Rectangle theBox = new Rectangle(15, 15, 200, 200);
e.Graphics.DrawRectangle(SystemPens.WindowText, theBox);
```

The second version of *DrawRectangle* accepts four integer values, as shown here:

```
int top = 15;
int left = 15;
int width = 200;
int height = 200;
e.Graphics.DrawRectangle(SystemPens.WindowText,
                left,
                top,
                width,
                height);
```

The integers passed as parameters represent (in order) the rectangle's left x-coordinate, the rectangle's top y-coordinate, the width of the rectangle, and the height of the rectangle.

The third version of *DrawRectangle* uses *float* parameters to specify the dimensions of the rectangle, as shown here:

```
float top = 15.0f;
float left = 15.0f;
float width = 200.0f;
float height = 200.0f;
e.Graphics.DrawRectangle(SystemPens.WindowText,
                         left,
                         top,
                         width,
                         height);
```

When you need to draw multiple rectangles, it's often more efficient to arrange your rectangles in an array and call one of two overloaded versions of the *DrawRectangles* method. As with the *DrawRectangle* method, the two overloaded versions of *DrawRectangles* differ only in how the drawing targets are passed as parameters. The *DrawRectangles* method accepts either *Rectangle* or *RectangleF* structures. The following version of *DrawRectangles* accepts an array of *Rectangle* structures:

```
Rectangle [] theBoxes = new Rectangle[] {
                        new Rectangle(15, 15, 200, 200),
                        new Rectangle(40, 30, 200, 200),
                        new Rectangle(100, 100, 200, 200),
                        new Rectangle(200, 100, 200, 200)
                        };
e.Graphics.DrawRectangles(SystemPens.WindowText, theBoxes);
```

Filling Rectangles

The *Graphics* class includes two methods that are used to fill rectangles: *FillRectangle* and *FillRectangles*. Each of these methods accepts a *Brush* object as a parameter; the *Brush* object is used to specify the color and pattern that fill the rectangle. For the examples in this section, we'll use a solid red brush that's part of the *Brushes* class. Creating a reference to this brush requires just one line of code:

```
Brush brush = Brushes.Red;
```

This code creates a brush that will fill a rectangle with a solid red color. Later in this chapter, in the section "Using Brushes," we'll look at the wide range of brushes that are available to you when developing with GDI+. For now, it's enough to know that the preceding code will create an object that turns everything it touches red.

There are four versions of the *FillRectangle* method. In addition to the brush passed to each version of *FillRectangle*, these methods enable you to describe the rectangle's boundaries in four different ways, just like the *DrawRectangle* method discussed in the previous section. In the first version of *FillRectangle*, you pass a *Rectangle* object that describes the area to be filled, as shown here:

```
Rectangle theBox = new Rectangle(15, 15, 200, 200);
e.Graphics.FillRectangle(Brushes.Red, theBox);
```

You can also pass *FillRectangle* a *RectangleF* value that describes the rectangle to be filled, as shown here:

```
RectangleF theBox = new RectangleF(15.0f, 15.0f, 200.0f, 200.0f);
e.Graphics.FillRectangle(Brushes.Red, theBox);
```

The remaining two versions of *FillRectangle* accept either integer or floating-point values as coordinates of the rectangle to be filled. As with *DrawRectangle*, these parameters follow the standard rectangle pattern: left x-coordinate, top y-coordinate, width, and height.

When filling multiple rectangles, you can take advantage of one of the two versions of the *FillRectangles* method, both of which accept an array of rectangles to be filled. These rectangles can be specified with either *Rectangle* or *RectangleF* structures. The following version of *FillRectangles* accepts *Rectangle* structures:

```
Rectangle [] theBoxes = new Rectangle[] {
                        new Rectangle(15, 15, 200, 200),
                        new Rectangle(40, 30, 200, 200),
                        new Rectangle(100, 100, 200, 200),
                        new Rectangle(200, 100, 200, 200)
                        };
e.Graphics.FillRectangles(Brushes.Red, theBoxes);
```

The companion CD includes a Windows Forms example named ClickRects that draws a series of rectangles in the form's client area. A new rectangle is drawn at the location of each mouse click in the client area. Figure 14-1 shows the ClickRects application after several rectangles have been drawn in the client area.

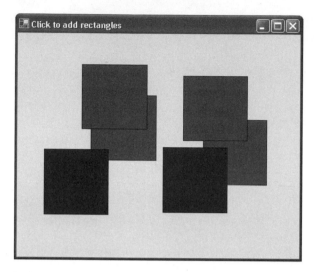

Figure 14-1. The ClickRects application after several rectangles have been drawn.

The relevant parts of the ClickRects source code are shown here:

```
public class MainForm : System.Windows.Forms.Form
{
    ArrayList _points = new ArrayList();
    readonly Size _rectSize = new Size(100, 100);
    Brush [] _brushes = new Brush[] { Brushes.Red,
                                      Brushes.Green,
                                      Brushes.Blue };
    Pen _edgePen = Pens.Black;
    ⋮
    [STAThread]
    static void Main()
    {
        Application.Run(new MainForm());
    }

    private void MainForm_Paint(object sender,
                          System.Windows.Forms.PaintEventArgs e)
    {
        int index = 0;
        foreach(Point pt in _points)
        {
            e.Graphics.FillRectangle(_brushes[index],
                            pt.X,
                            pt.Y,
                            _rectSize.Width,
                            _rectSize.Height);
```

```
          e.Graphics.DrawRectangle(_edgePen,
                                    pt.X,
                                    pt.Y,
                                    _rectSize.Width,
                                    _rectSize.Height);
          if(++index == 3)
              index = 0;
      }
  }

  private void MainForm_Click(object sender, System.EventArgs e)
  {
      _points.Add(PointToClient(MousePosition));
      Invalidate();
  }
}
```

The ClickRects application maintains an *ArrayList* collection that stores the location of each mouse click. When a *Click* event is handled in *MainForm_Click*, the location of the mouse click is added to *ArrayList* and the client area is invalidated. When the form receives a *Paint* event, a rectangle is displayed on the form at each location retrieved from the array.

Using Color with Windows Forms

Colors in the .NET Framework are based on four components. In addition to the three primary colors of red, green, and blue, a fourth value, called the *alpha component*, is used to specify the transparency of the color. Each of the four components is a single byte, which permits values between 0 and 255. In this section, we'll look at the various classes and structures that are used to work with color when programming with GDI+.

Creating Color Structures

Colors are represented in GDI+ by the *Color* structure, and when classes and methods work with colors, they work with an instance of the *Color* structure. The simplest approach to creating a *Color* instance is to create a named color through a static property. The *Color* structure exposes 140 named colors through static properties that return prebuilt *Color* objects. You create a *Color* value initialized to one of the named colors, like this:

```
Color newColor = Color.Red;
```

> **Note**   Although you can create an instance of the *Color* structure
> using the default constructor, the resulting *Color* object is pure black
> and can't be modified to represent a different color. Instead of using
> the default constructor, the .NET Framework provides several other
> ways to create *Color* instances, which we'll look at in this section.

There isn't space to list all 140 colors here, but the complete list of 140 colors is available in the MSDN online help, as well as through Microsoft IntelliSense when you're writing code with the Code Editor. All of the common color names such as *Red*, *Green*, *Blue*, and *Orange* are included, as are more exotic names such as *MintCream* and *PapayaWhip*. In addition, the *Transparent* property returns a *Color* structure that has the alpha component set to *0*, resulting in a transparent color.

Another way to create a *Color* instance is to invoke the static *FromArgb* method. There are four versions of this method. The first version accepts the four components that make up a *Color* object as parameters, as shown here:

```
Color sky = Color.FromArgb(100, 200, 200, 255);
```

The first parameter is the alpha component, followed by the red, green, and blue (RGB) components.

A second, commonly used version of the *FromArgb* method, shown in the following code, accepts only the three RGB color components and implicitly sets the alpha component to its maximum value, resulting in a fully opaque color:

```
Color sky = Color.FromArgb(200, 200, 255);
```

The third version of *FromArgb* is used to create a new *Color* instance from an existing *Color* object while changing only the alpha component, as shown here:

```
Color sky = Color.FromArgb(100, Color.PowderBlue);
```

This version of *FromArgb* is used later in this chapter, in the section "Creating Solid Brushes," to create a brush that provides a transparent blue wash over the client area.

The fourth and final version of the *FromArgb* method is used to create an instance of *Color* from a packed integer in the form *AARRGGBB*, as shown here:

```
Color sky = Color.FromArgb(0x64C8C8FF);
```

Color objects also can be created by calling the static *FromKnownColor* method. This method accepts a parameter from the *KnownColor* enumeration, which is discussed later in this chapter, in the section "Using the Current System Colors." The *FromKnownColor* method is used as follows:

```
Color sky = Color.FromKnownColor(KnownColor.PowderBlue);
```

Another way to create a *Color* object is to invoke the static *FromName* method. This method accepts a string parameter that must contain the name of a value from the *KnownColor* enumeration, as shown here:

```
Color sky = Color.FromName("PowderBlue");
```

Using Color Properties

The *Color* structure exposes the following four read-only properties that can be used to extract the component parts of a color:

- **A** Returns the alpha component of the color
- **R** Returns the red component of the color
- **G** Returns the green component of the color
- **B** Returns the blue component of the color

You can use these properties to extract the individual components in order to blend new colors, as shown here:

```
Color sky = Color.FromArgb(Color.PowderBlue.A/2,
                           Color.PowderBlue.R,
                           Color.PowderBlue.G,
                           Color.PowderBlue.B);
```

This code extracts the individual component colors and uses the *FromArgb* method to create a new color that's slightly more transparent by reducing the value of the alpha component.

Other useful non-static properties exposed by the *Color* structure include the following:

- **IsNamedColor** Boolean value that's *true* if the color value is one of the 140 named colors; otherwise, it's *false*.

- **IsKnownColor** Boolean value that's *true* if the color value is one of the colors from the *KnownColors* enumeration; otherwise, it's *false*.

- **IsSystemColor** Boolean value that's *true* if the color value is one of the property values from the *SystemColors* class; otherwise, it's *false*.

Using the Current System Colors

The Windows user interface enables the user to change predefined colors for elements with a Windows application. Through the Display Properties dialog box, the user can change many of the colors used for standard Windows elements, such as the color of the title bar, the color of windows, and the color of controls. This flexibility for users can make life difficult for application developers. For example, if you choose to display text or figures in a specific color, users who have redefined their color schemes might have difficulty using your application. For this reason, it's a good idea to take advantage of the user's color preferences whenever possible.

The *SystemColors* class encapsulates 26 system colors that are subject to modification by the user. This class provides access to colors via static properties, like this:

```
Color textColor = SystemColors.WindowText;
```

This code retrieves the user's preferred color for window text, whether it's *Black*, *BurlyBrown*, or *AntiqueWhite*. Table 14-3 lists the static *SystemColors* properties.

Table 14-3.   Read-Only Static Properties from the *SystemColors* Class

Property	Description
ActiveBorder	Border of the active window.
ActiveCaption	Title bar for the active window.
ActiveCaptionText	Text color in the active window's title bar.
AppWorkspace	Background color for Multiple Document Interface (MDI) application workspace.
Control	Control background color.
ControlDark	Shadow for 3-D controls.
ControlDarkDark	Darkest shadow for 3-D controls.
ControlLight	Highlight for 3-D controls.
ControlLightLight	Lightest highlight for 3-D controls.
ControlText	Text color for controls.
Desktop	Windows desktop color.
GrayText	Disabled text.
Highlight	Background for highlighted text.
HighlightText	Highlighted text color.

(continued)

**Table 14-3.   Read-Only Static Properties from the
    SystemColors Class**   *(continued)*

Property	Description
HotTrack	Hot track color that indicates a hot-tracked item. A hot-tracked item is executed when it is single-clicked.
InactiveBorder	Border of inactive windows.
InactiveCaption	Title bar for inactive windows.
InactiveCaptionText	Text color for inactive window's title bar.
Info	ToolTip background color.
InfoText	ToolTip text color.
Menu	Background color for menu items.
MenuText	Text color for menu items.
ScrollBar	Background color for scroll bars.
Window	Background color for windows.
WindowFrame	Window frame color.
WindowText	Text color for windows.

The *KnownColor* enumeration includes values that encompass the 26 colors exposed as static properties from the *SystemColors* class, as well as all 141 colors (including *Transparent*) that are exposed through static properties from the *Color* structure. A *KnownColor* value isn't more space-efficient than a *Color* value—they're both 32-bit values.

As mentioned, the *Color* structure includes the static *FromKnownColor* method, which can be used to translate a value from the *KnownColor* enumeration into a *Color* instance, as shown here:

```
Color textColor = Color.FromKnownColor(KnownColor.WindowText);
```

The Color Common Dialog Box

The Color common dialog box is included with every Windows installation. As with the File Open and File Save common dialog boxes discussed in Chapter 13, the Color common dialog box provides a common user interface for a fairly complex task. By leveraging the common dialog boxes in your application, you make life easier for the users of your application and you get a great deal of functionality with just a few lines of code. The basic Color dialog box is shown in Figure 14-2.

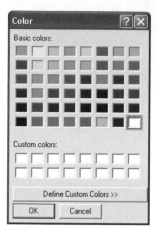

Figure 14-2. The basic form of the Color dialog box before expansion.

This dialog box enables the user to select from an array of predefined colors presented in the palette. The user can also expand the dialog box, as shown in Figure 14-3, which provides a wider selection of colors.

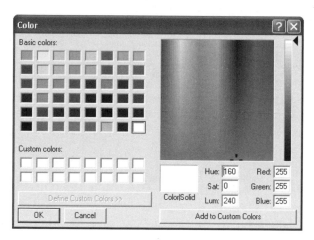

Figure 14-3. The Color common dialog box after expansion.

To display the Color common dialog box in its fully expanded state from the outset, set the *FullOpen* property to *true*, as shown here:

```
ColorDialog dlg = new ColorDialog();
dlg.FullOpen = true;
```

You interact with the Color common dialog box through the *ColorDialog* class, which works much like any other dialog box that's created in a Windows Form application, as shown here:

```
System.Windows.Forms.TextBox textBox;
    ⋮
ColorDialog dlg = new ColorDialog();
dlg.Color = textBox.BackColor;
if(dlg.ShowDialog() == DialogResult.OK)
{
    textBox.BackColor = dlg.Color;
    ⋮
}
```

As shown in this example, the color selected by the user is retrieved through the *Color* property. The *Color* property is also set before the dialog box is invoked, which enables the Color common dialog box to display the current color selection to the user. This is a common design pattern that improves the user's experience and often makes it much easier for the user to select a desirable color. For example, if the user wants to select a lighter or darker color, it's helpful to display the current color.

The current set of custom colors also can be preserved and passed to the dialog box before it's opened. The custom colors are exposed as the *CustomColors* property, which is typed as an array of integers. To retrieve the current set of custom colors, use code such as this:

```
int [] _customColors = null;
    ⋮
ColorDialog dlg = new ColorDialog();
if(dlg.ShowDialog() == DialogResult.OK)
{
    _customColors = dlg.CustomColors;
}
```

To set the custom colors shown in the dialog box using custom colors that have been previously saved, set the *CustomColors* property before the dialog box is displayed, as shown here:

```
int [] _customColors = null;
    ⋮
ColorDialog dlg = new ColorDialog();
dlg.CustomColors = _customColors;
if(dlg.ShowDialog() == DialogResult.OK)
{
    ⋮
}
```

The companion CD includes an enhancement to the SimpleEdit project initially created in Chapter 13. This version adds the capability for the user to change the colors of the client area and font. New menu items such as

Background Color and Foreground Color have been added to the View menu. The *Click* event handlers for the new methods are shown here:

```
private void viewBackgroundMenuItem_Click(object sender,
                                          System.EventArgs e)
{
    ColorDialog dlg = new ColorDialog();
    dlg.CustomColors = _customColors;
    dlg.Color = textBox.BackColor;
    if(dlg.ShowDialog() == DialogResult.OK)
    {
        textBox.BackColor = dlg.Color;
        _customColors = dlg.CustomColors;
    }
}

private void viewForegroundMenuItem_Click(object sender,
                                          System.EventArgs e)
{
    ColorDialog dlg = new ColorDialog();
    dlg.CustomColors = _customColors;
    dlg.Color = textBox.ForeColor;
    if(dlg.ShowDialog() == DialogResult.OK)
    {
        textBox.ForeColor = dlg.Color;
        _customColors = dlg.CustomColors;
    }
}
```

Both event handlers work in similar ways. First the *ColorDialog* object is instantiated, and then the current color context is passed to the dialog box's *CustomColors* and *Color* properties. If the user clicks OK to dismiss the dialog box, the appropriate color property for the *textBox* object is modified and the current set of custom colors is cached.

Using Brushes

As mentioned, brushes are used to fill areas with a color or a pattern. The *Brush* class is a base class for the following five concrete brush classes in the .NET Framework:

- **SolidBrush**   Fills an area with a solid color
- **TextureBrush**   Fills an area with an image
- **HatchBrush**   Fills an area with one of the predefined hatch patterns
- **LinearGradientBrush**   Fills an area with a linear gradient
- **PathGradientBrush**   Fills an area with a path gradient

The two most basic brushes, *SolidBrush* and *TextureBrush*, are found in the *System.Drawing* namespace. The remaining brushes are used for more advanced effects and are found in the *System.Drawing.Drawing2D* namespace.

The abstract *Brush* class serves as a base class for all *Brush* classes in the .NET Framework. Other classes that work with brushes generally accept parameters of the *Brush* type, allowing for a great deal of flexibility when you're filling a figure or a region.

Two classes serve as repositories for commonly used, prebuilt brushes: *SystemBrushes* and *Brushes*. The *SystemBrushes* class returns references to brushes matching the colors of specific components in the user interface as well as named colors. This class consists of a number of static methods that each return a *Brush* reference. In earlier examples in this chapter, references to *Brush* objects were created that were compatible with the colors selected by the user for the window client area. You can also create *Brush* references that follow other user preferences, as shown here:

```
Brush highlightBrush = SystemBrushes.Highlight;
```

This example creates a reference to a *Brush* object that's initialized to the user's preferred color for a highlighted background.

A complete list of the static *SystemBrushes* properties that are used to obtain brush references based on user color selections is provided in Table 14-4.

Table 14-4.   Properties Used to Obtain User-Centric Brush References

Method	Description
ActiveBorder	Border of the active window
ActiveCaption	Title bar for the active window
ActiveCaptionText	Text color in the active window's title bar
AppWorkspace	Background color for the MDI application workspace
Control	Control background color
ControlDark	Shadow for 3-D controls
ControlDarkDark	Darkest shadow for 3-D controls
ControlLight	Highlight for 3-D controls
ControlLightLight	Lightest highlight for 3-D controls
ControlText	Text color for controls
Desktop	Windows desktop color
Highlight	Background for highlighted text
HighlightText	Highlighted text color

(continued)

Table 14-4.   Properties Used to Obtain User-Centric Brush References *(continued)*

Method	Description
HotTrack	Hot track color
InactiveBorder	Border of inactive windows
InactiveCaption	Title bar for inactive windows
Info	ToolTip background color
Menu	Background color for menu items
ScrollBar	Background color for scroll bars
Window	Background color for windows
WindowText	Text color for windows

The properties from the *SystemBrushes* class in Table 14-4 are a subset of the properties available in the *SystemColors* class listed in Table 14-3. Specifically, colors that are rarely used to fill areas, such as *Color.InfoText*, aren't included. This doesn't prevent you from using these colors with brushes—it just means that you must take the extra step of creating a *Color* value and then using it to create the brush.

To create a reference to a brush based on a *Color* value, use the *FromSystem-Color* method, as shown here:

```
Brush infoBrush = SystemBrushes.FromSystemColor(SystemColors.InfoText);
```

An alternative to passing a named color to the *SystemBrushes* class is to use the *Brushes* class. The *Brushes* class is organized much like the *System-Brushes* and *Color* classes, in that it exposes a large number of static methods that are used to obtain *Brush* references. For example, if you need a red brush, you call the static *Brushes.Red* method, like this:

```
Brush stopBrush = Brushes.Red;
```

Because there's one static method in the *Brushes* class for each named color, there isn't space to list all the methods here. However, the *Brushes* class follows the same naming convention as the *Color* class, so if you know the named color, you can always obtain a reference to a *Brush* object directly, without extracting the color first.

Creating Solid Brushes

You've seen how references to the *Brush* class can be used along with the *Brushes* and *SystemBrushes* classes to fill rectangles and other areas. Although this is a good approach when creating brushes that are based on named colors or brushes that are consistent with the user's color preferences, it doesn't provide a way to create a brush that fills an area with the full range of possible colors. If you need to create a brush that has some degree of transparency or if you need a color other than the choices offered by the *Brushes* class, you'll need to use the *SolidBrush* class. There's just one constructor used to create *SolidBrush* objects, as shown here:

```
SolidBrush skyBrush = new SolidBrush(Color.FromArgb(99, 200, 210, 255));
```

The *SolidBrush* class exposes a single property, *Color*, that's used to get or set the brush's color.

```
// Make the brush more transparent.
skyBrush.Color = Color.FromArgb(50, 200, 210, 255);
```

Because the brushes returned from the *Brushes* and *SystemBrushes* classes are really *SolidBrush* objects, you can safely cast the returned reference to a *SolidBrush* object, as shown here:

```
SolidBrush skyBrush = (SolidBrush)Brushes.PowderBlue;
Color newColor = Color.FromArgb(100, skyBrush.Color);
skyBrush.Color = newColor;
```

In this case, the *skyBrush* object starts as a powder blue solid brush. The color is extracted, and the alpha component is changed to a more transparent value. After the *skyBrush.Color* property is set to the new color, the brush can be used to provide a sky blue wash effect over an area.

Using the *TextureBrush* Class

The *TextureBrush* class is used to represent a brush that fills an area with a pattern from an image. The brush can be constructed using the entire image or just a subset of the image; the image can also be rotated and scaled to suit your needs.

TextureBrush Constructors

There are seven versions of the *TextureBrush* constructor, but several of these differ only because they accept *RectangleF* instead of *Rectangle* parameters. The simplest version of the constructor accepts a single parameter—the image to be used for the brush—as shown here:

```
Image logo = Image.FromFile("C:\\windows\\winnt256.bmp");
TextureBrush br = new TextureBrush(logo);
```

As shown here, an *Image* object can be created by loading the image directly from a file. The *Image* class supports images in the Windows bitmap format as well as other common formats, such as GIF, TIFF, JPEG, and PNG.

Another version of the constructor is used to control how a space larger than the brush is filled. This behavior is controlled by a value from the *Wrap-Mode* enumeration that's passed as a parameter, as shown here:

```
TextureBrush br = new TextureBrush(logo, WrapMode.TileFlipXY);
```

The *WrapMode* enumeration values are listed in Table 14-5. These values are also used to control the behavior of *PathGradientBrush* constructors, which are discussed later in this chapter, in the section "Using the *PathGradient-Brush* Class."

Table 14-5.   *WrapMode* Enumeration Values

Value	Description
Clamp	No tiling. The image is displayed only once.
Tile	The default value. Tiles the brush image to fill the area.
TileFlipX	Tiles the brush image to fill the area, reversing the image horizontally in every second column.
TileFlipY	Tiles the brush image to fill the area, reversing the image vertically in every second row.
TileFlipXY	Combines the behavior of *TileFlipX* and *TileFlipY*. The image in every second column and every second row is reversed.

Often your brush needs only a subset of a larger image. Instead of cropping an image specifically for use with a *TextureBrush* object, you can simply select a subset of the image during construction. Two additional constructors are used to select a rectangular subset of the image—one constructor accepts a *Rectangle* parameter, and the other accepts a *RectangleF* parameter:

```
TextureBrush br = new TextureBrush(logo, new Rectangle(0,0,95,100));
TextureBrush br2 = new TextureBrush(logo, new RectangleF(0.0f,
                                                          0.0f,
                                                          95.0f,
                                                          100.0f));
```

A *TextureBrush* object created with either of these constructors will have its *WrapMode* property set to *WrapMode.Tile*. Although you can change the wrap mode through a property, it's usually easier to construct a brush with the proper characteristics from the beginning.

Two of the remaining constructors for the *TextureBrush* class enable you to select a rectangular subset of the image and define a wrap mode. The following code uses a *Rectangle* parameter to define the selected area of the image. A similar version accepts a parameter of type *RectangleF*.

```
TextureBrush br = new TextureBrush(logo, new Rectangle(0, 0, 95, 100));
```

The final pair of *TextureBrush* constructors are used with an *ImageAttributes* object that controls how the image is rendered.

TextureBrush Properties and Methods

The *TextureBrush* class exposes a number of methods and properties that can be used to manage a *TextureBrush* object. The commonly used properties exposed by the *TextureBrush* class include the following:

- **Image**   Returns a reference to the *Image* object associated with the brush

- **WrapMode**   Specifies the wrap mode for the brush

    The *TextureBrush* class also includes a number of methods that are used to manage a *TextureBrush* object. Two commonly used methods are used to rotate or scale the associated image.

- **RotateTransform**   Enables you to rotate the image by a specific amounts

- **ScaleTransform**   Enables you to scale the image to a smaller or larger size

    The following example loads one of the standard bitmaps shipped with Windows XP Professional, applies two transforms to it, and displays the image in the client area:

```
private void MainForm_Paint(object sender,
                        System.Windows.Forms.PaintEventArgs e)
{
    Image logo = Image.FromFile("C:\\windows\\winnt256.bmp");
    TextureBrush br = new TextureBrush(logo);
    br.RotateTransform(30.0f);
    br.ScaleTransform(.5f, .5f);
    br.WrapMode = WrapMode.TileFlipXY;
    e.Graphics.FillRectangle(br, ClientRectangle);
}
```

The results of running this code on a computer equipped with Windows XP Professional are shown in Figure 14-4.

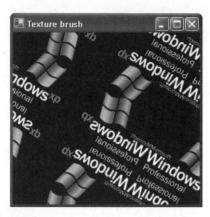

Figure 14-4.   A client area filled with a texture brush.

Filling Shapes with Patterns Using Hatch Brushes

The *HatchBrush* class is used to fill a region with one of 56 hatch patterns. Each hatch pattern is made from two colors: the background color and the foreground color. The *HatchBrush* class enables you to define these two colors and the style of the hatch pattern.

There are two ways to construct *HatchBrush* objects. The first constructor enables you to specify the style of the hatch pattern and the foreground color used to draw lines in the hatch bitmap, as shown here:

```
HatchBrush crossBrush = new HatchBrush(HatchStyle.Cross,
                                       Color.AliceBlue);
```

The second version of the constructor accepts an additional parameter that's used to specify the background color used when drawing the hatch pattern.

```
HatchBrush crossBrush = new HatchBrush(HatchStyle.Cross,
                                       Color.AliceBlue,
                                       Color.DarkOliveGreen);
```

In the following code, a *HatchBrush* object is created using the *Hatch-Style.Cross* hatch style and is then used to fill the client area of the form:

```
HatchBrush crossBrush = new HatchBrush(HatchStyle.Cross,
                                       Color.AliceBlue,
                                       Color.DarkOliveGreen);
e.Graphics.FillRectangle(crossBrush, ClientRectangle);
```

Figure 14-5 shows a simple Windows Forms application that uses this code to fill the client area.

Figure 14-5.   A client area filled with a *HatchBrush* object that uses the *Cross* style.

The companion CD includes a simple Windows Forms application called HatchSelection that enables you to select from all the hatch patterns. The main form from the HatchSelection application is shown in Figure 14-6.

Figure 14-6.   The main form from the HatchSelection example.

The main form in the HatchSelection application fills a combo box with the names of hatch patterns from the *HatchStyle* enumeration. When the name of a hatch style is selected, a *HatchBrush* object is created based on the selection and the panel that covers the lower half of the form has its client area invalidated, as shown on the following page.

```
private void hatchStyleCombo_SelectionChangeCommitted(object sender,
    System.EventArgs e)
{
    if(_panelBrush != null)
        _panelBrush.Dispose();
    switch((string)hatchStyleCombo.SelectedItem)
    {
        case "BackwardDiagonal":
            _panelBrush = new HatchBrush(HatchStyle.BackwardDiagonal,
                                        Color.White,
                                        Color.Black);
            break;

        case "Cross":
            _panelBrush = new HatchBrush(HatchStyle.Cross,
                                        Color.White,
                                        Color.Black);
            break;
            ⋮
    }
    panel.Invalidate();
}
```

The *Paint* event handler for the panel then uses the brush to fill its client area, as shown here:

```
private void panel_Paint(object sender,
                        System.Windows.Forms.PaintEventArgs e)
{
    if(_panelBrush != null)
        e.Graphics.FillRectangle(_panelBrush, panel.ClientRectangle);
}
```

Using the *LinearGradientBrush* Class

The *LinearGradientBrush* class creates brushes that fill an area with colors that transition from one hue to another. There are always two colors associated with a linear brush—these colors are found at the edges of the gradient, and the transition area is located between them.

There are several ways to create a *LinearGradientBrush* object. One approach is to create a *LinearGradientBrush* object that's exactly the size of the area to be filled. This will result in an area filled with a single gradient transition. Another approach is to create a *LinearGradientBrush* instance that's somewhat smaller than the area to be filled and then use the *WrapMode* enumeration to define how the brush will be tiled within the filled-in area.

There are eight versions of the *LinearGradientBrush* constructor. Many of these constructors are similar and differ only in accepting the *PointF* or *RectangleF* parameters instead of *Point* or *Rectangle* parameters, so conceptually there are only four ways to build a *LinearGradientBrush* object. The first two constructors accept two points that define the edges of the gradient boundary. Here *Point* structures are used to define the gradient edges:

```
// Create a gradient using Point structures.
LinearGradientBrush gradient = new LinearGradientBrush(new Point(0, 0),
                                                       new Point(0, 5),
                                                       Color.Red,
                                                       Color.Bisque);
e.Graphics.FillRectangle(gradient, ClientRectangle);
```

Alternatively, you can use *PointF* structures, as shown here:

```
// Create a gradient using Point structures.
LinearGradientBrush br = new LinearGradientBrush(new PointF(0.0f, 0.0f),
                                                 new PointF(0.0f, 5.0f),
                                                 Color.Red,
                                                 Color.Bisque);
e.Graphics.FillRectangle(br, ClientRectangle);
```

When you define the extent of the gradient in terms of *Point* or *PointF* structures, the defined points of the gradient are drawn in the pure colors and the area located between the points is drawn with a gradually changing color. Each color band in the gradient extends at right angles to a line drawn between the points. Using either of the constructors in the preceding code examples, a vertical line would connect the two points because they have the same first coordinate, so the gradient extends horizontally, as shown in Figure 14-7.

Figure 14-7.   A form filled with a simple gradient.

To create a gradient that extends at an angle, simply specify gradient edges that lie on the desired angle, as shown here:

```
LinearGradientBrush fader = new LinearGradientBrush(new Point(10, 10),
                                                    new Point(20, 20),
                                                    Color.Salmon,
                                                    Color.Bisque);
e.Graphics.FillRectangle(fader, ClientRectangle);
```

This code creates a *LinearGradientBrush* object that extends at a 45-degree angle.

The transition between gradient bands in these examples is fairly pronounced because the default *WrapMode* setting for *LinearGradientBrush* instances is *WrapMode.Tile*. There are a couple of ways to achieve a smoother effect. The first is simply to change *WrapMode.Tile* to *WrapMode.TileFlipXY*, as shown here:

```
fader.WrapMode = WrapMode.TileFlipXY;
```

The resulting gradient blends smoothly through as many iterations as required to fill the rectangle, as shown in Figure 14-8.

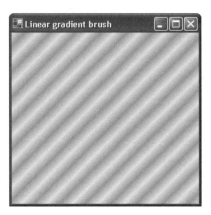

Figure 14-8. Using *WrapMode* to create a smooth gradient transition.

Another option for creating a smoother gradient is to create a gradient that has the same dimensions as the area you're filling. The next two *LinearGradient-Brush* constructors accept *Rectangle* or *RectangleF* structures that define the edges of the gradient. The version that uses a *Rectangle* structure is shown here:

```
LinearGradientBrush gradient = new LinearGradientBrush(ClientRectangle,
                                                       Color.Red,
                                                       Color.Bisque,
                                                       90.0f);
e.Graphics.FillRectangle(gradient, ClientRectangle);
```

The last parameter, *90.0f*, specifies the orientation of the gradient transition—in this example, the gradient extends horizontally, or 90 degrees.

This code results in a client area that's filled with a single gradient transition from top to bottom, as shown in Figure 14-9.

Figure 14-9.   Controlling the orientation of the gradient transition.

The final two constructors for the *LinearGradientBrush* class enable you to specify the orientation of the gradient with the *LinearGradientMode* enumeration. These two constructors accept either *Rectangle* or *RectangleF* structures that define the gradient's boundaries. In this example, a *Rectangle* structure is used to create a gradient brush that extends horizontally:

```
LinearGradientBrush gradient = new LinearGradientBrush(ClientRectangle,
                                    Color.Red,
                                    Color.Bisque,
                                    LinearGradientMode.Vertical);
e.Graphics.FillRectangle(gradient, ClientRectangle);
```

The *LinearGradientMode* enumeration values are listed in Table 14-6.

Table 14-6.   *LinearGradientMode* **Enumeration Values**

Value	Description
Horizontal	Specifies a gradient that fades horizontally
Vertical	Specifies a gradient that fades vertically
ForwardDiagonal	Specifies a gradient that fades from the upper-left corner to the lower-right corner
BackwardDiagonal	Specifies a gradient that fades from the upper-right corner to the lower-left corner

Using the *PathGradientBrush* Class

Like *LinearGradientBrush* objects, instances of the *PathGradientBrush* class are used to fill areas with a range of gradating colors. Unlike the *LinearGradient-Brush* class, however, the *PathGradientBrush* class offers more flexibility in the shape of the gradient brush. For example, a *PathGradientBrush* object can be used to create filled text patterns and other complex shapes built with graphics paths.

A *PathGradientBrush* object starts with a graphics path that's defined as either a *GraphicsPath* object or an array of points (either *Point* or *PointF*) that describe a polygon. The *GraphicsPath* class isn't covered in detail in this book—for our purposes, all you need to know about this class is that it stores a sequence of lines, curves, and shapes. Refer to the MSDN online help for more information about this class.

There are four constructors that create *PathGradientBrush* objects based on polygons defined by arrays of *Point* or *PointF*. For example, the following array of *Point* defines a triangle:

```
Point [] trianglePoints = new Point[] {  new Point(0, 0),
                                         new Point(0, 60),
                                         new Point(80, 60)};
```

The *trianglePoints* array can be passed to a *PathGradientBrush* constructor to create a brush based on the triangle, as shown here:

```
PathGradientBrush triBrush = new PathGradientBrush(trianglePoints);
```

No color information is defined in the constructor for the brush. By default, the brush will have a black center, with a gradient toward white at every point in the polygon. Another unique aspect of the *PathGradientBrush* class is that, unlike the behavior of the *TextureBrush* and *LinearGradientBrush* classes, its default *WrapMode* setting is *WrapMode.Clamp*. Figure 14-10 shows a form that has had its client area filled with the *triBrush* object created in the preceding code example.

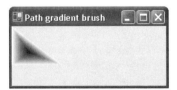

Figure 14-10.   A single iteration of a *PathGradientBrush* object, created with the default *WrapMode* setting.

As with other brushes, the wrap mode for a *PathGradientBrush* can be adjusted with the *WrapMode* property, as shown here:

```
triBrush.WrapMode = WrapMode.TileFlipXY;
```

By default, the center of the polygon is determined automatically by the *PathGradientBrush* class; this is the location that contains one of the colors in the gradient. You can adjust the location of the center gradient point with the *CenterPoint* property, which is typed as a *PointF* structure, as shown here:

```
triBrush.CenterPoint = new PointF(5.0f, 30.0f);
```

The color of the center gradient point is specified with the *CenterColor* property, as shown here:

```
triBrush.CenterColor = Color.AntiqueWhite;
```

Each point used to define the brush's polygon can have a different color defined for its gradient. The edge gradients are specified with the *Surround-Colors* property, which accepts an array of *Color* values. The following code creates a rectangular *PathGradientBrush* object and specifies a different color for each corner:

```
Point [] quadPoints = new Point[] {  new Point(0, 0),
                                     new Point(0, 60),
                                     new Point(80, 60),
                                     new Point(80, 0)
                              };
PathGradientBrush quadBrush = new PathGradientBrush(quadPoints);
quadBrush.WrapMode = WrapMode.TileFlipXY;
quadBrush.CenterColor = Color.Black;
quadBrush.SurroundColors = new Color[] {
                                        Color.Black,
                                        Color.White,
                                        Color.Gray,
                                        Color.AntiqueWhite
                                        };
e.Graphics.FillRectangle(quadBrush, ClientRectangle);
```

Figure 14-11 shows a form that's had its client area filled with a *Path-GradientBrush* object built using this code.

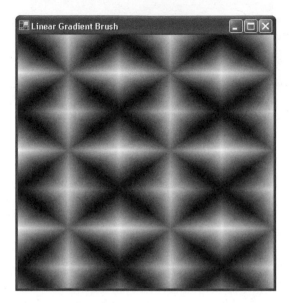

Figure 14-11.   A form filled with a tiled *PathGradientBrush* object.

Drawing with Pens

As mentioned, pens are used with the *Graphics* class to draw lines and other figures. In the examples earlier in this chapter, the *SystemPens* class has been used to obtain references to *Pen* objects initialized with the same color as client window text. In this section, we'll examine the *SystemPens* class more closely and you'll learn how to use the *Pens* class and the *Pen* class directly to create *Pen* objects in a variety of styles and colors.

Using the *SystemPens* and *Pens* Classes

Just like the *SystemBrushes* class discussed earlier in this chapter, the *System-Pens* class is used to create pens that match user interface components and system colors. The static properties exposed by the *SystemPens* class each return a reference to a shared *Pen* object. In earlier examples, *Pen* objects were created that were compatible with the window text color selected by the user. You can also create *Pen* objects that follow other user preferences, as shown here:

```
Pen highlightPen = SystemPens.HighlightText;
```

This example creates a *Pen* object that's initialized to the user's preferred color for highlighted text. A complete list of the static *SystemPens* properties used to create pens based on user preferences is provided in Table 14-7.

Table 14-7.   Properties Used to Create Pens Based on User Preferences

Method	Description
ActiveCaptionText	Text color in the active window's title bar
Control	Control background color
ControlDark	Shadow for 3-D controls
ControlDarkDark	Darkest shadow for 3-D controls
ControlLight	Highlight for 3-D controls
ControlLightLight	Lightest highlight for 3-D controls
ControlText	Text color for controls
GrayText	Disabled text color
Highlight	Background for highlighted text
HighlightText	Highlighted text color
InactiveCaptionText	Text color for inactive window's title bar
InfoText	ToolTip text color
MenuText	Text color for menu items
WindowFrame	Window frame color
WindowText	Text color for windows

The properties in Table 14-7 are similar to the properties exposed by the *SystemBrushes* class listed in Table 14-4. They differ because pens and brushes typically are used to draw with different color schemes. Pens are often used to draw lines and shadow effects, whereas brushes are often used to fill areas with a color or a pattern. For example, there's no *Window* property for the *SystemPens* class because pens aren't frequently used to draw in colors that match the client area. As with the *SystemBrushes* class, the *SystemPens* class can be used to create pens based on a *Color* value passed as a parameter to the *SystemPens.From-SystemColor* method, as shown here:

```
Pen clientAreaPen = SystemPens.FromSystemColor(SystemColors.Window);
```

All the *Pen* references you'll get from the *SystemPens* class (as well as from the *Pens* class, which we'll get to shortly) have an initial width of 1 pixel. You don't own the *Pen* objects, so you can't modify them. If you need alternative widths or styles, you'll need to create your pens using the *Pen* class, which will be discussed in the next section.

An alternative to passing a named color to the *SystemPens* class is to use the *Pens* class. The *Pens* class is organized much like the *SystemPens* class in that it exposes a large number of static methods that are used to create *Pen* objects. For example, to create a red pen, you call the static *Pens.Red* method, like this:

```
Pen warningPen = Pens.Red;
```

All told, there are 141 static methods in the *Pens* class, so again there isn't space to list them all here. The *Pens* class follows the same naming convention as the *Color* and *Brushes* classes, however, so if you know the named color, you can create your *Pen* object directly, without extracting the color first.

Using the *Pen* Class

The objective behind using the *SystemPens* and *Pens* classes is to obtain a reference to a *Pen* object. Up to now, you've seen the *Pen* class used to draw lines and figures; in this section, we'll examine the various methods and properties exposed by the *Pen* class that enable you to manage the characteristics of the lines drawn using a *Pen* object.

Creating Pens

In addition to using the *SystemPens* and *Pens* classes to fetch references to *Pen* objects, you can also create them using the *Pen* class directly. There are four constructors used to create *Pen* objects. These constructors enable you to specify a color or a brush that will be used to define the pattern drawn by the pen, as well as an optional width. The first constructor is used to create a pen of a specific color with an initial width of 1 pixel, as shown here:

```
Pen clearBluePen = new Pen(Color.FromArgb(40, 50, 50, 255));
```

You can also specify the width when constructing a *Pen* object with a *Color* value, as shown here:

```
Pen clearBluePen = new Pen(Color.FromArgb(40, 50, 50, 255), 20.0f);
```

Alternatively, you can use a *Brush* object to supply a pattern for your new *Pen*, using code such as this:

```
HatchBrush _horizontalBrickBrush = null;
HatchBrush _diagonalBrickBrush = null;
Pen        _diagonalThinBricks = null;
Pen        _horizontalThinBricks = null;
⋮
public MainForm()
{
    ⋮
    _horizontalBrickBrush = new HatchBrush(HatchStyle.HorizontalBrick,
                                           Color.Gray,
                                           Color.Firebrick);
```

```
_diagonalBrickBrush = new HatchBrush(HatchStyle.DiagonalBrick,
                                     Color.Gray,
                                     Color.Firebrick);
_diagonalThinBricks = new Pen(_diagonalBrickBrush);
_horizontalThinBricks = new Pen(_horizontalBrickBrush);
}
```

This code creates instances of *HatchBrush* with the *DiagonalBrick* and *HorizontalBrick* hatch styles and then uses the brushes to create two pens that are each 1 pixel wide. Because the width of the pens is much smaller than the brick pattern, the lines drawn with these pens will have a striped appearance. The fourth version of the *Pen* constructor enables you to specify a width for the pen that makes the brick pattern more apparent, as shown here:

```
Pen_diagonalThickBricks = new Pen(_diagonalBrickBrush, 10.0f);
Pen_horizontalThickBricks = new Pen(_horizontalBrickBrush, 10.0f);
```

Figure 14-12 shows an example using these *Pen* objects to draw figures in a Windows Form client area.

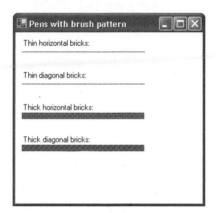

Figure 14-12.   Several pens initialized with hatch brushes.

Taking Advantage of Pen Styles

The *Pen* class exposes styles as properties that can be changed dynamically without having to re-create the *Pen* object each time a property needs to be altered. The most commonly used properties from the *Pen* class are as follows:

- ■ **Alignment**   Specifies the position of the drawn line in relation to the curve or figure coordinates.

- ■ **Brush**   Specifies a brush used to provide the pattern and color for this pen.

- ■ **Color**   Specifies a color used for this pen.

- **EndCap**   Specifies the shape rendered at the end of the line or curve, using a value from the *LineCap* enumeration. The default value is *LineCap.Flat*.

- **LineJoin**   Specifies how sequences of lines are joined, using a value from the *LineJoin* enumeration.

- **MiterLimit**   Specifies the maximum permitted ratio between line width and miter thickness before clipping occurs. This property applies only if the *LineJoin* property is set to *LineJoin.MiterClipped*. The default value is *10.0f*.

- **PenType**   Returns a value from the *PenType* enumeration that describes the *Pen* object.

- **StartCap**   Specifies the shape rendered at the start of the line, using a value from the *LineCap* enumeration. The default value is *LineCap.Flat*.

- **Width**   Specifies the width of the line drawn with the pen.

The *Alignment* property specifies how screen real estate is consumed by a line drawn with the pen. The default value of *PenAlignment.Center* draws the line centered over the line boundary. A value of *PenAlignment.Inset* draws the line inside the line that forms the boundary of a curve or a figure.

The *LineCap* enumeration is used by the *StartCap* and *EndCap* properties to draw the ends of each line. Some values in the *LineCap* enumeration include *Anchor* in their name, which indicates that the *LineCap* style draws an anchored end for the line. Anchor values cause the line end to be drawn wider than the line's width. This type of *LineCap* style is useful when you want to emphasize the endpoints of the line. To determine whether a *LineCap* style is one of the anchor values, you can use *AnchorMask*, a value from the *LineCap* enumeration, as shown here:

```
if((clearBluePen.EndCap & LineCap.AnchorMask) > 0)
{
    // EndCap has one of the anchor styles.
    ⋮
}
```

As mentioned, the *LineCap* enumeration is used to specify how the ends of each line are drawn. The *LineCap* enumeration values are provided in Table 14-8.

Table 14-8.   *LineCap* **Enumeration Values**

Value	Description
AnchorMask	A mask value used to test whether a *LineCap* value specifies an anchor cap.
ArrowAnchor	An arrow-shaped anchor is drawn for the line cap.
Custom	A custom end cap specified by the application is drawn.
DiamondAnchor	A diamond-shaped anchor is drawn for the line cap.
Flat	The default value; no cap is drawn.
NoAnchor	Same as *LineCap.Flat*; no anchor is drawn.
Round	A round line cap is drawn.
RoundAnchor	A large round line cap is drawn.
Square	A square line cap is drawn.
SquareAnchor	A large square anchor line cap is drawn.
Triangle	A triangle-shaped line cap is drawn.

The *LineJoin* property uses the values from the *LineJoin* enumeration to control how line endpoints are joined together when drawing figures with methods such as *DrawPolygon* or when several lines are drawn with a single call to the *DrawLines* method. This property isn't used when you're drawing multiple lines by making multiple calls to the *DrawLine method*. The *LineJoin* enumeration values are provided in Table 14-9.

Table 14-9.   *LineJoin* **Enumeration Values**

Value	Description
Bevel	The lines are joined in a beveled edge.
Miter	The lines are joined as if mitered, with the outside edges of the lines extended until they meet.
MiterClipped	The lines are extended just like the *LineJoin.Miter* style, except that the length of the mitered join is subject to clipping if it extends past the length allowed by the *Pen* object's *MiterLimit* property.
Round	The lines are joined with a rounded corner.

The *PenType* property returns a value from the *PenType* enumeration that describes how the *Pen* object determines its color or pattern. This read-only value contains information about the underlying brush or color that the *Pen* object is currently using. The *PenType* enumeration values are listed in Table 14-10.

Table 14-10.   *PenType* Enumeration Values

Value	Description
HatchFill	The pen uses a hatch brush.
LinearGradient	The pen uses a linear gradient brush.
PathGradient	The pen uses a path gradient brush.
SolidColor	The pen uses a color or a *SolidBrush* object.
TextureFill	The pen uses a texture brush.

Drawing Dashed Lines with Pens

The *Pen* class can be used to create pens that will draw dashed lines. There are three properties that are used to control how dashes are drawn.

- ■   ***DashOffset***   Specifies the distance from the start of the line to the start of the dash pattern

- ■   ***DashStyle***   Specifies the pattern of the dashes, using a value from the *DashStyle* enumeration

- ■   ***DashPattern***   Specifies an array of floating-point values that define a pattern of dots and dashes used when the *DashStyle* property is set to *DashPattern.Custom*

The *DashStyle* property uses values from the *DashStyle* enumeration to select from among predefined dash styles or to specify that a custom dash pattern is to be used. The *DashStyle* enumeration values are provided in Table 14-11.

Table 14-11.   *DashStyle* Enumeration Values

Value	Description
Custom	A dash style that's defined by the application
Dash	A line that's drawn with dashes
DashDot	A line with alternating dashes and dots
DashDotDot	A line drawn with a repeating sequence of a dash followed by two dots
Dot	A line that's drawn with dots
Solid	An unbroken line

The *DashPattern* property accepts an array of floating-point values, with each element alternatively specifying the length of each dash and space, like this:

```
clearBluePen.DashStyle = DashStyle.Custom;
clearBluePen.DashPattern = new float [] {   0.5f,
                                            0.3f,
                                            1.0f,
                                            0.5f };
```

The values passed to the *DashPattern* property are multiplied by the pen's width to determine the actual spacing of dashes and spaces.

Using Fonts

Fonts are GDI+ objects much like the pens and brushes discussed earlier in this chapter and are represented by the *Font* class. When text is displayed anywhere in a Windows Forms application, it's done using a font. Most of the time, you can display text without explicitly specifying a font because controls and forms are always associated with a default *Font* object. However, there are many occasions when it's useful to specify a particular font—perhaps you need to have some text that's shown with a heavier, bolder font, or perhaps you prefer that a label or a section of text use a particular size of font.

Fonts used in Windows Forms application follow two specifications:

- **TrueType**   A standard for fonts that was developed by Microsoft and Apple. This type of font was first used in Microsoft Windows 3.1. In the Font common dialog box, TrueType fonts are distinguished by a TT icon next to their name.

- **OpenType**   An extension of the TrueType specification that was developed by Microsoft and Adobe.

These are the only types of fonts available in a Windows Forms application. In particular, the older raster fonts available in Win32 SDK applications aren't supported.

Understanding the Vocabulary of Fonts

Working with fonts requires a unique vocabulary. A *typeface* is a specific style of drawing a character. Arial, Times New Roman, and Garamond are all names of typefaces. A collection of descriptions that describe how to draw a set of characters using the same display characteristics and the same typeface is a *font*. The font is traditionally referred to by its typeface name along with any style modifiers, as in Arial Bold and Garamond Italic.

Fonts can be *monospace* (sometimes called *fixed-pitch fonts*), such as Courier New and Lucida Console, or they can be *variable-pitched*, like Arial and Times New Roman. Characters drawn with a monospace font all have the same width, whereas in a variable-pitched font, the width of the characters varies on a character-by-character basis.

Serif fonts include an extra flourish at the end of strokes. Examples of serif fonts include Times New Roman, Courier New, and Garamond. *Sans serif fonts* don't have serifs and include fonts such as Arial and Helvetica.

The *FontStyle* enumeration is used to identify common variations in fonts, using the following values:

- *Bold*
- *Italic*
- *Regular*
- *Underline*
- *Strikeout*
- *Underline*

Values from the *FontStyle* enumeration can be combined, so to specify a bold-face italic font, you would use code like this:

```
FontStyle style = FontStyle.Bold | FontStyle.Italic;
```

Every font is part of a *font family*, which serves as a grouping for fonts that have the same typeface and similar styles. Variations of a font that differ based on their *FontStyle* characteristics are generally in the same font family. However, it's not unusual for one typeface to be shared by multiple font families—for example, there are several font families that use variations of the Arial typeface.

The *FontFamily* class is used to interact with the font families installed on a computer. There are three constructors used to create *FontFamily* objects. The first constructor accepts a value from the *GenericFontFamilies* enumeration and creates an instance of *FontFamily* that represents one of the generic font families, as shown here:

```
FontFamily monoFont = new FontFamily(GenericFontFamilies.Monospace);
```

This code creates a *FontFamily* object that represents a generic mono-space font family. The *GenericFontFamilies* enumeration values are provided in Table 14-12.

Table 14-12.   *GenericFontFamilies* **Enumeration Values**

Value	Description
Monospace	A monospace *FontFamily* such as Courier New
SansSerif	A *FontFamily* without serifs, such as Microsoft Sans Serif
Serif	A *FontFamily* with serifs, such as Times New Roman

The second *FontFamily* constructor enables you to specify the font family by name and create a *FontFamily* object to represent it, as shown here:

```
FontFamily arialFamily = new FontFamily("Arial");
```

The third *FontFamily* constructor is used to create a *FontFamily* object based on a font that's stored in an instance of *PrivateFontCollection*, which will be discussed in the next section.

In addition to the *FontFamily* constructors, you also can obtain references to *FontFamily* objects through static methods and properties exposed by the *FontFamily* class. The following static properties are used to obtain references to *FontFamily* objects that represent generic fonts:

- **GenericMonospace**   Returns a *FontFamily* object that refers to a generic monospace font, such as Courier New

- **GenericSansSerif**   Returns a *FontFamily* object that refers to a generic sans serif font, such as Microsoft Sans Serif

- **GenericSerif**   Returns a *FontFamily* object that refers to a generic serif font, such as Times New Roman

In the next section, you'll learn how to retrieve an array of *FontFamily* objects that represents all the installed fonts.

The *FontFamily* class exposes one non-static property—the *Name* property, which returns the name of the font family, as shown here:

```
FontFamily arialFamily = new FontFamily("Arial");
string familyName = arialFamily.Name;
```

The *FontFamily* class exposes several useful methods, including the *IsStyleAvailable* method. If you attempt to create a font with an unsupported style, an exception will be thrown. For example, some font families don't support the boldface or italic font styles. The *IsStyleAvailable* method provides a useful way to determine whether a specific font style is supported by a font family, as shown here:

```
if(arialFamily.IsStyleAvailable(FontStyle.Bold))
{
    // Font can be safely created.
    ⋮
}
```

Using the *FontCollection* Classes

The *FontCollection* base class is used to store a collection of fonts available for use. There are two sealed subclasses:

■   ***InstalledFontCollection***   Class that represents the collection of fonts that are installed on the user's computer

■   ***PrivateFontCollection***   Class that represents a collection of fonts used for the application only and not installed in the operating system's collection of installed fonts

The *InstalledFontCollection* class is useful when you want to determine whether a particular font family has been installed. If your application requires a specific font, you can use this collection to determine whether the font is available for use. The following code displays all the installed fonts in a message box:

```
static void Main()
{
    StringBuilder familyNames = new StringBuilder();
    InstalledFontCollection ifc = new InstalledFontCollection();
    FontFamily[] families = ifc.Families;
    foreach(FontFamily family in families)
    {
        familyNames.AppendFormat("{0}\n", family.Name);
    }
    MessageBox.Show(familyNames.ToString());
}
```

This example creates an instance of *InstalledFontCollection* and retrieves an array of *FontFamily* objects that represent all the fonts installed on the computer. Next the code iterates over the array of *FontFamily* objects and displays the names in a message box, as shown in Figure 14-13.

Figure 14-13. A message box displaying currently installed font families.

Font Metrics

Fonts are measured using a variety of metrics, including points, em sizes, and design units. In this section, these terms are defined, and you'll learn how to collect font metrics.

A good place to begin is with the *point*. A point is about 1/72 of an inch and is a common unit used to describe relative font sizes. On a computer screen, the point sizes don't refer to physical dimensions and are really useful only for comparison purposes. The default font size for Windows is 10 points, whereas the default font size for Windows Forms is 8.25 points. A common unit of measurement in Windows Forms is the *document unit*, which is 1/300 of an inch, or about 4.16 document units per point.

When working with font metrics, you'll often see references to the *em size*. An em is the point size of a given font. If the font is 10 points, the em size will be 10 points. A value of 2 ems is twice the size of the current font (for example, 20 points if the current font is 10 points).

The following methods from the *FontFamily* class can be used to collect information about font metrics:

■ ***GetCellAscent*** Returns the vertical size reserved for an *ascender* (the portion of a font drawn above the baseline) for a specified font style

- ***GetCellDescent***   Returns the vertical size reserved for a *descender* (the portion of a font drawn below the baseline) for a specified font style

- ***GetEmHeight***   Returns the height of an em for a specified font style

- ***GetLineSpacing***   Returns the spacing between lines for a specified font style

Creating Fonts Programmatically

There are 13 versions of the *Font* constructor. These constructors create *Font* objects based on combinations of the font family, the size of the font, desired font styles, and other parameters.

A common reason to create a new *Font* object is to change one of the *FontStyle* values associated with the font. For example, you might have a menu item that retains the current font family but changes the style to boldface or italic. The following version of the *Font* constructor enables you to create a *Font* object by passing an existing *Font* object as a template along with a new *FontStyle* value, as shown here:

```
Font = new Font(oldFont, newStyle);
```

The following code uses this version of the constructor to enable or disable the boldface style for the font:

```
private void ToggleBoldStyle()
{
    // Get the current font and style.
    Font oldFont = Font;
    // Flip the Bold style flag.
    FontStyle newStyle = Font.Style ^ FontStyle.Bold;
    // Use the old font and the new style to create a new Font object.
    Font = new Font(oldFont, newStyle);
    // Clean up.
    oldFont.Dispose();
    Invalidate();
}
```

This code toggles the boldface style for the text displayed in a form. First the current font is retrieved through the *Font* property. Next the form's font style is retrieved, and the *FontStyle.Bold* value is toggled using a bitwise XOR operation. The new *Font* object is created using the new *FontStyle* value. The great thing about using this approach is that there's no need to know anything about the current font—it's easy to write a generic method that works with any font that's currently assigned to a form or a control. The only problem with this approach is that font families aren't required to supply fonts that include every possible combination of styles available in the *FontStyle* enumeration. If you attempt to create a font with a style that doesn't exist, an exception will be thrown. To avoid an exception, use the *FontFamily.IsStyleAvailable* method to determine whether the new font style is supported, as described earlier.

The 12 remaining *Font* constructors can be arranged in six pairs, with one constructor in each pair accepting a *FontFamily* value as its first parameter, and the other constructor in each pair accepting the name of a font family as a string value. The first pair of constructors enables you to specify the font family and em size, as shown here:

```
FontFamily family = new FontFamily("Trebuchet MS");
Font labelFont = new Font(family, 20.0f);
Font statusFont = new Font("Garamond", 20.0f);
```

These two versions of the *Font* constructor create a *Font* object with default properties for the font style. The following pair of constructors enable you to specify values from the *FontStyle* enumeration that will be applied to the new *Font* object:

```
Font labelFont = new Font(family, 20.0f, FontStyle.Underline);
Font statusFont = new Font("Garamond", 20.0f, FontStyle.Bold);
```

Although these constructors enable you to specify a font style, remember that any constructor that accepts a *FontStyle* parameter will throw an exception if a font can't be created with the requested font style.

The next pair of constructors creates *Font* objects with measurement units set to a value other than the point size. The value passed as the *GraphicsUnit* parameter specifies which unit of measurement is used for the font size, as shown here:

```
Font labelFont = new Font(family,
                          20.0f,
                          GraphicsUnit.Document);
Font statusFont = new Font("Garamond",
                           20.0f,
                           GraphicsUnit.Document);
```

The next set of constructors combines the parameters of the previous two sets of constructors, enabling you to specify a *FontStyle* value and a value from the *GraphicsUnit* enumeration:

```
Font labelFont = new Font(family,
                          20.0f,
                          FontStyle.Underline,
                          GraphicsUnit.Document);
Font statusFont = new Font("Garamond",
                           20.0f,
                           FontStyle.Bold,
                           GraphicsUnit.Document);
```

Values from the *GraphicsUnit* enumeration are provided in Table 14-13.

Table 14-13.   *GraphicsUnit* Enumeration Values

Value	Measurement Unit
Display	1/75 inch
Document	1/300 inch
Inch	Inch
Millimeter	Millimeter
Pixel	Device pixel
Point	1/72 inch
World	World units

When creating a *Font* object, you can specify the desired character set using the following set of constructors:

```
// From WinGDI.h
const byte OEM_CHARSET = 255;
Font labelFont = new Font(family,
                     20.0f,
                     FontStyle.Underline,
                     GraphicsUnit.Point,
                     OEM_CHARSET);
Font statusFont = new Font("Garamond",
                     20.0f,
                     FontStyle.Bold,
                     GraphicsUnit.Point,
                     OEM_CHARSET);
```

Unfortunately, there isn't any enumeration supplied with the .NET Framework that represents the available values for character sets, so you have to look in the WinGDI.h header file from the Win32 Platform SDK and pull the values out manually, as was done for this example. You can download the Win32 Platform SDK from *http://msdn.microsoft.com/downloads/default.asp*.

The final set of *Font* constructors, shown in the following code, is used to specify whether the new *Font* object is a vertical font. The last parameter of these constructors is *true* if the font is a vertical font; otherwise, it's *false*.

```
Font labelFont = new Font(family,
                     20.0f,
                     FontStyle.Underline,
                     GraphicsUnit.Point,
                     OEM_CHARSET,
                     true);
```

```
Font statusFont = new Font("Garamond",
                           20.0f,
                           FontStyle.Bold,
                           GraphicsUnit.Point,
                           OEM_CHARSET,
                           true);
```

Managing Font Properties

The properties exposed by a font are read-only because changing any of the properties would result in a new font. The most commonly used properties are listed here:

- **Bold** Boolean value that's *true* for boldface fonts and *false* otherwise

- **FontFamily** Value from the *FontFamily* enumeration that identifies the font family for this font

- **Height** Height of the font

- **Italic** Boolean value that's *true* for italic fonts and *false* otherwise

- **Size** Size of the font

- **SizeInPoints** Size of the font in points, regardless of the current *Unit* property setting

- **Strikeout** Boolean value that's *true* for strikeout fonts and *false* otherwise

- **Style** Value that combines all values from the *FontStyle* enumeration that are applied to this font

- **Underline** Boolean value that's *true* for underlined fonts and *false* otherwise

- **Unit** Value from the *GraphicsUnit* enumeration that identifies the units used by the *Height*, *Width*, and *Size* properties

The Font Common Dialog Box

Adding support for selectable fonts to an application is easy using Microsoft Visual C# .NET and the .NET Framework. The companion CD includes a new version of the SimpleEdit example originally presented in Chapter 13. The version included in this chapter enables the user to select the font used to display the edited text. The code required to make this change spans just a few lines, as shown on the following page.

```
private void editFontMenuItem_Click(object sender, System.EventArgs e)
{
    FontDialog dialog = new FontDialog();
    dialog.Font = Font;
    if(dialog.ShowDialog() == DialogResult.OK)
    {
        Font = dialog.Font;
        Invalidate();
    }
}
```

This code is simple, but it improves the user's experience with the Simple-Edit application because the user is now free to use any available font when editing a text file. The *editFontMenuItem_Click* method starts by creating an instance of the *FontDialog* class and then passes the form's font to the common dialog box. As with the *ColorDialog* class, discussed earlier in this chapter, in the section "The Color Common Dialog Box," it's a good idea to pass the current context information (in this case, the font) to the dialog box before it's displayed to the user. This lets the user see the current settings before making changes.

Conclusion

This chapter examined using GDI+ to draw graphics in your Windows Forms applications. The *Point, Size,* and *Rectangle* structures are used throughout the GDI+ and Windows Forms classes to specify the shapes, locations, and sizes of graphical objects.

The key class used with GDI+ is the *Graphics* class, which exposes methods and properties for performing graphics operations, as well as for gathering information about the display. The *Graphics* class uses other classes to draw to the display. The *Brush* class and its descendant classes are used to fill areas, such as rectangles or ellipses. *Brush* objects can be created in a wide range of colors, or they can be created with various hatching styles, images, or graphics paths. The *Pen* class is used to draw lines and shapes such as rectangles. *Pen* objects can be created in a variety of styles and colors—they can even be created from an existing *Brush* object. The *Graphics* class uses the *Font* class to draw text.

In Chapter 15, we'll look at more Windows Forms controls and we'll also examine techniques for anchoring and docking controls.

15

Advanced Controls

In this chapter, we'll look at several more controls that are part of the Microsoft Windows Forms namespace. Although the chapter is titled "Advanced Controls," these controls aren't difficult to use or understand. On the contrary, the controls in this chapter enable you to add a large amount of functionality—often with just a few lines of code. For example, the *MonthCalendar* and *DateTimePicker* controls provide rich user interfaces for selecting the time and date but require almost no coding on your part.

We'll start by looking at the up-down controls and the *ProgressBar* control. The up-down controls come in two flavors: the *NumericUpDown* control works with numeric values, whereas the *DomainUpDown* control can be used to iterate and select almost any collection of objects. The *ProgressBar* control provides visual feedback to the user regarding the status of a task.

Next we'll examine the *PictureBox* and *ImageList* controls, which are used to work with images, and the *RichTextBox* control, which provides support for editing formatted text. We'll also look at the *TabControl* control, which helps you organize groups of controls to conserve space in your application's forms, and we'll discuss the *MonthCalendar* and *DateTimePicker* controls.

The chapter concludes with a discussion of anchoring and docking—two features that are exposed by all controls and that make it easy to position and dynamically resize controls in forms that are resizable.

Using Up-Down Controls

Up-down controls are commonly used in Windows Forms applications to enable the user to select from a range of incrementing values. An up-down control couples a *TextBox* control with a small scroll bar that's used to increment and decrement the contents of the *TextBox* control.

The *UpDownBase* class serves as an abstract base class for the two up-down control implementations provided in the *System.Windows.Forms* namespace.

- **NumericUpDown**   Enables the user to increment and decrement decimal values in a *TextBox* control

- **DomainUpDown**   Enables the user to iterate over an array of objects that are represented as strings

    Two commonly used properties are defined by the *UpDownBase* class.

- **ReadOnly**   A Boolean value that specifies whether the contents of the control are read-only. If *true*, the contents of the control can be changed only by using the up and down arrows.

- **UpDownAlign**   A value from the *LeftRightAlignment* enumeration (*LeftRightAlignment.Left* or *LeftRightAlignment.Right*) that specifies the positioning of the up and down arrows.

The following subsections describe the concrete controls that are derived from the *UpDownBase* class. The *NumericUpDown* and *DomainUpDown* controls have the same outward appearance and basic operation; however, they extend the base control in different ways to add functionality.

The *NumericUpDown* Control

The *NumericUpDown* control, the most common form of up-down control, is used to increment a numeric value that's displayed in the text box. The *NumericUpDown* control works with decimal values instead of integers; using the decimal type makes it possible to increment values that aren't whole numbers.

The current value of the control is obtained through the *Value* property, as shown here:

```
int age = Convert.ToInt32(ageUpDown.Value);
```

Because the *NumericUpDown* control works with decimal values, you must explicitly convert the *Value* property to an integer.

By default, the *NumericUpDown* control will display only whole-number values. To enable the display of floating-point values, you must specify the desired precision with the *DecimalPlaces* property, like this:

```
ageUpDown.DecimalPlaces = 3;
```

This example causes the control to display three decimal places to the right of the decimal point.

By default, values allowed by the *NumericUpDown* control will range from *0* through *100*. These limits are changed with the *Minimum* and *Maximum* properties, as shown in the following code:

```
interestRateUpDown.Minimum = 4.55M;
interestRateUpDown.Maximum = 12.35M;
```

In most cases, you'll want to increment and decrement values in the control by *1*, and this is the default setting. The *Increment* property is used to modify the rate of change for the control, as shown here:

```
interestRateUpDown.Increment = 0.1M;
```

When the value stored in the *NumericUpDown* control is changed using the up and down arrows, the *ValueChanged* event is raised. You can handle this event to take action when the contents of the control have been updated, as shown here:

```
private void interestRateUpDown_ValueChanged(object sender,
                                             System.EventArgs e)
{
    _rate = interestRateUpDown.Value;
    statusLabel.Text = string.Format("The current interest rate is {0}",
                                     _rate);
}
```

If the user enters a new value directly into the control, the *ValueChanged* event won't be raised; instead, you'll see a *TextChanged* event. If the control's *ReadOnly* property isn't set to *true*, you should handle this event as shown in the following code:

```
private void interestRateUpDown_TextChanged(object sender,
                                            System.EventArgs e)
{
    _rate = interestRateUpDown.Value;
    statusLabel.Text = string.Format("The current interest rate is {0}",
                                     _rate);
}
```

The *DomainUpDown* Control

The *DomainUpDown* control enables any collection of objects to be used as the underlying items in an up-down control. Each item in the collection must have a *string* representation, which means either that you're storing a collection of *string* objects or that each of your objects implements the *ToString* method.

For example, consider a simple *Sailboat* class, such as the one shown here (with the non-essential methods and fields filtered out):

```
public class Sailboat
{
    string _name;
    ⋮
    public Sailboat(string name)
    {
        _name = name;
    }
    ⋮
    public override string ToString()
    {
        return _name;
    }
}
```

Because the *Sailboat* class overrides the *ToString* method to return the name of the sailboat, an array of *Sailboat* objects can be placed into a *DomainUpDown* control, using code such as this:

```
Sailboat [] boats = new Sailboat [] {
                            new Sailboat("Pegasus"),
                            new Sailboat("Sayonara"),
                            new Sailboat("Stars 'n Stripes"),
                            new Sailboat("Black Magic")
                        };
domainUpDown.Items.AddRange(boats);
```

Because the *DomainUpDown* control works with collections of objects instead of decimal values, it doesn't use the *Value* property exposed by the *NumericUpDown* control. Instead, the following two properties are exposed for retrieving the currently selected object:

- **SelectedIndex**   Identifies the index of the currently selected item

- **SelectedItem**   Identifies a reference to the currently selected item

The ColorUpDown application, on the companion CD, is an example project that fills a *DomainUpDown* control with the names of values from the *KnownColor* enumeration. (See the Microsoft Developer Network [MSDN]

Library for a list of members.) When the user selects a new color, the client area of the form is changed to use the new color. The relevant code is shown here:

```
public class MainForm : System.Windows.Forms.Form
{
    ⋮
    public MainForm()
    {
        ⋮
        string [] colorNames = Enum.GetNames(typeof(KnownColor));
        knownColorUpDown.Items.AddRange(colorNames);
        knownColorUpDown.SelectedIndex = 0;
    }
    ⋮
    private void knownColorUpDown_SelectedItemChanged(object sender,
                                                    System.EventArgs e)
    {
        string currentColorName = (string)knownColorUpDown.SelectedItem;
        try
        {
            BackColor = Color.FromName(currentColorName);
        }
        catch(ArgumentException exception)
        {
            MessageBox.Show(exception.Message);
        }
    }
}
```

The handler for the *SelectedItemChanged* event catches the *Argument-Exception* exception to handle a specific case. One of the members of the *KnownColor* enumeration is *KnownColor.Transparent*, and the form's *BackColor* property can't be set to this value.

Using the *ProgressBar* Control

The *ProgressBar* control is used to provide visual feedback to the user regarding the status of a task, usually for tasks that exceed a short duration. For example, a *ProgressBar* control can be used to display the progress of a task that copies a number of files or populates a database table.

The *ProgressBar* control consists of a bar that's filled as an operation progresses. Because the progress bar is often used to display the percentage of a task that's been completed, the default minimum and maximum values are optimized for this common case. The default minimum value is set to *0*, and the default maximum value is set to *100*.

One reason to change the range of values for a *ProgressBar* control is to simplify working with a specific number of items. You can adjust the lower boundary with the *Minimum* property, as shown here:

```
progressBar.Minimum = 50;
```

The *Maximum* property is used to adjust the upper end of the range:

```
progressBar.Maximum = 125;
```

The following two methods are used to change the value displayed in the *ProgressBar* control:

- **PerformStep**   Updates the control's value by the amount specified by the *Step* property

- **Increment**   Updates the control's value by the amount specified in the method's parameter

Typically, you'll use the *PerformStep* method to increment the control a fixed number of times, as shown here:

```
private void timer_Tick(object sender, System.EventArgs e)
{
    progressBar.PerformStep();
    if(progressBar.Value == progressBar.Maximum)
    {
        // Timer period elapsed.
        ⋮
    }
}
```

In addition to *Maximum* and *Minimum*, commonly used properties exposed by the *ProgressBar* class include the following:

- **Value**   The current position of the progress bar

- **Step**   The amount that the progress bar is incremented when the *PerformStep* method is called

The following code uses the *Value* property to update a label control with the current progress:

```
progressBar.PerformStep();
progressLabel.Text = string.Format("{0}% complete", progressBar.Value);
```

You also can use the *Value* property to explicitly set a new value for the control, as shown here:

```
progressBar.Value = 75;
```

Using the *PictureBox* Control

The *PictureBox* control is used to simplify the work required to display images. Using a *PictureBox* control, you can simply create an instance of the *PictureBox* class and assign a few properties. Most of the work required to properly display the image is encapsulated by the *PictureBox* class.

The most important property exposed by the *PictureBox* class is the *Image* property, which is used to specify the image that's displayed in the control, as shown here:

```
pictureBox.Image = Image.FromFile(@"C:\Windows\winnt256.bmp");
```

In many cases, the image and the *PictureBox* control will be different sizes. The *SizeMode* property specifies how the image and the *PictureBox* control are sized in relation to each other. This property uses values from the *PictureBoxSizeMode* enumeration, listed in Table 15-1.

Table 15-1.   *PictureBoxSizeMode* Enumeration Values

Value	Description
AutoSize	The control is resized to fit the image.
CenterImage	The image is centered inside the control. If the image is larger than the control, the edges of the image are clipped.
Normal	The image is displayed in the upper-left corner of the control. If the image is larger than the control, the edges of the image are clipped.
StretchImage	The image is resized to fit the control.

Using the *ImageList* Control

The *ImageList* control is used to store images that are used by other Windows Forms controls. The *ImageList* control stores images as if they were stored on a roll of film. Unlike a roll of film, however, it's a simple matter to add images to and remove images from an *ImageList* control. Controls such as the *ToolBar* control (discussed in Chapter 17) use the *ImageList* control as a repository for the images they display. Other controls that interact with the *ImageList* control include the *ListView*, *TreeView*, and *Button* controls. (The *ListView* and *TreeView* controls are discussed in Chapter 16, and the *Button* control is discussed in Chapter 12.)

To create an instance of the *ImageList* control, you'll typically drag the control onto your form, just as you would any other control. Alternatively, you can create an *ImageList* object programmatically, by calling its default constructor, as shown here:

```
ImageList imageList = new ImageList();
```

The images contained in the *ImageList* control are accessed through the *Images* property, which returns a reference to an *ImageCollection* object, as shown here:

```
ImageList.ImageCollection collection = imageList.Images;
foreach(Image img in collection)
{
    ⋮
}
```

As with similar collections used with other controls, you'll rarely need to explicitly employ a reference to the *ImageCollection* class. Instead, you can use the *Images* property directly, as shown here:

```
foreach(Image img in imageList.Images)
{
    ⋮
}
```

Because the *ImageCollection* class exposes an indexer, you can treat the *Images* property as an array of *Image* objects, as shown in the following code:

```
myButton.BackgroundImage = imageList.Images[0];
```

Three versions of the *Add* method are used to add an image to an *ImageList* control. The first version of the *Add* method accepts a reference to an *Image* object, as shown here:

```
Image anImage = Image.FromFile(@"C:\Windows\winnt256.bmp");
imageList.Images.Add(anImage);
```

The second version of *Add* is more advanced, enabling you to specify a masking color for the image, as shown in the following code:

```
Image img = Image.FromFile(@"C:\Windows\winnt256.bmp");
int index = imageList.Images.Add(img, Color.Black);
pictureBox.Image = imageList.Images[0];
```

This code causes all the areas that are colored black in the original image to be displayed transparently in the *PictureBox* control. This version of *Add* also returns an integer representing the new image's index position in the *ImageList* control.

The third version of *Add* accepts a reference to an *Icon* object, as shown here:

```
imageList.Images.Add(myIcon);
```

To remove an image from the *ImageList* control, call the *RemoveAt* method, passing the index of the image to be removed, as shown here:

```
imageList.Images.RemoveAt(0);
```

To remove all images from an *ImageList* control, call the *Clear* method.

```
imageList.Images.Clear();
```

Three of the most commonly used properties exposed by the *ImageList* class are as follows:

- **ImageSize**   A *Size* value that specifies dimensions for images stored in the *ImageList* control

- **ColorDepth**   A value from the *ColorDepth* enumeration that specifies the number of bits per pixel allocated for the image color

- **TransparentColor**   The color that's treated as transparent when the image is rendered

The default value for the *ImageSize* property is 16 by 16 pixels. The *ImageSize* property will accept any value up to 256 by 256 pixels, as shown here:

```
imageList.ImageSize = new Size(256, 256);
```

The *ColorDepth* property accepts values from the *ColorDepth* enumeration, listed in Table 15-2.

Table 15-2.   *ColorDepth* Enumeration Values

Value	Description
Depth4Bit	4 bits per pixel
Depth8Bit	8 bits per pixel
Depth16Bit	16 bits per pixel
Depth24Bit	24 bits per pixel
Depth32Bit	32 bits per pixel

The following code changes the *ImageList* control's color depth to accept true-color (24-bit) images:

```
imageList.ColorDepth = ColorDepth.Depth24Bit;
```

Using the *RichTextBox* Control

The *RichTextBox* control is used to provide text editing support for text stored in Rich Text Format (RTF). The RTF standard was developed by Microsoft as an early specification for exchanging text that includes formatting information. The

WordPad application distributed with Windows uses a Microsoft Win32 *Rich-Text* control, which is the moral equivalent of the Windows Forms *RichTextBox* control.

The *RichTextBox* control shares a base class (*TextBoxBase*) with the *TextBox* control, which is discussed in Chapter 12. As with the *TextBox* control, text can be entered directly into the *RichTextBox* control by the user. Text can also be loaded into the control from a file or a stream, in either text or RTF format. Many of the properties and methods exposed by the *TextBox* control are also available through the *RichTextBox* control. The most commonly used properties include the following:

- *BackColor*

- *ForeColor*

- *Lines*

- *Multiline*

- *Scrollbars*

- *WordWrap*

Although these properties are shared by the *TextBox* and *RichTextBox* classes, in some cases the default values of the properties differ between the two control classes. For example, the default value for the *Multiline* property for a *TextBox* control is *false*, whereas the default value for a *RichTextBox* control is *true*. These differences reflect the typical usage scenarios for the controls. A *TextBox* control is often used for simple text input, and a *RichTextBox* control is typically used to contain text formatted with multiple styles.

Common Formatting Options

As it does for the *TextBox* control, the *ForeColor* property of the *RichTextBox* control specifies the color used to display text. Unlike the *TextBox* control, however, the *RichTextBox* control exposes properties that enable you to specify multiple formatting options for text. This feature enables you to create headings and bulleted lists and also allows you to emphasize sections of text using italic or boldface fonts. Two of the more commonly used properties that target selected text are listed here:

- ***SelectionColor***   Specifies the color used by the currently selected text

- ***SelectionFont***   Specifies the font used by the currently selected text

The following code uses the *SelectionColor* property to change the color for the currently selected text, using the *ColorDialog* class to obtain the color from the user:

```
private void editColorMenuItem_Click(object sender, System.EventArgs e)
{
    ColorDialog dlg = new ColorDialog();
    dlg.Color = richTextBox.SelectionColor;
    if(dlg.ShowDialog() == DialogResult.OK)
    {
        richTextBox.SelectionColor = dlg.Color;
    }
}
```

The following code uses the *FontDialog* class to get the user's choice of font and then applies the font to the currently selected text with the *Selection-Font* property:

```
private void editFontMenuItem_Click(object sender, System.EventArgs e)
{
    FontDialog dlg = new FontDialog();
    dlg.Font = richTextBox.SelectionFont;
    if(dlg.ShowDialog() == DialogResult.OK)
    {
        richTextBox.SelectionFont = dlg.Font;
    }
}
```

> **Note**   Both of the previous examples can be found in the RichText-BoxPad example application included on the companion CD.

Other properties enable you to specify the current list bullet style, text alignment, paragraph formatting, and other options. When no text is currently selected, new formatting options set using these properties will be applied to the current text insertion point, and any new text entered into the control will be formatted using the new properties.

When a text selection includes text that has conflicting formatting properties, the property will return a value that indicates that the selection uses multiple formatting options. For example, the *SelectionFont* property will return *null* if the selected text uses multiple fonts. The *SelectionColor* property returns *Color.Empty* when the selected text contains multiple colors.

Loading a *RichTextBox* Control from a File

When we worked with the *TextBox* control in Chapter 12, the *Text* property was used to fill the *TextBox* control with text. Although the *RichTextBox* control also exposes the *Text* property, it's often more convenient to fill the control directly using the *LoadFile* method, which fills the control directly from a file or a stream.

There are three versions of the *LoadFile* method. The first version accepts a string that contains the path to the file to be loaded, as shown here:

```
richTextBox.LoadFile(path);
```

This version of the *LoadFile* method assumes that the file contains RTF text. If the file contains text in another format, an *ArgumentException* exception will be thrown.

The second version of the *LoadFile* method also accepts a string for the file path, as well as a value from the *RichTextBoxStreamType* enumeration that's used to specify the type of file that's being loaded, as shown here:

```
richTextBox.LoadFile(path, RichTextBoxStreamType.RichText);
```

Values from the *RichTextBoxStreamType* enumeration are listed in Table 15-3.

Table 15-3.   *RichTextBoxStreamType* Enumeration Values

Value	Description
PlainText	The file is plain text.
RichNoOleObjs	The file contains RTF text, with spaces in place of OLE objects. This option is used only with the *SaveFile* method (discussed in the next section).
RichText	The file contains RTF text.
TextTextOleObjs	The file is in plain text format, with spaces in place of OLE objects. This option is used only with the *SaveFile* method.
UnicodePlainText	The file is in Unicode-encoded plain text.

The third version of *LoadFile* accepts a stream reference instead of a file path, as shown here:

```
FileStream fs = new FileStream(path, FileMode.Open);
richTextBox.LoadFile(fs, RichTextBoxStreamType.RichText);
```

Saving the Contents of a *RichTextBox* Control

The contents of a *RichTextBox* control can be written to a file or a stream with the *SaveFile* method. As with the *LoadFile* method, there are three versions of *Save-File*. The first version saves the contents of the control into an RTF file located at a location specified by the path, as shown here:

```
richTextBox.SaveFile(path);
```

The second version of the *SaveFile* method enables you to specify the file format, as shown in the following code, using values from the *RichTextBox-StreamType* enumeration. (See Table 15-3 earlier in this chapter.)

```
richTextBox.SaveFile(path, RichTextBoxStreamType.RichText);
```

The third version of *SaveFile* is used to write the contents of the *RichText-Box* control into a stream, as shown here:

```
FileStream fs = new FileStream(path, FileMode.Create);
richTextBox.SaveFile(fs, RichTextBoxStreamType.RichText);
```

Using *TabControl* Controls

A common way to conserve space in a dialog box or a form is to use the *Tab-Control* control. The *TabControl* control enables you to stack multiple *TabPage* objects in a single shared location; navigation between pages is performed by clicking the tab associated with each page. An example of a dialog box that uses this type of user interface is the Windows Display Properties dialog box, shown in Figure 15-1.

Figure 15-1.   Tabs used by the Display Properties dialog box.

> **Note** When programming with the Win32 SDK, this type of user interface is created using property sheets and property pages. The *TabControl* and *TabPage* controls are roughly equivalent to these Win32 controls.

Creating *TabPage* Objects

The *TabPage* class represents a single tabbed page in a *TabControl* control. A *TabPage* object is like a virtual form surface—when its tab is selected, controls contained in the *TabPage* object are displayed and will remain visible until a different tab is selected.

There are two approaches you can use to create an instance of a *TabPage* object. In this section, we'll go through the steps used to create a *TabPage* object programmatically. Later in this chapter, in the section, "Creating *Tab-Control* Controls with the Windows Forms Designer," you'll learn how to use the Windows Forms Designer to create *TabPage* objects.

The *TabPage* class has two constructors. The following code uses the default constructor, which creates a *TabPage* object without a caption:

```
TabPage hobbiesTab = new TabPage();
```

The second version of the *TabPage* constructor accepts a string parameter that's used as the tab caption, as shown here:

```
TabPage phoneTab = new TabPage("Phones");
```

Managing *TabPage* Objects Programmatically

As mentioned, the *TabControl* control serves as the container for all tabbed pages, and each tab is represented by a *TabPage* object. The *TabControl* class exposes its collection of *TabPage* objects through its *TabPages* property, which returns a reference to an instance of *TabPageCollection*, as shown here:

```
TabControl.TabPageCollection collection = tabControl.TabPages;
foreach(TabPage page in collection)
{
    ⋮
}
```

As with similar classes discussed earlier in Part III, you rarely need to refer to the *TabPageCollection* class directly. Instead, you can simply write your code as if the *TabPages* property was the collection, which results in more compact code, as shown here:

```
foreach(TabPage page in tabControl.TabPages)
{
    ⋮
}
```

Because the *TabPageCollection* class provides an indexer, you can access *TabPage* objects stored in the collection just as if they were in an array, like this:

```
tabControl.TabPages[0].Text = "Location";
```

To add a *TabPage* object to a *TabControl* programmatically, you use the *Add* or *AddRange* method. The *Add* method accepts a reference to the *TabPage* object to be added, as shown here:

```
TabPage phoneTab = new TabPage("Phones");
tabControl.TabPages.Add(phoneTab);
```

The *AddRange* method is used to add multiple pages to a *TabControl* control. The *AddRange* method accepts an array of *TabPage* objects, as shown in the following code:

```
TabPage [] pages = new TabPage [] {
                            new TabPage("Contact"),
                            new TabPage("Sports"),
                            new TabPage("Hobbies")
                };

tabControl.TabPages.AddRange(pages);
```

There are two ways to remove a *TabPage* object from a *TabControl* control. The first approach requires you to pass a *TabPage* reference to the *Remove* method, as shown here:

```
tabControl.TabPages.Remove(phoneTab);
```

If it's not convenient to pass a reference to *Remove*, you can remove a *TabPage* object by its position in the *TabPages* collection by passing its index to the *RemoveAt* method, as follows:

```
tabControl.TabPages.RemoveAt(0);
```

And finally, to remove all the *TabPage* objects associated with a *TabControl* control, use the *Clear* method, as shown here:

```
tabControl.TabPages.Clear();
```

Creating *TabControl* Controls with the Windows Forms Designer

Although you can create a *TabControl* control programmatically, the simplest approach is to use the Windows Forms Designer that's part of Microsoft Visual Studio .NET. Get started by dragging a *TabControl* control from the Toolbox window to your form. The control will initially be displayed as a rectangle with no visible tabs, as shown in Figure 15-2.

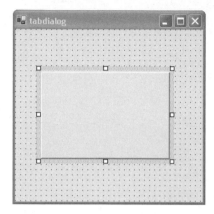

Figure 15-2.   A new *TabControl* control before tabs have been added.

To launch the TabPage Collection Editor, click the button next to the *Tab-Control* object's *TabPages* property in the Properties window. Initially, the TabPage Collection Editor is empty, as shown in Figure 15-3.

Figure 15-3.   The TabPage Collection Editor window before tabs have been added.

TabPage objects are added to the control's collection of tabs by clicking the Add button. After a tab is added to the collection, its properties can be managed from within the TabPage Collection Editor. A list of the tabs in the collection is provided on the left side of the editor, and a Properties window is displayed on the right, as shown in Figure 15-4.

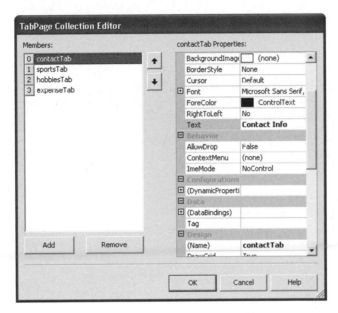

Figure 15-4.   Editing *TabPage* objects using the TabPage Collection Editor.

After a *TabPage* object has been added, controls can be added to the tab just as they are added to a dialog box.

Managing *TabControl* Controls

The *TabControl* class exposes additional properties that can be used to manage *TabControl* controls, including the following:

- **Alignment**   A value from the *TabAlignment* enumeration that specifies which edge of the *TabControl* control hosts the tabs

- **Appearance**   A value from the *TabAppearance* enumeration that specifies how tabs are drawn

- **Multiline**   A Boolean value that specifies whether multiple rows of tabs can be displayed

- **SelectedIndex**   The index of the currently selected tab

- *SelectedTab* A reference to the currently selected tab

- *SizeMode* A value from the *TabSizeMode* enumeration that specifies how tabs are sized

- *TabCount* The number of tabs contained by the control

The *Alignment* property enables you to specify which edge of the control will contain the tabs. Values from the *TabAlignment* enumeration are listed in Table 15-4.

Table 15-4. *TabAlignment* **Enumeration Values**

Value	Description
Bottom	Tabs are located along the bottom of the control.
Left	Tabs are located along the left edge of the control, and the *Multiline* property is automatically set to *true*.
Right	Tabs are located along the right edge of the control, and the *Multiline* property is automatically set to *true*.
Top	Tabs are located along the top edge of the control. This is the default value.

Be aware that if you select an alignment option other than *TabAlignment.Top*, your choices for the *TabAppearance* property will be limited. The following code uses the *Alignment* property to align the tabs across the bottom edge of the control:

```
tabControl.Alignment = TabAlignment.Bottom;
```

The *Appearance* property specifies how individual tabs are drawn. Values from the *TabAppearance* enumeration are listed in Table 15-5.

Table 15-5. *TabAppearance* **Enumeration Values**

Value	Description
Buttons	The tabs are drawn as buttons.
FlatButtons	The tabs are drawn as flat buttons. This setting requires the *Alignment* property to be set to *TabAlignment.Top*.
Normal	The tabs are drawn as tabs. This is the default setting.

As Table 15-5 indicates, the *TabAppearance.FlatButtons* value requires the *Alignment* property to be set to *TabAlignment.Top*. The following code uses the *Appearance* property to cause the tabs to be drawn as flat buttons:

```
tabControl.Appearance = TabAppearance.FlatButtons;
```

Occasionally, a *TabControl* control might contain more *TabPage* objects than can be displayed in a single row. The *Multiline* property specifies whether multiple rows of tabs can be displayed. If this value is *true*, multiple rows of tabs will be displayed, as shown in Figure 15-5.

Figure 15-5.   Multiple tab rows displayed in a *TabControl* control.

If the *Multiline* property is set to *false*, some tabs will be clipped so that a single row of tabs is displayed and navigation arrows will be provided to access the hidden tabs, as shown in Figure 15-6.

Figure 15-6.   A single tab row with navigation arrows.

The *SizeMode* property is used to specify how individual tabs are sized and is set to a value from the *TabSizeMode* enumeration, listed in Table 15-6. This property enables you to choose between displaying tabs that have a uniform size and displaying tabs that conserve space.

Table 15-6.   *TabSizeMode* Enumeration Values

Value	Description
FillToRight	The width of tabs is adjusted so that the tabs completely fill each row.
Fixed	The width of all tabs is the same.
Normal	The width of each tab is sized to hold the tab's contents.

The following code uses the *SizeMode* property to set all the tabs to a consistent size:

```
tabControl.SizeMode = TabSizeMode.Fixed;
```

Using the *MonthCalendar* Control

Two controls are available to enable the user to select the time and date. In this section, we'll examine the *MonthCalendar* control; in the next section, we'll look at the *DateTimePicker* control. The *MonthCalendar* control displays a calendar page that enables the user to select one or more dates. The user can scroll to additional months by using arrow buttons located at the top of the control.

The user selects a date from the *MonthCalendar* control by clicking the date displayed on the calendar page. By default, the user can select a range of dates. Initially, the user is allowed to select a range of up to seven dates. To change this behavior, use the *MaxSelectionCount* property, as shown in the following code, which restricts the user to selecting a single date at a time:

```
vacationCalendar.MaxSelectionCount = 1;
```

The following properties are used to get or set information about the currently selected dates in a *MonthCalendar* control:

- **SelectionStart**   A *DateTime* value that specifies the first selected date

- **SelectionRange**   A *SelectionRange* object that represents the dates selected in the control

- **SelectionEnd**   A *DateTime* value that specifies the last selected date

The *SelectionRange* class is used to model the relationship between the start and end dates. The *SelectionRange* class exposes the following two useful properties that shadow the properties available in the *MonthCalendar* class:

■   ***Start***   A *DateTime* value that represents the first date in the range

■   ***End***   A *DateTime* value that represents the last date in the range

If you're setting a selection range for a *MonthCalendar* control, there are three constructors you can use to create a *SelectionRange* object. The most commonly used version of the constructor uses two *DateTime* values passed as parameters to define the range for the new *SelectionRange* object. The following code creates a *SelectionRange* object that contains a one-week time range. This object is then used to set the selected date range for a *MonthCalendar* control.

```
SelectionRange range = new SelectionRange(DateTime.Now,
                                    DateTime.Now.AddDays(6.0));
vacationCalendar.SelectionRange = range;
```

The second version of the *SelectionRange* constructor creates an empty object, as shown here:

```
SelectionRange range = new SelectionRange();
```

After you create a *SelectionRange* object with this constructor, you'll need to use the *Start* and *End* properties to establish the endpoints for the range, as shown here:

```
SelectionRange range = new SelectionRange();
range.Start = DateTime.Now;
range.End = DateTime.Now.AddDays(3.0);
vacationCalendar.SelectionRange = range;
```

The third version of the constructor creates a new object by copying values from an existing *SelectionRange* object, as shown here:

```
SelectionRange defaultRange;
⋮
SelectionRange range = new SelectionRange(defaultRange);
```

The time period allowed for a *MonthCalendar* control is managed by two properties:

■   ***MinDate***   The earliest valid date for the control

■   ***MaxDate***   The latest valid date for the control

The following code restricts a *MonthCalendar* control to a two-week period. The user isn't allowed to scroll to other months and isn't allowed to select a date outside of the two-week period.

```
vacationCalendar.MinDate = DateTime.Now;
vacationCalendar.MaxDate = DateTime.Now.AddDays(14.0);
```

A single *MonthCalendar* control can display up to 12 months in a single grid. The dimensions of the calendar grid are set with the *CalendarDimensions* property, with the dimensions passed as a *Size* value, as shown here:

```
vacationCalendar.CalendarDimensions = new Size(2, 3);
```

This code creates a calendar that has two columns and three rows of months, as shown in Figure 15-7.

Figure 15-7.   A *MonthCalendar* control displaying a grid of six calendar months.

The *MonthCalendar* control can provide visual clues as to the current date. The *ShowToday* property is a Boolean value that specifies whether the date should be displayed at the bottom of the control. The default value for *ShowToday* is *true*. To prevent the current date from being displayed, set the property to *false*, as shown here:

```
vacationCalendar.ShowToday = false;
```

The *ShowTodayCircle* property specifies whether a circle is drawn around the current date. By default, this property is *true*, and the circle is drawn. To prevent the circle from being displayed, set this property to *false*, like this:

```
vacationCalendar.ShowTodayCircle = false;
```

By default, the date that's shown in the control is obtained from the system clock. The *TodayDate* property can be used to set the date explicitly, as shown in this code, which sets the calendar's date forward two days:

```
vacationCalendar.TodayDate = DateTime.Now.AddDays(2.0);
```

You can determine whether the date has been set explicitly with the *Today-DateSet* property, which returns *true* if the *TodayDate* property has been used to set the date, as shown here:

```
if(vacationCalendar.TodayDateSet)
{
    // Date has been explicitly set.
    ⋮
}
```

The *FirstDayOfWeek* property specifies the first day of the week displayed in the calendar, using one of these values from the *Day* enumeration:

- *Default*
- *Sunday*
- *Monday*
- *Tuesday*
- *Wednesday*
- *Thursday*
- *Friday*
- *Saturday*

This property is normally set to *Day.Default*, which displays Sunday as the first day of the week. The following code changes the calendar to display Monday as the first day of the week:

```
vacationCalendar.FirstDayOfWeek = Day.Monday;
```

The *ShowWeekNumbers* method is used to specify whether week numbers are displayed in the calendar. By default, this property is *false*; to enable week numbers, set this property to *true*, as shown in this code:

```
vacationCalendar.ShowWeekNumbers = true;
```

Another visual clue that's provided in the *MonthCalendar* control is the boldface rendering of special dates. Dates can be formatted in boldface on an individual basis, or they can be formatted in boldface on a repeating schedule so that the same dates appear in boldface for each month or are repeated for each year. A large number of methods and properties are dedicated to managing boldface dates. First let's look at the methods and properties that work with nonrepeating boldface dates:

- ***BoldedDates*** Property that specifies the current set of nonrepeating boldface dates

- **AddBoldedDate**   Method that adds a specific boldface date
- **RemoveBoldedDate**   Method that removes a specific boldface date
- **RemoveAllBoldedDates**   Method that removes all nonrepeating boldface dates

To set an initial set of boldface dates, assign an array of *DateTime* values to the *BoldedDates* property, as shown in the following code:

```
DateTime [] boldDates = new DateTime [] {
                                          DateTime.Now,
                                          DateTime.Now.AddDays(3.0),
                                          DateTime.Now.AddDays(6.0),
                                          DateTime.Now.AddDays(9.0)
                                        };
vacationCalendar.BoldedDates = boldDates;
```

You can also retrieve an array of *DateTime* values that represents the dates currently displayed in boldface, as shown here:

```
StringBuilder boldDateString = new StringBuilder();
foreach(DateTime day in vacationCalendar.BoldedDates)
{
    boldDateString.AppendFormat("{0}\n", day.ToShortDateString());
}
MessageBox.Show(boldDateString.ToString());
```

This code builds a string that contains the boldface dates from the *vacation-Calendar* object and displays the result in a message box.

When assigning new values with the *BoldedDates* property, be aware that any new assignment to *BoldedDates* will overwrite the existing values. If you want to preserve existing boldface dates, the simplest approach is to use the *AddBoldedDate* method, as shown here:

```
vacationCalendar.AddBoldedDate(DateTime.Now.AddDays(1.0));
```

This example adds a new boldface date, without overwriting any of the existing boldface dates.

To remove a specific boldface date, use the *RemoveBoldedDate* method, as shown here:

```
vacationCalendar.RemoveBoldedDate(DateTime.Now.AddDays(1.0));
```

Alternatively, you can remove all nonrepeating boldface dates with the *RemoveAllBoldedDates* method:

```
vacationCalendar.RemoveAllBoldedDates();
```

After you update any of the boldface dates, you must call the *UpdateBolded-Dates* method to ensure that the control draws the boldface dates properly, as shown here:

```
vacationCalendar.UpdateBoldedDates();
```

The *CalendarMonth* control also provides the following properties and methods used to manage dates that are repeated on a monthly or an annual basis:

■ **MonthlyBoldedDates**   Property that specifies the set of repeating dates that are displayed in boldface on a monthly basis

■ **AnnuallyBoldedDates**   Property that specifies the set of repeating dates that are displayed in boldface on an annual basis

■ **AddMonthlyBoldedDate**   Method used to add a date to be displayed in boldface on a monthly basis

■ **AddAnnuallyBoldedDate**   Method used to add a date to be displayed in boldface on an annual basis

■ **RemoveMonthlyBoldedDate**   Method used to remove a specific date that's displayed in boldface on a monthly basis

■ **RemoveAnnuallyBoldedDate**   Method used to remove a specific date that's displayed in boldface on an annual basis

■ **RemoveAllMonthlyBoldedDates**   Method used to remove all dates displayed in boldface on a monthly basis

■ **RemoveAllAnnuallyBoldedDates**   Method used to remove all dates displayed in boldface on an annual basis

These methods and properties work just like the nonrepeating boldface methods and properties discussed earlier except that these methods are used for dates that repeat on a monthly or an annual basis.

By default, the colors displayed by the *MonthCalendar* control are set to colors that fit in with the user's color preferences. However, the colors can be customized according to your needs. The following properties affect the color of the control:

■ **BackColor**   Specifies the color used for the background of the calendar page.

■ **ForeColor**   Specifies the color used to display the numbers for the calendar dates.

■ **TitleBackColor**   Specifies the background color used for the month caption. This color is also used for the text that heads the day columns.

- **TitleForeColor**   Specifies the foreground color used for the month caption.

- **TrailingForeColor**   Specifies the color used for dates that fall outside the displayed month.

Using the *DateTimePicker* Control

The *DateTimePicker* control offers a more compact user interface than the *MonthCalendar* control by displaying the current date in a text box that's similar to a drop-down combo box control. When the user clicks the down arrow, a *MonthCalendar* control is displayed. Unlike the *MonthCalendar* control discussed in the previous section, the *DateTimePicker* control displays only a single month at a time, as shown in Figure 15-8.

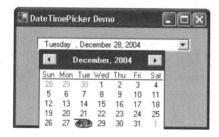

Figure 15-8.   A *DateTimePicker* control displaying a month calendar.

The date reflected by the control is available through the *Value* property, which is typed as a *DateTime* object, as shown here:

```
DateTime selectedDate = startTimeDatePicker.Value;
```

In addition to the *Value* property, which can be used to set or read the current status of the *DateTimePicker* control, the *Value* property's type has the following read-only properties, which can be used to retrieve time and date components:

- *Year*

- *Month*

- *Day*

- *DayOfWeek*

- *Hour*

- *Minute*

- *Second*

- *Millisecond*

Two additional properties are used to control the visual appearance of the *DateTimePicker* control:

- **ShowCheckBox** Specifies whether a check box should be displayed inside the control. When the check box is selected, the control is enabled. When the check box is cleared, the control appears to be disabled.

- **ShowUpDown** Specifies whether the down arrow should be replaced by an up-down control that's used to scroll individual components of the time and date.

The *DateTimePicker* control supports several formatting options for displaying the date and time. By default, the formatting displays the date in the long format, as in Thursday, May 13, 2004. (This format will vary slightly depending on the culture and date format preferences set by the user.) The display format is controlled by the control's *Format* property, using one of the values from the *DateTimePickerFormat* enumeration, listed in Table 15-7.

Table 15-7. *DateTimePickerFormat* **Enumeration Values**

Value	Description
Long	The date is displayed in the long format—for example, Thursday, May 13, 2004.
Short	The date is displayed in the short format—for example, 5/13/2004.
Time	The time is displayed in standard format—for example, 7:27:39 PM. This format is useful in combination with the *ShowUpDown* property set to *true*; without the *ShowUpDown* property set to *true*, the user can change the date but not the time.
Custom	The date and time are displayed in a custom format specified by the *CustomFormat* property.

To display the date in the short format, set the *Format* property to *DateTimePickerFormat.Short*, as shown here:

```
startTimeDatePicker.Format = DateTimePickerFormat.Short;
```

When the *Format* property is set to *DateTimePickerFormat.Custom*, you're expected to provide a custom format string. The *CustomFormat* property specifies the manner in which the date and time are displayed in the text portion of the control. The *CustomFormat* property is set to a string value that contains a combination of the values listed in Table 15-8.

Table 15-8.   Custom Format Strings for the _DateTimePicker_ Control

Value	Description
_d_	The one-digit or two-digit day
_dd_	The day displayed as two digits, with a leading zero added if needed
ddd	The three-character abbreviation for the day of the week
dddd	The full name of the day of the week
_h_	The one-digit or two-digit hour in 12-hour format
_hh_	The hour displayed as two digits in 12-hour format, with a leading zero added if needed
_H_	The one-digit or two-digit hour in 24-hour format
_HH_	The hour displayed as two digits in 24-hour format, with a leading zero added if needed
_m_	The one-digit or two-digit minute
_mm_	The minute displayed as two digits, with a leading zero added if needed
_M_	The month displayed as a one-digit or two-digit month number
_MM_	The month displayed as a two-digit month number, with a leading zero added if needed
MMM	The three-character abbreviation for the month
MMMM	The full name of the month
_s_	The one-digit or two-digit value for the seconds
_ss_	The seconds displayed as two digits, with a leading zero added if needed
_t_	A single letter that indicates AM or PM (A or P)
_tt_	Two letters that indicate AM or PM
_y_	The last digit of the year
_yy_	The last two digits of the year
yyyy	The full year

The following code sets the _DateTimePicker_ control to display both the time and date in a custom format:

```
startTimeDatePicker.Format = DateTimePickerFormat.Custom;
startTimeDatePicker.CustomFormat = "HH:mm:ss MMMM d, yyyy";
```

The custom format string passed to the _CustomFormat_ property can be a mixture of strings from Table 15-8 and text displayed in the control. You can take advantage of this capability to add new text to display a more descriptive string, as shown in the following code:

```
startTimeDatePicker.Format = DateTimePickerFormat.Custom;
startTimeDatePicker.CustomFormat = "'The time is' HH:mm:ss MMMM d, yyyy";
```

A control that uses this custom format is shown in Figure 15-9.

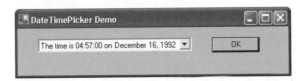

Figure 15-9.   A *DateTimePicker* control with a custom format.

Managing the Position and Size of Controls

At times, you need more than just the basic control positioning features we've examined thus far. We've looked at two techniques for sizing and positioning controls:

- At design time, controls are positioned and sized using the Windows Forms Designer.

- At run time, the location and size of a control are managed using the *Location* and *Size* properties.

Although these techniques are flexible, both approaches break down when you allow control containers to be resized. Writing code that manually resizes controls based on the size of the container is difficult—in fact, third-party controls that assist in resizing have always been among the most popular ActiveX controls. Controls and forms in the .NET Framework expose the following two properties that enable them to be dynamically resized or positioned as their containers are resized:

- ***Anchor***   Specifies which edges of the container control the size and position of the control

- ***Dock***   Specifies which edges of the container the control will be attached to

The following subsections describe the use of these properties in more detail, beginning with the *Anchor* property.

Anchoring Controls

The *Anchor* property for a control specifies how the control is positioned when its parent is resized. By default, a control is anchored to the top and left edges of its container; as the container is resized, the controls remain a fixed distance from the top and left edges of the container. The *Anchor* property can be set to one or more values from the *AnchorStyles* enumeration, listed in Table 15-9.

Table 15-9. *AnchorStyles* **Enumeration Values**

Value	Description
None	No anchoring.
Top	The control is anchored to the top edge of its container.
Bottom	The control is anchored to the bottom edge of its container.
Left	The control is anchored to the left edge of its container.
Right	The control is anchored to the right edge of its container.

The default *Anchor* property value for a control is shown here:

```
AnchorStyles.Top | AnchorStyles.Left
```

Figure 15-10 shows a simple example form that has two push button controls and a *TextBox* control.

Figure 15-10. Simple form before resizing.

If this form is resized, as shown in Figure 15-11, the controls on the form remain in their current locations. Ideally, the *TextBox* control would be resized to conform to the larger form that's now available. In addition, the OK and Cancel buttons should align at the right edge of the container. With the *Anchor* property, you can achieve this effect easily.

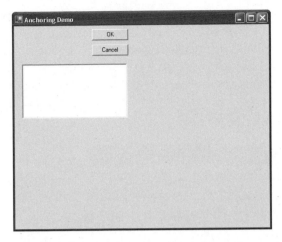

Figure 15-11.   After form resizing, controls remain fixed.

Instead of being anchored to only the top and left edges of its container, the *TextBox* control should be anchored to all of its container's edges, forcing the control to be resized as the form is resized. You can change the property programmatically using code such as this:

```
Anchor = AnchorStyles.Top | AnchorStyles.Right;
```

A much easier approach is to use the Windows Forms Designer to change the *Anchor* property graphically at design time. To do so, click the *Anchor* property in the Properties window and then click the drop-down arrow to display a graphical representation of the current *Anchor* property value, as shown in Figure 15-12.

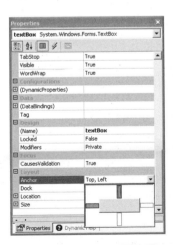

Figure 15-12.   Changing the *Anchor* property with the Windows Forms Designer.

In the graphical representation of the *Anchor* property, the gray bars that lead from the center of the box to the box's edges indicate that the *Anchor* property is set to *AnchorStyles.Top* and *AnchorStyles.Left*. You can toggle any of the anchor settings by clicking the associated bar. In Figure 15-13, the *TextBox* control's *Anchor* property has been changed so that the control is anchored to all sides of its container, and the push button controls have an *Anchor* property of *AnchorStyles.Top | AnchorStyles.Right*.

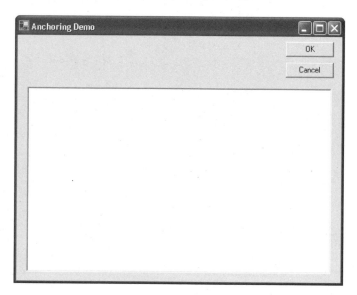

Figure 15-13.   Resizing the form with new *Anchor* properties for the controls.

Docking Controls

In some ways, the *Dock* property is similar to the *Anchor* property in that it too manages the interaction between a control and its container. The *Dock* property uses values from the *DockStyle* enumeration, listed in Table 15-10.

Table 15-10.   *DockStyle* **Enumeration Values**

Value	Description
None	No docking. This is the default style.
Top	The control is docked against the top edge of its container.
Bottom	The control is docked against the bottom edge of its container.
Left	The control is docked against the left edge of its container.
Right	The control is docked against the right edge of its container.
Fill	The control is docked against all edges of the container.

Unlike the *Anchor* property and the *AnchorStyles* enumeration, however, you never combine multiple values from the *DockStyle* enumeration. A control is docked against one side of its container, except for the special case of *DockStyle.Fill*, which causes the control to be resized to completely fill its container. When a control is docked, it's positioned so that the docked edge of the control is flush with an edge of the control's container; furthermore, the control is resized so that sides that are adjacent to the control's docked edge are also flush with the edges of the container. Figure 15-14 shows an example of a *TextBox* control that's docked against the bottom edge of its form.

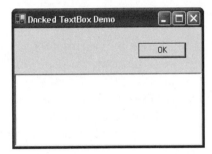

Figure 15-14.   *TextBox* control docked against bottom edge of a form.

The *Dock* property can be set programmatically, as shown in the following code:

```
Dock = DockStyle.Fill;
```

Like the *Anchor* property, the *Dock* property can also be set graphically using the Windows Forms Designer, as shown in Figure 15-15.

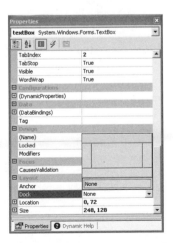

Figure 15-15.   The *Dock* property in the Windows Forms Designer.

Clicking the center button in the graphical representation of the *Dock* property selects *DockStyle.Fill*. Clicking any of the edge buttons selects the associated edge as the docking destination.

Conclusion

In this chapter, we've examined several of the controls that are used with Windows Forms. These controls offer a great deal of functionality that can be leveraged with a relatively small amount of code. For example, the *NumericUpDown*, *ProgressBar*, and *PictureBox* controls require almost no code if you're able to accept the default control behavior.

The *NumericUpDown* and *DomainUpDown* controls are used to iterate through a range of values. The *NumericUpDown* control works with numbers, whereas the *DomainUpDown* control can be used with almost any collection of objects. Another easy-to-use control is the *ProgressBar* control, which is used to provide a visual representation of the current status of a task. The *PictureBox* and *ImageList* controls simplify working with images. The *RichTextBox* control is similar to the *TextBox* control, except that it enables text contained inside the control to be formatted in multiple styles. The *TabControl* control is used to arrange groups of controls on individual pages—which can enable you to display a large number of controls while conserving space.

This chapter also explored anchoring and docking. All controls expose the *Anchor* and *Dock* properties, which are used to dynamically resize and position controls on a form. In Chapter 16, we'll look at three more controls: *ListView*, *TreeView*, and *Grid*. These controls use many of the features we've discussed in this chapter. For example, you'll often find these controls anchored or docked on a form. Also, the *TreeView* and *ListView* classes frequently use the *ImageList* control as an image container.

16

Grid, Tree, and List Controls

If you look at an average Microsoft Windows application, you'll notice that it uses not only stock controls such as buttons and text boxes, but also much more sophisticated controls. This chapter introduces you to three commonly used rich controls and describes how to effectively use these controls in your applications. Along the way, you'll see how easy it is to program controls with Microsoft Visual C# .NET.

Two of the controls we'll look at in this chapter—the *TreeView* control and the *ListView* control—are *common controls*, meaning that they ship with all versions of Windows and are available to any programming language, not only to Microsoft .NET Framework applications. Given that at one time or another most of the data in applications is presented either in list view or in a hierarchical tree view, you'll probably find yourself using these controls often in your applications.

Although it isn't a common control, the *DataGrid* control is bound to appear often in your Visual C# applications too. When listing data in read-only form isn't sufficient and real data editing is needed, this control will be your choice. The *DataGrid* control enables you to make various types of data available for editing, supports extensive style options, and (last, but not least) is easily put to use thanks to the Visual C# .NET Forms Designer. We'll look first at how to use the *DataGrid* control and then at the *TreeView* and *ListView* controls.

Using the *DataGrid* Control

Grid controls sold like hotcakes in the days of Microsoft Visual Basic 6, which included a simple grid control. With the advent of the .NET Framework, this grid control's reach has been extended to all programming languages and the control, now called the *DataGrid* control, has become much more powerful. In this section, you'll learn how to use the *DataGrid* control to display database data in a grid, display data hierarchically, and edit and navigate a database. You'll also learn how to customize the *DataGrid* control to suit your needs, and you'll even learn how to import XML data easily into a data grid for viewing and editing purposes.

Displaying Database Data

The *DataGrid* control is most commonly used to connect to database data. The concepts of database access are described in detail in Chapter 18, which discusses ADO.NET; here we'll concentrate on using the data access classes to populate data grids and not on how these classes work. As you'll see, ADO.NET isn't hard to use—you follow a few simple steps to bind a *DataGrid* control to database data.

In the following subsections, we'll develop a simple application that uses a *DataGrid* control to display data from a database.

Creating a Database Connection

The first thing you need when retrieving data from a database is, of course, a database connection. Although you can use the Data Adapter Configuration Wizard to create a new database connection, the process is easier to understand if you do it yourself the first time. To do so, start a new Windows Application project, open the Toolbox window, and drag a new *SqlConnection* object onto the form.

You now have a *sqlConnection1* object in the Forms Designer. Open the object's Properties window, and in the ConnectionString drop-down list, select New Connection. In the Data Link Properties window that appears, enter the defaults for the Microsoft Data Engine (MSDE) that's installed with the .NET Framework SDK samples, as follows:

- For the server name, select (local)\NetSDK.

- For the login information, select Use Windows NT Integrated Security.

- For the database, select Northwind.

> **Note**   For information about configuring MSDE and the .NET Framework SDK samples, select Microsoft .NET Framework SDK from the Start menu, and click Samples And QuickStart Tutorials.

The fully configured Connection tab is shown in Figure 16-1.

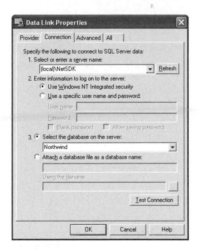

Figure 16-1.   Defining the connection properties.

Click OK to complete the database connection.

Configuring the Data Adapter

After the connection to the database is defined, we can use it to access any data in the Northwind database. To specify which data we're interested in, we'll use a data adapter, which enables us to define which data to retrieve. (You can also use a data adapter to update data; you'll learn how to do this in Chapter 18.)

To create a new *SqlDataAdapter* object, drag one from the Toolbox window onto the form. The Data Adapter Configuration Wizard will appear and will guide you through the creation of the *SqlDataAdapter* object. Because we've already defined a *SqlConnection* object, the wizard proposes to use that connection, which is perfectly fine with us. The wizard next prompts for a query type—here we'll stick with the default of using SQL statements.

The SQL statement you provide will specify what users will ultimately see in the data grid. To limit the number of columns in the data grid, enter the following SQL statement:

```
SELECT CustomerID, CompanyName, Address, City, PostalCode, Country
    FROM Customers
```

Using this information, the wizard will generate everything necessary for populating a dataset based on the SQL statement.

After you've created the *SqlDataAdapter* object, name it *sqldaCustomers*.

Generating a Dataset

Up to now, we haven't yet dealt with the data itself—only with how to connect to the database and specify the data to retrieve. The data representation on the client is called the *dataset*. In contrast to the ADO recordset, a dataset is tightly bound to the data it's representing. For this reason, you should create a specialized dataset for each *SqlDataAdapter* object. Because it's just a click away, this extra step doesn't really slow you down.

To create a *DataSet* object, simply select the *SqlDataAdapter* object you generated earlier and choose Generate Dataset from the Data menu. Give the dataset a descriptive name, such as *dsCustomers*, and then click OK. (Remember, ADO.NET is discussed at length in Chapter 18.)

Binding the Dataset to the Data Grid

Now that we've done the prerequisite work, we can concentrate on working with the data grid. To add a data grid to a form, simply drag the *DataGrid* control from the Toolbox window to the form. To bind the dataset you created in the previous section to the *DataGrid* control, you must set the following two properties of the control:

- **DataSource**   Specifies which *DataSet* object to bind to

- **DataMember**   Specifies which table (*DataTable* object) of the *DataSet* object the data grid should be bound to by default

Configuring the *DataMember* property of the *DataGrid* control is easy—your only choice is the *Customers table*.

The completed setup is shown in Figure 16-2.

Once the setup is complete, the *DataGrid* control immediately displays the columns it will have at run time. This neat feature is also useful in that it allows you to double-check your SQL commands.

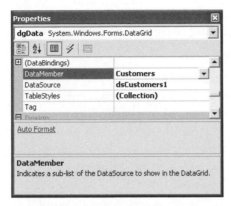

Figure 16-2.   Configuring the *DataSource* and *DataMember* properties for a data grid.

Loading Data into the Data Grid

At this point, the application can be compiled and started, but the data grid won't yet contain any data. Although you've defined everything from the connection to the dataset, nothing is loaded automatically. You must populate the dataset using the *Fill* method of the corresponding data adapter, as shown here:

```
dsCustomers1.Clear();
sqldaCustomers.Fill(dsCustomers1);
```

This code can be placed either in the constructor of the form or in a button event. When *Fill* returns, both the dataset and the data grid are populated, as shown in Figure 16-3.

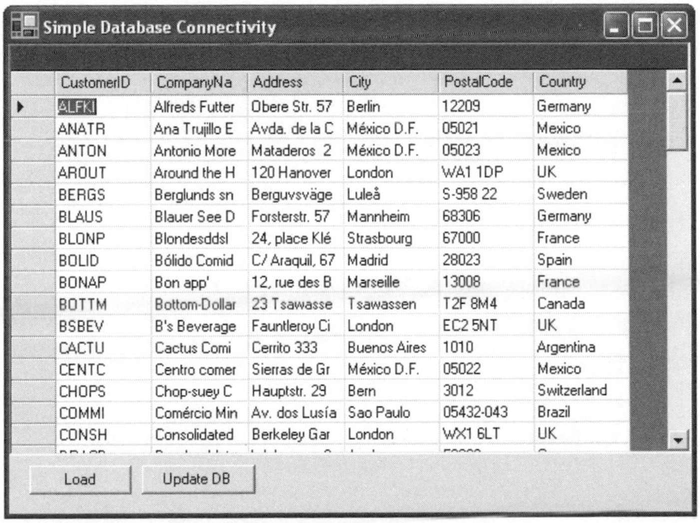

Figure 16-3.   The dataset displayed in the data grid.

The Update DB button shown in Figure 16-3 provides a clue as to what we'll look at next—editing data in the data grid and writing those changes back to the database.

Updating the Database with Data Grid Changes

As you play around with the data in the data grid, you'll notice that you can edit the data in a cell. But when you close the application or reload the dataset, all your changes are lost. This is because the dataset is a pure in-memory representation of the data and has no connection with the database from which you retrieved the data unless you explicitly tell the dataset to update the database with your changes.

The update operation is similar to filling a dataset—that is, you call a method on the corresponding data adapter. Actually, the update is a single line of code, as follows:

```
sqldaCustomers.Update(dsCustomers1);
```

To summarize, we've written a total of three lines of code for an application that can display and update customer data in a database. This is only the tip of the iceberg, however, with more to come in the following sections. If you want to familiarize yourself more with the current example, go to the Datagrid-DbconnSimple directory on the companion CD.

Displaying Hierarchical Data in Data Grids

You're not limited to displaying a single table in a data grid—it's also possible to display parent-child relationships. For example, with a single click, you can show all orders for a given customer and even drill down to all the line items (if you added that relationship as well). This capability has made *DataGrid* controls a powerful feature for database applications.

Preparing *SqlDataAdapter* Objects and the Dataset

The prerequisites for showing hierarchical data in a data grid are basically the same as for viewing nonhierarchical data. You'll need a database connection and a dataset, but here's the difference: for every hierarchy level (for example, Customers and Orders), you need a separate data adapter.

In addition to the connection and data adapter you created earlier in this chapter, create an additional *DataAdapter* object using the following SQL command:

```
SELECT OrderID, CustomerID, OrderDate, Freight, ShipAddress,
    ShipName, ShipCity, ShipPostalCode, ShipCountry
    FROM Orders
```

Name the new *DataAdapter* object *sqldaOrderHistory*.

To create the dataset, select both data adapters, choose Generate DataSet from the Data menu, and name the dataset *dsOrderHistory*. Because we're working with multiple tables in this example, we still have some work to do. The dataset still knows nothing about the relationship between the two tables—that is, which is the parent and which columns should be used to create the relationship.

To add this missing information, double-click *dsOrderHistory.xsd* in Solution Explorer. You're now in the XML Schema Designer (more on XML in Chapter 19), which displays definitions for the *Customers* and *Orders* tables. To define the relationship between these two tables, drag a *Relation* object from the Toolbox window to the *Orders* table. In the Edit Relation dialog box that appears, make sure that Parent Element is set to *Customers*, Child Element is set to *Orders*, and Key Fields and Foreign Key Fields are both set to *CustomerID*. Click OK to close the dialog box. The design will look something like Figure 16-4.

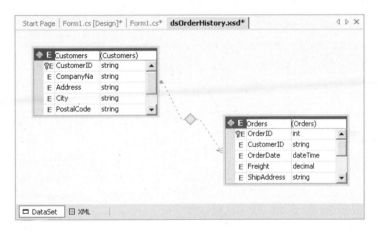

Figure 16-4.   Customers and Orders tables linked with a *Relation* object.

Save the changes to the schema, define the *DataGrid* control's *Data-Source* and *DataMember* properties as you did in the previous example, and populate the *dsOrderHistory* dataset using the following code:

```
dsOrderHistory1.Clear();
sqldaCustomers.Fill(dsOrderHistory1);
sqldaOrderHistory.Fill(dsOrderHistory1);
```

Finally, compile and run the application.

Navigating the Data Grid

The plus signs (+) displayed next to each record in the data grid enable you to drill down in the hierarchy that resides below the Customers table. Our example contains only one dependent child table, named Orders, accessible via the *CustomersOrders* relationship (unless you changed the default name of the relationship in the previous section). Clicking the relationship name changes your data grid to a view similar to that shown in Figure 16-5.

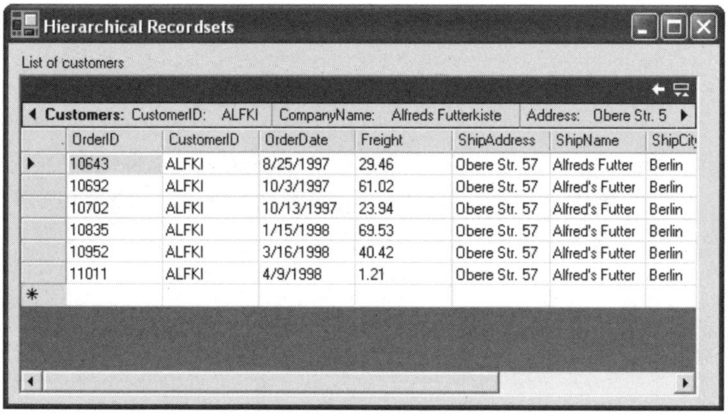

Figure 16-5. The Orders table expanded, with the Customers table information shown in the top row.

To return to the Customers table, click the left arrow in the top row. Although this drill-down capability can come in handy occasionally, it gets tiring when you need to view child records more frequently. In that case, you might consider linking multiple data grids.

Linking Multiple Data Grids

The relationship you specify in the XML Schema Designer not only allows for hierarchical display of data in a single data grid, but it also lets you link two separate data grids in such a way that when the active row is changed in the parent grid, the child grid automatically reflects the change by displaying the corresponding rows from the child table.

To see how easy this feature is to implement, add one more data grid to our existing form. Set the data grid's *DataSource* property to the existing dataset, and for the *DataMember* property, enter the following code:

```
Customers.CustomersOrders
```

This is the relationship between the parent and child tables of our dataset. Now whenever the row is changed in the parent data grid, the newly created child data grid will display the corresponding Orders table data, as shown in Figure 16-6.

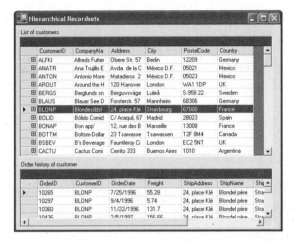

Figure 16-6. Selecting a customer in the parent data grid to automatically display the associated order information in the child grid.

You can verify that the child data displayed is correct by drilling down in the parent data grid—remember, it's still a hierarchical data grid.

Advanced Data Grids

Data grids are very flexible and can be used in a wide variety of applications. One potential use is to connect a data grid to an XML file instead of a database, which allows you to edit data before the data is uploaded to a server. Another powerful feature of data grids is their extensibility, which allows you to define the way data grids display data.

Connecting Data Grids to XML Data

As you'll see in Chapter 18 and Chapter 19, ADO.NET and XML are deeply intertwined. You can easily treat a dataset as XML data, and you can load XML data into a dataset.

To see how this works, take a look at this small XML data file, appropriately named SampleData.xml:

```
<?xml version="1.0" encoding="utf-8" ?>
<SnowReports Date="2/25/2002">
<Resort>
    <Name>Meribel</Name>
    <SnowHigh>120</SnowHigh>
    <SnowLow>43</SnowLow>
</Resort>
⋮
</SnowReports>
```

You'll find the complete listing of this file on the companion CD in the Data-gridXml directory. The tags describe what's contained in this XML file: snow reports from various ski resorts, with the date of the report in the root node and resort-specific information contained in the Resort node.

To import the XML file's contents into the data grid, the file first needs to be read and the data put into a dataset. Then the data binding of the data grid must be defined, which can be done using the *SetDataBinding* method. The code for these operations is shown here:

```
XmlDataDocument xdocSnowReports= new XmlDataDocument();
xdocSnowReports.DataSet.ReadXml(
    new StreamReader("SampleData.xml"), XmlReadMode.InferSchema);
dgLateXmlBound.SetDataBinding(xdocSnowReports.DataSet, "Resort");
```

The workhorse here is an instance of *XmlDataDocument*, which resides in the *System.Xml* namespace. The dataset of the *XmlDataDocument* object supports reading from an XML document, as well as the important task of automatically inferring a schema for the XML document. (We didn't create an .xsd file.) Once all loading is complete, the Resort table is bound to the data grid.

The dataset in this example contains multiple tables because the root node and the Resort nodes define separate levels of the hierarchy of the XML document—the root node is the topmost parent table, and the Resort nodes are records in the first child table. The other nodes in the Resort nodes are leaf nodes, and therefore they form columns in the Resort table, not tables of their own.

Being able to access the root node's attributes enables us to customize the data grid a bit more. One practical use for the date of the snow report would be to create a descriptive caption in the data grid, as shown here:

```
DataRow dr = xdocSnowReports.DataSet.Tables["SnowReports"].Rows[0];
string strCaption = dr["Date"].ToString();
this.dgLateXmlBound.CaptionText = "Snow report on " + strCaption;
```

You can customize the look and feel of your data grid in a number of ways. Probably the most important customization is defining table and column styles, which is covered next.

Defining Your Own Style

There are a number of good reasons for defining table and column styles. For example, you might not want to display all the columns that a table in a dataset offers; instead, you might want to show only a defined subset of columns. Another interesting possibility is to change how columns are rendered—for example, you can display check boxes for the True/False fields instead of text boxes. You can also adjust pure user interface settings, such as column width, background color, or font selection.

Applying table styles The first step in defining how a certain table from a dataset is rendered in the data grid is to create a new *DataGridTableStyle* object. To do so, select the *TableStyles* collection in the Properties window for the data grid. The DataGridTableStyle Collection Editor will open, and you can add your table style definitions there.

> **Note** This discussion refers to table styles in the plural because hierarchical data grids can display multiple tables (each with a different style) and data grids dynamically bound to various sources (such as XML files) can contain multiple tables (each with a different style).

Spend some time experimenting with changing the visual appearance of the table. In the end, one property controls whether your table style is applied: *MappingName*. You must set the *MappingName* property to the name of the table to which this style is to be applied (in the current example, the Resort table). If you enter the wrong name, it might take some time to find the error.

If you run your application now, the table styles you've specified will be applied. To limit which columns are displayed, which headers they show, or what kind of editing is provided, you'll have to go one level deeper—to the column styles.

Working with column styles To gain full control over how your data grid is displayed, you need to define each column with a column style. You can access the DataGridColumnStyle Collection Editor by clicking the *GridColumnStyles* collection in the respective *DataGridTableStyle* object. After you manually add all three columns of the snow report, the Collection Editor should look like Figure 16-7.

All three columns are defined as *DataGridTextBoxColumn* objects, with the *MappingName* property set to the respective XML tag name. Also modified are the *Width* and *HeaderText* properties. The sample application, including XML saving functionality, can be found on the companion CD in the directory DatagridXml.

Before we move on, we need to take a quick look at the *DataGridColumnStyle*-derived classes. The *DataGridColumnStyle* class provides you with a simple text box column and a Boolean column represented by a check box. However, nothing prevents you from creating your own column styles—for example, a drop-down list for lookup values from other tables. Sample implementations for such custom *DataGridColumnStyle*-derived classes can be found at *http://www.gotdotnet.com/*.

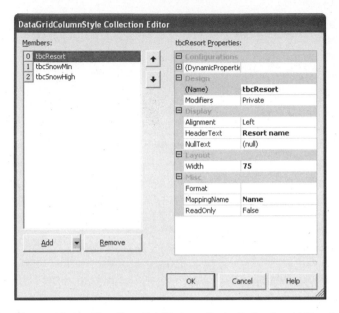

Figure 16-7.   The DataGridColumnStyle Collection Editor, in which you can add text box and Boolean columns.

Displaying Hierarchical Information in a *TreeView* Control

Every user has seen the *TreeView* control in action at least once—in Windows Explorer, various file dialog boxes, the Registry Editor, or the hundreds of other applications that use the *TreeView* control to display hierarchical information. Using the *TreeView* control used to be a bit painful in the pre–.NET Framework days—in C++, the control was hard to use, and in Visual Basic, you couldn't get to all the functionality. In the .NET Framework, however, you can keep things simple or get as fancy as the control will allow.

Designing a *TreeView* Control

To get a feel for what you can do with a *TreeView* control without writing a lot of code, you can use the Visual C# Forms Designer. With the Forms Designer, you can add items to a *TreeView* control, define its look and feel, and navigate the tree—from the end user's as well as the programmer's point of view.

Adding *TreeView* Items

The easiest way to start experimenting with a *TreeView* control is to manually add tree nodes at design time. Simply drag a *TreeView* control onto your form, and in the Properties window, open the *Nodes* collection. This will open the TreeNode Editor, shown in Figure 16-8.

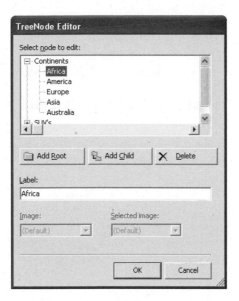

Figure 16-8.   Manually editing tree nodes using the TreeNode Editor.

You can add root or child nodes, as well as delete and edit tree nodes. When you've finished, take a look at the *InitializeComponent* method in your form's code to see what code was generated to build the tree. The code will be similar to the following:

```
this.tvSimple.Nodes.AddRange(new TreeNode[]
{
    new TreeNode("Continents", new TreeNode[]
    {
        new TreeNode("Africa"),
        new TreeNode("America"),
        new TreeNode("Europe"),
        new TreeNode("Asia"),
        new TreeNode("Australia")
    }),
    new TreeNode("SUV\'s", new TreeNode[]
    {
        new TreeNode("Hummer"),
        new TreeNode("Pinzgauer")
    })
});
```

This code has been made a little more readable than what you'll actually see in the *InitializeComponent* method, but it's the same as what the TreeNode Editor generates for you. Later examples show different ways to add tree nodes dynamically—without the help of the TreeNode Editor.

Setting Style Properties

A *TreeView* control can come in variety of styles. For example, it can be text only, as in the current example, or it can show images for each tree node. Table 16-1 lists some of the more important style properties for the *TreeView* control.

Table 16-1.   Important Style Properties of a *TreeView* Control

Property	Description
ShowLines	Specifies whether lines are to be drawn between nodes
ShowPlusMinus	Specifies whether plus or minus signs are to be shown before the nodes that can be expanded or collapsed
ShowRootLines	Specifies whether root nodes are to be connected with lines

You can experiment with these properties in Design view to see how the appearance of the control changes.

Navigating the *TreeView* Control

You now have a basic tree, without having written a line of code yourself. When your users start the application, they have a fully functional *TreeView* control that they can navigate by selecting, expanding, and collapsing nodes.

In addition to users being able to navigate the tree interactively, you can control the tree programmatically. This is where the *ExpandAll* and *CollapseAll* methods come into the picture; these two methods do exactly what their names imply. To demonstrate how these methods work, the example application Simple-Treeview, on the companion CD, creates two buttons that call the methods, as shown here:

```
private void cmdExpandAll_Click(object sender, System.EventArgs e)
{
    tvSimple.ExpandAll();
}

private void cmdCollapseAll_Click(object sender, System.EventArgs e)
{
    tvSimple.CollapseAll();
}
```

These two methods always act on the entire tree. Sometimes it's more appropriate to expand or collapse only a single branch of the tree, starting at a defined node. To do so, you can call the *ExpandAll* and *CollapseAll* methods on the currently selected node. The example application allows the user to expand or collapse the currently selected node via a shortcut menu, as shown here:

```
private void OnExpandNode(object sender, System.EventArgs e)
{
    TreeNode tn = tvSimple.SelectedNode;
```

```
        if (null == tn) return;
        tn.ExpandAll();
    }

    private void OnCollapseNode(object sender, System.EventArgs e)
    {
        TreeNode tn = tvSimple.SelectedNode;
        if (null == tn) return;
        tn.Collapse();
    }
```

Figure 16-9 shows this shortcut menu in action.

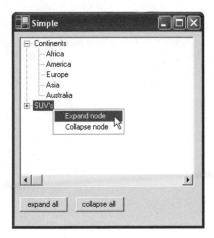

Figure 16-9.   Using a shortcut menu to enable the user to collapse or expand branches.

Generating Dynamic *TreeView* Controls

Most of the time, you use *TreeView* controls to display dynamic trees, not static trees that are fully defined at compile time, as in the previous section. Examples of dynamic trees include the file system's hierarchical structure, an XML file that has a tree structure, and even the Windows registry. For each of these cases, you determine the nodes dynamically and then add them to the *TreeView* control.

Because Windows Explorer is such a natural fit to show off *TreeView* controls (and *ListView* controls, as you'll see later in this chapter), you'll find numerous examples of Explorer look-alikes in various books and articles addressing this topic, both on line and off line. This section breaks with tradition, using the Windows registry as the base for a dynamic *TreeView* control.

In addition to creating a dynamic *TreeView* control, we'll also look more closely at the various classes in the *Microsoft.Win32* namespace. To follow along with the procedures in the following subsections, create a new project and add a *TreeView* control to its main form. The completed application can be found in the directory RegistryTree on the companion CD.

Adding Node Images

Each node in a *TreeView* control can be in one of two states: closed or open. You can represent those two states with images—for example, using closed and open folder bitmaps as is done by Windows Explorer.

> **Note** If you're not an accomplished graphic artist, you'll find some graphics to start out with at \Program Files\Microsoft Visual Studio .NET\Common7\Graphics. The samples in this chapter use the bitmaps provided in that directory, under bitmaps\Outline.

The easiest way to include such state images in a *TreeView* control is to add an *ImageList* object to the form. To do so, drag the object from the Toolbox window onto the form and in the Properties window, select the Images collection. The Image Collection Editor, shown in Figure 16-10, shows how easy it actually is.

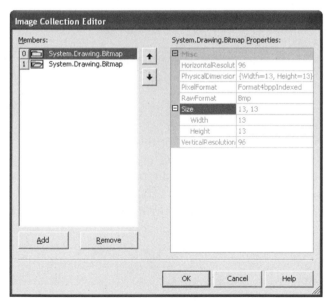

Figure 16-10. Using the Image Collection Editor to populate an *Image-List* object.

For this example, add the *Closed.bmp* and *Open.bmp* files (in that order) to the *ImageList* object. All that's left to do is set the *TreeView* control's *Image-List* property to the name of the *ImageList* object you just configured. With this task completed, you can start adding items to the *TreeView* control that refer to those state images.

Optimizing the Process of Adding Items to a *TreeView* Control

Whenever you add a new item to a *TreeView* control programmatically, the control is redrawn. This isn't exactly efficient, and thus it's good practice when you add multiple items to a *TreeView* control to do so in a block, as shown here:

```
tvRegistry.BeginUpdate();
    ⋮
tvRegistry.EndUpdate();
```

Calling *BeginUpdate* disables updates to the *TreeView* control; the updates are reenabled by calling *EndUpdate*. Between these two calls, you can add as many tree nodes as you want without causing rendering performance issues. The following practical example illustrates how the registry roots are added to a *TreeView* control:

```
public void RootNodes()
{
    tvRegistry.BeginUpdate();

    TreeNode tnHKCR = new TreeNode("HKEY_CLASSES_ROOT",0,1);
    tvRegistry.Nodes.Add(tnHKCR);
    AddBranch(tnHKCR);
        ⋮
    tvRegistry.SelectedNode = tnHKLM;
    tvRegistry.EndUpdate();
}
```

In total, the *RootNodes* method adds five registry roots to the *TreeView* control. For the sake of clarity, only one registry root is included in this code snippet. The calls to *BeginUpdate* and *EndUpdate* surround all *TreeView*-related work the method is doing—namely, creating a new *TreeNode* object and adding it to the *Nodes* collection of the *TreeView* object. By passing the name of the node and the index of the closed state as well as the index of the open state to the constructor, there's no need to set additional properties.

The *AddBranch* method is used to populate the next level in the branch. There's one good reason for doing this: prepopulating the entire tree would be too time-consuming. Therefore, we populate the tree as we go or, to be more precise, as the user navigates through the tree.

Handling *TreeView* Events

Because we've decided to populate the tree *just in time*—that is, when the user decides to expand a branch of the tree—only one event exactly fits the bill. Before we focus on this event, take a look at Table 16-2, which lists all the available *TreeView* events.

Table 16-2.   *TreeView* Events

Event	Description
AfterCheck	Fires after the node check box has been selected
AfterCollapse	Fires after a node has been collapsed
AfterExpand	Fires after a node has been expanded
AfterLabelEdit	Fires after the node label has been edited
AfterSelect	Fires after a node has been selected
BeforeCheck	Fires before the node check box is selected
BeforeCollapse	Fires before a node is collapsed
BeforeExpand	Fires before a node is expanded
BeforeLabelEdit	Fires before a label is edited
BeforeSelect	Fires before a node is selected
ItemDrag	Fires when an item is dragged onto the *TreeView* control

Of these events, the most important are *AfterCollapse*, *AfterExpand*, *AfterSelect*, *BeforeCollapse*, *BeforeExpand*, and *BeforeSelect*.

The event we'll be using to populate the tree just in time is *BeforeExpand*, which does some work just before the node is expanded for the user. The work that needs to be done is to create a list of all subkeys of the registry key that's going to be expanded. To do this, we create a new event handler for *BeforeExpand* and add the following code:

```
private void tvRegistry_BeforeExpand(object sender,
                                     TreeViewCancelEventArgs e)
{
    tvRegistry.BeginUpdate();
    foreach (TreeNode tn in e.Node.Nodes)
    {
        AddBranch(tn);
    }
    tvRegistry.EndUpdate();
}
```

At first glance, you might think that this code is just *BeginUpdate*, *AddBranch*, and *EndUpdate* and that you've seen all this before. But if you look more closely, one item in particular should spark your interest: *e.Node.Nodes*. We aren't just expanding on demand what the user wants to see. Instead, we're looking ahead one level, to a level the user doesn't yet see—all the user sees are the plus signs for expanding the nodes. If we don't expand one level ahead of the user, there won't be any plus signs, and no way for the user to drill any deeper!

One important method remains to be discussed—the often-called *AddBranch* method. The full code for the *AddBranch* method is shown here:

```
public void AddBranch(TreeNode tn)
{
    tn.Nodes.Clear();
    string strRegistryPath = tn.FullPath;

    RegistryKey regBranch = null;
    if (strRegistryPath.StartsWith("HKEY_CLASSES_ROOT"))
        regBranch = Registry.ClassesRoot;
    else if (strRegistryPath.StartsWith("HKEY_CURRENT_USER"))
        regBranch = Registry.CurrentUser;
    else if (strRegistryPath.StartsWith("HKEY_LOCAL_MACHINE"))
        regBranch = Registry.LocalMachine;
    else if (strRegistryPath.StartsWith("HKEY_USERS"))
        regBranch = Registry.Users;

    RegistryKey regSubKey = null;
    try
    {
        if (null != tn.Parent)
        {
            int nPosPathSeparator =
                strRegistryPath.IndexOf(this.tvRegistry.PathSeparator);
            string strSubkey =
                strRegistryPath.Substring(nPosPathSeparator + 1);
            regSubKey = regBranch.OpenSubKey(strSubkey);
        }
        else
            regSubKey = regBranch;
    }
    catch
    {
        return;
    }

    string[] astrSubkeyNames = regSubKey.GetSubKeyNames();
    for (int i=0; i < astrSubkeyNames.Length; i++)
    {
        TreeNode tnBranch = new TreeNode(astrSubkeyNames[i],0,1);
        tn.Nodes.Add(tnBranch);
    }
}
```

You can determine each node's position in the tree by looking at the node's *FullPath* property. In this example, the *FullPath* property is used to identify which portion of the registry is being expanded, and thus which root *RegistryKey* object must be used.

> **Note** Although you could store those *RegistryKey* objects in the *Tag* property of each node, performance-wise it might not be such a good idea to do so. Text comparison is extremely fast in the .NET Framework, and therefore these few checks are rather inexpensive compared to using thousands of tags.

After obtaining the root *RegistryKey* object, the subkey is opened. Because *FullPath* includes the root key, it must be removed from the subkey string first, before calling *OpenSubKey* on the root *RegistryKey*. Everything is encapsulated in a *try catch* block in case the user doesn't have enough permissions to open the intended branch.

Once the subkey is open and all the subkey names have been obtained using *GetSubKeyNames*, those names are added to the *TreeView* control. Remember that the callers of *AddBranch* are responsible for providing performance by wrapping the call in *BeginUpdate* and *EndUpdate* methods.

Implementing Your Own *TreeView* Control

When you're working on a larger-scale project, reusing components, or componentization in general, becomes more important. In the context of our *TreeView* example, this means that the *TreeView* control itself should know how to read the registry, should have no need for an external *ImageList* object, and should provide its own tree navigation. To accomplish this, you'll need to derive your own customized *TreeView* class.

Creating a *TreeView*-Derived Class

The intention of this exercise is to demonstrate how easily you can encapsulate functionality in your own control-derived classes—there's really no good excuse for not doing it. You can find the source code for this entire example in the RegistryTreeWithClass directory on the companion CD.

The first step is of course to open a new project and, within that project, add a new empty source file. In this file, you'll add your new *RegistryTreeClass* class, which is derived from *TreeView*. Add a constructor where you're going to place the *ImageList* object loading code, and override the *OnBeforeExpand* method, which handles the *BeforeExpand* method internally. That's all the new code you'll need; the rest of the code is reused from the preceding example. The result is shown here:

```
using System;
using System.Drawing;
using System.IO;
using System.Windows.Forms;
using Microsoft.Win32;

namespace RegistryTreeWithClass
{
    public class RegistryTreeClass: TreeView
    {
        public RegistryTreeClass()
        {
            ImageList = new ImageList();
            // Both images are embedded resources.
            ImageList.Images.Add(new Bitmap(GetType(), "CLOSED.BMP"));
            ImageList.Images.Add(new Bitmap(GetType(), "OPEN.BMP"));
            RootNodes();
        }

        protected override void OnBeforeExpand(TreeViewCancelEventArgs e)
        {
            base.OnBeforeExpand(e);
            BeginUpdate();

            foreach (TreeNode tn in e.Node.Nodes)
            {
                AddBranch(tn);
            }
            EndUpdate();
        }

        public void RootNodes()
        {
            BeginUpdate();

            TreeNode tnHKCR = new TreeNode("HKEY_CLASSES_ROOT", 0, 1);
            Nodes.Add(tnHKCR);
            AddBranch(tnHKCR);

                ⋮

            SelectedNode = tnHKLM;
            EndUpdate();
        }

        public void AddBranch(TreeNode tn)
```

(continued)

530 Part III   Programming Windows Forms

```
        {
             ⋮
        }
    }
}
```

The ellipses represent code that hasn't changed. In the constructor, you create the *ImageList* object and then load the images that are defined as embedded resources for the project. (The images are defined as an embedded resource by choosing Add Existing Item from the Project menu to add the image to your project and then setting the image's Build Action property to Embedded Resource.) The call to *RootNodes* completes the work done in the constructor.

In addition to no longer having to reference a control instance (*tvRegistry* is gone), the only important action to take is in *OnBeforeExpand*: don't forget to call the base class implementation. The resulting code is virtually the same as before, but it's embedded in a class waiting to be used in an application.

Using the *RegistryTreeClass* Class

The *RegistryTreeClass* class we just created isn't a perfect citizen in the component world, but it's a good one. The class isn't yet ready to be used in the Forms Designer, but Forms Designer can be used to add a *TreeView* control to your form. You can then simply change the class type in the declaration of the variable, as shown here:

```
public class MainForm : System.Windows.Forms.Form
{
    private RegistryTreeClass rtvRegistry;
```

Usually, you'll find *System.Windows.Forms.TreeView* used as a class type, but here it's been changed to *RegistryTreeClass*. Compile and run the application; the results will be similar to Figure 16-11.

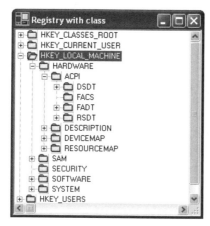

Figure 16-11.   The *RegistryTreeClass* class in action.

Code reuse is important; we'll return to this topic later in this chapter, in the section "RegistryViewer—*TreeView* and *ListView* Combined."

Using the *ListView* Control

As well known as the *TreeView* control is the *ListView* control. Every file dialog box features a *ListView* control as its most important control. Windows Explorer and the Registry Editor use it, as does any application that wants to list data in various ways. Chances are good that you'll want to use the *ListView* control in your own applications. The following subsections will guide you through the intricacies of the *ListView* control.

Implementing a *ListView* Control

Although there's designer support for *ListView* too, this time we'll start with writing code. The example used throughout this section is located in the folder ListviewDrives on the companion CD. It shows how a *ListView* control can be used to view the drives accessible on the local computer.

The Four Views

A *ListView* control supports four distinct ways to display its items: a small icons view, a large icons view, a list view, and a details view. Every user knows these views from Windows Explorer, and you can choose to support any or all of the views in your applications as you see fit. The following subsections describe what's necessary to support the four views.

Working with small and large icons   The small icons and large icons views are very similar—both require an *ImageList* object for the icons to be displayed alongside the *ListViewItem* object's text. The *ImageList* property for the small icons view is appropriately named *SmallImageList*, whereas the large icons view is controlled via the *LargeImageList* property. As with the *TreeView* control, you can set the *ImageList* properties in the Properties window at design time or programmatically at run time.

The process of creating an *ImageList* object from single images was shown earlier in this chapter, in the section "Designing a *TreeView* Control." There's another technique, however, that's faster and more convenient—placing all icon images in a single image strip. An example image strip is shown in Figure 16-12.

Figure 16-12.   A single image strip can contain all *ImageList* images.

If you've used Visual C++ to write Microsoft Foundation Classes (MFC) applications, you know what this is all about because that's how *CToolbar* works: you provide an image strip, a transparent color, and a size for the individual bitmaps in the image strip. Given that information, *CToolbar* extracts the button bitmaps and paints its toolbar. This is the way it works in *ImageList* objects too, as shown here:

```
lvDrives.LargeImageList = new ImageList();
Bitmap icoLarge = new Bitmap(GetType(), "LvIconsLarge.bmp");
icoLarge.MakeTransparent(Color.FromArgb(0xff, 0x00, 0xff));
Size sizeImages = new Size(32,32);
lvDrives.LargeImageList.ImageSize = sizeImages;
lvDrives.LargeImageList.Images.AddStrip(icoLarge);
```

You first create a new *ImageList* object for the view you're customizing. Then you load the image strip into a new *Bitmap* object and define the transparent color using the *MakeTransparentColor* method. Because images in an *ImageList* object have a default *Size* property value, you have to assign this property the size of the bitmaps in the image strip. Now all that's left to do is to assign the *Bitmap* object to the *ImageList* object, which is done by the *AddStrip* method.

When programming a *ListView* control that supports the small icons or large icons view, you typically load the *ImageList* objects in the constructor of your form or custom *ListView* control, or at the latest before you actually add items to the *ListView* control. You can add an item with an icon to your *ListView* control as follows:

```
ListViewItem lvi = new ListViewItem();
lvi.ImageIndex = 1;
lvi.Text = "Drive C:\\";
lvDrives.Items.Add(lvi);
```

The *ImageIndex* property is used for both the small icons and large icons views. To programmatically switch a *ListView* control to the small icons view, use the following code:

```
lvDrives.View = View.SmallIcon;
```

To switch to the large icons view, set the *View* property to *View.LargeIcon*.

Listing the contents   When you need to view a large number of items using multiple columns, the list view is what you're looking for. Enabling the list view is as simple as enabling any other view, as shown here:

```
lvDrives.View = View.List;
```

To display a small icon alongside the text of an item, set the *ImageIndex* property for each *ListViewItem* object in the *ListView* object. If this property is omitted, the list view displays text only, which can be desirable in certain applications.

Viewing details   The details view of a *ListView* control looks a lot like a read-only data grid. The details view has multiple columns, and you can sort on every column; however, you can't edit the data. Switching to the details view enables the user to display more detailed information about the properties of an item than might be available in one of the other views.

Before the details view works the way you want it to, you must do one thing: define the columns (their headers and sizes at least) that will be displayed. For example, to add two columns named Drive and Type, add the following code to the initialization of the *ListView* control:

```
lvDrives.Columns.Add("Drive", 100, HorizontalAlignment.Left);
lvDrives.Columns.Add("Type", 150, HorizontalAlignment.Left);
```

In this example, the second column is wider than the first one, and for both the text is left-aligned. (Other options are *Center* and *Right*.)

To switch to the details view, use the following code:

```
lvDrives.View = View.Details;
```

Figure 16-13 shows the details view for our sample application ListViewDrives.

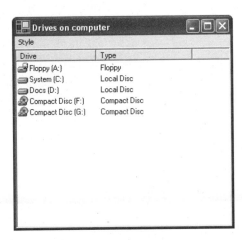

Figure 16-13.   The sample application ListViewDrives in details view.

Filling the *ListView* Control

A *ListView* control's *Items* collection contains any number of *ListViewItem* objects, which define how an element is shown in each of the four view styles. In its most simple form, a *ListViewItem* object can be added with the following command:

```
lvDrives.Items.Add(new ListViewItem(@"Drive C:\"));
```

This item has no image associated with it, only text. It would appear as an empty icon in both the small icons and large icons views. If you want to display an icon, you have to set the *ImageIndex* property of the *ListViewItem* object prior to adding the item, as shown here:

```
ListViewItem lvi = new ListViewItem(@"Drive C:\");
lvi.ImageIndex = 1;
lvDrives.Items.Add(lvi);
```

You could also pass the *ImageIndex* property via the constructor, as follows:

```
ListViewItem lvi = new ListViewItem(@"Drive C:\", 1);
```

The *ImageIndex* property is zero-based, like all other arrays in the .NET Framework. When switching to the small icons or large icons view, the second image is taken from the assigned *ImageList* object.

To put everything together, take a look at the ListviewDrives application on the companion CD. This application enumerates all drives on the local computer, reads drive name and drive type, and displays this information in a *ListView* control that can be switched between its four views using menu commands.

The filling of the *ListView* control is handled by the *ListDrives* function, as shown here:

```
protected void ListDrives()
{
    string[] drives = Directory.GetLogicalDrives();
    string strDriveType = "";
    for (int i=0; i < drives.Length; i++)
    {
        string strDriveName = Win32.GetVolumeName(drives[i]);
        ListViewItem lvi = new ListViewItem();

        // Note: Network drives show up as local.
        switch(Win32.GetDriveType(drives[i]))
        {
            case Win32.DRIVE_CDROM:
                strDriveType = "Compact Disc";
                lvi.ImageIndex = 1;
                break;
```

```
            case Win32.DRIVE_FIXED:
                strDriveType = "Local Disc";
                lvi.ImageIndex = 0;
                break;
            case Win32.DRIVE_REMOVABLE:
                strDriveType = "Floppy";
                lvi.ImageIndex = 2;
                break;
            default:
                goto case Win32.DRIVE_FIXED;
        }
        if (0 == strDriveName.Length) strDriveName = strDriveType;
        lvi.Text = strDriveName + " (" + drives[i].Substring(0, 2) + ")";
        lvi.SubItems.Add(strDriveType);
        this.lvDrives.Items.Add(lvi);
    }
}
```

A list of available drives can be obtained by calling the static *GetLogical-Drives* method. This method provides you with the drive letters but doesn't provide drive name or drive type. To get that information, you'll have to dig a little deeper—that is, you're forced to use platform invoke (P/Invoke) calls, which in this sample application are encapsulated in the *Win32* class, shown in the following code:

```
public sealed class Win32
{
    public const uint DRIVE_UNKNOWN     = 0;
    public const uint DRIVE_NO_ROOT_DIR = 1;
    public const uint DRIVE_REMOVABLE   = 2;
    public const uint DRIVE_FIXED       = 3;
    public const uint DRIVE_REMOTE      = 4;
    public const uint DRIVE_CDROM       = 5;
    public const uint DRIVE_RAMDISK     = 6;

    [DllImport("kernel32.dll")]
    public static extern uint GetDriveType(
        string lpRootPathName    // Root directory
        );

    [DllImport("kernel32.dll")]
    private static extern bool GetVolumeInformation(
        string lpRootPathName,
        StringBuilder lpVolumeNameBuffer,
        int nVolumeNameSize,
        ref int lpVolumeSerialNumber,
        ref int lpMaximumComponentLength,
        ref int lpFileSystemFlags,
```

(continued)

```
        StringBuilder lpFileSystemNameBuffer,
        int nFileSystemNameSize
        );

    public static string GetVolumeName(string strRootPath)
    {
        StringBuilder sbVolumeName = new StringBuilder(256);
        StringBuilder sbFileSystemName = new StringBuilder(256);
        int nVolSerial = 0;
        int nMaxCompLength = 0;
        int nFSFlags = 0;

        bool bResult = GetVolumeInformation(strRootPath,sbVolumeName,256,
            ref nVolSerial, ref nMaxCompLength,
            ref nFSFlags, sbFileSystemName, 256);

        if (true == bResult)
        {
            return sbVolumeName.ToString();
        }
        else
        {
            return "";
        }
    }
}
```

Using the information obtained by *GetVolumeName*, the application sets the *Text* property of the *ListViewItem* object to the volume name plus the drive letter. The call to *GetDriveType* is used to determine the *ImageIndex* value, as well as the text to be shown in the Type column in the details view. Because the *Text* property refers to the first column, additional column text is added using the following code:

```
lvi.SubItems.Add(strDriveType);
```

You can create almost as many subitems as you want, but don't go overboard with information. Instead, provide additional information to the user when an item is selected.

Handling Item Selection and Activation

The first action you as a developer are interested in is when the user selects or deselects an item in the *ListView* control. When this happens, the *SelectedIndexChanged* event is triggered. This event doesn't pass the selected items as parameters, however. You have to retrieve the selected items from the *SelectedItems* collection, as shown here:

```
private void OnSelItemChanged(object sender, System.EventArgs e)
{
    string strSelected = "";
    foreach (ListViewItem lvi in lvDrives.SelectedItems)
    {
        strSelected += " " + lvi.Text;
    }
    MessageBox.Show(strSelected);
}
```

If the *MultiSelect* property of the *ListView* control is set to *true*, this code returns all items that were selected; it returns a single item if this property is set to *false*. To verify whether anything was selected, check *lvDrives.SelectedItems.Count* for a value greater than 0. When the selection is complete, you can act on the selected items, depending on your application.

One way to act on selected items is through the *ItemActivate* event. This event is triggered by either a single click or a double click, depending on the *Activation* property setting. Table 16-3 shows all possible *ItemActivation* members.

Table 16-3.   *ItemActivation* **Enumeration Values**

Value	Description
OneClick	Item activation is triggered by a user single-clicking an item. Visual feedback is provided by changing the mouse pointer to a hand when the user hovers over an item.
Standard	The item is activated by a double click; however, the user is given no visual feedback.
TwoClick	The item is activated by a double click; the user gets visual feedback via an item text color change.

Remember, to find out which item was activated, use the *SelectedItems* collection, as described at the beginning of this section. The event arguments for the *ItemActivate* event don't provide you with this information.

RegistryViewer—*TreeView* and *ListView* Combined

As a final example, we'll create a registry viewer that combines the *RegistryTree-Class* class written earlier with a *ListView* control that displays the values for a given subkey. Figure 16-14 shows the completed application, which is located in the RegistryViewer folder on the companion CD.

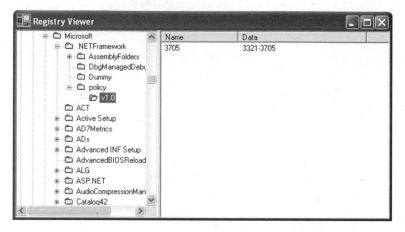

Figure 16-14. Using the RegistryViewer sample application to browse the local computer's registry.

Creating the User Interface

First you'll need to design the user interface. To do this, you need one *TreeView* control and one *ListView* control. Although you can't see the effect in Figure 16-14, this user interface adjusts to window size changes. This adjustment is accomplished using various docking styles and a splitter.

The first element to be placed on the form is the *TreeView* control. Set its docking style to *Left*, and add the splitter, which must have the same docking style. Then add the *ListView* control, whose docking style must be set to *Fill*. Next you need to configure the *ListView* control: in the Properties window, select Columns, and in the ColumnHeader Collection Editor, add columns named Name and Data. The Forms Designer should now look like Figure 16-15.

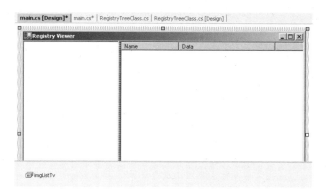

Figure 16-15. Designing the user interface of the RegistryViewer application.

One more thing can be taken care of immediately: changing the *TreeView* class to *RegistryTreeClass*. This class contains almost all of the application's functionality. The sole exception is that no data will appear in the *ListView* control unless we put it there.

Updating the Contents of the *ListView* Control

As mentioned, the *ListView* control's task is to show registry values (not keys) for the currently selected subkey. Therefore, to change the contents of the *ListView* control according to what's selected in the *TreeView* control, we have to react to an event—but which one? *BeforeExpand* is obviously the wrong choice; *AfterSelect* is definitely what we're looking for.

After you've wired up the *AfterSelect* event handler, you must open the subkey, just as you did earlier for the *TreeView* control. The following code shows the *AfterSelect* event handler, with the code to open the subkey omitted for clarity:

```
private void AfterSelect(object sender, TreeViewEventArgs e)
{
    ⋮
    string[] astrValueNames = regSubKey.GetValueNames();
    lvValues.Items.Clear();
    for (int j=0; j < astrValueNames.Length; j++)
    {
        object val = regSubKey.GetValue(astrValueNames[j]);
        ListViewItem lvi = new ListViewItem(astrValueNames[j]);
        lvi.SubItems.Add(val.ToString());
        lvValues.Items.Add(lvi);
    }
}
```

With this snippet of new code, we're all set. When the user selects a node in the RegistryViewer application, this code will first clear the *ListView* control of all old values and then fill the control with the values it found for the current subkey.

Conclusion

The grid, tree, and list controls will play a major part in your applications. The grid control is particularly important because most applications in production today are database applications. These controls are useful in their standard forms, but you can extend them to make them even more useful. For example, you can add custom items to a list or a tree, or you can create your own grid column styles. The ability to extend these controls allows you to make your applications more powerful.

With all the possibilities these controls offer, Visual C# does an outstanding job of providing programmers with access to all the control functionality, through the Forms Designer and the Collection Editor, as well as through numerous other helpful features. Don't forget that a peek under the hood—as simple as looking at the *InitializeComponent* method—can provide helpful insight into the inner workings of the control you're just about to use.

Chapter 17 concludes our discussion of Windows Forms programming with a look at topics that generally enhance the user's experience of your application, including the use of toolbars, drag and drop operations, and the clipboard. These features are a must for every modern application.

17

Enhancing Windows Forms

This chapter concludes our tour of Windows Forms. In this chapter, you'll learn how to enhance your Windows Forms applications by adding common functionality such as toolbars, clipboard support, and drag and drop capability. These features will improve the productiveness of your applications by providing shortcuts to frequently used functionality and by enabling reuse of existing data from other applications.

Most of the applications that you use every day use toolbars. Toolbars provide shortcuts to functionality hidden in menus; a toolbar can be especially handy for users who don't remember shortcut keys or who prefer pointing and clicking to typing. To be useful, your toolbars should be clearly structured and expose only regularly used functionality.

The clipboard and drag and drop capability also help the user to be more productive with your applications. With these features, users can easily copy data into an application or export data out of an application. Drag and drop even allows users to move data from one application to another or to link data. To make your applications truly successful, clipboard and drag-and-drop support should be included.

Adding Toolbars

Toolbars are an effective middle ground between using shortcut keys and plowing through menus to execute the desired command. Because they allow easy point-and-click access to the most frequently used features of your application, toolbars are considered a must by users.

In the following subsections, you'll learn how to create toolbars and format them to achieve the visual appearance you want. You'll also find a description of the various button styles you include in your toolbars to make users more productive.

Creating a Toolbar

The easiest way to add a toolbar to your application or form is to design the toolbar using the Microsoft Visual C# .NET Forms Designer. You first need to add two controls to your form: an *ImageList* control and the *ToolBar* control itself. When you drag the *ToolBar* control onto your form, it will automatically dock at the top of your form; the *ImageList* control is an invisible control that sits below the form.

You next need to add images to the *ImageList* control; these images will appear on the toolbar buttons. Visual Studio .NET includes images for toolbars—one set to match the Microsoft Office toolbar and one set to match Microsoft Windows 95. For this example, we'll use the Office-style bitmaps, which can be found in \Program Files\Microsoft Visual Studio .NET\Common7\Graphics\bitmaps\OffCtlBr\Small\Color. The bitmaps aren't stellar, but they'll get you off to a good start.

The example toolbar we're building is based on standard actions you'll find in almost any application: New, Open, Save, Cut, Copy, Paste, and Help. Each of these commands is represented by a single image file. You can use the Image Collection Editor to add and remove images to the control. To access it, click the ellipsis button next to the *Images* property in the Properties window of the *ImageList* control. The completed Image Collection Editor is shown in Figure 17-1.

With the images all defined, the final step is to create the buttons on the toolbar. To accomplish this, select Buttons in the Properties window for the *ToolBar* control to open the ToolBarButton Collection Editor. For every button, add one *ToolBarButton* object, as shown in Figure 17-2. You can use the Add and Remove buttons to add buttons to and remove buttons from the *ToolBar* control. To configure the properties for each button, use the pane on the right side of the editor.

Figure 17-1. Adding bitmaps to the *ImageList* control with the Image Collection Editor.

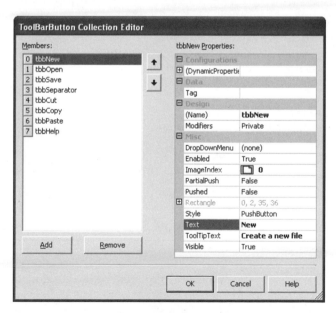

Figure 17-2. Defining buttons for the toolbar.

All properties that have been changed are displayed in boldface in this window. In this case, the properties that have been set are *Name* (the name of the *ToolBarButton* button), *ImageIndex* (the bitmap that will be used), *Text* (the text string displayed on the button), and *ToolTipText* (the text that will appear on mouseover).

> **Tip**   To display ToolTips, you must set the *ShowToolTips* property of the *ToolBar* control to *true*. If your ToolTips are missing, check this property setting first.

After you've defined all your buttons, you can view the completed toolbar in the Forms Designer. (We'll return to the subject of separators later in this chapter, in the section "Defining Toolbar Button Styles".) One final thing remains to be done: wire up an event handler to the toolbar so that we know which button was pressed. To do this, create a *ButtonClick* event handler and add the following code:

```
private void OnButtonClick(object sender,
    System.Windows.Forms.ToolBarButtonClickEventArgs e)
{
    ToolBarButton tbCurrent = e.Button;
    MessageBox.Show("You clicked button " + tbCurrent.Text);
}
```

The *ToolBarButtonClickEventArgs* class is simple to use because it includes only one property: *Button*. This property enables us to retrieve the instance of *ToolBarButton* that was clicked. This example uses the *Text* property to display a simple message box; your applications will likely respond with much more sophisticated actions.

Modifying the Toolbar's Appearance

A toolbar doesn't come in just one flavor—you can adapt it visually to suit your application's needs, or you can let your users decide at run time how they want the toolbar to appear. Table 17-1 lists the properties that influence how your toolbar is displayed.

Table 17-1.   *ToolBar* Properties for Visual Style

Property	Description
Appearance	Specifies how the toolbar is displayed. Allowed values are defined in the *ToolBarAppearance* enumeration. The default is *Normal*.
BorderStyle	Specifies the border style of the toolbar. Allowed values are defined in the *BorderStyle* enumeration. The default is *None*.
Divider	Specifies whether to display a divider between the toolbar and the menu bar. The default is *true*.

(continued)

Table 17-1.   *ToolBar* Properties for Visual Style   *(continued)*

Property	Description
TextAlign	Specifies the alignment for text on toolbar buttons. Allowed values are defined in the *ToolBarTextAlign* enumeration. The default is *Underneath*.
Wrappable	Specifies whether toolbar buttons can wrap to another line if the toolbar is too small to display all the buttons on the same line. The default is *true*.

> **Note**   Refer to the Platform SDK for a detailed discussion about the enumerations mentioned in Table 17-1.

The sample application ToolbarStyles, on the companion CD, was designed to let you experiment with visual changes to the toolbar. The application loads the *ImageList* and *ToolBar* controls dynamically in the constructor, after the call to *InitializeComponent*, as shown here:

```
// Initialize the ImageList object.
tbMain.ImageList = new ImageList();
Bitmap bmpImageStrip = new Bitmap(GetType(), "Toolbar.bmp");
bmpImageStrip.MakeTransparent(Color.FromArgb(0xff, 0x00, 0xff));
tbMain.ImageList.ImageSize = new Size(16, 15);
tbMain.ImageList.Images.AddStrip(bmpImageStrip);

// Create the toolbar buttons.
for (int i=0; i < astrTBarButtons.Length; i++)
{
    ToolBarButton tbb = new ToolBarButton();
    tbb.ImageIndex = i;
    tbb.ToolTipText = astrTBarButtons[i];
    tbMain.Buttons.Add(tbb);
}
```

The bitmap *Toolbar.bmp* is an embedded resource of the project. It sports a transparent background color, and the images aren't the standard 16-by-16 pixels, but 16-by-15 instead. The reason for this deviation is that this bitmap was taken from an existing Microsoft Foundation Classes (MFC) Windows application project that included a toolbar—a conversion task that you might be facing too.

With the bitmap loaded into the *ImageList* control, we can start adding *ToolBarButton* objects to the *ToolBar* control. The *astrTBarButtons* array is defined as follows:

```
string[] astrTBarButtons = { "New", "Open", "Save",
                             "Cut", "Copy", "Paste", "Print", "Help"};
```

The text is used for the *ToolTipText* property, and the index in the array matches the bitmap index in the *ImageList* control, which is used for the *Image-Index* property. With all buttons initialized, the application starts up, as shown in Figure 17-3.

Figure 17-3.   A standard toolbar with images only, no text, and a divider line between the menu bar and the toolbar.

On startup, the *Divider* property is automatically set to *true* and the *Appearance* property is set to *Normal*. To toggle the divider line, which is simply a line separating the toolbar and the menu bar, use the following code:

```
tbMain.Divider = !tbMain.Divider;
```

Another change that alters the look and feel of the toolbar considerably is switching from *Normal* to *Flat* appearance, as follows:

```
tbMain.Appearance = ToolBarAppearance.Flat;
```

The toolbar now looks like Figure 17-4.

To switch back to normal appearance, set the *Appearance* property to *ToolBarAppearance.Normal*.

The example toolbar in the previous section displayed additional text beneath the image on the toolbar button. To achieve this effect at design time, you can use the Properties window to set the *ToolBarButton* object's *Text* property to the text you want to display and then set the *TextAlign* property to the desired alignment—either centered underneath or displayed to the right of the bitmap.

Figure 17-4.   A flat toolbar with images only, no text, and a divider line between the menu bar and the toolbar.

You can also set these properties at run time. For example, the following code performs these tasks:

```
private void AddTextToToolBarButtons()
{
    for (int i=0; i < astrTBarButtons.Length; i++)
    {
        tbMain.Buttons[i].Text = astrTBarButtons[i];
    }
}
```

The *AddTextToToolBarButtons* method adds text to each *ToolBarButton* object contained in the *Buttons* collection. To display the text underneath the button image, you can set the *TextAlign* property to *Underneath*:

```
tbMain.TextAlign = ToolBarTextAlign.Underneath;
```

Your toolbar now looks like Figure 17-5.

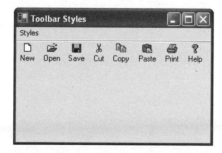

Figure 17-5.   A flat toolbar with text underneath the button images and a divider line between the menu bar and the toolbar.

To display text to the right of the image, set the *TextAlign* property to *Right*. Your toolbar will resemble Figure 17-6.

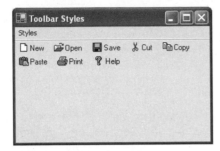

Figure 17-6. A flat toolbar with text to the right of the button images and a divider line between the menu bar and the toolbar.

So how do you revert to displaying images only at run time? The solution is to use the *RemoveTextFromToolBarButtons* method to remove all text from the *ToolBarButton* objects, as shown here:

```
private void RemoveTextFromToolBarButtons()
{
    for (int i=0; i < astrTBarButtons.Length; i++)
    {
        tbMain.Buttons[i].Text = "";
    }
    tbMain.Refresh();
}
```

The toolbar is now returned to normal, with no text displayed on the buttons.

Defining Toolbar Button Styles

You can also modify the appearance of the individual buttons on the toolbar. *ToolBarButton* objects come in four styles, with the push button style being the most familiar option. Table 17-2 lists the four styles available through the *ToolBarButtonStyle* enumeration.

Table 17-2. *ToolBarButtonStyle* Enumeration Values

Value	Description
DropDownButton	Displays a button with a drop-down arrow next to it. Clicking this arrow will display either a menu or another window.
PushButton	Displays a standard button.

(continued)

Table 17-2.   *ToolBarButtonStyle* Enumeration Values   *(continued)*

Value	Description
Separator	Displays a line or a space between buttons. Use separators to group buttons on your toolbar.
ToggleButton	Displays a button that remains depressed when clicked. When the user clicks the button again, it returns to its unpressed state.

The TBBStyle application, on the companion CD, demonstrates how each of these buttons works. This application sports a number of standard *PushButton* objects, two *Separator* objects to group the *PushButton* objects, one *ToggleButton* object that controls event handling, and one *DropDownButton* object that displays a shortcut menu. Figure 17-7 gives you an idea of how this application looks when executed.

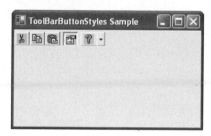

Figure 17-7.   A toolbar that uses all four button styles.

For simplicity, the bitmaps for these buttons are added manually to the *ImageList* control. The toolbar properties are set programmatically with the use of these three arrays, as shown here:

```
string[] astrTBB = {"Cut", "Copy", "Paste", "", "Messages", "", "Help"};
ToolBarButtonStyle[] atbbStyles = {ToolBarButtonStyle.PushButton,
    ToolBarButtonStyle.PushButton, ToolBarButtonStyle.PushButton,
    ToolBarButtonStyle.Separator, ToolBarButtonStyle.ToggleButton,
    ToolBarButtonStyle.Separator, ToolBarButtonStyle.DropDownButton };
int[] anImageIndex = { 0, 1, 2, 0, 4, 0, 3 };
```

The first array defines the text for the ToolTip, with an empty string used for the separators. The second array holds the styles for each button, and the third array defines which image to use from the *ImageList* object. Armed with this information, the application can go about creating the toolbar, as shown in the code listing on the following page.

```
for (int i=0; i < astrTBB.Length; i++)
{
    ToolBarButton tbb = new ToolBarButton();
    tbb.ImageIndex = anImageIndex[i];
    tbb.Style = atbbStyles[i];
    tbb.ToolTipText = astrTBB[i];
    if (tbb.Style == ToolBarButtonStyle.DropDownButton)
    {
        tbb.DropDownMenu = ddmDemo;
    }
    tbMain.Buttons.Add(tbb);
}
```

The drop-down arrow displays a demo shortcut menu, which is added to the form. When you click the arrow, the shortcut menu appears, as shown in Figure 17-8.

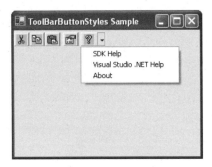

Figure 17-8. Clicking a drop-down arrow to display a shortcut menu.

The button to the left of the drop-down button is a toggle button. It can be either pressed or released, and you can use it to display the states of your application. For example, you can use a toggle button to specify whether your toolbar will process button clicks, as shown here:

```
private void OnButtonClick(object sender,
    System.Windows.Forms.ToolBarButtonClickEventArgs e)
{
    bool bShowMessages = tbMain.Buttons[4].Pushed;
    if (true == bShowMessages)
    {
        MessageBox.Show("Button " + e.Button.ToolTipText +
                    " was clicked");
    }
}
```

Toggle buttons have many practical uses. For example, you can use a toggle button to format text in boldface in a word processing application. As long as the button is depressed, all text is written in boldface. When the button is clicked again, the font returns to normal.

Using the Clipboard

You've no doubt written programs or at least parts of programs using the copy and paste approach, and so you know that the clipboard is a helpful feature for getting data from one place or application to another. That's what the clipboard is all about—easy and fast data transfer between applications.

Although you could create an internal clipboard handling mechanism for your own application only, users expect that when they execute a cut or copy command in one application, they can then paste that data into another application. Providing clipboard support is essential, and the following subsections show you how to use the clipboard effectively.

Copying to the Clipboard

All work related to the clipboard is performed using the *Clipboard* class. The *Clipboard* class isn't large—it supports only three methods, two to copy data to the clipboard and one to get at data on the clipboard. The two methods for putting data on the clipboard are shown in the following code. (The third method is discussed in the next section.)

```
public static void SetDataObject(object);
public static void SetDataObject(object, bool);
```

When you use the first method, data put on the clipboard is nonpermanent, which means that when your application closes, the last content you put on the clipboard is removed. The second method gives you a choice: setting the second Boolean parameter to *true* allows the data to remain on the clipboard even after your application quits, whereas setting it to *false* leads to the same behavior as the first method call—the data is removed on exit.

Any data you place on the clipboard replaces the data that was on the clipboard previously. For example, the following code replaces the contents of the clipboard with the string *Hello World*:

```
string strText = "Hello World";
Clipboard.SetDataObject(strText, true);
```

The data is copied to the clipboard; no object reference is kept to the original data. Therefore, the following code would be valid as well:

```
Clipboard.SetDataObject("Hello World", true);
```

As you know from other applications, you can copy various data formats, such as bitmaps, to the clipboard. This can be done in Visual C# too, as shown here:

```
Bitmap bmp2Clipboard = new Bitmap("pinz.jpg");
Clipboard.SetDataObject(bmp2Clipboard, true);
```

You can now go to your favorite paint program and paste the clipboard contents. The clipboard formats are well-defined (more on clipboard formats later in this chapter, in the section "Exploring Clipboard Formats"), and thus data can be retrieved by any application that uses the clipboard and accepts the format of the data that was put on the clipboard.

Retrieving Data from the Clipboard

Now that we've looked at copying data to the clipboard, let's look at how to retrieve data from the clipboard. For this job, we'll use the *Clipboard* class's third method, as follows:

```
public static IDataObject GetDataObject();
```

This method returns a data object (or to be more correct, an interface of type *IDataObject*) that represents the data waiting on the clipboard. To retrieve data from the clipboard, you'll use the following *IDataObject* methods (and their overloads) most often:

```
bool GetDataPresent(Type);
object GetData(Type);
```

When dealing with the clipboard, you always start by checking whether the data on the clipboard can be consumed by your application. For example, if you write a simple Notepad replacement, you want to paste text only, as shown here:

```
IDataObject data = Clipboard.GetDataObject();
if (data.GetDataPresent(typeof(string)))
{
    ⋮
}
```

After you've determined that the format on the clipboard can be accepted by your application, you get at the data by calling *GetData*. The following code snippet first checks for bitmap data format, then gets the bitmap from the clipboard, and then simply saves the result to disk:

```
IDataObject data = Clipboard.GetDataObject();
if (data.GetDataPresent(typeof(Bitmap)))
{
    Bitmap bmp = (Bitmap)data.GetData(typeof(Bitmap));
```

```
    bmp.Save(@"c:\cliptest.bmp");
    MessageBox.Show("Saved to c:\\cliptest.bmp");
}
else
{
    MessageBox.Show("Data not retrievable as bitmap");
}
```

Retrieving text from the clipboard is equally simple, as shown here:

```
IDataObject data = Clipboard.GetDataObject();
if (data.GetDataPresent(typeof(string)))
{
    string strData = (string)data.GetData(typeof(string));
    // Do processing.
    ⋮
}
```

The text and bitmap formats aren't the only clipboard formats available. In the next section, we'll examine the various clipboard formats in more detail.

Exploring Clipboard Formats

As mentioned, the clipboard isn't limited to sharing only textual or bitmap data. It can provide interchange for many more formats; these formats are fields from the *DataFormats* class. Table 17-3 lists the field names and their string values (used by the Win32 API).

Table 17-3. *DataFormats* Class Fields

Field	Value
Bitmap	*Bitmap*
CommaSeparatedValue	*Csv*
Dib	*DeviceIndependentBitmap*
Dif	*DataInterchangeFormat*
EnhancedMetafile	*EnhancedMetafile*
FileDrop	*FileDrop*
Html	*HTML Format*
Locale	*Locale*
MetafilePict	*MetaFilePict*
OemText	*OEMText*
Palette	*Palette*
PenData	*PenData*

(continued)

Table 17-3. *DataFormats* **Class Fields**   *(continued)*

Field	Value
Riff	*RiffAudio*
Rtf	*Rich Text Format*
Serializable	*WindowsForms10PersistentObject*
StringFormat	*System.String*
SymbolicLink	*SymbolicLink*
Text	*Text*
Tiff	*TaggedImageFileFormat*
UnicodeText	*UnicodeText*
WaveAudio	*WaveAudio*

Having 21 formats at your disposal isn't bad. (There are more, but these are the formats supported by the .NET Framework at this time.) But why are there so many formats dealing with textual data? The reason is that each of these formats is needed under different conditions. For example, Unicode came to the Windows scene a little later than standard ANSI text. If an application copies a Unicode string to the clipboard, you don't want an ANSI application to then paste the Unicode string. That's why the clipboard offers not only the format that was put on the clipboard, but also any applicable conversions.

To demonstrate that clipboard data can exist in various formats, the sample application ClipboardFormatsAvailable, on the companion CD, enumerates the formats that are available for pasting. Figure 17-9 shows the application enumerating formats for a string that was placed on the clipboard beforehand.

Figure 17-9. Viewing available clipboard formats.

The code for getting at the formats isn't complicated, as you can see:

```
private void cmdCheckClipboard_Click(object sender, System.EventArgs e)
{
    lbFormats.Items.Clear();
    IDataObject data = Clipboard.GetDataObject();

    string[] astrFormats = data.GetFormats(false);
    for (int i=0; i < astrFormats.Length; i++)
        lbFormats.Items.Add(astrFormats[i]);
}
```

All you need to do is call *GetFormats*. The Boolean parameter does make quite a difference, however. If you pass a value of *false*, as in this code, you get only formats that were put into the clipboard by the application, whereas passing *true* lets you also see the formats for which the clipboard can offer an automatic conversion. In this example, the native formats are *System.String*, *UnicodeText*, and *Text*; the additional convertible formats are *Locale* and *OEMText*. The native formats displayed include those that are put into the clipboard explicitly by the application that calls *SetDataObject*.

If you're interested in an application that automatically checks the clipboard for updates (the sample requires a button click to check for new data), take a look at the article "Tool for Viewing Drag and Drop and Clipboard Formats," located at *http://www.codeproject.com/csharp/clipboardformatviewer.asp*. This article shows you how to hook into the clipboard events, a feature that is currently not directly supported in the .NET Framework.

Your application can choose which data format it wants to retrieve by specifying the format string in the *GetData* call, as shown in the following code:

```
string strData = (string)Clipboard.GetData("Text", false)
```

Be sure to specify the second parameter, however. This parameter indicates whether your application will accept a converted format (*true*) or only a native format (*false*).

Storing the Same Data in Multiple Formats on the Clipboard

As you saw earlier in this chapter, in the section "Copying to the Clipboard," the clipboard can hold only one item at a time. So how do you store the same data in multiple formats on the clipboard? The answer lies in the *DataObject* class, which implements the *IDataObject* interface. Aside from the constructors, *DataObject* offers four interesting implementations of *SetData*, as shown here:

```
void SetData(object data);
void SetData(string format, object data);
void SetData(Type type, object data);
void SetData(string format, bool autoConvert, object data);
```

The interesting part is that you can call *SetData* multiple times with different formats specified and then put the *DataObject* on the clipboard, as shown in the following example. The ClipboardSetDataObject application, on the companion CD, contains the complete code listing.

```
string strText = "Hello World";
string strHtml = "<h1>Hello World</h1>";
DataObject data = new DataObject();
data.SetData(strText);
data.SetData(DataFormats.Html, strHtml);
data.SetData("My.Internal.Format","Some internal data");
Clipboard.SetDataObject(data, true);
```

Using this technique, you can choose to paste either text or HTML data; you probably won't use the custom format *My.Internal.Format*. Putting multiple formats on the clipboard is a cooperative approach, and it allows you to keep your custom formats on the clipboard too.

Working with Drag and Drop

Working with drag and drop isn't much different from working with the clipboard. The difference is that the data isn't first copied to an intermediary storage from which it can later be retrieved (multiple times); instead, it's directly transferred from one application to another by means of a mouse operation—the drag and drop operation.

The following subsections introduce you to the various concepts of drag and drop, including basic drag and drop operations and related events, dragging and dropping files, and implementing a drag and drop source.

Drag and Drop Basics

Our examination of the clipboard laid the foundation for working with drag and drop. You already know about the types of data that can be passed and how that data is handled through the *IDataObject* interface. We now have to look at how the drag and drop operation actually takes place between the initiator (the drag and drop *source*) and the recipient of the data (the drag and drop *target*).

The drag and drop operation involves the mouse and, less obviously, the keyboard. Depending on which keys are pressed, the drag and drop operation is either a copy, a move, or a link operation. Table 17-4 lists the operations and their modifier keys.

Table 17-4.   Drag and Drop Operations

Operation	Modifier Keys
Copy	The Ctrl key is pressed.
Link	The Shift and Ctrl keys are pressed during the drag and drop operation.
Move	No key is pressed.

In a copy operation, the data from the source is duplicated at the target. The move operation copies data to the target and removes it from the source. In addition to initially copying the data, the link operation provides a way for the target to update its data whenever the source changes.

These three operations are available to any control in a Windows Forms application. By default, none of these controls is enabled as a drag and drop target, however. You have to do that yourself, by setting the *AllowDrop* property to *true*. Although technically your control now allows drops, you can't yet perform a drag and drop operation.

To be able to accept drag and drop data, your control must implement a few events. Table 17-5 lists all drag and drop–related events; an explanation of which events must be implemented follows.

Table 17-5.   Drag and Drop–Related Control Events

Event	Description
DragDrop	Fires when the mouse button is released over the drop target
DragEnter	Fires when the mouse pointer is moved onto a control that has *AllowDrop* set to *true* during an ongoing drag and drop operation
DragLeave	Fires when the mouse pointer is moved out of a control during an ongoing drag and drop operation
DragOver	Fires when the mouse pointer is moved over a drag and drop control during a drag and drop operation
GiveFeedback	Enables the source to give visual feedback about the drag and drop operation by changing the mouse pointer style
QueryContinueDrag	Fires during a drag and drop operation and allows the source to determine whether the drag and drop operation should be cancelled

The first four events in this table are designed for drag and drop targets. *DragEnter* is called first, followed by *DragOver*, and then either *DragDrop* or *DragLeave*. To implement a target that accepts drops, you must implement *DragOver* and *DragDrop*. The other two events are optional; they just give you more information about when a drag and drop operation enters or leaves the control.

The *DragOver* event serves an important purpose in that it gives you the chance to modify how the drag and drop operation takes place—for example, whether you're going to accept the operation at all based on the data that's being offered. The information about the operation and your feedback is packaged in the *DragEventArgs* parameter that's passed to your implementation of *DragOver*. Table 17-6 lists the *DragEventArgs* properties and their types and accessibilities.

Table 17-6.   *DragEventArgs* Properties

Property	Type	Accessibility
AllowedEffect	*DragDropEffects*	*get*
Data	*IDataObject*	*get*
Effect	*DragDropEffects*	*get/set*
KeyState	*Int*	*get*
X	*Int*	*get*
Y	*Int*	*get*

With the exception of *Effect*, all of these properties are read-only. You can use the coordinates, data, allowed effects, and key states to determine whether to allow the drag and drop operation on your control. The kind of operation you allow is reported back to the application through the *Effect* property, which can be any value of the *DragDropEffects* enumeration, listed in Table 17-7.

Table 17-7.   *DragDropEffects* Enumeration Values

Value	Description
All	Combines *Copy*, *Move*, and *Scroll*
Copy	Allows data copying to the target
Link	Enables the target to link to data in the source
Move	Performs a move of data from the source to the target
None	Disallows the drop operation
Scroll	Indicates that the drop target is about to begin scrolling or is scrolling

A drag and drop source sets the *AllowedEffect* property, whereas the target can report back to the application through the *Effect* property. Most commonly, sources allow copy, link, and move operations. Depending on how sophisticated it is, the target will allow link, copy, and move operations or only copy and move operations.

Your application can determine what the source allows and what in general your target can accept. But what about the user's intentions, as expressed through the modifier keys? This information is passed in the *KeyState* property; the bit flags for each key are listed in Table 17-8.

Table 17-8.   *KeyState* Bit Flags

Bit Flag	Key
0x01	Left mouse button is pressed.
0x02	Right mouse button is pressed.
0x10	Middle mouse button is pressed.
0x04	Shift key is pressed.
0x08	Ctrl key is pressed.
0x20	Alt key is pressed.

You can check whether a certain key or button was pressed by ANDing the *KeyState* property with the bit flag, as follows:

```
if (0 != (e.KeyState & 0x01))
    ⋮
```

This information enables you to determine what *Effect* the user wants from your application. Combined with the data type your application can accept as a drag and drop target, you set the respective *DragDropEffects* values in your event handlers.

Enabling *FileDrop*

Almost any application supports the *FileDrop* operation in Windows Explorer. In this operation, the user selects one or more files and drags them over the target application. On release, the target application opens the files. To support this operation, you must implement the *DragOver* and *DragDrop* events, and of course the *AllowDrop* property must be set to *true*.

For demonstration purposes, the simple Notepad-like application FileDropTarget is included on the companion CD. This application contains a multiline *TextBox* control, with docking style set to *Full*. The *AllowDrop* property is set to *true*, which allows the application to be a drag and drop target. To enable *FileDrop*, we need to first implement the *DragOver* event, as shown here:

```
private void txtMain_DragOver(object sender, DragEventArgs e)
{
    if (e.Data.GetDataPresent(DataFormats.FileDrop))
    {
        e.Effect = DragDropEffects.Copy;
    }
}
```

Because this simple application supports *FileDrop* only, *DragDropEffects.Copy* is set only when data in *FileDrop* format is offered. When other data is dragged to this application, the no-drop mouse pointer will be displayed. Also note that we're not concerned with the modifier keys with a *FileDrop* operation.

When the user drops the files on the application, the *DragDrop* event is fired. For our sample application, the *DragDrop* event looks like this:

```
private void txtMain_DragDrop(object sender, DragEventArgs e)
{
    if (e.Data.GetDataPresent(DataFormats.FileDrop))
    {
        string[] strFiles =
            (string[])e.Data.GetData(DataFormats.FileDrop);
        StreamReader reader = new StreamReader(strFiles[0]);
        this.txtMain.Clear();
        this.txtMain.Text = reader.ReadToEnd();
        reader.Close();
    }
}
```

We need to perform a final check on the data that's being offered. If the data is in the specified Windows *FileDrop* format as the application expects, we can retrieve the associated data, which is a string array of file names. Because the application is a Single Document Interface (SDI) application, it opens only the first file and ignores the rest. (The user can drag more than one file.) If you were building Multiple Document Interface (MDI) applications, you would open all the files—so long as your application can open the file format used by the files.

Implementing a Drag and Drop Source

It's very common for applications to be drag and drop sources as well as drag and drop targets. One familiar application that works as a source and a target is Visual C#. For example, when you drag a control from the Toolbox onto a form, the Toolbox is the drag and drop source and the form is the drag and drop target.

You can make any control you build or use a drag and drop source. The DragDropSample application, on the companion CD, demonstrates a drag and drop source. As shown in Figure 17-10, the drag and drop source is the list box on the left, and the target is the text box on the right.

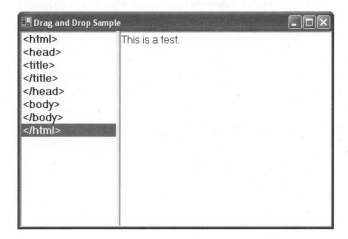

Figure 17-10.   An application that demonstrates a drag and drop source.

The user selects an item in the list box and drags it to the text box. When dropped, the text is pasted to the end of the text that already appears in the text box. How much work is involved in making this happen? To start with, take a look at how the *ListBox* object is filled:

```
this.lbDragDropSource.Items.Add("<html>");
    :
this.lbDragDropSource.Items.Add("</html>");
```

The data displayed in the *ListBox* object also serves as drag and drop data.

Because a drag and drop operation is in process as long as the mouse button is down, the ideal starting point for a drag and drop operation is the *Mouse-Down* event of the drag and drop source, as shown here:

```
private void lbDragDropSource_MouseDown(object sender, MouseEventArgs e)
{
    int nSelectedIndex = lbDragDropSource.SelectedIndex;
    string strItem = (string)lbDragDropSource.Items[nSelectedIndex];

    DragDropEffects dde = lbDragDropSource.DoDragDrop(strItem,
        DragDropEffects.Copy);

    if (DragDropEffects.None == dde)
        MessageBox.Show("Our drag and drop offer was not accepted");
}
```

Note that in this example, we don't care which mouse button was pressed; we simply handle any *MouseDown* event.

You need to determine what data you want the drag and drop source to offer. In this application, the data is the currently selected item in the list box, and the data is offered for copying through the call to *DoDragDrop*. This method won't return until either the data is accepted or the drag and drop operation is cancelled. You're notified what operation took place on your data by the return value of the method, which is of type *DragDropEffects*. A return value of *None* indicates that the drag and drop operation didn't take place because no one accepted the data.

Sometimes it might be desirable for your drag and drop source to influence the ongoing drag and drop operation. This can be done in the *QueryContinueDrag* event, as shown here:

```
private void lbDragDropSource_QueryContinueDrag(object sender,
    QueryContinueDragEventArgs e)
{
    // e.Action = DragAction.Cancel;
}
```

The *QueryContinueDragEventArgs* argument has three useful properties named *Action*, *EscapePressed*, and *KeyState*. This argument enables you to modify the drag and drop operation based on the internal state of your application or the key states that are passed through *EscapePressed* and *KeyState*. The *Action* property can be any value of the *DragAction* enumeration, listed in Table 17-9.

Table 17-9.   *DragAction* Enumeration Values

Value	Description
Cancel	Aborts the operation with no drop taking place
Continue	Continues the operation
Drop	Stops the operation with a drop

In our sample application, there's no need to actually make use of the event. We're fine with what our *TextBox* client does in its *DragOver* and *DragDrop* event handlers, as shown here:

```
private void txtMain_DragOver(object sender, DragEventArgs e)
{
    if (e.Data.GetDataPresent(typeof(string)))
    {
        e.Effect = DragDropEffects.Copy;
    }
}
```

```
private void txtMain_DragDrop(object sender, DragEventArgs e)
{
    if (e.Data.GetDataPresent(typeof(string)))
    {
        string strData = (string)e.Data.GetData(typeof(string));
        // Append text to the current text in the text box.
        txtMain.AppendText(strData);
    }
}
```

You can use the drag and drop source implemented in this section with any other drag and drop source application—for example, to drag and drop text into Visual C#.

Conclusion

The technologies discussed in this chapter and the functionality they provide are taken for granted by the user: users expect a toolbar, they expect copy and paste support, and they expect to be able to open a file they've dragged from Windows Explorer to your application. Fortunately, adding the necessary implementation is easy with Visual C#, especially compared to drag and drop implementation in the days before the .NET Framework.

Toolbars and menus should be created following the style guidelines of your operating system. Don't reinvent the wheel—people are used to the location of the Save button and to how the Cut, Copy, and Paste buttons look on the toolbar. The more standard your application's appearance, the easier it will be for your users to find their way in your application. A good application is easy to use.

This advice holds true for clipboard and drag and drop support as well. Users expect these features, and they expect them to work the way they're used to. Don't try to outsmart your users with your own private clipboard implementation—the average user won't be pleased. When implementing drag and drop, think of the big picture—drag and drop takes places not only between applications, but also between controls and even inside a control. Drag and drop can also make your applications easier to use.

Part IV

Data Access and XML

18

ADO.NET

Most of the applications you create access·or save data. Typically, this data is stored in a database or in some other type of storage mechanism, such as an XML file. Before the .NET initiative, you would use Microsoft ActiveX Data Objects (ADO) as a means of accessing and storing data. ADO.NET is the next step in this evolution of data access technology, integrating the data access capabilities of ADO with the Microsoft .NET Framework. As you'll see in this chapter, ADO.NET encompasses a number of changes to the data access technology and provides you with many more capabilities.

What's New in ADO.NET

ADO.NET has been redesigned from earlier versions of ADO to build more-scalable and better-performing data access applications. This section provides a general overview of some of these improvements.

The ADO.NET Disconnected Model

ADO.NET has been designed from the ground up to work with the data while disconnected from the data source. Data is retrieved from the data store and maintained at a local level, within ADO.NET structures. Because the data store doesn't have to maintain the data cursors or maintain connections while the data is being used by the client, the store can support more client users.

XML Integration

ADO.NET is very tightly integrated with XML. XML is used behind the scenes to maintain the data in datasets and to retain relationships and constraints within the data. In addition, data in ADO.NET can be easily persisted to XML data files for offline usage. In addition, data schemas are maintained in standard XML schemas for use by ADO.NET.

ADO.NET Datasets

ADO.NET has replaced the concept of recordsets with a new construct called *datasets*. Datasets greatly expand on the capabilities of recordsets. Recordsets can hold one table of data and are database-centric. Datasets, however, can hold multiple tables of data that can be related, with the relationships known and maintained by ADO.NET. Recordsets can write and read XML data from data streams. Datasets are designed to integrate directly with XML data. In addition, datasets operate with the data completely disconnected from the database but hold changes to the database so that the data can be updated whenever necessary.

.NET Data Providers

To access and manipulate data from the data store, you'll work through an existing data provider. The .NET data providers link the data store and your application. The .NET Framework includes two data providers for your use, depending on which data store you'll be accessing, as follows:

- **OLE DB .NET Data Provider**   Used to access any OLE DB–compliant data store

- **SQL Server .NET Data Provider**   Used to access Microsoft SQL Server 7 or later data stores

Each of the data providers holds an implementation of the following classes, which form the core of the provider:

- **_Connection_**   Used to establish the connection to the data store

- **_Command_**   Used to execute commands on the data store

- **_DataReader_**   Used to access data in a forward-only, read-only form

- **_DataAdapter_**   Used to access data in a read/write form and to manage updates of data

Table 18-1 lists the classes each .NET data provider includes. The OLE DB .NET Data Provider classes are located in the _System.Data.OleDb_ namespace, and the SQL Server .NET Data Provider classes are located in the _System.Data.SqlClient_ namespace.

Table 18-1.   Objects Included in .NET Data Providers

Class	OLE DB .NET Data Provider	SQL Server .NET Data Provider
Connection	_OleDbConnection_	_SqlConnection_
Command	_OleDbCommand_	_SqlCommand_
DataReader	_OleDbDataReader_	_SqlDataReader_
DataAdapter	_OleDbDataAdapter_	_SqlDataAdapter_

> **Note**   The examples in this chapter will use the SQL Server .NET Data Provider to work with the database. However, we could use the OLE DB .NET Data Provider just as easily.

Creating and Using Datasets

The _DataSet_ object lies at the heart of ADO.NET. Datasets are roughly analogous to recordsets in earlier versions of ADO. However, the dataset greatly extends and expands upon the concept of the recordset. Datasets are used to maintain local copies of the data, completely disconnected from the database.

To create an instance of the _DataSet_ object, call the _DataSet_ constructor, as shown in the following code. You can use the base constructor, which takes no parameters. You can also call the overloaded version of this constructor, which takes the name of the dataset as its parameter.

```
DataSet ds = new DataSet();
DataSet ds = new DataSet("myDataSet");
```

It's the job of the .NET data providers to fill the *DataSet* object with the appropriate data and to provide the interface to the database for that data. It's the function of the *DataSet* object to hold that data locally while the application is working on it and to maintain the data, including all changes, additions, and deletions. Any changes are then sent to the database through the *DataAdapter* object when its *Update* method is called. *DataAdapter* is covered in more detail later in this chapter, in the section "Using a *DataAdapter* Object to Populate a Dataset."

Data in the *DataSet* object is organized in a set of tables. These tables are built by the *DataTable* object. Using these tables, the *DataSet* object can hold a number of different sets of data, which might or might not be related. Each *DataTable* object consists of *DataRow* and *DataColumn* objects that hold the data.

After you've filled the dataset with your data, you'll need to parse through the data, retrieving the data you want. You can easily loop through the rows and columns in the dataset, as shown here:

```
foreach(DataRow row in ds.Tables[0].Rows)
{
    foreach(DataColumn col in row.Table.Columns)
        this.textBox1.Text = this.textBox1.Text
            + row[col].ToString() + "\t";
    this.textBox1.Text = this.textBox1.Text + "\n";
}
```

As you parse through the data, you might need to make changes to it. You can access the data values through the *DataRow* and *DataColumn* objects, assigning new values as necessary, as shown here:

```
foreach(DataRow row in ds.Tables[0].Rows)
    row[1] = "NewValue";
```

Adding Records

You can add new records to the dataset by creating a *DataRow* object using the *DataTable* object's *NewRow* method, as shown in the following code. This method will create an empty row with the same structure as other rows in the table. Values can be assigned to each of the columns in the row, and the newly created row can then be added to the *Rows* collection of the *DataTable* object.

```
DataRow row = ds.Tables[0].NewRow();
row["au_id"] = "123-45-6789";
row["au_lname"] = "MyLastName";
row["au_fname"] = "MyFirstName";
ds.Tables[0].Rows.Add(row);
```

Detecting "Dirty" Data

At times, you might need to determine whether any changes have been made to the current dataset that haven't been accepted or committed to the dataset. These changes can include data that's been modified, added, or deleted from the dataset that hasn't been accepted into the dataset. You can detect these changes by using the *HasChanges* method, which returns *true* if changes have been made but not accepted. You can then retrieve the *DataRow* objects that have changes by calling the *GetChanges* method, as shown here:

```
private void UpdateDataSet (DataSet ds)
{
    if(ds.HasChanges())
    {
        DataSet dirtyDS = ds.GetChanges();
        //Take action.
        ⋮
    }
    ⋮
}
```

Accepting Changes

Whenever you make changes to the dataset, the data is flagged as having been changed. The data changes can be retrieved and manipulated fairly easily, as you've seen. When you're sure that the changes made are correct and can be accepted into the current dataset, you can call the *AcceptChanges* method of the *DataSet* object, as shown here:

```
ds.AcceptChanges();
```

The *DataTable* and *DataRow* objects also have the *AcceptChanges* method, which allows you to commit all the changes made to the *DataTable* and *DataRow* objects. This is useful when you want to accept just the changes in a particular table or just a specific row of a table.

Accepting the changes to the dataset doesn't save those changes back to the database. Because the dataset maintains the data locally, changes you make to the data aren't automatically saved to the database. To save the data in the data store, you call the *Update* method of the *DataAdapter* object.

Binding to Data Components

With the new .NET components, you can easily bind many controls in both Windows Forms and Web Forms to a dataset so that the applications will show the contents of the current dataset in those controls.

The *DataGrid* control is an example of a control that can show the contents of multiple *DataTable* objects and multiple data rows in each table. In the grid, you can assign the dataset to which the grid will be bound to the *Data-Source* property of the *DataGrid* control, as shown in the following code. You can then assign a *DataTable* object within that dataset to the *DataMember* property of the *DataGrid* control. If you don't provide a value for the data source, the grid will display each of the *DataTable* objects in the dataset and allow the user to select the desired table.

```
dataGrid1.DataSource = ds;
dataGrid1.DataMember = "authors";
```

The other controls that are derived from the *System.Windows.Forms.Control* class can also be bound to a dataset. In these cases, you add the data binding to the *DataBindings* collection of the control, as shown here:

```
textBox1.DataBindings.Add(new System.Windows.Forms.Binding("Text",
    ds, "authors.au_lname"));
```

The *Binding* class referenced here is used to bind a property of a Windows Forms control to a field in a dataset. To perform a similar task in building an ASP.NET application, you can use the *System.Web.UI.DataBinding* class. Fortunately, for the standard controls, these tasks are taken care of automatically.

Persisting Data

When you're working with the dataset, you can save that data locally to an XML file so that the information can be persisted beyond the current session. This technique might be used if you have users who will retrieve data from the database, go off line, and then work with the database while traveling.

You save the data to an XML file using the *WriteXML* method of the *DataSet* object and specifying the file to which the data will be saved, as shown here:

```
ds.WriteXML("C:\mydata.xml");
```

When you restart the session, you can read that data back into the dataset using the *ReadXML* method.

```
ds.ReadXML("C:\mydata.xml");
```

Establishing a Connection to a Data Store

As mentioned, the *Connection* class is used to create and manage connections to your data stores in ADO.NET. In this section, you'll learn how to connect to a database, close a connection, control the connection pooling behavior, and perform a transaction.

Constructing *Connection* Objects

The *Connection* class provides two constructors, allowing you to create an instance of the *Connection* class in two ways. The first constructor takes no parameters. In this case, you'll need to define the connection string separately, by specifying it in the *ConnectionString* property, as shown in the following code. The connection string includes the source database names and other parameters to establish the connection. The default value is an empty string.

```
SqlConnection conn = new SqlConnection();
string sConnString = "data source=(local);initial catalog=pubs;" +
                     "user id=sa;password=;";
conn.ConnectionString = sConnString;
```

The second constructor will accept the connection string as its parameter, as shown here:

```
string sConnString = "data source=(local);initial catalog=pubs;" +
                     "user id=sa;password=;";
SqlConnection conn = new SqlConnection(sConnString);
```

Connecting to the Database

The first step in accessing the data store to retrieve data is to establish a connection to the database. After you instantiate a *Connection* object, you pass it the connection string that defines the data store to which you'll be connecting as a part of the initialization. You open the connection using the *Open* method of the object, as shown here:

```
string sConnString = "data source=(local);initial catalog=pubs;" +
                     "user id=sa;password=;";
SqlConnection conn = new SqlConnection(sConnString);
conn.Open();
```

Alternatively, you could instantiate the *Connection* object without the connection string and then add the connection string to the *ConnectionString* property of the object, as shown here:

```
string sConnString = "data source=(local);initial catalog=pubs;" +
                     "user id=sa;password=;";
SqlConnection conn = new SqlConnection();
conn.ConnectionString = sConnString;
conn.Open();
```

Pooling Connections with .NET Data Providers

To provide greater scalability in building data access components, ADO.NET data providers support connection pooling to the database. *Connection pooling* means that connections to the database are held and managed by ADO.NET. When a connection is opened, it will be retrieved from the connection pool, if connections are available, or a new connection will be opened, as shown in Figure 18-1.

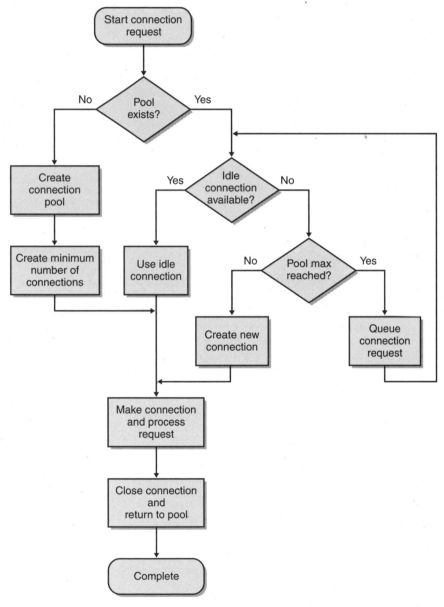

Figure 18-1. The connection pooling process.

As you can see in Figure 18-1, when a connection is opened to the data store, ADO.NET checks the connection string. It then looks to see whether there are any idle connections to the same data store with the identical connection string. If this is the first time a connection is being made to the data store with this connection string, a connection pool will be created and multiple database connections will be created to meet the minimum size requirements for the connection pool.

If the connection pool already exists and an idle connection is available, that connection will be used. If no idle connections are available and the pool hasn't yet reached the maximum number of connections, another connection will be created and used. This new connection will be added to the pool when it's released. If the connection pool has reached its maximum size, the connection request will be queued and serviced when a connection becomes available.

A connection is released and returned to the connection pool when the *Close* method is called. You'll learn how to close a connection later in this chapter, in the section "Closing the Connection."

> **Caution**   You must be extremely diligent about ensuring that you close all connections when you've finished using them. If you don't explicitly close the connections, they won't be placed in the pool and they won't be implicitly released when the *Connection* objects go out of scope or are cleaned during the garbage collection process.

You can control the way connection pools are created and maintained by passing parameters as a part of the connection string. By default, the SQL Server .NET Data Provider uses an implicit pooling model to provide connection pooling. The connection pool parameters for the *ConnectionString* property of the *SQLConnection* object are listed in Table 18-2.

Table 18-2.   Connection Pooling Configuration Parameters

Parameter	Default Value	Description
Connection Lifetime	*0*	Specifies the number of seconds after which the connection is destroyed. This parameter forces connections to be reestablished with the database and can be useful in load balancing. With a *0* value, the lifetime of the connection will never time out.

(continued)

Table 18-2.   Connection Pooling Configuration Parameters   *(continued)*

Parameter	Default Value	Description
Connection Reset	*true*	Specifies whether the connection is reset when it's removed from the pool.
Enlist	*true*	Specifies whether the pool should enlist the connection in the current transaction context of the creation thread.
Max Pool Size	*100*	Specifies the maximum number of connections held in the pool.
Min Pool Size	*0*	Specifies the minimum number of connections held in the pool.
Pooling	*true*	Specifies whether connections will be pooled.

For example, the following connection strings will result in two separate connection pools being created because the two connection strings are not identical:

```
string sConnString = "data source=(local);initial catalog=pubs;" +
                     "user id=pubAdmin;password=AdminPassword;";
string sConnString = "data source=(local);initial catalog=pubs;" +
                     "user id=pubUser;password=mypassword;";
```

In this case, the connection strings make use of two different users.

By default, the OLE DB .NET Data Provider makes use of OLE DB session pooling to provide data access scalability. More details are provided on OLE DB session pooling in the OLE DB Programmer's Reference in the Microsoft Developer Network (MSDN) Library (*http://msdn.microsoft.com/library*).

Initiating Transactions

The *Connection* object is also used to initiate transactions within the data store. These transactions are then managed and ended using the appropriate *Transaction* class (either *SqlTransaction* or *OleDbTransaction*). The *Connection* object initiates the transaction by calling the *BeginTransaction* method, as shown in the following code. This method returns the transaction object that will be used to commit or abort the completed transaction.

```
SqlTransaction trans = conn.BeginTransaction();
```

If you're using the SQL Server .NET Data Provider, the transaction will make use of SQL Server's *BEGIN TRANSACTION* implementation in Transact-SQL. If you're using the OLE DB .NET Data Provider, the OLE DB layer manages the transaction.

The *BeginTransaction* method is overloaded so that it can be initialized in several ways, depending on which data provider you're using. With both the SQL Server and the OLE DB data providers, you can initialize the object with no parameters or pass a single isolation level parameter. The transaction *IsolationLevel* enumeration values are listed in Table 18-3.

Table 18-3.   Transaction *IsolationLevel* Enumeration

Member	Description
Chaos	Changes from other transactions that have a higher level of isolation can't be overwritten.
ReadCommitted	Data is locked while it's being read but can be changed by other transactions before this transaction is completed.
ReadUncommitted	No locks are placed on the data while it's being read. In addition, locks by other transactions are ignored while the data is being read.
RepeatableRead	Data used in the query is locked so that other transactions can't update the data.
Serializable	A range lock is placed on the data so that other transactions can't change existing data or insert new data into the dataset.
Unspecified	An unknown isolation level is being used.

With the SQL Server .NET Data Provider, you can also provide a name for the transaction as a string, specify the isolation level of the transaction, or both in the *BeginTransaction* method, as shown here:

```
trans = conn.BeginTransaction(IsolationLevel.ReadCommitted,
    "MyTransaction");
```

Completing the Transaction

The *BeginTransaction* method returns a transaction object that will be used to manage and complete the transaction. Once the transaction is initiated, you'll need to either commit or roll back the transaction.

In practice, you'll typically provide a routine that will execute one or more SQL commands as part of the transaction, as shown in the code on the following page. If an error is raised by the database, the transaction will be rolled back and no changes will be recorded. However, if no error is reported, the transaction can be committed and the updates to the data will take place.

```
//Create a connection and open the connection to the database.
SqlConnection conn = new SqlConnection(sConnString);
conn.Open();
SqlTransaction trans = conn.BeginTransaction();

try
{
    //Execute SQL commands or other database transactions.
    :
    trans.Commit();
}
catch(Exception e)
{
    //Error handling, logging, reporting, and so on
    :
    trans.Rollback();
}
finally
{
    //Always close the connection!
    conn.Close();
}
```

Closing the Connection

As mentioned, when you've retrieved all the data you need, you should immediately release the connection to the database. A general rule of thumb is to
open the connection as late as possible and close it as early as possible. Two
methods are provided to release the connection.

- *Close*

- *Dispose*

The *Close* method, shown in the following code, is the recommended way
to release the connection. *Close* closes the database connection and returns the
connection to the connection pool so that it can be reused by the application.

```
SqlConnection conn = new SqlConnection(sConnString);
conn.Open();
//Do some work here.
conn.Close();
```

The *Dispose* method, shown in the following code, releases all the
resources associated with the connection. *Dispose* releases all the unmanaged
resources that are being used by the connection, and optionally it can release
the managed resources.

```
SqlConnection conn = new SqlConnection(sConnString);
conn.Open();
//Do some work here.
conn.Dispose();
```

Executing a Command

In general, the most efficient way to work with your data stores is to execute commands directly on the database server—that is, you allow the database server to handle all requests for the data directly. Doing this will allow the database server to do what it does best, and what it's designed for. Typically, when you're working with a database system, it will be able to optimize commands to be performed more efficiently. This is especially the case when you're working with stored procedures on the server rather than writing ad hoc queries.

ADO.NET lets you execute commands directly on the database server by initializing a *Command* object. The *Command* object is used to execute a variety of commands to the database server and to handle data that's returned as a result of those commands.

Constructing *Command* Objects

When you instantiate the *Command* object, you'll have the option of using one of four constructors. The first constructor doesn't provide any parameters, as shown here:

```
SqlCommand cmd = new SqlCommand();
```

This constructor sets the properties of the *Command* object to their default values. You'll learn how to change these values on your own in the following sections.

You can also initialize the object with the command text at the start, by providing it as a parameter in the constructor, as shown in the following code. The command text can be the name of the stored procedure, a table name, or a SQL statement.

```
SqlCommand cmd = new SqlCommand("myCommandText");
```

You can also add the *Connection* object that this *Command* object will use to the constructor, as shown in the following code. This will define the connection that the *Command* object will use to access the database.

```
SqlConnection conn = new SqlConnection();
//Initialize connection.
SqlCommand cmd = new SqlCommand("myCommandText", conn);
```

Last, if your commands are also going to be executed within the context of a transaction, you can initialize the command with the transaction object as well, as shown here:

```
SqlConnection conn = new SqlConnection();
//Initialize connection.
SqlTransaction trans = conn.BeginTransaction();
SqlCommand cmd = new SqlCommand("myCommandText", conn, trans);
```

Providing Command Text

When you create a *Command* object, you can initialize the object with command text, as shown in the previous section. You can also specify the text of the command using the *CommandText* property, as shown in the following code. As mentioned, the command text might be the name of a stored procedure, a table name, or a SQL statement.

```
SqlCommand cmd = new SqlCommand();
cmd.CommandText = "myStoredProcedureName";    //Stored procedure
cmd.CommandText = "authors"                   //Table name
cmd.CommandText = "SELECT * FROM authors"     //SQL statement
```

Associating with a Connection

You'll need to associate the *Command* object with a database connection, which the object will use to communicate with the database, as shown here:

```
SqlConnection conn = new SqlConnection();
//Initialize connection.
SqlCommand cmd = new SqlCommand("myCommandText");
cmd.Connection = conn;
```

As you can see from this code, if you don't initialize the *Command* object with the connection, you'll need to assign the *Connection* object to the *Command* object's *Connection* property.

Associating with a Transaction

If you want to execute the command within the context of a database transaction, you'll need to associate the *Command* object with a *Transaction* object. You can do so when you instantiate the object, as shown earlier in this chapter, in the section "Constructing *Command* Objects," or you can assign an existing transaction to the *Command* object's *Transaction* property, as shown here:

```
SqlConnection conn = new SqlConnection();
//Initialize connection.
SqlTransaction trans = conn.BeginTransaction();
SqlCommand cmd = new SqlCommand("myCommandText", conn);
cmd.Transaction = trans;
```

Configuring the Command Time-Out

Each command has an associated time-out value. If the command doesn't return a result within that time, a time-out error is triggered. This prevents the calling application from getting caught up in a command that takes too long to execute. When you create a *Command* object, you can set the time-out value using the *CommandTimeout* property, as shown in the following code. The default value for this property is 30 seconds.

```
SqlCommand cmd = new SqlCommand();
cmd.CommandTimeout = 60;
```

Specifying Command Types

Before you execute a command through the *Command* object, you'll need to specify the type of command that will be executed using the *CommandType* property. The available types are listed here:

- **StoredProcedure**   The text you've provided as the command is the name of the stored procedure on the server that will be executed. If the stored procedure requires parameters, you'll need to add the required parameters to the *Parameters* property of the *Command* object.

- **TableDirect**   The text you've provided is the name of a table in the data store. You can specify multiple tables by providing a comma-delimited list of tables without any spaces. In the case of multiple tables, a *JOIN* will be performed with the returned tables.

- **Text**   The text you've provided is an ad hoc SQL command. This is the default command type.

You can use the enumerated command types to specify the type of any *Command* object, as shown here:

```
SqlCommand cmd = new SqlCommand();
cmd.CommandText = "myStoredProcedureName";
cmd.CommandType = CommandType.StoredProcedure;
```

Passing Parameters

When you're making use of stored procedures in particular, you'll often pass parameters to the procedure to define how the command should be executed. You do this by creating and adding parameters and their associated values to the *Command* object. In ADO.NET, you use the *Parameter* object to create and add these parameters. You'll learn how to create and add parameters later in this chapter, in the section "Creating and Adding Parameters."

Each *Command* object has a *Parameters* property. This property holds a *SqlParameterCollection* or an *OleDbParameterCollection* object (depending on your data provider), which holds all the parameters for the *Command* object.

Specifying Parameter Direction

Each parameter you define will have an associated direction. This direction is specified in the *Direction* property of the *Parameter* object and indicates whether you're providing data to the stored procedure or you're expecting data to be returned from the procedure. The allowable directions are listed here:

- *Input*
- *InputOutput*
- *Output*
- *ReturnValue*

Specifying Parameter Types

The parameter type you'll use will be provided in either the *DbType* or the *SqlDbType* property of the *Parameter* object, for the OLE DB or SQL Server data provider, respectively. The *DbType* values are enumerated as follows:

AnsiString	*Decimal*	*Single*
AnsiStringFixedLength	*Double*	*String*
Binary	*Guid*	*StringFixedLength*
Boolean	*Int16*	*Time*
Byte	*Int32*	*UInt16*
Currency	*Int64*	*UInt32*
Date	*Object*	*UInt64*
DateTime	*SByte*	*VarNumeric*

The *SqlDbType* values are enumerated as follows:

BinInt	*Int*	*SmallMoney*
Binary	*Money*	*Text*
Bit	*NChar*	*TimeStamp*
Char	*NText*	*TinyInt*
DateTime	*NVarChar*	*UniqueIdentifier*
Decimal	*Real*	*VarBinary*
Float	*SmallDateTime*	*VarChar*
Image	*SmallInt*	*Variant*

> **Note**   Both *SqlDbType* and *DbType* are properties of the *SqlParameter* class. They're linked, so setting the *SqlDbType* will automatically set the *DbType* property. Likewise, setting the *DbType* will automatically set the *SqlDbType*.

Creating and Adding Parameters

To create a parameter, you can explicitly declare a *Parameter* object, set the required properties, and then add the parameter to the parameter collection of the *Command* object, as shown here:

```
SqlParameter parm = new SqlParameter();
parm.ParameterName = "@username";
parm.Direction = ParameterDirection.Input;
parm.SqlDbType = SqlDbType.Varchar;
parm.Value = "myParamValue";

cmd.Parameters.Add(parm);
```

This example code uses the base constructor of the *Parameter* object to create a parameter. It specifies the parameter's name using the *ParameterName* property in the form *@paramname*. Then it sets other property values using the *Direction*, *SqlDbType*, and *Value* properties of the *Parameter* object.

This object's constructor is overloaded, so you can initialize a new instance of the object in several ways. You can provide the parameter name and the value as the object's parameters, or you can provide the parameter name and the data type as the object's parameters. Both approaches are shown here:

```
SqlParameter parm = new SqlParameter("@username", "myParamValue");
SqlParameter parm = new SqlParameter("@username", SqlDbType.Varchar);
```

To add a parameter to the parameter collection, you can also perform most of these steps in a single line, by using another overloaded version of the *Add* method, as follows:

```
cmd.Parameters.Add("@username", SqlDbType.VarChar).Value
    = "MyParamValue";
```

Executing Commands

After the *CommandText* and *CommandType* properties and any required parameters have been defined and added to the command, you'll be able to execute the command. The *Command* object uses several different methods to execute commands, based on the type of command and expected return data.

ExecuteNonQuery

If your query isn't going to return a result set or any value other than the number of rows that were affected, you'll use the *ExecuteNonQuery* method, as shown here:

```
SqlCommand cmd = new SqlCommand();
cmd.CommandText = "updateUserStatus";
cmd.CommandType = CommandType.StoredProcedure;
recordsAffected = cmd.ExecuteNonQuery();
```

This example creates a *Command* object and uses the object with a stored procedure named *updateUserStatus*.

The result of the *ExecuteNonQuery* method for *INSERT*, *UPDATE*, and *DELETE* statements will be a report of the number of rows affected. For other types of statements, it will return −1 on successful execution.

ExecuteScalar

The *ExecuteScalar* method is typically used to execute a command that will return a value, as shown in the following code. In fact, the method is used to execute any command, and it returns the value in the first column of the first row of the result set.

```
SqlCommand cmd = new SqlCommand();
cmd.CommandText = "getInventoryLevel";
cmd.CommandType = CommandType.StoredProcedure;
inventoryLevel = cmd.ExecuteScalar();
```

ExecuteReader

The *ExecuteReader* method is used to execute the command and returns the result set as the *DataReader* object, as shown here:

```
SqlCommand cmd = new SqlCommand();
cmd.CommandText = "getProductList";
cmd.CommandType = CommandType.StoredProcedure;
SqlDataReader dr = cmd.ExecuteReader();
```

The *DataReader* object gives you fast and efficient access to data, in a forward-only, read-only mode. (*DataReader* is covered in more detail later in this chapter, in the section "Using a *DataReader* Object to Retrieve Data.")

Alternatively, you can specify how the *ExecuteReader* method should operate by providing a parameter to the method that defines the *CommandBehavior*. The available members of the *CommandBehavior* enumeration are listed in Table 18-4.

Table 18-4.   *CommandBehavior* **Enumeration Members**

Member	Description
CloseConnection	The connection is closed after the command has been executed.
Default	No behavior is defined. The command can return multiple result sets and can affect the database state.
KeyInfo	The command returns column and primary key information. It doesn't lock any rows of data.
SchemaOnly	The command returns column information and doesn't affect database state.
SequentialAccess	The command allows the *DataReader* object to load the data as a stream and retrieve data from large binary values using *GetBytes* or *GetChars* methods.
SingleResult	The command will return only a single result set.
SingleRow	The command will return only a single row in a single result set.

ExecuteXMLReader

The *ExecuteXMLReader* method is provided only by the SQL Server .NET Data Provider and will return the results as an *XMLReader* object. To return the data in XML format from Microsoft SQL Server 2000, the *CommandText* property usually specifies a SQL statement with the *FOR XML* clause, as shown here:

```
SqlCommand cmd = new SqlCommand();
cmd.CommandText = "SELECT * FROM authors FOR XML";
XMLReader reader = cmd.ExecuteXMLReader();
```

> **Note**   The *XMLReader* object keeps the associated SQL Server connection busy so that no other operations can be performed on the connection until *XMLReader* is closed.

Using a *DataReader* Object to Retrieve Data

The *DataReader* object is used to retrieve data in a forward-only, read-only stream. With it, you can get quick and efficient access to your data. To create a *DataReader* object, call the *ExecuteReader* method of the *Command* object instead of using a constructor. You can read each row of data in the current dataset using the *Read* method of the *DataReader* class. This method will return *true* as long as data is available to be read; it will return *false* if no more data is available.

The data from each column of the returned row can be read using the various *Get* methods. Each method returns a particular column as a particular data type. For example, the *GetSqlString* method of the *SqlDataReader* class returns a column as a *SqlString*, which represents a variable-length string. Similarly, the *GetSqlInt32* method returns the column value as a *SqlInt32*, which represents a 32-bit *integer*. Each of these methods takes the zero-based column ordinal as its parameter. For example, calling *GetSqlInt32(0)* will return the value of the first column in the current row as a 32-bit integer. The following code illustrates how to read data from SQL Server using the *DataReader* object:

```
SqlCommand cmd = new SqlCommand("SELECT * FROM authors");
    ⋮
SqlDataReader rdr = cmd.ExecuteReader();

While(rdr.Read())
{
    string firstCol = rdr.GetSqlString(0);
    int secondCol = rdr.GetSqlInt32(1);
    //Get other columns using the Get methods
    //and take action.
    ⋮
}
```

If the *DataReader* object holds multiple result sets, you can move to the next set of data by calling the *NextResult* method.

> **Note** Like the *XMLReader* object, the *DataReader* object also keeps the associated SQL Server connection busy so that no other operations can be performed on the connection other than closing *DataReader*.

Using a *DataAdapter* Object to Populate a Dataset

The *DataAdapter* class is the primary interface to the data set and the data provider. This class enables you to fill datasets, manage and maintain the data, and send updates back to the data store.

Constructing *DataAdapter* Objects

DataAdapter objects can be initialized with several different sets of data. The state of the data adapter after it's created will depend on which constructor is used. The first *DataAdapter* constructor doesn't accept any parameters, as shown in the following code. The data adapter is created, and all of its properties must be set individually.

```
SqlDataAdapter da = new SqlDataAdapter();
```

The second *DataAdapter* constructor accepts a *Command* object as a parameter, as shown in the following code. This *Command* object will be assigned to the *SelectCommand* property.

```
SqlDataAdapter da = new SqlDataAdapter(cmd);
```

The third *DataAdapter* constructor, shown in the following code, will accept a parameter that contains the command text of the objcct's *Select-Command* property. This command text will be used to create the *Command* object that will be assigned to the *SelectCommand* property. In addition, this constructor will accept a *SqlConnection* object, which will be used to connect to the database.

```
SqlDataAdapter da = new SqlDataAdapter(sSQLSelect, conn);
```

The fourth constructor, shown in the following code, accepts a parameter that contains the command text of the object's *SelectCommand* property. This command text will be used to create the *Command* object that will be assigned to the *SelectCommand* property. The constructor also accepts a connection string that defines the connection to the data source.

```
SqlDataAdapter da = new SqlDataAdapter(sSQLSelect, sConnString);
```

Associating Commands with the *DataAdapter*

The *DataAdapter* class uses a set of *Command* objects to manage the data. A *Command* object can be assigned to each of the properties related to the four major data operations, as follows:

- *SelectCommand*
- *InsertCommand*
- *UpdateCommand*
- *DeleteCommand*

The *SelectCommand* property is used to hold the *Command* object that will be used when data is selected from the data store, as shown here:

```
SqlCommand cmd = new SqlCommand("SELECT * FROM authors");
SqlDataAdapter da = new SqlDataAdapter();
da.SelectCommand = cmd;
```

The *InsertCommand*, *UpdateCommand*, and *DeleteCommand* properties hold *Command* objects that will be used when the *Update* method of the *DataAdapter* class is called, as shown in the following code. The *Update* method is discussed in detail later in this chapter, in the section "Updating Data." Any changes to the local dataset will be sent to the data store, using the set of commands that are associated with the *DataAdapter* object.

```
SqlCommand cmd = new SqlCommand("spInsertNewAuthor");
cmd.CommandType = CommandType.StoredProcedure;

cmd.Parameters.Add(new SqlParameter("@au_lname", SqlDbType.VarChar,
                                    40, "au_lname");
cmd.Parameters.Add(new SqlParameter("@au_fname", SqlDbType.VarChar,
                                    20, "au_fname");
SqlDataAdapter da = new SqlDataAdapter();
da.InsertCommand = cmd;
```

Filling Datasets

You can fill a dataset with data based on the *Command* object in the *SelectCommand* property by calling the *Fill* method, which is inherited from the *DbDataAdapter* class. The data to be filled will depend on the parameters you provide for this method. The most common parameters are shown here:

- *Fill(DataSet)*   Fills the dataset from the data store and names the resulting table in the dataset Table. If the *SelectCommand* property returns multiple result sets, subsequent tables will be named Table1, Table2, and so on. The following code shows how to create a *DataAdapter* object and fill rows in the dataset to match those in the data store:

  ```
  SqlDataAdapter da = new SqlDataAdapter();
  //Configure DataAdapter with commands and so on.
  ⋮
  DataSet ds = new DataSet();
  da.Fill(ds);
  ```

- *Fill(DataTable)*   Fills the data table from the data store, as shown here:

  ```
  SqlDataAdapter da = new SqlDataAdapter();
  //Configure DataAdapter with commands and so on.
  ⋮
  DataTable tbl = new DataTable("authors");
  da.Fill(tbl);
  ```

- *Fill(dataSet, srcTable)*   Fills the named table in the dataset from the data store, as shown here:

```
SqlDataAdapter da = new SqlDataAdapter();
//Configure DataAdapter with commands and so on.
    ⋮
DataSet ds = new DataSet();
DataTable tbl = new DataTable("authors");
ds.Tables.Add(tbl);
da.Fill(ds, "authors");
```

- *Fill(dataSet, startRecord, maxRecords, srcTable)*   Fills the named data table in the dataset, starting with the specified record and including the maximum number of records to retrieve, as shown here:

```
SqlDataAdapter da = new SqlDataAdapter();
//Configure DataAdapter with commands and so on.
    ⋮
DataSet ds = new DataSet();
DataTable tbl = new DataTable("authors");
ds.Tables.Add(tbl);
da.Fill(ds, 21, 10, "authors");
```

> **Note**   Behind the scenes, the *DataAdapter* object uses the *DataReader* object to fill the dataset with the current set of data, based on the *SelectCommand* property.

Updating Data

As mentioned, the dataset maintains data locally, disconnected from the data store. The data can be changed locally, with records being updated, added, or deleted. This won't result in the changes being made to the database, however. To save each of these changes, you'll need to call the *DataAdapter* object's *Update* method. This method will use the commands in the *InsertCommand*, *UpdateCommand*, and *DeleteCommand* properties to make the necessary changes in the database.

Like the *Fill* method described earlier, the *Update* method is overloaded and will function differently depending on which parameters you supply. The most common overloaded versions are shown on the following page.

- **Update(DataRow[])** Updates the data rows in the array of *DataRow* objects as provided, as shown here:

```
SqlDataAdapter da = new SqlDataAdapter();
//Configure DataAdapter with commands and so on.
    ⋮
DataSet ds = new DataSet();
da.Fill(ds);
//Do stuff.
DataRow[] dr = ds.Tables[0].Select(null, null,
    DataViewRowState.Added);
da.Update(dr);
```

- **Update(DataSet)** Updates the dataset, as shown here:

```
SqlDataAdapter da = new SqlDataAdapter();
//Configure DataAdapter with commands and so on.
    ⋮
DataSet ds = new DataSet();
da.Fill(ds);
//Do stuff.
da.Update(ds);
```

- **Update(DataTable)** Updates the data table, as shown here:

```
SqlDataAdapter da = new SqlDataAdapter();
//Configure DataAdapter with commands and so on.
    ⋮
DataTable tbl = new DataTable("authors");
Da.Fill(tbl);
//Do stuff.
da.Update(tbl);
```

- **Update(DataSet, srcTable)** Updates the identified table in the dataset, as shown here:

```
SqlDataAdapter da = new SqlDataAdapter();
//Configure DataAdapter with commands and so on.
    ⋮
DataSet ds = new DataSet();
DataTable tbl = new DataTable("authors");
ds.Tables.Add(tbl);
da.Update(ds, "authors");
```

Mapping Tables

Table mapping enables you to use column names in a *DataTable* object different from those in a data source. When the dataset is created and populated using the *DataAdapter* object, you can map the data tables in the dataset back to the original source tables in the database using the *DataTableMappings* collection, which is stored in the *TableMappings* property of the *DataAdapter* object. In most cases, you'll use the *Add* method of the collection to add a mapping to the dataset, providing the name of the source table in the database and the name of the data table in the dataset, as shown here:

```
SqlDataAdapter da = new SqlDataAdapter();
//Configure DataAdapter with commands and so on.
 ⋮
da.TableMappings.Add("authors", "LocalAuthors");
```

Using the Data Adapter Configuration Wizard

You can drag the *SqlDataAdapter* or *OleDbDataAdapter* object from the Data tab of the Toolbox window to a Web Form or a Windows Form in the Microsoft Visual Studio .NET integrated development environment (IDE) to launch the Data Adapter Configuration Wizard, shown in Figure 18-2. This wizard allows you to automatically configure the *DataAdapter* object so that it can be used by your application. Behind the scenes, the code for your application that initializes the *DataAdapter* object and the data connection is developed.

Figure 18-2.   The Data Adapter Configuration Wizard start page.

This wizard enables you to specify the data connection that the data adapter will use to access the database, as shown in Figure 18-3. The drop-down list displays any data connections that you've already created on this computer.

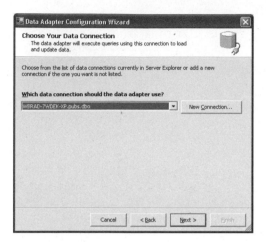

Figure 18-3. Choosing a data connection.

If the desired data connection isn't listed, you can create a new connection by clicking the New Connection button to display the Connection tab of the Data Link Properties dialog box. You can use this dialog box to configure the properties of the data connection.

On the next page of the wizard, shown in Figure 18-4, you specify whether the data adapter will use SQL statements or stored procedures to access the data.

Figure 18-4. Choosing a query type.

You have the following options:

- **Use SQL Statements**   Lets you create an ad hoc SQL *SELECT* statement. The wizard can then generate the *INSERT*, *UPDATE*, and *DELETE* commands.

- **Create New Stored Procedures**   Lets you create new stored procedures for each of the *SELECT*, *INSERT*, *UPDATE*, and *DELETE* commands.

- **Use Existing Stored Procedures**   Lets you select already existing stored procedures for the *SELECT*, *INSERT*, *UPDATE*, and *DELETE* commands.

If you choose to use SQL statements, the next page of the wizard will prompt you to write a SQL *SELECT* statement to retrieve the data you want from the database, as shown in Figure 18-5.

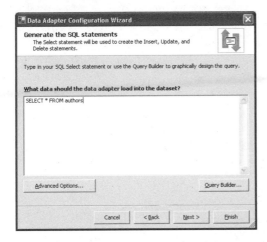

Figure 18-5.   Providing a SQL *SELECT* statement.

Based on the *SELECT* statement you create, the wizard will automatically generate the *INSERT*, *UPDATE*, and *DELETE* statements the data adapter will use.

If you decide to create the stored procedures, you'll begin by defining the SQL *SELECT* statement that will retrieve the data on a page similar to the one shown in Figure 18-5. Based on this statement, the wizard can build the new stored procedures, using the names you specify, as shown in Figure 18-6. The stored procedures will be created within the database, and the code to access those stored procedures will also be generated within your application.

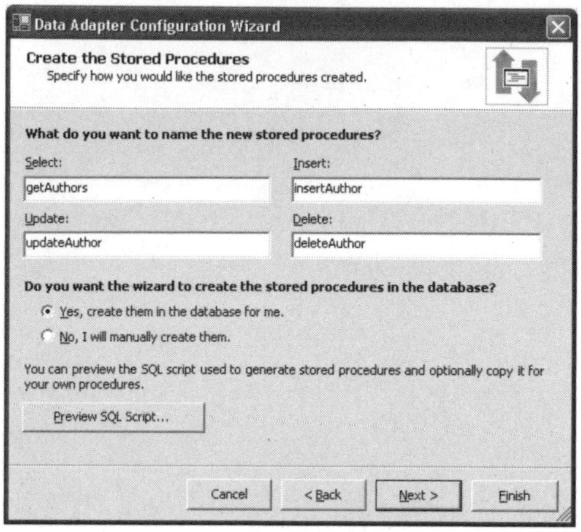

Figure 18-6. Creating the stored procedures.

If you choose to use existing stored procedures, you can select the stored procedures that will be used for the *SELECT*, *INSERT*, *UPDATE*, and *DELETE* commands, as shown in Figure 18-7.

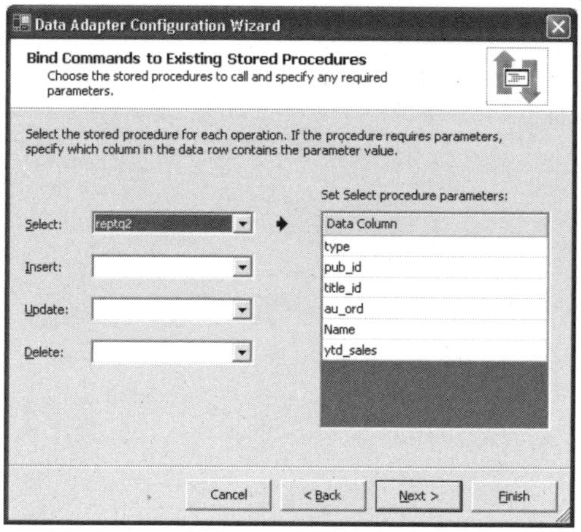

Figure 18-7. Selecting the stored procedures that will be used.

Finally the wizard will generate the appropriate code and stored procedures, if applicable. To confirm that the settings you've configured should be applied, click the Finish button, shown in Figure 18-8.

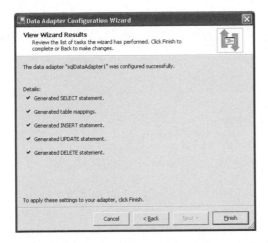

Figure 18-8.   Completing the data adapter configuration.

Conclusion

You now have an overview of ADO.NET as it can be used in your Microsoft Visual C# applications. The .NET Framework includes the *DataSet* object to work directly with the data. The object gives you the flexibility and control to represent the data in any way needed. The object can easily be bound to controls in either Windows Forms or Web Forms to tie the controls and datasets together. This allows you to build data entry screens quickly.

The .NET Framework also includes two data providers that are used to access data sources: the OLE DB .NET Data Provider and the SQL Server .NET Data Provider. Using the *Connection*, *Command*, *DataReader*, and *DataAdapter* objects included in each data provider, you can get complete access to your data.

The integration of .NET with XML means that the data in ADO.NET can easily be portable and persisted locally. You can retrieve information not just about the data contents, but about the data schema as well. In addition, you can easily read and write XML data documents.

This chapter has just brushed the surface, however. Entire books have been written on the subject, including *Microsoft ADO.NET (Core Reference)*, by David Sceppa (Microsoft Press, 2002).

19

XML

Extensible Markup Language (XML) has become the unquestionable standard for generically marking data to be shared. As XML continues to grow in popularity, so too do the number of ways in which XML is being implemented. XML can be used for a variety of purposes, from obvious tasks such as marking up simple data files and storing temporary data to more complex tasks such as passing information from one program or process to another. This chapter describes methods for reading and writing XML files, working with XML documents, using XML with datasets, editing raw XML data, and creating a schema for an XML file.

The Microsoft .NET Framework, and thus Microsoft Visual C# .NET, provides wide support for the use of XML in an open, standards-compliant manner. A number of XML classes and namespaces are available. In general, you'll find the classes you need in the *System.Xml* namespace. Within *System.Xml* are a number of other namespaces, including the following:

- *System.Xml.XPath*

- *System.Xml.Schema*

- *System.Xml.Xsl*

Which of these namespaces you'll want to include in your programs will depend on what you want to accomplish. For example, if you want to address parts of an XML document and manipulate strings and numbers, you should include the *System.Xml.XPath* namespace. *System.Xml.Schema* contains classes that enable you to perform schema mapping and validation. *System.Xml.Xsl* provides support for transforming XML-based data into HTML or other presentation formats. Most often you'll simply include *System.Xml*.

These namespaces contain a number of classes, which can be broken into four categories, as follows:

- Classes for performing basic XML parsing and writing operations
- Classes for editing XML in a document, node, or structure
- Classes for validating XML
- Classes for transforming XML

> **Caution**   Be aware that the names of XML classes provided by the .NET Framework generally begin with *Xml*—that is, *Xml* with a capital *X* and lowercase *m* and *l*. Visual C# .NET is case-sensitive, so it's easy to cause errors in your programs by using all capital letters for *Xml* in class names.

Reading and Writing XML

Reading and writing XML in Visual C# .NET programs is usually accomplished by using a class derived from the *XmlReader* and *XmlWriter* classes. These classes are abstract and therefore must be extended. This abstraction not only allows customized readers and writers to be created, but it also leaves the capability for these derived classes to be swapped in and out if needed. A few customized readers and writers are already available. Within the .NET Framework classes, you have access to the following classes, which are extensions of the *XmlReader* class:

- *XmlTextReader*
- *XmlValidatingReader*
- *XmlNodeReader*

In addition, you have access to the *XmlTextWriter* class, which is an extension of the *XmlWriter* base class.

The *XmlTextReader* and *XmlTextWriter* classes provide you with a quick and efficient means of reading and writing XML. These classes were created to be fast; however, that speed comes at a cost. You're provided with sequential, forward-only navigation to the raw data in the files. In addition, the classes provide the ability to read XML from a non-cached stream. The *XmlTextReader* and *XmlTextWriter* classes will be covered in the following sections.

Using *XmlTextWriter* to Create XML

You can write XML to a stream, the console, or a file using an *XmlTextWriter* object. The process of writing XML to a file is similar to the way other data is written to a file. You first open or create a file, then write the data to the file, and then flush the data stream to make sure everything is committed. When you've finished, you close the file. The methods of the *XmlTextWriter* object produce well-formed XML.

You can open a file at the same time you construct an *XmlTextWriter* object by passing the file name and an encoding parameter to the constructor. The encoding parameter, of type *System.Text.Encoding*, specifies the character encoding to generate. The following example shows one way to create an *XmlTextWriter* object:

XmlTextWriter *myWriterObj* = new XmlTextWriter(*filename, encoding*);

In this example, *myWriterObj* is the name of the *XmlTextWriter* object being created. The variable *filename* is the name of the XML file to be created. If the file already exists, it will be overwritten. The *encoding* parameter can be an instance of one of the following classes:

- *System.Text.ASCIIEncoding*
- *System.Text.UnicodeEncoding*
- *System.Text.UTF7Encoding*
- *System.Text.UTF8Encoding*

You can also pass a null reference for the *encoding* parameter, which causes *XmlTextWriter* to use UTF-8 encoding.

To create an *XmlTextWriter* object named *myWriter* and assign it to a file named myWriter.xml in the C:\Xmldata directory, you would use the following constructor:

```
XmlTextWriter myWriter = new XmlTextWriter(@"C:\Xmldata\myWriter.xml", null);
```

Once the *XmlTextWriter* object has been created and assigned, you can begin writing XML. You can write either a full XML document or fragments of XML—in either case, the *XmlTextWriter* object will work to ensure that the resulting XML is well-formed.

Your XML file should include the following items:

- XML declaration
- Comments
- Elements
- Subelements
- Attributes

We'll look at how to create each of these items in the sections that follow.

Creating an XML Declaration

If you're writing a complete XML document, you should start by writing an XML declaration at the beginning of your file. The *WriteStartDocument* method can be used to create this declaration. This method can be called with no parameters, as shown here:

```
myWriter.WriteStartDocument();
```

Calling this method starts a new XML document and writes the following text to your XML file or stream:

```
<?xml version="1.0" encoding="utf-8"?>
```

Adding Comments

Although comments aren't mandatory in XML, it's good practice to add them. To add a comment to your XML file using your *XmlTextWriter* object, you use the *WriteComment* method. This method takes the comment string as a parameter, as follows:

```
myWriter.WriteComment("comment text");
```

The result of calling this method is shown here:

```
<!--comment text-->
```

As you can see, the *WriteComment* method takes care of formatting the comment in the appropriate XML markup.

Writing Elements and Subelements

The most important section of an XML file is the area containing the elements. The primary data is stored in the elements. Elements can contain attribute names, values, and subelements.

In general, there are two techniques for creating elements: you can write the element and its value all at once, or you can start an element, write the element content, and then later close the element.

The *WriteElementString* method allows you to write an element and its value all at the same time. This method takes two parameters: the first is the name of the element you want to create, and the second is the value of the element. For example, to write *Gone with the Wind* as the value for a video element, you could use the following line of code:

```
myWriter.WriteElementString("Video", "Gone with the Wind");
```

Here's the resulting XML that would be written:

```
<Video>Gone with the Wind</Video>
```

As you can see, this method writes the video element's start tag, its content, and the end tag. If you want to create an element with subelements or if you want to add attributes to an element, you must open the element, write the tags and any other data, and then close the original element. The opening and closing of individual elements can be accomplished using the *WriteStartElement* and *WriteEndElement* methods.

The *WriteStartElement* method takes the name of the element as its parameter, resulting in just the start tag of the element being written. You can then create additional subelements and any other data. Last you'll call the *WriteEndElement* method with no parameters to create an end tag to close the element. The following code shows how the *Video* element can be created using this technique:

```
myWriter.WriteStartElement("Video");
myWriter.WriteString("Gone with the Wind");
myWriter.WriteEndElement();
```

> **Note**   *WriteEndElement* will close the last element that was opened, so you'll need to keep track of the elements you have open. You'll receive an exception if you try to write a closing element with no open elements.

Between the start and end tags of an element, you can write additional subelements, write the value of the element, or add attributes. To add subelements, you can use either of the techniques you just learned. To write the element value or attribute value, you can call the *WriteString* method, as shown in the previous example. This method writes a text string, passed as a parameter, directly to the XML file. You'll learn how to write attributes in the next section.

Adding Attributes

The *XmlTextWriter* class also supports the creation of attributes using the *Write-AttributeString* method. *WriteAttributeString* can be used to add an attribute to an XML element. The simple form of this method takes the attribute name and the attribute values as parameters. For example, an element for measuring time, named *Length*, could have an attribute to indicate what unit of measurement is being used. A video could be 120 minutes, or it could be 2 hours. The following code creates a *Length* element with an attribute:

```
myWriter.WriteStartElement("Length");
myWriter.WriteAttributeString("Measurement", "Minutes");
myWriter.WriteString("120");
myWriter.WriteEndElement();
```

The resulting XML from this code is shown here:

```
<Length Measurement="Minutes">120</Length>
```

As you can see, attribute values are enclosed in quotation marks in XML. If you need more control over your attribute definitions, you can use the *WriteStartAttribute* and *WriteEndAttribute* methods. These more advanced methods allow you to set the attribute prefix and namespace. For more information about these two methods, refer to the Microsoft Developer Network (MSDN) Library.

Adding Formatting and Spacing to an XML File

Just like C# code, XML doesn't require any fancy spacing or indentation; however, adding formatting and spacing can make your XML files easier to view. You might want to set the following four properties of the *XmlTextWriter* object when creating XML files:

- *Formatting*

- *Indentation*

- *IndentChar*

- *QuoteChar*

The *Formatting* property is set to either the default value of *Formatting.None* or *Formatting.Indented*. If you set this property to *Formatting.Indented*, you can then set values for *Indentation* and *IndentChar*. If you leave the default value of *Formatting.None*, any values specified for *Indentation* and *IndentChar* are ignored. *IndentChar* indicates which character to use for indenting the XML code. By default, the *XmlTextWriter* object uses a space character, but you can change this setting to any character you want to use for indentation. Keep in mind that, to ensure valid XML, you must use the white-space characters

0x9 (tab), 0x10 (linefeed), 0x13 (carriage return), or 0x20 (space). In addition to specifying an indentation character, you can set the distance of the indentation by specifying a number in the *Indentation* property, which defaults to 2.

The other property you can set is the *QuoteChar* property. This property is used for specifying which character to use to quote text such as attribute values. By default, the character used to quote text is the double quotation mark ("). You can change this to a single quotation mark (').

Closing the XML File or Stream

After you've written the elements, subelements, attributes, and other values to your XML file, you'll want to close things down. When closing down an *Xml-TextWriter* object, you should first end the document by calling the *WriteEnd-Document* method, as shown here:

```
myWriter.WriteEndDocument();
```

Calling this method will ensure that all open items are also closed. When all the elements are closed, you can then close the *XmlTextWriter* object by calling the *Close* method:

```
myWriter.Close();
```

Sample Application Using *XmlTextWriter*

The following listing illustrates many of the methods and properties for writing an XML file using *XmlTextWriter*. This listing creates a simple dialog box in which you can enter a video title, a star's name, the length of the video (assumption is minutes), and the rating of the video. This information is written to an XML file stored at C:\Videos.xml.

> **Note**   To save space, only a partial code listing is included here. For the complete listing, see the XMLWrite application on the companion CD. This listing doesn't include error handling, nor does it allow you to enter a dynamic file name. These features were removed to keep the listing short.

```
using System;
using System.Drawing;
using System.Collections;
using System.ComponentModel;
using System.Windows.Forms;
using System.Data;
using System.Xml;
using System.Text;
```

(continued)

```csharp
namespace MyXMLApplication
{

    /// <summary>
    /// Summary description for Form1.
    /// </summary>
    public class FrmVideo : System.Windows.Forms.Form
    {
        private System.Windows.Forms.Button btnAdd;
        private System.Windows.Forms.Button btnExit;
        private System.Windows.Forms.Label label1;
        private System.Windows.Forms.Label label2;
        private System.ComponentModel.IContainer components;
        private System.Windows.Forms.TextBox txtVideo;
        private System.Windows.Forms.TextBox txtLength;
        private System.Windows.Forms.ToolTip toolTip1;
        private System.Windows.Forms.TextBox txtStar;
        private System.Windows.Forms.ComboBox cmbRating;
        private System.Windows.Forms.Label label3;
        private System.Windows.Forms.Label label4;

        // Define an XmlTextWriter object.
        private XmlTextWriter xtw;

        public FrmVideo()
        {
            //
            // Required for Windows Form Designer support
            //
            InitializeComponent();

            // Create an XmlTextWriter object and initialize a few
            // properties.
            xtw = new XmlTextWriter(@"C:\Videos.xml", null);

            xtw.Formatting = Formatting.Indented;
            xtw.Indentation = 3;

            // Start the XML document.
            xtw.WriteStartDocument();

            xtw.WriteComment("Video Library");
            xtw.WriteComment(
                "This is a file containing a number of videos.");
            // Create the root element.
            xtw.WriteStartElement("VideoLibrary");
        }
```

```csharp
/// <summary>
/// Clean up any resources being used.
/// </summary>
protected override void Dispose( bool disposing )
{
    if( disposing )
    {
        if (components != null)
        {
            components.Dispose();
        }
    }
    base.Dispose( disposing );
}

#region Windows Form Designer generated code
/// <summary>
/// Required method for Designer support - do not modify
/// the contents of this method with the code editor.
/// </summary>
private void InitializeComponent()
{
    ⋮
}
#endregion

/// <summary>
/// The main entry point for the application.
/// </summary>
[STAThread]
static void Main()
{
    // Create the form to gather input.
    Application.Run(new FrmVideo());
}

private void btnExit_Click(object sender, System.EventArgs e)
{
    // Close the root element, and close the file.
    xtw.WriteEndElement();
    xtw.WriteEndDocument();
    xtw.Flush();  // Flush the stream.
    xtw.Close();  // Close the XmlTextWriter object.

    Application.Exit();
}

private void btnAdd_Click(object sender, System.EventArgs e)
```

(continued)

```
      {
          // Add the data on the screen to the XML file.
          // Start a Video element.
          xtw.WriteStartElement("Video");
          // Add a Title element.
          xtw.WriteElementString("Title", txtVideo.Text );
          // Start a Length element.
          xtw.WriteStartElement("Length");
          // Add the Measurement attribute to the Length element.
          xtw.WriteAttributeString("Measurement", "minutes");
          // Add the data to the Length element.
          xtw.WriteString(txtLength.Text );
          xtw.WriteEndElement();  // End Length element.
          xtw.WriteElementString("star", txtStar.Text);
          xtw.WriteElementString("rating", cmbRating.Text);
          xtw.WriteEndElement(); // End Video element.
          // Put insertion point back in first field.
          txtVideo.Focus();
          // Clear the fields on the screen.
          txtVideo.Text = "";
          txtLength.Text = "";
          txtStar.Text = "";
          cmbRating.Text = "";
      }
    }
}
```

The resulting dialog box is shown in Figure 19-1.

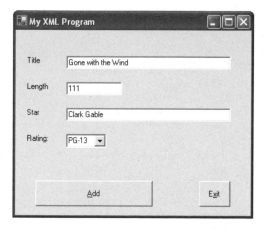

Figure 19-1. XMLWrite, a sample video application using *Xml-TextWriter.*

As you can see, this listing uses all the features we've been looking at, including formatting, elements, subelements, attributes, comments, and more.

Using *XmlTextReader* to Read XML

Reading a basic XML file is much less involved than creating one. As mentioned, the *XmlTextReader* class provides a fast, efficient way to read an XML file. *XmlTextReader* is limited to forward-only reading.

The technique for using *XmlTextReader* is similar to reading any other file. First you open the file, then you read information from the file, and last you close the file. Each time you read from the file, your location in the file moves forward. When you reach the end of the file, there's nothing more you can do.

Creating an *XmlTextReader* Object

You can open an XML file at the same time you create the *XmlTextReader* object. The following line of code creates an *XmlTextReader* object named *myReader* and points it to a file named *filename*. This file name can include a full path.

XmlTextReader myReader = new XmlTextReader("*filename*");

There are a number of other ways to create an *XmlTextReader* object. For example, you can create an *XmlTextReader* object that points to a stream containing XML. Refer to the MSDN Library for the different ways of creating *XmlTextReader* objects.

Reading Data

After you've opened an *XmlTextReader* object, you can read the data from it. A number of methods can be used to read data from an XML file. The more common methods are listed in Table 19-1.

> **Note**   The *XmlTextReader* object doesn't validate the data; it assumes that you're using standard XML (W3C's XML 1.0). This lack of data validation helps to ensure that you obtain the fastest speed.

Table 19-1.   *XmlTextReader* Methods for Reading Data

Method	Description
Read	Reads the next node within the XML file
ReadAttributeValue	Reads an attribute value
ReadBase64	Reads Base64 values
ReadBinHex	Reads BinHex values

(continued)

Table 19-1. *XmlTextReader* **Methods for Reading Data**   *(continued)*

Method	Description
ReadChars	Reads text characters
ReadElementString	Reads text-only elements
ReadEndElement	Reads an ending element
ReadInnerXml	Reads the entire contents of an XML node into a string
ReadOuterXml	Reads an entire XML node and its contents into a string
ReadStartElement	Reads a starting element
ReadString	Reads an element or a text node value into a string

The *Read* method gives you a lot of flexibility. This method reads each node in the XML file individually. You can then evaluate each item's type to determine what it is and what you can do with it. This evaluation can be done by comparing the value read from the *XmlTextReader* object with an *XmlNodeType* value. The possible *XmlNodeType* enumeration members are listed in Table 19-2.

Table 19-2. *XmlNodeType* **Enumeration Values**

Value	Description
XmlNodeType.Attribute	An attribute
XmlNodeType.CDATA	A CDATA section
XmlNodeType.Comment	An XML comment
XmlNodeType.Document	The document node, which is generally the root node
XmlNodeType.DocumentFragment	A document fragment of XML not associated with an actual document
XmlNodeType.DocumentType	The document type tag
XmlNodeType.Element	The start tag for an element
XmlNodeType.EndElement	The end tag for an element
XmlNodeType.EndEntity	The end tag for an entity (physically, an XML document is composed of units called *entities*)
XmlNodeType.Entity	An entity
XmlNodeType.EntityReference	An entity reference
XmlNodeType.None	Returned when the *Read* method of the *XmlTextReader* object hasn't been called

(continued)

Table 19-2. *XmlNodeType* **Enumeration Values**   *(continued)*

Value	Description
XmlNodeType.Notation	A notation in the document declaration
XmlNodeType.ProcessingInstruction	A processing instruction in the XML file
XmlNodeType.SignificantWhitespace	The significant white space (white space that's intended for inclusion in the delivered version of an XML document) in a mixed content model
XmlNodeType.Text	The text content in a node
XmlNodeType.Whitespace	The white space between the different markup items
XmlNodeType.XmlDeclaration	The declaration for the XML document

As you read data from an *XmlTextReader* object, you can determine whether it's important or unimportant to your application. As you read each item, you increment a pointer to the next item. As mentioned, you can't go back to a previous item when using *XmlTextReader* because reading is forward only.

Closing the *XmlTextReader* Object

After you've read the contents of a file, you should close it. Closing the file requires a simple call to the *XmlTextReader* object's *Close* method, as shown in the following code. Calling this method also releases resources held while reading.

```
myReader.Close();
```

Sample Application Using *XmlTextReader*

The following listing pulls together a simple Microsoft Windows–based application that reads an XML file using *XmlTextReader*. In this program, the file name is hard-coded to C:\Videos.xml; however, you could change this to any valid XML file name. The program cycles through the XML file using the *Read* method. With each read, the node's type is displayed, along with the value and name. The application also displays the data with formatting.

> **Note**   To save space, only a partial code listing is included here. For the complete listing, see the Read XML application on the companion CD.

```csharp
using System;
using System.Drawing;
using System.Collections;
using System.ComponentModel;
using System.Windows.Forms;
using System.Data;
using System.Xml;
using System.Text;

namespace ReadXML
{
    public class frmReadXML : System.Windows.Forms.Form
    {
        private System.Windows.Forms.TextBox txtNode;
        private System.Windows.Forms.Label lblNode;
        private System.Windows.Forms.Label label1;
        private System.Windows.Forms.Label label2;
        private System.Windows.Forms.TextBox txtValue;
        private System.Windows.Forms.TextBox txtName;
        private System.Windows.Forms.Button btnExit;
        private System.Windows.Forms.Button btnNext;
        /// <summary>
        /// Required designer variable.
        /// </summary>
        private System.ComponentModel.Container components = null;
        private System.Windows.Forms.Label txtDisplay;

        private XmlTextReader xtr = null;

        public frmReadXML()
        {
            // Required for Windows Form Designer support
            InitializeComponent();

            // Create XmlTextReader object.
            xtr = new XmlTextReader(@"C:\Videos.xml");
            // Don't ignore white space.
            xtr.WhitespaceHandling = WhitespaceHandling.All;
        }

        /// <summary>
        /// Clean up any resources being used.
        /// </summary>
        protected override void Dispose( bool disposing )
        {
            if( disposing )
            {
                if (components != null)
                {
```

```
                components.Dispose();
            }
        }
        base.Dispose( disposing );
    }


    #region Windows Form Designer generated code
    /// <summary>
    /// Required method for Designer support - do not modify
    /// the contents of this method with the code editor.
    /// </summary>
    private void InitializeComponent()
    {
        ⋮
    }
    #endregion


    /// <summary>
    /// The main entry point for the application.
    /// </summary>
    [STAThread]
    static void Main()
    {
        Application.Run(new frmReadXML());
    }


    private void button1_Click(object sender, System.EventArgs e)
    {
        if ( xtr != null)
            xtr.Close();

        Application.Exit();
    }


    private void btnNext_Click(object sender, System.EventArgs e)
    {
        StringBuilder str = new StringBuilder("Formatted: ");

        if (xtr.Read() == true)
        {
            txtNode.Text    = xtr.NodeType.ToString();
            txtName.Text    = xtr.Name.ToString();
            txtValue.Text   = xtr.Value.ToString();

            switch (xtr.NodeType)
            {
                case XmlNodeType.Element:
                    str.AppendFormat("<{0}>",xtr.Name);
                    break;
```

(continued)

```csharp
                    case XmlNodeType.Text:
                        break;
                    case XmlNodeType.CDATA:
                        str.AppendFormat("<![CDATA[{0}]]>",
                            xtr.Value);
                        break;
                    case XmlNodeType.ProcessingInstruction:
                        str.AppendFormat("<?{0} {1}?>",
                            xtr.Name, xtr.Value);
                        break;
                    case XmlNodeType.Comment:
                        str.AppendFormat("<!--{0}-->", xtr.Value);
                        break;
                    case XmlNodeType.XmlDeclaration:
                        //Console.Write("<?xml version='1.0'?>");
                        break;
                    case XmlNodeType.DocumentType:
                        str.AppendFormat("<!DOCTYPE {0} [{1}]",
                            xtr.Name, xtr.Value);
                        break;
                    case XmlNodeType.EntityReference:
                        str.Append(xtr.Name);
                        break;
                    case XmlNodeType.EndElement:
                        str.AppendFormat("</{0}>", xtr.Name);
                        break;
                    case XmlNodeType.Whitespace:
                        //Console.Write("{0}", xtr.Value );
                        break;
                }

                txtDisplay.Text = str.ToString();
            }
            else
            {
                // End of file
                txtValue.Text = "EoF";
                txtName.Text  = "EoF";
                txtNode.Text  = "Eof";
            }
        }
    }
}
```

This listing generates the dialog box shown in Figure 19-2.

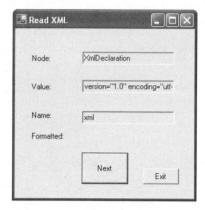

Figure 19-2.   Read XML, a sample application using *XmlTextReader*.

This listing reads through the Videos.xml file you created with the XML-Write application, which is listed earlier in this chapter, in the section "Sample Application Using *XmlTextWriter*." The code uses the *Read* method to read each XML node out of the file. Once a node has been read, the next few lines move node values to the fields on the screen.

```
txtNode.Text  = xtr.NodeType.ToString();
txtName.Text  = xtr.Name.ToString();
txtValue.Text = xtr.Value.ToString();
```

The node type is stored in the *NodeType* property of *xtr* (the *XmlText-Reader* object), the name of the node is stored in the object's *Name* property, and the node's value is stored in the object's *Value* property. As you click the Next button, you'll see each node displayed. You'll also notice that not all node types have both a name and a value.

After the screen values have been set, the node type in *xtr* is compared to the different *XmlNodeType* values via a *switch* statement. The *switch* statement formats the read XML data based on its type, and the information is displayed in the dialog box. When the end of the file is reached, the values in the dialog box are set to *EOF*.

Using the Document Object Model (DOM)

XmlTextReader and *XmlTextWriter* are great classes to use when you want fast, forward-only reading and writing; however, they're not perfect for every situation. You'll also find times when you want to deal with XML data using the Document Object Model (DOM).

The DOM allows you to load the structure of an XML document into memory. By loading the structure, you gain the ability to perform updates, insertions, and deletions within the XML document. Unfortunately, this gain comes at the cost of scalability. Because the *XmlTextReader* and *XmlTextWriter* classes read only part of the XML file into memory at a time, they're much more scalable.

The DOM is composed of the different items within an XML file. Each of these items is considered a node in the structure, as shown in Figure 19-3.

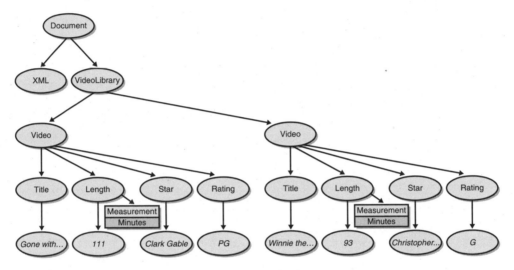

Figure 19-3.   The DOM for part of the Videos.xml file.

Figure 19-3 illustrates the nodes from the following XML file. This XML file is like the Videos.xml file created earlier in this chapter, in the section "Sample Application Using *XmlTextWriter*."

```xml
<?xml version="1.0"?>
<VideoLibrary>
   <Video>
      <Title>Gone with the Wind</Title>
      <Length Measurement="minutes">111</Length>
      <star>Clark Gable</star>
      <rating>PG</rating>
   </Video>
   <Video>
      <Title>Winnie the Pooh</Title>
      <Length Measurement="minutes">93</Length>
      <star>Christopher Robin</star>
      <rating>G</rating>
   </Video>
</VideoLibrary>
```

As you can see, the DOM has a tree structure. Each item in the file is a node in the tree, with subnodes attached below. The data is represented as nodes too and is separate from the elements. Using DOM-related classes within the .NET Framework, you can gain access to any of these nodes.

Working with XML Documents

When you use the DOM, you'll have the ability to read and write as well as navigate through an XML file. A number of classes can be used to access the DOM from Visual C# .NET and the .NET Framework. These classes are listed in Table 19-3.

> **Note**   The DOM support in the .NET Framework is based on the W3C DOM Level 2 Core XML specification. For more information about this specification, see *http://www.w3.org/TR/DOM-Level-2/core.html*.

Table 19-3.   Classes in the .NET Framework That Access the DOM

Class	Description
XmlNode	Used to create objects that can hold a single node of an XML document.
XmlDocument	Used to hold an entire XML document object. Allows document navigation as well as editing.
XmlDocumentFragment	Used to hold a fragment of XML. This XML fragment can be inserted into a document or used for other purposes.
XmlElement	Used to work with element type nodes within an XML document.
XmlNodeList	Represents an ordered collection of nodes within an XML document.
XmlNamedNodeMap	Used to access a collection of nodes either by name or by an index value.
XmlAttribute	Used to work with an attribute type node within an XML document.
XmlCDataSection	Used to work with a CDATA section.
XmlText	Used to hold the text content of an element or attribute.

(continued)

Table 19-3. Classes in the .NET Framework That Access the DOM *(continued)*

Class	Description
XmlComment	Used to work with comments.
XmlDocumentType	Used to hold information associated with the document type declaration.
XmlElement	Used to hold an XML document element.
XmlEntity	Used to hold an entity.
XmlEntityReference	Used to hold an entity reference node.
XmlNotation	Used to hold the notation declared within a Document Type Definition (DTD).
XmlProcessingInstruction	Used to hold a processing instruction.

The .NET Framework provides the *XmlDocument* class as the starting point for working with basic XML documents. This class will load the XML document into memory so that you can manipulate it.

Loading an XML Document into the DOM

To load an XML document into memory, you can use the *Load* method of the *XmlDocument* class, as shown here:

```
XmlDocument myDoc = new XmlDocument();
myDoc.Load(@"C:\Videos.xml");
```

The first line of code declares an *XmlDocument* object named *myDoc*. The file, Videos.xml, is then loaded into this *XMLDocument* object. Once loaded, the information can be viewed, updated, and saved.

The *Load* method has been overloaded so that you can also load from other sources. Possible sources include an *XmlReader* object, a *TextReader* object, a stream, and a URL or a file name.

In addition to the *Load* method, there's also a *LoadXML* method. The *LoadXML* method receives a string as a parameter. This string contains formatted XML that will be placed into the *XmlDocument* object. It's important to note that white space is ignored and DTD or schema information isn't validated. If these elements are important to you, you'll want to use the *Load* method.

Working with Document Data

Once the XML document has been loaded into memory, you can begin working with the information stored in the document. Because the entire file is in memory, you can navigate and manipulate the information in any manner you choose. A number of classes (listed earlier in this chapter, in Table 19-3) and methods are available to make this easy for you.

It's important to understand how the XML document is organized. Figure 19-3 earlier in this chapter showed the node structure for an XML document. In Figure 19-4, you see a portion of the same figure with additional information: references to some of the nodes.

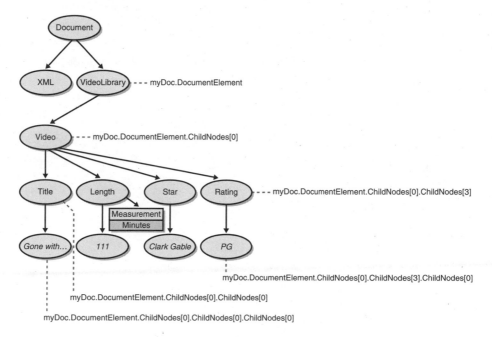

Figure 19-4.   Node access in an XML document.

Access to all of the elements is through the *XmlDocument* object you create. Within the *XmlDocument* object, you can access the root element using the *DocumentElement* property. From there, you can access each of the nodes and subnodes using *ChildNodes* arrays. Although the root element is accessed differently than the child nodes (using the *DocumentElement* property instead of the *ChildNodes* array), the properties and methods of both are virtually the same because both are types of *XmlNode* objects.

Notice also that nodes positioned at the same level are peers to each other. Peers can be accessed in the same manner—using the *ChildNodes* array. The difference is that each contains a different subscript. If a child node element has subnodes, use another *ChildNodes* array to access the subnodes, continuing for as many levels as there are subnodes. Once you've reached the level of the node you're interested in using, you can use other methods and properties to access the node's information.

Using *DocumentElement* with XML

You can use the *DocumentElement* property to get a glimpse of an XML document. The *DocumentElement* property returns an *XmlElement* object. This object has two properties that are great for getting a quick view of the XML in an XML document: *OuterXml* and *InnerXml*. Using the *OuterXml* property, all the XML will be returned, including the current node, as shown in the following code:

```
using System;
using System.IO;
using System.Xml;

public class Videos
{
    public static void Main()
    {
      //Create the XmlDocument object.
      XmlDocument myDoc = new XmlDocument();
      myDoc.LoadXml("<?xml version='1.0' ?>" +
                    "<Video><Title>Gone with the Wind</Title>" +
                    "<rating>PG</rating></Video>");

      Console.WriteLine(myDoc.DocumentElement.OuterXml);
    }
}
```

This code will return:

```
<Video><Title>Gone with the Wind</Title><rating>PG</rating></Video>
```

If you want all the XML within the current element but not the current element itself, you can use the *InnerXml* property. Changing the previous *WriteLine* statement to the following:

```
Console.WriteLine(myDoc.DocumentElement.InnerXml);
```

will result in the following output:

```
<Title>Gone with the Wind</Title><rating>PG</rating>
```

Saving a File from the DOM

After you've made changes to a file, you might want to save them. Remember, an *XmlDocument* object is stored in memory. When you make changes, they're made in memory, not in the file. You must save the *XmlDocument* object if you want to keep the changes. The *Save* method is used to update the file. In addition to assigning a file name or a URL, you can also save to an *XmlWriter* object, a *TextWriter* object, or a stream.

Sample Application Using the DOM

The following code is a program that loops through the first node of the Videos.xml file you created earlier in this chapter, in the section "Sample Application Using *XmlTextWriter*." It allows you to update the data, which is then saved back to a new file (NewVideos.xml).

> **Note**   To save space, only a partial code listing is included here. For the complete listing, see the XMLDoc application on the companion CD.

```
using System;
using System.Drawing;
using System.Collections;
using System.ComponentModel;
using System.Windows.Forms;
using System.Data;
using System.Xml;
using System.Text;

namespace ReadDataSet
{
    public class frmReadXML : System.Windows.Forms.Form
    {
        private System.Windows.Forms.Label label1;
        private System.Windows.Forms.Label label2;
        private System.Windows.Forms.TextBox txtValue;
        private System.Windows.Forms.TextBox txtName;
        private System.Windows.Forms.Button btnExit;
        private System.Windows.Forms.Button btnNext;
        /// <summary>
        /// Required designer variable.
        /// </summary>
        private System.ComponentModel.Container components = null;
        private System.Windows.Forms.Label txtDisplay;
```

(continued)

```csharp
    // Counter to loop through elements
    private int ctr = 0;
    private System.Windows.Forms.Button btnUpdate;

    XmlDocument myDoc = null;  // For XmlDocument object

    public frmReadXML()
    {
        //
        // Required for Windows Form Designer support
        //
        InitializeComponent();

        // TODO: Add any constructor code
        // after InitializeComponent call.

        // Allocate XmlDocument object.
        myDoc = new XmlDocument();

        // Load XML data.
        myDoc.Load(@"C:\Videos.xml");
    }

    /// <summary>
    /// Clean up any resources being used.
    /// </summary>
    protected override void Dispose( bool disposing )
    {
        if( disposing )
        {
            if (components != null)
            {
                components.Dispose();
            }
        }
        base.Dispose( disposing );
    }

    #region Windows Form Designer generated code
    /// <summary>
    /// Required method for Designer support - do not modify
    /// the contents of this method with the code editor.
    /// </summary>
    private void InitializeComponent()
    {
        ⋮
    }
    #endregion
```

```csharp
/// <summary>
/// The main entry point for the application.
/// </summary>
[STAThread]
static void Main()
{
    Application.Run(new frmReadXML());
}

private void btnExit_Click(object sender, System.EventArgs e)
{
    myDoc.Save(@"C:\newVideos.xml");
    Application.Exit();
}

private void btnNext_Click(object sender, System.EventArgs e)
{
    XmlNode aNode = myDoc.DocumentElement
        .ChildNodes[0].ChildNodes[ctr];

    if (++ctr >= myDoc.DocumentElement
        .ChildNodes[0].ChildNodes.Count)
        ctr = 0;

    txtName.Text    = aNode.Name;
    txtValue.Text   = aNode.ChildNodes[0].Value;
    txtDisplay.Text = aNode.InnerText;
}

private void btnUpdate_Click(object sender,
    System.EventArgs e)
{
    int tmp = 0;
// Need the previous value of the ctr variable.
    if (ctr == 0)
    {
        // Set tmp to the last element in the array (count - 1).
        tmp = myDoc.DocumentElement
            .ChildNodes[0].ChildNodes.Count - 1;
    }
    else
        tmp = ctr - 1;

// If Name of node is blank, skip update.
// Name of node will be blank when program starts.
    if( myDoc.DocumentElement
        .ChildNodes[0].ChildNodes[tmp].Name != "" )
    {
        myDoc.DocumentElement.ChildNodes[0]
```

(continued)

```
                        .ChildNodes[tmp].ChildNodes[0].Value =
                        txtValue.Text;
                    txtDisplay.Text = "Updated: "
                        + myDoc.DocumentElement.ChildNodes[0]
                        .ChildNodes[tmp].ChildNodes[0].Value;
                }
            }
        }
    }
```

This listing displays the form shown in Figure 19-5.

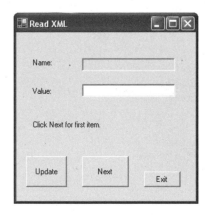

Figure 19-5. Sample XML DOM application.

Keep in mind that this application isn't particularly practical. It does illustrate some of the basic uses of *XmlDocument* objects as well as some of the basic navigation techniques, however. As you can see, the *Load* method is used to open the Videos.xml file from the root of the C drive. You can also see in the *btnExit_Click* event that the *Save* method is used to write the resulting XML to a file named NewVideos.xml, also on the root of C.

In the *btnNext_Click* event, an *XmlNode* object is created and assigned to a node within the document, as follows:

```
XmlNode aNode = myDoc.DocumentElement.ChildNodes[0].ChildNodes[ctr];
```

Within the *myDoc* object are the subnodes, or child nodes. The first subnode, *ChildNodes[0]*, is the first *Video* element. The first *Video* element contains the subnodes for each of the items within a video—in this example, there are four items: title, length, star, and rating. Using a counter, the *ctr* variable, you can loop through each of these items. For each of these subelements, you can then display a name and a value. Within the *btnNext_Click* event, the use of the *XmlNode* object makes the remaining code much simpler. You can easily work with the methods and properties. In the *btnUpdate_Click* event handler, instead of an *XmlNode* object, the values in the *XmlDocument* object, *myDoc*, are used. As you can see, both methods work—which you decide to use depends on your personal preferences.

A number of additional properties, methods, and events are used with the classes listed earlier in Table 19-3. Check the online help for additional information.

Using XML with Datasets

XML can also be used with datasets. The *DataSet* class, described in Chapter 18, has methods for both reading and writing XML. In this section, you'll learn how to place XML data in a dataset and how to write data from a dataset to an XML file.

Placing XML Data into a Dataset

To read data into a dataset, you use the *ReadXml* method of the *DataSet* class. This method can work with both XML and schema information. Consider the following XML file, which is like the one that was created using the Videos form presented earlier in this chapter, in the section "Sample Application Using *Xml-TextWriter*":

```
<?xml version="1.0" encoding="utf-8" ?>
<!--Video Library-->
<!--This is a file containing a number of videos.-->
<VideoLibrary>
    <Video>
        <Title>Gone with the Wind</Title>
        <Length Measurement="minutes">111</Length>
        <star>Clark Gable</star>
        <rating>PG</rating>
    </Video>
    <Video>
        <Title>The Matrix</Title>
        <Length Measurement="minutes">123</Length>
        <star>Keanu Reeves</star>
        <rating>R</rating>
    </Video>
    <Video>
        <Title>Vanilla Sky</Title>
        <Length Measurement="minutes">109</Length>
        <star>Tom Cruise</star>
        <rating>R</rating>
    </Video>
    <Video>
        <Title>Lord of the Rings</Title>
        <Length Measurement="minutes">168</Length>
```

(continued)

```
         <star>Frodo</star>
         <rating>PG-13</rating>
      </Video>
      <Video>
         <Title>Winnie the Pooh</Title>
         <Length Measurement="minutes">93</Length>
         <star>Christopher Robin</star>
         <rating>G</rating>
      </Video>
</VideoLibrary>
```

The listing for XMLWrite was hard-coded to store an XML file such as the preceding one at C:\Videos.xml. To read this file into a dataset, you should first instantiate a *DataSet* object, as shown here:

```
DataSet myDataSet = new DataSet();
```

After the object has been instantiated, you use the *ReadXml* method to load the XML data into the dataset, as follows:

```
myDataSet.ReadXml(@"C:\Videos.xml");
```

Once this command has been executed, the XML file is loaded into the dataset. You can then manipulate the data just as you can other data stored in a dataset. Refer to Chapter 18 for more information about working with datasets.

The following listing presents a simple form that contains a data grid that displays the primary data in the Videos.xml file:

```
using System;
using System.Drawing;
using System.Collections;
using System.ComponentModel;
using System.Windows.Forms;
using System.Data;

namespace ReadDataSet
{
    /// <summary>
    /// Summary description for Form1
    /// </summary>
    public class Form1 : System.Windows.Forms.Form
    {
        private System.Windows.Forms.DataGrid dataGrid1;
        /// <summary>
        /// Required designer variable
        /// </summary>
        private System.ComponentModel.Container components = null;

        public Form1()
        {
            //
```

```csharp
        // Required for Windows Form Designer support
        //
        InitializeComponent();

        // TODO: Add constructor code after InitializeComponent call.

        // Create the DataSet object.
        DataSet myDataSet = new DataSet();

        // Load XML data.
        myDataSet.ReadXml(@"C:\Videos.xml");

        // Bind the dataset to the data grid.
        dataGrid1.DataSource = myDataSet;
        dataGrid1.SetDataBinding(myDataSet, "Video" );
    }


    /// <summary>
    /// Clean up any resources being used.
    /// </summary>
    protected override void Dispose( bool disposing )
    {
        if( disposing )
        {
            if (components != null)
            {
                components.Dispose();
            }
        }
        base.Dispose( disposing );
    }


    #region Windows Form Designer generated code
    /// <summary>
    /// Required method for Designer support - do not modify
    /// the contents of this method with the code editor.
    /// </summary>
    private void InitializeComponent()
    {
        this.dataGrid1 = new System.Windows.Forms.DataGrid();
        ((System.ComponentModel.ISupportInitialize)
            (this.dataGrid1)).BeginInit();
        this.SuspendLayout();
        //
        // dataGrid1
        //
        this.dataGrid1.DataMember = "";
        this.dataGrid1.HeaderForeColor =
            System.Drawing.SystemColors.ControlText;
```

(continued)

```
        this.dataGrid1.Location = new System.Drawing.Point(16, 16);
        this.dataGrid1.Name = "dataGrid1";
        this.dataGrid1.Size = new System.Drawing.Size(496, 232);
        this.dataGrid1.TabIndex = 0;
        //
        // Form1
        //
        this.AutoScaleBaseSize = new System.Drawing.Size(5, 13);
        this.ClientSize = new System.Drawing.Size(528, 262);
        this.Controls.AddRange(new System.Windows.Forms.Control[] {
            this.dataGrid1});
        this.Name = "Form1";
        this.Text = "Read Data Set";
        ((System.ComponentModel.ISupportInitialize)
            (this.dataGrid1)).EndInit();
        this.ResumeLayout(false);

    }
    #endregion

    /// <summary>
    /// Main entry point for the application
    /// </summary>
    [STAThread]
    static void Main()
    {
        Application.Run(new Form1());
    }
  }
}
```

As you can see, the Videos.xml file is loaded into *myDataSet* using the *ReadXml* method. The next two lines of the listing connect the dataset to the data grid and specify which data will be displayed, as follows:

```
dataGrid1.DataSource = myDataSet;
dataGrid1.SetDataBinding(myDataSet, "Video");
```

In this case, the video information is displayed. The first line sets the data source for the data grid to the dataset you loaded with the XML data. The second line binds the Video data to the control. This binding will cause the Video data to be displayed as a table.

You can also display the video length information if you change the preceding data binding line to this:

```
dataGrid1.SetDataBinding(myDataSet, "Length" );
```

When the Videos.xml file was loaded, it was automatically broken into relational tables for you. You'll need to write the necessary code if you want to rejoin these tables when displaying the information.

Writing XML from a Dataset

Once you have data in a dataset, you can write it to an XML file by calling the *WriteXml* method. The *WriteXml* method of the dataset will take care of all the work for you. The following line of code will create a file named NewXml.xml from *myDataSet* in the root directory of the C drive:

```
myDataSet.WriteXml(@"C:\NewXml.xml");
```

You can also specify whether a schema should be included with the file. This is done by including an *XmlWriteMode* value as a second parameter to the *WriteXml* method call, as shown here:

```
myDataSet.WriteXml(@"C:\Filename", writeMode)
```

The *writeMode* parameter can be one of the following values:

- ***XmlWriteMode.DiffGram***   Writes the XML file as a DiffGram, which is a format used to identify current and original version of data elements.

- ***XmlWriteMode.IgnoreSchema***   Writes just the XML data. If the file contains no data, nothing is written.

- ***XmlWriteMode.WriteSchema***   Writes the XML data and the schema.

Using Visual C# .NET to Edit XML Files

Visual C# .NET provides tools for working directly with XML. At times, you'll find that you don't want to write a Visual C# .NET program to create an XML file—instead, you simply need an XML file to use in your program. In addition, you might find that viewing or editing a schema would be helpful. With Visual C# .NET, you can perform the following tasks:

- Create and edit raw XML data.
- View and edit a schema.
- Add XML data.

Creating and Editing XML Raw Data

You can add an XML file to an existing Visual C# .NET project. To do so, choose Add To Project from the File menu. You can then select XML File from the presented options. You also have options to add an XML schema, an XSL transformation (XSLT) file, or a schema file. XSLT is a language for transforming XML documents into other XML documents. XSLT is designed for use as part of XSL, which stands for *XML style sheet language*.

When you add an XML File template, a new file is added to your project with the following text contained in it:

```
<?xml version="1.0" encoding="utf-8" ?>
```

You're then free to add whatever XML markup you desire. The editor is XML-aware, so it will not only color code, but also provide end tags automatically.

Figure 19-6 shows the Videos.xml file displayed in the Visual C# .NET XML editor.

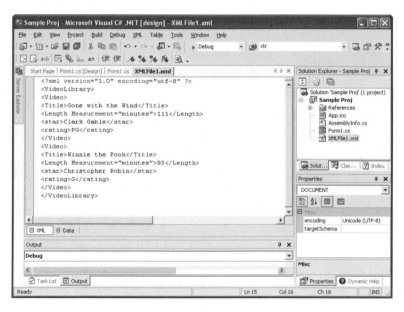

Figure 19-6.   The Videos.xml file in the Visual C# .NET XML editor.

Viewing and Editing the Schema

You can use Visual C# .NET to automatically create a schema for an XML file, or you can create an XML schema from scratch. To create a schema from scratch, you can either right-click an XML file (such as the one shown in Figure 19-6), or you can select XML from the menu. Either technique will display a menu of options, including the Create Schema option. Selecting Create Schema will automatically add a schema file to your project and include the schema for your XML file. Figure 19-7 shows the schema for the Videos.xml file.

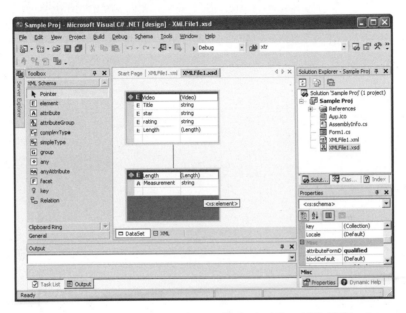

Figure 19-7.   The Videos.xml schema file in the Visual C# .NET schema editor (DataSet view).

> **Note**   When you create the schema for your file, the Visual C# .NET editor will automatically format your XML file.

Once you have a schema, you have the option to validate your XML data file. If your schema was automatically generated, your XML file will be valid; however, if you created or changed your schema using the schema editor, you should validate your XML data against it. This can be done within the XML editor. Choose Validate XML Data from the XML menu; any problems will be reported in the task list.

Figure 19-7 presented the schema in DataSet view. You can also view and edit the schema in an XML view. To switch views from within the schema editor, right-click the schema editor and choose View XML Source from the shortcut menu. You can also select the XML tab at the bottom of the schema editor window. Figure 19-8 shows the video schema in XML Source view.

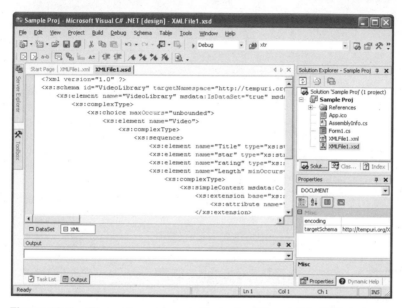

Figure 19-8. The video schema file in the Visual C# .NET schema editor (XML view).

Adding XML Data

If you need to add data to your XML file, you can use one other feature of the Visual C# .NET editor. From within the XML editor, you can select the View Data option by right-clicking the XML editor window or by clicking the editor's Data tab. A data table will appear, as shown in Figure 19-9, allowing you to enter data directly into your XML file.

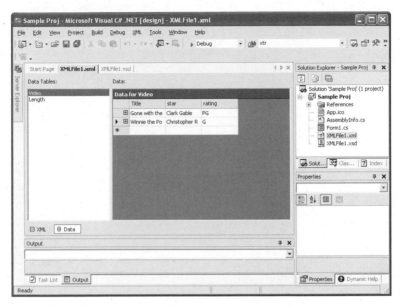

Figure 19-9.   Data view for adding XML data.

Conclusion

This chapter has covered a lot of ground, and yet it has only introduced the topic of working with XML using Visual C# .NET. An entire book could be written to address all the features and functionality of XML with Visual C# .NET.

You can access XML from a number of different classes. For fast access, the *XmlReader* and *XmlWriter* classes offer optimized solutions. For those times when you need to modify XML data, the classes that access the Document Object Model (DOM) are much better suited. Visual C# .NET has a number of built-in editors that can help you in the basic creation and manipulation of XML.

Visual C# .NET and the .NET Framework also provide functionality for manipulation of XML in a number of other ways, including support for transformations, style sheets, XPath, schema, and much more. The .NET Framework and Visual C# .NET documentation provide more information about these topics.

Part V

ASP.NET and Web Services

20

Web Forms

As a C# programmer, you'll probably want to create applications that run on the Web. How can you accomplish this? Along with new languages (including C#, of course) and a new Microsoft Windows Forms technology, the Microsoft .NET Framework has introduced a new technology for developing Web applications: Microsoft ASP.NET. ASP.NET works as an extension of the basic Web server facilities of Microsoft Internet Information Services (IIS), providing you with a .NET way to program Web pages. Using ASP.NET, you can develop Web server–based applications, including both the application user interface in the form of programmable HTML pages, known as Web Forms pages, and Web-based components, known as Web services. In this chapter, we'll concentrate on Web Forms pages—what they are, how they work, and how to program them. In Chapter 21, you'll learn how to create Web services as Web-based components.

ASP.NET and Web Forms are a big area of the .NET Framework. (Entire books have been devoted to both topics. See, for example, *Designing Microsoft ASP.NET Applications*, by Douglas J. Reilly [Microsoft Press, 2002] and Building Web Solutions with ASP.NET and ADO.NET, by Dino Esposito [Microsoft Press, 2002].) This chapter can't give you all of the in-depth information you need to become a Web Forms expert, but it will provide you with a thorough grounding in Web Forms. By the end of the chapter, you'll have a good grasp of what Web Forms are and how to create them.

Requirements for Working with ASP.NET

Web Forms pages have dependencies on technologies other than just the .NET Framework. For starters, you must be running IIS. (If the server is running Microsoft Windows NT 4, you need to have IIS version 4 or later.) Ideally, you'll have IIS running on your own computer. You can use IIS on another machine, but you'll need administrative privileges on that computer and read/write access to the Inetpub directory and its subdirectories. In either case, the computer running IIS must also have the .NET Framework installed so that IIS can call ASP.NET as needed. And the server must have Microsoft FrontPage Server Extensions installed.

Because we'll be looking at data access as well, you'll also need access to a database such as the Microsoft SQL Server or Microsoft Access database. (Again, ideally this database will be installed on your own computer.)

Features of ASP.NET

If you've done Web development using IIS, you've probably worked with the predecessor to ASP.NET—namely, Active Server Pages (ASP). Like ASP, ASP.NET provides a means to program Web pages on an IIS server (rather than in the browser or on the client). But ASP had a number of limitations—for example, it was constructed with interpreted code and didn't scale well—so when the Web development group began designing an update to ASP, they started from scratch.

The result, ASP.NET, isn't just an evolution of ASP; it's effectively an entirely new technology that improves on its predecessor in many ways, both small and large. The major features of ASP.NET are listed in the following subsections, with notes about why these features are important in making you a more effective Web developer and, for those familiar with ASP, a few notes about how these features are enhancements.

Separation of Logic from the User Interface

An ASP page is an HTML page in which you embed your server-side code using special delimiters (<% %>). The result, while functional, is somewhat messy, and sophisticated pages could involve extremely complex combinations of code and HTML. ASP.NET offers a much cleaner model in which the user interface—the page's static HTML text and its controls—is completely separate from the page's logic. Developing a Web Forms page is now much more like developing a form in Visual Basic or Visual C++, especially if you're working in Microsoft Visual Studio .NET. The result is a dramatic improvement in ease of programming and maintainability.

Compiled Pages

When a user requests a Web Forms page as part of your application, the page runs as compiled code. In ASP, code is in VBScript or Microsoft JScript, which both run as interpreted languages. The result of compiling is that your Web Forms pages are much more reliable code because compile-time errors are caught and type checking is enforced. In most cases, compiled pages also perform better.

Support for Multiple Languages

You can write the code for Web Forms pages in any common language runtime language you want. In this chapter, we'll concentrate on writing pages in C#, but if you work in an environment where different programmers have reasons to use different languages, that's no impediment to creating Web Forms. In fact, different components of your Web application can be written in different languages, but because they all share the same runtime environment, they interoperate perfectly.

Event-Driven Model

In any Web application, the client (the browser) and the server are almost completely separate and they communicate only the most rudimentary information back and forth. The server sends an HTML stream to the browser; the browser sends information back to the server when the user submits a form. Traditional Web programming is very linear: receive a request and construct an output stream, top to bottom, to send back to the browser. Compared to programming in the extremely rich message and event model of something like Windows, programming Web applications seems primitive. However, with ASP.NET, the page architecture of Web Forms emulates true events, so you can, in effect, create event handlers for a button click, a selection in a list box, and so on. This model brings the productivity of a tool such as Visual Basic to Web programming.

Improved Object Model

Web pages have traditionally had notoriously simplistic object models. Basically, on the server, you could read only the values of controls. By controlling the output stream, you could insert text or controls as needed. ASP.NET changes all that. A Web Forms page, all its controls, and related objects are full-featured .NET classes, and you can program them as you would any other .NET classes. The Web Forms classes also incorporate much of the base functionality of a Web page that you would otherwise have to tediously code by hand, such as reading and writing HTTP responses, maintaining control state during trips between the client and the server, and so on. The result is a supremely rich object model that allows you to manipulate objects for Web applications with the same sophistication you would use for Windows Forms or other components.

Scalability and Performance

In contrast to ASP, which doesn't scale easily, ASP.NET was specifically designed to allow you to create applications that would run as effectively on a small intranet as on a large commercial site. These features include compiled pages, a caching system for pages already served, and inherent support for multiple-processor machines and multiple-machine Web farms.

Security

ASP.NET provides two types of security. One is the authentication/authorization security that identifies users and grants them permission to use application resources. ASP.NET can rely on IIS, or you can implement your own such security, including interfacing with Microsoft .NET Passport and other models. As a part of the .NET Framework, ASP.NET also provides you with code-level security that allows you to control the context in which code runs.

Support for Tracing and Debugging

To help you iron out problems in developing your Web Forms pages, you can specify trace features that allow you to follow the flow as a page is constructed and rendered and to insert custom trace messages for your own code. In addition, if you're using Visual Studio, you can use the standard debugger when developing your Web Forms pages to set breakpoints, watch variables, and so on.

ASP Capability in ASP.NET

Although ASP.NET is very different from its predecessor, ASP, the ASP.NET development team went to some effort to maintain backward compatibility. If you have existing ASP pages, you can run them as-is in the ASP.NET environment. When ASP.NET sees the .asp extension on a page, it hands the page off to the old ASP engine (asp.dll), which processes the page as it would have before. A great benefit of this feature is that you can move an ASP application into ASP.NET and continue to run it while you convert it to ASP.NET or rewrite it.

If you want, you can convert, or *migrate*, existing ASP pages to ASP.NET. At its simplest, this migration consists of renaming the file with the .aspx extension. For the most part, ASP.NET recognizes old ASP syntax, including the unique <% %> delimiters for ASP in-line code. There are enough small changes in ASP.NET, however, that anything but the simplest ASP pages will probably require at least some minor tweaking, and in some cases, perhaps quite a lot. For starters, the programming languages for ASP pages—JScript and VBScript—have been replaced by .NET counterparts, with commensurate changes in syntax. (Obviously, there was no equivalent to C# in ASP.) There are additional issues to think about with COM interoperability, which includes access to ActiveX Data Objects (ADO) for data access, security, and so on.

In short, although ASP.NET does offer a decent measure of compatibility with ASP, it's not perfect. But the advantages of using Web Forms pages are so significant that if it's at all practical to do so, you should consider rewriting old ASP pages as Web Forms pages.

An Introduction to Web Forms

If you haven't done Web programming before, working with Web Forms generally requires some getting used to because Web programming differs in some fundamental ways from working with traditional Windows client applications. This section will introduce some of the basic concepts of Web Forms programming. As you move through the chapter, additional concepts will be presented.

Server-Based Programming

Web Forms (and ASP.NET in general) is a server-based technology—that is, all your code runs on the server. The client—the application's user interface—is the user's browser. The sequence goes something like this: First the user requests your Web Forms page. The browser then sends the request to the Web server (IIS), which calls on ASP.NET to process the page. The page's output is an HTML stream that's sent to the client, where it's out of your hands until the next time the user sends it back to you.

This is quite different from a Windows Form, in which you have complete control over how the form is displayed. In a Windows Form, your code runs in the client (the window) and you can monitor many different events while the user works, reacting more or less instantly to any user action. In a Web Form, the user interacts with the form in the browser by typing and clicking. It's only when the user has finished and clicks a button (typically) that the page is posted back to the server, where your code can run again.

Server-based processing has a number of advantages for Web applications. You already know that server-based processing allows you to use C# and

---

Client Scripting

ASP.NET doesn't prevent you from using client script (usually ECMA-Script—JavaScript or JScript—or VBScript) in your Web Forms page. In Microsoft Internet Explorer 4 and later, for example, you can use client script to program the page in the browser using Dynamic HTML (DHTML).

You can't use C# to program the browser, however, because C# runs only on the server. When the page is being processed on the server, ASP.NET runs your server-side C# code and then sends the page to the browser. If the page contains client script, ASP.NET ignores the client script and passes it through to the browser.

There are times when it's useful to include client script in a page, usually for enriching the user interface experience. A good example is a mouseover effect, which can be done only in client script. Certain Web Forms controls also rely on small snippets of client script. For example, the validation controls can take advantage of client script if the browser is Internet Explorer to perform validation in the client side before a request is sent to the server.

If you do want to program in client script, you're mostly on your own. The various browser scripting languages aren't .NET languages, so you can't take advantage of the facilities of the .NET Framework from client script. Visual Studio .NET provides only rudimentary support for client script in its Web Forms Designer. For information about programming Internet Explorer using client script, see the Windows script and DHTML Web sites at *http://msdn.microsoft.com/library/default.asp*.

the .NET Framework. Another important advantage is that the code is client-independent—it runs the same way no matter what type of browser your users might be using. (In contrast, trying to write a Web application that's client-specific can get complex, often involving multiple versions of the same page.) Yet another advantage is that your code is on the server, safe from scrutiny by users. When the code runs, it renders ordinary HTML, so users never see your code. Finally, when your code runs on the server, it has access to all the other resources that the server has access to, such as databases, message queuing, and other Windows facilities.

Postbacks and Round-Trips

Because your Web Forms code runs on the server, the form has to be posted back (submitted) to the server for any of your processing to happen. Therefore, Web Forms controls generally post the form back so that it can be reprocessed. In addition to using buttons, you can set list box, drop-down list, check box, and radio button controls to post back a Web Forms page.

Perhaps you can see the implication: the Web Forms page makes a round-trip to the server each time the user clicks a button, as shown in Figure 20-1. Compared to performing this action in a Windows Form, this is a comparatively expensive proposition in both time and processing resources. There's really no other choice, however—if you want to respond to the user's selection in a list box, the form needs to be sent to the server so that ASP.NET and your code can handle it.

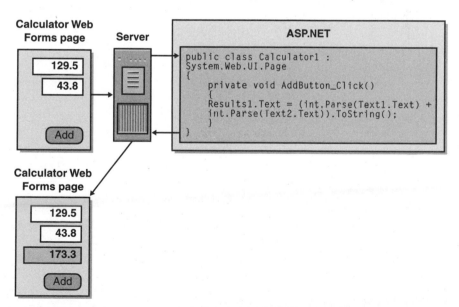

Figure 20-1.   The Web Forms page performing a round-trip to the server.

Posting forms to the server is an inherent part of all Web processing, not just ASP.NET. In fact, an advantage of Web Forms is that it handles a great deal of the work required to perform and process the information sent back and forth with each round-trip.

Disconnected Access and Page Regeneration

When ASP.NET gets a page request, it processes the page and your code, renders the page, and then discards it. If the user posts the page back, ASP.NET starts the process all over again: fetch, process, render, discard.

This might seem inefficient to you—if the user might post the page back, why not keep the page handy? The answer, again, has to do with the nature of how Web processing works. The Web is inherently a disconnected environment—the client and the server don't stay in continual contact. Instead, the client and the server communicate only long enough to exchange information. This model makes perfect sense for HTML pages, where the user might request a page from one Web site, spend some time reading it, and then perhaps jump to another Web site altogether. There's no good way (or reason) for the first Web site to maintain contact with the user until he or she moves to the next site.

At this level, Web Forms are really no different from HTML pages. The user requests a Web Forms page, and then who knows what the user might do next. To be efficient (in a counterintuitive sense), therefore, ASP.NET "discards" a page as soon as the page has been processed, freeing itself to handle the next request in the queue. (In fact, ASP.NET does cache pages it has processed because Web Forms pages are often posted back and reprocessed. Regardless of what ASP.NET does under the covers, however, you should treat Web Forms processing as if the page were being created from scratch each time.)

The fact that the page is regenerated each time has implications for how you program. For example, the page's initialize and load sequences run each time the page is requested. Controls on the page are reinstantiated with every round-trip. Remember that the page is requested not just when the user types in the page's URL, but each time the user clicks a button or performs another action that causes a postback. Compare this to a Windows Form: it's as if the *Load* event were fired and the controls re-created each time the user clicked a button.

Creating a Basic Web Forms Page

Before we get too bogged down in theory, let's create a Web Forms page and then examine what it is and how it works. Our first example will be a simple calculator application, but you'll be able to see in action some of the principles we've been looking at.

> **Note**   Because this section is an introduction to Web Forms pages, it goes into some detail about the mechanics of how to create the page. Subsequent sections won't be as detailed.

Creating the Project

We'll begin by creating a Web application project in Visual Studio .NET. To do so, follow these steps:

1. Open Visual Studio .NET. From the File menu, choose New and then choose Project to open the New Project dialog box.

2. Under Project Types, select Visual C# Projects, and under Templates, select ASP.NET Web Application.

3. In the Location box, delete the name *WebApplication1* and instead name your project *VisualCSharpCorRef*. (If you're not using IIS locally, substitute the appropriate server name for *localhost*.) The full path will look something like this:

   ```
   http://localhost/VisualCSharpCorRef
   ```

4. Click OK.

Visual Studio .NET creates your new Web application by generating a folder with the application name under the IIS default folder (usually \inetpub\wwwroot) and having IIS set a virtual folder pointing to that location. Visual Studio .NET also populates the new project with a handful of files. Of these, only three—WebForm1.aspx, WebForm1.aspx.cs, and WebForm1.aspx.resx—are actually Web Forms files. The rest are files used to manage the Web application.

Installing the Sample Project

On the companion CD, you can find a Visual Studio .NET project called VisualCSharpCorRef that contains source files for the examples you create in this chapter. To use the sample project, you need to do the following:

1. Install the project. It's designed to run on Visual Studio .NET with access to a local Web server.

2. Set access permissions so that you can run the data-bound pages.

3. Open the project in Visual Studio .NET.

Installing the Project

1. Copy the VisualCSharpCorRefDeploy.msi file to your computer, and double-click it to start the installation.

2. When you are prompted for a target location, accept the default of VisualCSharpCorRefInstall and the default port value of 80. The installation process creates a new folder underneath the IIS root (usually \inetpub\wwwroot) and copies the files to that folder.

Setting Permissions

The data-bound Web Forms pages in the project rely on an Access database (nwind.mdb) that is included with the files copied to the IIS folder. The data pages require read/write access to the nwind.mdb file as well as permission to create a new file (nwind.ldb) in the folder.

If you are using the FAT32 file system in Windows, you can access these files without a problem. However, if you are using NTFS file system, you must give your Web application explicit permission to write to the database and to the application directory. The installation process cannot set these permissions for you.

Using Windows Explorer, navigate to the IIS root (\inetpub\wwwroot), right-click the VisualCSharpCorRefInstall folder, and choose Properties. Click the Security tab, and then follow these steps:

1. Click Add, and then add the user name <*yourcomputer-name*>\ASPNET. For example, if your computer is named MyDevComputer, you would add the user named MyDevComputer\ASPNET. The ASPNET user is a local user (not a domain user) that is created automatically when ASP.NET is installed on your computer. By default, ASP.NET applications run within the context of this user.

Installing the Sample Project   *(continued)*

2.   Grant read and write privileges to the ASPNET user for the Visual-CSharpCorRefInstall folder.

Opening the Project

The final step is to open the project in Visual Studio .NET. Follow these steps:

1.   In Visual Studio .NET, from the File menu choose Open and then Project From Web. Visual Studio will prompt you for the URL of the server to open the project from. Since you have installed the project on your local server, you can accept the default of http://localhost.

2.   In the Open Project dialog box, open the VisualCSharpCorRef-Install folder and choose VisualCSharpCorRef.csproj.

You can then work with the project files. The first time you save a file, Visual Studio .NET will prompt you to create a solution file (.sln), since that is not part of the deployed project. You can create the file anyplace you like.

Moving the Nwind.mdb File

By default, the nwind.mdb file for the project is installed in the same folder as the Web Forms pages, which requires that you grant read and write privileges to that folder for run-time access. If you don't want to make that folder write accessible, you can move the nwind.mdb file to another folder and set permissions on that folder instead. If you move the nwind.mdb file, you must change the connection string for the OleDbConnection objects in the various Web Forms pages. This value is stored as a dynamic property value in the project's Web.config file. To change the connection string, open the Web.config file and in the <appSettings> element, edit the path stored in the element that starts with the following:

```
<add key="oleDbConnection1.ConnectionString" >
```

Creating the Calculator1 Web Forms Page

Visual Studio .NET creates a default Web Forms page (WebForm1) for you, but it's helpful to understand how to create a page from scratch. To do so, follow the steps on the following page.

1. Close WebForm1.aspx.

2. From the Project menu, choose Add Web Form to open the Add New Item dialog box.

3. Under Templates, make sure that Web Form is selected.

4. In the Name box, type the name *Calculator1* and click Open. A new blank Web Forms page named Calculator1.aspx is created and displayed in Web Forms Designer. In Solution Explorer, right-click Calculator1.aspx, and choose Set As Start Page from the shortcut menu. This makes the page the opening form in your application.

Adding Controls

You add controls to a Web Forms page in much the way you add controls to a Windows Form. By default, Web Forms pages are set to use a grid layout (xy-coordinates), so you can drag controls anywhere on the page. To add controls to the page, follow these steps:

1. From the View menu, choose Toolbox.

2. From the Web Forms tab of the Toolbox, drag the following controls onto the page and name them as indicated in the following table.

Control	Property Settings
TextBox	*ID*: *Number1TextBox*
	Text: (leave blank)
Label	*ID*: *OpLabel*
	Text: (leave blank)
TextBox	*ID*: *Number2TextBox*
	Text: (leave blank)
Label	*ID*: *ResultLabel*
	Text: (leave blank)
Button	*ID*: *AddButton*
	Text: +
Button	*ID*: *SubtractButton*
	Text: −
Button	*ID*: *MultiplyButton*
	Text: *

(continued)

Control	Property Settings
Button	*ID*: *DivideButton*
	Text: */*
Button	*ID*: *ClearButton*
	Text: *Clear*

Notice that each control has a small green arrow in the upper-left corner; this symbol tells you that the element is a control, not a static HTML element.

Figure 20-2 shows what the page will look like when you've finished dragging controls onto it. We'll look at how to add the static HTML text shown in this figure in the next section.

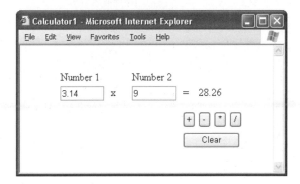

Figure 20-2.   The sample Web Forms page Calculator1.

Adding Static HTML Text

In addition to controls, you can add static HTML text to the page. Static HTML text is text that you don't need to program, so it doesn't need to be in a control. To add HTML text to your page, follow these steps:

1. From the HTML tab of the Toolbox, drag a *Label* control onto the form and position it as a label for the first text box you added earlier.

2. Select this new label, and then click it once. (Don't double-click it.) The label is now in edit mode, as indicated by the cross-hatched border.

3. Edit the label's text to read *Number 1*, and then click in a blank area of the page to unselect the label.

4. Repeat steps 1 through 3 to add a label above the second text box. Edit the text to read *Number 2*.

5. Create one more label like this, position it to the left of the *Result-Label* control, and set its text to **=** (equal sign).

The distinction between a control and static HTML text is an important one in Web Forms pages, and a difference that you don't find in Windows Forms. We'll go into this in more detail later in this chapter, in the section "Web Forms Controls."

Programming the Button Controls

To add functionality to the page, you need to add event handlers to the buttons. In the Visual Studio .NET Web Forms Designer, this process is similar to working with Windows Forms. To add event handlers to the button controls in our page, follow these steps:

1. Double-click the *AddButton* control. The Calculator1.aspx.cs file will open in the Code Editor, and the insertion point will be in a new, blank method (*AddButton_Click*).

2. Add the following lines of code:

```
private void AddButton_Click(object sender, System.EventArgs e)
{
    ResultLabel.Text = (double.Parse(Number1TextBox.Text) +
        double.Parse(Number2TextBox.Text)).ToString();
    OpLabel.Text = "+";
}
```

This code is relatively straightforward: it gets the values of the two *TextBox* controls, casts the values as doubles, adds them together, casts the result back to a string, and then sets the *Text* property of the *ResultLabel* control to the result of this operation. The code also displays an operator by setting the *Text* property of the *OpLabel* control.

3. Add handlers for the *SubtractButton*, *MultiplyButton*, and *DivideButton* controls by double-clicking each and adding code to perform the appropriate operation. You might also add code to ensure that users don't try to divide by zero. When you've finished, the three handlers will look like this:

```
private void SubtractButton_Click(object sender, System.EventArgs e)
{
    ResultLabel.Text = (double.Parse(this.Number1TextBox.Text) -
        double.Parse(Number2TextBox.Text)).ToString();
    OpLabel.Text = "-";
}
```

```
private void MultiplyButton_Click(object sender, System.EventArgs e)
{
    ResultLabel.Text = (double.Parse(Number1TextBox.Text) *
        double.Parse(Number2TextBox.Text)).ToString();
    OpLabel.Text = "x";
}

private void DivideButton_Click(object sender, System.EventArgs e)
{
    if((double.Parse(Number2TextBox.Text) != 0))
    {
        ResultLabel.Text = (double.Parse(Number1TextBox.Text) /
            double.Parse(Number2TextBox.Text)).ToString();
        OpLabel.Text = "/";
    }
    else
    {
        ResultLabel.Text = "Can't divide by zero!";
    }
}
```

4. Add a handler for the *ClearButton* control's *Click* event to reset the text boxes and operator label to empty strings, as shown here:

```
private void ClearButton_Click(object sender, System.EventArgs e)
{
    Number1TextBox.Text = "";
    Number2TextBox.Text = "";
    OpLabel.Text = "";
}
```

Running the Page

Now you're ready to run the page. To do so, press Ctrl+F5, which builds the project and runs it.

The browser opens with your page in it. Enter numbers in the text boxes, and click the operator buttons. If you watch the page's status bar, you'll see that each time you click a button, the page is reloaded—that is, it makes a round-trip to the server.

Examining the Calculator1 Web Forms Page

Now that you've created a Web Forms page, let's examine it more closely to learn how Web Forms work. In this section, we'll look separately at the .aspx file (the visible part of the page) and at the code for the page.

The .aspx File

The Web Forms page you just created is similar to an HTML page. If you open the Calculator1.aspx file in the Web Forms Designer and switch to HTML view by clicking the HTML tab at the bottom of the designer, you can see the "raw" HTML-like text of the .aspx file, which will be similar to Figure 20-3.

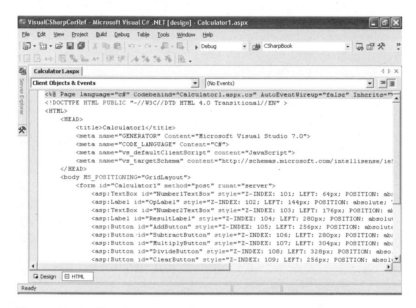

Figure 20-3.   The Calculator1 Web Forms page in HTML view.

The .aspx file differs from a standard HTML file in the following ways:

- The file extension is .aspx rather than .htm or .html. The extension is the trigger for a Web Forms page; when IIS sees that extension, it hands the page off to ASP.NET, which processes the page and your code.

- At the top of the page is an @ *Page* element, which is an ASP.NET processing directive. This links the .aspx file to the corresponding code file. See the next section for further details.

- The body contains a *Form* element, which was generated automatically by Visual Studio .NET. ASP.NET can process only the elements inside the *Form* element.

- The *runat* attribute of the *Form* element is set to *"server"*. This attribute is the key to server programming with ASP.NET. For ASP.NET to "see" any element, that element's start tag must contain *runat="server"*. ASP.NET treats anything in the page without *runat="server"*, including static HTML, as opaque text and simply passes the text on to the browser.

■ The controls you added to the form aren't standard HTML elements. Instead, they're declared as *asp:TextBox*, *asp:Label*, and *asp:Button* elements. These are the Web Forms controls recognized only by ASP.NET. These elements also have the attribute *runat="server"*.

■ The elements all have an *ID* attribute. This attribute provides the instance name by which you can refer to the element in code. For example, to refer to the label element in code, you use its ID (*Label1*).

■ The HTML labels are declared as *DIV* elements. Unlike the controls, these elements don't have the attribute *runat="server"*. They're static HTML elements, invisible to (and not programmable in) ASP.NET.

Note   If you're familiar with ASP, you might be surprised not to see any code in <% %> delimiters. ASP.NET does support <% %> syntax to enclose in-line code, but as a general rule, the controls on the page fulfill many of the same functions that used to be accomplished in ASP with in-line code.

Grid vs. Flow Layout

By default, the Web Forms Designer allows you to lay out elements by dragging in two dimensions. If you look at a page in HTML view, you'll see that each element has a style attribute that includes a *Left* (x) and *Top* (y) setting. This is why you had to drag the HTML *Label* controls onto the page—so that you'd have a container for static text. An alternative that we won't look at here is to set the page to Flow Layout mode, in which elements are laid out in standard HTML order, from top to bottom. The advantage of Flow Layout mode is that you can simply type static text directly in the page. The disadvantage is that it's much harder to position elements precisely, and developers usually end up putting elements in HTML tables. For a detailed discussion about Flow Layout mode, refer to the MSDN Library.

The Code

The .aspx file defines the visible elements of the page. The code for the page is in a separate file, Calculator1.aspx.cs. You can see the Calculator.aspx.cs file by clicking the Show All Files toolbar button in Solution Explorer and then opening the node for the Calculator1.aspx file. Open the Calculator1.aspx.cs file by double-clicking the file name in Solution Explorer. By looking at the code that the Web Forms Designer generates and the code that you've added, you can get a clear sense of how Web Forms pages are processed.

The most interesting thing to note is that your Web Forms page is a class (*Calculator1*) that inherits from the base *Page* class defined in *System.Web.UI*, as follows:

```
namespace VisualCSharpCorRef
{
    public class Calculator1 : System.Web.UI.Page
    {
        ⋮
    }
}
```

The class's namespace corresponds to your project—in this case, VisualCSharpCorRef.

When the page runs, ASP.NET creates an instance of your page class and runs it. As with any class, the page goes through an initialization process, performs its processing, and is then disposed of. As we've seen, the page goes through this cycle each time it's called—that is, with each round-trip.

In the Code Editor, open the node labeled Web Form Designer Generated Code. The page includes an override of the *OnInit* method. This method is called so that the page can initialize itself, which it does by calling a private *Initialize-Component* method. In the initialization code, shown here, you'll see statements that perform event wireup—that is, they bind page and control events to specific event handling methods. The keyword *this* refers to the current page instance.

```
private void InitializeComponent()
{
    this.DivideButton.Click += new
        System.EventHandler(this.DivideButton_Click);
    this.MultiplyButton.Click += new
        System.EventHandler(this.MultiplyButton_Click);
    ⋮
    this.Load += new System.EventHandler(this.Page_Load);
}
```

You don't have to write event wireup code yourself because when you use the Web Forms Designer in Visual Studio .NET, the event wireup code is part of the code that's generated when you double-click a control to create a handler.

> **Caution**   Don't change the code in the generated region, and don't add any of your own code. The code in this region is regenerated by the designer as necessary, and any changes you make might be lost.

When you compile a Web Forms page at design time in Visual Studio .NET, only the code-behind file is compiled. The .aspx file doesn't become part of the project assembly .dll file. When you deploy a Web Forms page, therefore, you deploy the .aspx file as-is. At run time, when the page is called, there's a second compilation step. In this second compilation, ASP.NET creates a new, temporary class from the .aspx file and code-behind files combined (specifically, the .aspx file inherits from the compiled code-behind file), and that's what actually runs.

Web Forms Controls

When we created the Calculator1 Web Forms page, we used special controls that are part of the Web Forms page architecture: the ASP.NET *server controls*. Server controls are the programmable elements in your page that provide you with the kind of behavior you expect from forms controls—programmable user interface, properties and methods, event-based programming, and so on—within the context of Web Forms. When a control runs, its specific job is to render some output, typically HTML, that's contributed to the page output.

> **Note**   A notable difference between a Web Forms page and a Windows Form is that every element in a Windows Form is a control or a component. In contrast, in a Web Forms page, only the elements you want to program against are server controls (or server-based components). The page can contain as much static HTML text as you want. If you don't need to program an element, don't use a server control. When the page is processed, ASP.NET ignores anything that isn't a server control and passes the page through to the browser.

Standard User Interface Controls

Many of the Web server controls fulfill almost the same roles in a Web Forms page that equivalent controls do in a Windows Form. Table 20-1 lists the Web server controls for a standard user interface.

Table 20-1.   Web Server Controls for Standard User Interface

Control	Description
Label	Displays text that can be changed programmatically.
Literal	Similar to the *Label* control, but more lightweight, with fewer properties.
TextBox	Allows entry of text or passwords. Supports single-line or multiline entry and display.
Button	Submits the page to the server. Is rendered as a standard Windows button.
LinkButton	Submits the page, but is rendered as a hyperlink.
ImageButton	Submits the page, but is rendered as a graphic.
HyperLink	Displays a hyperlink that can be configured programmatically.
DropDownList	Displays a drop-down list of static items or items added at run time.
ListBox	Displays a list box of static items or items added at run time.
CheckBox	Allows a boolean choice that can be set programmatically.
RadioButton	Displays a single radio button that can be set programmatically.
Image	Displays a graphic that can be set programmatically.
Panel	Provides an area on the page that can have its own settings (such as color) and that can act as the container for other controls.
Placeholder	Provides a container for other controls. Unlike the *Panel* control, has no properties of its own.

Controls for Displaying Data

All Web server controls can be bound to a data source—for example, you can bind a *TextBox* or a *ListBox* control to a data source. However, some controls exist only to display data; these controls are listed in Table 20-2. Data binding is discussed later in this chapter, in the section "Working with Data in Web Forms."

Table 20-2.   Web Server Data List Controls

Control	Description
DataGrid	Displays data from any data source (database, dataset, or other data structure) in a grid. Includes facilities for adding, sorting, and paging.
DataList	Displays data in a user-specified structure such as a table or a bulleted list. Supports editing.
Repeater	Displays data in a user-specified recurring structure such as a table, a bulleted list, or even a comma-delimited list.
CheckBoxList	Displays a group of check boxes that are typically bound to data.
RadioButtonList	Displays a group of radio buttons that are typically bound to data.

Validation Controls

You can add controls to a Web Forms page that automatically test what a user has typed into a text box, based on criteria that you specify. These controls are listed in Table 20-3.

Table 20-3.   Web Server Validation Controls

Control	Description
RequiredFieldValidator	Raises an error if a specific text control is left blank.
CompareValidator	Compares the value of a text control against a specified value using Boolean operators. Raises an error if the comparison returns *false*.
RangeValidator	Raises an error if the value in a text field falls outside a specified range.
RegularExpressionValidator	Raises an error if the value in a text field doesn't match a pattern specified using a regular expression.
CustomValidator	Calls custom logic and raises an error based on the return value.
ValidationSummary	Displays text of validation errors in one location.

Special-Purpose Controls

Among the Web server controls are a handful designed for specific functions, as described in Table 20-4.

Table 20-4.   Web Server Special-Purpose Controls

Control	Description
Calendar	Allows date display and selection
AdRotator	Displays randomly selected hyperlinked graphics supplied from a user-specified list
Table	Displays a table that can be configured dynamically at run time
Xml	Displays the contents of an XML file in the page, optionally after applying an XSLT transformation
CrystalReportViewer	Displays Crystal Report output in the page under programmatic control

Web server controls all derive from a base *WebControl* class defined in the *System.Web.UI.WebControls* namespace. This class provides basic properties for all the controls, such as their *BackColor*, *Width*, and *Enabled* properties. Each control class provides the additional members for the control.

When you add a Web server control to a page, the Web Forms Designer adds an instance of the control class to the page. For example, in the Calculator1 example, the Web Forms Designer added the following members for the buttons on the page:

```
public class Calculator1 : System.Web.UI.Page
{
    protected System.Web.UI.WebControls.Button SubtractButton;
    protected System.Web.UI.WebControls.Button AddButton;
    protected System.Web.UI.WebControls.Button MultiplyButton;
    protected System.Web.UI.WebControls.Button DivideButton;
    :
}
```

The page acts as the control's container. It has a *Controls* collection, which is a collection of the controls defined on the page.

Web Server Control Events

If you compare equivalent controls in Windows Forms and Web Forms, you'll notice that the Windows Forms controls have dozens of events. In contrast, Web Forms controls have fewer events. For example, the Windows Forms *Button* control has not just the *Click* event, but also drag and drop events, mouse events, move events, and so on. In contrast, the Web Forms *Button* control has, for most practical purposes, variations on only a single event: *Click*.

This discrepancy again underscores the different processing model for Web Forms. The basic purpose of a Web Forms button is to submit the page to the server, so the only event you really care about is something like the *Click* event. It doesn't make sense for the *Button* Web server control to expose (for example) a *Mouseover* event because you wouldn't want to send the page to the server each time the user moved the mouse over the button. You can use client script for these kinds of functions if you need them in your page.

In fact, to say that Web Forms pages have events at all is something of an artifice. In Web processing generally, when a page is submitted to the server, there's no real event. The browser simply sends a string (the HTTP request) to the server containing information such as the name of the process to call and the values of any controls on the page. The ASP.NET architecture takes this comparatively primitive information and translates it into a processing model that works much like true event handling in a Windows Form.

As mentioned, when you use the Visual Studio .NET Web Forms Designer to create an event handler for a control, the designer creates the event wireup and an event handling method. The method signature is the typical signature for events in the .NET Framework, passing a reference to the originating object and an instance of the appropriate event argument object. For example, this is the signature for a button's *Click* event:

```
private void AddButton_Click(object sender, System.EventArgs e){ }
```

When a *Button* server control is clicked, it immediately posts the page to the server. Not all Web server controls immediately post the page back, however. For example, the *DropDownList* and *ListBox* controls expose a *SelectedIndex-Changed* event that's raised to indicate that the user has selected something in the control. By default, when this event occurs, the page isn't immediately posted. Instead, the event is "cached" until another event posts the page, such as a *Button* control's *Click* event. Only when the page is posted is the *SelectedIndexChanged* event handler called, followed by the button's *Click* event.

All controls can post the page immediately and raise their event if you set their *AutoPostBack* property to *true*. This technique is useful, for example, when a user's selection in a list box affects the contents of other controls.

Creating a Web Forms Page with Control Events

To see some of the features of events in Web Forms, let's create a Web Forms page that exercises some Web server controls. The premise of this page is that you're choosing display attributes such as font, font size, and background for some text on the page. The page might look something like Figure 20-4.

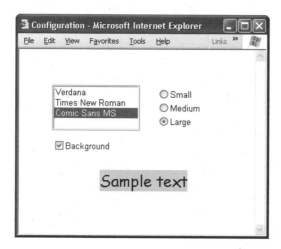

Figure 20-4. A Web Forms page that contains various Web Forms controls.

All the controls will post back, so you can see the effect of your choices immediately, and the page doesn't need a *Button* control.

Creating the Configuration Web Forms Page

Add a Web Forms page named Configuration to your Visual C# Web application project. Add the following controls, and set their properties as indicated in the following table.

Control	Property Settings
ListBox	*ID*: *FontsListBox*
	AutoPostBack: *True*
Checkbox	*ID*: *BackgroundCheckBox*
	AutoPostBack: *True*
	Checked: *False* (default)
	Text: *Background*

(continued)

Control	Property Settings
RadioButton	*ID*: *SmallRadioButton*
	AutoPostBack: *True*
	Checked: *False* (default)
	GroupName: *FontSize*
RadioButton	*ID*: *MediumRadioButton*
	AutoPostBack: *True*
	Checked: *True*
	GroupName: *FontSize*
RadioButton	*ID*: *LargeRadioButton*
	AutoPostBack: *True*
	Checked: *False* (default)
	GroupName: *FontSize*
Label	*ID*: *SampleLabelText*
	BackColor: *White*
	Font-Names: *Verdana*
	Font-Size: *Medium*
	Text: *Sample Text*

When you've finished, you'll have a page with an assortment of controls on it, most of which will cause the page to be posted to the server and therefore show an immediate effect when you change the controls' values.

Creating List Items for the *ListBox* Control

The *ListBox* control will contain three items that list the names of fonts. Because these are static items (and not, for example, read from a data source), you can create the items at design time in the Properties window. To create list items for the *ListBox* control, follow these steps:

1. Select the ListBox control, and press F4 to open the Properties window.

2. For the *Items* property value, click the ellipsis button to open the List-Item Collection Editor.

3. Click Add three times to add three items.

4. Select the first item in the Members list, and in the right-hand pane, set the *Text* property to *Verdana*.

5. Repeat step 4 for the other two items, setting their *Text* properties to *Times New Roman* and *Comic Sans MS*.

Figure 20-5 shows what the Collection Editor will look like when you've finished adding the three items.

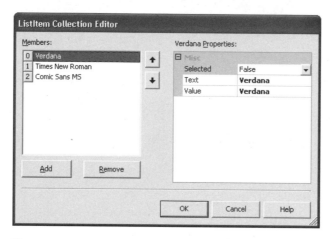

Figure 20-5. The ListItem Collection Editor, with three items added.

> **Note** You can use any fonts you want, but you must enter the exact names for the fonts.

6. Click OK to close the Collection Editor.

If you look at the page in HTML view in the designer, the control will look something like this:

```
<asp:ListBox id="FontsListBox"
    style="Z-INDEX: 101; LEFT: 70px; POSITION: absolute; TOP: 91px"
    runat="server" AutoPostBack="True">
    <asp:ListItem Value="Verdana">Verdana</asp:ListItem>
    <asp:ListItem Value="Times New Roman">Times New Roman</asp:ListItem>
    <asp:ListItem Value="Comic Sans MS">Comic Sans MS</asp:ListItem>
</asp:ListBox>
```

Creating the Event Handlers

You need an event handler for each control so that when the control's property value changes, the sample text in the *SampleLabelText* control is updated. In this section, we'll examine the event handler for each control that causes an automatic postback.

We can start by creating a handler for the *ListBox* control's *SelectedIndex-Changed* event and setting the *Font.Name* property of the label to the selected text. The handler will look like this:

```
private void FontsListBox_SelectedIndexChanged(object sender,
                                               System.EventArgs e)
{
    SampleLabelText.Font.Name = FontsListBox.SelectedItem.Text;
}
```

In the handler for the *CheckBox* control's *CheckedChanged* event, you want a handler that sets the *BackColor* property of the *Label* control if the check box is checked. The *BackColor* property must be set to a member of the *Color* structure. The code looks like this:

```
private void BackgroundCheckBox_CheckedChanged(object sender,
                                               System.EventArgs e)
{
    if (BackgroundCheckBox.Checked == true)
        SampleLabelText.BackColor = System.Drawing.Color.Red;
    else
        SampleLabelText.BackColor = System.Drawing.Color.White;
}
```

Because the page contains three grouped radio buttons, and because these buttons perform almost exactly the same task when clicked, you can create a single event handling method that will be called from all three radio buttons. To do so, follow these steps:

1. Select the first radio button (*SmallRadioButton*), and in the Properties window, click the Events toolbar button to display the control's events.

2. In the *CheckedChanged* event box, type *ResetFontSize*, which will create a handler with that name.

3. Select the *MediumRadioButton* control, and in its *CheckedChanged* event box, select ResetFontSize from the drop-down list.

4. Repeat step 3 for the *LargeRadioButton* control.

The *CheckedChanged* event of all three controls is now bound to the same method. In the event handler, test to see which radio button is checked and set the *SampleLabelText* control's *Font.Size* property accordingly. The *Font.Size* property is set to an instance of the *FontUnit* class. The code might look like this:

```
private void ResetFontSize(object sender, System.EventArgs e)
{
    if(SmallRadioButton.Checked)
```

(continued)

```
        SampleLabelText.Font.Size = new FontUnit("Small");
    else if (MediumRadioButton.Checked)
        SampleLabelText.Font.Size = new FontUnit("Medium");
    else if (LargeRadioButton.Checked)
        SampleLabelText.Font.Size = new FontUnit("Large");
}
```

In Solution Explorer, right-click the Configuration.aspx file and choose Build And Browse, and then use the controls to change the sample text.

HTML Server Controls and Other Controls for Web Forms Pages

In this chapter, you use the Web server controls, which are declared in the .aspx file with the *<asp:>* prefix (namespace identifier).

ASP.NET offers other types of controls that you can use on Web Forms as well. The most common alternative to Web server controls is HTML server controls. These are standard HTML elements that have been tagged so that ASP.NET recognizes them during page processing and creates server-side instances of them. You can turn any HTML element into a control by adding the attribute *runat="server"* and providing an ID you can use to refer to it in code. The following example shows a standard HTML text box (*Input* element) that's tagged as an HTML server control:

```
<input type="text" value="An HTML control" runat="server" id="Text1">
```

When the page runs, it will contain an instance of the *System.Web.UI.HtmlControls.HtmlInputText* class named *Text1*. HTML server controls essentially provide a server-programmable version of an HTML element. The element's attributes, such as *Value* and *Name*, map exactly to control properties, and there's no type checking of property values because they're all strings.

HTML server controls are useful if you're already familiar with the corresponding HTML elements. You can take an existing HTML page and turn it into a Web Forms page by simply changing the page extension to .aspx and tagging the HTML elements you need as server controls. HTML server controls are also useful if you want to specify exactly how the control is rendered.

You can use either Web server controls or HTML server controls (or both) in your page. There's some overlap between the two types. For example, buttons, text boxes, and check boxes are available as both Web server controls and HTML server controls. When there are similar controls of both types, they work almost the same.

HTML Server Controls and Other Controls for Web Forms Pages   *(continued)*

In general, unless you have a specific preference for HTML server controls, you should use Web server controls. And those aren't your only choices. The Web Forms page architecture is open, and third parties are free to create additional controls. For example, Microsoft offers a Mobile Internet Toolkit, which comes with a group of Web Forms controls that allow you to create pages for mobile devices.

Finally, you can also create your own server controls for specialized purposes. You can create user controls, which are essentially Web Forms pages that are configured so that you can embed them in other pages. It's also possible to create a custom control from scratch, deriving from specific Web Forms base classes and programming the control as you would a component, with its own properties, methods, events, and design-time behavior.

Maintaining State: Persisting Values Between Round-Trips

Because a page and its controls are regenerated each time the page makes a round-trip, the state of the page isn't preserved—that is, the value of its members is lost. This is a particularly subtle concept that's hard to get used to when you first program with Web Forms because it's so different from Windows Forms. Imagine that you have a page in which you've created a member to keep a count of the number of times the user clicks the Sumbit button. In a Windows Form, you initialize the variable at form load and then increment it whenever the user clicks the button. In a Web Form, the page, and thus the member you've created, is reinitialized each time the user clicks the button. You can increment the variable in the button click handler, but the value is never higher than 1.

Actually, the Web Forms page architecture does help you out somewhat. The page includes a property named *ViewState*. One of the last things a control does during page processing is store all the nondefault values of its properties in *ViewState*. The information stored in *ViewState* is rendered in the page as an HTML hidden field and is sent to the browser as part of the page. When the page is posted back to the server, during its initialization stage, the page reads the information back out of *ViewState* and plugs the values into the controls. The effect is that controls appear to be maintaining their state between round-trips.

However, if you create your own members during page processing, their values are not automatically saved in *ViewState*. If you need to persist values between round-trips, you have to do so yourself.

There are a couple of ways to persist state yourself. You can store values on the client by putting them in the page's *ViewState* property and then reading them back out when the page is posted. In this scenario, you use the page itself to persist values. Cookies are another possibility for persisting values on the client.

Alternatively, you can persist values on the server. ASP.NET provides two server-based caches that you can use as shared memory for your pages. The first is session state, which is a temporary cache available to a particular browser session (making it user-specific). The second is application state, which is a cache that's global to all pages in your application and to all separate users of the application. You can also use various .NET facilities to store values in a database, an XML file, a text file, or another storage medium available from server code.

No one strategy is best for all scenarios. Storing values in *ViewState* makes the page larger (and thus slower to load), which can affect performance if you store large values such as datasets. Storing values in *ViewState* is also less secure because users can see (and possibly modify) *ViewState* information. On the other hand, storing values in session or application state uses server memory. In particular, you need to use session state carefully because there's a different session state for every concurrent user of your application.

Creating a Web Forms Page That Persists Values

To illustrate how to use *ViewState* to persist values between round-trips, let's create a variation of the Calculator1 Web Forms page from earlier in this chapter. This variation will work a little bit more like a real calculator. Instead of two text boxes, it will have only one. You type in a value and then click an operator button. You then type the second (or third or fourth) number and click the operator button that you want to apply. The result is displayed in the text box, as shown in Figure 20-6.

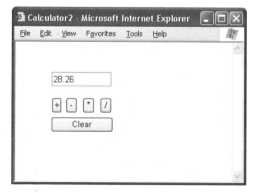

Figure 20-6.   The sample Web Forms page Calculator2.

> **Note**   Real calculators have individual buttons for each number. You could create individual number buttons here, but because clicking a button causes a round-trip to the server, that would be an impractical way to enter numbers.

This scenario requires that you store a running total, which we'll do by putting the total into *ViewState*. The page's *ViewState* property is an instance of the *StateBag* class, which in turn is implemented as a *Dictionary* object that allows you to store values in key-item pairs. You can assign values directly to *ViewState* using syntax such as the following:

```
ViewState["mystring"] = "a string value";
ViewState["myint"] = 42;
```

When you get values back out, they're typed as objects, so you need to cast them appropriately, as shown here:

```
string myvalue = (ViewState["mystring"]).ToString();
int i = int.Parse(ViewState["total"].ToString());
```

> **Note**   We could also store the running total in session state. For data this small, however, the extra space for storing *ViewState* information is insignificant, so we might as well not incur any server overhead by using session state.

When you enter the first number and click an operator button, you don't want to calculate a total yet. Instead, you want to wait until the second (or third or fourth) number is entered. The page needs to maintain a flag indicating whether this is a new calculation; this flag is set to *true* until after you've entered the first number. You have to store this flag in *ViewState* also.

Storing a running total and a new calculation flag introduces a new requirement. The first time the page runs, there's no running total to store, plus you have to initialize the flag. The *Page_Load* event is raised the first time the page runs as well as every time a button is clicked, so it's not sufficient to simply put the initialization logic in that handler. The solution is to check a page property named *IsPostBack*, which is set to *false* the first time the page runs and to *true* any time the page is running in response to a postback event.

Creating the Calculator2 Web Forms Page

This page is slightly simpler than the Calculator1 example. To create the page, add a Web Forms page named Calculator2 to your Visual C# Web application. Add the controls from the following table, and set their properties as indicated.

Control	Property Settings
TextBox	ID: *Number1TextBox*
	Text: (blank text)
Button	ID: *AddButton*
	Text: +
	CommandName: *Add*
Button	ID: *SubtractButton*
	Text:–
	CommandName: *Subtract*
Button	ID: *MultiplyButton*
	Text: *
	CommandName: *Multiply*
Button	ID: *DivideButton*
	Text: /
	CommandName: *Divide*
Button	ID: *ClearButton*
	Text: *Clear*

Notice that the *CommandName* property is set for all four of the operator buttons. The *CommandName* property gives you a way to pass command-specific information to a handler. As you'll see in the next section, we can create a single handler for all four buttons but still be able to tell easily which button was clicked.

Adding Code to the Calculator2 Web Forms Page

To add code to the Calculator2 page, open the code file for the page. (Right-click the page in Solution Explorer, and choose View Code from the shortcut menu.) Create two private member variables to hold the running total and the flag indicating whether this is a new calculation, as shown here:

```
private double StoredValue;
private bool NewCalculationFlag;
```

Now create the initialization logic in the *Page_Load* handler. If this is the first time the page is running (that is, if the page's *IsPostBack* property is *false*), you need to initialize the two keys in the *ViewState* property to hold the running total and the flag. However, if the page is being posted back, you need to read the keys back out of the *ViewState* property and into the member variables, as shown here:

```
private void Page_Load(object sender, System.EventArgs e)
{
    if(this.IsPostBack)
    {
        StoredValue = double.Parse(ViewState["total"].ToString());
        NewCalculationFlag =
            bool.Parse(ViewState["NewCalculationFlag"].ToString());
    }
    else
    {
        ViewState["total"] = 0;
        ViewState["NewCalculationFlag"] = true;
    }
}
```

When an operator button is clicked, the action that occurs depends on whether this is the first number in the calculation. If it is, all we need to do is store that number, our initial running total, because there's nothing to calculate yet. But if it's not the first number, we can do the calculation. The result is a new running total, which is displayed in the text box and is stored back into *ViewState*.

The logic for each button differs by only one line—the actual calculation—so it's reasonable to use a single handler for all of them. Create a handler named *Calculate* for the *AddButton* control's *Command* event (not the *Click* event). The *Command* event is similar to the *Click* event, except that it passes to the handler the value of the sender object's *CommandName* property. Bind the *Command* event of the remaining buttons to this same event. Refer to the section "Creating the Event Handlers," earlier in this chapter, for the procedure for creating a single handler for multiple buttons.

In the handler, check the *NewCalculationFlag* variable, and if it's *true*, clear the flag and store both the flag and the number from the text box in *ViewState*. Otherwise, get the running value out of *ViewState* and perform the calculation with the new value in the text box. To determine which operator button was clicked, test the *CommandName* property of the *CommandEventArgs* object passed in the handler. In the code on the following page, this is done with a *switch* statement.

```
private void Calculate(object sender,
                    System.Web.UI.WebControls.CommandEventArgs e)
{
    if(NewCalculationFlag)
    {
        ViewState["NewCalculationFlag"] = false;
        ViewState["total"] = Number1TextBox.Text;
    }
    else
    {
        switch(e.CommandName)
        {
            case("Subtract"):
            {
                StoredValue -= double.Parse(Number1TextBox.Text);
                break;
            }
            case("Add"):
            {
                StoredValue += double.Parse(Number1TextBox.Text);
                break;
            }
            case("Multiply"):
            {
                StoredValue *= double.Parse(Number1TextBox.Text);
                break;
            }
            case("Divide"):
            {
                if((double.Parse(Number1TextBox.Text) != 0))
                    StoredValue /= double.Parse(Number1TextBox.Text);
                break;
            }
        }
        ViewState["total"] = StoredValue;
        Number1TextBox.Text = StoredValue.ToString();
    }
}
```

Finally create a handler for the Clear button that resets the *ViewState* values to their initial state and that clears the *TextBox* control, as shown here:

```
private void ClearButton_Click(object sender, System.EventArgs e)
{
    Number1TextBox.Text = "";
    ViewState["total"] = 0;
    ViewState["NewCalculationFlag"] = true;
}
```

Working with Data in Web Forms

One of the primary reasons to create programmable Web pages at all is to work with data. Web Forms pages allow you to access, display, and edit data from a variety of sources.

As with other aspects of Web programming, data access in Web Forms is somewhat different than it is in Windows Forms or in other forms packages you might be familiar with. The most interesting differences are listed here:

- **Wide range of sources**   You can bind controls in a Web Forms page to everything from an array or a collection, to a database table, to an XML document. A data source needs only to implement the *IEnumerable* interface for it to be valid for data binding in Web Forms. For example, you can bind the contents of a control to a *DropDownList* or *ListBox* control elsewhere in the page. The most common source of data is databases, of course, and for that you typically use ADO.NET.

- **One-way data binding**   Data binding in Web Forms pages is read-only—that is, the data binding mechanism will fetch data from the source for you, but it doesn't automatically write changes back. You can certainly update data sources from Web Forms pages, but you have to provide code to do this yourself. The rationale for this initially surprising strategy is, once again, the differences in how Web applications work. A large majority of Web pages that work with data simply display it. Many fewer pages allow users to edit or enter data that needs to be saved. (Think about browsing commercial Web sites and how rarely you enter data.) Therefore, Web Forms pages don't incur the overhead of generating the extra code for updates when the code is used comparatively rarely.

- **Disconnected data access**   The inherently disconnected nature of Web Forms pages extends to data access as well. The page interacts with an external data source such as a database only long enough to fetch data or make an update, which promotes efficient use of database resources. But remember that the page is re-created with each round-trip. This could potentially mean having to refetch data each time. In particular, this can make the use of ADO.NET datasets a little problematic. We'll look at this topic in more detail in the sections that follow.

Multi-Tiered Data Access

In many applications, data access often isn't built into the presentation layer at all. Instead, data access is built into a business component that's called from the presentation layer.

In Web Forms applications, this business component would be a Web service. The Web service and its calling components usually exchange data in the form of an ADO.NET dataset. For example, a Web Forms page might call a Web service method to get customer information. The data will be sent back to the Web Forms page as a dataset. (Under the covers, the Web service and the calling component automatically serialize and deserialize the dataset as XML data in order to send it across the Web.)

Calling Web service methods to read and write data is slightly more involved than the basic data access discussed in this chapter, but not much. For details, see Chapter 21.

Creating the DataBinding_Simple Web Forms Page

To begin our examination of data binding, let's create the simplest possible scenario. Create a new Web Forms page named DataBinding_Simple. Use the Web Forms tab of the Toolbox to add a *ListBox* control and a *Button* control to the page. Name the *Button* control Submit. Create a *Page_Load* handler that looks like this:

```
private void Page_Load(object sender, System.EventArgs e)
{
    if (!this.IsPostBack)
    {
        ArrayList animals = new ArrayList();
        animals.Add("Dog");
        animals.Add("Cat");
        animals.Add("Goldfish");
        ListBox1.DataSource = animals;
        ListBox1.DataBind();
    }
}
```

When you run the page, the list box is filled in. Click the Submit button, and notice that the page makes its usual round-trip.

A number of data-binding features are illustrated here. First is that the data source here is simply an *ArrayList* object that you happen to create at run time.

Note also that you bind the *ListBox* control to the data source by setting its *DataSource* property.

The call to the control's *DataBind* method is important. In Web Forms pages, you specify data binding by setting various control properties (such as *DataSource* in this instance). But the actual data binding doesn't occur until the control's *DataBind* method is called. It's only then that the control performs whatever internal logic is required to read the data into the control. If the method isn't called, nothing happens. The *DataBind* method is part of the *System.Web.UI.Control* base class and is available for all Web server controls. You can call the method for an individual control or, because it applies to child controls, call the method for the page (*this.DataBind*), and the call will be cascaded to all controls on the page.

Finally, notice that the binding is set within a test for a postback—in this case, the data binding occurs only the first time the page is called. When you click the Submit button, this code is *not* being executed. If you didn't make this test, the data source would be re-created with each round-trip. For this trivial sample, it would make no difference, but when you're accessing a database, it can be very inefficient to perform a query every time the user clicks a button. After the first time the data source has been created and the *ListBox* control is bound to it, you don't need to rebind. The first time the page runs, the list items are created from the data. Thereafter, the control saves its state (the items) in *ViewState*.

Binding to an ADO.NET Dataset

To bind to a database, you generally use ADO.NET. In a Windows Form, this means that you create a dataset, read data into it from the database, and then bind the controls to dataset tables and columns. That way, you can read and write data while disconnected from the data source. For details, see Chapter 18.

You can use datasets in Web Forms pages as well, but there are some subtle differences. To demonstrate how a dataset is used, create a new page named DataBinding_Dataset1 or reuse the example page containing the *ListBox* control from the previous section. From the Data tab of the Toolbox, drag a data adapter (*SqlDataAdapter* or *OleDbDataAdapter*) control onto the page, and use the Data Adapter Configuration Wizard to configure the adapter to read a small table from a database you have access to. The following example assumes that you have access to the Categories table from the sample Northwind database included with Microsoft Access and SQL Server. If you're using a different database, you'll need to adjust accordingly. After the adapter has been configured, choose Generate Dataset from the Data menu and create a new dataset class named *dsCategories*. This will add an instance of the dataset named *dsCategories1* to your page.

Create a *Page_Load* handler that looks like this:

```
private void Page_Load(object sender, System.EventArgs e)
{
    if(!this.IsPostBack)
    {
        oleDbDataAdapter1.Fill(dsCategories1);
        ListBox1.DataSource = dsCategories1;
        ListBox1.DataMember = "Categories";
        ListBox1.DataTextField = "CategoryName";
        ListBox1.DataValueField = "CategoryID";
        ListBox1.DataBind();
    }
}
```

This is similar to the DataBinding_Simple example, except that you first fill the dataset and then bind the *ListBox* control to the dataset table. As before, you must call the *DataBind* method to get the control to read its data source.

The way the page in the DataBinding_Simple example is currently coded, the dataset is disposed of along with the page itself when the page has finished processing. This isn't a particularly intelligent way to use a dataset, which is after all designed to be an offline cache. In this example, the cache is thrown away as soon as it's filled.

There are two solutions to this dilemma. One is to bypass the dataset altogether and work directly against the database. The other is to save the dataset between round-trips.

Working Directly Against the Database

If the only thing you need to do is read data from the database and display it, you can often bypass the overhead of filling a dataset and use a data command instead. The data command allows you to directly execute a SQL statement—typically a *Select* command or a stored procedure—and read the results directly. If your command returns multiple records, you can read it with a data reader, which provides you with very fast, read-only, forward-only access to a result set.

The following example shows how you can use a data reader to get the same data that you got from the dataset in the DataBinding_Dataset1 example. The process requires more code because you have to create the reader, execute the command, and use the reader to fetch records, all manually. You also have to explicitly open and close the connection. (For the example, it's assumed that you have a connection in the page that's already configured to open the database you want to use.) All things considered, however, this code is more efficient.

```
private void Page_Load(object sender, System.EventArgs e)
```

```
    {
        if (!this.IsPostBack)
        {
            System.Data.OleDb.OleDbDataReader dreader;
            oleDbConnection1.Open();
            oleDbCommand1.CommandText =
                "Select CategoryId, CategoryName From Categories";
            dreader = oleDbCommand1.ExecuteReader();
            while(dreader.Read())
            {
                ListItem li = new ListItem();
                li.Text = dreader[1].ToString();
                li.Value = dreader[0].ToString();
                ListBox1.Items.Add(li);
            }
            dreader.Close();
            oleDbConnection1.Close();
        }
    }
```

Storing Datasets

Even though a data reader is more efficient in many cases, there are still times when you want to use a dataset, including the following:

■ When the page needs access to data in multiple tables

■ When you want to reuse the same data, such as in paging or filtering

■ When you're exchanging data with a Web service

If you do use a dataset, it's generally efficient to fill the dataset the first time the page runs and then store the dataset. The next time the page runs, you retrieve the dataset instead of requerying the database and refilling it. If this sounds familiar, it's because it's the same state management issue that comes up for other values you want to maintain between round-trips. You can store the dataset in *ViewState* on the client—in which case, the entire dataset is encoded in the page and sent to the browser and then sent back to you when the page is posted again. Alternatively, you can use a server-based state option for the dataset, such as session state. As before, there's no single recommended technique.

The following example shows how you can store a dataset in session state:

```
private void Page_Load(object sender, System.EventArgs e)
{
    if(this.IsPostBack)
    {
```

(continued)

```
            dsCategories1 = (dsCategories) Session["dsCategories"];
        }
        else
        {

            oleDbDataAdapter1.Fill(dsCategories1);
            Session["dsCategories"] = dsCategories1;
            ListBox1.DataSource = dsCategories1;
            ListBox1.DataMember = "Categories";
            ListBox1.DataTextField = "CategoryName";
            ListBox1.DataValueField = "CategoryID";
            ListBox1.DataBind();
        }

    }
```

Because objects stored in session state are typed as objects, you have to cast them when you get them out. Here we're using the generated dataset class *dsCategories*, which is the type for the instance *dsCategories1*.

The following code shows how to save the same dataset in *ViewState*. You can't store objects in *ViewState* that aren't serializable. Datasets aren't serializable, so you must go through the extra step of converting the dataset into a usable format. The usual solution is to call a dataset method that creates an XML representation of the dataset and store that. When the page is posted back, the XML is read back out of *ViewState* and converted back to dataset format. As usual, *ViewState* objects have to be cast from the object type to their true data type.

```
private void Page_Load(object sender, System.EventArgs e)
{
    if(this.IsPostBack)
    {
        System.IO.StringReader sr = new
            System.IO.StringReader((string)(ViewState["dsCategories"]));
        dsCategories1.ReadXml(sr);
    }
    else
    {
        oleDbDataAdapter1.Fill(dsCategories1);
        System.IO.StringWriter sw = new System.IO.StringWriter();
        dsCategories1.WriteXml(sw);
        ViewState["dsCategories"] = sw.ToString();
        ListBox1.DataSource = dsCategories1;
        ListBox1.DataMember = "Categories";
        ListBox1.DataTextField = "CategoryName";
        ListBox1.DataValueField = "CategoryID";
        ListBox1.DataBind();
    }

}
```

Working with List Data Controls

You can bind any server control to a data source, and in fact, you can bind any property of any control to data. For example, you can bind a *TextBox* control's *Text* property to a database column, but you can also bind its *BackColor*, *Width*, and other properties to suitable data sources. That aside, a number of Web server controls are specifically designed to help you display data: *Repeater*, *DataList*, and *DataGrid*. All three controls display multiple records—that is, lists of data. For detailed information about these controls, refer to the MSDN Library. We'll look at the *DataList* and *DataGrid* controls in more detail in the sections that follow.

The *DataList* Control

To give you an idea of the benefits of using templates to display data, let's work with the *DataList* control. Create a new Web Forms page named DataList. For the data, add a data adapter from the Data tab of the Toolbox and use the Data Adapter Configuration Wizard to point to a database and table. This example assumes that you're using the Categories table of the Northwind database, fetching the columns CategoryID and CategoryName. Drag a *DataSet* control onto the page, and reuse the *dsCategories* dataset class you defined earlier in this chapter, in the section "Binding to an ADO.NET Dataset." If the dataset isn't available in your project, generate a new dataset class and name it *dsCategories,* which will create an instance of the dataset named *dsCategories1* in the page.

Now drag a *DataList* control onto the page from the Web Forms tab of the Toolbox. You'll see only a gray rectangle that acts as a placeholder for the control. Because the *DataList* control has no inherent user interface, it's up to you to define what its output looks like.

Select the control, and in the Properties window, set the control's *Data-Source* property to *dsCategories1* (or whatever your dataset is named) and its *DataMember* property to *Categories*, which is the name of the data table in your dataset. You have now specified where the control will get the entire list of data from. In a moment, you'll specify individual data items.

Right-click the control, choose Edit Template from the shortcut menu, and then choose Item Templates to put the control into "template editing" mode. To define how the data is displayed, you drag controls into the Item Templates boxes. You can also type static text into the boxes. For example, from the Web Forms tab of the Toolbox, drag two *Label* controls into the ItemTemplate box and set their *Text* property to an empty string. Type parentheses around the second control so that it looks like Figure 20-7.

Figure 20-7. The *DataList* control in template editing mode, showing the two labels for the item template.

Although the ItemTemplate box appears somewhat cramped, you're free to drag as many controls into it as you need. You can also simply type carriage returns to make the box bigger. (You can also resize the *DataList* control if needed.) Basically, you're creating a region with whatever layout you want to use for each record. When the page runs, your layout will be repeated once for each record in the data source.

To display a specific data column, you data-bind the controls. Right-click the first label, and choose Properties on the shortcut menu to open the control's Properties window. Click the button in the (DataBindings) box to open the Data-Bindings dialog box. Under Bindable Properties, make sure Text is selected. Under Simple Binding, open the node for Container, and for DataItem, select CategoryName.

You've created a *data-binding expression* that will be resolved at run time. (You can see the expression in the disabled Custom Binding Expression box.) The expression is shown here:

```
DataBinder.Eval(Container, "DataItem.CategoryName")
```

This expression specifies that the control is getting its data from its container (the *DataList* control). As the *DataList* control is being processed, it fetches each data record in turn and makes the data available in its *DataItem* property. The expression indicates that this *Label* control should be bound at run time to the current *DataItem* object, extracting its *CategoryName* value.

Repeat the data binding process for the second label, binding it to the *CategoryID* value instead. Right-click the *DataList* control, and choose End Template Editing from the shortcut menu. Now the control finally looks like something—namely, the layout you specified in ItemTemplate.

Let's pretty things up a little, primarily to demonstrate the design-time features of the *DataList* control. Open the Properties window, choose the Auto Format link, and then choose a scheme.

Click the Property Builder link, which opens a builder that greatly simplifies setting the many properties supported by the *DataList* control. On the General tab, under Repeat Layout, set Columns to *2* to indicate that you want to display the data in two columns. On the Format tab, open the Items node and select Normal Items. Set the font to Verdana and the size to X-Small.

That's it for the layout. As with all data binding in Web Forms, you need to get your data and then explicitly call the control's *DataBind* method. Add code to the *Page_Load* handler that looks like the following, adjusting the names of your data objects as required:

```
private void Page_Load(object sender, System.EventArgs e)
{
    if(this.IsPostBack)
    {
        dsCategories1 = (dsCategories)Session["dsCategories"];
    }
    else
    {
        oleDbDataAdapter1.Fill(dsCategories1);
        Session["dsCategories"] = dsCategories1;
        DataList1.DataBind();
    }
}
```

Run the page, and you'll see that the data has been displayed exactly according to your layout. You can create much more sophisticated layouts by specifying a different layout such as the Alternating ItemTemplate (displayed every other record), a header and footer template, or a SeparatorTemplate. We won't cover these templates in this chapter. Refer to the MSDN Library for more information about these properties. To get some insight into editing data in a Web Forms page, let's move on to the *DataGrid* control.

The *DataGrid* Control

DataGrid is the most sophisticated of the Web server controls for working with data. Paradoxically, for simple data display, it's easier to work with than the *DataList* and *Repeater* controls, primarily because you don't have to define templates. In this section, you'll first learn how to use the *DataGrid* control as a read-only control for data. After that, you'll see what's involved in using it as a control for editing data. To some extent, the *DataGrid* control is the model of any kind of data update you do from a Web Forms page.

Creating the DataGrid Web page   To see how a *DataGrid* control works on a Web page, first create a new Web Forms page named DataGrid. Add a data connection, a data adapter, and a dataset as you did for the *DataList* control in the previous section. If you followed that example, this will give you a dataset that contains the Categories table from the Northwind database, with the columns CategoryID and CategoryName. The dataset class name is *dsCategories*, and the instance of the class in the page is named *dsCategories1*.

From the Web Forms tab of the Toolbox, drag a *DataGrid* control onto the page. In the Properties window, click the Auto Format link and specify a format for the grid. Then click the Property Builder link in the Properties window to configure the control for data access.

On the General tab, specify *dsCategories1* for the *DataSource* property and *Categories* for the *DataMember* property. In the Data Key Field box, choose *CategoryID*. This value will help you locate the appropriate record later when you want to update it.

On the Columns tab, clear the Create Columns Automatically At Run Time check box. If you leave this check box selected, the grid will render columns based on the data columns it finds in the data source. That would work fine in this case, but you want to customize the display a little bit, which requires that you define explicit columns instead. Under Available Columns, open the Data Fields node. Select CategoryID, and click the > button to copy the column to the Selected Columns list. Do the same for CategoryName. Your grid now has two columns. In the Selected Columns list, select CategoryID, and in the BoundColumn Properties section, select the Read Only check box. This setting will apply later, when you add editing to the grid.

Add a *Page_Load* handler using the same logic that you used for the *DataList* control. The handler will look something like this:

```
private void Page_Load(object sender, System.EventArgs e)
{
    if(this.IsPostBack)
    {
        dsCategories1 = (dsCategories)Session["dsCategories"];
    }
    else
    {
        oleDbDataAdapter1.Fill(dsCategories1);
        Session["dsCategories"] = dsCategories1;
        DataGrid1.DataBind();
    }
}
```

As usual, you're storing the dataset after filling it and restoring it with each round-trip. Run the page, and you'll see that the grid is filled with information from the Categories table.

There's no inherent way to edit the data displayed in the grid. The *DataGrid* control does offer editing capability, which works like this: You add an Edit button column to the grid, which then displays an Edit hyperlink in each row of the grid, as shown in Figure 20-8. When the user clicks one of these Edit links, that row is redisplayed with text boxes for the editable data and with Update and Cancel links in place of the original Edit link. When the user clicks Update, the data in that row is updated and the row is redisplayed in its normal mode.

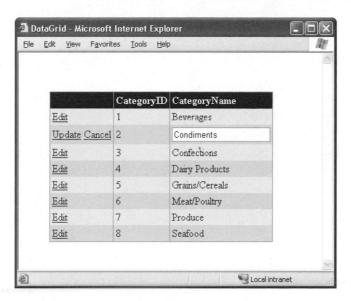

Figure 20-8. A *DataGrid* control with a row in edit mode, showing the Update and Cancel links.

Editing the data displayed in the grid   The rub is that you have to do most of the data editing work yourself. The *DataGrid* control displays the links automatically, and it raises events when users click the buttons. But you must code the switch to edit mode and, especially, the actual update. Fortunately, this isn't a particularly difficult task.

To add the edit buttons, select the grid again, open the Property Builder again, and go to the Columns tab. Under Available Columns, open the Button Column node and add an Edit, Update, and Cancel column to the Selected Columns list. If you want, use the arrows to the right to move the Edit button column to the first (that is, leftmost) position in the grid. Close the Property Builder, and notice that the *DataGrid* control now shows the Edit button column at design time.

When the user clicks a particular Edit button, an *EditCommand* event is raised for the grid. To put a specific row into edit mode, you need to set the *DataGrid* control's *EditItemIndex* property to the index of that row. How do you know which row the user clicked? The *DataGridComandEventArgs* object *e* for the *EditCommand* event contains the entire current row in the form of a *DataGridItem* object. You can work backward from this object and extract its

ItemIndex property to get the row offset in the grid. This sounds complicated, but it's actually quite simple. The code for the *EditCommand* handler almost always looks like this:

```
private void DataGrid1_EditCommand(object source,
    System.Web.UI.WebControls.DataGridCommandEventArgs e)
{
    DataGrid1.EditItemIndex = e.Item.ItemIndex;
    DataGrid1.DataBind();
}
```

After setting the grid's *EditItemIndex* property, you have to rebind it to cause it to be redisplayed in edit mode.

When the row is in edit mode, the Edit Button column contains Update and Cancel links. To cancel editing, you handle the *CancelCommand* event, set the grid's *EditItemIndex* to -1, and then rebind, as shown here:

```
private void DataGrid1_CancelCommand(object source,
    System.Web.UI.WebControls.DataGridCommandEventArgs e)
{
    DataGrid1.EditItemIndex = -1;
    DataGrid1.DataBind();
}
```

If you run the page now and try clicking the Edit button, you should see the row displayed with a *TextBox* control for the *CategoryName* field. (The *CategoryID* property shouldn't be displayed in a text box because you set it to be read-only when you first defined the column.) Clicking Cancel returns the row to display mode.

There's just one task left—namely, to handle an update. When the user clicks the Update button in edit mode, an *UpdateCommand* event is raised for the grid. You need to perform the following tasks:

1. Get the new or changed values of the *TextBox* controls in the editable row.

2. Use the new values to update the data source. In this case, you need to find the appropriate row in the dataset and copy the changed values into it. You then need to send the dataset changes back to the database.

3. Take the row out of edit mode and, as usual, rebind the grid. In this example, you also need to resave the dataset to session state because it has changes.

The code for the *UpdateCommand* handler is shown here:

```
private void DataGrid1_UpdateCommand(object source,
    System.Web.UI.WebControls.DataGridCommandEventArgs e)
{
    // Get the value of the editable TextBox in the third cell.
    TextBox tb = (TextBox) e.Item.Cells[2].Controls[0];
    String NewCategoryName = tb.Text;

    int categorykey = (int) DataGrid1.DataKeys[e.Item.ItemIndex];
    DataRow dr = dsCategories1.Categories.FindByCategoryID(categorykey);
    dr[1] = NewCategoryName;
    oleDbDataAdapter1.Update(dsCategories1);

    Session["dsCategories"] = dsCategories1;
    DataGrid1.EditItemIndex = -1;
    DataGrid1.DataBind();
}
```

When the row is in edit mode, it displays text boxes. To get their values, you have to dig fairly deeply into the *DataGrid* control's object model. Each row is an item containing a cell for each column. Each cell can contain controls, which you can access via the cell's *Controls* collection. For a simple scenario such as this one, the *TextBox* control is typically the first (and only) control in a given cell. The elements in the *Controls* collection are typed as objects, so you have to cast the object to a *TextBox* control. Then you can get the control's value.

The next task is to find and update the row in the dataset table that corresponds to the one being edited. It's usually not a good idea to assume that a row offset in the grid is the same as the row offset in a data table. (In this case, that's true, but in most cases it won't be.) The only reliable way to find the row in the data table is to find a match with the key of the row being edited. You can get the key of the current grid row by extracting it from the *DataGrid* control's *DataKeys* property, which contains a collection of the keys. This collection is available automatically as long as you set the grid's *DataKeyField* property (as you did when you first configured the grid), even if you don't display the key value in the grid. Once you have a key, you can use it to locate the data table row. You could loop through the table looking for a match, for example. In this case, you're using a typed dataset, in which each table exposes a *FindBy<key>* method. In the preceding code, the data table row is found by calling the *FindByCategoryID* method of the Categories table, passing it the key. Once you've got the data table row, you can set its columns to the new values you got earlier.

After updating the dataset, you propagate changes back to the database by calling the data adapter's *Update* method, which executes the appropriate SQL statements. Finally, because the dataset has changed, you need to make a new copy of it in session state. Then take the row out of edit mode and rebind the grid to show the new data in display mode.

Conclusion

ASP.NET and Web Forms provide you with a powerful way to create programmable Web pages in C#. Web Forms are server-based, meaning that the code runs on the server, producing HTML output that's sent to the browser. When users click a button in a Web Forms page, it sends the page to the server for processing—that is, it makes a round-trip. Because of the inherently stateless nature of the Web, you need to understand how the page and its controls maintain their values between round-trips and how you must do the same for values you want to preserve. Web server controls provide Web Forms pages with rich, consistent objects that you can work with using a standard event-driven model.

To access data in Web Forms, you can use datasets as you do in Windows Forms, but it's often more efficient to execute database commands directly. To display data in lists, you use the *Repeater*, *DataList*, and *DataGrid* controls. For the *Repeater* and *DataList* controls, you define templates in which you arrange controls and static text to specify the layout of each data item. The *DataGrid* control is the richest of the Web Forms data list controls; it provides you with the ability to add editing, although you must implement some of the logic yourself.

Web Forms and ASP.NET are complex areas in their own right, and the information in this chapter has provided only an overview of what they're for and how they work. For more in-depth information about Web Forms, refer to the MSDN Library.

21

SOAP and Web Services

In the .NET world, components are built by people with expertise in a given area and are placed close to the data that the components will work on. Other applications seeking access to that functionality or data can simply call the services of the needed components. This is the base concept of Web services: functionality is developed and hosted by experts and made available to those who need it.

In the world of the Internet, however, Web services have no way of knowing how a calling application is written, in what language it's written, or on what operating system it's running. Instead, these services must be available to any application that calls them. To ensure that the services are interoperable with any calling applications, Web services in the Microsoft .NET Framework make use of XML and the Simple Object Access Protocol (SOAP).

Understanding SOAP

SOAP is an XML-based messaging protocol that allows messages and components to be executed via an HTTP connection. The SOAP specification can be found at *http://www.w3.org/tr/soap*. By using the SOAP specification, applications can easily communicate and execute commands remotely. Because SOAP is XML-based, the applications can be on disparate systems. One application doesn't care about which operating system the other application runs on or which language it was developed in. As long as the SOAP specification is supported, the two applications can exchange messages. Those messages will contain the appropriate commands, parameters, and results.

Understanding Web Services

A Web service is an application that exposes functionality to clients, providing some service or access to data in a controlled manner. In many ways, Web services are analogous to the Distributed Component Object Model (DCOM) objects that many Microsoft developers are used to working with. The main difference, however, is that Web services are accessed through standards-based, open interfaces such as SOAP and HTTP.

As Web services are created, they'll be "owned" by the experts who develop them, whether the services are publicly available or private. These services can be called by applications on your local network or from across the Internet. Commands and messages will be received from client applications, and the results can be returned to the calling application. The applications can be written in any language and hosted on any operating system.

A .NET Web service is a Web application that consists of a number of *pages*, or *access points*, that are used to call functions. When you create a Web service project, the Microsoft Visual Studio .NET integrated development environment (IDE) creates a virtual Web directory that holds the project files. This section briefly describes the makeup of a Web service.

The *WebService* Directive

A Web service can include a number of access points, each defined by an .asmx file. This file is used to describe the Web service class that's being called. Within the file is a single *WebService* directive that identifies the page as a Web service, the language used to code the service, the location of the code for the Web service, and the Web service class name, as shown here:

```
<%@ WebService Language="c#" Codebehind="Service1.asmx.cs"
Class="WebService1.Service1" %>
```

The application code can then be found within the page identified by the *Code-behind* attribute of the directive.

Deriving from the *System. Web. Services. WebService* Class

Within the code file that the *Codebehind* attribute of the *WebService* directive identifies, a Web service class will be defined. This class will be the primary access point for this particular Web service component. It is identified by the *Class* attribute in the *WebService* directive and will inherit the *System.Web.Services.WebService* class, as shown here:

```
public class Service1 : System.Web.Services.WebService
{
    //All of the Web service code
}
```

By using this as the base class, the Web service will gain access to the standard Microsoft ASP.NET objects, including the following:

- **Application**   Holds application-level data, available to all users
- **Server**   Contains useful Web service utility functions and data
- **Session**   Holds user-specific data and session information
- **User**   Accesses information about the current user, if the user is authenticated

From the Web service class, you'll develop the code to support the functions you'll need. You'll write functions as you would in any other application so that they can be available to the Web service clients.

Using the *WebService* Attribute

When you use the Web service class as an access point, you can provide further documentation for your Web service. This documentation will be made available when the component is accessed through the discovery process, by accessing the Web service page and passing it the *wsdl* parameter (*http://localhost/WebService1/Service1.asmx?wsdl*). See the section "Identifying Web Services Using Discovery," later in this chapter, for a detailed description of the discovery process. In the Visual Studio .NET IDE, when you add the Web reference and click the View Documentation link, you'll see a dialog box similar to the one shown in Figure 21-1.

Figure 21-1. The Visual Studio .NET Add Web Reference dialog box, which allows you to browse for Web services.

To provide this additional documentation, you'll attach the *WebService* attribute to the Web service class by adding a tag to the line prior to the class declaration, as shown in the following code. The *WebService* attribute provides documentation based on the property settings that you supply.

```
[ WebService(
    Description="This is a sample Web service, with default names.",
    Namespace="http://www.mysite.com/", Name="My Web Service Name"
) ]
public class Service1 : System.Web.Services.WebService
{
    //All of the Web service code
}
```

The properties for the *WebService* attribute can include the following:

- **Description**   Provides a description of the Web service
- **Name**   Specifies a name for the Web service
- **Namespace**   Specifies an XML namespace for the Web service

Using the *WebMethod* Attribute

Any public method in the Web service class can be made available directly through the Web service. To make a method available, you simply add a line prior to the method definition, designating the method as a Web service method. You'll do this using the *WebMethod* attribute, as shown here:

```
[WebMethod(
    Description="A sample WebMethod that returns 'Hello World'",
    EnableSession=false)]
public string HelloWorld()
{
    return "Hello World";
}
```

This attribute can be expanded with the following properties, which give more information about the method:

- ■ *BufferResponse*   Specifies whether the response will be buffered.

- ■ *CacheDuration*   Specifies the number of seconds the response will be held in the cache.

- ■ *Description*   Provides a description of the method, for documentation.

- ■ *EnableSession*   Specifies whether the method retains session state information.

- ■ *MessageName*   Specifies the name used for the Web service method in the data being passed to and from the method. The default is the name of the method.

- ■ *TransactionOption*   Specifies whether the method supports transactions.

Creating a Web Service

To create a Web service within the Visual Studio .NET IDE, start the New Project Wizard by choosing New from the File menu and then choosing Project (or by clicking the New Project button on the Start Page). In the New Project Wizard, select ASP.NET Web Service from the templates available for Visual C# projects. Then enter a location that specifies the Web server and the virtual directory where Visual Studio .NET will create the Web service. Figure 21-2 shows the New Project Wizard, with a default value for the location of the new Web service.

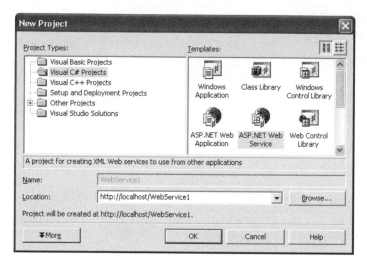

Figure 21-2. The New Project Wizard, which you can use to create a new Web service project.

After you've entered a location for your new Web service and clicked the OK button, Visual Studio will connect to the specified Web server and create the Web site, with the virtual directory you've provided, as shown in Figure 21-3.

Figure 21-3. Creating a directory on the Web server as the home of your new Web service.

The resulting Web service will contain the following files by default:

- **AssemblyInfo.cs** Contains assembly information for the Web service
- **Global.asax** Contains references to the global Web application page and code, including .cs and .resx files
- **Service1.asmx** Contains references to the Web service page access point and code, including .cs and .resx files
- **Web.config** Contains Web application configuration settings

- **WebService1.csproj**   Contains project settings and references to the Visual Studio project support files, including the .webinfo file

- **WebService1.vsdisco**   Contains the Web service dynamic discovery support document

Creating Web Service Classes

The Service1.asmx file and its associated pages are created automatically and include a reference to the default Web service class. This class will make use of the *System.Web.Services* namespace and will inherit the *System.Web.Services.WebService* class. At any time, you can create a new Web service class by choosing Add Web Service from the IDE Project menu. You'll be prompted to create the new Web service, as shown in Figure 21-4.

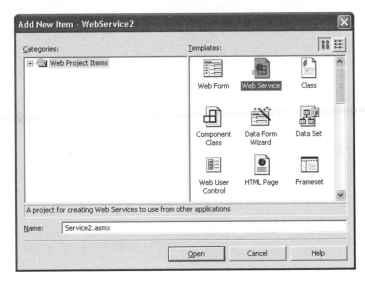

Figure 21-4.   Adding a Web service to your existing project.

Creating Web Methods

There's very little difference between writing functionality for a Web service and writing functionality for any other application—in both cases, you create public methods that will be called from the application. These can be simple methods that return some data or the result of an action, as shown in the following examples:

```
[WebMethod]
public string HelloWorld()
{
```

(continued)

```
        return "Hello World";
    }


[WebMethod(Description="This method will return the current time",
    EnableSession=false)]
public string CurrentTime()
{
    return System.DateTime.Now.ToString();
}


[WebMethod(Description="Adds two integers and returns the result",
    EnableSession=false)]
public long Add(int x, int y)
{
    return (long)(x + y);
}
```

As with any other methods you write, the Web service methods could be more involved and could return more complex data. For example, you might create a method that returns an ADO.NET dataset containing data that the user requests, as shown here:

```
[WebMethod(Description="Retrieves a list of authors in a dataset",
    EnableSession=false)]
public System.Data.DataSet getAuthors()
{
    string connString = "data source=(local);"
        + "initial catalog=pubs;"
        + "user id=sa;password=;"
        + "persist security info=True;"
        + "packet size=4096";
    System.Data.SqlClient.SqlConnection conn =
        new System.Data.SqlClient.SqlConnection(connString);
    System.Data.SqlClient.SqlCommand cmd =
        new System.Data.SqlClient.SqlCommand();
    cmd.CommandText = "SELECT * FROM authors";
    cmd.Connection = conn;
    System.Data.SqlClient.SqlDataAdapter da =
        new System.Data.SqlClient.SqlDataAdapter();
    da.SelectCommand = cmd;
    System.Data.DataSet ds = new System.Data.DataSet();
    da.Fill(ds);
    return ds;
}
```

Identifying Web Services Using Discovery

Once you've created Web services, they'll be available for use by developers. But you still have to provide a way for your developers to identify the services that exist. This process is called *discovery*. Through discovery, developers will be able to view the Web services and their available methods. Discovery makes use of a standard XML-formatted document that identifies which Web services are available and how the server should detect those services. There are two types of discovery: *static* and *dynamic*. This section describes both types of discovery, how to advertise the existence of your Web service to other developers, and the language that's used to describe Web services.

Using Static Discovery

Static discovery is used when a static discovery file exists. The file holds details about the services available on a site and has an extension of .disco. The static discovery file is an XML-formatted file that provides links to individual .disco files or to the services themselves. The root node of the document is *<discovery>*. The file contains *<contractRef>* or *<discoveryRef>* tags that hold the pertinent information about each service, as shown in the following code:

```
<?xml version="1.0"?>
<discovery xmlns="http://schemas.xmlsoap.org/disco/">
    <contractRef ref="myprofile.wsdl"
        xmlns="http://schemas.xmlsoap.org/disco/scl/"/>
    <contractRef ref="myservices.wsdl"
        xmlns="http://schemas.xmlsoap.org/disco/scl/"/>
</discovery>
```

The *<contractRef>* tag is used to specify a URL that will return the Web Services Description Language (WSDL) information for your Web service. (The section "Understanding WSDL," later in this chapter, provides additional information about WSDL.) You can use *<discoveryRef>* tags to identify the location of other discovery files.

Using Dynamic Discovery

Alternatively, you can use dynamic discovery to enable ASP.NET to dynamically detect the Web services on your site. This is done by providing a dynamic discovery file, which has the extension .vsdisco in the virtual directory with your Web services. The root node of the document will be *<dynamicDiscovery>*. The document can contain tags that will be used to exclude paths from the search for Web services, as illustrated in the example on the following page.

```
<?xml version="1.0" encoding="utf-8" ?>
<dynamicDiscovery xmlns="urn:schemas-dynamicdiscovery:disco.2000-03-17">
<exclude path="_vti_cnf" />
<exclude path="_vti_pvt" />
<exclude path="_vti_log" />
<exclude path="_vti_script" />
<exclude path="_vti_txt" />
<exclude path="Web References" />
</dynamicDiscovery>
```

Advertising Your Discovery Pages

Although the static and dynamic discovery pages provide information about the existing Web services on your site, they do little to advertise their existence to other developers. How will developers make use of your services if they don't know the services exist? If you want to make your Web services available to others, you can advertise them using the Universal Description, Discovery, and Integration (UDDI) services.

The UDDI specification defines a standard for publishing and discovering information about Web services. UDDI sites are Web services on which you can register your own Web services and search for other Web services. These directories can include the following four types of information about the services:

- Business information

- Service information

- Binding information

- Information about specifications for services

This information can be accessed programmatically and can be used to generate the proxy stubs that provide local references for your projects.

> **Tip**   You can get more information about UDDI, register your Web services, or search for other Web services at *http://www.uddi.org* or *http://uddi.microsoft.com*.

Understanding WSDL

Microsoft and IBM jointly developed WSDL to provide a standard way of documenting the messages that a Web service will send and receive. These messages define the methods and outputs of the Web services. These methods are known as the *contract* that's offered by the service. The contract specifies the message schemas that will be accepted and returned from the service.

> **Note** WSDL is explained in detail in the Microsoft Developer Network (MSDN) article "Web Services Description Language (WSDL) Explained," by Carlos Tapang, which can be found at *http://msdn.microsoft.com/library/default.asp?url=/library/en-us/dnwebsrv/html/wsdlexplained.asp*.

Browsing a Web Service

Once you've created and built a Web service, you can easily browse the contents of the service through a Web browser by navigating to the URL of the Web service page. When you browse to a page without providing any parameters, the Web service will display its discovery information and other documentation if you provided it in the *WebService* attribute, as shown in Figure 21-5.

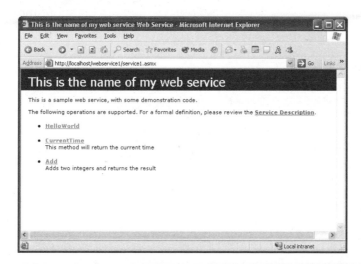

Figure 21-5. Browsing a Web service by browsing to the .asmx file.

This page will give you a quick look at the public methods of the Web service that have been exposed as Web methods. Further, if you've provided a *Description* property for the *WebMethod* attribute, that information will be displayed here. By clicking the link to any of these methods, you'll load a page that displays the details of the particular method, as shown in Figure 21-6.

Figure 21-6. Displaying the details for a Web service method.

This page is divided into four sections labeled *Test*, *SOAP*, *HTTP GET*, and *HTTP POST*. In the Test section, you'll find input boxes that can be used to pass any required parameters to the Web service method. Click the Invoke button to call the method and display the results in a second browser window, as shown in Figure 21-7.

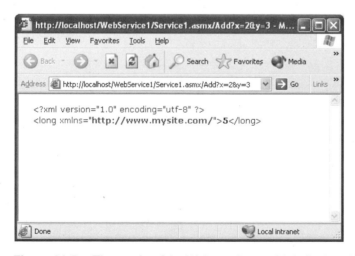

Figure 21-7. The results of the Web service method, displayed in a second browser window.

In addition, the Web service method page displays the XML schemas used to send and receive data from the Web service via the SOAP, HTTP GET, and HTTP POST protocols. (See the next section for more information about these protocols.)

Consuming a Web Service

After a Web service has been created, you can access and make use of it. You can consume the Web service using one of three protocols that the service is configured to respond to, as follows:

- HTTP GET
- HTTP POST
- SOAP

This section examines accessing a Web service method using these protocols.

Using the HTTP GET Protocol

The HTTP GET protocol is the simplest of the protocols. To consume the page, you simply make a call to the Web service name and pass the required parameters to the service as parameters in the query string, as shown here:

```
http://localhost/WebService1/Service1.asmx/Add?x=5&y=2
```

This call will return an XML document that includes the results of the service. The schema that's returned will depend on the particular method that's called.

The Web service supplies a contract that identifies how each protocol will be used to access the service. The contract for the HTTP GET method is shown here:

```
HTTP GET
The following is a sample HTTP GET request and response.
The placeholders shown need to be replaced with actual values.

GET /webservice1/service1.asmx/Add?x=string&y=string HTTP/1.1
Host: localhost

HTTP/1.1 200 OK
Content-Type: text/xml; charset=utf-8
Content-Length: length

<?xml version="1.0" encoding="utf-8"?>
<long xmlns="http://www.mysite.com/">long</long>
```

> **Note**   This is the same process that was used to browse the Web service, as described earlier in this chapter, in the section "Browsing a Web Service."

Using the HTTP POST Protocol

The HTTP POST protocol is similar to the HTTP GET protocol—with both protocols, you call the Web service page and post the parameters to the page as required. The following HTML code creates a Web page that allows you to access the *Add* Web service method described earlier in this chapter, in the section "Creating Web Methods":

```
<HTML>
<BODY>
<FORM ACTION="/WebService1/Service1.asmx/Add" METHOD=POST>
<INPUT NAME="x">
<BR>
<INPUT NAME="y">
<P>
<INPUT TYPE=SUBMIT>
</FORM>
</BODY>
</HTML>
```

The Web service method will write the results back to the page as an XML document, as shown here:

```
<?xml version="1.0" encoding="utf-8" ?>
<long xmlns="http://www.mysite.com/">5</long>
```

The Web service supplies a contract that identifies how each protocol will be used to access the service. The contract for the HTTP POST method is shown here:

```
HTTP POST
The following is a sample HTTP POST request and response.
The placeholders shown need to be replaced with actual values.

POST /webservice1/service1.asmx/Add HTTP/1.1
Host: localhost
Content-Type: application/x-www-form-urlencoded
Content-Length: length

x=string&y=string
HTTP/1.1 200 OK
Content-Type: text/xml; charset=utf-8
```

```
Content-Length: length

<?xml version="1.0" encoding="utf-8"?>
<long xmlns="http://www.mysite.com/">long</long>
```

Using the SOAP Protocol

More than likely, you'll most often access the Web service using SOAP. SOAP allows you to directly call components and execute methods. The Web service will return the data as an XML document, with the results passed back through the SOAP return function.

The Web service supplies a contract that identifies how each protocol will be used to access the service. The contract for the SOAP method is shown here:

```
SOAP
The following is a sample SOAP request and response.
The placeholders shown need to be replaced with actual values.

POST /webservice1/service1.asmx HTTP/1.1
Host: localhost
Content-Type: text/xml; charset=utf-8
Content-Length: length
SOAPAction: "http://www.mysite.com/Add"

<?xml version="1.0" encoding="utf-8"?>
<soap:Envelope xmlns:xsi="http://www.w3.org/2001/XMLSchema-instance"
xmlns:xsd="http://www.w3.org/2001/XMLSchema"
xmlns:soap="http://schemas.xmlsoap.org/soap/envelope/">
  <soap:Body>
    <Add xmlns="http://www.mysite.com/">
      <x>int</x>
      <y>int</y>
    </Add>
  </soap:Body>
</soap:Envelope>
HTTP/1.1 200 OK
Content-Type: text/xml; charset=utf-8
Content-Length: length

<?xml version="1.0" encoding="utf-8"?>
<soap:Envelope xmlns:xsi="http://www.w3.org/2001/XMLSchema-instance"
xmlns:xsd="http://www.w3.org/2001/XMLSchema"
xmlns:soap="http://schemas.xmlsoap.org/soap/envelope/">
  <soap:Body>
    <AddResponse xmlns="http://www.mysite.com/">
      <AddResult>long</AddResult>
    </AddResponse>
  </soap:Body>
</soap:Envelope>
```

Referencing a Web Service in the Visual Studio .NET IDE

To make use of a Web service in an application, you start by creating a reference to the Web service. To do so, choose Add Web Reference from the Project menu to open the Add Web Reference dialog box, in which you can search for the Web service, as shown in Figure 21-8. To search your local server, click the Web References On Local Web Server link. To search the UDDI services at Microsoft, click the appropriate links. Or you can type the URL of the Web service's discovery file in the Address bar.

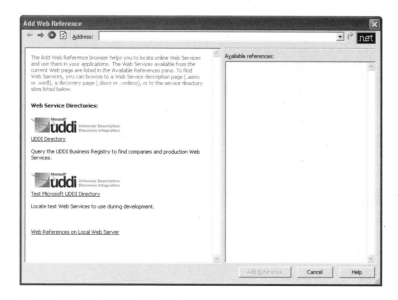

Figure 21-8.   The Add Web Reference dialog box.

If you click the Web References On Local Web Server link, the IDE will start a dynamic discovery of the Web services on your local machine, based on the *http://localhost/default.vsdisco* page. A list of the existing Web services on your system will be displayed in the right pane of the Add Web Reference dialog box, as shown in Figure 21-9.

If you click one of the Web service links, you'll see detailed information about the Web service and you'll be able to view the Web service contract and documentation, as shown in Figure 21-10. If this is the Web service you want to reference and use in your application, you can add the reference to your project by clicking the Add Reference button.

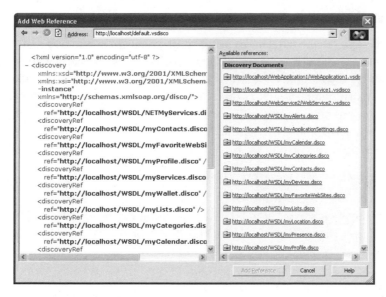

Figure 21-9.   Browsing the local server to display the available Web services.

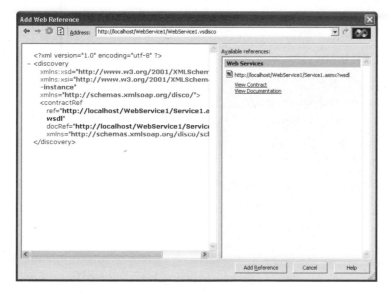

Figure 21-10.   Displaying detailed information about the Web service.

Generating a Web Service Proxy

If you want to make calls to an application other than one that you have on the local server, you'll need to generate a proxy class for the Web service. This proxy is used to identify the Web service and its methods. You can also specify the means by which you'll connect to and communicate with the service. Fortunately, you can generate this proxy class automatically, using the Wsdl.exe tool included in the .NET Framework SDK, which is a part of Visual Studio .NET. To build the proxy, simply run the following command:

```
wsdl http://localhost/webservice1/service1.asmx?wsdl
```

Of course, you'll want to replace the URL shown here with the particular URL for the Web service you'll be accessing on the remote host. This command will create a proxy class file with the name of the Web service and with the extension .cs (indicating that it's a C# file).

To specify other details about the proxy, you can use optional command-line parameters, including the following:

- **/language:<*language*>** Language of the proxy class. Use cs, vb, or js for C#, Visual Basic, or JScript. C# is the default.

- **/protocol:<*protocol*>** Protocol to use in accessing the service. Use SOAP, HTTP-GET, or HTTP-POST. SOAP is the default.

- **/username:<*username*>** User name to use when accessing the service to get WSDL information.

- **/password:<*password*>** Password to use when accessing the service to get WSDL information.

- **/domain:<*domain*>** Domain to use when accessing the service to get WSDL information.

- **/namespace:<*namespace*>** Namespace of the generated proxy class. The global namespace is the default.

- **/out:<*outputfile*>** Output file name for the proxy class. The name of the Web service is used as the default.

Based on the optional parameters, you could generate a Web service proxy class that communicates with a service using the HTTP POST protocol and authenticates itself using the username *bob* and the password *opensesame* by using the following command line:

```
wsdl /protocol:HTTP-POST /username:bob /password:opensesame
    http://localhost/webservice2/service1.asmx?wsdl
```

After the proxy class has been created, you can add it to your project and call it just like any other class in the project. Within the proxy class is the code required to access the Web service, call the desired methods with the needed parameters, and retrieve the necessary results.

Deploying Web Services

After you've created a Web service, you might need to deploy it from your development system onto production machines. Fortunately, in the .NET Framework, deploying applications, including Web services, is a simple process. To do so, you'll copy the following Web service files from your development system to a directory on the production machine:

- **The .asmx files**   The Web service access point files
- **The .disco or .vsdisco files**   Optional discovery files
- **The web.config file**   Optional Web configuration files for the Web service
- **The \bin directory**   The compiled Web service application

Securing Web Services

Because Web services are hosted within Internet Information Services (IIS) as ASP.NET applications, you can use ASP.NET to provide security. This means that securing a Web service application requires the same thought and configuration as securing any other ASP.NET application. And you can take advantage of either the ASP.NET Web configuration files or the IIS configuration settings to apply some basic security to the Web service.

As calling applications attempt to access your service, you might want to authenticate them to identify the user. This will enable you to restrict access to just those users that you want to allow. The basic techniques for authenticating your Web service users include the following:

- Standard IIS authentication (basic authentication, digest authentication, and Windows integrated security)
- Client digital certificates
- Internet protocol security
- Custom authentication

We'll look at each of these techniques in the following subsections.

Configuring IIS Authentication

You can easily configure IIS to include any of the authentication options by following these steps:

1. Open the Internet Information Services Manager.

2. Select the Web site and application that you want to secure.

3. Right-click on the application, and choose Properties from the shortcut menu.

4. In the Properties dialog box, click the Directory Security tab.

5. Click the Edit button in the Anonymous Access Authentication Control area. This will open the Authentication Methods dialog box, shown in Figure 21-11.

Figure 21-11. Managing directory security with the Authentication Methods dialog box, which is accessible from the Internet Information Services Manager.

6. Clear the Anonymous Access check box.

7. Select any of the other authentication methods you want to support, and click OK.

This authentication technique will require fewer programmatic changes in your Web service, but it will require some additional planning. Users should all map to users on the local server, in the local domain, or in the local active directory. This probably doesn't lend itself easily to a site with an extremely large number of users.

The calling application will need to be responsible for passing the proper user authentication information to your service. If you're writing the calling application, you should generate a Web service proxy class, as described earlier in this chapter, in the section "Generating a Web Service Proxy." After the proxy class has been added to your application, you can perform the following tasks:

1. Create *NetworkCredential* objects to hold your credentials.

2. Add the *NetworkCredential* objects to a *CredentialCache* object.

3. Save the *CredentialCache* object to the *Credentials* property of the Web service proxy class.

From there, you can proceed to call the Web service as usual. The following code illustrates how to implement these steps:

```
private void btnAddNumbers_Click(object sender, System.EventArgs e)
{
    MyWebService ws = new MyWebService();
    //Establish credentials to log on to Web service.
    CredentialCache credCache = new CredentialCache();
    NetworkCredential creds = new NetworkCredential("myusername",
        "mypassword", "mydomain");
    credCache.Add(new Uri(math.Url), "Basic", credentials);
    ws.Credentials = creds;
    //Call Web service method.
    txtResult.Text = ws.Add(5, 2).ToString();
}
```

Using Digital Certificates

Another authentication technique that might work nicely if your Web service is to be used in a business-to-business scenario that requires relatively few client users is to issue each of the clients a digital client certificate. This certificate can be used by IIS to automatically authenticate the user. The user can then also be mapped to a local machine or domain user if necessary.

If you're developing the calling application, you'll want to ensure that you send the client certificate as part of your call to the Web service. Assuming that you have a client certificate stored in a file named Clientcert.cer, follow these steps in your application code to use the certificate:

1. Create an instance of the *X509Certificate* class.

2. Use the *CreateFromCertFile* method to load the client certificate.

3. Add the client certificate to the *ClientCertificates* property of the Web service proxy class.

From there, you'll be able to call the Web service methods as usual. The following example illustrates how to implement these steps:

```
private void btnAddNumbers_Click(object sender, System.EventArgs e)
{
    MyWebService ws = new MyWebService();

    X509Certificate x509 =
        X509Certificate.CreateFromCertFile(@"C:\Clientcert.cer");
    ws.ClientCertificates.Add(x509);

    txtResult.Text = ws.Add(5, 2).ToString();
}
```

Setting Internet Protocol Security

Additionally, you can restrict access to your Web services by restricting the IP addresses that can gain access to your site. This is accomplished through IIS, by configuring the Directory Security tab of the Properties dialog box. Click the Edit button in the IP Address And Domain Name Restrictions area to specify the particular IP addresses that will be allowed to access your site.

This technique lends itself to services that will be used by a small and well-defined set of calling applications. This could be useful for services you're establishing for your corporate users or for business partners, where the IP addresses or IP address ranges are known.

Providing Custom Authentication

Another option is to provide a custom authentication scheme. For example, you might require the calling application to pass in a user name and password to authenticate the user. Or you might simply identify the user by placing a cookie on his or her system. There are a myriad of other options, all of which will require custom coding and implementation in your Web service. Many will also require that you establish a database of users.

Conclusion

Creating a Web service involves many of the same concepts and tasks you face when building any kind of application. You define the functionality and provide the logic necessary to create the service. You create classes, access other components, and utilize resources to complete the tasks. The code resembles the code within other applications.

However, by making the few modifications we've examined in this chapter, you can create a component that can be accessed remotely from anywhere on your local network or the Internet. Your Web service won't know anything about the calling application. It will simply provide a function and return a result. The Web service can be accessed using several of the standards-based protocols, such as SOAP or HTTP.

Likewise, building the consuming application that will make use of the Web service is similar to building any other application. The consuming application can treat the Web service as though it were a local component with which the application will communicate. The .NET Framework allows you to establish a proxy that can be referenced within the project.

This accessibility creates additional concerns, such as securing the Web service for your users. Using the tools provided by the operating system, IIS, and the .NET Framework, you'll be able to apply the desired level of security to your service to ensure that only those users that you authorize will gain access to your services.

Index

Send feedback about this index to *mspindex@microsoft.com*.

Symbols and Numbers

– (subtraction) operator, 106
-- (decrement) operator, 106–7, 273
! (exclamation mark) after top-level menu items, 391
! (negation) operator, 102, 104
!= (inequality) operator, 103
% (modulo (remainder)) operator, 106
%= (remainder assignment) operator, 111
& (ampersand)
  prefixing a character in caption text, 331
  prefixing a letter in a menu item's text caption, 393
& (AND (full evaluation)) operator, 104, 105
& (AND) operator, 107, 108–9
& (address of) operator, 114, 292
&& (AND (short-circuit)) operator, 104, 125
  overloading, 123–25
  tracing the Visual C# .NET compiler, 124–25
&= (bitwise-AND assignment) operator, 111, 112
* (multiplication) operator, 102, 106
* (pointer indirection) operator, 114
* (unsafe context) operator, 292
*= (multiplication assignment) operator, 111
.(dot operator). *See* dot operator (.)
… (ellipsis) after popup menu items, 391
/ (division) operator, 102, 106
/* and */, beginning and ending comment blocks, 26
/= (division assignment) operator, 111
:: (scope resolution) operator, 39, 114
?: (conditional) operator, 102, 112
@ (at sign) operator, indicating a string literal, 92
[] (index) operator, 114, 117
[] (subscript) operator, 193
∧ (XOR (exclusive OR)) operator, 104, 105, 107, 110
∧= (bitwise-XOR assignment) operator, 111, 112
{ } (curly braces)
  enclosing controlled statements, 134
  enclosing unsafe code, 290
| (bitwise OR operator), combining
  MessageBoxOptions values, 314
| (OR (full evaluation)) operator, 104, 105
| (OR) operator, 107, 109–10, 189, 314
|| (OR (short-circuit)) operator, 104, 123–25
|= (bitwise-OR assignment) operator, 111, 112
+ (addition) operator, 92, 106, 166
++ (increment) operator, 102, 106–7, 273
+= (addition assignment) operator, 110, 111, 166
< (less than) operator, 103, 104
<% %> delimiters, 651

<< (left shift) operator, 107, 108
<<= (left-shift assignment) operator, 111
<= (less than or equal to) operator, 103, 104
= (assignment) operator, 103, 110, 111
–= (subtraction assignment) operator, 110, 111, 166–67, 340
== (equality) operator, 92, 103
> (greater than) operator, 103, 104
-> (member access) operator, 39, 114
-> (unsafe context) operator, 292
>= (greater than or equal to) operator, 103, 104
>> (right shift) operator, 107, 108
>>= (right-shift assignment) operator, 111
~ (tilde), indicating a destructor, 55
~ (complement) operator, 107, 110
( ) (cast) operator, 114
( ) (parentheses), altering the precedence of operators, 116
3–D controls, shadow for, 440
32–bit color values, representing in the .NET Framework, 322

A

A property, exposed by the Color structure, 439
Abort method of a thread, 271
Aborted member of the ThreadState enumeration, 270
AbortRequested member of the ThreadState enumeration, 270
AbortRetryIgnore value of the MessageBoxButtons enumeration, 312
AboveNormal priority for a thread, 272
abstract classes, 42, 67
abstract declarations, 195
abstract indexers, 195
abstract keyword, 42, 56
abstract methods, 42, 55–56
AcceptButton property, 341
AcceptChanges method of the DataSet object, 571
AcceptsReturn property of the TextBox class, 346
AcceptsTab property of the TextBox class, 346
access points, 684
access protection level for indexers, 209
accessibility, 58–61
accessibility levels, 38
Action property of the QueryContinueDragEventArgs argument, 562

strong-named assemblies, 9, 119
struct keyword, 76
struct types, 85
structure members, 60
structure types. *See* structures; types
structures, 34, 76
  allocating on the stack, 77
  creating instances of, 77
  declaring, 76
  declaring as unsafe, 291
  declaring value types as, 120
  inheritance and, 76
  inheriting an interface with an indexer, 198
style properties of a TreeView control, 522
Style property
  of a font, 473
  of the StatusBarPanels class, 416
styles, defining for tables and columns, 518–20
subclasses, 41
subelements, adding to an XML file, 601
submenus, adding menu items with, 397
subnodes in the DOM structure, 615
subscript operator ([]), 193
SubtractButton control, 648
subtraction assignment (–=) operator, 111, 166–67
subtraction operator (–), 106, 166–67
subtraction with assignment operator (–=), 340
Sunken value in the StatusBarPanelBorderStyle
  enumeration, 417
.suo file, 303
SuppressFinalize method, 96, 98, 99
SurroundColors property, 457
Suspend method of a thread, 270
Suspended member of the ThreadState enumeration, 270
SuspendRequested member of the ThreadState
  enumeration, 270
switch clause, 137
Switch objects, 249
  controlling in an application's configuration file,
  249–51
  creating simple, 249–50
switch statement, 133, 137–40, 613
switches, controlling output with, 249–51
symbols, 239
synchronization, 273–84
synchronization events, blocking threads, 280
synchronization problems in multithreaded
  applications, 273–75
synchronization wrappers, 284
Synchronized method, 283–84
SyncRoot property of the ICollection interface, 220, 282,
  284
system colors, using the current, 440–41

System namespace, referencing, 63
system services, providing access to, 15–16
System value in the FlatStyle enumeration, 329
System.Array class, 87
System.Attribute class, 179, 181
SystemBrushes class, 445
SystemBrushes properties, 445–46
System.Collections namespace, 305
System.Collections.Specialized namespace, 234
SystemColors class, 440–41
System.ComponentModel namespace, 305
System.Convert class, 126
System.Data namespace, 305
SystemDefault value from the LinkBehavior
  enumeration, 350
System.Delegate class, 162
System.Diagnostics namespace, 238
  classes for trace and debug messages, 245
  classes providing access to the call stack, 241
System.Drawing namespace, 305
System.GC class, 99–100
System.MulticastDelegate class, 162, 166
System.Object class, 44
SystemPens class, 458–59
SystemPens properties, 458–59
System.Threading namespace, 275
System.Threading.Thread class, 268
System.ValueType class, 85
System.Windows.Forms namespace, 299, 305
System.Xml namespace, 597
System.Xml.Schema namespace, 597, 598
System.Xml.XPath namespace, 597, 598
System.Xml.Xsl namespace, 597, 598

T

TAB key, 346
TabAlignment enumeration, 492
TabAppearance enumeration, 492
tabbed-document mode of Visual Studio .NET, 12
TabControl controls, 487–94
  creating with the Windows Forms Designer, 489–91
  managing, 491–94
TabCount property, 492
Table control in Web server, 656
table styles, 519
TableDirect command type, 581
TableMappings property, 591
tables
  in a DataSet object, 570
  mapping, 590–91
TabPage class, 488
TabPage Collection Editor, 490–91

About the Author

Mickey Williams is the founder of Codev Technologies, which provides tools for Windows developers and consulting services for mission-critical systems. Active with object-oriented development since the 1980s, he has written many books about Windows programming tools and frequently speaks at conferences in the United States and Europe. An expert in Microsoft .NET development technologies, Williams is an instructor for .NET Experts, where he teaches courses on the .NET Framework, XML, and SOAP. He also writes the biweekly ".NET Nuts and Bolts" column for CodeGuru.com.

Propeller

A ship's propeller operates in much the same way as an airplane propeller. In the ship propeller, however, each blade is very broad (from leading to trailing edge) and very thin. The blades are usually built of copper alloys to resist corrosion. The speed of sound in water is much higher than the speed in air, and because of the high frictional resistance of water, the top speed never approaches the speed of sound. Although efficiencies as high as 77 percent have been achieved with experimental propellers, most ship propellers operate at efficiencies of about 56 percent. Clearance is also less of a problem on ship propellers, although the diameter and position of the propeller are limited by the loss in efficiency if the propeller blades come anywhere near the surface of the water. The principal problem of ship-propeller design and operation is cavitation, the formation of a vacuum along parts of the propeller blade, which leads to excessive slip, loss of efficiency, and pitting of the blades. It also causes excessive underwater noise, a serious disadvantage on submarines.*

At Microsoft Press, we use tools to illustrate our books for software developers and IT professionals. Tools very simply and powerfully symbolize human inventiveness. They're a metaphor for people extending their capabilities, precision, and reach. From simple calipers and pliers to digital micrometers and lasers, these stylized illustrations give each book a visual identity, and a personality to the series. With tools and knowledge, there's no limit to creativity and innovation. Our tagline says it all: *The tools you need to put technology to work.*

The manuscript for this book was prepared and galleyed using Microsoft Word. Pages were composed by Microsoft Press using Adobe FrameMaker+SGML for Windows, with text in Garamond and display type in Helvetica Condensed. Composed pages were delivered to the printer as electronic prepress files.

Cover Designer:	Methodologie, Inc.
Interior Graphic Designer:	James D. Kramer
Principal Compositor:	Elizabeth Hansford
Interior Artist:	Rob Nance
Principal Copy Editor:	Holly M. Viola
Indexer:	Richard Shrout

Get the *in-depth architectural information* you need about the hottest object-oriented programming language for Microsoft .NET.

Inside C#, Second Edition
U.S.A. $49.99
Canada $72.99
ISBN: 0-7356-1648-5

Take a detailed look at the internal architecture of the groundbreaking C# language with this architectural reference—**now fully updated** with the latest information about the Microsoft® .NET platform and Microsoft Visual Studio® .NET. It's packed with new sample code and demo applications to show you exactly how to develop with C#. You'll explore this advanced language and its design parameters and construction to gain a complete understanding of how it works—and why it works that way.

microsoft.com/mspress

Get step-by-step instruction plus
.NET development software
—all in one box!

Everything you need to start developing powerful applications and services for Microsoft .NET is right here in three economical training packages. DELUXE LEARNING EDITIONS give you powerful Microsoft .NET development software—Visual C# .NET Standard, Visual Basic .NET Standard, and Visual C++ .NET Standard—along with Microsoft's popular *Step by Step* tutorials to help you learn the languages. Work at your own pace through easy-to-follow lessons and hands-on exercises. Then apply your new expertise to full development software — not simulations or trial versions. DELUXE LEARNING EDITIONS are the ideal combination of tools and tutelage for the Microsoft .NET Framework—straight from the source!

Microsoft® Visual C#™ .NET Deluxe Learning Edition
U.S.A. $119.99
Canada $173.99
ISBN: 0-7356-1633-7

Microsoft Visual Basic® .NET Deluxe Learning Edition
U.S.A. $119.99
Canada $173.99
ISBN: 0-7356-1634-5

Microsoft Visual C++® .NET Deluxe Learning Edition
U.S.A. $119.99
Canada $173.99
ISBN: 0-7356-1635-3

Get ahead of the development curve with this **first look** at the Microsoft **C#** language specifications.

U.S.A. **$29.99**
Canada $43.99
ISBN: 0-7356-1448-2

C# is a modern, object-oriented language that enables programmers to quickly build a wide range of applications for the new Microsoft® .NET platform. Get a head start on developing in C# with this first printed look at the complete C# language specifications. Based on beta content, this MSDN® title includes:

> Information about the essential features and basic concepts of the C# language, plus in-depth analysis of the lexical structure of the language.

> Details about types, variables, conversions, expressions, statements, namespaces, classes, structures, arrays, interfaces, enumerators, delegates, exceptions, and attributes.

> Details on how C# simplifies coding by omitting pointers as a data type—and lets you get closer to the hardware by declaring and operating on pointers in unsafe code.

> A list of attributes used for creating programs that interoperate with COM programs, plus a list of other key references.

microsoft.com/mspress

Get a **Free**
e-mail newsletter, updates,
special offers, links to related books,
and more when you
register on line!

R egister your Microsoft Press® title on our Web site and you'll get
a FREE subscription to our e-mail newsletter, *Microsoft Press
Book Connections.* You'll find out about newly released and upcoming
books and learning tools, online events, software downloads, special
offers and coupons for Microsoft Press customers, and information
about major Microsoft® product releases. You can also read useful
additional information about all the titles we publish, such as detailed book descriptions, tables of contents and indexes, sample
chapters, links to related books and book series, author biographies,
and reviews by other customers.

Registration is easy. Just visit this Web page and fill in your information:

http://www.microsoft.com/mspress/register

Microsoft®

Proof of Purchase

Use this page as proof of purchase if participating in a promotion or rebate offer on
this title. Proof of purchase must be used in conjunction with other proof(s) of
payment such as your dated sales receipt—see offer details.

Microsoft® Visual C#™ .NET (Core Reference)
0-7356-1290-0

CUSTOMER NAME

Microsoft Press, PO Box 97017, Redmond, WA 98073-9830

MICROSOFT LICENSE AGREEMENT
Book Companion CD

IMPORTANT—READ CAREFULLY: This Microsoft End-User License Agreement ("EULA") is a legal agreement between you (either an individual or an entity) and Microsoft Corporation for the Microsoft product identified above, which includes computer software and may include associated media, printed materials, and "online" or electronic documentation ("SOFTWARE PRODUCT"). Any component included within the SOFTWARE PRODUCT that is accompanied by a separate End-User License Agreement shall be governed by such agreement and not the terms set forth below. By installing, copying, or otherwise using the SOFTWARE PRODUCT, you agree to be bound by the terms of this EULA. If you do not agree to the terms of this EULA, you are not authorized to install, copy, or otherwise use the SOFTWARE PRODUCT; you may, however, return the SOFTWARE PRODUCT, along with all printed materials and other items that form a part of the Microsoft product that includes the SOFTWARE PRODUCT, to the place you obtained them for a full refund.

SOFTWARE PRODUCT LICENSE

The SOFTWARE PRODUCT is protected by United States copyright laws and international copyright treaties, as well as other intellectual property laws and treaties. The SOFTWARE PRODUCT is licensed, not sold.

1. **GRANT OF LICENSE.** This EULA grants you the following rights:

   a. **Software Product.** You may install and use one copy of the SOFTWARE PRODUCT on a single computer. The primary user of the computer on which the SOFTWARE PRODUCT is installed may make a second copy for his or her exclusive use on a portable computer.

   b. **Storage/Network Use.** You may also store or install a copy of the SOFTWARE PRODUCT on a storage device, such as a network server, used only to install or run the SOFTWARE PRODUCT on your other computers over an internal network; however, you must acquire and dedicate a license for each separate computer on which the SOFTWARE PRODUCT is installed or run from the storage device. A license for the SOFTWARE PRODUCT may not be shared or used concurrently on different computers.

   c. **License Pak.** If you have acquired this EULA in a Microsoft License Pak, you may make the number of additional copies of the computer software portion of the SOFTWARE PRODUCT authorized on the printed copy of this EULA, and you may use each copy in the manner specified above. You are also entitled to make a corresponding number of secondary copies for portable computer use as specified above.

   d. **Sample Code.** Solely with respect to portions, if any, of the SOFTWARE PRODUCT that are identified within the SOFTWARE PRODUCT as sample code (the "SAMPLE CODE"):

      i. **Use and Modification.** Microsoft grants you the right to use and modify the source code version of the SAMPLE CODE, *provided* you comply with subsection (d)(iii) below. You may not distribute the SAMPLE CODE, or any modified version of the SAMPLE CODE, in source code form.

      ii. **Redistributable Files.** Provided you comply with subsection (d)(iii) below, Microsoft grants you a nonexclusive, royalty-free right to reproduce and distribute the object code version of the SAMPLE CODE and of any modified SAMPLE CODE, other than SAMPLE CODE, or any modified version thereof, designated as not redistributable in the Readme file that forms a part of the SOFTWARE PRODUCT (the "Non-Redistributable Sample Code"). All SAMPLE CODE other than the Non-Redistributable Sample Code is collectively referred to as the "REDISTRIBUTABLES."

      iii. **Redistribution Requirements.** If you redistribute the REDISTRIBUTABLES, you agree to: (i) distribute the REDISTRIBUTABLES in object code form only in conjunction with and as a part of your software application product; (ii) not use Microsoft's name, logo, or trademarks to market your software application product; (iii) include a valid copyright notice on your software application product; (iv) indemnify, hold harmless, and defend Microsoft from and against any claims or lawsuits, including attorney's fees, that arise or result from the use or distribution of your software application product; and (v) not permit further distribution of the REDISTRIBUTABLES by your end user. Contact Microsoft for the applicable royalties due and other licensing terms for all other uses and/or distribution of the REDISTRIBUTABLES.

2. **DESCRIPTION OF OTHER RIGHTS AND LIMITATIONS.**

   - **Limitations on Reverse Engineering, Decompilation, and Disassembly.** You may not reverse engineer, decompile, or disassemble the SOFTWARE PRODUCT, except and only to the extent that such activity is expressly permitted by applicable law notwithstanding this limitation.

   - **Separation of Components.** The SOFTWARE PRODUCT is licensed as a single product. Its component parts may not be separated for use on more than one computer.

   - **Rental.** You may not rent, lease, or lend the SOFTWARE PRODUCT.

   - **Support Services.** Microsoft may, but is not obligated to, provide you with support services related to the SOFTWARE PRODUCT ("Support Services"). Use of Support Services is governed by the Microsoft policies and programs described in the user manual, in "online" documentation, and/or in other Microsoft-provided materials. Any supplemental software code provided to you as part of the Support Services shall be considered part of the SOFTWARE PRODUCT and subject to the terms and conditions of this EULA. With respect to technical information you provide to Microsoft as part of the Support Services, Microsoft may use such information for its business purposes, including for product support and development. Microsoft will not utilize such technical information in a form that personally identifies you.

- **Software Transfer.** You may permanently transfer all of your rights under this EULA, provided you retain no copies, you transfer all of the SOFTWARE PRODUCT (including all component parts, the media and printed materials, any upgrades, this EULA, and, if applicable, the Certificate of Authenticity), **and** the recipient agrees to the terms of this EULA.

- **Termination.** Without prejudice to any other rights, Microsoft may terminate this EULA if you fail to comply with the terms and conditions of this EULA. In such event, you must destroy all copies of the SOFTWARE PRODUCT and all of its component parts.

3. **COPYRIGHT.** All title and copyrights in and to the SOFTWARE PRODUCT (including but not limited to any images, photographs, animations, video, audio, music, text, SAMPLE CODE, REDISTRIBUTABLES, and "applets" incorporated into the SOFTWARE PRODUCT) and any copies of the SOFTWARE PRODUCT are owned by Microsoft or its suppliers. The SOFTWARE PRODUCT is protected by copyright laws and international treaty provisions. Therefore, you must treat the SOFTWARE PRODUCT like any other copyrighted material **except** that you may install the SOFTWARE PRODUCT on a single computer provided you keep the original solely for backup or archival purposes. You may not copy the printed materials accompanying the SOFTWARE PRODUCT.

4. **U.S. GOVERNMENT RESTRICTED RIGHTS.** The SOFTWARE PRODUCT and documentation are provided with RESTRICTED RIGHTS. Use, duplication, or disclosure by the Government is subject to restrictions as set forth in subparagraph (c)(1)(ii) of the Rights in Technical Data and Computer Software clause at DFARS 252.227-7013 or subparagraphs (c)(1) and (2) of the Commercial Computer Software—Restricted Rights at 48 CFR 52.227-19, as applicable. Manufacturer is Microsoft Corporation/One Microsoft Way/Redmond, WA 98052-6399.

5. **EXPORT RESTRICTIONS.** You agree that you will not export or re-export the SOFTWARE PRODUCT, any part thereof, or any process or service that is the direct product of the SOFTWARE PRODUCT (the foregoing collectively referred to as the "Restricted Components"), to any country, person, entity, or end user subject to U.S. export restrictions. You specifically agree not to export or re-export any of the Restricted Components (i) to any country to which the U.S. has embargoed or restricted the export of goods or services, which currently include, but are not necessarily limited to, Cuba, Iran, Iraq, Libya, North Korea, Sudan, and Syria, or to any national of any such country, wherever located, who intends to transmit or transport the Restricted Components back to such country; (ii) to any end user who you know or have reason to know will utilize the Restricted Components in the design, development, or production of nuclear, chemical, or biological weapons; or (iii) to any end user who has been prohibited from participating in U.S. export transactions by any federal agency of the U.S. government. You warrant and represent that neither the BXA nor any other U.S. federal agency has suspended, revoked, or denied your export privileges.

DISCLAIMER OF WARRANTY

NO WARRANTIES OR CONDITIONS. MICROSOFT EXPRESSLY DISCLAIMS ANY WARRANTY OR CONDITION FOR THE SOFTWARE PRODUCT. THE SOFTWARE PRODUCT AND ANY RELATED DOCUMENTATION ARE PROVIDED "AS IS" WITHOUT WARRANTY OR CONDITION OF ANY KIND, EITHER EXPRESS OR IMPLIED, INCLUDING, WITHOUT LIMITATION, THE IMPLIED WARRANTIES OF MERCHANTABILITY, FITNESS FOR A PARTICULAR PURPOSE, OR NONINFRINGEMENT. THE ENTIRE RISK ARISING OUT OF USE OR PERFORMANCE OF THE SOFTWARE PRODUCT REMAINS WITH YOU.

LIMITATION OF LIABILITY. TO THE MAXIMUM EXTENT PERMITTED BY APPLICABLE LAW, IN NO EVENT SHALL MICROSOFT OR ITS SUPPLIERS BE LIABLE FOR ANY SPECIAL, INCIDENTAL, INDIRECT, OR CONSEQUENTIAL DAMAGES WHATSOEVER (INCLUDING, WITHOUT LIMITATION, DAMAGES FOR LOSS OF BUSINESS PROFITS, BUSINESS INTERRUPTION, LOSS OF BUSINESS INFORMATION, OR ANY OTHER PECUNIARY LOSS) ARISING OUT OF THE USE OF OR INABILITY TO USE THE SOFTWARE PRODUCT OR THE PROVISION OF OR FAILURE TO PROVIDE SUPPORT SERVICES, EVEN IF MICROSOFT HAS BEEN ADVISED OF THE POSSIBILITY OF SUCH DAMAGES. IN ANY CASE, MICROSOFT'S ENTIRE LIABILITY UNDER ANY PROVISION OF THIS EULA SHALL BE LIMITED TO THE GREATER OF THE AMOUNT ACTUALLY PAID BY YOU FOR THE SOFTWARE PRODUCT OR US$5.00; PROVIDED, HOWEVER, IF YOU HAVE ENTERED INTO A MICROSOFT SUPPORT SERVICES AGREEMENT, MICROSOFT'S ENTIRE LIABILITY REGARDING SUPPORT SERVICES SHALL BE GOVERNED BY THE TERMS OF THAT AGREEMENT. BECAUSE SOME STATES AND JURISDICTIONS DO NOT ALLOW THE EXCLUSION OR LIMITATION OF LIABILITY, THE ABOVE LIMITATION MAY NOT APPLY TO YOU.

MISCELLANEOUS

This EULA is governed by the laws of the State of Washington USA, except and only to the extent that applicable law mandates governing law of a different jurisdiction.

Should you have any questions concerning this EULA, or if you desire to contact Microsoft for any reason, please contact the Microsoft subsidiary serving your country, or write: Microsoft Sales Information Center/One Microsoft Way/Redmond, WA 98052-6399.